Big Data and Computational Intelligence in Networking

Big Data and Computational Intelligence in Networking

Edited by

YULEI WU
FEI HU
GEYONG MIN
ALBERT Y. ZOMAYA

CRC Press is an imprint of the
Taylor & Francis Group, an **informa** business

CRC Press
Taylor & Francis Group
6000 Broken Sound Parkway NW, Suite 300
Boca Raton, FL 33487-2742

First issued in paperback 2020

ISBN-13: 978-0-367-57244-0 (pbk)
ISBN-13: 978-1-4987-8486-3 (hbk)

Library of Congress Cataloging-in-Publication Data

Names: Wu, Yulei, editor.
Title: Big data and computational intelligence in networking / Yulei Wu, Fei Hu, Geyong Min, Albert Y. Zomaya.
Description: Boca Raton, FL : CRC Press, [2018] | Includes bibliographical references and index.
Identifiers: LCCN 2017028407| ISBN 9781498784863 (hardback : acid-free paper) | ISBN 9781315155678 (e-book) | ISBN 9781498784870 (e-book) | ISBN 9781351651721 (e-book) | ISBN 9781351642200 (e-book)
Subjects: LCSH: Big data. | Cloud computing. | Computer networks--Management. | Computational intelligence.
Classification: LCC QA76.9.B45 W824 2018 | DDC 005.7--dc23
LC record available at https://lccn.loc.gov/2017028407

Visit the Taylor & Francis Web site at
http://www.taylorandfrancis.com

and the CRC Press Web site at
http://www.crcpress.com

Big Data and Computational Intelligence in Networking

Edited by
YULEI WU
FEI HU
GEYONG MIN
ALBERT Y. ZOMAYA

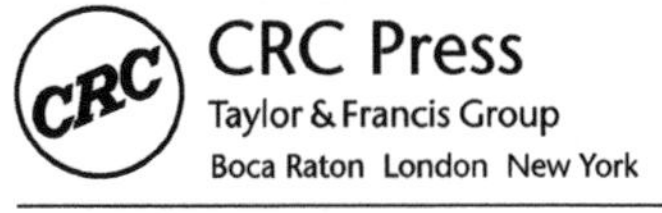

CRC Press
Taylor & Francis Group
Boca Raton London New York

CRC Press is an imprint of the
Taylor & Francis Group, an **informa** business

CRC Press
Taylor & Francis Group
6000 Broken Sound Parkway NW, Suite 300
Boca Raton, FL 33487-2742

First issued in paperback 2020

ISBN-13: 978-0-367-57244-0 (pbk)
ISBN-13: 978-1-4987-8486-3 (hbk)

Library of Congress Cataloging-in-Publication Data

Names: Wu, Yulei, editor.
Title: Big data and computational intelligence in networking / Yulei Wu, Fei Hu, Geyong Min, Albert Y. Zomaya.
Description: Boca Raton, FL : CRC Press, [2018] | Includes bibliographical references and index.
Identifiers: LCCN 2017028407| ISBN 9781498784863 (hardback : acid-free paper) | ISBN 9781315155678 (e-book) | ISBN 9781498784870 (e-book) | ISBN 9781351651721 (e-book) | ISBN 9781351642200 (e-book)
Subjects: LCSH: Big data. | Cloud computing. | Computer networks--Management. | Computational intelligence.
Classification: LCC QA76.9.B45 W824 2018 | DDC 005.7--dc23
LC record available at https://lccn.loc.gov/2017028407

Visit the Taylor & Francis Web site at
http://www.taylorandfrancis.com

and the CRC Press Web site at
http://www.crcpress.com

Contents

Preface

Recent years have witnessed a deluge of network data propelled by the emerging online social media, user-generated video contents, and global-scale communications, bringing people into the era of big data. Such network big data holds much critical and valuable information including customer experiences, user behaviors, service levels, and other contents, which could significantly improve the efficiency, effectiveness, and intelligence on the optimization of the current Internet, facilitate the smart network operation and management, and help service providers and content providers reduce capital expenditure (CapEx) and operational expenditure (OpEx) while maintaining a relatively high-level quality of service (QoS) and quality of experience (QoE).

Typical examples of network intelligence received from network big data include rapid QoE impairment detection and mitigation, optimization of network asset utilization, proactive maintenance, rapid outage restoration, and graceful disaster recovery. These aims can be achieved from high-level computational intelligence based on emerging analytical techniques such as big data processing, Web analytics, and network analytics employing software tools from advanced analytics disciplines such as machine learning, data mining, and predictive analytics. The computational intelligence for big data analysis is playing an ever-increasingly important role in supporting the evolution of the current Internet toward the next-generation intelligent Internet.

However, the unstructured, heterogeneous, sheer volume and complex nature of network big data pose great challenges on the computational intelligence of these emerging analytical techniques due to high computational overhead and communication cost, non-real-time response, sparse matrix-vector multiplications, and high convergence time. It is therefore of critical importance to understand network big data and design novel solutions of computational intelligence, scaling up for big data analytics of large-scale networks to automatically discover the hidden and valuable information available for smart network operations, management, and optimization. This has been established as a new cross-discipline research topic in computer science, requiring anticipation of technical and practical challenges faced by mixed methods across multiple disciplines.

In this book, we have invited world experts in this area to contribute the chapters that cover the following four parts:

1. *Part 1: Basics of Networked Big Data*: This part helps understand the properties, characteristics, challenges, and opportunities of networked big data, geospatial data, and wireless big data. This part covers the following:

    a. *Mathematical properties*: A variety of aspects related to networks, including their topological and dynamical properties, as well as their applications to real-world examples

    b. *Geospatial data and geospatial semantic web*: Challenges and opportunities of the geospatial semantic web brought for sharing and utilizing big geospatial data

    c. *Big data over wireless networks*: Typical scenarios, various challenges, and potential solutions for wireless transmission of big data

2. *Part 2: Network Architecture for Big Data Transmissions*: This part presents new proposals and network architectures to ensure efficient big data transmissions and streaming big data processing.

    a. *Big data transfer*: Challenges of bandwidth reservation service for efficient big data transfer and the potential solutions

    b. *Internet of Things (IoT)*: A dynamic and independent Cloud computing architecture based on a service-oriented architecture for IoT devices, to allow users to freely transfer their IoT devices from one vendor to another

    c. *Streaming big data processing*: How to maximize QoS and minimize OpEx when performing task scheduling and resource allocation in geo-distributed Clouds

3. *Part 3: Analysis and Processing of Networked Big Data*: This part explains how to perform big data analytics based on emerging analytical techniques such as big data analytics, Web analytics, network analytics, and advanced analytics disciplines such as machine learning, data mining, and predictive analytics. This part covers the following areas:

    a. *Alternating direction method of multiplier (ADMM)*: Its applications to large-scale network optimizations

    b. *Dynamic network management and optimization*: Rethink of current network analysis, management and operation practices; impact of

network evolution on the computation of key network metrics; hyperbolic big data analytics

c. *Predictive analytics and smart retrieval*: Utilize the network big data by performing a data, information, knowledge, and wisdom (DIKW) hierarchy to the product of its processes
d. *Recommendation systems*: Key challenges and solutions for data sparsity problem, data scale issue, and cold-start problem
e. *Coordinate gradient descent methods*: Unconstrained convex minimization problems with differentiable objective function in network problems
f. *MapReduce*: Data locality and dependency analysis; dependency-aware locality for MapReduce
g. *Distributed machine learning*: Big data and big models for network big data; how to parallelize parameter updates on multiple workers; how to synchronize concurrent parameter updates performed by multiple workers
h. *Big graph*: Big graph decomposition; real-time and large-scale graph processing; big data security

4. *Part 4: Emerging Applications of Networked Big Data*: This part covers some emerging applications on the following:

   a. *Intelligent mall shopping*: Location-based mobile augmented reality applications; using network data to enable intelligent shopping; robust feature learning in cold-start heterogeneous-device localization; learning to query in the cold-start retailer content
   b. *Network anomaly detection*: How to efficiently use network big data to perform accurate anomaly detection
   c. *Transportation*: Advances of spatial network big data (SNBD) techniques; challenges posed by SNBD in transportation applications and the potential solutions
   d. *Biomedical and social media domain*: Graph as a representation schema for big data; graph-based models and analyses in social text mining, and bioinformatics and biomedical
   e. *Smart manufacturing*: Big data characteristics in manufacturing; data collection and data mining in manufacturing; applications of big data in manufacturing.

This book presents the state-of-the-art solutions to the theoretical and practical challenges stemming from the leverage of big data and its computational intelligence in supporting smart network operation, management, and optimization. In particular, the technical focus covers the comprehensive understanding of network big data, efficient collection and management of network big data, distributed and scalable online analytics for network big data, and emerging applications of network big data for computational intelligence.

Targeted audiences: This book targets both academia and industry readers. Graduate students can select promising research topics from this book that are suitable for their thesis or dissertation research. Researchers will have a deep understanding of the challenging issues and opportunities of network big data and can thus easily find an unsolved research problem to pursue. Industry engineers from IT companies, service providers, content providers, network operators, and equipment manufacturers can get to know the engineering design issues and corresponding solutions after reading some practical schemes described in some chapters.

We have required all chapter authors to provide as much technical detail as possible. Each chapter also includes references for readers' further studies and investigations. If you have any comments or questions on certain chapters, please contact the chapter authors for more information.

Thank you for reading this book. We wish that this book will help you with the scientific research and practical problems of network big data.

Contributors

Assad Abbas
North Dakota State University
Fargo, North Dakota

Reem Y. Ali
Department of Computer Science
University of Minnesota
Minneapolis, Minnesota

Mehdi Bahrami
Cloud Lab
University of California, Merced
Merced, California

Hong Cao
Analytics & Enterprise Intelligence
Ernst & Young Advisory Pte. Ltd
Singapore

Xiaoyi Fan
School of Computing Science
Simon Fraser University
Burnaby, British Columbia, Canada

Vishrawas Gopalakrishnan
Department of Computer Science and Engineering
State University of New York
Buffalo, New York

Lin Gu
Huazhong University of Science and Technology
Wuhan, China

Venkata M.V. Gunturi
Department of Computer Science
Indraprastha Institute of Information Technology
Delhi, India

Y. B. Guo
Department of Mechanical Engineering
University of Alabama
Tuscaloosa, Alabama

Chengyu Hu
China University of Geosciences
Wuhan, China

Fei Hu
Electrical and Computer Engineering
University of Alabama
Tuscaloosa, Alabama

Chengqiang Huang
University of Exeter
Exeter, United Kingdom

Zhe Jiang
Department of Computer Science
University of Alabama
Tuscaloosa, Alabama

Vasileios Karyotis
School of Electrical and Computer Engineering
National Technical University of Athens (NTUA)
Athens, Greece

Samee U. Khan
North Dakota State University
Fargo, North Dakota

Joonseok Lee
Google Research
Video Understanding Team, Machine Perception
Mountain View, California

Seunghak Lee
Human Longevity, Inc.,
San Diego, California

Weidong Li
Department of Geography & Center for Environmental Sciences and Engineering
University of Connecticut
Storrs, Connecticut

Nan Lin
Department of Mathematics
Washington University in St. Louis
St. Louis, Missouri

Jiangchuan Liu
School of Computing Science
Simon Fraser University
Burnaby, British Columbia, Canada

Z. Y. Liu
Department of Mechanical Engineering
University of Alabama
Tuscaloosa, Alabama

Yu Lu
Electrical and Computer Engineering
University of Alabama
Tuscaloosa, Alabama

Xiaoqiang Ma
School of Electronic Information and Communications
Huazhong University of Science and Technology
Wuhan, China

Immanuel Manohar
Electrical and Computer Engineering
University of Alabama
Tuscaloosa, Alabama

Norashidah Md. Din
Universiti Tenaga Nasional
Selangor, Malaysia

Geyong Min
University of Exeter
Exeter, United Kingdom

Ion Necoara
Automatic Control and Systems Engineering Department
University Politehnica Bucharest
Bucharest, Romania

Guo Ren
China University of Geosciences
Wuhan, China

Shashi Shekhar
Department of Computer Science
University of Minnesota
Minneapolis, Minnesota

Mukesh Singhal
Cloud Lab
University of California, Merced
Merced, California

Eleni Stai
School of Computer & Communication Sciences
École Polytechnique Fédérale de Lausanne
Lausanne, Switzerland

Marcello Trovati
Department of Computer Science
Edge Hill University
Ormskirk, United Kingdom

Yulei Wu
University of Exeter
Exeter, United Kingdom

Liqun Yu
Department of Mathematics
Washington University in St. Louis
St. Louis, Missouri

Zuo Yuan
University of Exeter
Exeter, United Kingdom

Aziyati Yusoff
Universiti Tenaga Nasional
Selangor, Malaysia

Salman Yussof
Universiti Tenaga Nasional
Selangor, Malaysia

Deze Zeng
China University of Geosciences
Wuhan, China

Aidong Zhang
Department of Computer Science and Engineering
State University of New York
Buffalo, New York

Chuanrong Zhang
Department of Geography & Center for Environmental Sciences and Engineering
University of Connecticut
Storrs, Connecticut

Tian Zhao
Department of Computer Science
University of Wisconsin-Milwaukee
Milwaukee, Wisconsin

Vincent W. Zheng
Advanced Digital Sciences Center
Singapore

Michelle Mengxia Zhu
Department of Computer Science
Montclair State University
Montclair, New Jersey

Yujia Zhu
University of Exeter
Exeter, United Kingdom

Albert Zomaya
The University of Sydney
Sydney, Australia

Liudong Zuo
Computer Science Department
California State University, Dominguez Hills
Carson, California

I

BASICS OF NETWORKED BIG DATA

Chapter 1

A Survey of Big Data and Computational Intelligence in Networking

Yujia Zhu, Yulei Wu, and Geyong Min

University of Exeter
Exeter, United Kingdom

Albert Zomaya

The University of Sydney
Sydney, Australia

Fei Hu

University of Alabama
Tuscaloosa, Alabama

CONTENTS

1.1 Introduction

With the rapid development of computing capabilities and storage techniques, there is no doubt that we are facing a series of opportunities and challenges brought about by the big data era. Simply put, big data not only injects wisdom into decision-making and performance improvement but also poses a great threat to traditional data processing techniques. For example, NeteaseMusic is a popular musical software among Chinese teenagers and it is well known for a particular function, Daily Recommendation, which aims to provide users with the songs in which they may be interested. It tracks what songs individual users listen to most frequently and what pages they look at; it usually develops some relevant tags for each song, such as “sad,” “pleasure,” “Country music,” and “Quiet.” Besides these tags, it is able to utilize some initial information like similar singers and albums. This software develops algorithms to better understand the customers by taking advantage of the digital data mentioned above. Customers can respond to each song with "like" or "dislike" by highlighting, or not, a heart tag beneath the song. This process is similar to a training process in machine learning. According to these valuable data, indicating users' preference NeteaseMusic can recommend songs to users with very high accuracy.

The success of NeteaseMusic can showcase the benefits that big data brings—smarter decisions and better predictions. By utilizing it appropriately, we can explore some fresh areas so far dominated by intuition and gut. Big data spreads to every aspect in people's daily lives, changing long-standing ideas about the value of experience, the nature of expertise, and the practice of management [1].

Networking has become an indispensable part of the modern world, providing convenient access to the Internet, remote communication, information exchange, etc. As mentioned above, big data also has a great influence on networking. The amount of data has exploded in recent years, with a transformation from traditional simple-structured physical networks to complex-structured virtual networks. Considering network management, a novel method is to collect unstructured system logs (which can reach the magnitude of terabytes (TB) per day) and analyze these valuable data to evaluate system performance or tackle faults. So far, we have explored what opportunities networked big data brings, but the challenges are also significant. In the next chapter, a variety of challenges will be discussed.

1.2 Comprehensive Understanding of Networked Big Data

Networked big data, in fact, is not simply another way of saying "analytics" or large amount of data. In addition to the common features of veracity and value, networked big data has higher volume, velocity, and variety compared with other forms of big data.

1. *Volume*: According to a recent report from IBM, 2.5 quintillion bytes of data are created every day [2]. The Web includes various sources of data like cookies, browsing history, and so on, which makes it an extraordinary data set. Many search engines like Google and Yahoo are responsible for dealing with billions of user access requests every day. When entering the keyword "big data" in Google Chrome, about 341,000,000 results are returned in 0.59 seconds (as of May 2017).

2. *Velocity*: The large volume of data has increased the complexity of processing and storing, while for some applications, real-time or nearly real-time data analysis is much more important given the high speed of data creation. Given troubleshooting in networks, this has been an open question in academic and industrial fields. From traditional faults in the

hardware components like routers or links down to virtual machines, there are a number of fault management tools such as HP Openview and OpenNMS, which focus on real-time fault localization or prediction. Thus, how to quickly and accurately handle faults in order to reduce human intervention is critical to making a company more competitive.

3. *Variety*: Networked big data comes from various sources: for instance, messages, images or videos from social networks, event logs and configuration parameters from systems, measurements from sensors, and many more. Specifically speaking, every second, on average, around 6000 tweets are posted on Twitter, which corresponds to over 350,000 tweets sent per minute, 500 million tweets per day, and around 200 billion tweets per year [3]. On 4 October 2012, the first presidential debate between President Barack Obama and Governor Mitt Romney triggered more than 10 million tweets within 2 hours [4]. A vast number of users post tweets in various formats such as texts, images, or videos contributing to data diversity.

1.2.1 Challenges for networked big data

A network application in the era of big data usually involves data sources from different geographically distributed data centers. Thus, in addition to the general nature of big data such as large volume, high velocity, and high variety, networked big data possesses many unique features, which are summarized below. These unique features also bring some research issues of networked big data, as shown in Figure 1.1.

1.2.1.1 Distributed and decentralized data collection and storage

An emerging wave of Internet deployments, most notably the Internet of Things (IoT) [5] and the integration of IoT and fog computing [6], often depend on a distributed networking system to collect data from geographically distributed

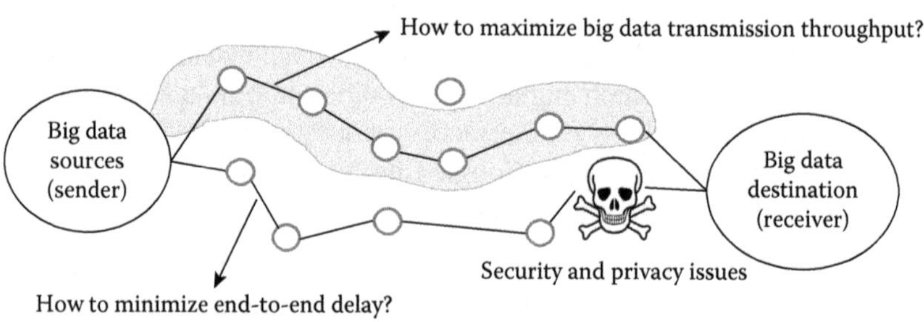

Figure 1.1: Networked big data: Research issues.

sources, such as sensors and data centers. For example, visualizing data collected within the IoT are geo-related and sparsely distributed. Internet geographic information system (GIS)-based solutions are required to cope with this challenge. Apache Hadoop [7] is well known for its distributed storage and processing of big data. Hadoop Distributed File System (HDFS) [8] is the core part of the storage system in Hadoop, which is a distributed file system that stores data on commodity machines, providing very high aggregate bandwidth across the clusters. HDFS was inspired by Google file system (GFS) [9], which is the most widely adopted mechanism for distributed file systems.

1.2.1.2 Distributed and parallel data processing

In light of the way the networked big data are collected, it is straightforward to process these data in a distributed and parallel manner. There have been several well-known frameworks available for distributed big data processing, e.g., Apache Hadoop [7], Apache Storm [10], Apache Spark [11], and Apache Flink [12]. Hadoop is the first major big data processing framework that provides batch processing based on its MapReduce processing engine. Since it heavily leverages permanent storage, each task involves multiple instances of reading and writing operations. When using Hadoop, time should not be a significant factor. In contrast to batch processing, stream processing systems compute over data as it enters the system, and thus could well serve the processing with near real-time demands. Storm is the first major stream processing framework for big data analytics that focuses on extremely low latency, but does not provide a batch processing mode. Apache Spark provides a hybrid processing system, where it is a batch processing framework with stream processing capabilities. Spark focuses on speeding up batch processing workloads by offering full in-memory computation and processing optimization. It provides a good candidate for those with diverse processing workloads. Apache Flink offers a stream processing framework with the support for traditional batch processing models. It treats batch processing as an extension of stream processing by reading a bounded data set off persistent storage.

1.2.1.3 More complex and evolving relationships among data

Under the distributed and decentralized control of large volume, heterogeneous, autonomous sources, big data seeks to explore the complex and ever-changing relationship among data. Apart from the great challenges that large volume poses to big data, how to effectively extract the relationships underneath data has attracted particular attention not only in academic but also in industrial fields. People establish friendship circles based on common hobbies, biological relationships, and many more in human society, while these social connections also exist in the cyber world. For example, a majority of social networks recommend people or messages by utilizing social functions such as friend-connections and followers. Mining the correlations between users' behavior and preference can reveal some underlying but valuable information for these social network operators. In this dynamic world, there is no doubt that these relationships evolve all the time, temporally and spatially. Another example is troubleshooting in networks, where topology graphs can be regarded as spatial information while key performance indicators (KPI) or traffic records represented in time series can be regarded as temporal information. Kimura et al. [13] once claimed that log messages should be characterized as spatial-temporal data, since event logs are usually generated from distributed hosts, routers, or switches spanning across several geographical locations (spatial information) and include timestamps indicating generating time (temporal information). Based on deep insights of spatial-temporal features of logs, they proposed two novel techniques, statistical template extraction (STE) and log tensor factorization (LTF), to capture particular patterns of log messages which provide useful knowledge into root cause analysis.

1.2.1.4 Heterogeneous data representation

Traditional data mining algorithms usually require inputs to be homogeneous, that is to say, inputs should possess similar formats. However, as mentioned above, big data comes from heterogeneous sources, making traditional mining algorithms inapplicable to handle this problem in the forthcoming big data revolution. Most objects and data in the real world are of multiple types and interconnected, forming complex, heterogeneous but often semistructured information networks [14]. There are three main challenges that make mining heterogeneous networks a new game:

1. Information propagates across heterogeneous nodes and links.
2. Rich semantic information should be carefully and effectively parsed to extract the representative network structures.
3. User demands should be taken into consideration to automatically select the right relationships.

Sun and Han [14] proposed a novel semistructured heterogeneous network modeling focusing on the objects and the interactions among them. In this way, rich semantic information and valuable schema-level information can be retained. A directed graph with an object-type mapping function and a link-type mapping function is utilized to represent the heterogeneous information networks effectively.

1.2.2 Requirement engineering of networked big data for computational intelligence

Intelligent computation techniques can be translated into "machine learning" algorithms that are employed in a range of computing tasks where designing and programming explicit algorithms with good performance is difficult or unfeasible. There is a large amount of research taking place to combine advanced machine learning techniques with networked big data analysis. Shang et al. [15] suggested a novel fault diagnosis model of computer networks based on rough set and back-propagation (BP) neural networks. They retrieved faults as a series of rules and reduced them to a minimum diagnosis rules by rough set theory; then a neural network was designed to learn from these rules in order to identify and localize faults quickly and accurately. Sankaran et al. [16] designed a hardware framework embedded with a machine learning coprocessor to emphasize intrusion detection in case of attacks unknown for the signature library. They chose a vector space model with a K-nearest neighbors (K-NN) classifier and a radial basis function (RBF)-based classifier, concluding that machine learning processors enable improvement in energy saving, processing speed, and detection accuracy, especially dealing with big data sets. Chung et al. [17] addressed the significant advantages that deep neural networks (DNNs) demonstrate in pattern recognition applications, regardless of the biggest drawback of computation resource consumption and training time reaching a tenfold addition compared to traditional techniques. In order to cope with this, a data-parallel Hessian-free second-order optimization algorithm is used to train DNN and implemented by a large-scale speech task on Blue Gene/Q computer system due to the excellent interprocessor communication ability of this system. The results show that performance on Blue Gene/Q scales up to 4096 processes lossless in accuracy and that enables the training of DNN using billions of inputs in just a few hours.

1.2.3 Representation and modeling of networked big data

Networked big data possesses unstructured, semistructured, and structured formats. This nature hinders its representation and modeling, which are of paramount importance in the process of big data analytics. Several existing representation and modeling methods have been reported in the current literature, e.g., graph representation, dynamic representation, and matrix representation [18].

1.2.3.1 Graph representation

Graphs consisting of nodes and edges can be applied to a variety of situations. For example, in social networks, nodes can be regarded as individuals and connected edges representing two users build a relationship. Network topology can be represented as nodes for hosts (or switches, routers) and edges for links among them. With a rapid increase in the amount of data, the corresponding scale of graphs dramatically expands to even millions of nodes and edges. Coping with such large graphs can be an extremely complex task considering efficiently extracting valuable underlying knowledge encoded into graphs. There are a lot of techniques to simplify and refine graphs summed up in three categories: graph spectra [19], graph summarization, and graph compression.

Graphs can be represented by an adjacency matrix and mapped into its spectrum domain, filtering out small elements by exploiting application-aware thresholds. Finally, a smaller graph can be obtained by means of an inverse transform. Sahneh et al. [20] utilized Laplacian spectra to represent transition rate graphs in spreading process modeling of complex networks.

The original concept of graph summarization comes from the database community [21] and aims to provide users with small and informative graphs based on attributes and relationships of interest.

Shi et al. [22] addressed an Influence Graph Summarization (IGS) problem abstracting individual influence from complex citation networks. They proposed a summarization scheme based on matrix factorization techniques to handle this problem and tested it on real-world citation networks to prove that this method outperforms the previous method in visual effects and quantitative IGS objective optimization.

Redundancies are hidden in nodes belonging to similar communities; graph compression in fact focuses on identifying communities. Lim et al. [23] discovered the importance of hubs or high-degree nodes disconnecting graphs, gradually removed them from graphs and finally acquired a smaller giant connected component. This compression method proves more suitable for real-world issues than a conventional "caveman community."

1.2.3.2 Dynamic representation

Graph representation can be regarded as a static representation of valid network topology and properties, while in practice a large number of networks are dynamically characterized. How to efficiently represent dynamic features of networks such as topology and configuration has received notable attention from researchers and practitioners. A majority of current approaches take advantage of visualization techniques. Burch et al. [24] chose a series of timesteps and represented each stage as a single graph contributing to a dynamic and hierarchically organized graph set for visualization. Mashima et al. [25] visualized user traffic on radio station and TV-viewing patterns from an Internet Protocol Television (IPTV) service under the assistance of a geographic map metaphor in coping with large-scale dynamic data sets.

1.2.3.3 Tensor

Although many studies have been performed on networked big data processing, very few have addressed the problems of representing the various formats of data with a simple model and extracting the core data sets that are smaller but still contain valuable information. Kuang et al. [26] targeted these issues and proposed a unified tensor model to represent data with various formats. With the help of tensor extension operators, the authors represented the various types of data as subtensors and merged them to a unified tensor. They further devised an incremental high-order singular value decomposition method (IHOSVD) to extract the core tensor, which is able to update the orthogonal bases and compute the new core tensor by recursively applying the incremental matrix decomposition algorithm. In comparison with the traditional approaches of data dimensionality reduction—e.g., principal component analysis (PCA) [27], incremental singular value decomposition (SVD) [28], and dynamic tensor analysis (DTA) [29], which are mainly used for low dimension reduction—IHOSVD is particularly suitable for handling high-dimensional data and extracting the core data sets from streaming networked big data with a relatively low time consumption.

1.2.4 Security and privacy issues on networked big data

Every day, people surf the Internet, browse websites, post messages, and share personal information like cookies through their own digital devices. This can pose a potential threat to privacy issues through identity theft, online banking abuse, password leakage, and so on. Information security suffers from the proliferation of devices connected to the Internet and connected with each other. Big data security issues are related to a set of risk areas, which includes information lifecycle, data creation, and collection processes. Despite complex initial characteristics, ultimately, the objective remains the same as traditional data types, devoted to preserving confidentiality, integrity, and availability. Due to user/data mobility requirements, conventional security measures such as firewalls are no longer suitable for big data scenarios. Cloud Security Alliance (CSA) [30], a non-profit organization with a mission to promote the use of best practices for providing security assurance within Cloud Computing and provide education on the uses of Cloud Computing to help secure all other forms of computing, has created a Big Data Working Group, which has focused on the major challenges to implement secure Big Data services. According to CSA, security and privacy challenges can be categorized according to four aspects: infrastructure security (e.g., secure distributed computation using MapReduce), data privacy (e.g., data mining that preserves privacy/granular access), data management (e.g., secure data provenance and storage), and integrity and reactive security (e.g., real-time monitoring of anomalies and attacks).

When considering reasonable solutions to secure networked big data, in-depth inquiry should be focused on different data sources, complex relationships, and unstructured data formats. Encryption, masking, and tokenization are regular approaches for sensitive data protection. Modern security networking issues gradually expand from enterprise to the public Cloud. The internal behavior model of Cloud computing consists of a big data storage service retrieval layer (where users match and invoke resources from Cloud service packages according to specific demands), a data refinement task decomposition layer (where complex tasks will be split and disseminated to proper locations to maximize resource leveraging rate), a Cloud computing optimization combination evaluation layer (which will optimize and integrate results under thoughtful resource utilizing plans to achieve the best Quality of Service (QoS) target), and a big data Cloud computing algorithm selection layer (where optimal execution strategy will be selected according to different requirements). Considering these features of Cloud computing systems, a four-level security framework was proposed by Cui [31], involving copyright authentication, virtual task decomposition, collaborative network password protection, disaster recovery scheme development, and so on.

1.2.5 Wireless big data

First, as demonstrated in Ref. [32], wireless big data can be simply explained as a wide range of massive data generated, collected, and stored in wireless networks by wireless devices and users. Wireless big data has a significant influence over network deployment and service quality, and poses a big challenge to traditional solutions due to its dynamic data sets and stochastic nature. Lijun et al. [32] categorized wireless big data through two aspects: socioecological and specific application. From the socioecological perspective, big data can be explained as three types: primordial wireless big data (data sets generated by massive wireless network users such as wireless access behavior), derived wireless big data (spectrum, transmission, access, and network data served for reliable communication such as resource allocation of transmission signals), and developing wireless big data (data collected from performance testing and evaluation processes). From the specific application perspective, categories can be simply described as cellular networks, Wi-Fi hotspots, smart grids, wireless sensor networks (WSNs), IoT, and so on.

Researches have explored massive efficient data representation as a solution in wireless networking domain. He et al. [33] proposed a unified data analytic model based on the random matrix theory for tackling problems of dynamic data collected from multiple sources. A variety of data types such as signaling data, traffic data, and heterogeneous data are studied to evaluate model performance in mobile cellular networks. As demonstrated in Ref. [34], large-scale random matrices are applied to model distributed spectrum sensing and network monitoring in a multiple-input multiple-output (MIMO) system. According to specific features such as the large scale and the heterogeneous nature which indicate complex interrelationships among data, unstructured data should be taken into consideration as demonstrated in Ref. [34]. A number of subtensors are leveraged to transform various data types into unified tensor representation, then dimension reduction is implemented by SVD method, and, finally, a real case study is simulated on intelligent transportation to evaluate the performance of the proposed model.

Considering separate temporal, spatial characteristics, and complicated spatial-temporal interconnection relationships of wireless big data, some novel and effective methods are studied in recent research, including time series analysis, machine learning techniques, and game theory. The authors in Ref. [35] proved the potential value of time series analysis in traffic pattern recognition tasks. Regular behavior patterns are extracted to predict future patterns. Deep learning, developed from conventional neural networks, has become a powerful tool in modeling high-level data representation. In Ref. [36], Apache Spark, a distributed framework supporting deep learning, is utilized to apply deep learning to wireless communication with millions of records. Game theory contributes to intelligent rational decision-making in many fields such as economics, psychology, computer science, and so on. The authors in Ref. [37] introduced a network management approach based on a multiple cognitive agent-based divide-and-conquer strategy and the Markovian game-theoretic model.

Apart from data itself, one factor that cannot be neglected is the wireless channel, which conveys information from end to end. Two commonly accepted methods are deterministic model and stochastic simulation. The former requires enormous spectrum resources consumption, while the latter lacks precision assurance. It is important to seek a balancing point between them to build an accurate channel impulse response (CIR) environment. Network design and optimization is another key factor to achieve energy saving, scalability, and flexibility. Moreover, a wide range of applications such as user mobility analysis and smart grid, making use of wireless big data, can be found in the survey [32].

1.3 Network Architecture for Big Data Transmissions

Without the foundation of a strong, robust, and flexible network, no reliable data can be obtained, resulting in big losses in academic and industrial fields. For example, business enterprises may lose clients due to data loss considering individual demands, and researchers cannot have access to big data centers distributed across worldwide. A vast amount of network architecture is designed to ensure scalability and flexibility during the data transmission phase. In this chapter, various aspects related to this topic will be discussed.

1.3.1 Novel collection protocols for networked big data

As mentioned above, networked big data usually comes from geographic distributed sources. Hence, how to collect valuable network information efficiently and securely has been an open research problem recently. The main research field of this topic concentrates on WSNs or ad hoc networks utilizing sensors to capture useful information. Two examples of this are outlined below. Guo et al. [38] proposed a novel and secure mechanism for collecting information from Internet of Vehicles (IoV, an extension of IoT contributing to unified management in smart transportation), such as vehicle location, speed, and driving route. IoV basically consists of vehicle nodes (which are responsible for data collection), sink nodes (which are responsible for data transfer), and big data center (which is responsible for data integration and management). The main challenges for this ad hoc network are dynamic topological nodes modeling due to high-speed moving vehicles and users' privacy preservation policy assurance. First, vehicles should be registered in a data center before connecting to the network, after which a single sign-on algorithm is utilized to associate authenticated vehicles with the big data center. Finally, a secure information collection scheme is applied with lots of operational functions, such as integrity, to protect messages against modification or destruction.

Given a more general application scenario in WSNs, a traditional data collection process selects relay nodes (closer to the sink) to transfer the data, which are from the nodes beyond the communication range of sink node, to the sink node, resulting in faster energy consumption of the relay nodes that are easily disconnected from networks [39]. In order to tackle this, mobile data collectors (MDC), roaming over the whole sensing field while pausing at some points to collect data in short-range communication for energy saving, are brought into use. Three stages collaboratively contribute to data collection using MDC in WSN [40]:

1. *Discovery*: Sensors identify the mobile collector existing in their communication range.
2. *Data transfer*: Ensure maximum data throughput in minimal contact time.
3. *Routing*: The collected data from multiple nodes is forwarded toward the sink or base station.

There are two common strategies in data collection protocols using MDC: mobile sink and mobile relay nodes protocols. The mobile sink is characterized by the moving sink which moves in a predesigned path and sends a message to sensors in its communication range. Sensors receiving the message will identify the sink and respond to it with collected data. The mobile relay nodes try to strike a balance between the tour length of the mobile relay and the relay hop count of the sensors in data aggregation to save energy [41].

1.3.2 Efficient management of networked big data and distributed data systems

Network logs, which usually consist of timestamps and messages, can reveal the health condition and performance degradation of networks. However, due to the unstructured text messages of network logs generated by vendor-specific rules and their extremely high generating velocity, this still remains an open challenge. Kimura et al. [13] tackled these obstacles by building two novel techniques: STE and LTF. STE is responsible for automatically extracting primary log templates from unstructured messages by utilizing clustering, and LTF aims to build a statistical model capturing spatial-temporal patterns of log messages. Such spatial-temporal patterns provide useful insights into understanding the impacts and root cause of hidden network events. Wang et al. [42] proposed an efficient learning algorithm to extract indexable fault signatures that encode temporal evolution of events generated by a network fault as well as topological relationships among the nodes where these events occur. With the help of novel spatial-temporal indexing structures, efficient and online signature matching can be successfully implemented.

Network traffic or data traffic, which is defined as the amount of data moving across a network by a given path in a unit time, can also usually be leveraged to perform fault localization. Hajji et al. [43] built a normal network operation baseline based on the stochastic approximation of the maximum likelihood function. Network traffic is under monitoring by agents and a large deviation from the baseline indicates a network anomaly.

A distributed system can be a communication protocol, a database, or a computer application divided across multiple processing elements intercommunicating through a wired or wireless data network, mainly aiming at improving computing ability in this big data era. Wang and Lemmon [44] proposed a distributed event-triggering scheme that was applied in distributed network control systems (consisting of numerous coupled subsystems which are geographically distributed and exchange information over a communication network) coping with packet loss and transmission delays. A subsystem broadcasts its state information to its neighbors only when the local state error exceeds a specified threshold. It is able to make broadcast decisions using its locally sampled data. It can also locally predict the maximal allowable number of successive data dropouts (MANSD) and the state-based deadlines for transmission delays.

The authors in Ref. [45] concentrated on bandwidth utilization and processing cost reduction in distributed data systems by minimizing the amount of internal data updates. The key characteristic is to rely on frequent updates instead of immediate updates to synchronize values among interdependent data fields scattered across the system. A data committal is postponed to guarantee that all the impacted data fields will always be fully synchronized.

1.3.3 Context-aware networked big data processing for computational intelligence

Dey [46] first made a definition of "context" as "any information that can be used to characterize the situation of an entity." Considering a specific scenario in cyberspace, context awareness, originated from ubiquitous computing (which seeks to solve linking changes in computer systems' environment), refers to the ability of mobile devices to sense and react according to their surroundings. Sophisticated and general context models have been proposed to adapt interfaces, tailor the set of application-aware data, increase the precision of information retrieval, discover services, make the user interaction implicit, or build smart environments [47]. For instance, a context-aware mobile phone may sense that it is currently in the library and that the user has entered the reading room. Hence, this smart phone may conclude that noise is forbidden in this area and turn off the phone's ringtones automatically.

As for next generation network management, context awareness is an indispensable feature to obtain smarter systems and ensure that user demands are satisfied in advance regardless of evolving environment. Special infrastructures such as middleware, libraries, toolkits, and frameworks are needed to implement context-aware applications during the development process. Among all the infrastructures, middleware outperforms others in terms of providing plenty of context cycle functionalities including acquisition, modeling, reasoning, and distribution in a regular way with special abstractions. Bilen and Canberk [48] proposed a middleware infrastructure based on binary context tree modeling technique (priority rule and stack data structure are used to represent context attributes in a well-structured and standard format). They implemented this approach in an exemplary smart workplace scenario and showed 12% better time efficiency and 50% more devices connected to the distributed access point.

The rapid increase in the number of mobile devices users poses a new challenge to build proper relationships between "things," "people," "places," and "data." The authors in Ref. [49] introduced a flexible and powerful framework called Context-Aware Networks for the Design of Connected Things (CANthings) to enrich IoT eco-systems. Self-adaption is addressed to enhance reliable communication between different devices with changing environments.

1.4 Analysis and Processing of Networked Big Data

Networked big data is usually collected from a wide range of geographically distributed data centers under decentralized control, hence demonstrating heterogeneous and distributed characteristics that increase the complexity for data analytics and processing. Six parts of this research area will be explored, which are categorized as distributed machine learning algorithms, data mining techniques, online prediction, sparse matrix vector multiplication (SpMV), high-performance analytics platform, and scalable and efficient networking architectures and algorithms for computing and storage, respectively.

1.4.1 *Distributed machine learning algorithms for networked big data*

Machine learning paradigms are dedicated to uncovering new knowledge hidden behind historical data, providing proof for data-driven predictions and decisions in a wide range of fields. As for networked big data analytics, a variety of machine learning algorithms such as decision trees, Bayesian networks, and expert systems (including rule-based, case-based, and model-based reasoning) are studied in recent research topics. The most extraordinary advantage of decision trees is the interpretable ability for network operators to gain a better understanding of network management with less manual effort. A spam detection scheme in social networks based on decision trees and K-NN algorithms is proposed in Ref. [50]. A real data set from Twitter is labeled manually and feature selection methods are then leveraged to extract useful features to feed into the decision tree classifier for distinguishing spam tweets from normal ones. Several performance metrics including F-measure, true positive rate (TPR), and false positive rate (FPR) are selected to evaluate the efficiency of the proposed scheme via a well-known machine learning tool named Weka. Bayesian network (BN), which is different from conventional deterministic models, is a probabilistic graphical model that represents a set of random variables and their conditional dependencies via a directed acyclic graph (DAG) to implement uncertain knowledge inference. The authors in Ref. [51] introduced a novel challenge to extend classic BN generating methods to data-intensive computing environments. They tackled this problem by proposing a parallel and incremental approach learning from massive, distributed, and evolving data. First, a MapReduce-based (aiming to provide users with resource allocation in distributed manner) scoring and search scheme is exploited to compute marginal probabilities of various subsets according to each sample, and then a set of candidate graphic structures will be generated and optimal network structure can be learned by the hill climbing search. Experiments on two real-world belief networks revealed the accuracy and effectiveness of this BN incremental learning scheme from performance metrics such as execution time and speedup. Expert systems mimic thinking patterns of human experts and transform professional experience into a knowledge base understandable by computers to achieve intelligent reasoning and decision-making. In [52], an expert system was built according to environment data collected from campus WSNs to assist authorities in choosing the right options for campus development. Subasinghe and Kodithuwakku [53] proposed an expert system based on the hidden Markov model (HMM), recognizing user behavior patterns to identify risky unauthorized clients with respect to their activity logs accumulated for years in social networks.

1.4.2 Distributed data mining with networked big data

As interdisciplinary subfields of computer science, it is difficult to give a precise definition of the difference between data mining and machine learning. They have a lot of overlaps in algorithms at the intersection of artificial intelligence and statistics. From the data analytics perspective, machine learning focuses on knowledge prediction from historical experience, while data mining aims at knowledge discovery from massive data sets. In other words, data mining utilizes similar techniques to extract patterns also known as unsupervised learning such as clustering, associate rule mining for dependencies. Data mining is a commonly accepted method for processing networked big data, including anomaly detection, fault diagnosis, and so on.

The authors in Ref. [54] proposed an intrusion detection system, which is key for assurance in integrity, availability, and confidentiality of computing resources. Averaged one-dependence estimators (AODE), a recent enhancement of the naïve Bayesian method, averages all models generated by a traditional one-dependence estimator and is utilized to classify attack types based on the NHL-KDD data set. High detection rate with low False Alarm Rate (FAR) demonstrated the effectiveness of this proposed approach.

A Network failure log (NFL) stores valuable information about network performance, such as CPU usage rate, execution error, configuration updates, and so on. However, due to the unstructured format and high volume of NFLs, powerful and efficient data mining methods are needed to handle them. The authors in Ref. [55] addressed the importance of proactive self-healing mechanisms in low latency, high Quality of Experience (QoE), and minimal recovery time. To achieve this goal, five data mining approaches—K-means clustering, fuzzy C-means clustering, local outlier factor, local outlier probabilities, and self-organizing maps—are implemented on an NFL data set to extract typical hidden spatial-temporal patterns which are then exploited for future trend prediction. Experiments indicated that SOM outperforms other algorithms in terms of sum of squared errors.

With the increasing popularity of mobile devices like smart phones and laptops in recent years, intelligent resource management in worldwide wireless networks has attracted public attention. Latif and Adnan [56] investigated a variety of ANN frameworks to develop base-station intelligent agents which enable real-time forecasts of on-demand resources scheduling. Training examples in this literature came from a 6-month wireless traffic data set acquired from the Pakistan Telecommunication Company Ltd. Regular behavior patterns were discovered within traffic data and stored for future analysis to achieve satisfactory QoS.

1.4.3 Online prediction with networked big data

Big data-driven analysis plays a crucial role in the networking area, where real-time prediction is addressed to ensure stability and reliability. Traffic flow data contains rich treasure with respect to intelligent system management and minimal recovery time for business use, while complex and evolving associations make it a challenging task to undertake proactive traffic analysis. Accuracy and timeliness are two key factors considering efficient and appropriate traffic data processing. A common online traffic data prediction framework including two modules (offline distributed training [ODT] and online parallel prediction [OPP]) is introduced in Ref. [57]. The offline training phase takes inputs as a large amount of historical data and outputs refined correlations of these input data.

Then current observed data combined with correlations extracted from ODT are utilized to generate online predictions based on a novel computing model in the OPP module. The empirical study on real-world traffic flow data proves its superiority over other benchmark methods in terms of accuracy, speedup, scale-up, and size-up.

The IoT is a global infrastructure capable of integrating the physical world into cyberspace and contributes to improved efficiency, accuracy, and economic benefit in addition to less human intervention. The authors in Ref. [58] proposed an online QoS provisioning algorithm for bandwidth allocation of heterogeneous home networks. General regression neural networks (GRNN) is selected to implement online service response prediction based on previous transactions' storing bandwidth usage and corresponding service feedback. Experiments indicate that the simplicity, effectiveness, and efficiency of the algorithm are well suited for dynamic environments.

Routing scheme selection is one of the most considerable tasks when talking about network design. In [59], accurate online flow size prediction was proven helpful for routing, load balancing, and scheduling improvement in network simulations, although this task must be done in a real-time manner due to evolving flow patterns. Three online predictors based on neural networks, Gaussian process regression, and Bayesian moment matching are implemented on three real traffic data sets to evaluate the predictive nature of a set of features.

Detecting hot topics has a significant influence for topic recommendation and public opinions guidance in online social networks. A continuous temporal User topic participant (UTP) model was investigated in Ref. [60]. Users' interests, friendship circles, and unexpected events were used to model dynamic user behavior patterns for predicting hot topics in online social networks.

1.4.4 Sparse matrix vector multiplication on distributed architectures for networked big data

SpMV is one of the most widely used kernels in scientific computing [61] due to its outstanding performance of multiple applications in economic modeling and information retrieval. However, sparse representations suffer from higher instruction and storage overheads. The authors in Ref. [61] introduced shortcomings of conventional implementations on single-core cache-based microprocessor systems and proposed multicore parallel optimization solutions to overcome these obstacles. As mentioned in Ref. [62], SpMV was especially suitable for machine learning applications handling massive unstructured data (rapidly approaching TB range). They modified conventional algorithm into two distinct phases: a scaled matrix is generated in the first stage and then reduced in the next stage. Irregular big data sets are utilized on a large-scale POWER8 SMP system demonstrating comparable performance to a 256-node cluster. Networked big data, which is usually characterized as unstructured, large-volume, heterogeneous, and distributed data, can be transformed into matrix formation by using feature selection methodology such as SVD and nonnegative matrix factorization (NMF) [63] presented a lossy data compression algorithm based on SVD in a smart distributed system. A significant amount of data transmitted through communication networks is discarded and then accurately reconstructed.

The paper [64] introduced a nonsmooth NMF algorithm for learning sparse representation of observed data. Experiments in cyberspace and real-world data proved the effectiveness and efficiency of the proposed scheme compared to other benchmarks.

1.4.5 High-performance analytics platform for networked big data

There are a variety of high-performance computing (HPC) platforms, widely applied in areas of economics, computer networks, and so on. For example, SAP HANA [65], a new generation of in-memory database as well as an integrated analytics platform, provides higher processing speed and accuracy. The authors in Ref. [66] took advantage of the HANA platform to implement a real-time event analysis and monitoring system (REAMS) since logs reflect system status and users' behaviors, both internal and external, thus ensuring system reliability and security. They collected user events, especially logon and logoff events from multiple sources, and stored in a unified format for further efficient analysis. The Cloud environment is extremely suitable for streaming data analysis due to many aspects. For example, Cloud deployment on virtual machines provides application portability, platform independence, and dynamic resource allocation for specific tasks. Moreover, Cloud-based tools enable rich performance information collection and application optimization. Chef [67], Puppet [68], and Ansible [69] are currently widely used Cloud automation tools for single Cloud provider application deployment, while GEANT network infrastructure [70], a Zero touch provisioning, operations, and management (ZTPOM) concept implementation, allows inter-Cloud service delivery and provisioning. As for some specific applications in networked big data platform deployment, considering a currently growing phenomenon that cybercriminals spread malicious payloads through spam, AlMahmoud et al. [71] proposed a privacy-preserving collaborative spam detection platform (Spamdoop) built on top of a standard MapReduce facility. Network designers often use simulators to pre-evaluate the performance of a designed network with artificial network traffic prior to actual deployment. The authors in Ref. [72] introduced a novel method for modeling network traffic patterns of big data platforms, extracting communication behaviors, and replaying them instead of packet traces. Experiments proved the reliability and scalability of this methodology when compared to real traffic.

1.5 Conclusions

Networked big data shares many common characteristics with traditional big data while also posing its own unique challenges. Much research work has been involved in tackling the issues raised, and some significant progress has also been achieved. However, there are still several unsolved and open problems, such as data correlation in virtual network environment, which motivates researchers to gain deeper insights in this field.

References

[1] McAfee, A., and E. Brynjolfsson. Big data: The management revolution. *Harvard Business Review* 90(10), 60–68, 2012.

[2] IBM. *What is big data: Bring big data to the enterprise*. Available from: http://www-01.ibm.com/software/data/bigdata/ (accessed March 3, 2016).

[3] Available from: www.internetlivestats.com/twitter-statistics/

[4] *Twitter Blog, Dispatch from the Denver Debate*. Available from: http://blog.twitter.com/2012/10/dispatch-from-denver-debate.html (accessed October, 2012).

[5] Ma, H. Internet of Things: Objectives and scientific challenges. *Journal of Computer Science and Technology* 26(6), 919–924, 2011.

[6] Bonomi, F., R. Milito, J. Zhu, and S. Addepalli. Fog computing and its role in the Internet of Things. In *Proceedings of the first edition of the MCC Workshop on Mobile Cloud Computing (MCC'12)*, pp. 13–16, 2012.

[7] Available from: http://hadoop.apache.org

[8] Available from: https://hadoop.apache.org/docs/r1.2.1/hdfs_design.html

[9] Ghemawat, S., H. Gobioff, and S.-T. Leung. The Google file system. *ACM SIGOPS Operating Systems Review* 37(5), 29–43, 2003.

[10] Available from: http://storm.apache.org

[11] Available from: http://spark.apache.org

[12] Available from: https://flink.apache.org

[13] Kimura, T., et al. Spatio-temporal factorization of log data for understanding network events. INFOCOM, 2014 Proceedings IEEE. IEEE, 2014.

[14] Sun, Y., and J. Han. Mining heterogeneous information networks: A structural analysis approach. *ACM SIGKDD Explorations Newsletter* 14(2), 20–28, 2013.

[15] Shang, Z., et al. Fault diagnosis of computer network based on rough sets and BP neural network. In 2012 8th International Conference on Wireless Communications, Networking and Mobile Computing (WiCOM), IEEE, 2012.

[16] Sankaran, R., and R.A. Calix. On the feasibility of an embedded machine learning processor for intrusion detection. In 2016 IEEE International Conference on Big Data (Big Data), IEEE, 2016.

[17] Chung, I.-H., et al. Parallel deep neural network training for big data on blue gene/q. *IEEE Transactions on Parallel and Distributed Systems* 28(6), 1703–1714, 2017.

[18] Yu, S., M. Liu, W. Dou, X. Liu, and S. Zhou. Networking for big data: A survey. *IEEE Communications Surveys & Tutorials* 19(1), 531–549, 2017.

[19] Van Mieghem, P. *Graph spectra for complex networks*. Cambridge, UK: Cambridge University Press, 2010.

[20] Sahneh, F.D., C. Scoglio, and P. Van Mieghem. Generalized epidemic mean-field model for spreading processes over multilayer complex networks. *IEEE/ACM Transactions on Networking* 21(5), 1609–1620, 2013.

[21] Tian, Y., R.A. Hankins, and J.M. Patel. Efficient aggregation for graph summarization. In *Proceedings of the 2008 ACM SIGMOD International Conference on Management of Data*, ACM, 2008.

[22] Shi, L., et al. Vegas: Visual influence graph summarization on citation networks. *IEEE Transactions on Knowledge and Data Engineering* 27(12), 3417–3431, 2015.

[23] Lim, Y., U. Kang, and C. Faloutsos. Slashburn: Graph compression and mining beyond caveman communities. *IEEE Transactions on Knowledge and Data Engineering* 26(12), 3077–3089, 2014.

[24] Burch, M., et al. Parallel edge splatting for scalable dynamic graph visualization. *IEEE Transactions on Visualization and Computer Graphics* 17(12), 2344–2353, 2011.

[25] Mashima, D., S. Kobourov, and Y. Hu. Visualizing dynamic data with maps. *IEEE Transactions on Visualization and Computer Graphics* 18(9), 1424–1437, 2012.

[26] Kuang, L., F. Hao, L.T. Yang, M. Lin, C. Luo, and G. Min. A tensor-based approach for big data representation and dimensionality reduction. *IEEE Transactions on Emerging Topics in Computing* 2(3), 280–291, 2014.

[27] Abdi, H., and L.J. Williams. Principal component analysis. *Wiley Interdisciplinary Reviews: Computational Statistics* 2(4), 433–459, 2010.

[28] Brand, M. Incremental singular value decomposition of uncertain data with missing values. In *Proceedings of the 7th European Conference on Computer Vision (ECCV)*, pp. 707–720, 2002.

[29] Sun, J., D. Tao, and C. Faloutsos. Beyond streams and graphs: Dynamic tensor analysis. In *Proceedings of the 12th ACM SIGKDD International Conference on Knowledge Discovery and Data Mining (KDD)*, pp. 374–383, 2006.

[30] Available from: https://cloudsecurityalliance.org/

[31] Cui, H.-T. Research on the model of big data serve security in cloud environment. In 2016 IEEE International Conference on Computer Communication and the Internet (ICCCI), IEEE, 2016.

[32] Lijun, Q., Z. Jinkang, and Z. Sihai. Survey of wireless big data. *Journal of Communications and Information Networks* 2(1), 1–18, 2017.

[33] He, Y., et al. Big data analytics in mobile cellular networks. *IEEE Access* 4, 1985–1996, 2016.

[34] Kuang, L., et al. A tensor-based approach for big data representation and dimensionality reduction. *IEEE Transactions on Emerging Topics in Computing* 2(3), 280–291, 2014.

[35] Xu, F., et al. Big data driven mobile traffic understanding and forecasting: A time series approach. *IEEE Transactions on Services Computing* 9(5), 796–805, 2016.

[36] Alsheikh, M.A., et al. Mobile big data analytics using deep learning and apache spark. *IEEE Network* 30(3), 22–29, 2016.

[37] Yang, C. Learning methodologies for wireless big data networks: A Markovian game-theoretic perspective. *Neurocomputing* 174, 431–438, 2016.

[38] Guo, L., et al. A secure mechanism for big data collection in large scale Internet of vehicle. *IEEE Internet of Things Journal* 4(2), 601–610, 2017.

[39] Mukherjee, R., S. Roy, and A. Das. Survey on data collection protocols in wireless sensor networks using mobile data collectors. In 2015 2nd International Conference on Computing for Sustainable Global Development (INDIACom), IEEE, 2015.

[40] Di Francesco, M., S.K. Das, and G. Anastasi. Data collection in wireless sensor networks with mobile elements: A survey. *ACM Transactions on Sensor Networks (TOSN)* 8(1), 7, 2011.

[41] Zhao, M., and Y. Yang. Bounded relay hop mobile data gathering in wireless sensor networks. *IEEE Transactions on Computers* 61(2), 265–277, 2012.

[42] Wang, T., et al. Learning, indexing, and diagnosing network faults. *Proceedings of the 15th ACM SIGKDD International Conference on Knowledge Discovery and Data Mining*, ACM, 2009.

[43] Hajji, H., B.H. Far, and J. Cheng. Detection of network faults and performance problems. *Proceedings of the Internet Conference*, 2001.

[44] Wang, X., and M.D. Lemmon. Event-triggering in distributed networked control systems. *IEEE Transactions on Automatic Control* 56(3), 586–601, 2011.

[45] Benzing, A., B. Koldehofe, and K. Rothermel. Bandwidth-minimized distribution of measurements in global sensor networks. In IFIP International Conference on Distributed Applications and Interoperable Systems, Springer, Berlin, 2014.

[46] Dey, A. Understanding and using context. *Personal and Ubiquitous Computing* 5, 4, 2001. doi: 10.1007/s007790170019.

[47] Bolchini, C., et al. A data-oriented survey of context models. *ACM Sigmod Record* 36(4), 19–26, 2007.

[48] Bilen, T., and B. Canberk. Binary context tree based middleware for next generation context aware networks. In 2015 3rd International Conference on Future Internet of Things and Cloud (FiCloud), IEEE, 2015.

[49] Davoudpour, M., et al. "CANthings": Context-aware networks for the design of connected things. World Automation Congress (WAC), 2014, IEEE, 2014.

[50] Goyal, S., R.K. Chauhan, and S. Parveen. Spam detection using KNN and decision tree mechanism in social network. In 2016 4th International Conference on Parallel, Distributed and Grid Computing (PDGC), IEEE, 2016.

[51] Yue, K., et al. A parallel and incremental approach for data-intensive learning of Bayesian networks. *IEEE Transactions on Cybernetics* 45(12), 2890–2904, 2015.

[52] Nurhayati, O.D., M.N. Prasetyo, and E.D. Widianto. Expert system for campus environment indexing in wireless sensor network. In 2015 2nd International Conference on Information Technology, Computer, and Electrical Engineering (ICITACEE), IEEE, 2015.

[53] Subasinghe, K.D.B.H., and S.R. Kodithuwakku. A big data analytic identity management expert system for social media networks. In 2015 IEEE International WIE Conference on Electrical and Computer Engineering (WIECON-ECE), IEEE, 2015.

[54] Sultana, A., and M.A. Jabbar. Intelligent network intrusion detection system using data mining techniques. In 2016 2nd International Conference on Applied and Theoretical Computing and Communication Technology (iCATccT), IEEE, 2016.

[55] Hashmi, U.S., A. Darbandi, and A. Imran. Enabling proactive self-healing by data mining network failure logs. In 2017 International Conference on Computing, Networking and Communications (ICNC), IEEE, 2017.

[56] Latif, M.A., and M. Adnan. ANN-based data mining for better resource management in the next generation wireless networks. In 2016 International Conference on Frontiers of Information Technology (FIT), IEEE, 2016.

[57] Xia, D., et al. A map reduce-based nearest neighbor approach for big-data-driven traffic flow prediction. *IEEE Access* 4, 2920–2934, 2016.

[58] Hwang, W.-J., et al. Quality of service management for home networks using online service response prediction. *IEEE Internet of Things Journal* 2017.

[59] Poupart, P., et al. Online flow size prediction for improved network routing. In 2016 IEEE 24th International Conference on Network Protocols (ICNP), IEEE, 2016.

[60] Wang, C., X. Xin, and J. Shang. When to make a topic popular again? A temporal model for topic re-hotting prediction in online social networks. *IEEE Transactions on Signal and Information Processing Over Networks* 2017.

[61] Williams, S., et al. Optimization of sparse matrix–vector multiplication on emerging multicore platforms. *Parallel Computing* 35(3), 178–194, 2009.

[62] Buono, D., et al. Optimizing sparse matrix-vector multiplication for large-scale data analytics. In *Proceedings of the 2016 International Conference on Supercomputing*, ACM, 2016.

[63] de Souza, J.C.S., T.M.L. Assis, and B.C. Pal. Data compression in smart distribution systems via singular value decomposition. *IEEE Transactions on Smart Grid* 8(1), 275–284, 2017.

[64] Yang, Z., et al. A fast non-smooth nonnegative matrix factorization for learning sparse representation. *IEEE Access* 4, 5161–5168, 2016.

[65] Plattner, H. *A course in in-memory data management: The inner mechanics of in-memory databases*. Berlin: Springer, 2013, pp. 445–461.

[66] Cheng, F., et al. Analyzing boundary device logs on the in-memory platform. In High Performance Computing and Communications (HPCC), 2015 IEEE 7th International Symposium on Cyberspace Safety and Security (CSS), 2015 IEEE 12th International Conference on Embedded Software and Systems (ICESS), 2015 IEEE 17th International Conference on, IEEE, 2015.

[67] Available from: https://www.chefio/chef/

[68] Available from: https://puppetlabs.com/

[69] Available from: http://docs.ansible.com/ansible/

[70] Available from: http://www.geant.org/Networks/Pan-European_network/Pages/Home.aspx

[71] AlMahmoud, A., et al. Spamdoop: A privacy-preserving big data platform for collaborative spam detection. *IEEE Transactions on Big Data*, 2017.

[72] Xie, Z., et al. Modeling traffic of big data platform for large scale datacenter networks. In 2016 IEEE 22nd International Conference on Parallel and Distributed Systems (ICPADS), IEEE, 2016.

Chapter 2

Some Mathematical Properties of Networks for Big Data

Marcello Trovati
Edge Hill University
Ormskirk, United Kingdom

CONTENTS

2.1 Introduction

Research in big data has been the focus of numerous research communities, resulting in the advance of novel theories and applications to address the crucial challenges arising from the *Four V*s, namely, volume, velocity, variety, and veracity [1]. The continuous creation of data from both structured and unstructured sources requires the use of cutting-edge techniques to fully harness the potential embedded in data, to provide effective tools in the assessment and extraction of actionable information.

In this chapter, we will discuss some mathematical approaches based on the topological properties of data, and a specific application to the automated extraction of Bayesian networks from textual sources. The evaluation results show the potential of this approach, which in turn could be applied to a wider range of topics to advance the current understanding of data science and its applications.

2.2 Topological Properties of Big Data

Big data, as discussed above, is characterized by the lack of structure, huge size, as well as evolving properties. As a consequence, data points are often described within vector spaces, whose dimensions and complexity largely depends on the corresponding datasets. However, when these are very large, methods based on explicit geometric properties of the single points are typically computationally ineffective. For example, in the majority of clustering approaches, assessing the mutual distances between points can lead to a slow evaluation, especially when analyzing large datasets embedded in multidimensional spaces.

Topology aims to understand invariant properties of spaces, providing a *global* classification of spaces, as opposed to attempting to assess their *local* properties. This can provide a powerful approach to big data where a very fine granularity might prove counterproductive. Broadly speaking, rather than observing each point and its interactions with its neighbors, considering their "shape" allows a better approach to their investigation. In other words, features such as holes and number of components provide a set of tools to classify the corresponding datasets.

Topological data analysis (TDA) is an emerging research field, which aims to apply theoretical approaches in topology to data science [3]. Since topology does not need to specifically consider a coordinate system to incorporate the dataset, it allows greater flexibility and the utilization of approaches that can be applied to a wider set of scenarios.

2.2.1 Homology theory

The fundamental component of homology is the concept of *simplicial complexes* [2], which are based on the process of covering a shape with joined, nonoverlapping polyhedra. More specifically, an n–simplex, denoted by Δ_n, is defined as the complete graph on $(n+1)$ vertices associated with a collection of $n+1$ points in $\mathbb{R}^n$. The subset of the vertices of the simplex is called an n-face, and two simplices are properly situated if their intersection is either empty or a face of both simplices. More formally, a simplicial complex K is defined as a finite set of simplices so that for all simplices $S \in K$, a face s of S satisfies the condition that $s \in K$. It also has the property that if $S_1, S_2 \in K$, then S_1 and S_2 are properly situated. Geometrically speaking, simplicial complexes triangulate the shape created by a dataset. In other words, they provide an approximation of the actual shape, without losing any topological information. This is similar to taking a picture of our favorite landscape, as this will produce a good approximation of the real image depending on the quality of our camera. Triangulation follows the same idea: often we do not need a faithful representation of the data, but an accurate enough version of it. Furthermore, this clearly enhances the computational efficiency.

The fundamental question is: *how do we associate the most suitable triangulation*? The aim is to achieve a triangulation that captures the shape of data, without creating a trivial or useless simplicial complex. Let's take the shape of a doughnut defined by a set of data points, as depicted in Figure 2.1.

If we join any two of them by an edge when they are close enough (according to the euclidean distance), then how close do they need to be? If their distance has to be within a very small range, then we might end up with a trivial

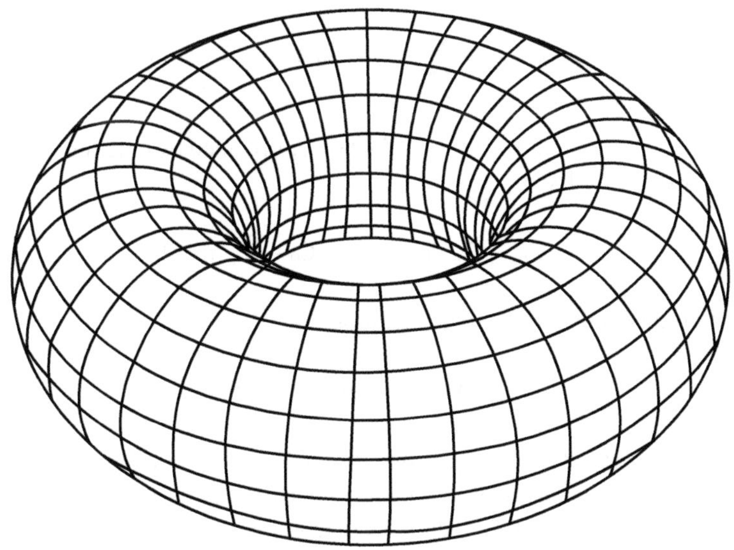

Figure 2.1: A doughnut (image publicly available from Wikipedia Commons).

representation, i.e., totally disconnected. On the other hand, if they can be far away from each other, we might have the opposite situation, i.e., they are all connected creating a complete graph. In either case, we lose the important feature of a doughnut, the hole in the middle. There has been extensive research on this topic with triangulations defined by Voronoi diagrams, Delaunay triangulations, as well as Vietoris-Rips and Čech complexes [2]. In particular, the Vietoris-Rips complex is based on the property that if the distance between every couple of points is at most d, then they will be connected. Similarly, a Čech complex is constructed based on balls with a specific radius, so that points are connected if they fall within the same ball. As discussed above, the identification of the most efficient triangulation is essential in analyzing large datasets, which is the focus of current research [4]. More formally, the Vietoris-Rips triangulation is based on a space in $\mathbb{R}^n$, a distance d, and a positive number ϵ. The construction of a simplicial complex is then carried out iteratively, by assuming that each point is associated with a $0-$complex and any two points x_1 and x_2 such that $d(x_1,x_2) < \epsilon$, are connected by a $1-$simplex between them. The process can be extended to n points if they are all within a distance ϵ, or in other words, if $d(x_i,x_j) < \epsilon$ for $1 \leq i \neq j \leq n$. Current research shows that Vietoris-Rips complexes are more computationally efficient with respect to Čech triangulation [2].

Another important concept in homology is *chains* of p–simplices defined as a linear combination $\sum_{i=1}^{p} \alpha_i p_i$, for some coefficients α_i. Let $s = \{v_0, \ldots, v_p\}$ be a simplicial; we define the *boundary map* as $D_p s = \sum_{j=1}^{p-1} \alpha_j$, or in other words we omit the pth element of p. For a chain C_p, when then have that D_p: $C_p \rightarrow C_{p-1}$, such that

$$D_p(C_p) = \sum_{j=0}^{i} (-1)^j \langle s_0, s_1, \ldots, \tilde{s}_j, \ldots, s_i \rangle$$

where $\langle s_0, s_1, \ldots, \tilde{s}_j, \ldots, s_i \rangle$ is the $j-$face of C_p obtained by deleting its jth vertex. In other words, we have

$$C_p \rightarrow C_{p-1} \rightarrow \cdots \rightarrow C_0 \rightarrow C_{-1} \rightarrow 0 \tag{2.1}$$

The homology is then defined as the quotient

$$H_i(X, \mathbb{R}) = \ker D_p / \operatorname{Im} D_{p+1}$$

A crucial property of homology is that it is defined as a functor, which guarantees that topologically equivalent spaces have corresponding isomorphic homology groups [3]. Furthermore, it measures discontinuity between different components. As a consequence, the assessment of homological properties of specific datasets is increasingly drawing attention as it has been shown to enhance the current understanding of data science [5].

2.2.2 Network theory

Simplicial complexes are closely related to networks, especially when they are embedded onto the plane.

As discussed in the previous section, data points naturally create networks based on their topological properties. However, not only can geometric properties define such networks, but also they can be populated by any other dataset based on one or more relation types among its elements. In fact, the concept of big data refers to a multitude of data, which may or may not exhibit a structure defined on a specific geometry. For example, textual sources contain semantic relations, which generate, once analyzed, a hierarchical structure among the different parts of the text corpora. Furthermore, relations can also be constructed to identify specific types of connections between concepts. This will be discussed in Section 2.3.

Network theory provides a set of tools to mathematically investigate the mutual relationships among data, where the network topology, defined as the level of connectedness of its nodes, identifies both the global and local properties of the system they model. A variety of techniques and approaches have, therefore, been developed within several interdisciplinary research fields including mathematics, computer science, biology, and the social sciences [7]. Furthermore, properties associated with the dynamical properties of networks allow the investigation of the overall behavior of the system under specific parameters.

2.2.2.1 Scale-free and small-world networks

The mostly investigated and used network topologies are scale-free and small-world networks [7]. These, in fact, are widely utilized to model a variety of complex systems.

World Wide Web links, biological and social networks often exhibit a scale-free structure, which is characterized by a degree distribution following a power law, or in other words:

$$p_k \approx k^{-\gamma} \tag{2.2}$$

where p_k is the fraction of nodes with degree k, and typically $2 < \gamma < 3$. Equation 2.2 implies that scale-free networks are likely to have large hubs, or in other words, they have a degree much larger than the average node degree. In particular, the tail of the node degree distribution, associated with large values for k, differs from purely random networks [7]. Furthermore, scale-free networks tend to have a large number of small degree nodes, which are, again, rare in random networks (Figure 2.2).

Small-world networks are characterized by the property that the majority of nodes have a relatively small degree, and that each node can be reached from any another one with a small number of "jumps," in terms of the number of edges linking them [7]. They were first observed by Milgram's famous small-world

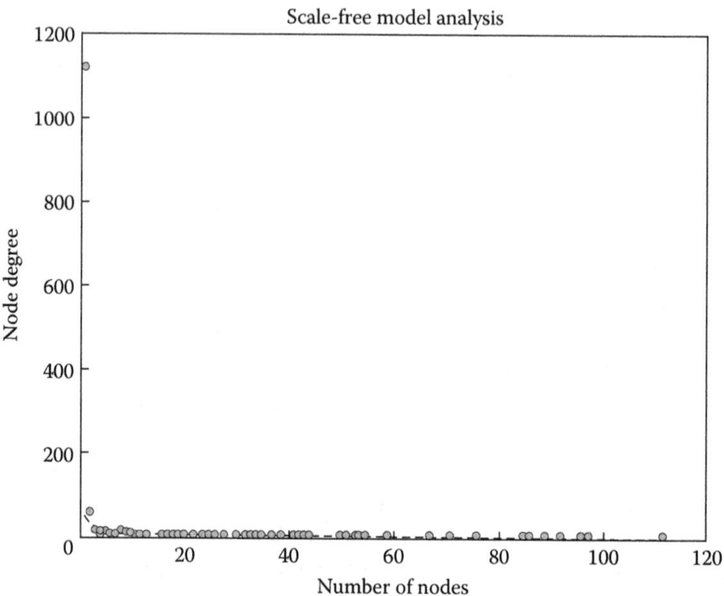

Figure 2.2: A scale-free network (Reproduced from James, I.M. History of Topology, *ScienceDirect*, v, 1999. With permission.).

experiment, which measured the average path length of social networks among a sample of people in the United States [8].

Small-world networks were first investigated as a class of random graphs, which tend to have a small average shortest path length, and a small clustering coefficient. However, small-world networks were soon grouped into a different type of network due to a higher clustering coefficient, compared to random networks. This motivated the introduction of the Watts and Strogatz model, which has proved successful in modeling a variety of real-world scenarios [9].

Broadly speaking, both scale-free and small-world networks differ from purely random networks in terms of a higher predictability of their global behavior, as their topology can be utilized to identify properties, which would be difficult to investigate otherwise. In the next section, we will discuss an application of the theoretical properties discussed above.

2.3 Extraction of Bayesian Networks

The decision-making process has seen unprecedented challenges posed by big data. The need to provide tools and algorithms to harness the wealth of information captured by data is becoming increasingly crucial in a variety of fields. However, the lack of structure and volume characterizing big data often prevents full utilization of the available data [1].

There are a variety of existing approaches to decision-making, and Bayesian networks (BNs) offer an effective tool to understand the various components of a system and their mutual dependencies. In fact, they provide an efficient and agile modeling framework with numerous applications including business analysis, medical decision support tools, intelligence extraction, and many more [6].

Formally, BNs are graphical models used to identify dependence and independence relationships among random variables, which define a complex decisional system. They are defined as directed, acyclic networks $G = G(V,E)$, where $V = \{v_i\}_{i=1}^n$ is the set of nodes, and $E = \{e_{v_i,v_j}\}_{v_i \neq v_j \in V}$ is the set of edges between nodes connected by dependency relations. Note that the directionality of the network implies that $e_{v_i,v_j} \neq e_{v_j,v_i}$, and no loops (a directed path starting and ending from the same node) are allowed, which ensure the creation of consistent BNs based on Bayes' Rule [16]. BNs consist of a quantitative layer defined by the factorization of the joint probability distribution of all the variables in the network, and by a qualitative one, which includes the properties of the underlying system. The most common example of BNs is the depiction of chance having wet grass on any given day, subject to the following assumptions:

1. A cloudy sky is associated with a higher probability of rain.
2. The sprinkler system is activated depending on whether the sky is cloudy.
3. Both the sprinkler system and rain have a direct impact on the probability of having wet grass.

The corresponding BN is depicted in Figure 2.3.

The edges $e_{v_i,v_j} \in E$ are associated with a conditional probability based on the direction of the edge, that is $P(v_j|v_i)$, which provides a probabilistic layer

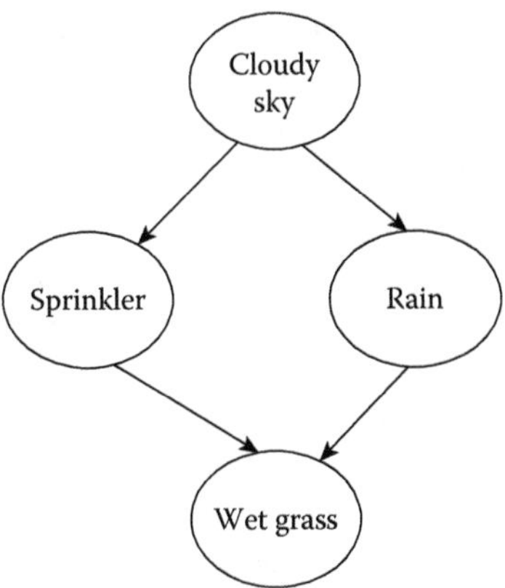

Figure 2.3: Example of a Bayesian network.

to the corresponding BN to enable reasoning over the probabilistic information. The investigation of the different components of a BN is usually carried out via explicit data analysis, or via literature review and expert assessment. These tasks tend to be time-consuming and complex when carried out manually, depending on the type, size, and complexity of the corresponding datasets. In particular, unstructured datasets provide a further challenge as relevant information is often embedded into data with a potentially contradicting and ambiguous structure. Text corpora are unstructured datasets, which are often used to extract BNs, and there is well-established research in this field see [15] for an overview. The majority of approaches focus on the lexico-syntactic properties of text to identify specific relationships between concepts and their mutual relations, such as causation, dependency, and independence. However, the intrinsic ambiguity and subtlety of human language negatively impacts on the accuracy of any information extraction method [14].

The aim of this section is to discuss the mathematical approach introduced in [1], which allows an investigation and analysis of information from large textual sources to semiautomatically populate fragments of BNs.

2.3.1 Text mining

The understanding of the human language is the focus of text mining (TM), where linguistic and semantic properties are investigated to understand the connections between the different parts in the corresponding text fragments [14]. There are a variety of approaches in TM, which broadly speaking are based on grammatical and syntactic rules, as well as statistical properties of the different textual components. The former are defined by text patterns, which are constructed to identify textual fragments containing information relevant to particular information extraction tasks, and mapped onto definite knowledge representation schemes [13]. Text patterns and the linguistic properties of text identify the hierarchical structure of the various concepts embedded in the corresponding textual fragments, which can be utilized to provide an insight into the different relationships between concepts. On the other hand, the statistical properties related to large text corpora give a further insight into specific properties, which could be missed by simply using a text pattern approach. In fact, the distribution and occurrence of words and concepts allows the investigation and prediction of their related properties [14].

More specifically, grammar-based approaches in TM are based on first the identification of the *tokenization* of sentences, whose output is the fragmentation of the corresponding sentences into words. Subsequently, an ordered tree representing the hierarchical syntactic structure of a sentence is produced, called the parsing tree.

Furthermore, the identification of the syntactic structure of text allows a better extraction of the relations between different entities [14] (Figure 2.4).

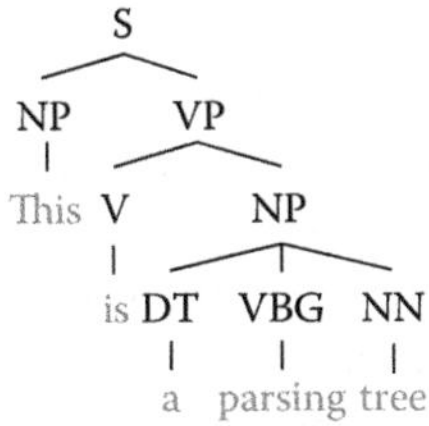

Figure 2.4: The parsing tree of the sentence "This is a parsing tree."

Depending on the type and scope of extraction, a variety of relations can be determined. For example, if we consider the above example again, the sentence "*the sprinkler system and rain have a direct impact on the probability of having wet grass*" suggests that the condition of having wet grass is directly linked with the sprinkler system and rain. This is clearly an important step in creating BNs.

2.3.2 Automatic extraction of Bayesian networks from text

The topological and probabilistic constraints of BNs are by no means trivial, and as a consequence the assessment and identification of the most appropriate network structure is often carried out manually. Depending on the size and complexity of the data investigated, the manual process of constructing BNs is likely to be very time-consuming and not efficient. There is, therefore, the risk of only addressing limited datasets, which is in contrast to the increasing need for intelligence extraction tools for big data. The automated extraction of BNs would particularly address this point, and it would provide a valuable tool to discover knowledge embedded into unstructured and complex data. However, as discussed above, any TM approach tends to target specific textual forms resulting in limited accuracy and recall of actionable information. As a consequence, the integration of the analysis of the properties associated with the relational network created by text analysis, with its topological features, can provide a deep insight into the definition of the most suitable and accurate BNs modeling complex scenarios.

The use of text patterns of the form `(NP1, keyword, NP2)` (where `NP1` and `NP2` are the *noun phrases* of a sentence containing the head nouns, and `keyword` can be a specific keyword or verb joining the two noun phrases) naturally creates a relational network. In particular, its nodes refer to the concepts associated to the nouns contained in the noun phrases, connected by an edge, depending on the type of the corresponding keyword. The type of relations that are relevant to the construction of BNs are dependency (including causality) and independence relations. For example, in the sentence "*uncertainty in the property market will cause a rise in the cost of average family house*," the two main concepts, *uncertainty in the property market*, and *rise in the cost of average family house*, are linked by the keyword *cause*, which suggests a dependency type of relation. This will therefore translate into an edge between them. On the other hand, *an increased number of working hours is not linked with better performance* specifies that the two concepts *increased number of working hours* and *better performance* are independent, and so no edge between them will be present.

In order to achieve an optimal textual information extraction, a semantically precise set of text pattern rules should be utilized. Usually causal relationships, which are a subgroup of dependence relationships, are associated with very effective textual rules with a limited ambiguity level [16]. However, causal statements are less likely to be present due to their much stronger implications, as well as where causality is implicit [16].

The nodes in the relational network discussed above represent different concepts, which are identified during the text analysis process. There are multiple aspects to consider in this task, which include avoiding duplication of similar concepts, as well as the context of the extraction. Broadly speaking, semantically equivalent concepts, such as synonyms, should be merged to ensure a meaningful BN. Refer to Ref. [14] for an overview. Furthermore, probabilistic information needs to be identified, and the combination of qualitative and quantitative information available from unstructured datasets raises several challenges. The assessment and ranking of specific keywords (and their combinations), when describing probability, can provide a useful insight into the structure of the corresponding relationships (Figure 2.5).

Figure 2.5 depicts the main components of the approach discussed [1], which includes:

- Two specific ontologies have been defined, according to the semantic properties of concepts, as well as probabilistic and statistical terms. These were populated from Wikipedia identified by a query related to general statistical and probabilistic terminology. This process created

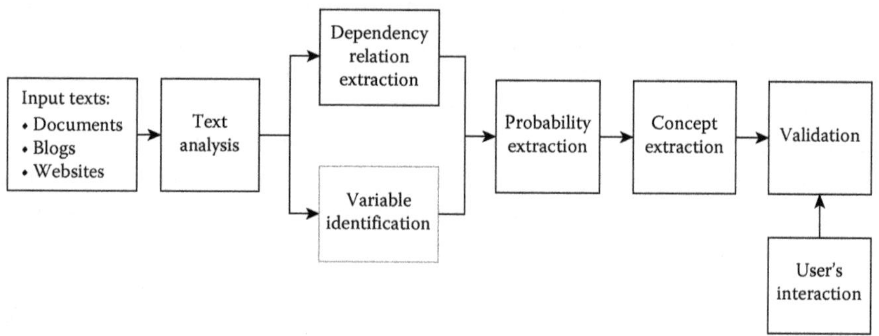

Figure 2.5: The architecture described in Section 2.3.2.

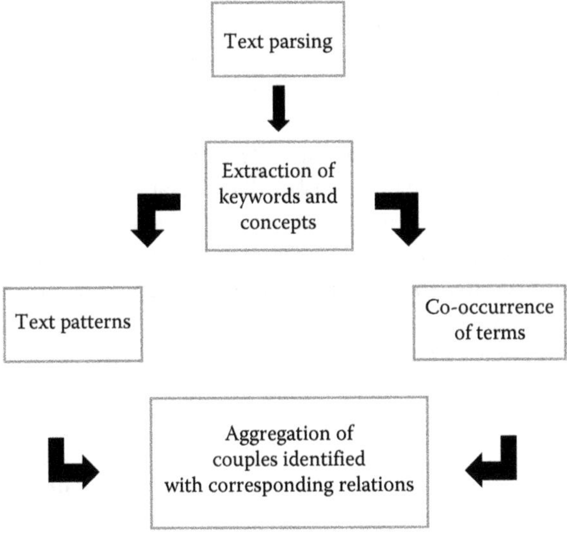

Figure 2.6: The specific components of the text analysis.

over 2300 terms likely to occur in text fragments containing information related to uncertainty and probabilistic states, which included semantically equivalent terminology derived from WordNet [10].

Open Biological and Biomedical Ontologies [11] was used to extract over 60,000 concepts related to the biomedical sector.

- A text analysis, as depicted in Figure 2.6, was carried out to identify specific probabilistic and statistical terms and general concepts, including synonyms, antonyms, meronyms, etc.
- Specific text patterns have been defined for extracting probabilistic relationships between concepts.
- The output of the extraction, including couples of concepts linked by a probabilistic relationship, can be of probabilistic dependence or independence type, as discussed above.
- Finally, any newly extracted concept and probabilistic information were merged into the above ontologies.

2.3.3 Extraction of probabilistic information

As discussed above, a BN is based on the conditional probability between any two concepts. However, a full extraction of conditional probabilities tends to be based on lexical and semantic properties that are either difficult to capture, or they produce a high level of inaccuracies [1]. As a consequence, we focused on an approximated version of conditional probability. More specifically, any probabilistic information should focus on the shared concepts, and on the nature of the mutual relationships between nodes, or in other words whether they are known and explicitly retrievable probabilistic relationships.

For two nodes $A, B \in V$ associated with two concepts, let S_A and S_B be their respective subsets of nodes, which are connected to them. Intuitively, any two concepts are linked depending on the number of common attributes and further concepts they share. Therefore, $P(A,B)$ is based on the proportion of neighbors they share, or in other words, on the following parameter:

$$\ell(A,B) = \frac{|S_A \cap S_B|}{|S_A \cup S_B|} \tag{2.3}$$

Define $\mathcal{R}$ to be the finite set of relations associated with edges with a specified relation type in the semantic network, where the "empty" relation $\emptyset$ is associated with edges with an unspecified relations type. Let R_{S_A} and R_{S_B} be two subsets of $\mathcal{R}^{|S_A|}$ and $\mathcal{R}^{|S_B|}$, respectively, only containing the probabilistic dependence relationships in $\mathcal{R}$. If a relation is extracted with a specific probabilistic type, this gives a better insight into its nature and veracity rather than an unknown relationship. As a consequence, we also need to consider the following parameter:

$$\tilde{R}_A = \frac{|R_{S_A}|}{|S_A|} \tag{2.4}$$

Clearly, $\tilde{R}_A$ evaluates how many edges from the nodes in S_A have an associated type. Furthermore, we also need to determine how many shared connections between A and B have the same type. This is carried out via the following parameter:

$$\tilde{T}(S_A, S_B) = \frac{|R_{S_A} \cap R_{S_B}|}{|S_A \cap S_B|} \tag{2.5}$$

Note that we assume that Equations 2.4 and 2.5 are always defined. In other words, their corresponding denominators are never 0. In fact, in Equation 2.5, if $|S_A \cap S_B| = 0$, it implies that $|R_{S_A} \cap R_{S_B}| = 0$, which is the trivial case. As a consequence, we assume that in such case $\tilde{T}(S_A, S_B) = 0$.

We can also easily see that both $\tilde{R}_A$ and $\tilde{T}(S_A, S_B)$ take values ranging between 0 and 1.

We then define the *probabilistic relationship measure* $\tilde{p}(A,B)$ between A and B as:

$$\tilde{p}(A,B) = w_1 \ell(A,B) + w_2 \tilde{R}_A + w_3 \tilde{T}(S_A, S_B) \tag{2.6}$$

where $\sum_{i=1}^{3} w_i = 1$, and $0 \leq w_i \leq 1$, for $i = 1,2,3$, are the *context parameters*. These usually depend on the context of the discovery process, and they can be

Algorithm 2.1 Measure of Probabilistic Relationship

1: Evaluate $\ell(A,B)$
2: Evaluate $\tilde{R}_A$
3: Evaluate $\tilde{T}(S_A, S_B)$
4: Determine the context parameters following the constraints $\sum_{i=1}^{3} w_i = 1$, and $0 \leq w_i \leq 1$, for $i = 1,2,3$

determined by considering specific concepts whose conditional probability is known, or at least it is assumed to fall into a specific interval. More specifically, the method utilized in this chapter focuses on the fact that contextual probabilistic information can be assessed by considering concepts that are semantically linked. However, not all such semantic relations are suitable. In fact, synonyms such as "car" and "automobile" even though are semantically equivalent, they might not be equivalent from a probabilistic point of view. In fact, one term might be used instead of the other depending on the origin of the textual source, such as "corpora" in British and American English.

There is extensive research on the relationships between concepts linked by hypernym/hyponym relations [17]. In particular, a term that is a hyponym of another term is likely to co-occur. For example, *adenocarcinoma* might be considered as a hyponym of *cancer*. Furthermore, a type of cancer is a hyponym of cancer. Therefore, $P($`cancer`, `cancer_of_`<TYPE>$)$, where <TYPE> is a specific type of cancer, is assumed to have a conditional probability greater than 0.8. Subsequently, all the parameters in Equation 2.6 can be calculated by considering suitable text corpora.

This process is shown in Algorithm 2.1.

Subsequently, once the network is fully populated, a simple search algorithm to identify the possible BNs is utilized to identify meaningful BNs [1]. In fact, depending on the network topology, more than one BN can be identified. In particular, only the edges associated with a probability equal to or greater than the threshold of 0.2 were kept, while the others were removed. The output of this process is a table of connected concepts, with their linking probability.

2.3.4 Evaluation

The context parameters w_i for $i = 1,2,3$ have been determined as discussed above. In fact, we isolated the two following concepts:

- `cancer` and `cancer_of_`<TYPE>,
- `infection` and `infection_of_`<TYPE>,

where <TYPE> is a specific type of cancer or infection, such as breast cancer, prostate cancer, throat infection, etc.

Subsequently, we assumed that P(`cancer, cancer_of_<TYPE>)>0.8`. From the dataset we identified, we evaluated all the components of (Equation 2.6) which identified all the context parameters. Their average was then calculated to fully populate Equation 2.6, namely $w_1 = 0.46$, $w_2 = 0.31$, and $w_3 = 0.33$. The above process was applied to approximately 250 articles and 400 abstracts from the biomedical sector, freely available from PubMed [12]. As discussed in [6], both semantic and extracted connections between the different concepts created a relational network $G(V,E)$, with approximately 750 nodes and 1200 edges. Furthermore, such network exhibits a scale-free structure as shown in Figure 2.7. The method discussed in [6] gave $\gamma = 2.1$, as defined in Equation 2.2, which is consistent with real-world scale-free networks.

Finally, fragments of BNs were created for specific concepts and assessed by a group of experts. Table 2.1 shows a selection of such evaluation. The experts evaluated approximately 80 concepts, which were subsequently compared with the automated extraction of the corresponding relationships within specific BNs. This generated a recall of 73% and a precision of approximately 61%. In particular, approximately 20 possible BNs, based on the topological and probabilistic constraints discussed above, were identified. The manual evaluation highlighted that all of them were acceptable, even though only half were deemed useful to represent relevant knowledge. This is due to the fact that the approach discussed

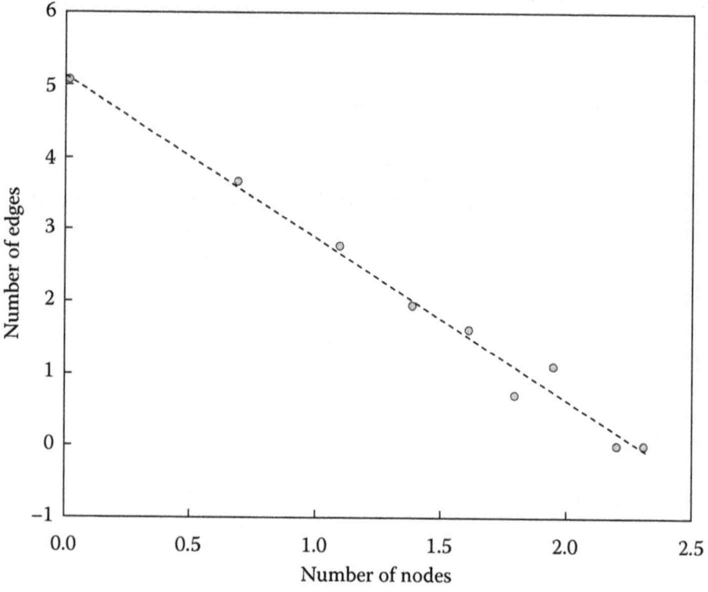

Figure 2.7: The log graph of the scale-free network discussed in Section 2.3.4, depicting the number of edges versus the number of nodes.

Table 2.1 A selection of the concepts used in the evaluation as in Section 2.3.4

Concept *A*	**Concept *B***	$\tilde{p}(A, B)$	**Expert's assessment**
Cancer	Diet	0.59	0.6–0.7
Heart attack	Aspirine	0.45	0.4–0.6
Organophosphate	Pyrethroid	0.21	0.2–0.5
Symptom	Disease	0.69	0.8–0.9

in this section only provides consistency in populating BNs, and users' and general contextual preferences are not considered. This is, however, the focus of current research efforts [1,6].

2.4 Conclusion

This chapter focuses on a selection of some emerging theoretical approaches within big data, and on a specific application to extract BNs from text. The utilization and integration of network and topology theory provide a set of tools, which allow the assessment and discovery of knowledge embedded in unstructured datasets. Big data has created challenges as well as new opportunities, which, if fully exploited, can advance the current state of the art in knowledge representation and discovery.

References

[1] Trovati, M., Hayes, J., Palmieri, F., and Bessis, N. Automated extraction of fragments of Bayesian networks from textual sources, *Applied Soft Computing*, 60, pp. 508–519, 2017.

[2] Janich, K. *Topology*, Springer, 1984.

[3] Lum, P. Y., Singh, G., Lehman, A., Ishkanov, T., Vejdemo-Johansson, M., Alagappan, M., Carlsson, J., and Carlsson, G. *Extracting insights from the shape of complex data using topology*, Scientific Reports 3, Article number 1236, 2013.

[4] Tamal K. Dey, F. F., and Y. Wang. Graph induced complex on point data. *Proceedings of the 9th Annual Symposium on Computational Geometry*, Rio de Janeiro, Brazil, 2013.

[5] Carlsson, G. Topology and data, *Bulletin of the Mathematical Society*, 46, 2, pp. 255–308, 2009.

[6] Trovati, M. and Bessis, N. *An influence assessment method based on co-occurrence for topologically reduced big data sets.* Soft Computing, 2015.

[7] Albert, R. and Barabasi, A. L. Statistical mechanics of complex networks. *Reviews of Modern Physics*, 74, 47, 2002.

[8] Milgram, S. *The individual in a social world.* New York: McGraw-Hill, 1984.

[9] Watts, D. J. and Strogatz, H. S. Collective dynamics of small-world networks, *Nature*, 393, pp. 440–442, 1998.

[10] Fellbaum, C. *WordNet: An electronic lexical database.* Cambridge, MA: MIT Press, 1998.

[11] The Open Biological and Biomedical Ontologies. http://www.obofoundry.org/ (accessed March 2016).

[12] Pubmed, http://www.ncbi.nlm.nih.gov/pubmed (accessed March 2016).

[13] Laporte, E. Symbolic natural language processing. In *Applied combinatorics on words.* Lothaire Ed.: Cambridge University Press, pp. 164–209, 2005.

[14] Manning, C. D. and Schutze, H. *Foundations of statistical natural language processing.* Cambridge, MA: MIT Press, 1999.

[15] Sanchez-Graillet, O. and Poesio, M. *Acquiring Bayesian networks from text.* Lisbon, Portugal: LREC, 2004.

[16] Pearl, J. *Probabilistic reasoning in intelligent systems: Networks of plausible inference.* San Francisco, CA: Morgan Kaufmann Publishers Inc., 1998.

[17] Dias, G., Mukelov, R., and Cleuziou, G., Mapping General-Specific noun relationships to WordNet Hypernym/Hyponym Relations, *Proceedings of the 16th International Conference, EKAW*, September 29–October 3, Acitrezza, Italy, pp. 198–212, 2008.

Chapter 3

Big Geospatial Data and the Geospatial Semantic Web: Current State and Future Opportunities

Chuanrong Zhang and Weidong Li
University of Connecticut
Storrs, Connecticut

Tian Zhao
University of Wisconsin-Milwaukee
Milwaukee, Wisconsin

CONTENTS

3.1 Big Geospatial Data

Because of technology development, data sets are rapidly growing in data volume. Many technologies such as ubiquitous information-sensing mobile devices, aerial sensory technologies, cameras, social media networks, remote sensing imagery, and wireless sensor networks are increasingly used to gather various data sets. Large volumes of data are being created and continue to increase every day. A large part of big data can be georeferenced. In fact, 80% of big data are geospatial data [1]. Geospatial data contain information about a physical object that can be represented by numerical values in a geographic coordinate system. Geospatial data represents the location, size, and shape of an object on earth such as a school, house, sea, park or county. Remote sensing, global positioning system (GPS), geographic information system (GIS), and volunteered geographic information (VGI) are major modern geospatial technologies to collect and handle geospatial data. In recent years, these geospatial technologies have generated large volumes of geospatial data about things and human beings, which are available for better understanding our coupled human and environmental systems.

Remote sensing is the science of deriving information about an object from measurements made at a distance from the object, i.e., without actually coming in contact with it [2]. Remote sensing data are undergoing rapid growth because of recent advances in remote sensing techniques. Every day many spaceborne and airborne sensors from many different countries collect a massive amount of remotely sensed data. Remote sensing devices have been widely used to observe our planet from different angles and perspectives for different purposes. The remote sensing data collected by a single satellite data center are dramatically increasing by several terabytes per day [3]. Global archived remotely sensed data would probably exceed 1 exabyte based on the statistics of the Open geospatial consortium (OGC). A huge amount of remotely sensed data are now freely available from the National Aeronautics and Space Administration (NASA) Open Government Initiative. One of NASA's archives, the Earth Science Data and Information System (ESDIS), holds 7.5 petabyte of data with nearly 7000 unique data sets and a million users in 2013. Remotely sensed images include a variety of data from multiple sources (laser, radar, optical, etc) and are multitemporal (collected on different dates) and multiresolution (from high resolution to medium and coarse resolution). The advent of high-resolution earth observation has led to the high dimensionality of remotely sensed data. Large-scale environmental monitoring research has generated multitemporal and multisensor remotely sensed data at multiple scales: local, regional, and global. Those remotely sensed data are used for different applications such as global climate change, urban planning, and natural disaster management. Large remote sensing applications overwhelmed with massive remotely sensed data are regarded as typical big geospatial data-intensive challenges [4].

GPS is an electronic system that uses satellites to determine the position of an object such as a vehicle or a person. GPS technology has been developed to provide precise positional and velocity data and global time synchronization for air, sea, and land travel. Advances in GPS technologies have helped to generate a big volume of geospatial information for different applications. A growing number of cell phones, personal digital assistants (PDAs), digital cameras, and other handheld devices use GPS technology to provide users with information based on their locations. For example, GPS-enabled devices and mobile applications have generated huge volumes of health data by capturing daily activities of patients. A GPS-enabled tracker can produce a large volume of health data by recording inhaler usage by asthmatics. For another example, GPS has been extensively used for generating data tracking of suspected criminals and for land surveying.

GPS plays many important roles in bridging a variety of Web applications and end users. The availability of smartphones with built-in GPS and developments of web technology called Web 2.0 allows end users to produce, visualize, and analyze "mashups" of data from different sources over the Web. Many GPS-enabled web applications have been created. Nowadays, many websites provide web services based on users' geographic location. Innovative GPS-enabled device use will continue to grow as a means to help gain insights into different applications through real-time data generation and complex data analytics that would otherwise be hard to piece together. GPS has been and will continue to be used in many fields such as transportation. For example, raw GPS logs have been used to understand transportation modes such as walking and driving, which is a type of human behavior data that can provide pervasive computing systems with more contextual information of a user's mobility [5]. For another example, GPS-equipped taxis have been regarded as mobile sensors probing the travel speed of each road [6]. GPS-enabled navigation devices can integrate real-time traffic patterns and alerts with navigation maps and suggest the best routes to drivers.

Advances in GPS, Web mapping, cellular communications, and wiki technologies have led to VGI. VGI is a special case of user-generated content with explicit or implicit embedded geospatial information. VGI is created by volunteers through crowdsourcing, and represents a new phenomenon arising from Web 2.0 technologies [7,8]. VGI is dramatically altering the way in which ordinary citizens can create digital geospatial data. VGI enables both experts and amateur enthusiasts to create and share geospatial information. Complementing the traditional authoritative geographic information collected by government agencies or private organizations, VGI has become another popular source of geospatial data for many applications in recent years. For example, there were more than 20 million geographic features in the database of Wikimapia in 2014 [9], which is more than many of the world's largest gazetteers.

VGI is more than just a new type of data; it establishes a new paradigm for continuous monitoring of the changing landscape, behaviors, and social interactions [10]. Many VGI data sets are available at very fine spatial and temporal resolutions. VGI collects data using three main methods: (1) by using geo-aware mobile devices, (2) by annotating geographic features using Geoweb mapping interfaces, and (3) by extracting or inferring location information from ambient geospatial data in social media (such as photos, videos, blog posts, and tweets) [11,12]. Examples of VGI include OpenStreetMap, Geolocated Twitter "tweet" data sets, Wikimapia, Microsoft's Virtual Earth, and Foursquare Venue data.

VGI data sets may have the following characteristics: (1) large in volume, (2) subject to dynamic changes and updates, (3) collected through crowdsourcing architectures using different devices and technologies, and (4) contain a mixture of structured and unstructured information. By making it possible for more people to produce more data in digital form, VGI can dramatically increase the volume of existing geospatial data. With a high and increasing degree of heterogeneity, VGI may create shifts in the content and characteristics of existing geospatial data. Compared with authoritative geospatial data, VGI data sets face challenges such as data quality, accuracy, and validity. However, VGI may provide good data sources for augmenting, updating, or completing existing authoritative spatial databases. VGI calls for new procedures and infrastructures for handling distributed big geospatial data.

GIS is a system designed to capture, store, manipulate, analyze, manage, and present all types of geospatial data. GIS has been applied to many different application areas for geospatial analysis and decision-making such as climate change, disaster response, banking, retail and E-commerce, political campaigns, insurance, and fraud analysis. Currently, several commercial desktop GIS software systems dominate the geographical information (GI) industry, such as Esri ArcGIS, Hexagon Geospatial Geomedia, MapInfo Professional, Global Mapper, Manifold GIS, GE Smallworld, Bentley Map, Golden Software MapViewer, and Clark Laboratories IDRISI. Recently, many free, open-source GIS packages have been developed such as GRASS GIS, gvGIS, ILWIS, JUMP GIS, MapWindow GIS, QGIS, SAGA GIS, and uDig. The development of the World Wide Web creates a unique environment for developing GIS. Besides many of commercial Internet GIS programs such as Esri's ArcGIS Online, a number of open-source Web map servers, such as GeoServer, MapGuide Open Source, Mapnik, and MapServer, have been developed to offer better tools for managing geospatial data over the Web. These online GIS programs have freed many users from the need to store large geospatial data sets on their own servers. It is possible to perform basic spatial data analyses and transmit data back to the office by using these online GIS programs.

However, as the size of geospatial data sets increases, these conventional GIS software packages, which are normally based on single central processing unit (CPU) architecture and single-user interfaces, face tremendous challenges for managing big geospatial data. The existing GIS framework and tools, either desktop or web-server based, do not support (1) shared access to terabyte-scale data, (2) real-time collaborative spatial analysis of massive data, or (3) user-friendly integration between big geospatial data access and spatial analysis [13,14]. Big geospatial data need new GIS tools and software to search, sift, and sieve data from multiple and disparate data sources for spatial analysis. New GIS tools and software should be developed to extend the capabilities of the traditional GIS over new technologies, such as the Cloud, embedded sensors, mobile and social media, and thus can access disparate big geospatial data in real time for geospatial data analysis. New GIS tools and systems should support geospatial analysis of big unstructured data in real time and be able to aggregate terabytes or more geospatial data sets for better understanding of spatial patterns, trends, or relationships.

3.2 Geospatial Semantic Web

Although the recent developments of the aforementioned geographic information technologies and the proliferation of cost effective and ubiquitous positioning technologies (GPS) have enabled capturing spatially oriented data at an unprecedented scale and rate and have proven useful for gathering information, the increasing volumes of geospatial data present problems for transparent geospatial data exchange and sharing because of heterogeneous semantic problems.

To facilitate the exchange and sharing of geospatial data built on initial expenditures, spatial data infrastructures (SDIs) have been developed in many countries in the past two decades. SDIs based on open standards and OGC web service technologies offer the potential to overcome the heterogeneous problems of legacy GIS databases and facilitate sharing geospatial data in a cost-effective way. The fast development of SDIs and OGC web service technologies has undoubtedly improved the sharing and synchronization of big geospatial information across diverse sources.

However, literature about SDI shows that there are limitations in the current SDIs, and it might be still difficult to find proper data from the current SDIs and big data sources. Current SDIs only emphasize technical data interoperability via web services and standard interfaces and cannot resolve semantic heterogeneity problems in big geospatial data sharing. However, differences in semantics used in diverse big data sources are one of the major problems in big geospatial data sharing and data interoperability. Second, with the currently implemented SDIs, it is only possible to search and access geospatial data and services by metadata keywords and it is impossible to directly search and access geospatial data and services based on their content [15]. This causes a problem for novice portal users who may not know which keywords to use or may not even know they should try many keywords [16]. In addition, a keyword-based search may have a low recall if a different terminology is used and/or a low precision if terms are homonymous [17]. On the other hand, the keyword search may sometimes bring an overwhelming number of search results. As a result, users may have to spend a lot of time sifting through undesirable query results before finding the desired data set [16]. Third, although SDIs aim to make discovery and access to distributed geographic data more efficient, the catalog services currently used in SDIs for discovering geographic data do not allow expressive queries and also do not take into account more than one data source that might be required to answer a question [18]. It is not possible to automatically discover several data sources that only in combination can provide the information required to answer a given question. However, it is unrealistic to expect that one web service or one data source can fulfill exactly the needs of a user's request. Therefore, SDIs need a semantic-based approach that can reason about a service's capability to a level of detail that permits their automatic discovery and composition. In addition, SDIs and the many geospatial portals have large amounts of geospatial data that tend to be only available for download but not for analysis due to the lack of a comprehensive data science environment.

The concept of the geospatial semantic web (GSW) was proposed to overcome semantic heterogeneity problems of geospatial data [19,20]. The GSW is an extension of the current Web, where geospatial information is given well-defined meaning by applied ontology and thus geospatial contents can be discovered, queried, and consumed automatically by software [20]. The GSW aims to add computer-processable meaning (semantics) to the geospatial information on the World Wide Web.

Semantic heterogeneity refers to disagreements about meaning, interpretation, or intended use of the same or related data. By associating spatial data content from the Web with ontologies that would supply context and meaning, the vision of GSW is to extract geospatial knowledge from the Web regardless of geospatial data formats or sources; thus it can facilitate transparent geospatial data exchange, sharing, and query. For example, the GSW will be able to search for needed geospatial information not based on keywords, but on data contents and context, e.g., understanding what the word "near" means based on different spatial data contents and context.

Figure 3.1 illustrates a GSW architecture for geospatial data sharing [21]. For instant remote data access and exchange, the ontology-based web services are used to access and manipulate geospatial data over the Web from heterogeneous databases. The architecture is based on service-oriented architecture (SOA) and is essentially a collection of ontology-based OGC web services, which communicate with each other by simple data passing or coordinating some activities. It has four major elements: service provider, service broker, service client, and ontology server. The service provider supplies the ontology-based geospatial data the service client searches and integrates the ontology-based geospatial data from the service providers, and the service broker provides a registry for the available ontology-based web services. The ontology server ensures semantic interoperability of ontologies from the service providers and clients.

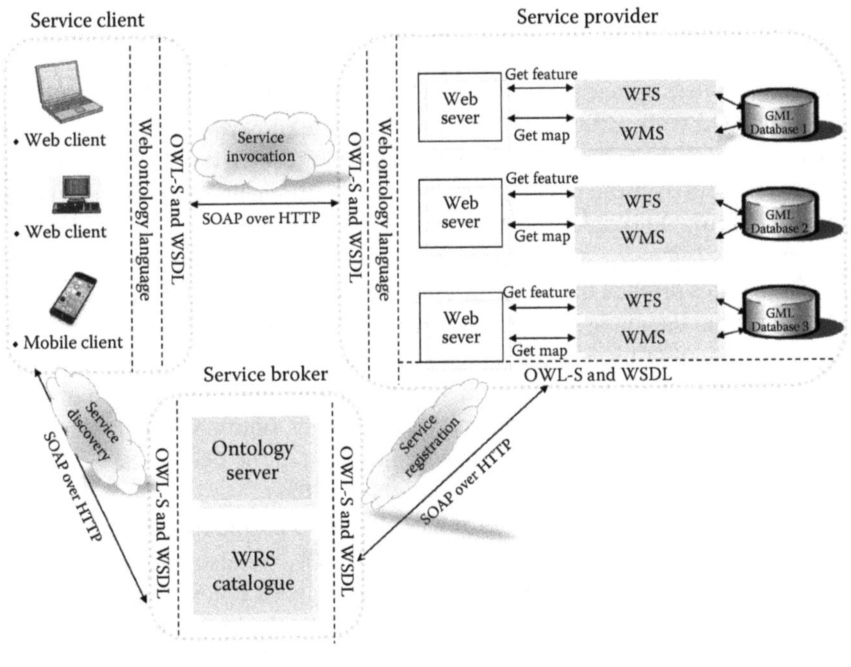

Figure 3.1: A geospatial semantic web architecture.

Based on the work in geospatial ontologies, some recent research focuses on how to query heterogeneous spatial data over the Web through ontologies. Many studies involve the concepts and feasibility of the GSW. However, many of these studies are at the initial stage of proposing frameworks for making queries in the GSW using the concept of global ontology and local ontology, or ontology integrations. There is still a long way to go to realize the aforementioned goals of GSW particularly for big geospatial data. There are many challenges to implement a workable GSW system. The major challenges and future directions of the GSW in the context of big geospatial data will be discussed in the following sections.

3.3 Challenges and Future Directions of Geospatial Semantic Web in the Context of Big Geospatial Data

3.3.1 Ontology

The introduction of big geospatial data from diverse sources over the Web makes semantic heterogeneous problem more complex. It becomes a greater challenge to share, integrate, analyze, and manage big geospatial data because of the semantic heterogeneity. An ontology defines and represents the concepts in a domain and uses a shared vocabulary to represent knowledge. When ontologies are populated with valid data, they can provide a knowledge base that supports the analytics of these data. Ontologies are used to resolve the semantic heterogeneous problem over the GSW, and ontology development forms the backbone of the GSW [16]. Ontologies offer the potential to address the semantic challenges presented by big geospatial data.

Ontologies provide the semantic congruity, consistency, and clarity to support big geospatial data analysis and knowledge extraction. Ontologies may make it possible to exploit big geospatial data in the context of their relationships with other existing data. Ontology quality and ontology matching are important for big geospatial data querying and sharing. However, ontology quality and ontology matching remain a challenge for development of the GSW. The challenge is further exacerbated with the big geospatial data effect.

Big geospatial data not only introduce efficiency problems for accessing, integrating, and querying ontology data from the GSW, but also create visualization problems for communicating and representing large, complex, and varied domain ontologies and knowledge. The high variety and velocity of the big geospatial data means a large number of concepts, properties, and domain knowledge bases. Exploration with the large number of concepts, relationships, and attributions of ontologies with high complexity for big geospatial data is difficult because of the mismatch/gap between users' or developers' understanding of large domain ontologies for big geospatial data over the GSW.

Ontology quality may be the most important challenge for sharing big geospatial data over the GSW. Although some studies have created specific application ontologies, currently these ontologies are typically built by a small number of people, in most cases by researchers, using ontology tools and editors such as Protégé. For example, the United States Geological Survey (USGS) has been working on developing ontologies for The National Map for many years and has published RDF triple data derived from The National Map to support geospatial knowledge queries [22–24]. These ontology tools and editors supporting ontological modeling have been improved over the last few years and many functions are available now, such as ontology consistency checking, import of existing ontologies, and visualization of ontologies. Manual ontology building for big geospatial data has proven to be a very difficult and error-prone task and becomes the bottleneck of knowledge acquiring processes from big geospatial data. It is especially challenging to build high-quality large ontologies for big geospatial data. For instance, it is unrealistic for nondomain experts to use these tools to build high-quality ontologies for a variety of big geospatial data. Although transformation algorithms have been proposed by Zhang et al. [21] to automatically transform existing Unified modeling language (UML) to Web Ontology Language (OWL) so as to avoid errors and provide a cost-efficient method for the development of high-quality ontologies, there are many issues yet to be resolved due to the differences between UML and OWL. It is extremely challenging to develop the automatic transform approaches for building high-quality large ontologies for big geospatial data.

Ontology matching is another important challenge for sharing big geospatial data over the GSW. On the GSW, different users communicate and collaborate based on what different ontologies connected with different knowledge expressions mean. The differences between ontologies from varied sources can be handled by ontology matching. Ontology matching is a solution to the semantic heterogeneity problem over the Web by finding correspondences between semantically related entities of ontologies, and is inevitable for ensuring interoperability of big geospatial data. The past several years have witnessed impressive progress in the development of ontology matching tools. However, there are many issues still to be solved for reliable ontology matching for sharing big geospatial data over the GSW.

The first issue is that ontology matching needs to work on a larger scale. In the era of big geospatial data, ontology matching needs fast algorithms to analyze and integrate a large set of ontologies. However, existing ontology matching tools have not demonstrated that they can handle a large set of ontologies. The second issue is that the performance of existing ontology matching tools needs to be improved. For dynamic sharing and utilizing of big geospatial data over GSW, performance is particularly important because users cannot wait too long for the Web to respond. However, large ontology matching may become a bottleneck for dynamic big geospatial data applications if the matching techniques perform slowly. The third issue is missing background knowledge. Missing background knowledge is one important reason for the failure of large ontology matching for big geospatial data applications. Ontologies are developed with specific background knowledge and in a specific context. However, the background knowledge and context information may not be available for matching tools. The lack of background knowledge and context information may generate ambiguities and thus increase uncertainties and errors of large ontology matching. Strategies are needed to resolve the missing background knowledge and context information in large ontology matching.

In addition, the lack of sufficient metadata annotations of large ontologies for big geospatial data is also a challenge. While ontologies are important for semantic interoperability and communication among big geospatial data sources, ontologies are always developed by groups or individuals in isolation. There is a lack of metadata annotations of ontologies, which causes difficulty for large ontology matching and sharing. The various ontologies without metadata are usually developed using different techniques. There is no enforced standard convention for describing the contents and context of large ontologies. However, metadata annotations of large ontologies should facilitate ontology discovery and matching for sharing big geospatial data over the GSW.

Finally, it is a challenge to provide a dynamic ontology matching support infrastructure at the Web scale for sharing and utilizing big geospatial data. The matching life cycle is strongly related to the ontology life cycle: as soon as ontologies evolve, new matching tools have to be produced following the ontology evolution. This may be achieved by recording the changes made to ontologies and transforming these changes into matching processes, which can be used for computing new matching that will update the previous ones.

In general, nowadays web sites are no longer static web pages serving contents and images; they have become more responsive, adaptive, and dynamic. There is inherent uncertainty in the ontology creation, maintenance, and matching processes particularly for sharing and utilizing big geospatial data. The use of newer data formats in big geospatial data (many of which are without schema) makes it harder to use existing ontology creation, matching, and alignment techniques for big geospatial data applications. Under these conditions, existing approaches for ontology creation, maintenance, and matching need to be modified and new perspectives should be considered for solving this problem. Since the existing approaches based on deterministic assumptions will not perform well in situations that are nondeterministic, probabilistic methods based on approximate sampling of big geospatial data may be explored to overcome this problem.

In dynamic settings of big geospatial data sources, it is natural that data are constantly changing. Thus, approaches that attempt to automatically tune and adapt ontology creation and match solutions to the settings in which an application operates are of high importance. However, it is hard to perform automatic tuning and adapting of large ontologies. It is too cumbersome for one person or a small group of people to resolve the problem. Many people need to work together for creating high-quality, large ontologies and matching correct large ontologies. Crowd sourcing and other collaborative and social approaches that allow easy sharing and reusing ontologies may be used to aid large ontology creating and matching.

3.3.2 GeoSPARQL queries

The GeoSPARQL protocol was proposed by the OGC as an extension of SPARQL for querying geographic RDF data. GeoSPARQL queries are dominated by spatial join operations due to the fine-grained nature of the RDF data model. Lack of spatial indices causes additional performance problems for GeoSPARQL queries. One reason for the poor performance problems is caused by the way that spatial attributes are stored in RDF data sets. Spatial attributes are usually stored as string literals that conform to certain formats such as WKT or GML. The GeoSPARQL query engine that implements spatial operators and filter functions has to parse these strings to recover the spatial coordinates for spatial computation. A naïve implementation of a spatial operator or a filter function in GeoSPARQL treats its spatial inputs as plain strings and has to parse the strings to retrieve spatial contents such as x and y coordinates. Repeated parsing of the spatial inputs imposes a very large runtime overhead. The second reason for the poor performance problems is due to the lack of parallelization. Since spatial objects are not indexed, a GeoSPARQL query engine cannot partition ontology data into subsets to be processed in parallel. As a result, a GeoSPARQL query can only be processed as a single-threaded program. Even with precomputed spatial indices, partitioning spatial ontology data is not easy since the targeted data may not be evenly distributed in the indices.

In fact, different parallel approaches have been widely used for improving the query performance for a long time as reported in literature. However, past research on improving query performance using parallelization has been centered on relational databases [25–27]. Optimizing techniques for parallel relational databases do not specialize on the triple model of RDF and triple patterns of SPARQL queries for query engines based on the RDF- and SPARQL-specific properties [28]. Although there are studies to query heterogeneous relational databases using SPARQL and parallel algorithms [29,30], parallel relational databases have inherent limitations such as scalability. A SPARQL query can be parallelized by treating each triple statement in the query as a parallel task and the results of all the triple statement subqueries can be joined together after all the parallel tasks have completed [28]. Unfortunately, this approach does not work efficiently when spatial predicates exist in the triple statements. There are also studies to propose methods for efficiently parallelizing joint query of RDF data using MapReduce systems [31].

However, to the best of our knowledge, there are only a few studies that deal with parallelizing spatial join computations to support efficient spatial RDF queries, which is an important issue for the development of a GSW [20]. Zhao et al. [32] proposed a query strategy to improve the query performance of a geospatial knowledge base by creating spatial indexing on-the-fly to prune the search space for spatial queries and by parallelizing the spatial join computations within the queries. Their initial experiments show that the proposed strategy can greatly reduce the runtime costs of GeoSPARQL queries through on-the-fly spatial indexing and parallel execution. Zhang et al. [33] introduced a MapReduce-based parallel approach for improving the query performance of a geospatial ontology for disaster response. Their approach makes full use of data/task parallelism for spatial queries and focuses on parallelizing the spatial join computations of GeoSPARQL queries. The results of initial experiments show that the proposed approach can reduce individual spatial query execution time by taking advantage of parallel processes. Their proposed approach, therefore, may afford a large number of concurrent spatial queries in disaster response applications.

Although some insights into how the execution of GeoSPARQL queries can be improved through a parallel process have been gained based on the aforementioned studies, these results are limited since they were based on the use of a small- and a medium-sized spatial data sets. To implement a workable GSW system for big geospatial data for efficient spatial knowledge queries, more studies are needed. Spatial queries from big geospatial data are complex and time-consuming. The geospatial data objects are normally nested and more complex than other data types. They are stored as multidimensional geometry objects, for example points, lines, and polygons. Spatial queries are based not only on the value of alphanumeric attributes but also on the spatial location, extent, and measurements of spatial objects in different reference systems. Therefore, spatial query processing over big geospatial data requires intensive disk I/O accesses and spatial computation. The I/O and computation capabilities of traditional GIS, VGI, and SDI can hardly meet the high performance requirement of spatial queries or spatial analyses over big geospatial data. While the emerging key value store (KVS) systems, such as Bigtable, HBase, and Cassandra, are proved to be helpful for some I/O intensive applications, these KVS systems cannot process spatial queries efficiently because the data in KVSs are organized regardless of geographic proximity and are indexed by a key-based structure rather than a spatial index.

Spatial analysis for big geospatial data involves complex queries such as spatial cross-matching, overlaying of multiple sets of spatial objects, spatial proximity computations between objects, and queries for spatial pattern discovery. These queries often involve millions or billions of spatial objects and heavy geometric computations, which not only are used for computing measurements or generating new spatial objects, but also as logical operations for topology relationships. Therefore, novel approaches are needed to support efficient parallel execution of GeoSPARQL queries. Future studies may explore how to improve the performance of GeoSPARQL queries in distributed platforms using Cloud-based web services and cluster platforms. Future studies should focus on studying (1) how to implement extensions to the RDF query engine (such as Jena) to build and cache spatial indices on-the-fly and (2) how to utilize distributed and paralleled computing resources including computing clusters (through libraries such as Spark) and graphic processing units (GPUs) to accelerate GeoSPARQL.

3.3.3 Geospatial indexing

Performing a spatial query of a knowledge base of the GSW can be very inefficient if it contains a large number of spatial objects. Spatial indexing algorithms such as R-tree [34], quadtree [35], and KD-tree [36] are used in traditional spatial databases to improve query performance. These methods may be used to improve query performance over the GSW in the context of big geospatial data. With spatial indexing, spatial queries of big geospatial data over GSW can be answered more efficiently since the computation involves far fewer spatial objects.

There are three important spatial indexing algorithms in literature: R-tree, quadtree, and KD-tree. All three algorithms can be used to reduce the runtime costs of range queries, spatial joins, and K-nearest neighbors (K-NN) queries of geospatial objects. However, quadtree and KD-tree may be more suitable for indexing point objects, while R-tree and its variations work well for all types of spatial objects including lines and polygons.

R-tree and its variations are the preferred algorithms for spatial indexing [37,38]. R-tree performs well for all kinds of spatial objects including points, lines, and polygons It is a height-balanced tree where each spatial object is inserted into the tree leaf using its minimum bounding rectangle (MBR) as a guide. Each node of a R-tree has a MBR that encloses the MBRs of its children. The number of the children of each node is maintained within a range so that if there is an overflow of children at a node, then the node is split into two, and if there is an underflow, then two or more nodes are merged. If the insertion of a spatial object causes the root node to split, then the tree will grow by adding a new root.

R-tree is a dynamic tree whose shape depends on the order in which the spatial objects are inserted. The MBRs of the children of a node may also overlap so that search operations may require recursive descent into multiple children of a node. Various heuristics can be applied to subtree insertion and node splitting.

Quadtree is a tree data structure where each tree node has four children with each child representing a quadrant in a two-dimensional space. Quadtree for points can be constructed by recursively adding tree nodes until each leaf contains at most one point. To search a quadtree for the points within a range, the tree nodes can be recursively searched and only quadrants that intersect the range will be visited. For each visited leaf quadrant, the points of the leaf that are within the range will be returned.

The height of a quadtree depends on the smallest distance between two points. The time complexity of searching the nearest neighbor of a point using a quadtree is linear to the depth of the tree. Quadtrees may not be balanced, however, and the shape depends on the distribution of spatial objects. In extreme cases, the depth of a quadtree can be linear to the number of points. The advantage of the quadtree approach is its simplicity and it can be efficient for evenly distributed points.

A common type of quadtree is the region quadtree, which divides the space into four equally-sized quadrants. Region quadtrees are suitable for indexing points. There are other types of quadtrees (with more complexity) for indexing lines and polygons.

KD-tree is a binary tree with a k-dimensional point in each node. For a node at depth d, the dimension d *modulo* k of the node's point is used as the key to separate the node's subtrees. A value at each dimension (such as the medium value of the data points) needs to be chosen for data separation. Finding one nearest neighbor in a balanced KD-tree of randomly distributed points takes log time on average. However, in general, multiple subtrees of each node may be explored in a nearest neighbor search. To search a KD-tree for points within a range, the splitting hyperplane may be used to decide which subtrees to visit.

There are some challenges in introducing spatial indexing to the GSW such as how to retrofit an ontology query engine to build spatial indices and how to take advantage of the spatial indices in answering spatial queries. An ontology query engine such as Jena can be modified to build spatial indices when spatial ontology data are initially loaded. To implement this, the query engine should provide the means to identify the ontology class whose instances are spatial objects that should be indexed. In addition, when new ontology instances are added or updated, the related spatial indices should be updated as well. Extensions to spatial ontology constructs may be needed to ensure that the ontology data are written in formats that can be parsed and indexed by the query engine.

Answering ontology queries using spatial indices is more intricate since each query may or may not involve spatial attributes that can be processed with indices. There are several possible implementations. One choice is to implement low-level extensions to the ontology query engine to intercept calls to spatial functions or predicates of a query and generate results using spatial indices if available. Another choice is to analyze the entire query first, separate the spatial components of the query, and then attempt to answer it with spatial indices. The third choice is to build spatial indices on demand when answering queries such as those that contain operators corresponding to spatial joins, and cache the indices for subsequent use.

3.3.4 Spatial join

Queries over the GSW may require joining two or more types of spatial objects. In spatial databases, spatial join algorithms are used to improve runtime performance and the same algorithms can also be applied to improve query performance over the GSW. The choice of these algorithms depends on whether one or more spatial indices are present.

Nested loop is the simplest approach to join two sets of spatial objects and it works with or without spatial indices [39]. It simply takes one from each of the two sets of spatial objects via nest loops to check which pairs satisfy the join conditions. The set of objects that are indexed should be placed in the inner loop so that the index can be used to check the spatial join relation for each object of the outer loop. The advantage of this approach is that it is very simple, does not require indices, and is efficient for small sets of spatial objects. This algorithm can be easily parallelized. The disadvantage is that it can be very slow for large data sets where the spatial relation is costly to compute.

Hierarchical traversal algorithms can be used if both sets of objects are indexed using R-tree or similar data structures [40]. The basic algorithm takes two sets of tree nodes as inputs. For each pair of nodes with one from each set, it compares the MBRs of the nodes to determine whether or not they are disjoint. If they are not, then the algorithm recursively calls itself with the children of the nonleaf nodes as inputs. The recursion stops when both nodes are leaves and returns the pair of leaves that are related by the spatial join predicate. This approach is very efficient when the MBRs of an R-tree do not have many overlaps. Like a nest loop, this algorithm is parallelizable. The drawback is the requirement of available indices on both sets of input objects, which may not be possible when the input sets are dynamically generated.

The plane sweep algorithm does not use spatial indices [41]. The algorithm works by sweeping along one dimension (e.g., x-dimension) so that if an MBR of a set is detected, it becomes active and is inserted into a sweep structure for that set. Once the sweep line passes an MBR, it is removed from the corresponding sweep structure. Each MBR in one sweep structure is compared with the active MBR of the other set to find out whether or not they are spatially related using other dimensions (e.g., y-dimension). The plane sweep algorithm works for smaller data sets that can be fitted into memory. The advantage of the approach is that it does not require indices and it is more scalable than the nested loop algorithm when the objects are evenly distributed. The drawback is that it requires all objects to fit in memory for efficient processing. Therefore, its applicability is limited by the size of the memory and the sizes of the data sets.

For larger data sets, the *partition-based spatial merge-join* algorithm may be used. This algorithm recursively partitions the pair of input data sets into pairs of smaller sets until each pair can fit in memory such that the plane sweep algorithm can be applied. The partition can be based on a grid but MBRs that intersect grid lines must be duplicated.

To improve performance, the spatial join process can be split into two steps: filtering and refinement. The filtering step approximates the spatial join using the MBRs to obtain a set of candidate pairs and the refinement step checks spatial relations of the candidate pairs to obtain the final result. The filtering step processes more pairs of spatial objects but it is efficient to compute join relations for MBRs. The refinement step spends more time on computing the join relations of candidate pairs using their exact geometries though it involves a smaller number of spatial object pairs. The aforementioned spatial join algorithms can be used for the filtering step.

3.3.5 Distributed geospatial computing

Spatial computation such as spatial indexing, K-NN, searching, range query, and spatial joins is very expensive for large spatial data sets. To improve performance, several systems have been developed to implement spatial computation over distributed platforms such as computing clusters and Cloud-based servers. Two of these systems—Hadoop-GIS [42] and SpatialHadoop [43]—are directly based on the Hadoop framework, which provides a distributed file system that supports

MapReduce computation over a large number of computing nodes. The other two systems, GeoSpark [44] and SpatialSpark [45], are based on a more recent framework, Spark, which provides better performance than Hadoop due to its in-memory capability. The crucial abstraction in Spark is a resilient distributed data set (RDD), which is used to hold distributed data.

All the aforementioned four systems have implemented spatial computation such as K-NN, range queries, and spatial join. All systems provide distributed spatial indexing capability, which can greatly improve the performance of some spatial operations. SpatialHadoop supports spatial indexing as an integrated component of the Hadoop distributed file system, which can optimize skewed spatial data distributions. However, GeoSpark has better performance than SpatialHadoop over spatial joins with or without indexing. It is unclear how SpatialSpark compares with other systems due to its limited number of implementations.

The challenging issues with implementing distributed spatial computation focus on distributed indexing of spatial data on the computing nodes and revision of sequential spatial algorithms to use the MapReduce framework. Memory consumption of Spark-based systems is also a challenging issue. There are at least four choices with spatial indexing over the MapReduce framework. One is to only build an index and use it through other frameworks. The second choice is to build an index on demand. The third choice is to build a global index on the distributed data sets. The last choice is to have both a global index and a local index for each local data set. Hadoop-GIS builds global indices but has local indices on demand, while SpatialHadoop builds both global and local indices. GeoSpark builds global indices but local indices are based on needs. When partitioning data over spatial indices such as R-tree, one must consider spatial objects across the boundaries of the partitions. A common solution is to replicate the spatial objects for all partitions with boundaries that overlap the objects. However, the subsequent computation is needed to remove the duplicated objects from the results. Implementing range queries, K-NN, and spatial joins on MapReduce frameworks seems straightforward with or without spatial indices as the algorithms can be made data parallel. These frameworks demonstrate that spatial computation can be made scalable with respect to the number of computing nodes. This makes it possible to support spatial computation on very large spatial data sets of GSW.

Other than MapReduce based frameworks, GPUs, multicore CPUs, and vector processing units (VPUs) have been used in accelerating spatial computation in the literature. Examples include building R-tree indices and using R-tree indices for spatial querying [46], point in polygon, point to polygon computation [47], spatial join [48], and spatial-temporal aggregation [49]. The experiments in these studies have revealed the potential of many-core processing units such as GPU and VPU in reducing the runtime cost of certain data-parallel geospatial computation. The main burden of taking advantage of the computing power of GPU and VPU is the more complex programming interface provided by these platforms when compared with MapReduce frameworks. There is also the cost of copying data between CPU and GPU memory, which, if occurs frequently, can substantially diminish the performance gain.

While the aforementioned researches have demonstrated the effectiveness of scalable spatial computation over distributed systems, more work is needed to improve the query performance of large geospatial data sets over the GSW. The primary challenge is how to distribute the geospatial data within a knowledge base over computing nodes to enable global and local spatial indices and to distribute the spatial computation workload. One possible research direction is to have virtual representation of spatial objects within a geospatial knowledge base while storing the concrete data in original distributed servers. This requires modification to the ontology query engine to redirect the spatial computation of a query that involves virtual spatial objects to the distributed servers and to integrate the results with that of the rest of the query. Another possible direction is to partition the geospatial knowledge base over distributed servers, perform an ontology query over each computing node, and then integrate the results. The nonspatial portion of the knowledge may need to be replicated across the computing nodes so that the results of the ontology query at each computing node are completed except the geospatial data, which needs to be joined.

3.4 Conclusion

Modern geospatial technologies such as remote sensing, GPS, GIS, and VGI have been used to collect and handle geospatial data. In recent years, these geospatial technologies have generated large volumes of geospatial data about things and human beings. Although recent development of geographic information and Internet technologies has enabled accessing and sharing big geospatial data, we still face huge challenges for transparent geospatial data exchange and sharing because of the lack of fast and interoperating algorithms and tools along with heterogeneous semantic problems. The concept of a GSW was proposed to overcome semantic and spatial computation limitations. However, there is still a long way to go to support efficient query of big geospatial data over the GSW. In this chapter, we investigated the challenges and opportunities of GSW brought for sharing and utilizing big geospatial data. Ontologies provide the semantic congruity, consistency, and clarity for support of big geospatial data analysis and knowledge extraction. However, ontology quality and ontology matching remains a challenge for development of the GSW. The challenge is further exacerbated with the big geospatial data effect. It is very inefficient to query big geospatial data using the standard semantic web query language (GeoSPARQL) because the data in the knowledge base of the GSW are no longer indexed to support efficient big geospatial data query. A new query strategy is needed to reduce the runtime costs of GeoSPARQL query through on-the-fly spatial indexing and parallel execution. Three important spatial indexing algorithms in the literature—R-tree, quadtree, and KD-tree—can be used to improve query performance from big geospatial data sources over GSW. However, quadtree and KD-tree may be more suitable for indexing point objects, while R-tree and its variations may work well for all types of spatial objects including lines and polygons. To get the needed information from big geospatial data sources over the GSW, spatial queries may require joining two or more types of spatial objects. The spatial join algorithms for spatial databases may be used to obtain the needed information from big geospatial data sources over the GSW. The choice of these algorithms depends on whether one or more spatial indices are present. To improve performance, several systems such as Hadoop-GIS, SpatialHadoop, GeoSpark, and SpatialSpark have been developed to implement spatial computation over distributed platforms such as computing clusters and Cloud-based servers. Each of these implemented distributed geospatial computing systems has its own advantages and disadvantages. However, the challenge still exists to implement distributed spatial computation for sharing and utilizing big geospatial data over the GSW.

In summary, although big geospatial data are available for better understanding our coupled human and environmental systems, there are still many challenges of GSW techniques for sharing and utilizing big geospatial data. New methods for the GSW and distributed spatial computing are needed to make full use of available big geospatial data.

References

[1] Morais, C.D. (2012). Where is the Phrase "80% of Data is Geographic" From?. http://www.gislounge.com/80-percent-data-is-geographic/ (accessed October 4, 2016).

[2] Campbell, J. B., & Wynne, R. H. (2011). *Introduction to remote sensing*. New York: Guilford Press.

[3] Gamba, P., Du, P., Juergens, C., & Maktav, D. (2011). Foreword to the special issue on "Human settlements: A global remote sensing challenge". *IEEE Journal of Selected Topics in Applied Earth Observations and Remote Sensing*, 4(1), 5–7.

[4] Ma, Y., Wu, H., Wang, L., Huang, B., Ranjan, R., Zomaya, A., & Jie, W. (2015). Remote sensing big data computing: Challenges and opportunities. *Future Generation Computer Systems*, 51, 47–60.

[5] Zheng, Y., Chen, Y., Li, Q., Xie, X., & Ma, W. Y. (2010). Understanding transportation modes based on GPS data for web applications. *ACM Transactions on the Web (TWEB)*, 4(1), 1.

[6] Zheng, Y., Liu, F., & Hsieh, H. P. (2013, August). U-Air: When urban air quality inference meets big data. *Proceedings of the 19th ACM SIGKDD International Conference on Knowledge Discovery and Data Mining*, KDD'13, August 11–14, pp. 1436–1444, Chicago, IL: ACM.

[7] Goodchild, M. F. (2007). Citizens as sensors: The world of volunteered geography. *GeoJournal*, 69(4), 211–221.

[8] Sui, D., Elwood, S., & Goodchild, M. (Eds.). (2012). *Crowdsourcing geographic knowledge: Volunteered geographic information (VGI) in theory and practice*. Dordrecht: Springer Science & Business Media.

[9] Gao, S., Li, L., Li, W., Janowicz, K., & Zhang, Y. (2014). *Constructing gazetteers from volunteered big geo-data based on Hadoop. Computers, Environment and Urban Systems*, The Netherlands: Elsevier.

[10] Jiang, B., & Thill, J. C. (2015). Volunteered geographic information: Towards the establishment of a new paradigm. *Computers, Environment and Urban Systems*, 53, 1–3.

[11] Cinnamon, J., & Schuurman, N. (2013). Confronting the data-divide in a time of spatial turns and volunteered geographic information. *GeoJournal*, 78(4), 657–674.

[12] Stefanidis, A., Crooks, A., & Radzikowski, J. (2013). Harvesting ambient geospatial information from social media feeds. *GeoJournal*, 78(2), 319–338.

[13] Wang, S. (2010). A CyberGIS framework for the synthesis of cyberinfrastructure, GIS, and spatial analysis. *Annals of the Association of American Geographers*, 100(3), 535–557.

[14] Wang, S., Anselin, L., Bhaduri, B., Crosby, C., Goodchild, M. F., Liu, Y., & Nyerges, T. L. (2013). CyberGIS software: A synthetic review and integration roadmap. *International Journal of Geographical Information Science*, 27(11), 2122–2145.

[15] Farrugia, J., & Egenhofer, M. J. (2002, May). Presentations and Bearers of Semantics on the Web. *FLAIRS Conference*, pp. 408–412, FL: AAAI.

[16] Wiegand, N., & García, C. (2007). A task–based ontology approach to automate geospatial data retrieval. *Transactions in GIS*, 11(3), 355–376.

[17] Lutz, M. (2007). Ontology-based descriptions for semantic discovery and composition of geoprocessing services. *Geoinformatica*, 11(1), 1–36.

[18] Lutz, M., & Kolas, D. (2007). Rule–based discovery in spatial data infrastructure. *Transactions in GIS*, 11(3), 317–336.

[19] Egenhofer, M. J. (2002, November). Toward the semantic geospatial web. *Proceedings of the 10th ACM International Symposium on Advances in Geographic Information Systems*, pp. 1–4, New York: ACM.

[20] Zhang, C., Zhao, T., & Li, W. (2015b). *Geospatial semantic web*. Springer International Publishing, Switzerland, p. 194.

[21] Zhang, C., Li, W., & Zhao, T. (2007). Geospatial data sharing based on geospatial semantic web technologies. *Journal of Spatial Science*, 52(2), 35–49.

[22] Varanka, D. E. (2011). Ontology patterns for complex topographic feature types. *Cartography and Geographic Information Science*, 38(2), 126–136.

[23] Usery, E. L., & Varanka, D. (2012). Design and development of linked data from the national map. *Semantic Web*, 3(4), 371–384.

[24] Varanka, D. E., & Usery, E. L. (2015). An applied ontology for semantics associated with surface water features. *Land Use and Land Cover Semantics: Principles, Best Practices, and Prospects*, pp. 145–170, Boca Raton, FL.

[25] Kitsuregawa, M., Tanaka, H., & Moto-Oka, T. (1983). Application of hash to data base machine and its architecture. *New Generation Computing*, 1(1), 63–74.

[26] DeWitt, D. J., Gerber, R., Graefe, G., Heytens, M., Kumar, K., & Muralikrishna, M. (1986). GAMMA—A High Performance Dataflow Database Machine. In *Proceedings of the 12th International Conference on Very Large Data Bases*, August 25–28, pp. 228–237, San Francisco, CA: Morgan Kaufmann.

[27] Boral, H., Alexander, W., Clay, L., Copeland, G., Danforth, S., Franklin, M., ... Valduriez, P. (1990). Prototyping Bubba, a highly parallel database system. *IEEE Transactions on Knowledge and Data Engineering*, 2(1), 4–24, IEEE Educational Activities Department Piscataway, NJ.

[28] Groppe, J., & Groppe, S. (2011, March). Parallelizing join computations of SPARQL queries for large semantic web databases. *Proceedings of the 2011 ACM Symposium on Applied Computing*, pp. 1681–1686, New York: ACM.

[29] Castagna, P., Seaborne, A., & Dollin, C. (2009). *A parallel processing framework for RDF design and issues*. HP Labs, Bristol, Technical Report.

[30] Wang, J., Miao, Z., Zhang, Y., & Zhou, B. (2009, June). Querying heterogeneous relational database using SPARQL. *Eighth IEEE/ACIS International Conference on Computer and Information Science, ICIS 2009*, pp. 475–480, IEEE.

[31] Ravindra, P., Kim, H., & Anyanwu, K. (2011, May). An intermediate algebra for optimizing RDF graph pattern matching on MapReduce. *Extended Semantic Web Conference*, pp. 46–61, Springer, Berlin.

[32] Zhao, T., Zhang, C., Anselin, L., Li, W., & Chen, K. (2015). A parallel approach for improving Geo-SPARQL query performance. *International Journal of Digital Earth*, 8(5), 383–402.

[33] Zhang, C., Zhao, T., Anselin, L., Li, W., & Chen, K. (2015a). A MapReduce based parallel approach for improving query performance in a geospatial semantic web for disaster response. *Earth Science Informatics*, 8(3), 499–509.

[34] Guttman, A. (1984). *R-trees: A dynamic index structure for spatial searching*, Vol. 14(2), pp. 47–57, New York: ACM.

[35] Samet, H., & Webber, R. E. (1985). Storing a collection of polygons using quadtrees. *ACM Transactions on Graphics (TOG)*, 4(3), 182–222.

[36] Bentley, J. L. (1975). Multidimensional binary search trees used for associative searching. *Communications of the ACM*, 18(9), 509–517.

[37] Sellis, T., Roussopoulos, N., & Faloutsos, C. (1987). The R+-Tree: A dynamic index for multi-dimensional objects. In *Proceedings of the 13th VLDB (Very Large Data Bases) Conference*, Brighton, 1987, September 01–04, pp. 507–518, San Francisco, CA: Morgan Kaufmann.

[38] Beckmann, N., Kriegel, H. P., Schneider, R., & Seeger, B. (1990). The R*-tree: An efficient and robust access method for points and rectangles. *ACM SIGMOD Record*, 19(2), 322–331.

[39] Mishra, P., & Eich, M. H. (1992). Join processing in relational databases. *ACM Computing Surveys (CSUR)*, 24(1), 63–113.

[40] Brinkhoff, T., Kriegel, H. P., & Schneider, R. (1993, April). Comparison of approximations of complex objects used for approximation-based query processing in spatial database systems. *Ninth International Conference on Data Engineering, Proceedings*, pp. 40–49, Washington, DC: IEEE Computer Society.

[41] Arge, L., Procopiuc, O., Ramaswamy, S., Suel, T., & Vitter, J. S. (1998). Scalable sweeping-based spatial join. *VLDB*, 98, 570–581.

[42] Aji, A., Wang, F., Vo, H., Lee, R., Liu, Q., Zhang, X., & Saltz, J. (2013). Hadoop GIS: A high performance spatial data warehousing system over MapReduce. *Proceedings of the VLDB Endowment*, 6(11), 1009–1020.

[43] Eldawy, A., & Mokbel, M. F. (2015, April). SpatialHadoop: A MapReduce framework for spatial data. *2015 IEEE 31st International Conference on Data Engineering*, pp. 1352–1363, Seoul, South Korea: IEEE.

[44] Yu, J., Wu, J., & Sarwat, M. (2015, November). GeoSpark: A cluster computing framework for processing large-scale spatial data. *Proceedings of the 23rd SIGSPATIAL International Conference on Advances in Geographic Information Systems*, November 03–06, 2015, p. 70, Bellevue, WA: ACM.

[45] Zhang, J., You, S., & Gruenwald, L. (2015c). Large-scale spatial data processing on GPUs and GPU-accelerated clusters. *SIGSPATIAL Special*, 6(3), 27–34.

[46] You, S., Zhang, J., & Gruenwald, L. (2013). Parallel spatial query processing on GPUs using R-trees. *Proceedings of the 2nd ACM SIGSPATIAL International Workshop on Analytics for Big Geospatial Data*, Orlando, Florida, November 4, pp. 23–31, New York: ACM.

[47] Zhang, J., & You, S. (2014). Large-scale geospatial processing on multi-core and many-core processors: Evaluations on CPUs, GPUs and MICs. *CoRR*, abs/1403.0802.

[48] You, S., Zhang, J., & Gruenwald, L. (2015). Large-scale spatial join query processing in cloud. *31st IEEE International Conference on Data Engineering Workshops (ICDEW)*, Seoul, South Korea, pp. 34–41, IEEE.

[49] Zhang, J., You, S., & Gruenwald, L. (2014). Parallel online spatial and temporal aggregations on multi-core CPUs and many-core GPUs. *Information Systems*, 44, 134–154.

Chapter 4

Big Data over Wireless Networks (WiBi)

Immanuel Manohar and Fei Hu
University of Alabama
Tuscaloosa, Alabama

CONTENTS

4.1 Introduction

Big data is generally characterized by the four Vs, namely, volume, variety, veracity, and velocity, as shown in Figure 4.1. The terms are briefly discussed below:

Volume: This refers to the large amount of storage space needed for big data. The volume of big data depends on the applications and types of data under consideration. Different types of data would require different technologies for handling them. The same volume of two different types of data (e.g., XML and multimedia) would require vastly different processing techniques to analyze them.

Variety: This refers to structure of the data. There are three major types, i.e., structured, semistructured and unstructured. Structured data can be stored and referenced from a table and has a formal structure. This category consists of around 5% of the total content in big data applications. Semistructured data does not adhere to a formal structure but still has certain hierarchies or tags, and has its own structure. For example, XML documents have semistructured architecture. This category also accounts for about 5–10% of big data. Unstructured data does not have regular structure, e.g., multimedia data such as video and audio, financial time series, market survey responses, etc. different varieties are illustrated in Figure 4.2.

Veracity: The huge data set may be highly redundant, and one might need to scan huge quantities of data to extract the essential information from it. Other data sets might contain essential information in an already condensed form. While the former has lower veracity, the latter has higher veracity.

Velocity: This describes the rate of data gathering. Big data typically requires fast data collection speed.

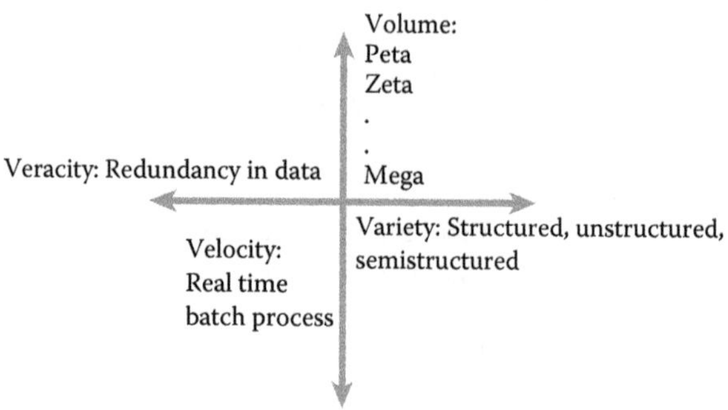

Figure 4.1: The four Vs of big data [1].

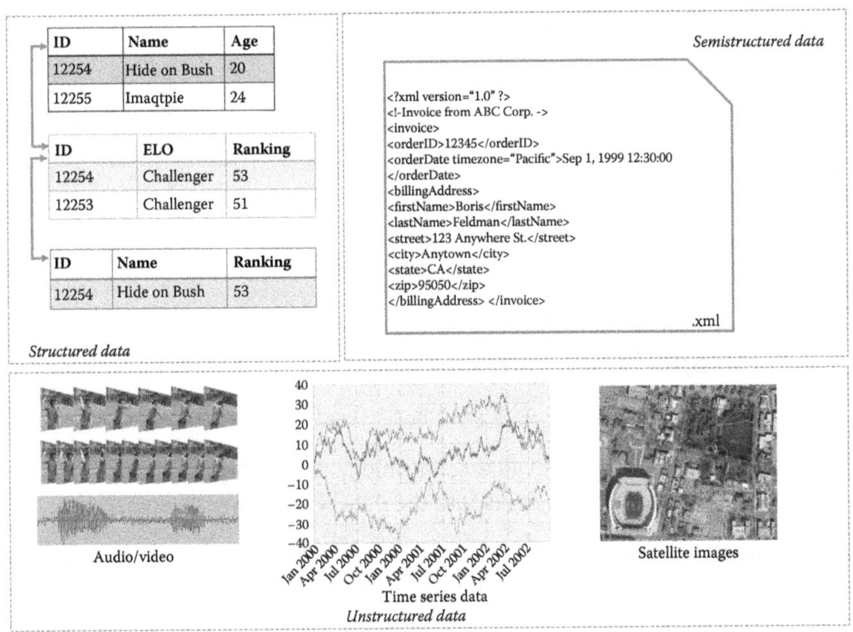

Figure 4.2: Examples of three different data types. Structured data has a relational model associated with it and can be organized as a table; semistructured does not have a well-defined structure, but still has an inherent structure based on tags and hierarchies as expressed in the graph. Three examples of unstructured data are also provided in this figure.

With the increasing use of wireless networks, more and more wireless applications require the efficient transmission of big data. A few examples of wireless systems for big data (WiBi) include:

1. *Homeland security via drones*: Here, a swarm of drones captures video, audio and other data by using various sensors, and send the gathered information to a common node for processing and information extraction. With ever more sophisticated sensors, the amount of data gathered increases rapidly and enters the big data domain. This could be used for homeland security systems, weather monitoring, or remote and hazardous area surveillance.

2. *Smart cities*: With increasing integration of the cities' cyber infrastructure into the wireless grid, the concept of smart cities will become a reality, and we can easily gather information for better traffic flow control and comprehensive surveillance for security and disaster response services.

4.2 Big Data Representations

With big data being collected in various forms, sizes, and rates, the need for a standard form of representing such data arises. Here we will discuss two typical forms used to represent big data:

1. Big graph
2. Big table (tensors)

4.2.1 *Graph-based representation*

There are two main reasons why graphs are used to represent big data:

1. Graphs can model and abstract problems with a high degree of flexibility. This leads to good insights into the data when using data analytics.
2. Graph operations could be done in a highly distributed manner, which helps with the scalability of big data operations.

The use of graphs helps with finding the correlations among seemingly disparate data. To represent structured and semistructured data as a graph, we can use the nodes to represent the various entities in the structured or semistructured data such as Name, Id etc., and use edges to connect one node to another one, as well as to other subfields. An example of representing structured and semistructured data as a graph is shown in Figure 4.3. Much research is currently under way to represent various forms of unstructured data as graphs and use them for analytics. This is called graph signal processing wherein images, video, and other unstructured data are represented as graphs upon which classical signal processing operations, such as graph Fourier transform, could be applied to extract useful patterns. An example of expressing an image as a graph is shown in Figure 4.4. After segmenting an image into various regions based on some preferred properties, a graph is constructed. Each node in the graph corresponds to a segmented region of the image and has the specific signal value associated with it, and the edges of the graph are used to connect different regions based on some distance measure functions between the segments. An illustration is shown in Figure 4.4. Similar techniques are used to represent 3D three-dimensional point Clouds, videos, etc.

4.2.2 *Tensor-based representation* [2]

Recently, tensors have gained popularity in representing big data. A tensor is basically a matrix of more than two dimensions. These extra dimensions help tensors to represent all types of data and more comprehensively represent the the relationships between the various forms of data. We use tensors to represent

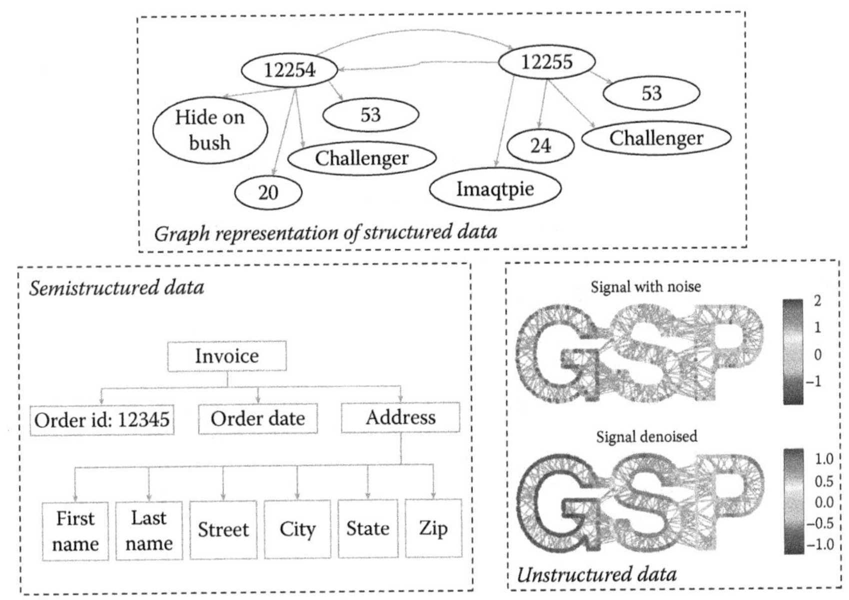

Figure 4.3: Graph-based representation of structured and semistructured data from Figure 4.2 and unstructured data taken from the Graph Signal Processing toolbox (https://lts2.epfl.ch/gsp/).

big data instead of using general matrices because, unlike matrices, tensors can represent and exploit fairly complex relationships among data.

This can be seen from the following example: Suppose machine A needs to send three vectors $v_1, v_2 = 2v_1$, and $v_3 = 3v_2$ to machine B. If the vectors are looked at individually, the redundancy between v_1, v_2, and v_3 goes unexploited in the communication process. When arranged as a matrix, $V = [v_1, v_2, v_3]$, we can see the rank of the matrix is only 1 and thus, by using any dimension reduction decomposition such as singular value decomposition (SVD), we can reduce the amount of data to be transmitted by approximately three times. Note in the above example, representing the data as a two-dimensional tensor helps to reveal the interrelationship between those one-dimensional tensors. Similar interesting relationships could be exploited by using a higher dimension of tensors when needed.

Another example of the tensor is a video and audio sequence with each frame stacked up as shown in Figure 4.4. The video tensor is of dimension $X \times Y \times 3 \times T$, where X and Y correspond to the resolution of the video per frame, 3 corresponds to R (Red) G (Green) and B (Blue) frame, and T corresponds to the frames at different time instants. The audio information could also be combined with the video tensor by associating each frame in the video with a segment of the audio clip, which results in a combined $X \times Y \times Z \times 3 \times T \times A$ where A is the dimension (number of samples) of the audio clip. Analyzing the video and audio clip combined in the same tensor gives more intuition into the contents of the video. For example, a bomb explosion can result in an increased amplitude in the audio clip with the location of the explosion lighting up in the video frame. Correlating both gives crucial defense-related information in war zones. Such relationship could be exploited when representing the data as a combined huge tensor instead of disjointed matrices and vectors. Figure 4.4 gives an illustration of the construction of the tensors for structured, semistructured and unstructured data, and it also shows how to combine them to make a joint tensor.

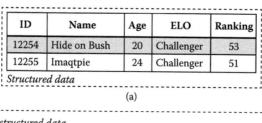

ID	Name	Age	ELO	Ranking
12254	Hide on Bush	20	Challenger	53
12255	Imaqtpie	24	Challenger	51

Structured data

(a)

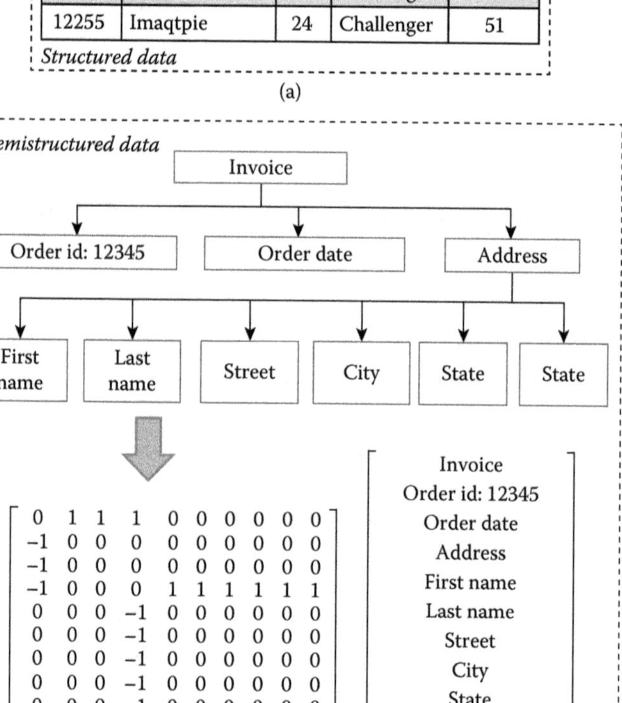

(b)

Figure 4.4: Tensor representation for examples in Figure 4.2. (a) Structured data tensor. (b) Tensor representation for semistructured data. *(Continued)*

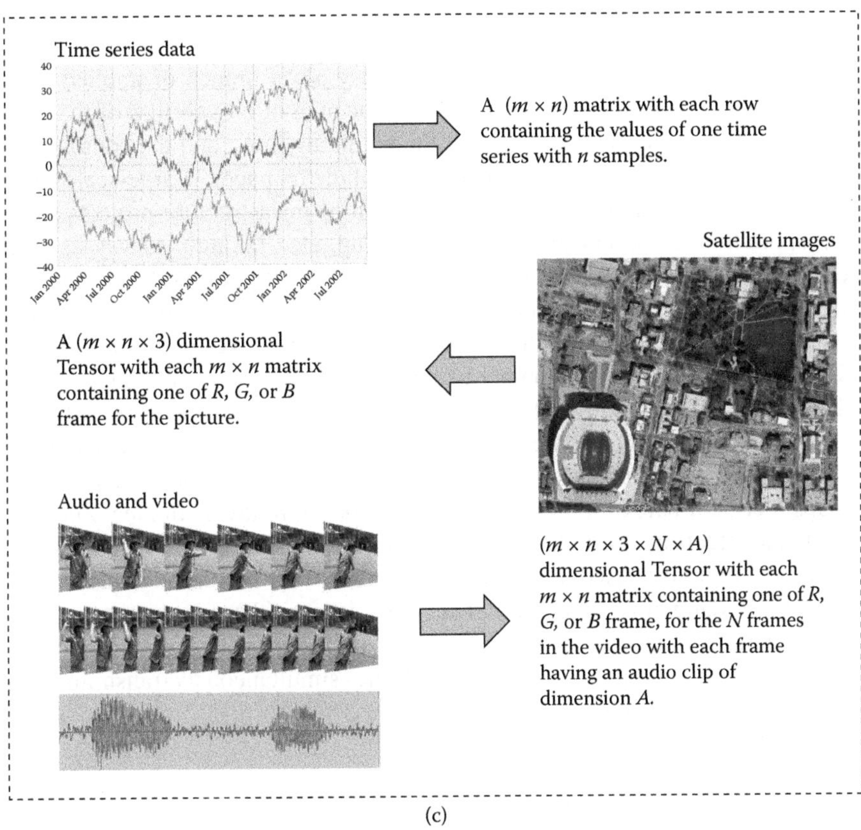

(c)

Figure 4.4 (Continued): Tensor representation for examples in Figure 4.2. (c) Tensors for unstructured data.

4.3 Wireless Transmission for Big Data (WiBi)

First we discuss the various big data wireless transmission scenarios encountered in practice, a few of which are covered in Subsection 4.3.1. Then we discuss on the various challenges which are covered in Subsection 4.3.2. Finally interesting techniques for dealing with wireless transmission of big data are detailed in Subsection 4.3.3.

4.3.1 WiBi scenarios

WiBi scenarios are emerging in various applications like surveillance, data gathering, remote monitoring, Internet of Things (IoT), and massive sensing.

4.3.1.1 Land surveying

Surveying is defined by Webster's Dictionary as "a branch of applied mathematics that is concerned with determining the area of any portion of the earth's surface, the lengths and directions of the bounding lines, and the contour of the surface and with accurately delineating the whole on paper." Large-scale surveying is done for planning and implementation of infrastructure projects such as transportation, electrical lines, urban planning, etc. Taking a survey using traditional methods takes days or even months. Recently, drone-based surveying has been implemented wherein a drone maps and captures the x, y, z coordinates of the land with very high resolution of 3 cm/pixel within a few hours. This results in millions of points gathered by the drone over a huge distance. This information is transmitted by the drone to a base station wirelessly. After some postprocessing, a completed survey of the land is obtained. An example of a completed survey undertaken by SCOPIX is shown in Figure 4.5. This survey maps a critical part of a remote vulnerable coastal roadway in New Zealand to study the effects of coastal erosion forces. In certain scenarios, constant mapping of critical regions is used to monitor any slip in the land near the roads to predict potentially dangerous landslides. The WiBi scenario here is the transportation of the data from the drone to the processor on the ground. Future implementation scenarios could involve a swarm of drones simultaneously transmitting such huge data from various regions of the map.

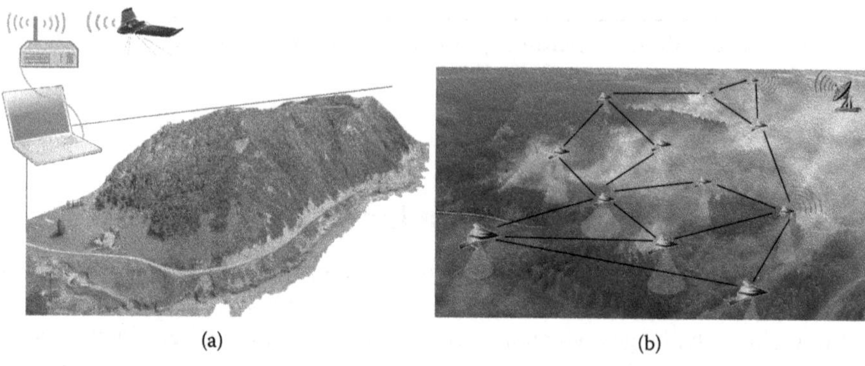

Figure 4.5: WiBi scenarios. (a) Drone-based survey, wherein a drone captures the layout of the land and communicates wirelessly to a receiver, which then sends the data to a PC for further processing. The pictures are courtesy of SCOPIX, and the image is of a vulnerable coastal road used to study coastal erosion. (b) Intelligence gathering using drones (photo courtesy of Jose Insenser).

4.3.1.2 Intelligence gathering

Intelligence gathering refers to areas where multiple wireless sources are used to gather huge bulks of data to be processed for gaining knowledge. Another example implementation is the use of a swarm of drones to monitor a region of interest to gather defense-related intelligence. This might be a swarm of drones capturing video and audio information from different zones in a battlefield. These drones then communicate the information to an area center, which then relays the information back to the base station for further processing. WiBi here is the distributed information gathering network that pools resources to process the data to be transmitted. The huge amounts of data gathered might be processed at the nodes themselves or shared with other nodes for parallel processing. There are some interesting challenges associated with this. Those challenges will be addressed in Subsection 4.3.2. An illustration of this scenario is shown in Figure 4.5.

4.3.1.3 Internet of Things and massive sensing

Huge amounts of data can be gathered in smart cities. The goal is to determine the optimal routing algorithms for distributed processing of such data, while delivering critical information to the destination. The destination then determines the optimal control strategies based on the measured data. One applications is optimal routing of vehicular traffic. The sensors along the roads collect the transportation-related data from various sectors of the roadways, and the data is then transmitted wirelessly to a central hub for processing. The hub then sends out control information.

4.3.2 Challenges in WiBi

There are various challenges when it comes to transmitting huge quantities of data through wireless channels. The factors that affect the wireless transmission include:

1. Distribution of big data pieces to be transmitted:

   ■ Big data might be organized into various files. The problem then is to schedule the file transfer. The question then arises, what is the optimal level of pipelining, parallelism, and concurrency to be used [3]. This is illustrated in Figure 4.6 (adapted from [3]). If the data is organized as one big tensor or graph, how do you break it up for transmission? The answers to these questions depend on various factors which will be explained later.

2. The condition of the channel:

   ■ When transmitting wirelessly, the channel conditions do not remain constant and have high variability. For big data transmission, constant high throughput is necessary for successful transmission of

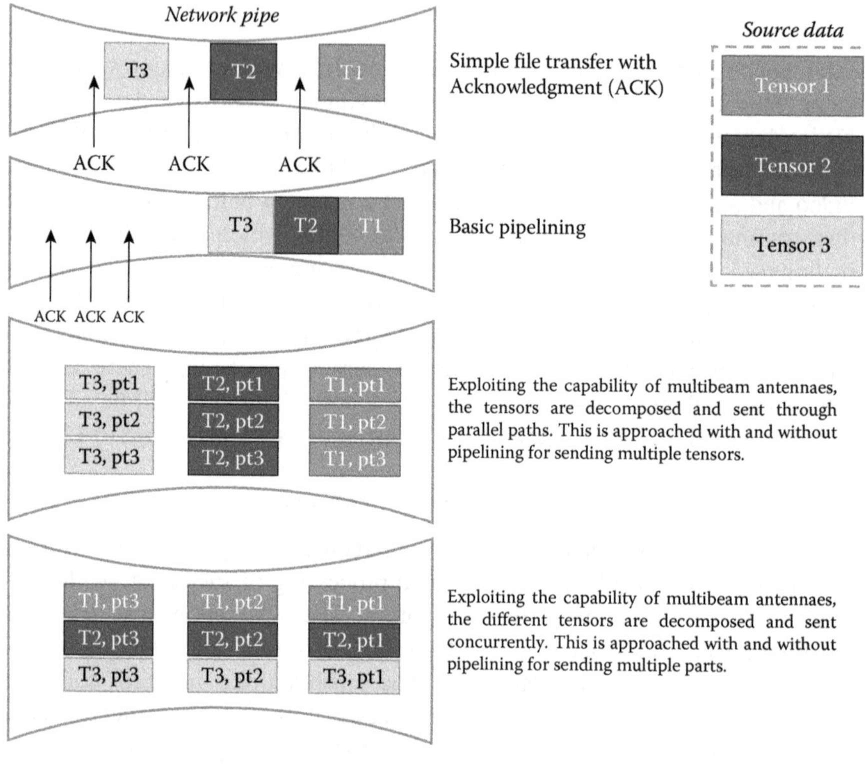

Figure 4.6: Illustration of pipelining, parallelism, and concurrency (Adapted from [3]).

data. In such a scenario, the routing protocols developed need to be robust enough to handle loss of a transmission node.

3. Distributed processing of data:

   - In most cases, the gathered data could not be handled by a single node in the network, and it is often wise to distribute the computational load to multiple nodes. Algorithms that help to achieve such a purpose is of huge interest. A few examples will be studied in the next section. An illustration is shown in Figure 4.11b.

4.3.3 *WiBi solutions*

Since WiBi is relatively new, most research in the field is in the nascent stage with the potential for various innovations in the field. There have been a few recent research articles discussing the solutions to some of the above posed challenges [4]. We suggest some solutions to these here.

4.3.3.1 Pipelining parallelism and concurrency

To effectively transmit big data that is organized into files of varying sizes, the algorithms to set levels of pipelining, parallelism, and concurrency can be developed. The concept of pipelining [3] is to successively transfer files without waiting for the "*226 Transfer successful*" message as illustrated in Figure 4.6. Pipelining helps with the problem of transferring a large number of small files. It prevents data channel idleness between successive transfers and helps keep the TCP window size from going to 0 (which can happen when the idle data channel time is higher than the round trip time [RTT]). The number of files to be sent successively without waiting for acknowledgment is referred to as the pipelining level (pp). An optimal pipelining level depends on bandwidth delay product (BDP) and file size (FS). If FS > BDP, pipelining is not effective. BDP is calculated using the bulk TCP disk and the average RTT is used for the delay. The optimal pipelining level for such a scenario is given by [3]:

$$pp_{opt} = \left\lceil \frac{BDP}{FS} \right\rceil - 1$$

It was found that with the optimal pipelining level set, the transfer of small files with optimal pipelining is similar to the transfer of a big file with no optimization. Hence, parallelism and concurrency levels are set after determining the optimal pipelining level.

Parallelism helps split a single large file using multiple TCP streams for transmission. This helps to achieve multiples of the throughput of a single TCP stream. The throughput of a single TCP stream's Band Width (BW) is given by the Mathis equation as [3]:

$$BW = \frac{MSS \times C}{RTT \times \sqrt{p}}$$

where MSS is the maximum segment size, C is a constant, p is the packet loss. Thus, as the packet loss increases, the throughput decreases. If there are n TCP streams, the aggregate throughput (BW_{agg}) increases to [3]

$$BW_{agg} \leq \frac{MSS \times C}{RTT} \left[\frac{1}{\sqrt{p_1}} \frac{1}{\sqrt{p_2}} \cdots \frac{1}{\sqrt{p_n}} \right] = n \frac{MSS \times C}{RTT \times \sqrt{p}} \tag{4.1}$$

However, as the number of parallel streams increases, the packet loss rate also increases in conventional networks, and hence an optimal parallelism level needs to be set. As a rule of thumb, as the network capacity increases, higher parallelism and concurrency levels could be set.

By using the above idea, when transporting big tensors/graphs, the optimal breakup of the big dataset into smaller blocks could be determined for a wireless network.

4.3.3.2 Channel conditions

Wireless networks suffer from unstable connections. This might be due to the mobility of different nodes in the network, jamming sources along the path, etc. Much research has attempted to find effective routing algorithms for such scenarios. There are many challenges in terms of maintaining the high throughput needed for big data transfers. One possible solution is the use of MIMO or multibeam antennas.

Multibeam antennas have multiple directional beams which direct the antenna radiation within a small angle, and all the beams can either transmit or receive simultaneously (thus increasing the bandwidth). The also increases the probability of finding reliable routing paths to transfer data.

An illustration of a multibeam antennae is shown in Figure 4.7. With a multibeam antenna, the routing in the case of jamming or node mobility is easier as there are multiple parallel paths that could be established to ensure the reliability

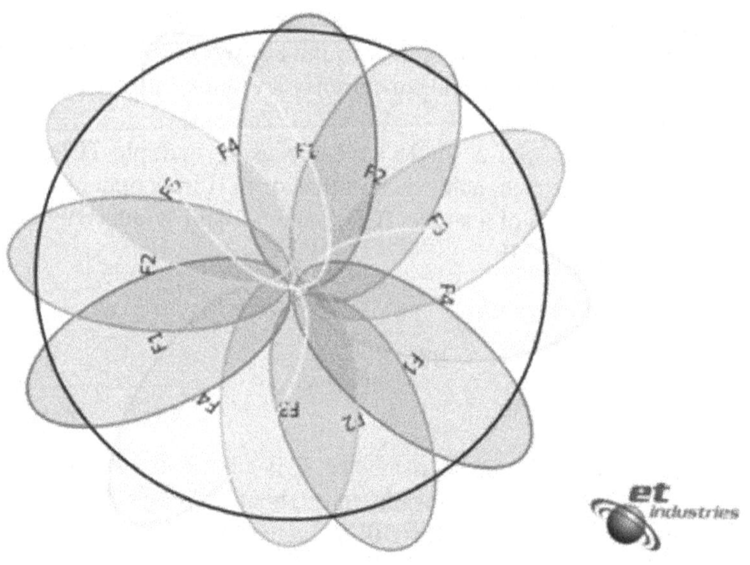

Figure 4.7: The cell site coverage of ETI's smart multibeam antenna system. (Courtesy of Electromagnetic Technologies Industries.)

of connections. This also helps to increase the number of parallel TCP streams that in turn increase the aggregate bandwidth, as shown in Equation 4.1.

There are many routing protocols that have been developed for handling jamming, node mobility, etc., in a transmission scenario as shown in Figure 4.8.

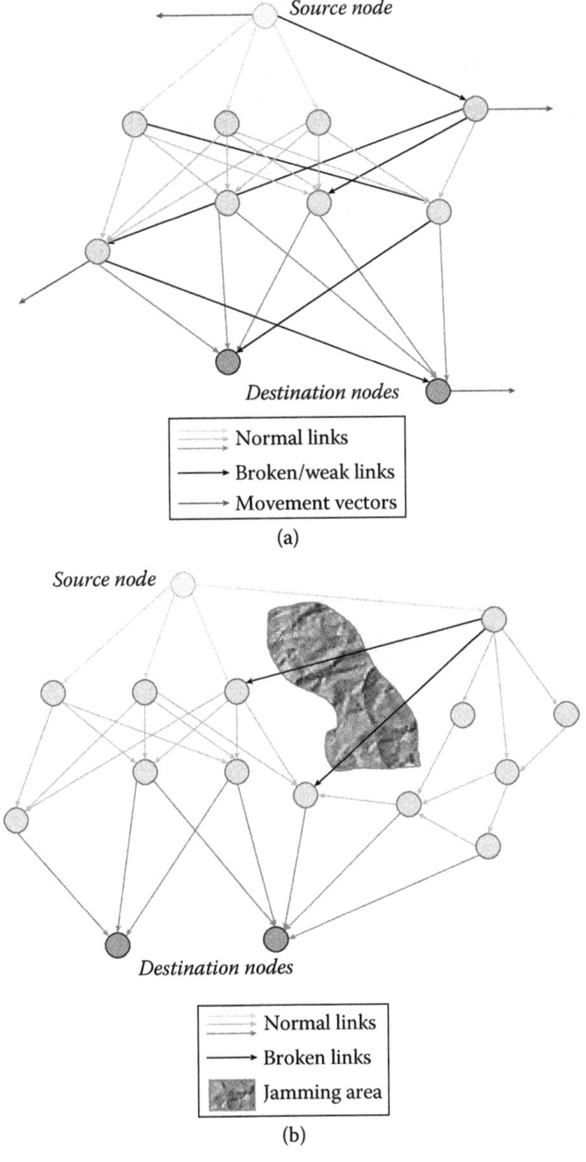

Figure 4.8: An example of robust routing for big data transmission using multibeam antennas. (a) Disruption due to node mobility. (b) Disruption due to signal jamming.

4.3.3.3 *Distributed processing of data*

Due to the high volumes of data, it is often impossible for one node to handle the entire load. The processing goal might be to compress the data efficiently, or to extract relevant information from the node, or a combination of both. There are a few ways of handling data in these scenarios.

4.3.3.4 *Distributed source coding* [5,6]

We can compress the data based on the Slepian–Wolf theorem [5,6]. Consider two statistically correlated *i.i.d.* random sequences: X and Y. Assuming a separate encoder is used for encoding both X and Y, the convention is to encode X at rate $R_X \geq H(X)$ and Y at rate $R_Y \geq H(Y)$. Thus the combined rate is $R_X + R_Y = H(X) + H(Y)$. Now, assuming the data is jointly decoded as shown in Figure 4.9a, according to the Slepian–Wolf theorem, the achievable rate is $R_X \geq H(X|Y)$ and $R_Y \geq H(Y|X)$ with the combined rate $R_X + R_Y \geq H(X,Y)$. This is shown in Figure 4.9b. This means that the source can transmit correlated

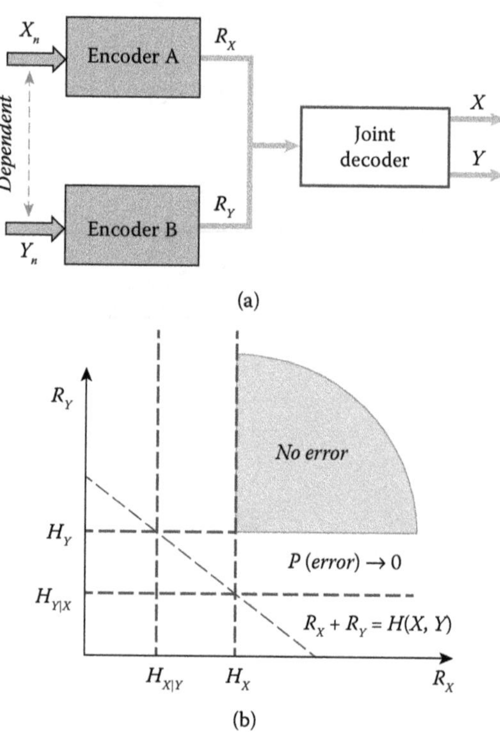

Figure 4.9: (a) Illustration of distributed source coding and (b) illustration of Slepian–Wolf theorem [5,6].

information X and Y generated at the same time to different nodes. Due to the computational complexity of encoding distributed to various nodes along the network, a scalable implementation is needed for lossless transmission of big data. Currently some codecs for distributed video coding have been developed, such as PRISM, the Stanford's pixel domain and transform domain architecture. These tools help to distribute the coding complexity from the video generation node to the rest of the nodes in the network. More general coding types could also be designed for matrices and tensors in a similar manner.

4.3.3.5 Using distributed tensor decomposition [2]

With data represented as a tensor we can perform tensor decomposition, followed by transmission of such tensors using multibeam antennas. Different models of tensor decomposition can be explored that best suit these transmission scenarios. The goal is to decompose the tensor such that the data is split into smaller chunks of varying priorities. These chunks are then transmitted using a routing protocol that exploits these priorities to deliver the best possible quality to the receiver. Figure 4.10 illustrates the process. One of the main concerns in this approach is the complexity of tensor decomposition: the higher the complexity, the higher the computational load on the sender, which would in turn delay the transmission. Here are a few ways of overcoming such an issue:

1. If the data is streaming with time (see Figure 4.11a), we could recursively use the decomposition performed in the past to update the new decomposition metrics.
2. Using the most effective algorithms that are of lower complexity we could reduce the computation time.

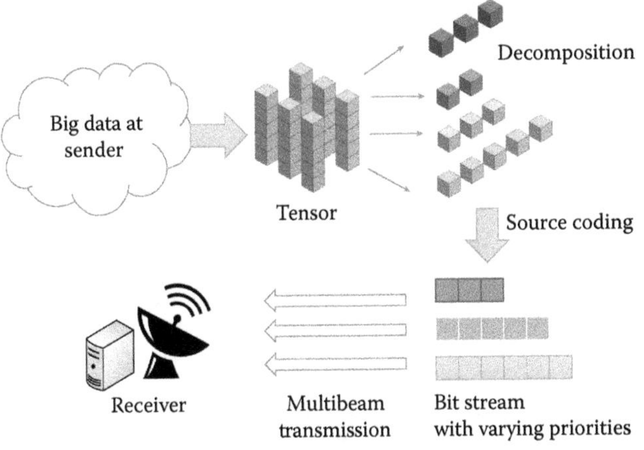

Figure 4.10: Illustration of proposed analysis scheme.

3. Using the algorithms that can distribute the computational complexity from the sender to various nodes in the network would help speed up the transmission, as illustrated in Figure 4.11b.

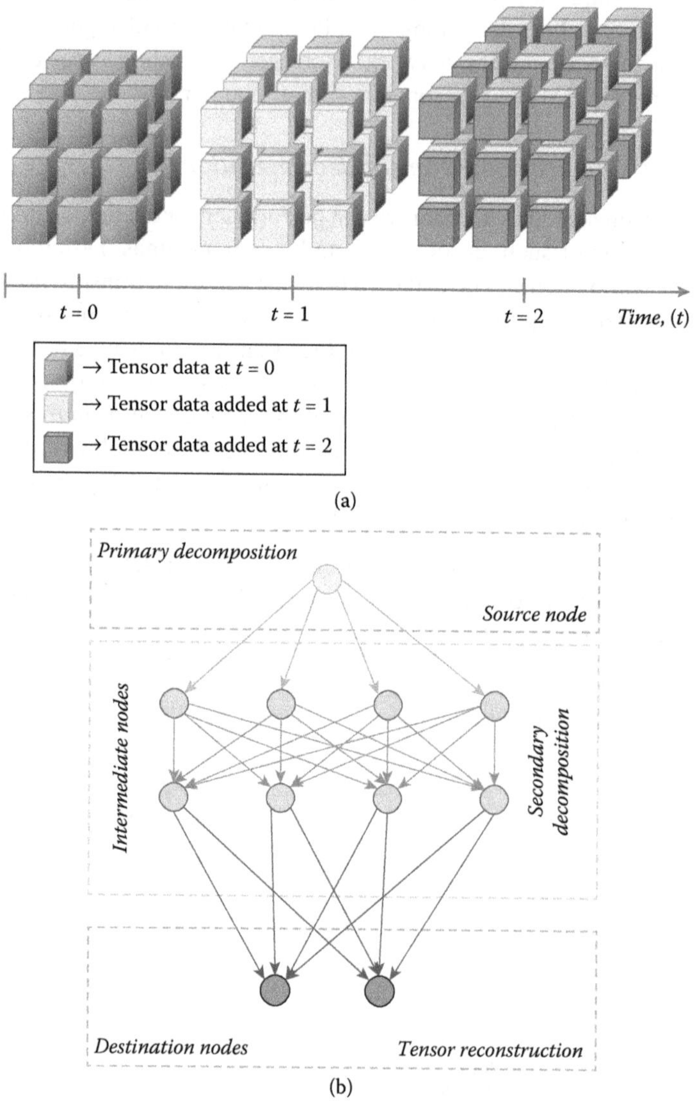

Figure 4.11: Illustration of streaming big data and distributed decomposition. (a) Each timestep increases the amount of data along one dimension of the six-dimensional tensor. (b) Primary node decomposes tensors into four parts which is followed by further decomposition along the network nodes based on need.

There are two different scenarios we consider here for big data transmission.

Scenario A: A single big data streaming source transmits data to single or multiple destinations. Refer to Figure 4.12a.

Scenario B: Big data is generated from multiple sources which communicate with each other to form a single stream to send to the destination. Refer to Figure 4.12b.

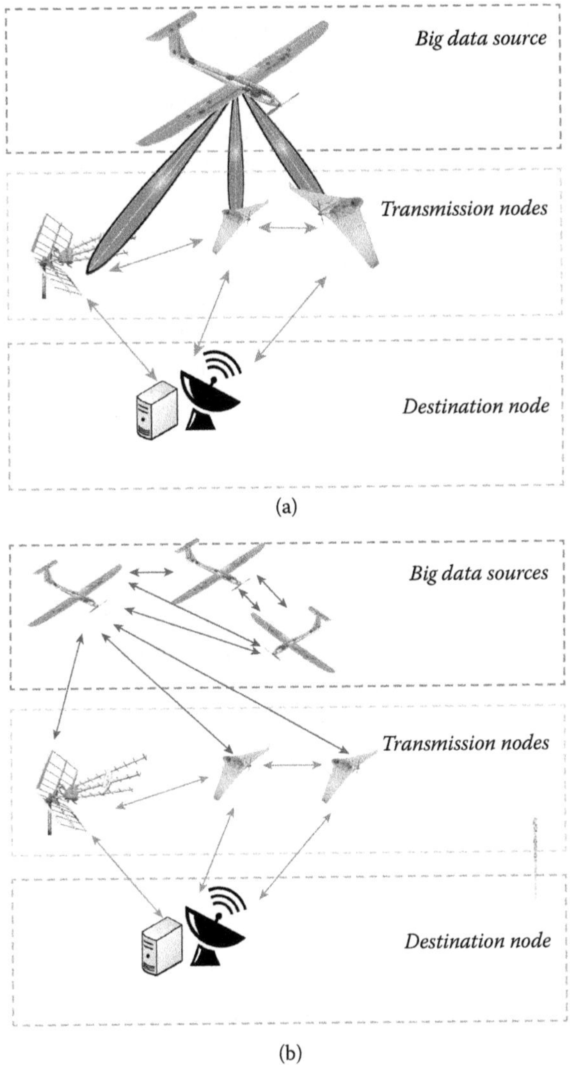

Figure 4.12: Example multibeam transmission scenarios. (a) Scenario A and (b) Scenario B.

In Scenario A all the data that needs to be transmitted is in a single node. The problem here is to find a good tensor decomposition that recursively updates its estimates with time such that the best data reconstruction accuracy occurs at the destination. The tensor decomposition algorithm should be designed to be scalable to huge data volumes. We may need to use distributed computation where each node in the network path is employed to compute the stages of the tensor decomposition. In scenario B, the data is distributed among multiple sources, and the goal is to have limited communication among sources by ensuring that all the data captured by different sources are consolidated with the minimum resources and then transmitted to the destination through intermediate nodes. Here the algorithms again should be scalable to handle huge volumes of structured data through the help of distributed processing.

One of the advantages of tensor representation and decomposition is its scalability to tera- or even petabyte levels with fault tolerance and distributed computational capabilities.

One particular decomposition of interest is the Tucker decomposition or higher order singular value decomposition (HOSVD) [2]. Let the tensor of interest be $\boldsymbol{T} \in \mathbb{R}^{I_1 \times I_2 \times \cdots \times I_N}$; the goal is to decompose $\boldsymbol{T}$ into a core tensor $\boldsymbol{G} \in \mathbb{R}^{R_1 \times R_2 \times \cdots \times R_N}$ where $R_i \leq I_i$, $i = 1, 2, \ldots, N$ and orthogonal matrices $B_i \in \mathbb{R}^{I_i \times R_i}$, $i = 1, 2, \ldots, N$ along with an error tensor $\boldsymbol{E} \in \mathbb{R}^{I_1 \times I_2 \times \cdots \times I_N}$.

We can achieve this by using singular value decomposition (SVD). Let $T \in \mathbb{R}^{I_1 \times I_2}$ be the matrix to be decomposed, then the SVD of the matrix is of the form:

$$T = B_1 G B_2 \tag{4.2}$$

where $G \in \mathbb{R}^{R_1 \times R_2}$ is a diagonal matrix, and B_1 and B_2 are orthogonal matrices $B_1 \in \mathbb{R}^{I_1 \times R_1}$ and $B_2 = \mathbb{R}^{R_2 \times I_2}$. If T is full row/column rank, then $R_1 = I_1$ and $R_2 = I_2$; if T is of rank $r < \min(I_1, I_2)$, then $R_1 = R_2 = r$, and the matrix B_1 is said to span the subspace spanned by T. If the low-rank matrix, T, gets corrupted by noise, then it has full row/column rank,

$$\tilde{T} = T + E \tag{4.3}$$

where $E \in \mathbb{R}^{I_1 \times I_2}$ is a full rank matrix of noise. The goal of the dimension-reducing algorithm is to determine the rank r of T using $\tilde{T}$ and also to determine an estimate of $B_1 \in \mathbb{R}^{I_1 \times r}$ that spans T using $\tilde{T}$.

Let

$$\tilde{T} = \tilde{B}_1 \tilde{G} \tilde{B}_2 \tag{4.4}$$

be the SVD of $\tilde{T}$. The top $\hat{r}$ singular values of $\tilde{T}$ that are higher than a set threshold are used to determine the rank of T, and the first $\hat{r}$ columns of $\tilde{B}_1$ are taken as the subspace that spans T.

Note that HOSVD is basically a SVD achieved by unfolding the tensor $\boldsymbol{T}$ into a matrix $T_{(i)} \in \mathbb{R}^{I_i \times I_1 I_2 \cdots I_{i-1} I_{i+1} \cdots I_N}$ and finding the B_i that spans $T_{(i)}$ using SVD for all $i = 1, \ldots, N$. Thus, we basically determine the subspace spanned by a matrix corrupted by noise when we determine the subspace of a tensor corrupted by noise. Based on different preferences, various constraints could be imposed on B_i, $\boldsymbol{G}$, and $\boldsymbol{E}$, similar to the orthogonality constraint imposed on B_i by SVD. In practical scenarios, the dimension $R_i \ll I_i$, and this helps to reduce the size of the tensor. Some algorithms to compute SVD such as LAPACK's SGESVD/SGESDD, enable parallel computation and hence reduce the time and load on a single processor. The computational complexity is $O(NI_1I_2 \cdots I_N) \asymp O(NI^N)$ where $O(\cdot)$ refers to order notation, and the symbol $\asymp$ denotes equivalence in order.

The above algorithm needs to be repeated for every change in tensor data such as the streaming updates illustrated in Figure 4.11a. A method to handle such a scenario is given in [1] where a recursive implementation of HOSVD is proposed. Other recent innovations to find the latent subspace of a matrix could also be adapted to be used with tensors. There are many matrix decomposition algorithms that could also be easily extended to tensors, like the Grassmannian robust adaptive subspace tracking algorithm (GRASTA) which is highly efficient with streaming data.

Tensor decomposition help infer useful information about the data. In a video tensor, the subspace detected by the tensor decomposition gives the information on the background and the noise matrix gives foreground information. There are also decomposition algorithms that come with the possibility of constraining the noise. They have certain useful characteristics like sparsity.

4.4 Conclusion

In this chapter, we covered the various ways to represent big data and introduced the concept of wireless big data transmission (WiBi). We explored the various interesting methods through which WiBi is implemented, listed a few challenges in the WiBi scenario, and posed some solutions to address the issues in WiBi.

References

[1] L. Kuang, F. Hao, L. T. Yang, M. Lin, C. Luo, and G. Min, A tensor-based approach for big data representation and dimensionality reduction, *IEEE Transactions on Emerging Topics in Computing*, vol. 2, no. 3, pp. 280–291, 2014.

[2] A. Cichocki, Era of big data processing: A new approach via tensor networks and tensor decompositions. In *International Workshop on Smart Info-Media Systems in Asia (SISA-2013)*, Nagoya, Japan, 30 September–2 October, 2013.

[3] E. Yildirim, E. Arslan, J. Kim, and T. Kosar, Application-level optimization of big data transfers through pipelining, parallelism and concurrency, *IEEE Transactions on Cloud Computing*, vol. 4, no. 1, pp. 63–75, 2016.

[4] S. Bi, R. Zhang, Z. Ding, and S. Cui, Wireless communications in the era of big data, *IEEE Communications Magazine*, vol. 53, no. 10, pp. 190–199, 2015.

[5] R. Puri, A. Majumdar, P. Ishwar, and K. Ramchandran, Distributed video coding in wireless sensor networks, *IEEE Signal Processing Magazine*, vol. 23, no. 4, pp. 94–106, 2006.

[6] J. He, L. Balzano, and A. Szlam, Incremental gradient on the grassmannian for online foreground and background separation in subsampled video. In *2012 IEEE Conference on Computer Vision and Pattern Recognition (CVPR)*, IEEE, 2012, pp. 1568–1575.

II

NETWORK ARCHITECTURE FOR BIG DATA TRANSMISSIONS

Chapter 5

Efficient Big Data Transfer Using Bandwidth Reservation Service in High-Performance Networks

Liudong Zuo
California State University
Carson, California

Michelle Mengxia Zhu
Montclair State University
Montclair, New Jersey

CONTENTS

Sheer volumes of data, now frequently termed as "big data," are being generated from various emerging applications of large-scale simulations, scientific experiments, and global-scale communications. Such extremely large amounts of data are normally generated at one data center and then need to be transferred to distributed data centers for data storage and analysis, within which fast, predictable, and reliable data transfer with guaranteed performance has become crucial to ensure success. Fortunately, reserving bandwidth as needed along selected paths in high-performance networks (HPNs) has proved to be an effective way to satisfy the requirements of such high-demanding data transfer. In this chapter, we first present the introduction and background of bandwidth reservation service in HPNs for big data transfer along with the challenges. The related works, and concepts and mechanisms of bandwidth reservation strategies are provided in Section 5.2 and Section 5.3, respectively. We show our algorithm's design and illustration through simple examples for easy comprehension in Section 5.4, and conclude our work in Section 5.5.

5.1 Introduction

In extreme-scale computations, big data is continuously being generated. For example, the Large Hadron Collider (LHC),* the world's largest and most powerful particle accelerator, can generate up to 30 petabytes of data per year. Attributes of such large volumes of data can be described using the 5Vs model: volume, variety, velocity, veracity, and vinculation. Processing the data sets in the big data domain is normally beyond the ability of commonly used software tools and single data processing centers within a tolerable elapsed time. Hence, big data sets usually need to be transferred from the data generating site to remote high-performance computing sites either for the necessary computing and storage power or for collaborative data analysis and knowledge discovery purpose [1–3]. Fast, predictable, and reliable data transfer with guaranteed performance has become crucial to ensure success, especially when the data sets needing to be transferred are time-sensitive. However, today's default best effort network cannot meet the needs of such high-demanding data transfer since

*http://home.web.cern.ch/about/computing

all competing data flows are treated equally and cannot provide any type of quality of service (QoS) [4]. Fortunately, next-generation research and education high-performance networks (HPNs), such as the Energy Sciences Network (ESnet) [5], are developed to address such concerns. These HPNs have dedicated large bandwidth links between sites and allow data transfers to reserve bandwidth as needed in the dedicated links, thus guaranteeing predictive and reliable data transfer. For example, the big data sets generated by LHC are currently transferred from the data generating center to remote data centers using the On-demand secure circuits and advance reservation system (OSCARS), the bandwidth reservation service provided by ESnet.*

Besides the widely used ESnet, other similar networks providing bandwidth reservation service have been developed or are currently underway. These networks include Internet2 [6], User controlled lightpaths (UCLP) [7], the UltraScience Net (USN) [8], the circuit-switched high-speed end-to-end transport architecture (CHEETAH) [9], the Dynamic Network System (DYNES) [4], and the dynamic resource allocation via generalized multi-protocol label switching (GMPLS) optical networks (DRAGON) [10].

In such HPNs, a management framework, called a control plane, is usually used to coordinate the network infrastructures, such as the core switches, the edge devices, and backbone routers [4]. The control plane is responsible for setting up the bandwidth reservation paths, reserving bandwidth on the reservation paths, and releasing the reserved bandwidth when the corresponding data transfers are completed. When a user would like to transfer data from a source end-site to a destination end-site using the bandwidth reservation service, he/she needs to create a bandwidth reservation request (BRR) and then send it to the HPNs. Typically, the following parameters are specified in the BRR: the source end-site, the destination end-site, the data size, the maximum local area network (LAN) bandwidth of the source and destination end-sites, the data available time, and the data transfer deadline. After receiving the BRR from the user, the control plane of the HPN tries to identify one path that satisfies all data transfer requirements and constraints defined in the BRR, and then makes a bandwidth reservation on it and returns the bandwidth reservation option. If multiple such paths exist, the control plane would choose the most appropriate one. If the control plane cannot identify any path that can satisfy all data transfer requirements and constraints, then one bandwidth reservation failure notice will be sent to the user.

The challenges of the bandwidth reservation service arise from both the users and the bandwidth reservation service providers. Besides the data transfer deadline requirement, users sometimes also want to achieve other data transfer performance parameters. For example, they might want to achieve the earliest data transfer completion time (ECT) and the shortest data transfer duration (SD). For highly critical applications such as national security data, users would want to achieve the maximum data transfer reliability, while for budget

* http://www.es.net/about/

constrained users, they would want to achieve the minimum data transfer cost requirement [4,11–13]. From the perspective of the bandwidth reservation service providers, all BRRs in one batch should be scheduled concurrently in the HPNs for high bandwidth resource utilization and throughput purposes. Sometimes users and the bandwidth reservation service providers might have requirement conflicts. For example, bandwidth reservation service providers sometimes would like to achieve the best average data transfer performance parameters of multiple BRRs in one batch, namely the global BRR optimality. However, each individual user oftentimes would like to achieve the best reservation options for his/her BRR, namely local single BRR optimality, and such local single BRR optimality does not usually lead to the global BRR optimality [14].

5.2 Related Work

Because of the solid performance and wide use of the bandwidth reservation service for big data transfer in reality, various problem classifications regarding bandwidth reservation service have been studied and multiple algorithms have been proposed. We conducted a survey about these problems and algorithms as follows.

The design, architecture, implementation, and coordinated use of OSCARS were outlined in [15]. Herms and Lukas investigated the problem of admission failure caused by bandwidth reservation saturation in a wireless mesh network [16]. A protocol was developed to guarantee consistent data exchange between neighboring stations and prevent admission failures using the well-known two-phase commit protocol. The problem of admission failure in a certain level was addressed by making the bandwidth reservation in a single hop instead of the common approach of the hop-by-hop reservation of bandwidth for individual routes. Admission control and scheduling for bulk data transfer were discussed in Ref. [17] to improve the network resource utilization and reduce the BRR rejection rate.

Sahni et al. focused on how to compute a dedicated channel from a source node to a destination node in a network under different requirements [8]: (1) a specified bandwidth in a specified time slot, (2) the highest available bandwidth in a specified time slot, (3) the earliest available time with a specified bandwidth and duration, and (4) all available time slots with a specified bandwidth and duration. Among these four scheduling problems, the first and third problems can be solved using the classical breadth-first search, the second one falls in the scope of problems solvable using Dijkstra's shortest path algorithm, and the solution to the fourth one is essentially a variant of Bellman–Ford algorithm.

To optimize network resource utilization, Dharam and Wu proposed a bandwidth reservation solution that integrates a routing algorithm and a preemption scheme by exploring the interactions between advance and immediate reservations [18]. Rajah et al. studied the problem of improving the network resource utilization and lowering the request rejection ratio [17]. This problem was regarded as an optimization problem in making admission control and scheduling decisions. A cohesive optimization-based framework consisting of reservation requests, multipath routing and bandwidth assignment was designed, and multiple algorithms were proposed. Balman et al. studied the problem of achieving ECT and SD for one single reservation request within an HPN, and proposed an optimal polynomial-time algorithm [11]. Given a specific reservation request, the proposed algorithm computes the reservation path and yields the reservation option with ECT and SD. Wu and Lin considered four types of advance bandwidth scheduling problems from the combination of different paths and bandwidth constraints [4]: (1) fixed path with fixed bandwidth, (2) fixed path with variable bandwidth, (3) variable path with fixed bandwidth, and (4) variable path with variable bandwidth. All these four problems aim to achieve the ECT for one single BRR within an HPN. Detailed problem complexity analysis and algorithm design were given for each problem.

Bandwidth scheduling algorithms can be categorized into two groups: (1) instant scheduling algorithm, which schedules one single BRR at a time and (2) periodical scheduling algorithm, which schedules multiple BRRs accumulated within a time period at a time. For example, the scheduling algorithms proposed in [4,11,18] are instant scheduling algorithms. A periodical scheduling problem is normally more difficult than an instant scheduling problem since its subject is multiple BRRs instead of one single BRR. However, a periodical scheduling algorithm may schedule these multiple BRRs in some order other than the BRRs receiving order, which could lead to a better overall scheduling performance than the first in, first out (FIFO) strategy used by an instant scheduling algorithm. Zuo et al. studied the problem of scheduling multiple BRRs with different priorities in an HPN [12,20]. In the study, two optimal algorithms were proposed, and for each BRR the proposed algorithms identify and return the bandwidth reservation options with ECT and SD to the users. Several trimming techniques and strategies are used to narrow down the search space for each BRR to improve the BRR scheduling efficiency.

Sharma et al. investigated the problem of accommodating as many BRRs as possible while minimizing the total time to finish all data transfers on one reservation path [13]. This problem was proven as a NP-hard problem and a polynomial-time heuristic algorithm was proposed. The proposed algorithm tries to identify the optimal reservation option for each reservation request to achieve the minimal total data transfer time of multiple reservation requests. The problems of scheduling as many concurrent BRRs as possible over one dedicated channel in an HPN while achieving the average ECT and the average SD of scheduled BRRs were studied in Ref. [14]. Both problems were proven as NP-hard problems and heuristic algorithms were proposed. The above problems were studied in more depth and wider breadth in Ref. [21] and were further proven as

NP-complete problems. More efficient heuristic algorithms were proposed. Zuo et al. investigated the problem of scheduling all BRRs in one batch over different paths of scheduling HPNs while achieving their best average data transfer performance parameters [22]. Two specific data transfer performance parameters were studied: ECT and SD. The corresponding problems were proven as NP-complete problems and efficient scheduling algorithms were proposed.

As shown above, we have done extensive research regarding big data transfer using bandwidth reservation service on HPNs. Our research can be incorporated into the real bandwidth reservation service, such as OSCARS, to improve the bandwidth reservation and data transfer performance. According to [4,23], changing the reserved bandwidth value for a data transfer during the transfer process is an extremely expensive and time-consuming operation. Hence, the reserved bandwidth for a BRR in this chapter is constrained as a fixed value throughout the entire data transfer duration.

5.3 Mathematical Models and Bandwidth Reservation Concepts

Suppose we have an example HPN, the topology of which, G, is shown on the left side of Figure 5.1. Suppose G receives a BRR at time point 0, the received BRR tries to transfer $36Gb$ data from v_s to v_d within time interval [0,10s], and the specified maximum LAN bandwidth is $12Gb/s$. It is easy to see that G consists of four nodes, namely v_s, a, b, and v_d, and four edges, namely $v_s - a$, $a - v_d$, $v_s - b$, and $b - v_d$. The available bandwidth table of each edge in G within time interval

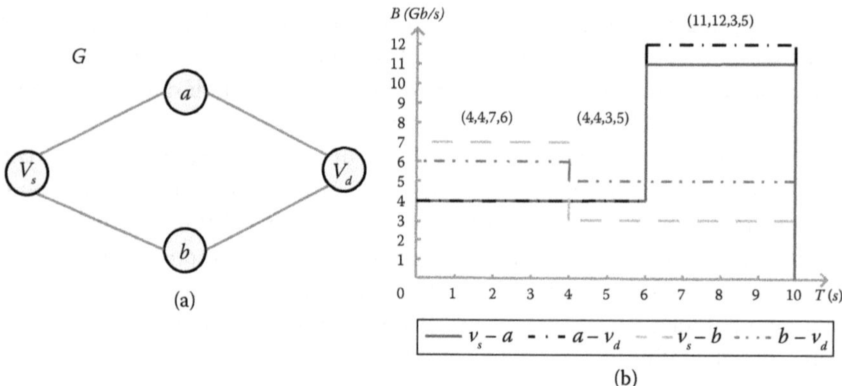

Figure 5.1: (a) Topology of an HPN and (b) the available bandwidth table of each edge within time interval [0,10s].

Table 5.1 Parameters introduced in Section 5.3

Parameters	Definitions
v_s	Source node
v_d	Destination node
B^{max}	Maximum LAN bandwidth constraint
D	Size of data to be transferred
t^S	Earliest data transfer start time
t^E	Latest data transfer end time (deadline)
P	Data transfer/bandwidth reservation path
B	Reserved bandwidth
t^s	Data transfer start time
t^e	Data transfer end time
ts^s	Start time of timestep ts
ts^e	End time of timestep ts
tw^s	Start time of timewindow tw
tw^e	End time of timewindow tw
$B(e,ts_i)$	Available bandwidth of edge e within timestep ts_i
$B(e,tw_j)$	Available bandwidth of edge e within timewindow tw_j
$B(p,tw_j)$	Available bandwidth of path p within timewindow tw_j
t^{min}	Minimum data transfer duration

[0,10*s*] is shown on the right side of Figure 5.1. Note that many parameters will be introduced in this section. For convenience, we tabulate these parameters in Table 5.1.

In general, the topology of an HPN can be modeled as a graph $G(V,E)$, where V and E represent the set of nodes and the set of edges, respectively. For the example HPN shown in Figure 5.1, $V = \{v_s, a, b, v_d\}$ and $E = \{v_s - a, a - v_d, v_s - b, b - v_d\}$. A BRR can be represented as $(v_s, v_d, D, B^{max}, [t^S, t^E])$, where v_s, v_d, B^{max}, and D denote the source node, the destination node, the maximum LAN bandwidth, and the total size of data to be transferred from the earliest data transfer start time t^S to the latest data transfer finish time (deadline) t^E, respectively [2,11,12,21]. For example, the BRR received by G at time point 0 can be represented as $(v_s, v_d, 36Gb, 12Gb/s, [0, 10s])$.

As noted in Section 5.2, bandwidth scheduling algorithms can be categorized into two groups: instant scheduling algorithms and periodical scheduling algorithms. For an instant scheduling algorithm, we only need to identify the topology of the scheduling HPN within the user-predefined data transfer time interval, namely $[t^S, t^E]$. For example, for the received BRR $(v_s, v_d, 36Gb, 12Gb/s, [0, 10s])$, we only need to focus on the topology of the HPN within time interval $[0, 10s]$ and if above BRR can be successfully scheduled. The topology of the HPN beyond time interval $[0, 10s]$ has nothing to do with the scheduling feasibility of above BRR. However, for a periodic scheduling algorithm, its subject is multiple BRRs accumulated within a time interval. We need to identify the least time interval containing user-predefined data transfer intervals of all BRRs. Suppose we have a BRR batch *LBRR* containing multiple BRRs accumulated within a time interval, we can use the following two equations to find out the earliest data transfer start time T^S and the latest data transfer deadline T^E of all BRRs:

$$T^S = min\left(t_0^S, t_1^S, \ldots, t_{|LBRR|-1}^S\right) \tag{5.1}$$

and

$$T^E = max\left(t_0^E, t_1^E, \ldots, t_{|LBRR|-1}^E\right) \tag{5.2}$$

where t_i^S and t_i^E represent the earliest data transfer start time t^S and the data transfer deadline t^E of brr_i, $brr_i \in LBRR$. Time interval $[T^S, T^E]$ would be the time interval that contains user-predefined data transfer intervals of all BRRs. For example, if we receive another BRR at time point $4s$ with the following representation $(v_s, v_d, 40Gb, 10Gb/s, [6s, 12s])$, then using Equations (5.1) and (5.2), we have time interval $[0, 12s]$. We then need to identify the topology of the scheduling HPN within the above time interval and try to schedule these two received BRRs.

Edge $e \in E$ an initial bandwidth capacity, which is the maximum amount of bandwidth that we can reserve on that edge at any time point. For example, suppose the initial bandwidth capacity of edge $v_s - a$ in Figure 5.1 is $11Gb/s$, then we can reserve at most $11Gb/s$ on edge $v_s - a$ at any time point. However, for edge $e \in E$, its available bandwidth varies over time as is being reserved and released in a dynamic manner. For example, as we can see from Figure 5.1, the available bandwidth of edge $v_s - a$ within time interval $[0, 6s]$ is $4Gb/s$ and we have reserved $11Gb/s - 4Gb/s = 7Gb/s$ for one or multiple BRRs within $[0, 6s]$. The available bandwidth of edge $v_s - a$ within time interval $[6s, 10s]$ becomes $11Gb/s$, its initial bandwidth capacity again, after the reserved bandwidth is released. It is not difficult to see that such dynamism of the edges and the entire HPN increases the difficulty of scheduling given BRRs and making bandwidth reservation for them. On the contrary, it would be much easier for us to compute the scheduling options for given BRRs if the whole HPN is static at least within a certain period and timepoint, timestep, and timewindow are defined for that purpose.

We can find out all timepoints within the scheduling HPN using the following strategy: Iterate through edge set E and for each edge $e \in E$, identify all time points when the available bandwidth of e changes, and then put these time points in priority queue LTP within which all elements are unique and sorted in increasing order. For example, following above strategy, G in Figure 5.1 has four timepoints 0, $4s$, $6s$ and $10s$, so we have $LTP = \{0, 4s, 6s, 10s\}$.

Suppose scheduling network G has n timepoints within certain time interval as follows:

$$LTP = \{tp_0, tp_1, \cdots, tp_{n-1}\} \tag{5.3}$$

A timestep is defined as a time interval in the form of $[tp_i, tp_{i+1}]$, where $0 \leq i < n-1$ [14]. With above definition, the timestep list, represented by LTS, can be easily identified:

$$LTS = \{[tp_0, tp_1], \cdots, [tp_i, tp_{i+1}], \cdots, [tp_{n-2}, tp_{n-1}]\} \tag{5.4}$$

It is easy to see that $LTS = n-1$. For convenience, timestep i is denoted as ts_i, namely $ts_i = [tp_i, tp_{i+1}]$. A timestep can also be defined as the longest time interval during which the available bandwidths of all edges remain unchanged [2,12,20]. For convenience, we also represent timestep i as $[ts_i^s, ts_i^e]$, where ts_i^s and ts_i^e denote the start time and end time of the corresponding time interval ($ts_i^s = tp_i$ and $ts_i^e = tp_{i+1}$), respectively. For example, it is easy to see that there are three timesteps in G: $ts_0 = [0, 4s]$, $ts_1 = [4s, 6s]$, and $ts_2 = [6s, 10s]$. We represent available bandwidth of edge e within ts_i as $B(e, ts_i)$ or $B(e, [ts_i^s, ts_i^e])$. For example, available bandwidth of edge $v_s - a$ within timestep $ts_0 = [0, 4s]$ is $4Gb/s$, so we have $B(v_s - a, ts_0) = 4Gb/s$. To make the available bandwidth table of edges in G easier to read, we use a quadruple denoted as $(B(v_s - a, ts_i), B(a - v_d, ts_i), B(v_s - b, ts_i), B(b - v_d, ts_i))$ without units to describe available bandwidths of edge $v_s - a$, $a - v_d$, $v_s - b$ and $b - v_d$ within timestep ts_i. For example, within timestep $ts_0 = [0, 4s]$, available bandwidths of these four edges are $4Gb/s$, $4Gb/s$, $7Gb/s$ and $6Gb/s$, respectively, so the corresponding quadruple is $(4, 4, 7, 6)$ as shown in Figure 5.1.

A timewindow is defined as a time interval consisting of one timestep or more consecutive timesteps [2,12,20]. Timewindow j, denoted as tw_j, can be represented as $[tw_j^s, tw_j^e]$, where tw_j^s and tw_j^e denote the start time and end time of the corresponding time interval, respectively. For example, with the three timesteps in G, namely $ts_0 = [0, 4s]$, $ts_1 = [4s, 6s]$ and $ts_2 = [6s, 10s]$ (they are also timewindows), we can derive three more timewindows: $[0, 6s]$, $[0, 10s]$, and $[4s, 10s]$. Given n timepoints, the time interval between any two consecutive timepoints is a timestep and that between any two different timepoints is a timewindow. According to the theory of combination, the total number of timewindows is $C(n, 2) = \frac{n \cdot (n-1)}{2}$ [12]. Given timewindow tw_j consisting of timesteps $ts_{j'}, ts_{j'+1}, \cdots, ts_{j''}$, the available bandwidth of edge e within tw_j, $B(e,tw_j)$ or $B(e,[tw_j^s,tw_j^e])$, is defined as its minimum available bandwidth across all timesteps of tw_j, namely

$$B(e,tw_j) = min\big(B(e,ts_{j'}),B(e,ts_{j'+1}),\cdots,B(e,ts_{j''})\big) \tag{5.5}$$

For example, timewindow $[0,6s]$ consists of $ts_0 = [0,4s]$ and $ts_1 = [4s,6s]$. Available bandwidths of edge $v_s - b$ within timestep ts_0 and ts_1 are $B(v_s - b,ts_0) = 7Gb/s$ and $B(v_s - b,ts_1) = 3Gb/s$, respectively. Following Equation 5.5, the available bandwidth of $v_s - b$ within timewindow $[0,6s]$, $B(v_s - b,[0,6s])$, is $min\,(B(v_s - b,ts_0),B(v_s - b,ts_1)) = min(7Gb/s,3Gb/s) = 3Gb/s$. From the definition of the available bandwidth of an edge within a timewindow, it is easy to see that G can be treated as static within a timewindow [11].

We use $B(p,tw_j)$ or $B(p,[tw_j^s,tw_j^e])$ to represent the available bandwidth of path p in G within timewindow tw_j. If path p consists of edges e_k, e_{k+1}, $\cdots$, $e_{k'}$, we represent path p as $e_k - e_{k+1} - \cdots - e_{k'}$. The available bandwidth of path p within timewindow tw_j is limited by the bottleneck edge on p, namely the edge with the minimum available bandwidth on p within tw_j [12]. We have

$$B(p,tw_j) = min\big(B(e_k,tw_j),B(e_{k+1},tw_j),\cdots,B(e_{k'},tw_j)\big) \tag{5.6}$$

For example, path $v_s - b - v_d$ consists of edges $v_s - b$ and $b - v_d$. Using Equation 5.6, we have the available bandwidth of path $v_s - b - v_d$ within timewindow $[0,10s]$, $B(v_s - b - v_d,[0,10s])$, equals $min\big(B(v_s - b,[0,10s]), B(b - v_d,[0,10s])\big) = min(3Gb/s,5Gb/s) = 3Gb/s$. Because of the constraint of B^{max}, it is easy to see that the maximum bandwidth that we can reserve on p within tw_j is $min\,(B(p,tw_j),B^{max})$.

For a given BRR, if all of its requirements and constraints can be satisfied by a reservation option, we say that the given BRR can be successfully scheduled. The reservation option is referred to as a qualified reservation (QR), denoted by $(P,B,[t^s,t^e])$, where P, B, t^s and t^e represent the data transfer/bandwidth reservation path, the reserved bandwidth, data transfer start time, and data transfer end time, respectively [2,12,20]. It is easy to see that $B \le B^{max}$, $t^S \le t^s < t^e \le t^E$, and $(t^e - t^s)\cdot B = D$ [12]. Multiple QRs can normally be made for one BRR. For example, for the given BRR $(v_s,v_d,36Gb,12Gb/s,[0,10s])$, we can make infinite QRs on path $v_s - a - v_d$ and $v_s - b - v_d$ within $[0,10s]$. However, sometimes we are interested in several special QRs. For example, as noted in Section 5.1, users oftentimes want to achieve additional data transfer performance parameters besides the required data transfer deadline, and two common such additional parameters are ECT and SD. We are then interested in QRs with above two data transfer parameters. Among these infinite QRs for the received BRRs $(v_s,v_d,36Gb,12Gb/s,[0,10s])$, the one with ECT and that with SD are denoted as QRECT and QRSD, respectively [2,12,20]. As we will see in Section 5.4, the QRECT of the received BRR at time point 0 is $(v_s - b - v_d, 4Gb/s, [0, 9s])$ with an ECT of $9s$ and the QRSD is $(v_s - a - v_d, 12Gb/s, [6s, 9.27s])$ with the SD of $(9.27s - 6s) = 3.27s$. We will introduce a scheduling algorithm that can successfully identify the QRECT and QRSD for one given BRR in Section 5.4.

Since the topology of an HPN might change from time to time, the QRECT and QRSD of a BRR are actually relative to time points. For the same BRR at different time points, its QRECT and QRSD might be different. For example, the QRECT for BRR $(v_s, v_d, 36Gb, 12Gb/s, [0, 10s])$ at time point 0 is $(v_s - b - v_d, 4Gb/s, [0, 9s])$. Suppose at time point $4s$, available bandwidths of both edge $v_s - b$ and edge $b - v_d$ within time interval $[4s, 10s]$ increase to $12Gb/s$. In this case, the QRECT for the given BRR becomes $(v_s - b - v_d, 12Gb/s, [4s, 7s])$, which is also its QRSD at time point $4s$. In this chapter, the QRECT and QRSD of a BRR are defined as its QRECT and QRSD at the time point when the scheduling algorithm starts processing that BRR.

Suppose we are trying to schedule a given BRR within timewindow tw_j, we know that the data can only be transferred within the overlapped time interval between the user-predefined time interval of the given BRR and timewindow tw_j. It is not hard to see that the overlapped time interval has the form $[max(t^S, tw_j^s), min(t^E, tw_j^e)]$. If the given BRR can be successfully scheduled within timewindow tw_j, the reserved bandwidth on the data transfer path within the overlapped time interval should be no less than $\frac{D}{min(t^E, tw_j^e) - max(t^S, tw_j^s)}$, namely within tw_j, v_s and v_d should be connected by at least one path with the available bandwidth no less than $\frac{D}{min(t^E, tw_j^e) - max(t^S, tw_j^s)}$ [2,12,20]. Hence, removing those edges with available bandwidths less than $\frac{D}{min(t^E, tw_j^e) - max(t^S, tw_j^s)}$ does not affect the scheduling feasibility of the given BRR within tw_j. For example, for BRR $(v_s, v_d, 36Gb, 12Gb/s, [0, 10s])$ within timewindow $[6s, 10s]$, the minimum bandwidth to be reserved is $\frac{36Gb}{(10s - 6s)} = 9Gb/s$. We can remove edge $v_s - b$ and $b - v_d$ since their available bandwidths within timewindow $[6s, 10s]$, $3Gb/s$ and $5Gb/s$, do not meet the minimum bandwidth requirement of $9Gb/s$.

Under the maximum LAN bandwidth constraint, the reserved bandwidth is upper limited by B^{max}. We can derive that the minimum data transfer duration of a BRR equals $\frac{D}{B^{max}}$, denoted as t^{min} [2,11,12,20]. If a BRR can be successfully scheduled within timewindow tw_j, the duration of the overlapped time interval $(max(t^S, tw_j^s), min(t^E, tw_j^e))$ must be no less than t^{min}, namely $(min(t^E, tw_j^e) - max(t^S, tw_j^s)) \geq t^{min}$. For example, for BRR $(v_s, v_d, 36Gb, 12Gb/s, [0, 10s])$, $t^{min} = \frac{36Gb}{12Gb/s} = 3s$. It is easy to see that the given BRR cannot be scheduled within timewindow $[4s, 6s]$ since its duration is $(6s - 4s) = 2s$, less than the minimum data transfer duration requirement of $3s$. Removing redundant edges within a timewindow and filtering timewindows using t^{min} can greatly improve the overall BRR scheduling speed and efficiency, which will be shown in Section 5.4.

5.4 Introduction and Illustration of One Bandwidth Reservation Algorithm

As shown in Section 5.2, we have done extensive research and studied many different problems regarding big data transfer using bandwidth reservation service in an HPN environment. In this section, we focus on the algorithm design and illustration of one bandwidth reservation algorithm we proposed in [12], followed by more discussions regarding several different aspects of the algorithm.

5.4.1 Algorithm design

As we know, users oftentimes would like to achieve additional data transfer parameters besides deadline. The most common one is the ECT. Here we show one bandwidth reservation algorithm proposed previously in our work [12] to identify the QRECT for one single BRR. Please refer to Algorithm 5.1 for the detailed algorithm design and pseudocode. In the worst case, its complexity is $O\left(|LBRR| \cdot |LTP|^2 \cdot (|E| + |V| \cdot \log |V| + \log |LTP|)\right)$.

5.4.2 Algorithm explanation

A brief explanation of Algorithm 5.1 is provided as follows.

After the operations stated in Line 1, identify the timewindow list TW for brr as shown in Lines 2–8 and then iterate through timewindow list TW. For $tw \in TW$, use Equation 5.5 to compute the available bandwidths of all edges and then prune edges with available bandwidths less than $\frac{D}{min(t^E, tw^e) - max(t^S, tw^s)}$ from E. If G becomes disconnected, and v_s and v_d are in two different components, the iteration of TW continues; otherwise, we use modified Dijkstra's algorithm to identify the path with the largest available bandwidth from v_s to v_d. Suppose the returned path is pb. If pb can finish the data transfer of brr within the time interval overlapping between tw and brr, namely time interval $\left(max\left(t^S, tw^s\right), min\left(t^E, tw^e\right)\right)$, the corresponding QR is created as shown in lines 17–20. We record the BRR with the ECT, namely QRECT, during the timewindow iteration. After the TW iteration, if $qr \neq NULL$, we know that brr can be successfully scheduled and we would update the available bandwidths of edges on the data transfer path by performing the operation stated in Line 25. If $qr = NULL$, that means we cannot identify any QR for the input BRR, and we will return $NULL$.

5.4.3 Algorithm illustration

We use BRR $(v_s, v_d, 36Gb, 12Gb/s, [0, 10s])$ to illustrate Algorithm 5.1 along with the example HPN shown in Figure 5.1.

Algorithm 5.1 Bandwidth Reservation Algorithm

INPUT: $G(V,E)$ and a BRR *brr*.
OUTPUT: The QRECT of *brr* if *brr* can be successfully scheduled, or $NULL$ otherwise.

Draw the current topology G of the HPN within $[t^S, t^E]$. Create a priority queue LTP containing all timepoints within $[t^S, t^E]$ without duplicates, in ascending order. Initialize timewindow list $TW = NULL$, QR $qr = NULL$ and $ect = \infty$;
for $j = 1$ to $|LTP| - 1$ **do**
    for $i = 0$ to $j - 1$ **do**
        if $min\left(LTP[j], t^E\right) - max\left(LTP[i], t^S\right) \geq t^{min} = \frac{D}{B^{max}}$ **then**
            Add timewindow $(LTP[i], LTP[j])$ to TW;
        end if
    end for
end for
for $tw \in TW$ **do**
    Prune edges with available bandwidths less than $\frac{D}{min(t^E, tw^e) - max(t^S, tw^s)}$ from E;
    if G becomes disconnected, and v_s and v_d are in two different components **then**
        continue;
    end if
    Use modified Dijkstra's algorithm to identify the path with the largest available bandwidth from v_s to v_d, suppose the returned path is pb;
    $l = min\left(t^E, tw^e\right) - max\left(t^S, tw^s\right)$;
    if $min\left(B(pb,tw), B^{max}\right) \cdot l \geq D \&\& max\left(t^S, tw^s\right) + \frac{D}{min(B(pb,tw), B^{max})} < ect$ **then**
        $sTime = max\left(t^S, tw^s\right)$;
        $b = min\left(B(pb,tw), B^{max}\right)$;
        $eTime = sTime + \frac{D}{b}$;
        $qr = (pb, b, [sTime, eTime])$;
        $ect = eTime$;
    end if
end for
if $qr \neq NULL$ **then**
    Add $sTime$ and $eTime$ to LTP, suppose $tp_i = sTime$ and $tp_j = eTime$. Decrease the available bandwidths of edges on pb by b within timesteps $[tp_i, tp_{i+1}]$, $[tp_{i+1}, tp_{i+2}]$, $\ldots$, $[tp_{j-1}, tp_j]$;
end if
Return qr.

With the given topology G of the HPN, the priority queue containing all time points within $[0,10s]$ in ascending order is $LTP = \{0,4s,6s,10s\}$. For $(v_s, v_d, 36Gb, 12Gb/s, [0,10s])$, $t^{min} = \frac{36Gb}{12Gb/s} = 3s$. Following lines 2–8, we have timewindow list $TW = ([0,4s],[0,6s],[0,10s],[4s,10s],[6s,10s])$. Iterate through TW. For timewindow $[0,4s]$, prune edges with available bandwidths less than $\frac{D}{min(t^E,tw^e)-max(t^S,tw^s)} = \frac{36Gb}{4s-0} = 9Gb/s$ from E. It is easy to see that all of these four edges will be removed. After removal, G becomes disconnected, and v_s and v_d are in two different components. We continue to the next timewindow $[0,6s]$. After computation, we know that all edges will also be removed. Within timewindow $[0,10s]$, prune edges with available bandwidths less than $\frac{36Gb}{10s-0} = 3.6Gb/s$ from E. Edge $v_s - b$ will be removed, and we use modified Dijkstra's algorithm to identify the path with the largest available bandwidth from v_s to v_d. After computation, the returned path is $v_s - a - v_d$. We have $B(v_s - a - v_d, [0,10s]) = 4Gb/s$, $l = min(10s,10s) - max(0,0) = 10s - 0 = 10s$ and $min(4Gb/s, 12Gb/s) \cdot 10s = 40Gb > 36Gb$; we know that path $v_s - a - v_d$ can finish the data transfer of brr and provide a valid QR within timewindow $[0,10s]$. The data transfer start time is $sTime = max(0,0) = 0$ and the reserved bandwidth is $b = min(4Gb/s, 12Gb/s) = 4Gb/s$, so the data transfer end time is $eTime = 0 + \frac{36Gb}{4Gb/s} = 9s$. The corresponding QR is $qr = (v_s - a - v_d, 4Gb/s, [0,9s])$. After the iteration of timewindows $[4s,10s]$ and $[6s,10s]$, we know that we cannot find any QR with an earlier data transfer completion time. After the iteration of all timewindows in TW, it is easy to see $qr \neq NULL$, we then add 0 and $9s$ to LTP. Timepoint 0 has already been in LTP while timepoint $9s$ is a new timepoint. Timestep $[6s,10s]$ will be split into two timesteps: $[6s,9s]$ and $[9s,10s]$. We then decrease the available bandwidths of edge $v_s - a$ and $a - v_d$ within timesteps $[0,4s]$, $[4s,6s]$ and $[6s,9s]$ by $4Gb/s$. Timepoints priority queue LTP becomes $\{0,4s,6s,9s,10s\}$. Finally, $qr = (v_s - a - v_d, 4Gb/s, [0,9s])$ will be returned as the QRECT for the received BRR $(v_s, v_d, 36Gb, 12Gb/s, [0,10s])$. After successfully scheduling above BRR, Figure 5.2 shows the available bandwidth table of edges in G.

For data transfer parameter SD, we only need to make some slight change to Line 12 of Algorithm 5.1: change $max\left(t^S, tw^s\right) + \frac{D}{min(B(pb,tw),B^{max})} < ect$ to $\frac{D}{min(B(pb,tw),B^{max})} < ect$, and then the returned QR should be the QRSD for the input BRR. For example, for the same BRR $(v_s, v_d, 36Gb, 12Gb/s, [0,10s])$, the identified QRSD should be $(v_s - a - v_d, 11Gb/s, [6s, 9.27s])$ with the data transfer duration of $9.27s - 6s = 3.27s$.

5.4.4 More discussion

Line 14 of Algorithm 5.1 uses modified Dijkstra's algorithm to identify the path with the largest available bandwidth. Actually, the shortest-widest path is a better option here. The shortest-widest path refers to the path with the largest available

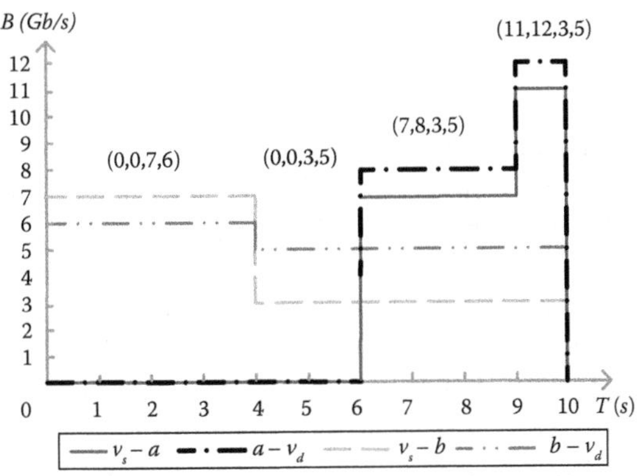

Figure 5.2: Available bandwidth table of edges in G after successfully scheduling BRR (v_s, v_d, 36Gb, 12Gb/s, [0,10s]).

bandwidth among all paths connecting the same source and destination node. If there are multiple paths with the same largest available bandwidth, then the one with the least length is returned. If several such paths exist, one is randomly selected and returned. For a BRR, its data transfer uses bandwidth resources of the scheduling HPN. If we can successfully schedule the received BRR on different paths with the same data transfer performance parameter, we should choose the path with the least length because the whole data would go through the least number of edges and use the minimum bandwidth resources. Again, from the perspective of the bandwidth reservation service providers, the more BRRs can be successfully scheduled within a certain time interval the better, because they would like to achieve high bandwidth resource utilization and throughput purposes most of the time.

Different paths might be returned under different circumstances. For example, sometimes we would like to return the path with the least length, the widest-shortest path and some other paths.

Algorithm 5.1 only processes one BRR at a time, so it is an instant scheduling algorithm. Periodic scheduling algorithms process multiple BRRs accumulated within a time interval. Processing these multiple BRRs in a certain order instead of FIFO order might give us an overall better scheduling performance. For example, if we would like to achieve a higher BRR scheduling ratio, namely the percentage of the BRRs that can be successfully scheduled within the batch, then we would like to sort the BRRs by their data sizes in an increasing order. The BRR scheduling ratio will be increased most of the time because after the sort, the BRRs with the least data sizes to be transferred will be processed first. After having the timewindow list TW for each BRR, we can also sort the timewindows according to some criteria along with other techniques to achieve a shorter overall algorithm execution time. Using such techniques will not decrease the time complexity of the scheduling algorithm; however, the average actual algorithm execution time could normally be decreased. Nowadays, the most widely used bandwidth reservation service within the global research and networking community is provided by ESnet, where the OSCARS software is deployed with multidomain, high-bandwidth virtual circuits. To mimic the real ESnet scenario, we performed our simulation experiments using the topology data gathered from ESnet. Our intensive experiments on simulated ESnet showed that our algorithms have much better overall BRR scheduling performance than similar scheduling algorithms. For example, Figures 5.3 and 5.4 from our published work [12] show the execution time and BRR scheduling success ratio comparison between our proposed algorithm FECT and the other two algorithms, namely Naïve-ECT and FRA-ECT, respectively. Naïve-ECT tries to identify the QRECT for the input BRR through searching the entire solution space neither using any trimming techniques nor sorting BRRs or timewindows, while FRA-ECT uses several trimming techniques to narrow down the solution space. For detailed algorithm designs, illustrations and experiment comparison results, please refer to our published work [12].

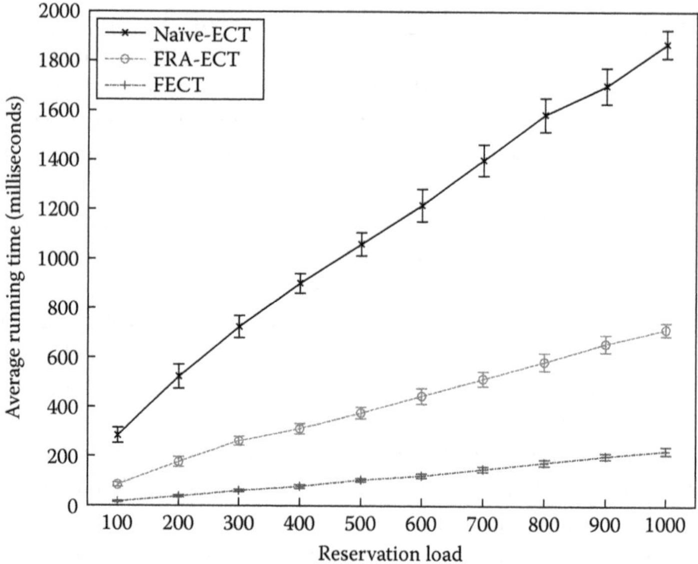

Figure 5.3: Comparison of running time between Naïve-ECT, FRA-ECT, and FECT.

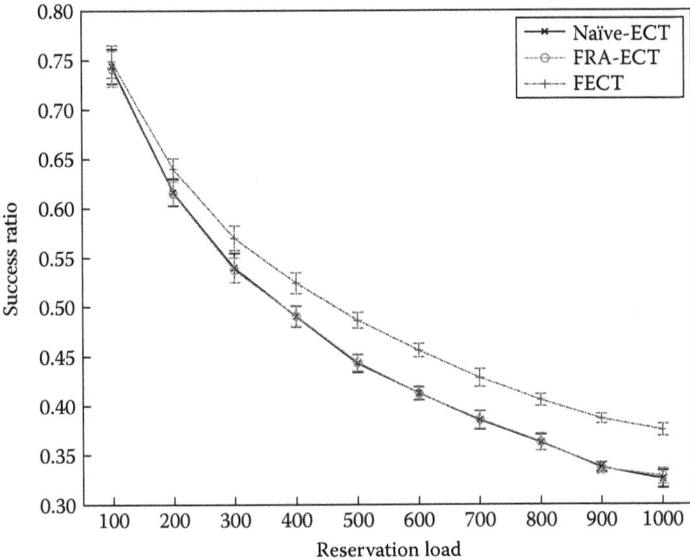

Figure 5.4: Comparison of success ratio between Naïve-ECT, FRA-ECT, and FECT.

5.5 Conclusion

Extremely large amounts of data, now frequently termed as big data, are being generated from various emerging applications of large-scale simulations, scientific experiments, and global-scale communications. Such data sets normally are generated at one data center and then need to be transferred over long distances to different sites for remote operations such as data archival, synthesis, and analysis. Thus, it has become a critical task to make the data transfer in a fast and reliable way, which goes beyond the capability and capacity of the traditional networks such as the Internet. To address this challenge, next-generation research and education dedicated HPNs are being developed to allow data flows to reserve bandwidth as needed in their dedicated channels. This strategy guarantees predictive and reliable data transfer, and is widely used in extreme-scale computations. In this chapter, we first presented the introduction and background of bandwidth reservation service in HPNs for big data transfer along with the challenges, followed by the related works. Detailed bandwidth reservation mechanisms and concepts were provided. We then showed one of our proposed bandwidth scheduling algorithms with illustration through simple examples for easy comprehension. Two experiment performance figures were included to show the scheduling comparison between our algorithm and the other two similar algorithms.

We are currently studying a problem regarding big data transfer reliability using the bandwidth reservation service in an HPN environment. In the future, we plan to cooperate with network service providers to implement and integrate our efficient and novel scheduling algorithm in a real network such as ESnet and GENI for performance evaluation purposes. We also plan to extend our work to data transfer and bandwidth scheduling in the Cloud computing environment.

References

[1] T. Shu, C. Wu, and D. Yun, Advance bandwidth reservation for energy efficiency in high-performance networks, in *IEEE 38th Conf. Local Comput. Netw.*, Oct. 2013, Sydney, NSW, pp. 541–548.

[2] L. Zuo, M. Khaleel, M. Zhu, and C. Wu, On fixed-path variable-bandwidth scheduling in high-performance networks, in *2013 IEEE Int. Conf. Green Comput. and Commun.*, Aug. 2013, Beijing, China, pp. 23–30.

[3] N. Rao, Q. Wu, S. Ding, S. Carter, W. Wing, A. Banerjee, D. Ghosal, and B. Mukherjee, Control plane for advance bandwidth scheduling in ultra high-speed networks, in *25th IEEE Int. Conf. Comput. Commun. Proc.*, Apr., 2006, Barcelona, Spain, pp. 1–5.

[4] Y. Lin and Q. Wu, Complexity analysis and algorithm design for advance bandwidth scheduling in dedicated networks, *IEEE/ACM Trans. Netw.*, vol. 21, no. 1, pp. 14–27, Feb. 2013.

[5] N. Charbonneau, V. M. Vokkarane, C. Guok, and I. Monga, Advance reservation frameworks in hybrid ip-wdm networks, *IEEE Commun. Mag.*, vol. 49, no. 5, pp. 132–139, 2011.

[6] R. Summerhill, The new internet2 network, in *6th Global Lambda Integrated Facility*, Sep., 2006, Tokyo, Japan.

[7] J. Recio, E. Grasa, S. Figuerola, and G. Junyent, Evolution of the user controlled lightpath provisioning system, in *Proc. of 2005 7th Int. Conf. Transparent Opt. Netw.*, vol. 1, July 2005, Barcelona, Spain, pp. 263–266.

[8] S. Sahni, N. Rao, S. Ranka, Y. Li, E.-S. Jung, and N. Kamath, Bandwidth scheduling and path computation algorithms for connection-oriented networks, in *6th Int. Conf. Netw.*, 2007, Martinique, France, p. 47.

[9] X. Zheng, M. Veeraraghavan, N. Rao, Q. Wu, and M. Zhu, Cheetah: Circuit-switched high-speed end-to-end transport architecture testbed, *IEEE Commun. Mag.*, vol. 43, no. 8, pp. 11–17, 2005.

[10] T. Lehman, J. Sobieski, and B. Jabbari, Dragon: A framework for service provisioning in heterogeneous grid networks, *IEEE Commun. Mag.*, vol. 44, no. 3, pp. 84–90, Mar. 2006.

[11] M. Balman, E. Chaniotakisy, A. Shoshani, and A. Sim, A flexible reservation algorithm for advance network provisioning, in *Proc. of the 2010 ACM/IEEE Int. Conf. High Perform. Comput. Netw. Storage Anal.*, 2010, New Orleans, LA, pp. 1–11.

[12] L. Zuo, M. M. Zhu, and C. Wu, Fast and efficient bandwidth reservation algorithms for dynamic network provisioning, *Physical Journal*, 23(3), 420–444, 2015.

[13] S. Sharma, D. Katramatos, and D. Yu, End-to-end network qos via scheduling of flexible resource reservation requests, in *Proc. of 2011 Int. Conf. High Perform. Comput. Netw. Storage Anal.*, 2011, Seatle, WA, pp. 1–10.

[14] L. Zuo, M. M. Zhu, and Q. Q. Wu, Concurrent bandwidth scheduling for big data transfer over a dedicated channel, *Int. J. Commun. Netw. Distri. Syst.*, vol. 15, no. 2/3, pp. 169–190, 2015.

[15] C. P. Guok, D. W. Robertson, E. Chaniotakis, M. R. Thompson, W. Johnston, and B. Tierney, A user driven dynamic circuit network implementation, in *IEEE Global Commun. Conf. Workshops*, Dec. 2008, New Orleans, LA, pp. 1–5.

[16] A. Herms and G. Lukas, Preventing admission failures of bandwidth reservation in wireless mesh networks, in *2008 IEEE/ACS Int. Conf. Comp. Sys. and App.*, Mar. 2008, Doha, Qatar, pp. 1094–1099.

[17] K. Rajah, S. Ranka, and Y. Xia, Advance reservations and scheduling for bulk transfers in research networks, *IEEE Trans. Paral. Distrib. Syst.*, vol. 20, no. 11, pp. 1682–1697, Nov. 2009.

[18] P. Dharam and Q. Wu, Advance bandwidth reservation with delay guarantee in high-performance networks, in *21st Int. Conf. Comput. Commun. Netw.* Jul., 2012, Munich, Germany, pp. 1–7.

[19] Y. Lin and Q. Wu, On design of bandwidth scheduling algorithms for multiple data transfers in dedicated networks, in *Proc. 4th ACM/IEEE Symp. Archi. Netw. Commun. Syst.*, 2008, San Jose, CA, pp. 151–160.

[20] L. Zuo and M. M. Zhu, Toward flexible and fast routing strategies for dynamic network provisioning, in *27th Int. Paral. Distri. Process. Symp. PhD Forum*, May 2013, Cambridge, MA, pp. 2222–2225.

[21] L. Zuo and M. M. Zhu, Improved scheduling algorithms for single-path multiple bandwidth reservation requests, in *10th IEEE Int. Conf. Big Data Sci. Eng. (IEEE BigDataSE-16)*, Aug. 2016, Tianjin, China.

[22] L. Zuo and M. M. Zhu, Concurrent bandwidth reservation strategies for big data transfers in high-performance networks, *IEEE Trans. Netw. Serv. Manage.*, vol. 12, no. 2, pp. 232–247, 2015.

[23] S. Sharma, D. Katramatos, D. Yu, and L. Shi, Design and implementation of an intelligent end-to-end network QoS system, in *Proc. Int. Conf. High Perform. Comput. Netw. Storage Anal.*, 2012, Salt Lake City, UT, pp. 1–11.

Chapter 6

A Dynamic Cloud Computing Architecture for Cloud-Assisted Internet of Things in the Era of Big Data

Mehdi Bahrami and Mukesh Singhal

University of California, Merced
Merced, California

CONTENTS

6.1 Introduction

This chapter describes a convergence of two recent and popular paradigms, Cloud computing and the Internet of Things (IoT). These two paradigms define a new cost-effective model for a network of devices that are connected through the Internet. In this section, we define these two paradigms, and the advantages of each that follow when we plan to collect a large amount of data and process big data. The processing of big data efficiently in the Cloud environment is an opportunity to use a variety of IoT devices to transfer raw data to intelligent data.

6.1.1 Cloud computing paradigm

Cloud computing uses virtualization technology to provide virtual services to users [1]. Virtualization technology has been known about since operating systems were introduced in the 1960s, but although this is not a new paradigm, the method of using virtualization technology is new—it provides virtual services to multitenant users in order to offer cost-effective IT services to Cloud users. The virtual services include storage and processing units in the Cloud, and are shared among all Cloud users.

The Cloud enables users to increase or decrease the capacity of virtual storage, and the number of virtual processing machines on demand. The Cloud vendor bills Cloud users based on a pay-per-use model. This dynamic resource allocation allows users to support any number of user requests without paying additional costs to maintain a large number of processing machines, and a massive amount of data. Cloud computing has become popular to both startup businesses and corporations, because startup businesses can begin with low investment, and the corporations could save maintenance costs when the number of user requests is decreased.

Since Cloud vendors maintain all storage and processing units, the Cloud users do not need to pay for additional maintenance costs, or even recovery costs in a disaster situation. The Cloud vendors also deploy global backup servers to prevent users' data loss.

6.1.2 Internet of Things (IoT) paradigm

The IoT [2] paradigm is an opportunity for businesses to have a network of small computing sensor devices for detecting the environment such as reading the current temperature of the environment, for predicting maintenance, and recently IoT sensors are being used in self-driving cars. Usually IoT devices use Internet protocol (IP) for connecting to the Internet, and it allows them to send data to the servers directly. IP allows each device to connect to the Internet without any local server, or a complicated IT infrastructure and the IoT devices are able to send their sensor results to any server around the world. The IoT devices use the IPsec protocol [3] in order to securely transfer their data to the server(s); however, they have limited resources such as their lack of power, low-speed CPUs, and the small amount of storage.

6.1.3 Convergence of IoT and the Cloud (Cloud-assisted IoT)

The convergence of Cloud and IoT devices, Cloud-assisted IoT, enables IoT devices to outsource their data to Cloud computing systems. The Cloud allows users to process the outsourced data with multiple virtual CPUs. Currently, several Cloud vendors offer particular platforms and Cloud services for IoT devices. For instance, Microsoft recently introduced the Azure IoT Suite during the *Convergence 2015* conference, which provides a platform for developing IoT devices on Microsoft Cloud Azure.

Another advantage of Cloud-assisted IoT is providing a hub between all IoT devices from around the world to collaborate with each other while using the Cloud as the main connection.

Finally, big data analytic tools [1] is another advantages of the Cloud that offers analytics services on collected raw data from IoT devices. Some of these tools are open-source, and are freely available to users to process complex queries on raw big data collected from IoT devices. Some of these analytic tools and services have been summarized in our previous study [1].

The rest of the chapter is organized as follows: the next section describes the architecture issue of Cloud-assisted IoT as one of the major challenges that faces users when they want to use different Cloud platforms. Section 6.3 describes a service-oriented architecture (SOA) [4] that allows different Cloud vendors to define a generic and dynamic platform in order to facilitate users' transformation for data, applications, and IoT devices. Section 6.4 describes some of the advantages of the proposed architecture, such as standardization between heterogeneous Cloud platforms by using the proposed architecture and security of the proposed architecture, and it reviews a case study of implementation of data security on the proposed architecture. Section 6.5 reviews related works, and finally, Section 6.6 concludes this chapter.

6.1.4 Big data

IoT offers a new set of tools, sensors, and devices that can be controlled through the Internet. In the era of big data, collecting data, processing, and analysis of data are key points. Moving to IoT in the Cloud environment allows us to achieve all these key points when each small computing machine (IoT device) generates daily reports of human activities. Collecting a large amount of data can be accomplished in the Cloud environment by employing Cloud-based databases (i.e., NoSQL databases) when users only pay per usage. In addition, there are several analysis tools that provide an analysis service on big data by using a pool of computing machines in the Cloud environment. In order to transfer bulk raw data of IoT devices to valuable data, we can process the content by using a large number of processors where the number of machines can be increased/decreased on demand. Using intelligent computation tools also raises interest in Cloud-based systems because computation on big data causes several limitations on traditional computing machines. The question is how can a variety of heterogeneous IoT devices be able to use a unique Cloud computing environment to efficiently collect big data and intelligently process it.

6.2 Challenges in Cloud-Assisted IoT

Currently, we do not have an acceptable standard between Cloud computing systems [5], and even between major key Cloud vendors, such as Microsoft and Amazon. So, each Cloud vendor offers its own platform to the users. The provided services differ from one vendor to another because each of them uses their unique set of inputs, outputs, and processes to provide Cloud services. These different services from different Cloud vendors offer heterogeneous Cloud services to users. Although the heterogeneous Cloud vendors accept major programming languages, transferring data and applications from one vendor to another, or returning applications and data back to the user's in-house IT department is difficult because each Cloud vendor uses its own platform, or uses its own application programming interface (API). If a user wishes to transfer data and applications to another platform, he/she needs to modify the codes, and sometimes needs to redevelop the applications or databases. The dependency of IoT devices to a particular Cloud platform causes several subissues as follows:

1. **Flexibility issue [5]:** This does not allow IoT devices to properly use all functions when the devices are moved to another platform.
2. **Customization issue [6]:** This arises when a vendor is not able to customize a Cloud platform for supporting different users' requests.
3. **Security issue [7]:** If a Cloud platform provides specific security protocols to IoT devices, the security of IoT devices can be compromised when

the devices are transferred to another platform. This issue originates when the security of an IoT device relies on the particular Cloud platform. In this case, the application on the Cloud-side (server-side) needs to be redeveloped in order to protect the IoT device. For instance, if an IoT devices uses a handshake protocol in order to submit its data to the Cloud and it is transferred to another vendor, the handshake protocol needs to be redesign for the new Cloud vendor.

6.3 Solution: A Dynamic Cloud Computing Architecture for Cloud-Assisted IoT

As a result of lack of standardization between Cloud vendors, each Cloud vendor offers their own Cloud architecture which means we have heterogeneous systems for IoT devices. For instance, if a user uses an IoT device that relies on IBM Cloud, it is difficult, or even impossible to use the device with other Cloud vendors, such as Microsoft Azure. Sometimes, it requires a redevelopment of database and applications in order to transfer IoT devices from one vendor to another.

Since we have heterogeneous Cloud platforms, it is not cost-effective to modify all Cloud platforms to provide standard services between different Cloud platforms. In our previous study, we proposed a dynamic Cloud computing architecture (DCCSOA) [5] based on SOA [4]. Figure 6.1 illustrates how the DCCSOA facilitates deployment of multiple IoT devices on the top of a Cloud vendor. In this figure, each component is connected to others as a service. The SOA's feature allows the architecture to implement on the top of heterogeneous Cloud platforms without requiring additional modification on each Cloud platform. Each Cloud vendor with different platforms is able to define different templates on the top of their Cloud services. A template is an interface that interacts with one or more Cloud services. A Cloud vendor is able to define different templates in order to customize their services to a variety of users. DCCSOA provides a flexible Cloud architecture that supports both the Cloud vendor, and the vendors' users. On the user side, the users can freely transfer data and applications from one vendor to another with minimal modification costs while a network of IoT devices uses DCCSOA's unique interface on the top of heterogeneous Cloud computing systems. On the vendor side, Cloud vendors are able to customize their platforms based on DCCSOA with minimal modifications in order to provide a unique and standard service to the users. On both sides (client side and vendor side), the level of modification is a key parameter of the provided architecture.

On the one hand, less modification on the user side's IoT device means more standardization between heterogeneous Cloud platforms and more independent Cloud services, and on the other hand, less modification on the architecture

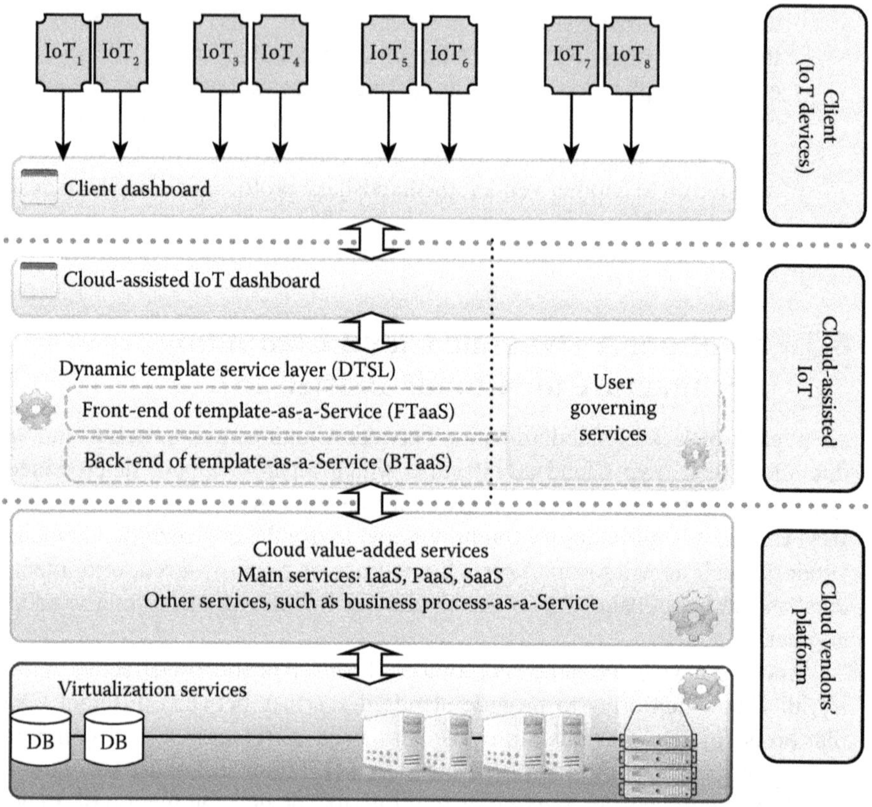

Figure 6.1: The proposed architecture of DCCSOA for Cloud-assisted IoT.

means offering a cost-effective model that supports a variety of user requests with minimal costs for customization.

The proposed architecture for Cloud-assisted IoT is divided into three layers as follows:

1. **Cloud vendor:** This layer shows the implementation of a Cloud vendor. Different Cloud vendors offer heterogeneous Cloud architecture in this level. Each Cloud vendor offers a variety of Cloud services which are called value-added services. For instance, Infrastructure-as-a-Service (IaaS) provides virtual infrastructures, such as virtual storage and virtual CPU to users, Platform-as-a-Service (PaaS) offers a development and deployment environment to implement applications, and Software-as-a-Service (SaaS) provides preinstalled applications on the Cloud. Recently, a new variety of Cloud services has also been deployed in Cloud computing

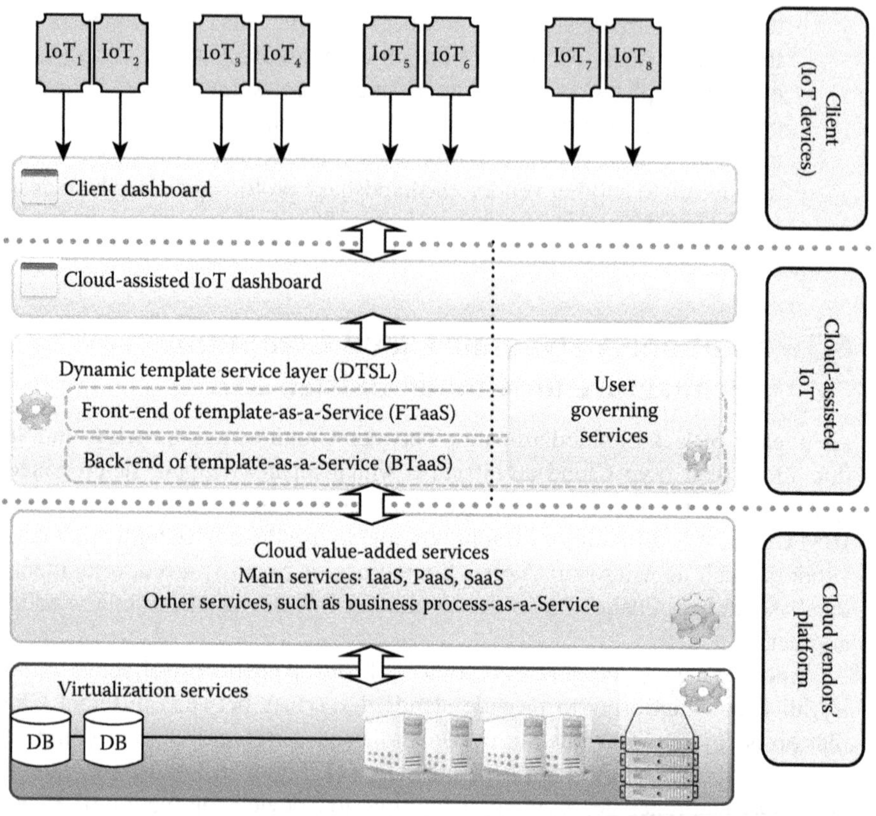

defined as *-as-a-Service (*aaS) [5]. A list of different Cloud services have been summarized in Ref. [1].

In this level, DCCSOA allows any type of Cloud services with heterogeneous platforms and different interfaces to be offered by a Cloud vendor.

2. **Cloud-assisted IoT:** This layer provides a generic interface on the top of heterogeneous Cloud platforms to the client side. The dynamic template service layer (DTSL) is divided into two sublayers as follows:

   - Front-end-template-as-a-Service (FTaaS) that provides a generic interface for Cloud services. Clients are able to access this layer though a platform, or even as a preinstalled application on the Cloud.
   - Back-end-template-as-a-Service (BTaaS) that binds each service at FTaaS as a generic interface to a particular Cloud value-added service. A template (T) defines a generic interface for a service s (K_s) based on the required input/output of the given service s as follows:

   $$T(K_s) = \sum_{i=1}^{m} input_{k,i} + \sum_{j=1}^{n} input_{k,j} \tag{6.1}$$

   where $K \in \{P\}$ and P is a set of different Cloud platforms which are heterogeneous, and each given service s has m number of input parameters and n number of output parameters.

   A Cloud vendor defines dynamically several different templates on demand at DTSL. Each template integrates with one or multiple value-added Cloud services. Cloud vendors can set up, configure, and provide different templates to their customers based on different value-added service layers in a Cloud computing system.

3. **Client:** End-user applications that include software and IoT devices are located in this layer. If an IoT vendor offers Cloud-assisted storage and computing units, the vendor can use the dashboard component (as illustrated in Figure 6.1) to have collaboration/interactions with the Cloud vendor on one side, and their customer on the other side. An IoT vendor who uses Cloud vendor infrastructure to provide IoT services can use heterogeneous Cloud vendors while using a generic interface (a defined template) at the top of each Cloud vendor.

The following equation defines a service at FTaaS which is required to pass a satisfaction function $\mathcal{S}$ to propose a generic service on the top of heterogeneous Cloud vendors [8].

$$\exists s \in FTaaS \mid \mathcal{S}at(s) \tag{6.2}$$

where s is a service at *FTaaS* and $\mathcal{S}at$ is a satisfaction function which is defined as follows:

$$Sat(s) : \mathcal{R} \rightarrow \mathcal{O} \tag{6.3}$$

where $\mathcal{R}$ is a finite set of requirements of r, and $\mathcal{O}$ is a finite set of corresponding output for each requirement in $\mathcal{R}$.

The generic service (*UI*) can be defined as follows:

$$UI(s) \rightarrow Sat(s_1)^\wedge Sat(s_1)^\wedge Sat(s_k) \tag{6.4}$$

At the implementation level, the following code [8] describes how a client is able access a template without being concerned about the location of the data source and other related configurations. The client accesses the data source in this example through FTaaS which is defined as a web service (FTaaS_Service_Ref). Although the query and data privacy method were implemented at BTaaS, it is possible to process both processes at FTaaS or even at the client side. In this example, the procedure enables a client access to data sources by calling the *GetDataList* procedure from the web service, and finally, the procedure returns the result on an object, *DataGridView*.

Data access at client-side through FTaaS

```
FTaaS_Service_Ref.Service1Client FTS = new TaaS_Service_Ref.Service1Client();
DataSet ds = FTS.GetDataList();
DataGridView.DataSource = ds.Tables[0];
DataGridView.DataBind();
```

As shown in this example, DCCSOA allows users to interact with a template at FTaaS that provides Cloud services. The user does not need to have any knowledge of Cloud value-added services because they are implemented at BTaaS. This independency would be a great opportunity for IoT users who use different IoT devices as it allows them to freely transfer their data and applications from one vendor to another.

6.4 Big Data Processing on DCCSOA for Cloud-Assisted IoT

In this study, we consider each IoT device sends data to Cloud vendors. The data is processed through FTaaS and the corresponding BTaaS, then it is submitted to the Cloud. Big data is defined by four characteristics—volume, velocity, variety, and veracity [1]. We describe the requirements of each of these characteristics as well as our recommended solutions to maintain these characteristics based on the proposed Cloud-assisted IoT architecture.

6.4.1 Volume

Big data is characterized by extremely high volume data which is indicated by the size of data. Regularly, each IoT device generates a small portion of big data; however, by periodically generating small data and collecting all data from a large number of devices, we will have a large volume of data. Processing big data on a Cloud computing server might be a challenge; however, different tools allow a Cloud vendor to store and process this big data. For instance, different NoSQL Cloud-based databases allow users to store structured and unstructured data in the Cloud without any concerns about speed of data retrieval.

6.4.2 Velocity

Velocity indicates the speed of data processing in terms of response time. The response time could be a batch, real-time, or stream response time. When we consider the velocity only for a portion of data which is generated by an IoT device in a short period of time, it is not a challenge but if we consider a long-term data collection from a large number of IoT devices, it is a challenge to achieve a response time of processing the data in a timely manner. In this case, sometimes it requires a Cloud computing system to support a real-time response. The real-time response requires a high-performance computing (HPC) system. In Section 6.4, we discuss a similar challenge for mobile users who need data privacy. We use a graphics processing unit (GPU) rather than a CPU that allows 1000s of threads to run a portion of the task when each thread is processed on a GPU core. In this case, the proposed architecture is able to efficiently process a request by parallelizing the task and splitting the task among multiple GPU cores. In order to offer this type of service (i.e., a real-time system), we may bind a BTaaS to a set of GPUs and provide a function as an interface at FTaaS. Therefore, any task submitted to the function at FTaaS will be able to be processed in real time at its corresponding BTaaS when the task actually runs on thousands of GPU cores. Some similar studies for implementing parallel tasks on the Cloud can be found in [9,10]. These systems can be connected to BTaaS to perform HPC on Cloud computing.

6.4.3 Variety

Variety represents heterogeneity/diversity in data which is collected from different IoT devices. Another challenge is analyzing the variety of data including structured, unstructured, and semistructured data. We have a variety of IoT devices and they might generate a set of video files, text files, JSON-based output files that include structured data such as database, semistructured data such as text and even unstructured data, such as multimedia (e.g., voices, images, videos). When we are using Cloud computing, it is capable of processing of a variety of formats. Some Cloud-based tools that allow users to analyze a variety of data [1], such as Talend [1] which is a data integration, data management, enterprise application integration, and big data software tool. Similar Cloud-based tools are available to solve the variety issue where each tool can be bound to BTaaS and the functionalities of each application can be exposed to the users at FTaaS. For instance, if Talend is bound to BTaaS, it can provide data integration at the DTSL layer but each function or multiple functions of data integration can be implemented in an FTaaS layer. Flexibility in defining services through defining multiple FTaaS allows Cloud vendors to support a variety of data types for IoT devices.

6.4.4 Veracity

Veracity is the level of accuracy of data. For example, a sensor that generates data may provide a wrong value (e.g., an IoT device which reports inaccurate temperature). The proposed architecture is able to verify the accuracy of collected data when a minimum of two similar IoT devices are located in the same environment and they are connected to an FTaaS (e.g., two IoT devices that measure the temperature are connected to FTaaS). The architecture allows the veracity of data to be reviewed on the edge (which is also the purpose of fog computing [11]) at FTaaS. In this scenario, if the value of collected data from two sensors are not the same, then an intelligent application might review the history of each device to see which device provided the correct result, or we can cross check the received data at FTaaS. Reviewing data at FTaaS allows us to remove additional overheads on the back end of a Cloud computing system. Therefore, the veracity of data can be accomplished without entering the back end (BTaaS). In this example, the accurate data can be collected at BTaaS and can be stored in the Cloud.

6.4.5 Advantages of DCCSOA for Cloud-assisted IoT

The proposed architecture provides several advantages to the Cloud vendor, IoT vendors, and their end users that include standardization, customization, and security which are described in the following.

6.5 Standardization

One of the major issues in Cloud computing is a lack of standardization between different Cloud platforms and as we discussed earlier, it causes a vendor lock-in issue that does not allow IoT devices, their data, and applications to freely transfer to another Cloud vendor. DCCSOA provides a dynamic service layer (DTSL) to enable different vendors to offer a generic platform through defining the same FTaaS in different Cloud platforms. When different Cloud vendors provide the same FTaaS to their customers, the customers are able to transfer their data and applications from one vendor to another, or they can even transfer data and applications to their own IT department. It also allows IoT devices to use all functions while transferring from one vendor to another.

In addition, the standardization between different Cloud platforms in DCCOSA can be extended to heterogeneous IoT devices by using a generic template that enables a Cloud platform to interact with different IoT devices where each IoT device has specific I/O features.

Adding standardization between Cloud platforms enables portability features for user applications and data in the Cloud.

For example, Figure 6.2 illustrates how three different groups of IoT users use two heterogeneous Clouds. Users are able to subscribe to different templates (T_1, T_2, and/or T_3). Users interact with templates from the FTaaS layer of DTSL, and each template binds to one or more Cloud service layers in any Cloud platform. For instance, IoT Customer Group 1 uses template T_1 to access the SaaS layer which is provided by the first Cloud vendor, $SaaS_a$. As illustrated in Figure 6.2, T_3 provides different PaaS from both vendors, $PaaS_a$ and $PaaS_b$.

The templates enable the vendor to have flexibility in offering a generic Cloud service. Although defined templates in Figure 6.2 bind to similar Cloud services from both vendors, each template can be bound to different services from different Cloud vendors. For instance, T_1 can be bound to $SaaS_a$ and $PaaS_b$.

In addition, the number of templates can be added/reduced on demand. If a Cloud vendor has an attractive service that brings more users, then the vendor can define a new template that covers the new user group needs for the new service.

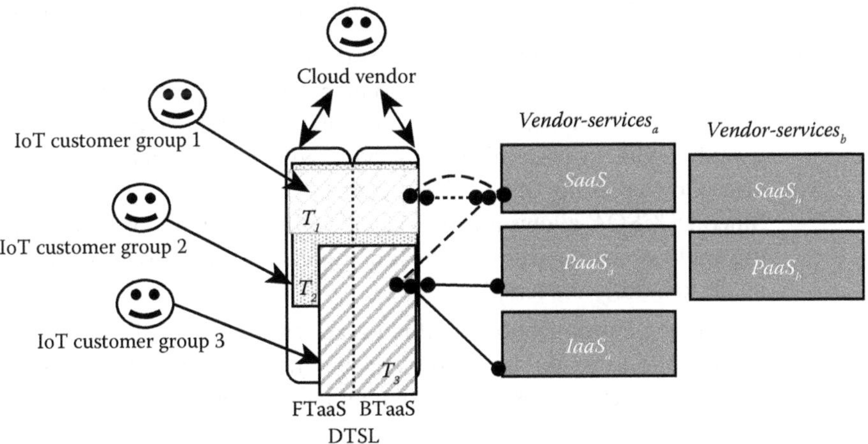

Figure 6.2: One snapshot of DTSL and its interaction with two heterogeneous Cloud platforms.

6.5.1 Customization of architecture

Customization is one of the major issues of Cloud architectures [5]. For instance, a third party who designs services for a Cloud vendor could not customize defined services. This issue causes other related issues such as the lack of usability of Cloud computing [6] that emphasizes the integration issue in Cloud computing systems.

The proposed architecture includes a dynamic layer (DTSL) that allows Cloud vendors to customize their Cloud architecture on demand because a vendor is able to define a template for a particular service. Although the template binds to a particular service at the BTaaS layer, it provides a generic and customized service at the FTaaS layer. When a Cloud vendor defines a new template that interacts with several Cloud services, it enables users to have an integrated service from different Cloud services. This integrated service cannot be only customized by Cloud vendors or their partners; it can also be provided as a generic service on the top of heterogeneous Cloud platforms. In addition, offering an integrated service could attract a variety of groups of users. For instance, if a Cloud vendor offers a message service that allows different applications to contact each other, and a virtual private network (VPN), the Cloud vendor can integrate these services and customize them into a template. In this case, a user is able to subscribe to the template and only subscribe to the template.

Customization of Cloud services can be completed at different levels as follows:

- Low-level customization that customizes services at the implementation level where the Cloud developer implements a system. This level of customization is not a cost-effective, practical method for both Cloud vendors and users because each individual application needs to be modified.
- High-level customization customizes the Cloud services at the architecture level that adopts new and customizes existing Cloud services. If the architecture implements on the top of existing architecture, it allows a Cloud vendor to customize the service with minimal modifications. It also allows existing applications to be used without any modifications. Since DCCSOA allows a Cloud vendor to modify a template, the existing applications can be run without modification and a Cloud vendor only needs to modify the template.

As a result, the customization of Cloud services is a practical model if both Cloud vendors and users do not need extensive modifications. DTSL removes the additional modification costs by using templates.

6.5.2 Data security

Data security emphasizes authentication for accessing data and applications and it protects data against an adversary from internal/external access to data.

Data privacy is another challenge in Cloud computing that emphasizes who are authorized to use the outsourced data in the Cloud [7].

Both data security and privacy schemas can be implemented as an FTaaS. More details on data privacy is described in the following section. The implementation of the security schemes as an FTaaS allows vendors, or users, to use standard security schemas on the top of heterogeneous Cloud computing platforms without additional computation overhead.

6.5.3 Data privacy

Data privacy is the one of the key challenges for Cloud users because users have to outsource their data to the Cloud in order to use the advantages of Cloud computing. However, outsourcing data to Cloud computing servers or performing computation on data in the Cloud environment raises a challenge for users—how is the Cloud vendor protecting user data against anyone from inside the Cloud, including the third parties of Cloud vendors? In order to protect user data privacy, we previously developed a lightweight data privacy method (DPM) that allows users to make a confusion file from an original file, and then user can submit it to the Cloud. The method can be run on a mobile device [7] to protect personal files, or it can be used as a proxy server [12] to protect user data when they wish to use Cloud databases.

In addition, DPM can be processed at FTaaS to provide user data privacy at BTaaS for the stored data in the Cloud. In order to process data faster to maintain both efficiency of service and data privacy, we can use a parallelization of DPM. The implementation of parallel computing algorithms was transferred from massive server machines to small personal computers when open forums and corporations introduced new platforms that allow users to have efficient parallel computing in the Cloud or even on personal computers [13]. For instance, the CUDA platform uses a GPU which was introduced by NVIDIA. This platform enables a user (even a mobile user) to process a procedure in parallel that needs intensive computation [13]. The GPU-based computing paradigm of parallel computing allows a device to use one or multiple GPUs to perform heavy computations where each GPU consists of thousands of small, low-speed cores. Regularly, each submitted task to a core is a repeated computing process so that each instruction does not need heavy computation.

GPU-based computation improves the performance of processing complex methods by parallelizing small tasks of a complex method on each GPU core. When we have a large amount of data, then we can use the parallel model of the DPM to process data faster and more efficiently by using a GPU rather than a CPU.

Let us describe DPM in more detail in the remainder of this section. We explain how DPM can be used in the proposed Cloud-assisted IoT in order to process a large volume of data when we consider velocity as the key parameter.

DPM must process data not only efficiently to save on computation, but also it needs to maintain the velocity of data. The parallel implementation of DPM uses pseudorandom permutation (PRP) which is the key module of many methods, such as encryption and simulations. PRP is defined as follows [13]:

$$F \text{ is mapping } \{0,1\}^n \times \{0,1\}^s \rightarrow \{0,1\}^n \tag{6.5}$$

F is a PRP if:

$$\text{(i) } \forall K \textit{ where } K \in \{0,1\}^s,\ F \text{ is a bijection of } \{0,1\}^n \rightarrow \{0,1\}^n \tag{6.6}$$

$$\text{(ii) } \forall K \textit{ where } K \in \{0,1\}^s\ F_K(x) \text{ is an effective algorithm} \tag{6.7}$$

$$\text{(iii) } D : \Pr(D^{F_K}(1^n) = 1) - \Pr\ (D^{f_n}(1^n) = 1)\ | < \varepsilon(s),\ \textit{where } K \leftarrow \{0,1\}^s[R3] \tag{6.8}$$

where $\Pr(\cdot)$ is the probability of raising the input event.

The main function for generating a pseudonumber is defined as follows:

$$F_{k+1} = \mu F_k(1 - F_K) \tag{6.9}$$

where $P \in \{0,1\}$ and μ is a parameter of this equation.

In the classic chaos system problem, if μ is selected between $3.569945 \leq \mu \leq 4$, and with an initial value of $F_0 = [0,1]$, F provides a complex chaos model [2]. F uses a set ξ to provide a nonconvergent, nonperiodic pseudorandom number [2]:

$$\xi = \{P_k\}_{k=0}^{\omega} \tag{6.10}$$

where ω is maximum number of an original content.

In addition, DPM can be run at BTaaS that allows a Cloud vendor to protect user data privacy.

A different scenario of DPM can be considered. For instance, we implemented DPM for a mobile healthcare system in the Cloud [8] that enables users to outsource their sensitive healthcare data to the Cloud while it preserves data privacy, and compatibility with the Health Insurance Portability and Accountability (HIPPA) Act for data privacy. We defined a template called the eHealth-Template (T_{eH}) for electronic healthcare systems. T_{eH} is divided into the front-end template ($FTaaS_{eH}$) and the back-end template ($BTaaS_{eH}$). $FTaaS_{eH}$ provides a generic interface with standard services and $BTaaS_{eH}$ binds specific Cloud value-added services to the generic service interfaces at $FTaaS_{eH}$. A user accesses generic and a generic Cloud service interfaces through an eHealth Client Application. The platform for the healthcare system can be simply transferred from a vendor V_1 to another V_2 by using the same $FTaaS_{eH}$ in another Cloud but with a different definition of $BTaaS_{eH}$.

6.6 Related Work

To the best of our knowledge, we could not find standardization and customization on the Cloud for IoT devices. However, a limited study has been conducted on Cloud architecture, service customization, and standardization between Clouds. In this section we review the major studies.

Tsai et al. provided SOCCA [14] which is a combination of enterprise SOA style and Cloud style, and Zhang et al. provided CCOA [15] architecture based on SOA with a scalable service feature, but these Cloud architectures do not provide customization on each service layer. Another study is *Cloud reference architecture* (CRA) [16] which is developed by NIST. This architecture has five primary actors as follows: Cloud consumer, Cloud provider, Cloud broker, Cloud auditor, and Cloud carrier. CRA does not define how Cloud vendors customize their services, or even standardization between heterogeneous Cloud platforms. Finally, the last group of related work is some outcomes from open-source projects. For instance, OGF Open cloud computing interface [17], Cloud Computing Interoperability Forum (CCIF),* Deltacloud [18], DMTF,† Open Stack [18], Open Cloud Consortium‡ and Open cloud computing interface (OCCI)§ [19]. Although these projects provide a common interface for different Cloud platforms, the outcomes of these projects are limited to some key Cloud vendors, such as Amazon which provides a high risk [20] of modification needs. However, DCCSOA allows vendors to not only customize their services, it also provides a low-cost model for standardization across different Cloud platforms. The vendors are not required to modify their platform and they can provide an extension layer on top of their Cloud platform.

6.7 Conclusion

In the era of big data, using Cloud computing gives several advantages to users to not only collect a large volume of data from the IoT but also process data efficiently through a variety of tools. The combination of Cloud computing and the IoT paradigms allows users to sense environment through IoT devices, to outsource data directly from IoT devices to the Cloud, and compute a massive amount of raw data on the Cloud. Although the Cloud-assisted IoT are providing a cost-effective model for users, we do not have an acceptable standard among Cloud vendors for supporting different IoT devices and that causes heterogeneous Cloud platforms. This causes lock-in issues for users that do not allow users to freely transfer their data and applications from one vendor to another,

---

* http://www.cloudforum.org/

† http://dmtf.org/standards/cloud

‡ http://opencloudconsortium.org

§ http://occi-wg.org/about

or even return to their IT department. In this chapter, we proposed a dynamic Cloud computing architecture which is designed based on a SOA that allows Cloud vendors to offer a generic interface (FTaaS) to their users that supports heterogeneous Cloud platforms at the corresponding BTaaS. The SOA-based feature of the architecture allows Cloud vendors to define a generic interface with minimal modifications on their platforms in order to avoid additional costs. The proposed architecture uses a dynamic layer (DTSL) to offer vendor services and it is divided into the front-end layer (FTaaS), and the back-end layer (BTaaS) which binds each generic service to a particular service in a Cloud computing system. The proposed architecture allows heterogeneous platforms to provide generic and standard services to the users with minimal modifications on the vendor side. The proposed architecture provides independency and customization ability to Cloud vendors as well as for the users. The proposed architecture can protect user data privacy through a lightweight data privacy method. We also described the definition of big data and what are the key requirements for supporting big data including collecting a massive volume of data, and the velocity of processing of big data in the Cloud.

References

[1] Bahrami, Mehdi, and Mukesh Singhal, The role of cloud computing architecture in big data, in *Information Granularity, Big Data, and Computational Intelligence*, Vol. 8, pp. 275–295, Chapter 13, W. Pedrycz and S.-M. Chen (eds.), Springer, 2015. http://goo.gl/0LxxlH (accessed March 9, 2017).

[2] Gubbi, Jayavardhana, et al. Internet of Things (IoT): A vision, architectural elements, and future directions. *Future Generation Computer Systems* 2013; 29(7): 1645–1660.

[3] Doraswamy, Naganand, and Dan Harkins. *IPSec: The New Security Standard for the Internet, Intranets, and Virtual Private Networks*. 2nd ed. Upper Saddle River, NJ: Prentice Hall Professional, 2003.

[4] Perrey, Randall, and Mark Lycett. Service-oriented architecture, in *2003 Symposium on Applications and the Internet Workshops, 2003, Proceedings*, IEEE, 2003, pp. 116–119.

[5] Bahrami, Mehdi, and Mukesh Singhal. DCCSOA: A dynamic cloud computing service-oriented architecture, in *Information Reuse and Integration (IRI), 2015 IEEE International Conference on*, Aug. 13–17, IEEE, San Francisco, CA, 2015, pp. 158–165.

[6] IDC Enterprise Panel, 3Q09. Retrieved on 15 June 2014 at http://blogs.idc.com/ie/?p=730

[7] Bahrami, Mehdi, and Mukesh Singhal. A light-weight permutation based method for data privacy in mobile cloud computing, in *2015 3rd IEEE International Conference on Mobile Cloud Computing, Services, and Engineering (IEEE Mobile Cloud 2015)*, 30 March–3 April 2015, IEEE, San Francisco, CA, 2015, http://ieeexplore.ieee.org/abstract/document/7130886/

[8] Bahrami, Mehdi, and Mukesh Singhal. DCCSOA: A dynamic Cloud computing service-oriented architecture, in *Information Reuse and Integration (IRI), 2015 IEEE International Conference on*, October 14–17 2015, IEEE, pp. 158–165, http://ieeexplore.ieee.org/abstract/document/7454539/

[9] Suttisirikul, Kiatchumpol, and Putchong Uthayopas. Accelerating the cloud backup using GPU based data deduplication, in *2012 IEEE 18th International Conference on Parallel and Distributed Systems (ICPADS)*, IEEE, Singapore, 2012, http://ieeexplore.ieee.org/abstract/document/6413608/

[10] Oikawa, Minoru, et al. DS-CUDA: A middleware to use many GPUs in the Cloud environment, in *2012 SC Companion: High Performance Computing, Networking, Storage and Analysis (SCC)*, November 10–16, IEEE, Salt Lake City, UT, 2012, http://ieeexplore.ieee.org/abstract/document/6495928/

[11] Bonomi, Flavio, et al. Fog computing: A platform for Internet of Things and analytics, in N. Bessis and C. Dobre (eds.), *Big Data and Internet of Things: A Roadmap for Smart Environments*, Switzerland: Springer International Publishing, 2014, DOI: 10.1007/978-3-319-05029-4_7.

[12] Bahrami, Mehdi, and Mukesh Singhal. CloudPDB: A light-weight data privacy schema for cloud-based databases, in *2016 International Conference on Computing, Networking and Communications (ICNC)*, February 15–18, IEEE, Kauai, HI, 2016.

[13] Bahrami, Mehdi, Dong Li, Mukesh Singhal and Ashish Kundu. An efficient parallel implementation of a light-weight data privacy method for mobile cloud users, in *Proceedings of ACM-IEEE SIGHPC SC'16 – DataCloud 2016*, Novermber 14, IEEE Press, Piscataway, NJ, 2016.

[14] Tsai, Wei-Tek, Xin Sun, and Janaka Balasooriya. Service-oriented cloud computing architecture, in *2010 7th International Conference on Information Technology: New Generations (ITNG)*, April 2–14, IEEE, Las Vegas, NV, 2010, http://ieeexplore.ieee.org/abstract/document/5501650/

[15] Zhang, Liang-Jie, and Qun Zhou. CCOA: Cloud computing open architecture, in *IEEE International Conference on Web Services, 2009* (ICWS 2009), July 6–10, 2009, IEEE, Los Angeles, CA, 2009, http://ieeexplore.ieee.org/abstract/document/5175875/

[16] Liu, Fang, et al. *NIST cloud computing reference architecture*. NIST Special Publication 500: 292, National Institute Standards and Technology, U.S. Department of Commerce, 2011, http://imtdocs.alberta.ca/NIST_Cloud_Computing_Reference_Architecture.pdf

[17] Metsch, Thijs, and Andy Edmonds. Open cloud computing interface–infrastructure, in *GFD-R in the Open Grid Forum Document Series*, Open Cloud Computing Interface (OCCI) Working Group, Muncie (IN), 2010.

[18] Bist, Meenakshi, Manoj Wariya, and Amit Agarwal. Comparing delta, open stack and Xen Cloud Platforms: A survey on open source IaaS, in *2013 IEEE 3rd International Advance Computing Conference (IACC)*, February 22–23, IEEE, Ghaziabad, India 2013.

[19] Grossman, Robert L., Yunhong Gu, Joe Mambretti, Michal Sabala, Alex Szalay, and Kevin White. An overview of the Open Science Data Cloud. In *Proceedings of the 19th ACM International Symposium on High Performance Distributed Computing (HPDC '10)*. ACM, New York, 2010, pp. 377–384.

[20] J. Shayan et al. Identifying benefits and risks associated with utilizing cloud computing. *International Journal of Soft Computing and Software Engineering [JSCSE]* 2013; 3(3), 416–421.

Chapter 7

Bicriteria Task Scheduling and Resource Allocation for Streaming Big Data Processing in Geo-Distributed Clouds

Deze Zeng, Chengyu Hu, and Guo Ren
China University of Geosciences
Wuhan, China

Lin Gu
Huazhong University of Science and Technology
Wuhan, China

CONTENTS

7.1 Introduction

With broad consensus that we are entering the era of big data, big data process or analytics have attracted much attention from both academia and industry. Big data is characterized by the 3Vs, i.e., volume, velocity, and variety, of which volume is the most recognized. As a result, batch-oriented big data processing frameworks like MapReduce first appeared. Besides "volume," velocity is another important characteristic that cannot be ignored. As a result, streaming big data processing (SBDP) has also become prevalent to deal with various big data like social media streams, sensor data streams, log streams, and stock exchanges streams, and has shown its great potential in unearthing valuable insights of data to improve decision-making, minimize risk, and develop new products and services. For example, each store of supermarket chains may generate a large amount of continuous data covering stock sales, customer information, environment information, etc. All these data need to be processed in real-time for efficient supermarket management. By the effort of both researchers and engineers, several dataflow-based programming architectures, e.g., Twitter's Storm [1,2] and LinkedIn's Spark [3], have been developed to support SBDP.

To support big data processing, a large amount of resource is required. Fortunately, the recent development in Cloud computing has inspired vast deployment of large-scale datacenters. Public Cloud service providers such as Amazon, Google, and Microsoft have also released various public Cloud services to tenants. These datacenters are usually distributed at different geographic regions across the globe. For example, Google owns 13 data centers over eight countries in four continents [4]. The potential of the public Cloud has been increasingly attracting individuals and organizations to move their data and services from local areas to the Internet for reliability, security, and cost benefits. Modern datacenters usually adopt virtualization technology. A tenant can rent the required resources in the form of virtual machines (VMs). In the popular Infrastructure-as-a-Service (IaaS) Cloud service provision model, virtual computing resources can be acquired and released on demand. The public Cloud appears to be the perfect infrastructure for realizing the SBDP service, by dynamically adjusting the virtual resources to the current conditions.

As a result, with the consideration of ever-growing resource demands of SBDP, it is natural to build SBDP services on the geo-distributed datacenters. Streaming big data is characterized by both large volume and high velocity. After deploying SBDP onto the public Cloud, the data explosion will result in an increase of data traffic between datacenters. Since most public Clouds today rely on Internet service providers (ISPs) to connect their geo-distributed datacenters, interdatacenter traffic is usually significantly more expensive than intradatacenter [5–7]. For example, Amazon's EC2* charges \$0.120–0.200/GB for interdatacenter transfer across geographic regions, \$0.01/GB in the same region, and free of charge for intradatacenter traffic, at the time of writing. Greenberg et al. [8] have revealed that communication cost is up to around 15% of the overall operational expenditure incurred for a Cloud provider. In particular, Chen et al. [9] have pointed out that interdatacenter traffic accounts for up to 45% of the total traffic going through datacenter egress routers. Different from conventional stream processing [10,11] (e.g., queries processing in wireless sensor networks) where each task is attached to a single server (i.e., one-to-one), Cloud-based SBDP is characterized by that each task can be supported by multiple replicated VMs (i.e., one-to-many) and the locations of VMs are also optional. However, we cannot arbitrarily deploy VMs as a certain computation cost must also be paid for the deployment of VMs. For example, renting a t2.nano VM with 1 vCPU, 0.5GB memory from Amazon EC2 costs \$0.0065 per hour, at the time of writing.

Hence, to avoid making big data equivalent to "big price" it is significant to investigate how to deploy the VMs so as to lower both communication cost and deployment cost for SBDP. According to the above discussion, it can be conjectured that if the SBDP VMs are judiciously placed, the overall cost can be potentially minimized. Actually this problem has already been widely addressed in the literature [7,12–17]. However, we notice that existing studies mainly take QoS as a predetermined requirement in their problem. For SBDP, the QoS can be measured in terms of the final result generation rate [18]. The higher the rate, the higher the QoS. The overall cost and QoS are two contradictory factors; lowering

*http://aws.amazon.com/ec2/pricing/

the overall cost usually implies degrading the QoS, and vice versa. Load shedding [18] therefore is an effective means to control the data rate so as to balance the overall cost and QoS. In addition, instead of considering a single-objective optimization, it is also significant to investigate a bicriteria optimization problem that jointly takes overall cost and QoS into consideration. In this chapter, we are motivated to investigate such a bicriteria problem by considering task scheduling and resource allocation for SBDP in geo-distributed datacenters. Our main contributions are summarized as follows:

- To our best knowledge, we are the first to investigate the bicriteria optimization problem for SBDP in geo-distributed datacenters. In particular, we try to simultaneously optimize the overall cost and the QoS, with joint consideration of flow scheduling, load shedding, and VM placement.
- We formally describe the bicriteria optimization problem as a multiple objective integer programming (MOIP) problem.
- We further propose an improved NSGA-II algorithm, by adopting a nondominated sorting mechanism and elitist strategy, to address the MOIP problem. Experimental results validate the high efficiency of our algorithm.

The rest of the chapter is organized as follows. Section 7.2 gives some background and preliminaries on SBDP. Section 7.3 introduces the system model for the optimization problem to be studied in this chapter. The MOIP formulation is presented in Section 7.4. Section 7.5 introduces our improved NSGA-II algorithm. The effectiveness of our proposal is verified by experiments in Section 7.6. Finally, Section 7.7 concludes our work.

7.2 Background, Preliminaries, and Related Work

In this section, we briefly introduce some representative big data processing frameworks in Clouds, with a special emphasize on SBDP. Then we present some pioneering work related to our study.

7.2.1 Background and preliminaries

With the advent of big data, many novel programming frameworks have been proposed. The most well-known one is MapReduce advocated by Google. The design goal of MapReduce is to provide a simple and powerful interface that enables automatic parallelization and distribution of large-scale computations on large clusters of commodity PCs [19]. With the ability of exploring large-scale computation resources, MapReduce therefore is suitable and actually has already been widely used, for dealing with big volumes of data in Clouds, i.e., one-step batch processing. However, one notorious disadvantage of MapReduce is its inefficiency for multistep tasks as lots of I/O processing is required. Unlike batch data processing, streaming data processing cannot be simply split and processed in a parallel manner like the MapReduce model. In batch data processing, the source data are stored in a local file system or database while, in streaming data processing, the data flow into the computation unit at a very fast speed and must be processed immediately. With respect to the task sequences and interdependencies, if we continue to use the "process-write" model in batch processing, the I/O communication cost will be extremely high due to the large involvement of intermediate I/O operations.

To address the limitation of MapReduce for multistep tasks like streaming processing, AMPLab at UC Berkeley developed an open-source framework Apache Spark.* Different from MapReduce, Spark allows users to load data into a clusters memory. By such means, it is possible to perform multiple steps for a single task without redundant I/O operations; therefore, it is suitable for SBDP. Although generally Spark can be regarded as the first framework supporting streaming data processing, it is still a general-purpose engine for big data processing and not specifically designed for streaming processing. Even without I/O operations, to read and write data is still very time-consuming and cannot catch up with the speed of data processing. To deal with the ever-growing demands on real-time streaming data processing, more specific streaming big data oriented solutions have been proposed.

Twitter Storm [20] is a free and open-source distributed real-time computation system for SBDP like real-time analytic, online machine learning, and so on. Storm is fast, scalable, fault-tolerant, and easy to set up. Two basic primitives, i.e., "spouts" and "bolts" are provided to developers for SBDP. Spouts transform the raw data stream into a new one in a distributed way. For example, a spout may receive sensing data from a sensor network and emit them as a new stream. The bolt works as the consumer of streams, performs operations, and then produces result streams for the next bolt without writing them back to the file system. Various operations such as computation, filter, and data aggregations are supported.

7.2.2 Related work

7.2.2.1 SBDP

SBDP is rapidly expanding in many science and engineering domains, including physical, biological, and social sciences, bringing not only high convenience but also high challenges to both academia and industry. To support efficient data processing and analysis, service providers need to characterize the features of the different big data services and propose new processing models [21,22].

* http://spark.apache.org/

Many theoretical researches and practical applications have been proposed in recent years.

For example, [23] presented a knowledge-based solution for big data analytics to overcome two fundamental issues of SBDP: data heterogeneity and advanced processing capabilities. Destounis et al. [24] proposed a distributed backpressure algorithm to adaptively allocate data center resources, aiming to accelerate the big data computations of query streams. Agerri et al. [25] leveraged SBDP models to improve the effectiveness and efficiency of distributed language processing across multiple machines by adopting parallel architectures. In the field of healthcare, Ta et al. [26] took advantage of SBDP to improve the quality of healthcare services by providing real-time decisions and lowering the service cost. They also proposed a generic healthcare stream analytic architecture by using open source big data frameworks with distributed real-time computing and storage systems that can effectively process large amount of healthcare data at rapid rates. Zhu et al. [27] explored the large volume of traffic streaming data and present a framework with two algorithms that can be used in different time-sensitive scenarios such as surveillance on suspect trackers for specific vehicles. Zhang et al. [28] focused on social computing to provide real-time solutions in the circumstance of massive data volumes and evolving application scenarios. An emotion-based social computing platform for streaming big data is proposed to provide sentiment analysis as the foundation of social computing and enable both real-time SBDP on off-line big data with high performance and low risk. Agarwal et al. [29] introduced an advanced stream analytics framework especially for continuously updating web-generated log streams in a high rate and volume, to provide useful insight of large scale web-based applications and derive web usage patterns.

7.2.2.2 Task scheduling and resource allocation

The geo-distributed datacenters are running rich and complex tasks to support a variety of user requirements. To improve the service performance and guarantee the QoS at the same time, task scheduling and resource allocation algorithm in a Cloud platform is a fundamental issue in achieving efficient Cloud services [30,31].

Generating an optimal task scheduling solution usually comes with a high computational complexity; [32] proposed a new method to generate suboptimal or sufficiently good schedules for smooth multitask workflows on Cloud platforms. To further reduce the tail completion time for typical Cloud applications, Dogar et al. [33] designed and implemented a decentralized task-aware scheduling system namely Baraat, which schedules tasks in a FIFO order but avoids head-of-line blocking by dynamically changing the level of multiplexing in the network. Tillenius et al. [34] took into consideration both task interdependencies and Cloud resource conditions, such as memory and bandwidth usages. They also provided a set of tools to detect task resource sensitivity and predicted the performance improvements of proposed resource-aware scheduling for multicore-based computer architectures. Panda et al. [35] presented three task scheduling algorithms for a heterogeneous Cloud environment, aiming to minimize the makespan and maximize the average Cloud utilization at the same time. In Ref. [36], a resource-aware hybrid scheduling algorithm for different types of applications for heterogeneous distributed computing is proposed, especially for modern high-performance computing systems.

However, present task scheduling and resource allocation solutions are mostly based on batch data processing, thus cannot be directly applied to SBDP. This motivates us to investigate the problem of task scheduling and resource allocation for SBDP in geo-distributed datacenters.

7.3 System Model

In this section, we introduce the system model. For the convenience of the readers, the major notations used in this chapter are listed in Table 7.1.

7.3.1 Geo-distributed computing environment

Recent information and communication technology (ICT) development has stimulated the deployment of a large-scale computing environments with

Table 7.1 Notations

Constants	
$G_s = (V_s, E_s)$	Geo-distributed server graph
C_{mn}	The interserver communication capacity between $m, n \in V_s$
P_{mn}	The interserver unit cost between $m, n \in V_s$
R_s	Storage capacity of server $s \in V_s$
C_s	Computation capacity of server $s \in V_s$
P_s	Unit VM deployment cost of $s \in V_s$
S	Producer set as $S \subset V_t$
F_s	Source data generation rate at producer $s \in S$
$G_t = (V_t, E_t)$	SBDP task graph
$G_v = (V_v, E_v)$	Extended SBDP task graph
$\delta(v)$	$\delta(v) \in V_s$, corresponding server of vertex $v \in V_v$
$i(v)$	Parent node set of vertex $v \in V_v$
$o(v)$	Child node set of vertex $v \in V_v$

geo-distributed servers, in either a Cloud computing or fog computing environments. We denote these geo-distributed servers by a graph $G_s = (V_s, E_s)$, consisting of server set V_s and their interconnections E_s. An edge $e_{mn} \in E_s, m, n \in V_s$ is weighted with C_{mn} and P_{mn} denoting the interserver communication capacity and unit cost between servers m and n. A server $s \in V_s$ has a limited storage capacity R_s and a computation capacity C_s. Deploying a VM on server s requires a unit cost P_s. For tractability, both the communication capacity and the computation capacity are normalized in terms of the flow value. Therefore, a limited number of VMs can be hosted and a limited amount of flow can be processed by a server.

7.3.2 SBDP graph

We represent a SBDP task by a loop-free directed acyclic graph (DAG) $G_t = (V_t, E_t)$, where vertex set V_t includes all the subtasks and edge set E_t denotes the data flow relationship between these subtasks. The vertices in V_t are classified into three categories, *producer*, *operator*, and *consumer*, according to their roles in the task. Data streams enter the system at the producers and exit at the consumer. The producers are also geo-distributed. We denote the producer set as $S \subset V_t$. A producer $s \in S$ generates source raw data at rate F_s. Without loss of generality, we assume that there is only one consumer $d \in V_t$ as the final data aggregation point. The semantics of the SBDP is determined by the operators as well as their topology. An operator receives input data flows from its parent subtasks and generates output flows to its child subtasks. A producer can be viewed as a special task without input flows and similarly a consumer can be viewed as one without output flows. An edge $e_{uv} \in E_t, u, v \in V_t$ denotes that a certain data flow goes from u to v. An operator $u \in V_t$ exists in the computing environment as a VM. Note that one operator may have a number of VM replicas with the same processing function.

7.4 A Multiobjective Integer Programming Problem Formulation

In this section, we propose an extended SBDP graph such that the flow relationships between any subtasks can be described using a unified graph, without knowing the final VM placement decision. After that, the problem is formulated into an MOIP problem.

7.4.1 Extended SBDP graph construction

As one operator may have multiple VMs placed in different servers, we expand the SBDP graph to an extended version $G_v = (V_v, E_v)$ to represent all VM placements based on the task graph G_t and the G_s. The construction process from

SBDP graph to extended SBDP graph is as follows. In the extended SBDP graph, the producers and consumers remain the same as in the SBDP graph. However, for each operator, $|V_s|$ VMs are generated, where $|\cdot|$ is the cardinality function. Therefore, we can denote a VM $v \in V_v$ in the extended SBDP graph using two subscripts $\eta(v)$ and $\delta(v)$, denoting the corresponding producer in the SBDP graph and the server in server graph, respectively. To reserve the semantics of the original SBDP, the connections between these VMs still follow the connections in the original SBDP graph. For example, if there is an edge from $m \in V_t$ to $n \in V_t$ in the SBDP graph, each VM of m will be connected to all VMs of n. Note that the edges are weighted according to their representing connections in the server graph. Figure 7.1 gives an example of an extended SBDP graph constructed from an SBDP graph and a server graph.

7.4.2 VM placement constraints

In SBDP, the streams are actually processed by the VMs of each operator. Traditionally, communication cost aware VM placement is usually formulated as

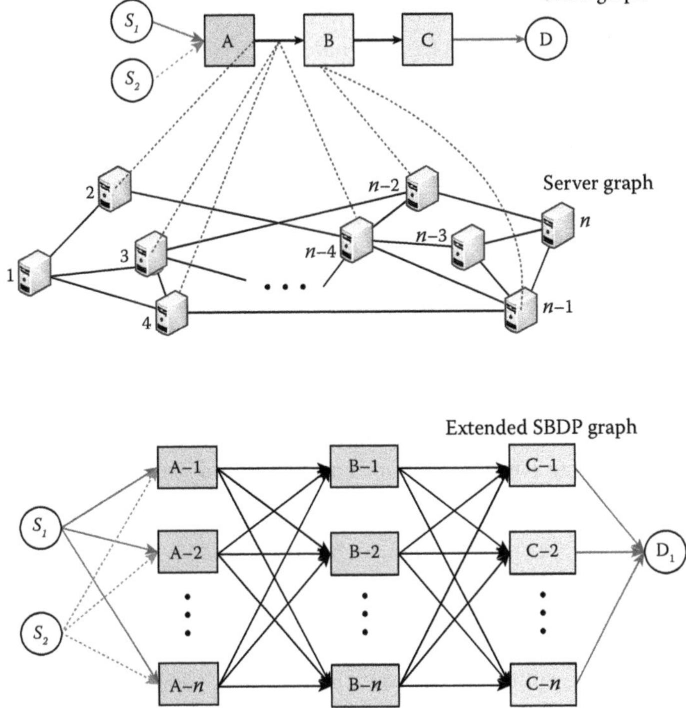

Figure 7.1: Illustration of an extended SBDP graph.

a quadratic optimization problem (e.g., [17,37]), which is with high computation complexity. With the help of an extended SBDP graph, we can transform the VM placement problem into a VM selection problem by exploring the flow relationship between VMs.

To place a VM into a server is equivalent to selecting one corresponding virtual VM in set V_v. That is, if virtual VM $i \in V_v$ is selected, it means that a VM for task $\eta(i)$ is placed in server $\delta(i)$. We define a binary variable x_i to denote whether VM $i \in V_v$ is selected or not as

$$x_i = \begin{cases} 1, \text{ if VM } i \text{ is selected} \\ 0, \text{ otherwise} \end{cases}$$

The total resource requirements of all VMs placed in server m should not exceed its resource capacity R_m. Hence, we have

$$\sum_{\substack{i \in V_v \\ \delta(i)=m}} x_i \cdot r_i \leq R_m, \forall m \in V_s \tag{7.1}$$

In G_v, the flow constraints of any VM v can be represented by the relationships between the input flows from its parents $i(v)$ and output flows to its children $o(v)$. Let λ_{uv} denote the flow rate between any two VNF instances u, v on edge $e_{uv} \in E_v$.

If flow rate generated from a VM v is larger than 0, it indicates that the VM must be actually placed in server $\delta(v)$, $x_v = 1$. The relationship between x_v and the output flow rate f_{uv} can be therefore described as

$$\frac{\sum_{u \in i(v)} f_{uv}}{L} \leq x_v \leq \sum_{u \in i(v)} f_{uv} \cdot L, \forall v \in V_v \tag{7.2}$$

where L is an arbitrary large number.

Taking load shedding into consideration, for each intermediate VM, the input flows from its input (or parent) nodes and its output (or child) nodes follow the relationship

$$\sum_{u \in i(v)} f_{uv} \geq \sum_{w \in o(v)} f_{vw}, \forall v \in V_v \tag{7.3}$$

to ensure the flow conservation.

Note that the source data flow is from the producers. As a result, the flow injected into the system will not exceed the source data generation rate. Therefore, we have

$$f_{sv} \leq F_s, \forall s \in S, e_{sv} \in E_v \tag{7.4}$$

The amount of flow that can go through a link is limited by the link capacity, as

$$\sum_{\substack{e_{uv}\in E_v,\\ \delta(u)=m,\delta(v)=n\\ \text{or } \delta(u)=n,\delta(v)=m}} f_{uv} \leq C_{mn}, \forall e_{mn} \in E_s \tag{7.5}$$

Besides, the total amount of flow that can processed by a server is also limited by its computation capacity, as

$$\sum_{\substack{e_{uv}\in E_v\\ \delta(v)=n}} f_{uv} \leq C_n, \forall n \in V_s \tag{7.6}$$

7.4.3 A multiple objective integer programming problem formulation

We are interested in (1) minimizing the overall cost, including both the communication cost between VMs and deployment cost and (2) maximizing the QoS. The overall cost can be calculated as

$$\text{Cost} = \sum_{e_{uv}\in E_v} f_{uv}P_{\delta(u)\delta(v)} + \sum_{i\in V_v} x_i P_{\delta(i)} \tag{7.7}$$

For streaming big data processing, the QoS can be measured in terms of the final result rate received by the consumer d. As a result, the QoS can be represented by

$$\text{QoS} = \sum_{u\in i(d)} f_{ud} \tag{7.8}$$

By summing up all above, we get the following MOIP problem:

MOIP:

$$\begin{aligned}
\min : & \sum_{e_{uv}\in E_v} f_{uv}C_{\delta(u)\delta(v)} + \sum_{i\in V_v} x_i C_{\delta(i)} \\
\max : & \sum_{u\in i(d)} f_{ud} \\
\text{s.t.} : & (7.1),(7.2),(7.3),(7.4),(7.5),(7.6) \\
& x_i \in \{0,1\}
\end{aligned}$$

To tackle this problem, we design a heuristic algorithm in the next section.

7.5 Algorithm Design

7.5.1 Pareto optimization

For bicriterion resource allocation and task scheduling problems, we propose an variation of the NSGA-II approach which employs matrix-structure chromosomes to encode the flow path and flow rate. Before detailing our algorithm, we introduce the Pareto optimization approach. Generally, a multiobjective optimization problem can be described as:

$$\begin{aligned} \min: f(\mathbf{x}) &= f_1(\mathbf{x}),\ldots,f_n(\mathbf{x}) \\ \text{s.t.: } g_i(\mathbf{x}) &> 0, i=1,2,\cdots,k \\ e_j(\mathbf{x}) &= 0, j=1,2,\cdots,l \end{aligned} \tag{7.9}$$

where $\mathbf{x} = (x_1,x_2,\ldots,x_n)^T$, $\mathbf{x} \in \mathbf{X}$. $\mathbf{X}$ is a set of feasible solutions or decision space. A feasible solution $\mathbf{x}$ is a Pareto solution if it meets two conditions: (1) it satisfies k inequality constraints $g_i(x)$ and l quality constraints $e_j(x)$ and (2) it is not possible to improve one objective without making at least one of the others worse.

In Figure 7.2, there are two conflicting objective functions f_1 and f_2 for a minimization problem. The solutions $A{\sim}H$ are nondominated Pareto solutions, e.g., $f_1(A) < f_1(H)$ and $f_2(A) > f_2(H)$. Solution C dominates J because $f_1(C) < f_1(J)$ and $f_2(C) < f_2(J)$.

7.5.2 A variation of NSGA-II

We present our heuristic algorithm for the bicriteria problem. The algorithm, as shown in Algorithm 7.1, mainly includes encoding and the initial population, crossover and mutation operation, and fitness function evaluation.

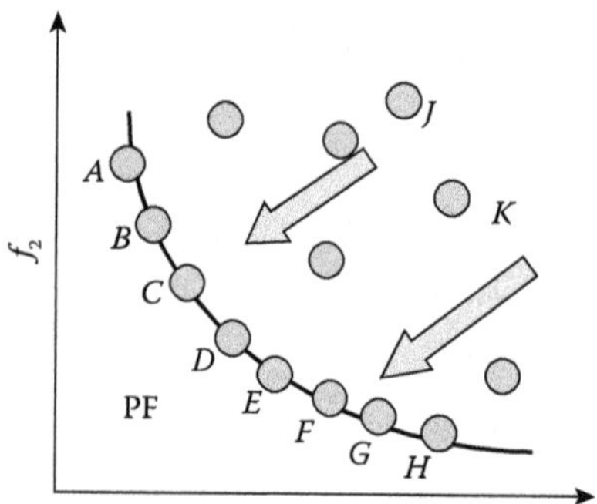

Figure 7.2: Pareto solution illustration. *A–H* are nondominated solutions and *J* and *K* are dominated solutions.

Algorithm 7.1 Heuristic Algorithm for Bicriteria Scheduling and Allocation

Require: $Population_{size}; ProblemSize, P_{crossover}, P_{mutation}.$
Ensure: $Children.$
  $Population \leftarrow InitializePopulation(Population_{size}, ProblemSize)$
  $EvaluateFitnessFunction(Population)$
  $FastNondomiatedSort(Population)$
  $Children \leftarrow SelectParentsByRank(Population, Population_{size})$
  $Children \leftarrow CrossoverAndMutation(Children, P_{crossover}, P_{mutation})$
  while *not reach maximum iteration* **do**
    $EvaluateFitnessFunction(Children)$
    $Union \leftarrow Merge(Poulation, Children)$
    $Fronts \leftarrow FastNondomiatedSort(Union)$
    $Parents \leftarrow \emptyset$
    $Front_L \leftarrow \emptyset$
    for each $Front_i \subseteq Fronts$ **do**
      $CrowdingDistance(Front_i)$
      if $Size(Parents) + Size(Front_i) > Population_{size}$ **then**
        $Front_L \Leftarrow i$
        $Break()$
      else
        $Parents \leftarrow Merge(Parents, Front_i)$
      end if
    end for
    if $Size(Parents) < Population_{size}$ **then**
      $Front_L \leftarrow SortByRankandDistance(Front_L)$
      for P_1 to $Population_{size}$ **do**
        $Parents \leftarrow P_i$
      end for
    end if
    $Children \leftarrow SelectParentsByRankandDistance(Parents, Population_{size})$
    $Population \leftarrow Children$
    $Children \leftarrow CrossoverAndMutation(Children, P_{crossover}, P_{mutation})$
  end while

First, a random parent *population* is created. Each chromosome in the population is initialized without violation of all of the constraints in **MOIP**. Then, we evaluate the fitness function and make a fast nondominated sorting. Each solution is then assigned with a fitness (or rank) equal to its nondomination level (1 is the best level, 2 is the next best level, and so on).

Second, selection, crossover, and mutation operator are carried out. Thereby, a new children population is generated. We merge the parent and children populations into a temporary population *Union*. Subsequently, we make a fast nondominated sorting on the *Union* population. From the sorting results, we select the good chromosomes into the parents and then make another crossover and mutation operation until the stop condition is satisfied.

The trade-off between the communication cost and QoS is minimized by the nondominated sorting technique. The Pareto set is generated by Algorithm 7.1. The choice of one solution over the other depends on user needs.

7.5.2.1 Encoding and initial population

Before applying our heuristic population-based algorithm, it is necessary to encode the flow path and flow rate. In our algorithm, we random generate the flow path matrix and flow rate matrix in different stages. The encoding scheme is presented in Algorithm 7.2:

Algorithm 7.2 Encoding and initial chromosomes

Require: *NumProducer, NumServer, NumConsumer, ServerCapacity, LinkCapacity.*
Ensure: *FlowPathsandFlowRates.*

```
% generate flow path and rate from producer to server
for i = 1 to NumProducer do
    random generate a binary vector;
    random allocate flow rate according to the flow path;
end for
% generate flow path and rate from server to server
for i = 1 to Server do
    random generate a binary vector;
    Server ← 0, if no flow pass the server;
    random allocate flow rate according to the flow path;
end for
% generate flow path from server to consumer
for i = 1 to NumConsumer do
    generate a binary vector;
end for
```

Let us take Figure 7.3a as an example to explain our encoding scheme. In Figure 7.3a, $S1, S2$ are two producers and A, B, C are three geo-distributed servers. Each task will be processed in two phases. We can see that the task from producer $S1$ first goes to servers A and B. Another task from source $S2$ goes to servers A and C. The two tasks should be processed concurrently in the first phase. Next, servers A and C will continually process the task in the second phase. Some tasks in servers A and C may be sent to server B according to the load balancing decision. After all the tasks are completely finished, the results flow into the consumer D.

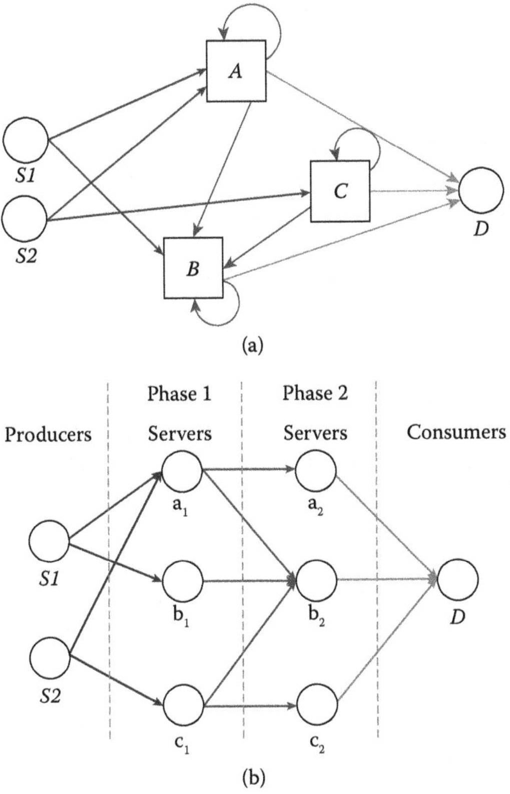

Figure 7.3: (a) The flow paths from producers to consumer and (b) phase division. Illustration of encoding and initial population.

Our encoding scheme for the case in Figure 7.3a is shown in Figure 7.3b. As the tasks are processed in three stages, and the flow path is encoded individually in each stage. At last, we combine each part into a complete chromosome.

In our algorithm, the flow paths and rates in the next stage have a close relationship with the former; the total input flow rate must be greater than the output one. In order to generate a legal route, we first randomly generate the flow path from producers to servers, then from servers to servers, and finally from servers to consumers. Accordingly, the chromosome is encoded as follows:

$$\begin{pmatrix} 1 & 1 & 0 \\ 1 & 0 & 1 \end{pmatrix} \tag{7.10}$$

$$\begin{pmatrix} 1 & 1 & 0 \\ 0 & 1 & 0 \\ 0 & 1 & 1 \end{pmatrix} \tag{7.11}$$

$$\begin{pmatrix} 1 \\ 1 \\ 1 \end{pmatrix} \tag{7.12}$$

Similarly, we randomly generate the flow rate according to the flow path. At the same time, we check the flow rate and keep it satisfying all of the constraints shown in **MOIP**. A legal chromosome consists of six matrices $\{LkProd, LkServ, LkCons; flowProd, flowServ, flowCons\}$, where the former matrices are 0-1 matrix and the last three matrices are real number matrices.

7.5.2.2 Crossover and mutation operations

To generate a second generation population of solutions, we randomly select one solution from the nondominated set and an individual in the current population as a pair of "parents." By producing a "child" solution using the single-point crossover, a new solution is created and typically shares many of the characteristics of its "parents." In our scheme, we first determine the cross point. The matrix from the beginning of the chromosome to the first crossover point is copied from one parent. The part from the first to the second crossover point is copied from the second parent and the rest is copied from the first parent. For example, consider two parents, chromesome1 and chromesome2 as

$$\begin{pmatrix} LkProd1 & LkServ1 & LkCons1 & flowProd1 & flowServ1 & flowCons1 \\ \mathbf{LkProd2} & \mathbf{LkServ2} & \mathbf{LkCons2} & \mathbf{flowProd2} & \mathbf{flowServ2} & \mathbf{flowCons2} \end{pmatrix} \tag{7.13}$$

If the cross point is selected between LkProd and LkServ, the offsprings after the crossover operation are as follows:

$$\begin{pmatrix} \mathbf{LkProd2} & LkServ1 & LkCons1 & flowProd1 & flowServ1 & flowCons1 \\ LkProd1 & \mathbf{LkServ2} & \mathbf{LkCons2} & \mathbf{flowProd2} & \mathbf{flowServ2} & \mathbf{flowCons2} \end{pmatrix} \tag{7.14}$$

After the crossover operation, we make a mutation operation on the offspring. The method is to randomly select some bits in the matrix and then invert them.

It is obviously that crossover and mutation are likely to produce some illegal offspring that violate the constraints. Therefore, we make a further adjustment on these offspring to guarantee their validity.

7.5.2.3 Fitness function evaluation

As each chromosome contains information of the flow path and flow rate at different stages, it is easy to compute the fitness function. In order to solve this problem using the Pareto method, we convert the problem of maximization of QoS to a minimization problem. The bicriteria optimization problem then becomes

$$f_1 = \sum_{i}^{NumProducer} LkProd \times C_{ps} + \sum_{i}^{NumServer} LkServ \times C_{ss} + \sum_{i}^{NumConsumer} LkCons \times C_{sc} + \sum_{i \in V_v} x_i C_{\delta(i)} \tag{7.15}$$

$$f_2 = \sum_{i}^{NumProducer} flowProd - \sum_{i}^{NumConsumer} flowCons \tag{7.16}$$

where C_{ps}, C_{ss}, and C_{sc} are the communication cost of each path from producers to the consumer.

The fitness function f_1 is the overall cost with the consideration of both communication cost and VMs placement cost. Function f_2 is the difference between the whole flow rate output from producers and the overall flow rate input to consumer.

7.6 Experimental Results and Discussion

In this section, we present the performance evaluation results of our proposed algorithm.

7.6.1 Data and experiment settings

In our experiment, we simulate a Cloud computing environment with a number of geo-distributed servers that vary in the range of $[10,50]$. Each server is with a computation capacity from 10 Mbps to 50 Mbps and a storage capacity from 20 MB to 50 MB. The number of producers is randomly set within [3,10] and each producer is with a flow rate within [1 Mbps, 80 Mbps]. We assume that each task must be processed in $3 \sim 5$ stages before it arrives at consumers, and each VM needs a storage resource from 1 MB to 10 MB and its deployment cost is varied in $[10,50]$. We generate the communication cost for each link according to an uniform distribution, varying in $[1,10]$. Specially, the communication cost between VMs in one physical server is set as 0. Each link is with a limited communication capacity varying in [8 MB–50 MB]. We set the population size as 500, crossover rate as 0.9, mutation rate as 0.1, and maximum number of iterations as 50.

7.6.2 Summary of results and discussion

In our experiments, a fast nondominated sorting method is used to generate Pareto solutions and fronts. For multiobjective optimization problem, in order to identify solutions of the first nondominated front in a population of size N, each individual will be compared with the others to determine whether it is dominated.

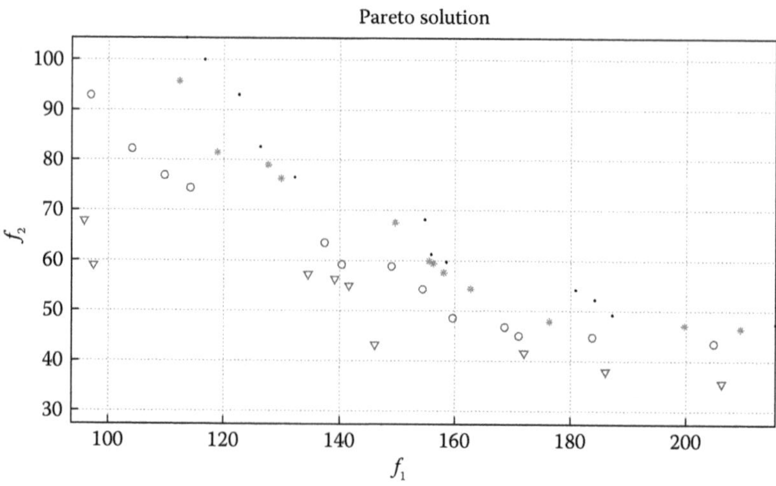

Figure 7.4: Pareto solutions in different clusters.

This requires $O(MN)$ comparisons for each solution, where M is the number of the first nondominated level in the population. If we obtain multilevels Pareto solutions, the total complexity is $O(MN^2)$. As shown in Figure 7.4, we get four level Pareto solutions in one iteration. Every solution is nondominated in the same level, but the solution in the first level will dominate the second level, and so on.

In Figure 7.5, black squares are Pareto solutions of the first iteration and red circles are Pareto solutions of the last iteration. We can see that QoS and overall cost are obviously contradictory. That is, if the overall cost increases, the QoS will be higher, and vice versa. In addition, we can see that the quality of the Pareto solution can be improved as the evolution proceeds.

The population size is an important factor in the quality of Pareto solutions, as shown in Figure 7.6.

We can see that the smaller the population size, the worse the quality. When the population size is 500, the quality of the solution is the best. Furthermore, we find that the numbers of Pareto solutions are similar when the population sizes are 100 and 500. This is because that the number of Pareto solutions is related to the specific problem.

7.7 Conclusion

In this chapter, we introduce the evolution of big data processing from static bulk data processing to dynamic streaming data processing. Some representative

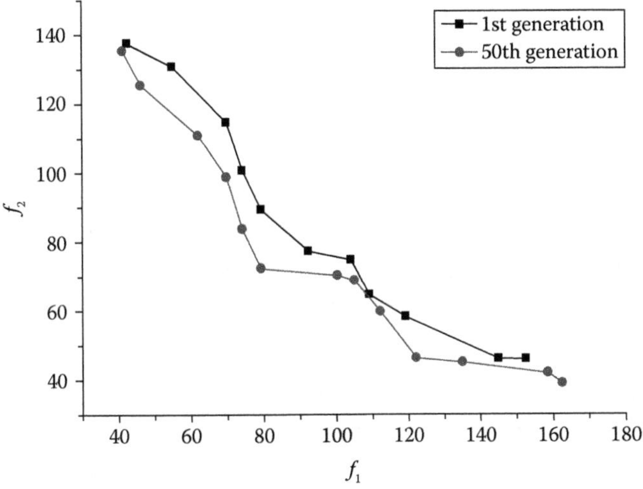

Figure 7.5: Pareto fronts for different generations.

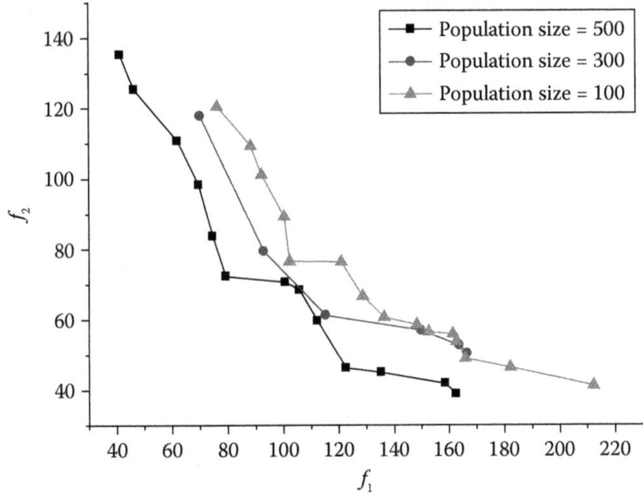

Figure 7.6: Pareto fronts for different population sizes.

SBDP platforms are introduced. To explore the flexibility of Cloud computing for SBDP, we further discuss a bicriteria problem on how to deploy VMs and balance workloads among the deployed VMs so as to improve the QoS and lower the overall cost at the same time. An MOIP formulation is presented to describe our problem. To address this problem, we then propose a heuristic NSGA-II algorithm with careful design of encoding, crossover, and mutual operations according to the inherent characteristics of our VM placement and workload balancing problem. Extensive simulation-based studies validate the correctness and efficiency of our design.

References

[1] G. Lee, J. Lin, C. Liu, A. Lorek, and D. Ryaboy, The unified logging infrastructure for data analytics at Twitter, *Proceedings of the VLDB Endowment*, August 27–31, vol. 5, no. 12, Istanbul, Turkey, 2012, pp. 1771–1780.

[2] G. Mishne, J. Dalton, Z. Li, A. Sharma, and J. Lin, Fast data in the era of big data: Twitter's real-time related query suggestion architecture, in *Proceedings of the 2013 International Conference on Management of Data*, June 22–27, ACM, New York, 2013, pp. 1147–1158.

[3] M. Zaharia, M. Chowdhury, T. Das, A. Dave, J. Ma, M. McCauley, M. J. Franklin, S. Shenker, and I. Stoica, Resilient distributed datasets: A fault-tolerant abstraction for in-memory cluster computing, in *Proceedings of the 9th USENIX Conference on Networked Systems Design and Implementation*, April 3–5, USENIX Association, Lombard, IL, 2013, pp. 2–2.

[4] Data center locations, http://www.google.com/about/datacenters/inside/locations/index.html (accessed December 2016).

[5] Z. Zhang, M. Zhang, A. G. Greenberg, Y. C. Hu, R. Mahajan, and B. Christian, Optimizing cost and performance in online service provider networks, in *Proceedings of the USENIX NSDI*, March 30–April 1, Boston, MA, 2010, pp. 33–48.

[6] P. Bodík, I. Menache, M. Chowdhury, P. Mani, D. A. Maltz, and I. Stoica, Surviving failures in bandwidth-constrained datacenters, in *Proceedings of the ACM SIGCOMM 2012 Conference on Applications, Technologies, Architectures, and Protocols for Computer Communication*, August 13–17, ACM, Helsinki, Finland, 2012, pp. 431–442.

[7] K. Yin Chen, Y. Xu, K. Xi, and H. Chao, Intelligent virtual machine placement for cost efficiency in geo-distributed cloud systems, in *2013 IEEE International Conference on Communications (ICC)*, June 9–13, Budapest, Hungary, 2013, pp. 3498–3503.

[8] A. Greenberg, J. Hamilton, D. A. Maltz, and P. Patel, The cost of a cloud: Research problems in data center networks, *SIGCOMM Computer Communication Review*, vol. 39, no. 1, pp. 68–73, 2008.

[9] Y. Chen, S. Jain, V. Adhikari, Z.-L. Zhang, and K. Xu, A first look at inter-data center traffic characteristics via Yahoo! datasets, in *2011 Proceedings IEEE INFOCOM*, April 10–15, Shanghai, China, 2011, pp. 1620–1628.

[10] M. Cherniack, H. Balakrishnan, M. Balazinska, D. Carney, U. Cetintemel, Y. Xing, and S. B. Zdonik, Scalable distributed stream processing, in *Proceedings of the 2003 CIDR Conference*, January 5–8, vol. 3, Asilomar, CA, 2003, pp. 257–268.

[11] L. Tian and K. M. Chandy, Resource allocation in streaming environments, in *7th IEEE/ACM International Conference on Grid Computing*, September 28–29, IEEE, Barcelona, Spain, 2006, pp. 270–277.

[12] J. Jiang, T. Lan, S. Ha, M. Chen, and M. Chiang, Joint VM placement and routing for data center traffic engineering, in *2012 Proceedings IEEE INFOCOM*, March 25–30, Orlando, FL, 2012, pp. 2876–2880.

[13] K. You, B. Tang, and F. Ding, Near-optimal virtual machine placement with product traffic pattern in data centers, in *2013 IEEE International Conference on Communications (ICC)*, June 9–13, Budapest, Hungary, 2013, pp. 3705–3709.

[14] H. Ballani, K. Jang, T. Karagiannis, C. Kim, D. Gunawardena, and G. OShea, Chatty tenants and the cloud network sharing problem, in *Proceedings of the 10th USENIX Conference on Networked Systems Design and Implementation*, USENIX Association, April 2–5, Lombard, IL, 2013, pp. 171–184.

[15] W. Fang, X. Liang, S. Li, L. Chiaraviglio, and N. Xiong, VMPlanner: Optimizing virtual machine placement and traffic flow routing to reduce network power costs in cloud data centers, *Computer Networks*, vol. 57, no. 1, pp. 179–196, 2013.

[16] X. Li, J. Wu, S. Tang, and S. Lu, Lets stay together: Towards traffic aware virtual machine placement in data centers, in *Proceedings of the 33rd IEEE International Conference on Computer Communications (INFOCOM)*, April 27–May 2, Toronto, Canada, 2014, pp. 1842–1850.

[17] L. Wang, F. Zhang, J. Arjona Aroca, A. Vasilakos, K. Zheng, C. Hou, D. Li, and Z. Liu, GreenDCN: A general framework for achieving energy efficiency in data center networks, *IEEE Journal on Selected Areas in Communications*, vol. 32, no. 1, pp. 4–15, 2014.

[18] N. Tatbul, U. Çetintemel, and S. Zdonik, Staying FIT: Efficient load shedding techniques for distributed stream processing, in *Proceedings of the 33rd International Conference on Very Large Data Bases*, ser. VLDB '07,

VLDB Endowment, September 23–28, University of Vienna, Austria, 2007, pp. 159–170.

[19] J. Dean and S. Ghemawat, MapReduce: Simplified data processing on large clusters, *Communications of the ACM*, vol. 51, no. 1, pp. 107–113, 2008.

[20] A. Toshniwal, S. Taneja, A. Shukla, K. Ramasamy, J. M. Patel, S. Kulkarni, J. Jackson, et al., Storm@Twitter, in *Proceedings of the 2014 ACM SIGMOD International Conference on Management of Data*, June 22–27, Snowbird, UT, ACM, New York, 2014, pp. 147–156.

[21] X. Wu, X. Zhu, G. Q. Wu, and W. Ding, Data mining with big data, *IEEE Transactions on Knowledge and Data Engineering*, vol. 26, no. 1, pp. 97–107, 2014.

[22] N. Marz and J. Warren, *Big Data: Principles and Best Practices of Scalable Realtime Data Systems*, 1st ed., Greenwich, CT, Manning Publications Co., 2015.

[23] C. Esposito, M. Ficco, F. Palmieri, and A. Castiglione, A knowledge-based platform for big data analytics based on publish/subscribe services and stream processing, *Knowledge-Based Systems*, vol. 79, pp. 3–17, 2015.

[24] A. Destounis, G. S. Paschos, and I. Koutsopoulos, Streaming big data meets backpressure in distributed network computation, in *IEEE INFOCOM 2016—The 35th Annual IEEE International Conference on Computer Communications*, April 10–15, San Francisco, CA, 2016, pp. 1–9.

[25] R. Agerri, X. Artola, Z. Beloki, G. Rigau, and A. Soroa, Big data for natural language processing: A streaming approach, *Knowledge-Based Systems*, vol. 79, pp. 36–42, 2015.

[26] V.-D. Ta, C.-M. Liu, and G. W. Nkabinde, Big data stream computing in healthcare real-time analytics, in *2016 IEEE International Conference on Cloud Computing and Big Data Analysis (ICCCBDA)*, July 5–7, Chengdu, China, 2016, pp. 37–42.

[27] M. Zhu, C. Liu, J. Wang, X. Wang, and Y. Han, Instant discovery of moment companion vehicles from big streaming traffic data, in *2015 International Conference on Cloud Computing and Big Data (CCBD)*, June 17–19, Huangshan, China, 2015, pp. 73–80.

[28] L. Zhang, J. Zhao, and K. Xu, Emotion-based social computing platform for streaming big-data: Architecture and application, in *2016 13th International Conference on Service Systems and Service Management (ICSSSM)*, June 24–26, Kunming, China, 2016, pp. 1–6.

[29] S. Agarwal and B. R. Prasad, High speed streaming data analysis of web generated log streams, in *2015 IEEE 10th International Conference on Industrial and Information Systems (ICIIS)*, December 18–20, University of Peradeniya Peradeniya, Sri Lanka, 2015, pp. 413–418.

[30] A. A. Chandio, K. Bilal, N. Tziritas, Z. Yu, Q. Jiang, S. U. Khan, and C.-Z. Xu, A comparative study on resource allocation and energy efficient job scheduling strategies in large-scale parallel computing systems, *Cluster Computing*, vol. 17, no. 4, pp. 1349–1367, 2014.

[31] A. Hameed, A. Khoshkbarforoushha, R. Ranjan, P. P. Jayaraman, J. Kolodziej, P. Balaji, S. Zeadally, et al., A survey and taxonomy on energy efficient resource allocation techniques for cloud computing systems, *Computing*, vol. 98, no. 7, pp. 751–774, 2016.

[32] F. Zhang, J. Cao, K. Li, S. U. Khan, and K. Hwang, Multi-objective scheduling of many tasks in cloud platforms, *Future Generation Computer Systems*, vol. 37, pp. 309–320, 2014, special Section: Innovative Methods and Algorithms for Advanced Data-Intensive Computing Special Section: Semantics, Intelligent Processing and Services for Big Data Special Section: Advances in Data-Intensive Modelling and Simulation Special Section: Hybrid Intelligence for Growing Internet and its Applications.

[33] F. R. Dogar, T. Karagiannis, H. Ballani, and A. Rowstron, Decentralized task-aware scheduling for data center networks, in *Proceedings of the 2014 ACM Conference on SIGCOMM*, ser. SIGCOMM '14, August 17–22, Chicago, IL, ACM, New York, 2014, pp. 431–442.

[34] M. Tillenius, E. Larsson, R. M. Badia, and X. Martorell, Resource-aware task scheduling, *ACM Transactions on Embedded Computing Systems*, vol. 14, no. 1, pp. 5:1–5:25, 2015.

[35] S. K. Panda and P. K. Jana, Efficient task scheduling algorithms for heterogeneous multi-cloud environment, *The Journal of Supercomputing*, vol. 71, no. 4, pp. 1505–1533, 2015.

[36] M.-A. Vasile, F. Pop, R.-I. Tutueanu, V. Cristea, and J. Koodziej, Resource-aware hybrid scheduling algorithm in heterogeneous distributed computing, *Future Generation Computer Systems*, vol. 51, pp. 61–71, 2015, special Section: A Note on New Trends in Data-Aware Scheduling and Resource Provisioning in Modern HPC Systems.

[37] K. LaCurts, S. Deng, A. Goyal, and H. Balakrishnan, Choreo: Network-aware task placement for cloud applications, in *Proceedings of the 2013 Conference on Internet Measurement Conference*, October 23–25, Barcelona, Spain, ACM, New York, 2013, pp. 191–204.

ANALYSIS AND PROCESSING OF NETWORKED BIG DATA

Chapter 8

The ADMM and Its Application to Network Big Data

Nan Lin and Liqun Yu

Washington University in St. Louis
St. Louis, Missouri

CONTENTS

The alternating direction method of multiplier (ADMM) is a distributed convex optimization algorithm that solves a wide range of convex optimization problems. It was first introduced in the 1970s and has become popular in recent years due to its capability of solving large-scale optimization problems arising from the modern statistics and machine learning fields. In this chapter, we review the ADMM algorithm together with some of its variants. We show that many network applications can be expressed as optimization problems on connected graphs and solved effectively and efficiently by the ADMM. Besides its wide range of applications, the ADMM is also scalable to modern-scale network big data by utilizing the computing power of modern distributed computing frameworks. We investigate different ways of parallelizing the ADMM for the distributed model fitting problems and present the consensus ADMM for distributed network analyses. Then, as a separate but closely related topic, we spare an independent section for a discussion on solving the ADMM subproblems, where a special technique for avoiding expensive numerical methods in the ADMM updates are shown. To end this chapter, we present the network lasso as an example of the ADMM for network applications.

8.1 Introduction to the ADMM Algorithm

The ADMM was first introduced by [1,2] in the 1970s as a general convex optimization algorithm. It enjoys ease of applicability and has proven to produce great empirical performances for a broad range of problems. It became popular recently due to its capability of solving large-scale optimizations that are now becoming more and more common in practice. In this section, we give a brief overview of the ADMM and also present some of its variants.

8.1.1 The ADMM algorithm

The ADMM solves the following general optimization problem:

$$\min_{x,z} \{f(\boldsymbol{x}) + g(\boldsymbol{z})\} \quad \text{s.t. } A\boldsymbol{x} + B\boldsymbol{z} = \boldsymbol{c} \tag{8.1}$$

where $\boldsymbol{x} \in \mathbb{R}^m$, $\boldsymbol{z} \in \mathbb{R}^n$ are the parameters of interest, $A \in \mathbb{R}^{s\times n}$, $B \in \mathbb{R}^{s\times(p+1)}$ are constant matrices, $\boldsymbol{c} \in \mathbb{R}^s$ is a constant vector, and f and g are the convex objective functions. The ADMM solves (8.1) by iteratively minimizing its *augmented Lagrangian*

$$L_\rho(\boldsymbol{x},\boldsymbol{z},\boldsymbol{u}) := f(\boldsymbol{x}) + g(\boldsymbol{z}) + \boldsymbol{u}^T(A\boldsymbol{x} + B\boldsymbol{z} - \boldsymbol{c}) + \frac{\rho}{2}||A\boldsymbol{x} + B\boldsymbol{z} - \boldsymbol{c}||_2^2$$

in the primal variables $\boldsymbol{x}$ and $\boldsymbol{z}$ and updating the dual variable $\boldsymbol{u}$ via dual ascent, where ρ is the tunable augmentation parameter. Specifically, the ADMM carries out the following updates at iteration k:

$$\begin{aligned}
\boldsymbol{x}^{k+1} &:= \arg\min_{\boldsymbol{x}} f(\boldsymbol{x}) + \frac{\rho}{2}||A\boldsymbol{x} + B\boldsymbol{z}^k - \boldsymbol{c} + \boldsymbol{u}^k/\rho||_2^2 \\
\boldsymbol{z}^{k+1} &:= \arg\min_{\boldsymbol{z}} g(\boldsymbol{z}) + \frac{\rho}{2}||A\boldsymbol{x}^{k+1} + B\boldsymbol{z} - \boldsymbol{c} + \boldsymbol{u}^k/\rho||_2^2 \\
\boldsymbol{u}^{k+1} &:= \boldsymbol{u}^k + \rho(A\boldsymbol{x}^{k+1} + B\boldsymbol{z}^{k+1} - \boldsymbol{c})
\end{aligned} \tag{8.2}$$

In general, the updates in (8.2) are easily solvable compared to (8.1), although sometimes they may not have closed form solutions and require approximation or iterative methods.

The formulation (8.1) is general enough to cover a wide range of problems in statistics, machine learning, engineering, finance, etc. As a matter of fact, the ADMM has been intensively used in these fields for a broad range of applications. A partial list of applications can be found in Refs. [3–11]. We strongly encourage interested readers to explore the applications of ADMM in their own research fields.

As a motivating example, let us consider the statistical model fitting problems. Under such a scenario, the function f is usually the loss function related to the data and g is the regularization on model parameters. One of the most commonly used models is the ℓ_1-penalized linear regression (LASSO, [12]),

$$\min_{\boldsymbol{\beta}\in\mathbb{R}^p} ||\boldsymbol{y} - X\boldsymbol{\beta}||_2^2 + \lambda||\boldsymbol{\beta}||_1 \tag{8.3}$$

which can be written into the following equivalent ADMM form

$$\min_{\boldsymbol{\beta},\boldsymbol{\gamma}\in\mathbb{R}^p} ||\boldsymbol{y} - X\boldsymbol{\beta}||_2^2 + \lambda||\boldsymbol{\gamma}||_1 \text{ s.t. } \boldsymbol{\beta} = \boldsymbol{\gamma}$$

where $\boldsymbol{y} \in \mathbb{R}^n$ is the response vector, $X \in \mathbb{R}^{n\times p}$ is the design matrix, $\boldsymbol{\beta} \in \mathbb{R}^p$ is the model coefficient vector, and $||\cdot||_p$ denotes the ℓ_p norm. Following (8.2), the problem (8.3) is then solved by iteratively carrying out the updates

$$\begin{aligned}
\beta^{k+1} &:= \arg\min_{\beta} \|y - X\beta\|_2^2 + (u^k)^T\beta + \frac{\rho}{2}\|\beta - \gamma^k\|_2^2 \\
\gamma^{k+1} &:= \arg\min_{\gamma} \frac{\rho}{2}\|\gamma - \beta^{k+1} - u^k\|_2^2 + \lambda\|\gamma\|_1 \\
u^{k+1} &:= u^k + \rho(\beta^{k+1} - \gamma^{k+1})
\end{aligned} \tag{8.4}$$

where the β-update is a least square problem and the γ-update can be solved by soft-thresholding

$$\gamma^{k+1} = \left(\beta^{k+1} + u^k - \frac{\lambda}{\rho}\mathbf{1}_p\right)_+ \left(-\beta^{k+1} - u^k - \frac{\lambda}{\rho}\mathbf{1}_p\right)_+ \tag{8.5}$$

The ADMM algorithm (8.2) has $O(1/k)$ convergence rate (k is the iteration number) for general convex problems. Faster convergence rate can be achieved with stronger assumptions, e.g., the strong convexity of the functions $f(\cdot)$ and $g(\cdot)$, and/or full-column rank conditions on the matrices A and B. It is worth mentioning that, the ADMM was originally designed only for convex problems, but was later extended to many noncovex problems, with the convergence established under more strict assumptions compared to the convex case. We refer the readers to Ref. [13] for a comprehensive review of the ADMM algorithm.

8.1.2 Some variants: Stochastic and online ADMM algorithms

Several stochastic and online variants of ADMM have been proposed for improvement of computational efficiency and streaming data processing. In this section, we present some stochastic and online ADMM algorithms while refer readers to Refs. [14–19] as a nonexclusive list for a deeper investigation.

8.1.2.1 Stochastic ADMM

In (8.2), the updates (usually the $\boldsymbol{x}$-update) sometimes have no closed form and require iterative methods. This results in a double loop algorithm where the inner loop consists of the iterative method for the updates and the outer loop consists of the ADMM iterations. This can be computationally demanding. To address this issue, stochastic versions of ADMM were proposed. The idea is to linearize the $\boldsymbol{x}$-update in (8.2) so that it has a closed form solution.

In Ref. [16], a basic version of stochastic ADMM was proposed. At iteration k, the $\boldsymbol{x}$-update is linearized at $\boldsymbol{x}^k$ from the previous iteration:

$$\boldsymbol{x}^{k+1} := \arg\min_{\boldsymbol{x}} \langle f'(\boldsymbol{x}^k), \boldsymbol{x}\rangle + \frac{\rho}{2}\|A\boldsymbol{x} + Bz^k - \boldsymbol{c} + \boldsymbol{u}^k/\rho\|_2^2 + \frac{\|\boldsymbol{x} - \boldsymbol{x}^k\|_2^2}{2(k+1)} \tag{8.6}$$

where the last term penalizes the divergence between the solutions from two subsequent iterations. In Ref. [19], the $\boldsymbol{x}$-update (8.6) is further linearized as

$$\boldsymbol{x}^{k+1} := \arg\min_{\boldsymbol{x}} \langle f'(\boldsymbol{x}^k), \boldsymbol{x}\rangle + \rho\langle A\boldsymbol{x}^k + B\boldsymbol{z}^k - \boldsymbol{c} + \boldsymbol{u}^k/\rho, \boldsymbol{x}\rangle + \frac{\|\boldsymbol{x}-\boldsymbol{x}^k\|_2^2}{2(k+1)} \tag{8.7}$$

A more complicated stochastic version was proposed in Ref. [17]. Assume that we have n data samples and

$$f(\boldsymbol{x}) = \sum_{i=1}^{n} \ell_i(\boldsymbol{x})$$

where each ℓ_i is the loss function corresponding to the ith sample. At time t, an index $k(t) \in \{1,2,\ldots,n\}$ is randomly selected. Then we define

$$\tau_i(t) = \begin{cases} t & i = k(t) \\ \tau_i(t-1) & \text{otherwise} \end{cases}$$

The $\boldsymbol{x}$-update (8.7) is then replaced by

$$\begin{aligned} \boldsymbol{x}^{k+1} := \arg\min_{\boldsymbol{x}} & \left\{ \sum_{i=1}^{n} \langle f'(\boldsymbol{x}^{\tau_i(t)}), \boldsymbol{x}\rangle + L\|\boldsymbol{x} - \boldsymbol{x}^{\tau_i(t)}\|_2^2 \right\} \\ & + \rho\langle A\boldsymbol{x}^k + B\boldsymbol{z}^k - \boldsymbol{c} + \boldsymbol{u}^k/\rho, \boldsymbol{x}\rangle \end{aligned} \tag{8.8}$$

where L is a constant. Essentially Equation 8.8 means that instead of linearizing all ℓ_i, $i = 1,2,\ldots,n$ at the same point $\boldsymbol{x}^k$, we linearize ℓ_i at the $\boldsymbol{x}$ value when the sample i was last visited. Compared to Equations 8.6 and 8.7, Equation 8.8 results in a faster convergence rate.

8.1.2.2 *Online ADMM for data stream*

The standard formulation of ADMM in (8.1) and (8.2) corresponds to the batch setting where we assume the function f is deterministic. For example, in statistical model fitting, e.g., (8.3), this means that the whole data $(X, \boldsymbol{y})$ are collected before fitting the model. Besides being computationally inefficient and challenging for storage when X is large, this assumption is also unrealistic in practice. Especially in network applications, data are collected in a streaming fashion, with new data coming in every day or even every second. An ideal scenario is to update results, e.g., $\boldsymbol{x}, \boldsymbol{z}$ in (8.1) or $\boldsymbol{\beta}$ in (8.3), on the fly and only store variables (x, z, and y) instead of historical data.

Under data streaming scenarios, the problem (8.1) is reformulated as follows,

$$\min_{\boldsymbol{x},\boldsymbol{z}} \sum_{t=1}^{T} (f_t(\boldsymbol{x}) + g(\boldsymbol{z})) \quad \text{s.t. } A\boldsymbol{x} + B\boldsymbol{z} = \boldsymbol{c} \tag{8.9}$$

At time T, $f(\boldsymbol{x}) = \sum_{t=1}^{T} f_t(\boldsymbol{x})$ and f_t only corresponds to a single data sample or a small batch of samples. For example in (8.3), the problem can be reformulated as

$$\min_{\beta,\gamma} \sum_{t=1}^{T} (\|\boldsymbol{y}_t - X_t\boldsymbol{\beta}\|_2^2 + \|\boldsymbol{\gamma}\|_1) \quad \text{s.t. } \boldsymbol{\beta} = \boldsymbol{\gamma}$$

where $(X_t, \boldsymbol{y}_t)$ is a single sample or a batch of samples collected at time t.

In Ref. [14], the online ADMM (OADM) algorithm was proposed to solve (8.9). At time t, we consider solving

$$(\boldsymbol{x}_{t+1}, \boldsymbol{z}_{t+1}) = \arg \min_{A\boldsymbol{x}+B\boldsymbol{z}=\boldsymbol{c}} f_t(\boldsymbol{x}) + g(\boldsymbol{z}) + \eta B_\phi(\boldsymbol{x}, \boldsymbol{x}_t) \tag{8.10}$$

where $\eta \geq 0$ is the learning rate and $B_\phi(\boldsymbol{x}, \boldsymbol{x}_t) \geq \frac{\alpha}{2}\|\boldsymbol{x} - \boldsymbol{x}_t\|_2^2$ (for some constant α) is the Bregman divergence. The problem (8.10) itself can be solved by the ADMM iteratively so that the constraint is exactly satisfied, but this results in a double loop algorithm, which is computationally unappealing. The OADM solves (8.10) by only one pass through the ADMM iteration. The intuition is that, instead of requiring $(\boldsymbol{x}_t, \boldsymbol{z}_t)$ to satisfy the linear constraint for every t, OADM only requires the constraint to be satisfied in the long run. Specifically, the problem (8.9) is written into the following form:

$$\min_{\boldsymbol{x}_t, \boldsymbol{z}_t} \sum_{t=0}^{T} f_t(\boldsymbol{x}_t) + g(\boldsymbol{z}_t) \quad \text{s.t. } \sum_{t=1}^{T} \|A\boldsymbol{x}_t + B\boldsymbol{z}_t - \boldsymbol{c}\|_2^2 = o(T)$$

so that the cumulative constraint violation grows at a sublinear rate, i.e., $o(T)$.

The augmented Lagrangian of (8.10) at time t is

$$L_{\rho t}(\boldsymbol{x}, \boldsymbol{z}, \boldsymbol{u}) = f_t(\boldsymbol{x}) + g(\boldsymbol{z}) + \boldsymbol{u}^T(A\boldsymbol{x} + B\boldsymbol{z} - \boldsymbol{c}) + \eta B_\phi(\boldsymbol{x}, \boldsymbol{x}_t) + \frac{\rho}{2}\|A\boldsymbol{x} + B\boldsymbol{z} - \boldsymbol{c}\|_2^2$$

and at time t the OADM consists of just one pass through the following updates:

$$\begin{aligned}
\boldsymbol{x}_{t+1} &:= \arg\min_{\boldsymbol{x}} f_t(\boldsymbol{x}) + \boldsymbol{u}_t(A\boldsymbol{x} + B\boldsymbol{z}_t - \boldsymbol{c}) + \frac{\rho}{2}\|A\boldsymbol{x} + B\boldsymbol{z}_t - \boldsymbol{c}\|_2^2 + \eta B_\phi(\boldsymbol{x}, \boldsymbol{x}_t) \\
\boldsymbol{z}_{t+1} &:= \arg\min_{\boldsymbol{z}} g(\boldsymbol{z}) + \boldsymbol{u}_t(A\boldsymbol{x}_{t+1} + B\boldsymbol{z} - \boldsymbol{c}) + \frac{\rho}{2}\|A\boldsymbol{x}_{t+1} + B\boldsymbol{z} - \boldsymbol{c}\|_2^2 \\
\boldsymbol{u}_{t+1} &:= \boldsymbol{u}_t + \rho(A\boldsymbol{x}_{t+1} + B\boldsymbol{z}_{t+1} - \boldsymbol{c})
\end{aligned} \tag{8.11}$$

In Ref. [14], the authors only considered the case where each iteration only processes one sample. Since in (8.10) and (8.11) there is no limitation on how many samples f_t can depend on, the OADM can be naturally applied to the more general case where each iteration takes a batch of data.

8.2 Distributed Model Fitting with ADMM

Besides being easily applicable to a wide range of problems, another main advantage of ADMM is its ease of parallelization and hence the ability to solve large-scale problems. Many network applications involve large amounts of data collected and stored distributedly across a network. In this section, we show how the ADMM is parallelized under the distributed model fitting context, which is commonly encountered in network applications. Two ways of parallelization, i.e., splitting across examples and splitting across features, are presented. Following this, we introduce the block-splitting ADMM recently proposed by [20]. The block-splitting ADMM offers a more flexible parallelization scheme by enabling splitting across both examples and features, which is appealing when both the sample size and feature dimension are large.

8.2.1 ADMM for distributed model fitting

This part follows Chapter 8 of Ref. [13]. We start with the problem setup then discuss how the ADMM is parallelized.

8.2.1.1 Problem setup

A general convex model fitting problem can be written as

$$\min_{\boldsymbol{\beta}\in\mathbb{R}^p} l(X\boldsymbol{\beta}-\boldsymbol{y})+r(\boldsymbol{\beta}) \tag{8.12}$$

where $X \in \mathbb{R}^{n\times p}$ is the design matrix, $\boldsymbol{b} \in \mathbb{R}^n$ is the response vector, $l(\cdot)$ is the loss function, and $r(\cdot)$ is the regularization. In practice, the loss function l is often additive, i.e.,

$$l(X\boldsymbol{\beta}-\boldsymbol{y}) = \sum_{i=1}^{n} l_i(\boldsymbol{x}_i^T\boldsymbol{\beta}-y_i)$$

where $\boldsymbol{x}_i$ denotes the ith row of X (ith sample). The regularization $r(\cdot)$ is also assumed to be additive. For example, $r(\cdot)$ can be the ℓ_2-norm or Lasso [12]. Specifically,

$$r(\boldsymbol{\beta}) = \sum_{j=1}^{p} r(\beta_j)$$

8.2.1.2 Splitting across examples

Here we discuss how to solve problem (8.12) in parallel with a large number of samples (large n) and a moderate number of features (relatively small p).

First, we partition X and $\boldsymbol{y}$ by rows:

$$X = \begin{bmatrix} X_1 \\ \vdots \\ X_N \end{bmatrix}, \quad \boldsymbol{y} = \begin{bmatrix} y_1 \\ \vdots \\ y_N \end{bmatrix}$$

where each $X_i \in \mathbb{R}^{n_i \times p}$ ($\sum_{i=1}^N n_i = n$) denotes a block (subset) of data. Next, we write problem (8.12) into the following equivalent form:

$$\min_{\boldsymbol{\beta}_i, z \in \mathbb{R}^p} \sum_{i=1}^{N} l_i(X_i\boldsymbol{\beta}_i - \boldsymbol{y}_i) + r(z) \quad \text{s.t. } \boldsymbol{\beta}_i = z,\ i = 1, 2, \ldots, N \tag{8.13}$$

Problems (8.12) and (8.13) are equivalent since we force each local $\boldsymbol{\beta}_i$ equal to a global z. A direct application of (8.2) to (8.13) results in the following update:

$$\begin{aligned} \boldsymbol{\beta}_i^{k+1} &:= \arg\min_{\boldsymbol{\beta}_i \in \mathbb{R}^p} l_i(X_i\boldsymbol{\beta}_i - \boldsymbol{y}_i) + \rho/2\|\boldsymbol{\beta}_i - z^k + \boldsymbol{u}_i^k/\rho\|_2^2 \\ z^{k+1} &:= \arg\min_{z} r(z) + (N\rho/2)\|z - \bar{\boldsymbol{\beta}}^{k+1} - \bar{\boldsymbol{u}}^k/\rho\|_2^2 \\ \boldsymbol{u}_i^{k+1} &:= \boldsymbol{u}_i^k + \boldsymbol{\beta}_i^{k+1} - z^{k+1} \end{aligned} \tag{8.14}$$

where $\bar{\boldsymbol{\beta}}^{k+1} = (1/N)\sum_{i=1}^N \boldsymbol{\beta}_i^{k+1}$ and $\bar{\boldsymbol{u}}^{k+1} = (1/N)\sum_{i=1}^N \boldsymbol{u}_i^{k+1}$, and $\boldsymbol{x}$, z, A and B in (8.1) corresponds to $(\boldsymbol{\beta}_1 T, \ldots, \boldsymbol{\beta}_N^T)^T$, z, I_{Np}, and $-[I_p \ldots I_p]^T \in \mathbb{R}^{Np \times p}$, respectively.

The first update in (8.14) can be carried out in parallel for each data block. In practice, the data blocks X_i, $i = 1, \ldots, N$ are distributed across N computing nodes with each computing node i storing data block i and carrying out updates with subscript i. The second update requires gathering variables to form the average. Notice that (8.14) does not require $r(\cdot)$ to be separable.

8.2.1.3 Splitting across features

In (8.12), when sample size n is not too large but the dimension p is high, the ADMM can be parallelized in a different way. First, the data matrix is partitioned across columns, $X = [X_1 \ldots X_N]$ with $X_i \in \mathbb{R}^{n \times p_i}$ ($\sum_{i=1}^N p_i = p$). The features are also split correspondingly, $\boldsymbol{\beta} = (\boldsymbol{\beta}_1^T, \ldots, \boldsymbol{\beta}_N^T)^T$. Problem (8.12) is then written as

$$\min_{\boldsymbol{\beta}} l\left(\sum_{i=1}^{N} X_i\boldsymbol{\beta}_i - \boldsymbol{y}\right) + \sum_{i=1}^{N} r(\boldsymbol{\beta}_i)$$

or equivalently,

$$\min_{\boldsymbol{\beta}, z_i} l\left(\sum_{i=1}^{n} z_i - \boldsymbol{y}\right) + \sum_{i=1}^{N} r(\boldsymbol{\beta}_i) \quad \text{s.t. } X_i\boldsymbol{\beta}_i - z_i = 0,\ i = 1, \ldots, N \tag{8.15}$$

Applying (8.2) to (8.15) with some algebraic manipulation gives the following updates:

$$\begin{aligned}
\beta_i^{k+1} &:= \arg\min_{\beta_i} r(\beta_i) + (\rho/2)\|X_i\beta_i - X_i\beta_i^k - \bar{z}^k + \overline{X\beta}^k + u^k/\rho\|_2^2 \\
\bar{z}^{k+1} &:= \arg\min_{\bar{z}} l(N\bar{z} - \beta) + (N\rho/2)\|\bar{z} - \overline{X\beta}^{k+1} - \bar{u}^k/\rho\|_2^2 \qquad (8.16)\\
u^{k+1} &:= u^k + \overline{X\beta}^{k+1} - z^{k+1}
\end{aligned}$$

where $\bar{z} = (1/N)\sum_{i=1}^N z_i$, $\bar{u} = (1/N)\sum_{i=1}^N u_i$, and $\overline{X\beta} = (1/N)\sum_{i=1}^N X_i\beta_i$.

The β_i-update in (8.16) can be carried out in parallel where the update with subscript i is conducted on a local machine i that stores the ith block of features. The second and third updates involves aggregation across different blocks of features. Notice that the formulation (8.16) does not require the loss function $l(\cdot)$ to be separable.

8.2.2 Flexible parallelization via block splitting

Section 8.2.1 showed how the ADMM is parallelized across examples or features. In Ref. [20], a block splitting formulation of ADMM that can be parallelized across both examples and features was proposed. In modern big data applications, the data sometimes are not only big in size (large n), but also high dimensional (large p). The block splitting ADMM is especially appealing for such problems. The rest of this section follows [20].

The block splitting aims to solve the following problem:

$$\min_{x\in\mathbb{R}^m, z\in\mathbb{R}^n} \{f(x) + g(z)\} \quad \text{s.t. } x = Az \qquad (8.17)$$

where $A \in \mathbb{R}^{m\times n}$, and functions f and g are assumed to be block separable, i.e.,

$$f(x) = \sum_{i=1}^{M} f_i(x_i) \quad g(z) = \sum_{j=1}^{N} g_j(z_j)$$

where $x = (x_1^T,\ldots,x_M^T)^T$ and $z = (z_1^T,\ldots,z_M^T)^T$. And $x_i \in \mathbb{R}^{m_i}$, $z_j \in \mathbb{R}^{n_j}$ with $\sum_{i=1}^M m_i = m$ and $\sum_{j=1}^N n_i = n$. Correspondingly,

$$A = \begin{bmatrix} A_{11} & A_{12} & \ldots & A_{1N} \\ A_{21} & A_{22} & \ldots & A_{2N} \\ \vdots & \vdots & \ddots & \vdots \\ A_{M1} & A_{M2} & \ldots & A_{MN} \end{bmatrix} \quad \text{with } A_{ij} \in \mathbb{R}^{m_i\times n_j}$$

As a result of the block splitting above, problem (8.17) is written as

$$\min_{x\in\mathbb{R}^m, z\in\mathbb{R}^n} \sum_{i=1}^{M} f_i(x_i) + \sum_{j=1}^{N} g_j(z_j) \quad \text{s.t. } x_i = \sum_{j=1}^{N} A_{ij}z_j,\ i = 1,\ldots,M \qquad (8.18)$$

Setting $\boldsymbol{r} = X\boldsymbol{\beta} - \boldsymbol{y}$, the distributed model fitting problem (8.12) is a special case of (8.18) with $\boldsymbol{x} = \boldsymbol{r} + \boldsymbol{y}$, $\boldsymbol{z} = \boldsymbol{\beta}$, $f(\boldsymbol{x}) = l(\boldsymbol{x} - \boldsymbol{y}) = l(\boldsymbol{r})$, $f_i(\boldsymbol{x}_i) = l(\boldsymbol{x}_i - \boldsymbol{y}_i) = l(\boldsymbol{r}_i)$, $g(\cdot) = g_j(\cdot) = r(\cdot)$, and $A = X$.

Problem (8.18) can be further written as

$$\begin{aligned} &\min_{\boldsymbol{x}\in\mathbb{R}^m, \boldsymbol{z}\in\mathbb{R}^n} \sum_{i=1}^{M} f_i(\boldsymbol{x}_i) + \sum_{j=1}^{N} g_j(\boldsymbol{z}_j) \\ &\quad \text{s.t. } \boldsymbol{z}_j = \boldsymbol{z}_{ij},\ \boldsymbol{x}_i = \sum_{i=1}^{N} \boldsymbol{x}_{ij}, \quad i = 1,\ldots,M \\ &\quad \boldsymbol{x}_{ij} = A_{ij}\boldsymbol{z}_{ij}, \quad i = 1,\ldots,M,\ j = 1,\ldots,N \end{aligned} \tag{8.19}$$

or equivalently,

$$\begin{aligned} &\min_{\boldsymbol{x}\in\mathbb{R}^m, \boldsymbol{z}\in\mathbb{R}^n} \sum_{i=1}^{M} f_i(\boldsymbol{x}_i) + \sum_{j=1}^{N} g_j(\boldsymbol{z}_j) + \sum_{i=1}^{M}\sum_{j=1}^{N} I_{ij}(\boldsymbol{x}_{ij}, \boldsymbol{z}_{ij}) \\ &\quad \text{s.t. } \boldsymbol{z}_j = \boldsymbol{z}_{ij},\ \boldsymbol{x}_i = \sum_{i=1}^{N} \boldsymbol{x}_{ij}, \quad i = 1,\ldots,M \end{aligned} \tag{8.20}$$

where I_{ij} is the indicator function of the graph of A_{ij}, i.e.,

$$I_{ij}(\boldsymbol{x}_{ij}, \boldsymbol{z}_{ij}) = \begin{cases} 0 & \text{if } \boldsymbol{x}_{ij} = A_{ij}\boldsymbol{z}_{ij} \\ \infty & \text{otherwise} \end{cases}$$

Problem (8.20) can be solved by the formulation of ADMM for the generic convex constrained optimization problem

$$\min_{w} \varphi(w) \quad \text{s.t. } w \in \mathcal{C} \tag{8.21}$$

where $\varphi(\cdot)$ is a convex function and $\mathcal{C}$ is a closed convex set. Moving the constraint to the objective function, we have the following equivalent problem:

$$\min_{w} \varphi(w^{1/2}) + I_{\mathcal{C}}(w^1) \quad \text{s.t. } w^{1/2} = w^1 \tag{8.22}$$

where $I_{\mathcal{C}}(\cdot)$ is the indicator function of $\mathcal{C}$. Denoting the value of $w^{1/2}$ at kth iteration as $w^{k+1/2}$ and the value of w^1 at kth iteration as w^{k+1}, from (8.2), problem (8.22) is solved by

$$\begin{aligned} w^{k+1/2} &:= \mathbf{prox}_{\varphi}(w^k - \tilde{w}^k) \\ w^{k+1} &:= \arg\min_{w^1} I_{\mathcal{C}}(w^1) + (\rho/2)\|w^1 - (w^{k+1/2} + \tilde{w}^k)\|_2^2 \\ &= \Pi_{\mathcal{C}}(w^{k+1/2} + \tilde{w}^k) \\ \tilde{w}^{k+1} &:= \tilde{w}^k + w^{k+1/2} - w^{k+1} \end{aligned} \tag{8.23}$$

where $\mathbf{prox}_{\varphi}(v) = \arg\min_w \left(\varphi(w) + (\rho/2)\|w - v\|_2^2\right)$, $\Pi_{\mathcal{C}}$ is the projection onto $\mathcal{C}$, and $\tilde{w}$ is the dual variable equivalent to $\boldsymbol{u}$ in (8.2). Applying (8.23) to (8.20) with w consisting of $\boldsymbol{x}$, $\boldsymbol{z}$, $(\boldsymbol{x}_{ij},\ \boldsymbol{z}_{ij})$, $i = 1,\ldots,M$, $j = 1,\ldots,N$, and $\varphi(w) = \sum_{i=1}^{M} f_i(\boldsymbol{x}_i) + \sum_{j=1}^{N} g_j(\boldsymbol{z}_j) + \sum_{i=1}^{M}\sum_{j=1}^{N} I_{ij}(\boldsymbol{x}_{ij},\boldsymbol{z}_{ij})$, we have the following updates:

$$
\begin{aligned}
\boldsymbol{x}_i^{k+1/2} &:= \mathbf{prox}_{f_i}(\boldsymbol{x}_i^k - \tilde{\boldsymbol{x}}_i^k) \\
\boldsymbol{z}_j^{k+1/2} &:= \mathbf{prox}_{g_j}(\boldsymbol{z}_j^k - \tilde{\boldsymbol{z}}_j^k) \\
(\boldsymbol{z}_{ij}^{k+1/2}, \boldsymbol{x}_{ij}^{k+1/2}) &:= \Pi_{ij}(\boldsymbol{z}_{ij}^k - \tilde{\boldsymbol{z}}_{ij}^k, \boldsymbol{x}_{ij}^k - \tilde{\boldsymbol{x}}_{ij}^k) \\
\boldsymbol{z}_j^{k+1} &:= \left(\boldsymbol{z}_j^{k+1/2} + \sum_{i=1}^{M} \boldsymbol{z}_{ij}^{k+1/2}\right)/(M+1) \\
\boldsymbol{x}_i^{k+1} &:= \boldsymbol{x}_i^{k+1/2} - \left(\boldsymbol{x}_i^{k+1/2} - \sum_{j=1}^{N} \boldsymbol{x}_{ij}^{k+1/2}\right)/(N+1) \\
\boldsymbol{x}_{ij}^{k+1} &:= \boldsymbol{x}_{ij}^{k+1/2} + \left(\boldsymbol{x}_i^{k+1/2} - \sum_{j=1}^{N} \boldsymbol{x}_{ij}^{k+1/2}\right)/(N+1) \\
\tilde{\boldsymbol{z}}_j^{k+1} &:= \tilde{\boldsymbol{z}}_j^k + \boldsymbol{z}_j^{k+1/2} - \boldsymbol{z}_j^{k+1} \\
\tilde{\boldsymbol{x}}_i^{k+1} &:= \tilde{\boldsymbol{x}}_i^k + \boldsymbol{x}_i^{k+1/2} - \boldsymbol{x}_i^{k+1} \\
\tilde{\boldsymbol{z}}_{ij}^{k+1} &:= \tilde{\boldsymbol{z}}_{ij}^k + \boldsymbol{z}_{ij}^{k+1/2} - \boldsymbol{z}_j^{k+1}
\end{aligned}
\tag{8.24}
$$

where Π_{ij} denotes the projection onto $\{(\boldsymbol{c},\boldsymbol{d}) \in \mathbb{R}^{m+n} | \boldsymbol{d} = A_{ij}\boldsymbol{c}\}$. The formulation (8.24) involves some simplification process, and we refer the readers to Ref. [20] for technical details.

In (8.24), each of the M $\boldsymbol{x}_i^{k+1/2}$-updates, N $\boldsymbol{z}_j^{k+1/2}$-updates, and the MN $(\boldsymbol{z}_{ij}^{k+1/2}, \boldsymbol{x}_{ij}^{k+1/2})$-updates can be carried out in parallel on different machines, so do the updates in the last three equations of (8.24). The fourth to sixth lines of (8.24) involve aggregation and hence communication between different machines. In Ref. [20], the communication details are described with graphs, and parallel implementation of (8.24) on Amazon EC2 is also presented in the simulation part. We refer interested readers to Ref. [20] for details.

8.3 Distributed ADMM: The Optimization on Network Big Data

In network applications, data are often collected and stored across a distributed network consisting of computing nodes from different locations. For many of these applications, the problems to be solved can be reduced to distributed model fitting across a connected network. This results in optimizing a global object function which is a combination of local objective functions known by the local computing nodes only. For example, in spam filtering, emails are distributed across user computers or the Cloud. The goal is to build a spam filter that detects spam. This involves building a classifier by minimizing some global loss function (e.g., number of misclassifications for all users), which is a sum of local loss function (number of misclassifications for each user).

Due to the distributed nature of network applications, it is often unrealistic to collect and process all data in a single computer. On the one hand, transferring local data to a center results in a huge communication overhead. On the other hand, in most real applications the data are almost surely too large for a single computer to store or process. Hence, algorithms that are capable of solving problems collectively over the network are required for such applications.

The ADMM is one such algorithm. In the previous section, we presented the parallelization of ADMM for distributed model fitting problems. The distributed model fitting problem is a special case of a generic problem in network applications called the *consensus* problem. In this section, we present several versions of the distributed ADMM algorithms for optimization over network big data that solve the consensus problem in different ways. The distributed ADMM is communication efficient and flexible to the network topology.

8.3.1 The consensus problem

Consider the optimization

$$\min_{\boldsymbol{x}} f(\boldsymbol{x}) = \sum_{i=1}^{N} f_i(\boldsymbol{x}) \tag{8.25}$$

where the goal is to find a global variable $\boldsymbol{x}$ that minimizes the global object function f that can be split into N objective functions $f_1, \ldots, f_N$. Equivalently, we solve

$$\min_{\boldsymbol{x}} \sum_{i=1}^{N} f_i(\boldsymbol{x}_i) \quad \text{s.t. } \boldsymbol{x}_i = z,\ i = 1, 2, \ldots, N \tag{8.26}$$

Problem (8.26) is called the *global consensus* by the fact that all local variables $\boldsymbol{x}_i$, $i = 1, \ldots, N$ are forced to agree with the global variable z. Sometimes, we consider adding certain regularization on the global variable z, which results in the regularized consensus problem

$$\min_{\boldsymbol{x}} \sum_{i=1}^{N} f_i(\boldsymbol{x}_i) + g(z) \quad \text{s.t. } \boldsymbol{x}_i = z,\ i = 1, 2, \ldots, N \tag{8.27}$$

where g is the regularization function.

A direct application of (8.2) to (8.26) and (8.27) gives us the following updates

$$
\begin{aligned}
\boldsymbol{x}_i^{k+1} &:= \arg\min_{\boldsymbol{x}_i} f_i(\boldsymbol{x}_i) + \frac{\rho}{2}||\boldsymbol{x}_i - \boldsymbol{z} + \boldsymbol{u}^k/\rho||_2^2 \\
\boldsymbol{z}^{k+1} &:= \frac{1}{N}\sum_{i=1}^{N}(\boldsymbol{x}_i^{k+1} + \boldsymbol{u}_i^k/\rho) \\
\boldsymbol{u}_i^{k+1} &:= \boldsymbol{u}_i^k + \rho(\boldsymbol{x}_i^{k+1} - \boldsymbol{z}^{k+1})
\end{aligned}
\tag{8.28}
$$

and

$$
\begin{aligned}
\boldsymbol{x}_i^{k+1} &:= \arg\min_{\boldsymbol{x}} f_i(\boldsymbol{x}_i) + \frac{\rho}{2}||\boldsymbol{x}_i - \boldsymbol{z} + \boldsymbol{u}^k/\rho||_2^2 \\
\boldsymbol{z}^{k+1} &:= \arg\min_{\boldsymbol{z}} g(\boldsymbol{z}) + \frac{N\rho}{2}||\boldsymbol{z} - \bar{\boldsymbol{x}}^{k+1} - \bar{\boldsymbol{u}}^k/\rho||_2^2 \\
\boldsymbol{u}_i^{k+1} &:= \boldsymbol{u}_i^k + \rho(\boldsymbol{x}_i^{k+1} - \boldsymbol{z}^{k+1})
\end{aligned}
\tag{8.29}
$$

respectively, where the upper bar denotes the average over $i = 1,2,\ldots,N$.

In practice, the f_i functions are often only known to a local agent i (e.g., local processors or computing nodes), and solving the consensus problem involves minimizing the global objective cooperatively across local agents. For example, the distributed model fitting problem (8.13) in Section 8.2 is a special case of consensus problem with f_i being the local loss function l_i, which depends on the ith block of data, and is hence only known to agent i that stores the local data X_i and $\boldsymbol{y}_i$.

The consensus problem finds its application in many fields, e.g., in signal processing and wireless communication; see Chapter 7 of Ref. [13] and the references therein.

8.3.1.1 An extension: The asynchronous consensus ADMM

In (8.28) and (8.29), the updates are synchronized. Each agent i conducts the $\boldsymbol{x}_i$ and $\boldsymbol{u}_i$-updates and sends the result to the *master*. After receiving updates from all agents, the master updates $\boldsymbol{z}$ with the aggregated $\boldsymbol{x}$ and $\boldsymbol{u}$ values from across agents $1,2,\ldots,N$. The master then sends the updated $\boldsymbol{z}$ to each agent for the next iteration. This can be problematic in practice. Since the master cannot proceed without receiving updates from all agents, the overall performance is decided by the slowest agent in the network. The master and all other agents have to wait for the slowest agent to finish its updates before they can proceed to the next iteration.

To address this issue, an asynchronous version of the consensus ADMM (8.26) and (8.27) was proposed in Ref. [21]. In the asynchronous consensus ADMM, the master and each agent keep their own timeline. The master keeps the master clock k which starts at 1 and increases by 1 after each $\boldsymbol{z}$-update; agent i keeps its worker clock k_i which also starts at 1 and increases by 1 after each

$\boldsymbol{u}_i$-update. For the master node, it does not have to wait until all agents to finish their work. Instead, it can proceed after receiving updates from at least S $(1 \leq S \leq N)$ agents. In practice, S can be much smaller than N. The master then carries out the z-update with the S updated $\boldsymbol{x}_i$, $\boldsymbol{u}_i$ values and $N-S$ outdated $\boldsymbol{x}_i$, $\boldsymbol{u}_i$ values. The updated z value is then sent back only to the S agents that sent their updates to the master in the latest iteration, and each of the remaining $N-S$ agents that did not send updates to the master uses the latest z value it received. For agent i, denoting the latest z-value it received as $\tilde{z}_i$, then each agent i updates $\boldsymbol{x}_i$ and $\boldsymbol{u}_i$ with the outdates $\tilde{z}_i$. To make sure that the asynchronization works, a constraint called *bounded delay condition* is imposed. The bounded delay condition requires that updates from each agent have to be served at least once every τ iterations, where $\tau \geq 1$ is a user-defined parameter. A counter τ_i is kept by the master for each agent i. Each τ_i increases as the master clock k increases. But once the master receives the updates from agent i, the corresponding τ_i is reset to 1. The bounded delay condition guarantees the freshness of the updates from each agent.

The convergence of the asynchronous consensus ADMM was analyzed in Ref. [21]. The convergence rate of $O(\frac{N\tau}{TS})$ is established, where T denotes the iteration number. Decreasing S and increasing τ result in a slower convergence rate but may benefit from faster speed when there are slow agents in the network, as indicated by the simulations in Ref. [21].

8.3.2 Distributed ADMM for the consensus problem

In the previous section, we showed how the ADMM is applied to solving the consensus problem. The problem formulation (8.26) and (8.28) or (8.27) and (8.29) results in a centralized network topology where all agents communicate with a center (master). The centralized network topology may incur communication inefficiency and instability. On the one hand, the center is overloaded with communication with the whole network, and establishing a direct connection between all agents and the center can be expensive or unrealistic in practice. On the other hand, the performance of such a centralized network depends crucially on the center. The entire network is at stake if anything goes wrong inside the center. To increase robustness of the network and improve communication efficiency, several distributed consensus ADMM formulations were proposed. The word "distributed" means decentralization, i.e., all computing nodes in the network are treated equally and there is no master role in the network. The topic of the limitation of centralization and the prospect of decentralization is far beyond the scope of this chapter; we strongly recommend readers to the book by Kevin Kelly [22], which provides profound insights about the connection between decentralization and the emergence of machine intelligence. In the following, we present the distributed consensus ADMM algorithm.

8.3.2.1 Problem formulation

We follow the distributed ADMM formulation of Ref. [23]. Consider a network represented by an undirected connected simple graph with N nodes and M edges, $G = \{V, E\}$, where V and E denote the sets of nodes (agents) and edges (connection between agents) of the network, respectively. We assume nodes are ordered from 1 to N and denote the edge between nodes i and j as e_{ij} $(i < j)$. To simplify the notation, we assume the functions f_i in (8.25) are univariate and replace the notation of variable $\boldsymbol{x}$ by x for the remainder of this section.

To concisely represent the distributed ADMM formulation, we define the *edge-node incidence matrix* of the network G as a matrix $A \in \mathbb{R}^{M \times N}$, with each row corresponding to an edge and each column corresponding to a node. The row corresponding to the edge e_{ij}, denoted by $[A]^{e_{ij}}$, has 1 in its ith coordinate, -1 in its jth coordinate, and 0 for other coordinates. Specifically, the elements of A are given by

$$[A]_k^{e_{ij}} = \begin{cases} 1 & \text{if } k = i \\ -1 & \text{if } k = j \\ 0 & \text{otherwise} \end{cases}$$

Now instead of requiring all local x_i's in (8.25) to be equal to a global z, we only require local variables x_i's to be equal to variables of its neighboring nodes. This requirement is represented concisely as

$$\min_{\boldsymbol{x} = (x_1, \ldots, x_N)^T} \sum_{i=1}^{N} f_i(x_i) \quad \text{s.t. } A\boldsymbol{x} = 0 \tag{8.30}$$

Since the graph G is connected, problem (8.30) is equivalent to (8.25) and (8.26).

8.3.2.2 The distributed consensus ADMM

For each node i in network G, we partition its neighbors into the *predecessors* and the *successors*, defined by $P(i) = \{j \mid e_{ij} \in E,\ i > j\}$ and $S(i) = \{j \mid e_{ij} \in E,\ i < j\}$. In Ref. [23], the authors applied the ADMM to (8.30) with the variables updated in a sequential order from x_1 to x_N. This results in the distributed ADMM algorithm as follows:

$$\begin{aligned} x_i^{k+1} &:= \arg\min_{x_i} f_i(x_i) + \frac{\rho}{2} \sum_{j \in P(i)} \left\| x_j^{k+1} - x_i - \frac{1}{\rho} u_{ji}^k \right\|_2^2 + \frac{\rho}{2} \sum_{j \in S(i)} \left\| x_j^k - x_i - \frac{1}{\rho} u_{ij}^k \right\|_2^2 \\ u_{ji}^{k+1} &:= u_{ji}^k - \rho(x_j^{k+1} - x_i^{k+1}) \end{aligned} \tag{8.31}$$

where each agent i updates x_i and the u_{ji} it owns, i.e., u_{ji} for all $j \in P(i)$.

For the formulation (8.31), the x_i-update and u_{ji}-update only rely on the x_j values from its neighboring nodes in the network, and hence the communication is only between neighboring nodes, i.e., the communication is decentralized.

8.3.2.3 *Decentralization on colored networks*

One drawback of the formulation (8.31) is that, the variables are updated sequentially. Each agent finishes its own update and sends the results to its successors, and an agent cannot proceed before receiving updates from all its predecessors. This node-by-node updating mechanism may require significant amount of time for each iteration of ADMM. To allow for certain amount of parallelization, a different version of distributed ADMM was proposed in Ref. [24].

The distributed ADMM formulation of Ref. [24] relies on the existence of a *coloring scheme* for the network. To be specific, a coloring scheme is an assignment of colors to the nodes in the network in a way that no adjacent nodes have the same color. In practice, we want to use as few colors as possible for a network.

Assume that there are C colors in the coloring scheme. Without loss of generality, we assume that the nodes are ordered such that the first C_1 nodes have color 1, the next C_2 nodes have color 2, and so on. The variables $\boldsymbol{x} = (x_1, \ldots, x_N)^T$ and the edge-node matrix A are split accordingly:

$$\boldsymbol{x} = (\underbrace{x_1, \ldots, x_{C_1}}_{\bar{\boldsymbol{x}}_1}, \ldots, \underbrace{x_{N-C_N+1}, \ldots, x_N}_{\bar{\boldsymbol{x}}_C})^T$$

and

$$A = [A_1, \ldots, A_C]$$

Problem (8.30) is then written as

$$\min_{\boldsymbol{x}} \sum_{c=1}^{C} \sum_{i \in \mathcal{C}_c} f_i(x_i) \quad \text{s.t. } A_1\bar{\boldsymbol{x}}_1 + \ldots + A_C\bar{\boldsymbol{x}}_C = 0 \tag{8.32}$$

where $\mathcal{C}_c$ is the set consisting of the indices of nodes with color c.

Compared to the standard ADMM in (8.1), the problem (8.32) is called the *extended ADMM* since there are more than two sets of variables when $C > 2$. The extended ADMM algorithm solves (8.32) by the following updates,

$$\begin{aligned}
\bar{\boldsymbol{x}}_1^{k+1} &:= \arg\min_{\bar{\boldsymbol{x}}_1} L_\rho(\bar{\boldsymbol{x}}_1, \bar{\boldsymbol{x}}_2^k, \ldots, \bar{\boldsymbol{x}}_C^k; \boldsymbol{u}^k) \\
&\vdots \\
\bar{\boldsymbol{x}}_C^{k+1} &:= \arg\min_{\bar{\boldsymbol{x}}_C} L_\rho(\bar{\boldsymbol{x}}_1^{k+1}, \ldots, \bar{\boldsymbol{x}}_{C-1}^{k+1}, \bar{\boldsymbol{x}}_C; \boldsymbol{u}^k) \\
\boldsymbol{u}^{k+1} &:= \boldsymbol{u}^k + \rho \sum_{c=1}^{C} A_c \bar{\boldsymbol{x}}_c^{k+1}
\end{aligned} \tag{8.33}$$

where L_ρ is the Lagrangian

$$L_\rho(\bar{\boldsymbol{x}}_1,\ldots,\bar{\boldsymbol{x}}_C;\boldsymbol{u}) = \sum_{i=1}^{N} f_i(x_i) + \boldsymbol{u}^T(A_1\bar{\boldsymbol{x}}_1 + \ldots + A_C\bar{\boldsymbol{x}}_C) + \frac{\rho}{2}\|A_1\bar{\boldsymbol{x}}_1 + \ldots + A_C\bar{\boldsymbol{x}}_C\|_2^2$$

Explicitly, we have

$$\bar{\boldsymbol{x}}_c^{k+1} = \arg\min_{\bar{\boldsymbol{x}}_c} \sum_{i\in\mathcal{C}_c} f_i(x_i) + \boldsymbol{u}^{k^T} A_c\bar{\boldsymbol{x}}_c + \frac{\rho}{2}\left\| A_c\bar{\boldsymbol{x}}_c + \sum_{d<c} A_d\bar{\boldsymbol{x}}_d^{k+1} + \sum_{d>c} A_d\bar{\boldsymbol{x}}_d^{k}\right\|_2^2 \tag{8.34}$$

Denoting the set of nodes neighboring i as $\mathcal{N}_i$ and $D_i = |\mathcal{N}_i|$ and utilizing the fact that nodes with the same color are not adjacent to each other, the $\bar{\boldsymbol{x}}_c$-update ($c = 1,2,\ldots,C$) (8.34) can be simplified as

$$\bar{\boldsymbol{x}}_c^{k+1} = \arg\min_{\bar{\boldsymbol{x}}_c} \sum_{i\in\mathcal{C}_c}\left(f_i(x_i) + v_i^k x_i + \frac{D_i\rho}{2}x_i^2\right) \tag{8.35}$$

where

$$v_i^k := \gamma_i^k - \rho\sum_{j\in\mathcal{N}_i, j<i} x_j^{k+1} - \rho\sum_{j\in\mathcal{N}_i, j>i} x_j^k \quad \text{with } \gamma_i^k = \sum_{j\in\mathcal{N}_i, j<i} u_{ji}^k - \sum_{j\in\mathcal{N}_i, j>i} u_{ji}^k$$

Notice that the update (8.35) can be parallelized for nodes with color c:

$$x_i = \arg\min_{x_1} f_i(x_i) + v_i^k x_i + \frac{D_i\rho}{2}x_i^2 \quad \text{for } i\in\mathcal{C}_c$$

Since the x_i updates do not depend directly on $\boldsymbol{u}$, the $\boldsymbol{u}$ update can also be simplified to

$$\gamma_i^{k+1} = \gamma_i^k + \rho\sum_{j\in\mathcal{N}_i}(x_i^{k+1} - x_j^{k+1}),\ i = 1,2,\ldots,N$$

which is carried out in parallel for $i = 1,2,\ldots,N$.

If we take a close look at the update (8.35), we can find that the communication is still only between neighboring nodes. The difference between (8.34) and (8.31) is that instead of updating variables sequentially node-by-node, (8.35) updates variables color-by-color, with the updates inside each color being completely parallel. As a result, if we can find a coloring scheme that contains only a few colors (compared to the number of nodes), the computational speed can be significantly improved.

In this section, two versions of distributed ADMM algorithms are presented. We finish this section by mentioning that there are other versions of distributed ADMM algorithms, and encourage readers to explore these. For example, Ref. [25] applies a simple distributed ADMM for optimization in modern communication networks, Ref. [26] proposed an online version of distributed ADMM for network applications.

8.4 Solving the ADMM Updates

An iteration of the ADMM consists of several updates, each of which is a subproblem that solves a small optimization problem. In practice, how efficiently the subproblems are solved is crucial to the performance of ADMM. Until now, we have put aside this very important part of the ADMM, i.e., how to solve the ADMM updates. Intentionally or unintentionally, we have treated the updates of ADMM as a black box, with the belief that these subproblems are guaranteed to be solved accurately and efficiently. In many real applications, however, the ADMM updates can be highly nontrivial and expensive to solve. This is typical when no closed form solutions are available for the subproblems. Meanwhile, the performance of the ADMM heavily depends on the accuracy and efficiency of the solutions of the subproblems. Especially in the distributed case, e.g., (8.14) and (8.16), where each computing node in the network may only have very limited computing power, efficient algorithms for the ADMM subproblems crucial.

When closed form solutions do not exist, one usually resorts to iterative numerical methods for the ADMM updates. Numerical methods, including Newton's method (see Section 3.3 of Ref. [27]) and the coordinate descent (CD) (see Section 9.3 of Ref. [27]), can be applied to a wide range of optimization problems, but may entail significant computational cost. In this section, we present an alternative approach for efficiently solving the ADMM updates. Following the unwrapping ADMM proposed in Ref. [28], we show that by writing problems into specific ADMM forms, the solutions of the resulted updates can be obtained without numerical methods. To be concrete, we use the model fitting problem (8.12) for illustration throughout this section. Similar ideas may be applied to a broader range of problems.

8.4.1 Solving the updates with iterative methods

Naïvely, problem (8.12) can be formulated into the ADMM form

$$\min_{\boldsymbol{\beta},z} \{l(X\boldsymbol{\beta}-\boldsymbol{y})+r(z)\} \quad \text{s.t. } \boldsymbol{\beta}=z \tag{8.36}$$

Applying (8.2) to (8.36) gives us the following updates:

$$\begin{aligned}
\boldsymbol{\beta}^{k+1} &:= \arg\min_{\boldsymbol{\beta}\in\mathbb{R}^p} l(X\boldsymbol{\beta}-\boldsymbol{y})+(\rho/2)\|\boldsymbol{\beta}-z^k+\boldsymbol{u}^k/\rho\|_2^2 \\
z^{k+1} &:= \arg\min_{z} r(z)+(\rho/2)\|z-\boldsymbol{\beta}^{k+1}-\boldsymbol{u}^k/\rho\|_2^2 \\
\boldsymbol{u}^{k+1} &:= \boldsymbol{u}^k+\boldsymbol{\beta}^{k+1}-z^{k+1}
\end{aligned} \tag{8.37}$$

In (8.37), the solution of z-update is usually presented as the *proximal* mapping:

$$\boldsymbol{\beta}^{k+1} := prox_r(\boldsymbol{\beta}^{k+1}-\boldsymbol{u}^k/\rho,\rho)$$

where the proximal mapping for a function f is defined as

$$prox_f(\boldsymbol{v}, \rho) := \arg\min_{\boldsymbol{x}} f(\boldsymbol{x}) + (\rho/2)\|\boldsymbol{x} - \boldsymbol{v}\|_2^2$$

The proxy can usually be efficiently evaluated with explicit solutions for a wide range of penalty functions $r(\cdot)$. On the other hand, in the $\boldsymbol{\beta}$-update the coordinates of $\boldsymbol{\beta}$ are coupled and hence closed form solutions are not available except when the loss function $l(\cdot)$ is quadratic. Depending on the form of the loss function, either Newton's method or CD can be applied to solve the β-update. This results in a double-loop algorithm that could be time consuming.

8.4.2 Reformulating the problem to avoid iterative methods

The unwrapping ADMM [28] suggests that, if a problem can be written into the following form:

$$\min_{\boldsymbol{x},\boldsymbol{y}} f(\boldsymbol{y}) \quad \text{s.t. } \boldsymbol{y} = D\boldsymbol{x} \tag{8.38}$$

with $f(\cdot)$ being a decomposible function, i.e., $f(\boldsymbol{y}) = \sum_{i=1}^{s} f_i(y_i)$ for $\boldsymbol{y} \in R^s$, then it can be efficiently solved by the ADMM. To be specific, the ADMM solution for (8.38) is

$$\begin{aligned}
\boldsymbol{x}^{k+1} &:= \arg\min_{\boldsymbol{x}} \|D\boldsymbol{x} - \boldsymbol{y}^k + \boldsymbol{u}^k\|_2^2 = (D^T D)^{-1} D^T(\boldsymbol{y}^k - \boldsymbol{u}^k) \\
\boldsymbol{y}^{k+1} &:= \arg\min_{\boldsymbol{y}} f(\boldsymbol{y}) + (\rho/2)\|\boldsymbol{y} - D\boldsymbol{x}^{k+1} - \boldsymbol{u}^k/\rho\|_2^2 \\
\boldsymbol{u}^{k+1} &:= \boldsymbol{u}^k + D\boldsymbol{x}^{k+1} - \boldsymbol{y}^{k+1}
\end{aligned} \tag{8.39}$$

and when $f(\boldsymbol{y})$ is decomposable, the $\boldsymbol{y}$-update is coordinate-wise decoupled and simple solutions are readily available.

As an application of the unwrapping ADMM, problem (8.12) can be reformulated into the following unwrapped form,

$$\min_{\boldsymbol{\beta},\boldsymbol{z}} g(\boldsymbol{z}) \quad \text{s.t. } D\boldsymbol{\beta} - \boldsymbol{z} = (0, \ldots, 0, \boldsymbol{y}^T)^T \in \mathbb{R}^{p+n} \tag{8.40}$$

where $D = \begin{pmatrix} I_p \\ X \end{pmatrix}$ and $g(\boldsymbol{z}) = \sum_{i=1}^{p+n} g_i(z_i)$ with

$$g_i(z_i) = \begin{cases} r(z_i) & \text{for } i \le p \\ l(z_i) & \text{for } i > p \end{cases}$$

Then (8.39) results in

$$
\begin{aligned}
\boldsymbol{\beta}^{k+1} &:= (D^T D)^{-1} D^T \left\{ z^k + (0,\ldots,0,\boldsymbol{y}^T)^T - \boldsymbol{u}^k/\rho \right\} \\
z_i^{k+1} &:= \arg\min_{z_i} r(z_i) + (\rho/2)(z_i - \boldsymbol{d}_i \cdot \boldsymbol{\beta}^{k+1} - u_i)^2, \ i = 1,2,\ldots,p \\
z_j^{k+1} &:= \arg\min_{z_j} l(z_j) + (\rho/2)(z_j - \boldsymbol{d}_j \cdot \boldsymbol{\beta}^{k+1} - u_j)^2, \ j = p+1,,\ldots,p+n \\
\boldsymbol{u}^{k+1} &:= \boldsymbol{u}^k + D\boldsymbol{\beta}^{k+1} - z^{k+1} - (0,\ldots,0,\boldsymbol{y}^T)^T
\end{aligned}
\tag{8.41}
$$

where $\boldsymbol{d}_j$ denotes the jth row of matrix D.

Compared to (8.37), the updates in (8.41) are decomposed into coordinate-wise optimizations, where the solutions are easily achievable without iterative methods. Also, the unwrapping ADMM facilitates a natural parallel implementation, where the z- and $\boldsymbol{u}$-updates can be completely parallelized, and the matrix evaluation $D^T D = I_p + \sum_{i=1}^{N} X_i^T X_i$ only needs to be computed separately across the network and aggregated once before the iteration starts (the data are split by rows with X_i being the ith subsample).

The unwrapping ADMM enjoys easy implementation and low computational cost, but may be restrictive because not all problems can be written into the unwrapped form (8.38). Furthermore, as commented by Ref. [29], a more difficult subproblem of ADMM at each iteration helps make more progress toward the global minimum and may hence converge faster. Compared to (8.37) where time-consuming numerical methods are applied to solve the subproblems, the unwrapping ADMM may result in a slower convergence in practice.

8.5 An Application: The Network Lasso

Recently, an algorithm called the *network lasso* was proposed in Ref. [30] for clustering and optimization in large networks. As shown in Ref. [30], the network lasso optimization problem can be efficiently solved by the ADMM. In this section, we present the network lasso and its optimization as an application of the ADMM algorithm.

8.5.1 Problem setup

Consider a network $\mathcal{N}$ consisting of the vertex set $\mathcal{V}$ and the edge set $\mathcal{E}$. The network lasso solves the following optimization problem on network $\mathcal{N}$:

$$
\min \sum_{i \in \mathcal{V}} f_i(\boldsymbol{x}_i) + \lambda \sum_{(j,k) \in \mathcal{E}} w_{jk} \|\boldsymbol{x}_j - \boldsymbol{x}_k\|_2 \tag{8.42}
$$

where $\boldsymbol{x}_1,\ldots,\boldsymbol{x}_m \in \mathbb{R}^p$ are the effective variables with $m = |\mathcal{V}|$, i.e., the cardinality of the set $\mathcal{V}$. Each node i on the network is considered as a local agent with local variable $\boldsymbol{x}_i$. The convex functions f_i are the local cost functions for agent i. The second term in the network lasso (8.42) is a generalization of the group lasso [31] that penalizes the differences of variables between neighboring nodes. It encourages some variables to be exactly the same, i.e., $\boldsymbol{x}_j = \boldsymbol{x}_k$ for some $(j,k) \in \mathcal{E}$. The constants $w_{jk} \geq 0$ adjust for the relative weights of the edges in the network, and the penalization parameter $\lambda \geq 0$ balances the node objectives and the level of consensus across the network.

The network lasso (8.42) is very similar to the consensus problem (8.25) or (8.26). Both of them conduct optimizations on a connected network consisting of local agents with local cost functions. There are two differences between the consensus problem and network lasso. First, the consensus problem tries to find a global consensus where all agents share the same decision variable. Although in (8.26) we introduced a separate variable for each node, those variables are forced to reach global consensus by the constraint $\boldsymbol{x}_i = z$. In network lasso, each node i has its own variable $\boldsymbol{x}_i$, and consensus is only encouraged (not forced) between neighboring nodes. Second, while the consensus only tries to find a variable that optimizes the objective function across the network, the network lasso facilitates clustering on the network at the same time, i.e., nodes that have the same decision variable form a natural cluster on the network.

Compared to the consensus problem, the flexibility of allowing local variables makes the network lasso appealing to problems where heterogeneity exists across potential clusters of a network. A general setting where one may find the network lasso useful is distributed statistical learning. Under the statistical learning context, the variable $\boldsymbol{x}_i$ represents the parameters for the local statistical model i that depends on the data resident at node i, and the objective function f_i represents the loss for the model over the data at node i. The ℓ_2-penalty on the differences of adjacent nodes encourage neighboring nodes to have similar or the same model parameters, which allows us to build models at each node that borrow statistical power from the neighboring nodes.

8.5.2 The ADMM solver

The network lasso problem (8.42) is a convex optimization problem and can be efficiently solved for small networks via generic convex optimization algorithms. For large networks (p, m, and $n = |\mathcal{E}|$ are large), [30] proposed a distributed and scalable ADMM solver for (8.42) that guarantees the global convergence.

By introducing new variables z_{ij} as a copy of $\boldsymbol{x}_i$ at each edge $(i,j) \in \mathcal{E}$, problem (8.42) is written into the following equivalent form:

$$\begin{aligned} &\min f_i(\boldsymbol{x}_i) + \lambda \sum_{(j,k)\in\mathcal{E}} w_{jk}\|z_{jk} - z_{kj}\|_2 \\ &\text{s.t. } \boldsymbol{x}_i = z_{ij},\ i = 1,\ldots,m,\ j \in N(i) \end{aligned} \tag{8.43}$$

where $N(i)$ is the index set of the neighbors of node i. Then we have the Lagrangian

$$L_\rho(\boldsymbol{x},\boldsymbol{z},\boldsymbol{u}) = \sum_{i\in\mathcal{V}} f_i(\boldsymbol{x}_i) + \sum_{(j,k)\in\mathcal{E}} \Big\{ \lambda w_{jk}\|\boldsymbol{z}_{jk} - \boldsymbol{z}_{kj}\|_2 - \frac{\rho}{2}\left(\|\boldsymbol{u}_{jk}\|_2^2 - \|\boldsymbol{u}_{kj}\|_2^2\right)$$
$$+ (\rho/2)\left(\|\boldsymbol{x}_j - \boldsymbol{z}_{jk} + \boldsymbol{u}_{jk}\|_2^2 - \|\boldsymbol{x}_k - \boldsymbol{z}_{kj} + \boldsymbol{u}_{kj}\|_2^2\right) \Big\} \quad (8.44)$$

and the following updates at iteration k:

$$\boldsymbol{x}_i^{k+1} = \arg\min_{\boldsymbol{x}_i} \left(f_i(\boldsymbol{x}_i) + \sum_{j\in N(i)} \frac{\rho}{2}\|\boldsymbol{x}_j - \boldsymbol{z}_{ij}^k + \boldsymbol{u}_{ij}^k\|_2^2 \right) \quad \text{(node } i\text{)}$$

$$\boldsymbol{z}_{ij}^{k+1}, \boldsymbol{z}_{ji}^{k+1}$$
$$= \arg\min_{\boldsymbol{z}_{ij},\boldsymbol{z}_{ij}} \Big(\lambda w_{jk}\|\boldsymbol{z}_{jk} - \boldsymbol{z}_{kj}\|_2 \quad (8.45)$$
$$+ \frac{\rho}{2}\left(\|\boldsymbol{x}_i^{k+1} - \boldsymbol{z}_{ij} + \boldsymbol{u}_{ij}^k\|_2^2 - \|\boldsymbol{x}_j^{k+1} - \boldsymbol{z}_{ji} + \boldsymbol{u}_{ji}^k\|_2^2\right)\Big) \quad \text{(edge } (i,j)\text{)}$$

$$\boldsymbol{u}_{ij}^{k+1} = \boldsymbol{u}_{ij}^k + \left(\boldsymbol{x}_i^{k+1} - \boldsymbol{z}_{ij}^{k+1}\right) \quad \text{(edge } (i,j)\text{)}$$

In (8.45), the $\boldsymbol{x}$-updates can be solved via numerical methods. When f_i's are decomposable, the solutions can be easily obtained via the proxy operator. The $\boldsymbol{z}$-updates have closed form solutions given by

$$\boldsymbol{z}_{ij}^{k+1} = \theta(\boldsymbol{x}_i^{k+1} + \boldsymbol{u}_{ij}^k) + (1-\theta)(\boldsymbol{x}_j^{k+1} + \boldsymbol{u}_{ji}^k)$$
$$\boldsymbol{z}_{ji}^{k+1} = (1-\theta)(\boldsymbol{x}_i^{k+1} + \boldsymbol{u}_{ij}^k) + \theta(\boldsymbol{x}_j^{k+1} + \boldsymbol{u}_{ji}^k)$$

where

$$\theta = \max\left(1 - \frac{\lambda w_{ij}}{\rho\|\boldsymbol{x}_i^{k+1} + \boldsymbol{u}_{ij}^k - (\boldsymbol{x}_j^{k+1} + \boldsymbol{u}_{ji}^k)\|_2}, 0.5\right)$$

The ADMM enables easy parallelization for the network lasso. In (8.45), updates with subscript i are independently calculated at node i, and updates with subscript ij are also calculated independently at edges (i,j). The parallelized ADMM solver gives the network lasso the scalability for clustering and optimization on large networks.

8.6 Conclusion

In this chapter, we presented the ADMM algorithm and its applications to large-scale network optimizations. Compared to traditional convex optimization algorithms, the ADMM enjoys two major advantages. First, it is a general purpose optimization tool that has been found useful for a broad scope of research fields and applications, with comparable and often better performances to domain-specific algorithms. Second, under a general context, the updates of ADMM often lend themselves to parallel implementations, which facilitate the parallel implementations of the ADMM and grant it the strength to solve large-scale problems. Throughout this chapter, we have seen that the flexible formulation of the ADMM enables it to represent a variety of problems on the network. This flexibility, combined with its easy parallelization, the ADMM among the most powerful tools for large-scale network analysis. We did not go deep into the detailed implementation of the ADMM in this chapter. Here we only point out that the ADMM computation naturally falls into the MapReduce computation paradigm [32] and can be implemented in modern distributed computing frameworks like Hadoop [33] and Spark [34]. We refer the readers to Chapter 10 of Ref. [13] for a detailed discussion of implementing ADMM under distributed computing environments.

References

[1] D. Gabay and M. Bertrand, A dual algorithm for the solution of nonlinear variational problems via finite element approximation, *Computers & Mathematics with Applications*, vol. 2, pp. 17–40, 1976.

[2] R. Glowinski and A. Marroco, Sur l'approximation, par éléments finis d'ordre un, et la résolution, par pénalisation-dualité d'une classe de problémes de Dirichlet non linéaires, *Revue Française d'automatique, Informatique, Recherche Opérationnelle. Analyse Numérique*, vol. 9, pp. 41–76, 1975.

[3] J. Bien, J. Taylor and R. Tibshirani, A lasso for hierarchical interactions, *Annals of Statistics*, vol. 41, no. 3, pp. 1111, 2013.

[4] S. Forouzan and A. Ihler, Linear approximation to ADMM for MAP inference, *Asian Conference on Machine Learning,* October 2013, pp. 48–61.

[5] J. Bien and R. Tibshirani, Sparse estimation of a covariance matrix, *Biometrika*, vol. 98, no. 4, pp. 807–820, 2011.

[6] R. Chartrand and B. Wohlberg, A nonconvex ADMM algorithm for group sparsity with sparse groups, *2013 IEEE International Conference on Acoustics, Speech and Signal Processing*, May, IEEE, 2013.

[7] J. F. Yang and Y. Zhang, Alternating direction algorithms for $\ell 1$ problems in compressive sensing, *SIAM Journal on Scientific Computing*, vol. 33, no. 1, pp. 250–278, 2011.

[8] B. Wahlberg, S. Boyd, M. Annergren and Y. Wang, An ADMM algorithm for a class of total variation regularized estimation problems, *IFAC Proceedings Volumes*, vol. 45, no. 16, pp. 83–88, July 2012.

[9] C. Shen, T.H. Chang, K.Y. Wang, Z. Qiu and C.Y. Chi, Distributed robust multicell coordinated beamforming with imperfect CSI: An ADMM approach, *IEEE Transactions on Signal Processing*, vol. 60, no. 6, pp. 2988–3003, 2012.

[10] J. Liu, P. Musialski, P. Wonka, and J. Ye, Tensor completion for estimating missing values in visual data, *IEEE Transactions on Pattern Analysis and Machine Intelligence*, vol. 35, no. 1, pp. 208–220, 2013.

[11] P. Das, N. Johnson and A. Banerjee, Online lazy updates for portfolio selection with transaction costs, *Proceedings of the 27th AAAI Conference on Artificial Intelligence*, June 2013, AAAI Press, pp. 201–208.

[12] R. Tibshirani, Regression shrinkage and selection via the lasso, *Journal of the Royal Statistical Society, Series B*, vol. 73, no. 3, pp. 273–282, 2011.

[13] S. Boyd, N. Parikh, E. Chu, B. Peleato and J. Eckstein, Distributed optimization and statistical learning via the alternating direction method of multipliers, *Foundations and Trends in Machine Learning*, vol. 3, no. 1, pp. 1–122, 2011.

[14] H. Wang and A. Banerjee, Online alternating direction method, *Proceedings of the 29th International Conference on Machine Learning*, pp. 1119–1126, 2012.

[15] T. Suzuki, Dual averaging and proximal gradient descent for online alternating direction multiplier method, *Proceedings of the 30th International Conference on Machine Learning*, pp. 392–400, 2013.

[16] H. Ouyang, N. He and A. Gray, Stochastic ADMM for nonsmooth optimization, *NIPS 5th Workshop on Optimization for Machine Learning*, 2012.

[17] W. Zhong and J. Kwok, Fast stochastic alternating direction method of multipliers, *Proceedings of The 31st International Conference on Machine Learning*, pp. 46–54, 2014.

[18] P. Zhao, J. Yang, T. Zhang and P. Li, Adaptive stochastic alternating direction method of multipliers, *Proceedings of the 32nd International Conference on Machine Learning*, pp. 69–77, 2015.

[19] X. Zhang and Z. Luo, A unified primal-dual algorithm framework based on Bregman iteration, *Journal of Scientific Computing*, vol. 46, no. 1, pp. 20–46, Jan. 2011.

[20] N. Parikh and S. Boyd, Block splitting for distributed optimization, *Mathematical Programming Computation*, vol. 6, no. 1, pp. 77–102, Springer, 2014.

[21] R. Zhang and J. Kwok, Asynchronous distributed ADMM for consensus optimization, *International Conference on Machine Learning*, pp. 1701–1709, 2014.

[22] K. Kelly, *Out of Control: The New Biology of Machines, Social Systems, and the Economic World*, Basic Books, 1994.

[23] E. Wei and A. Ozdaglar, Distributed direction method of multiplier, *51st IEEE Conference on Decision and Control*, pp. 5445–5450, 2012.

[24] J. Mota, J. Xavier, P. Aguiar and M. Püschel, D-ADMM: A communication-efficient distributed algorithm for separable optimization, *IEEE Transactions on Signal Processing*, vol. 61, no. 10, pp. 2718–2723, IEEE, 2013.

[25] L. Liu and Z. Han, Multi-Block ADMM for big data optimization in modern communication networks, arXiv preprint arXiv:1504.01809, 2015.

[26] S. Hosseini, A. Chapman and M. Mesbahi, Online distributed ADMM on networks, arXiv preprint arXiv:1412.7116, 2014.

[27] J. Nocedal and J. Wright, *Numerical Optimization*, Springer-Verlag, 2014.

[28] T. Goldstein, B. Taylor, K. Barabin and K. Sayre, Unwrapping ADMM: Efficient Distributed Computing via Transpose Reduction, Arxiv Preprint 1504.02147, 2015.

[29] A. Ramdas and R. Tibshirani, Fast and flexible ADMM algorithms for trend filtering, *Journal of Computational and Graphical Statistics*, vol. 25, no. 3, pp. 839–858, Aug. 2016.

[30] D. Hallac, J. Leskovec and S. Boyd, Network lasso: Clustering and optimization in large graphs, *Proceedings of the 21th ACM SIGKDD International Conference on Knowledge Discovery and Data Mining*, pp. 387–396, 2015.

[31] M. Yuan and Y. Lin, Model selection and estimation in regression with grouped variables, *Journal of the Royal Statistical Society: Series B*, vol. 68, no. 1, pp. 49–76, 2006.

[32] J. Dean and S. Ghemawat, MapReduce: simplified data processing on large clusters, *Communications of the ACM*, vol. 50, no. 1, pp. 107–113, 2008.

[33] T. White, *Hadoop: The Definitive Guide*, O'Reilly Media, Inc., Sebastopol, CA, 2012.

[34] M. Zaharia, M. Chowdhury, M. Franklin, S. Shenker and I. Stoica, Spark: cluster computing with working sets, In *Proceedings of the 2nd USENIX Conference on Hot Topics in Cloud Computing*, 2010, p. 10.

Chapter 9

Hyperbolic Big Data Analytics for Dynamic Network Management and Optimization

Vasileios Karyotis
National Technical University of Athens (NTUA)
Athens, Greece

Eleni Stai
École Polytechnique Fédérale de Lausanne
Lausanne, Switzerland

CONTENTS

Massive numbers of devices, growing user populations and voluminous amounts of produced/exchanged information are expected in the complex cyber-physical networks of the future. The new scales of operation give rise to a big network data era, where multi-layer networks form and users become content producers/consumers (prosumers). The challenges associated with the forthcoming networking environments require radical rethinking of current network analysis, management and operation practices. This chapter will focus on this effort, and more specifically on reinventing the machinery for computing key network metrics that allow improving network management/operation, while also developing more efficient overlay applications within demanding operational environments. Special attention is given to the impact of network evolution on the computation of such metrics, an aspect relatively neglected until recently. In order to efficiently compute key metrics associated with social or structural features of the network and track them when the infrastructure evolves, a big data analytics methodology, denoted as Hyperbolic Data Analytics (HDA), is applied. HDA is based on the embedding of graphs in the hyperbolic space, leading to more efficient management/operation, typically by exploiting hidden network structure. HDA is a characteristic example of developing computational intelligence over big network data and exploiting them for improving/optimizing both infrastructures and applications/services. HDA will provide the means for computing efficiently network analysis metrics, the evolution of which indicates the evolution of the corresponding network's structure.

The rest of the chapter is organized as follows. Section 9.1 introduces the problems addressed within their broader research field, while Section 9.2 presents the background on the HDA methodology employed in this chapter. Section 9.3 presents an efficient computation of complex network related metrics indicating the dependencies between entities of a big network data environment, while Section 9.4 investigates the application of HDA techniques for analyzing evolving and large-scale topologies. Finally, Section 9.5 recapitalizes the content presented and provides some indications for future work.

9.1 Introduction

Complex communication networks of the future are expected to consist of various heterogeneous sub-networks, overlaying each other and carrying unprecedented amounts of information [1]. Each of these sub-networks can be either a technological (physical) network, or a user-dictated (cyber) topology created by social or other types of interactions. Modern networking systems will consist of interdependent cyber-physical topologies with massive numbers of diverse sensory, relay and control devices, as well as their users with their social relations (cyber-physical networking systems). Such interdependence and amount of anticipated information will lead to more demanding scales of operation that will require more efficient handling, management and solution tools to address them.

Within these networking systems, all entities (devices, users and their interrelations) produce/consume data and even data can generate additional data (by correlating relevant ones), leading to the emergence of big network data environments [2]. In order to address the specific requirements of the big data environment of each complex (cyber-physical) topology, the methodologies of the future will need to be more efficient, targeted and scalable. This is especially true with respect to the efficient computation of various network metrics based on which the analysis and management of the network can be performed. For instance, computing efficiently and accurately the values of different distance and path-based centrality metrics in large-scale complex networks, e.g., betweenness, closeness, or traffic load centralities, is required for efficient design, optimization, management and monitoring of the infrastructures in terms of their traffic-carrying abilities and routing operations, as well as analyzing accurately the impact of the infrastructures on overlay services.

In this chapter, we focus on the efficient computation of such network metrics within big data environments, taking also into account the case where the network evolves over time. We apply a big data analytics framework, denoted as hyperbolic data analytics (HDA) [2], which can handle the required computation of network metrics in large-scale environments efficiently. With emphasis on routing, traffic/information relay, and in general distance and path-based applications in big data environments, we demonstrate HDA for the computation of relevant distance and path-based related metrics. The presented approach casts the computation as a network analysis problem and then exploits network embedding in hyperbolic metric space to perform the required computations, e.g., computations of distance and path-based centrality metrics. The framework allows exploiting "hidden" features of the underlying physical and cyber structures for improving precision in computations/approximations, while exploiting well-known properties of the hyperbolic space.

Furthermore, the aforementioned approach is taken one step ahead, by reconsidering it under the effect of network evolution, i.e., as the network topology varies with time, a very challenging aspect emerging in all modern complex cyber-physical networks. As networks and user behaviors vary with time, so will the paths connecting them along with the information/traffic carried through them, thus, calling for more adaptive and responsive approaches within the big network data environments mentioned above. The impact of evolution on the network will be investigated from an HDA perspective, especially considering the network structure, e.g., small-world, scale-free, random networks, etc. [3]. In more detail, the network evolution can be tracked via the network feature vector (NFV) methodology proposed in Ref. [4], which is based on the computation of key network metrics for the characterization of the network structure. In this chapter, on one hand we extend the NFV methodology for big network environments by combining it with HDA, while on the other hand, we study the emerging issues of applying the HDA methodology for tracking network evolution. Thus, we enable its use in such environments and eventually provide the tools for infusing computational intelligence in the big network data analytics of the future.

We should also note that even though our analytics approach (HDA) will be demonstrated especially for routing mechanisms (due to the selected network metrics), it can be straightforwardly extended in other fundamental networking operations, allowing for various extensions. It can be even applied in other application settings, e.g., web marketing [2], where the underlying cyber-physical system consists of customers and products of an online shop and problems such as targeted product recommendation can be investigated.

9.2 Big Data Analytics as Network Analysis

As mentioned already, modern networking systems inherently constitute multilayer cyber-physical networks, where physical devices interconnect socially linked users. Massive amounts of data are generated by the developed applications/services, the users and the physical devices. This volume of data consists of information to be exchanged, sensory data relevant to the monitoring and analysis of the systems, or control data aimed at responding to variations of the system environment. Analyzing such data in order to improve the infrastructures, services and operations, can be very demanding. In many cases, it is desired to analyze types of data, e.g., data related to the analysis of the infrastructure, which regard other types of data as well, e.g., data exchanged by devices, users, etc. This is characteristic for various network metrics for networking systems, e.g., those related with the routing operations. For example, in order to compute path-related centrality metrics, such as traffic load centrality [5,6], the topology needs to be analyzed (network-related data), while also considering the amount of traffic carried by each network node (user exchanged data). This is a typical example of big network data analytics problems and targeted methodologies are required to address similar ones.

General problems that fall under the big data analytics (BDA) category pose several challenges, described in various works in the literature [7]. However, despite the proliferation of BDA, and even though multiple perspectives have been employed, e.g., data mining, signal processing, machine-learning, etc., traditional analytics methodologies cannot completely address the full spectrum of challenges posed by network analytics problems as the ones described above. It seems that a new balance among flexibility-accuracy-scalability is yet to be achieved by new techniques. On one hand, BDA approaches need to be generic and applicable as piecemeal solutions to broad classes of problems. At the same time, current trends and products in analytics demand that solutions should be targeted towards the peculiarities of various applications and services they are addressing.

Given that, we advocate that a possible solution to achieving this balance, is a recently proposed analytics methodology, denoted by hyperbolic data analytics (HDA). HDA relies on graph embedding in hyperbolic metric spaces, i.e., a transformation of the original network to a more convenient form, depending on the application. This allows solving various BDA problems, e.g., network metric computations, via network problems that can be solved more efficiently in the embedded network. In the rest of this section, we present this approach in more detail.

9.2.1 Hyperbolic data analytics

Following the direction described above, the HDA framework exploits features of the hyperbolic geometry [8]. Apart from the computation of network metrics (network topology analysis), the framework can be employed in pure data analytics as well, by casting data dependencies into a network form and analyzing the corresponding data graph. General applications of interest in this case may include network economics, and product marketing [2]. The presented HDA technique can be seamlessly combined with traditional data mining, machine learning and other techniques to further increase performance and conserve computational resources (Figure 9.1).

The core concept of HDA is to embed the graph under analysis in hyperbolic space, as shown in the middle of Figure 9.1. This graph maybe the network to be analyzed, or a data graph representing dependencies among data items. Regarding the first, the analyzed graph can be of any type, e.g., random, scale-free, small-world, and can be either a physical, cyber or combination topology of the

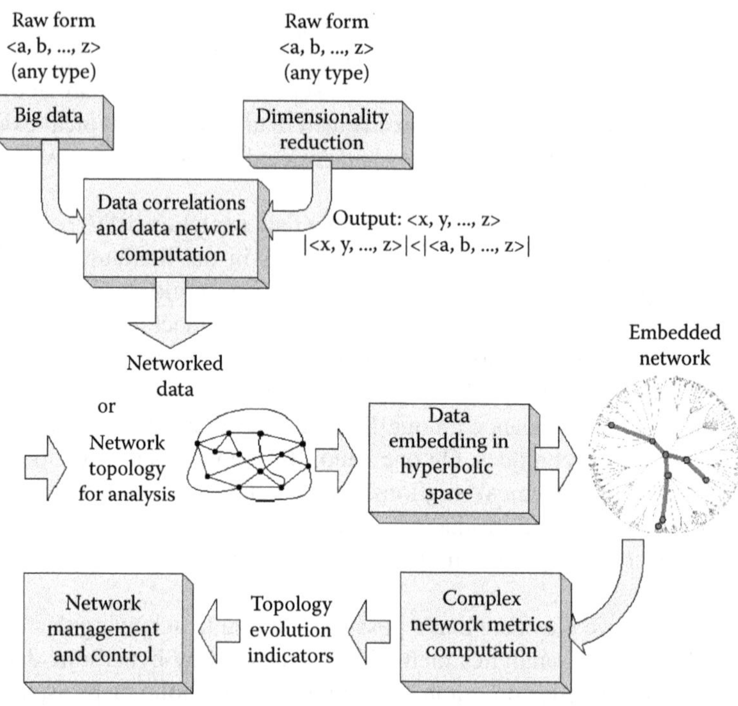

Figure 9.1: Hyperbolic Data Analytics (HDA) framework for network management and control.

layers that the networking system consists of. If the network represents the data graph, the data are eventually assumed available in network form, representing some (probably hierarchical) structure among them. To ensure this, a data correlations and network estimation phase precedes the embedding (top of Figure 9.1). Relations among data can be identified via various clustering, similarity-based (e.g., hyperbolic distance, interior product, cosine, Pearson, Kullback–Leibler divergence [9]) or inference techniques [10] and the correlations are reflected in the data graph, where nodes correspond to data items and links to their relations.

The embedding of the graph (network or data graph) in hyperbolic space consists of assigning hyperbolic coordinates to each 'data item' (network node) under consideration. The embedding allows exploiting hyperbolic distances and techniques already established over the hyperbolic geometry, e.g., greedy routing [11], etc., for solving the emerging network problem, e.g., routing or search problem. HDA accounts for efficient data embedding in hyperbolic space, exploiting its features. The latter can take place using any of the embedding techniques, i.e., Rigel, greedy or HyperMap, presented in Section 9.2.2.

In case of pure data analytics, an optional dimensionality reduction step of the analyzed data, e.g., either using techniques over hyperbolic space [12] or using traditional techniques [10], can be performed prior to or in parallel with data network estimation and data embedding. Depending on the application, this stage could aid in the scalability and efficiency of application-specific analytics that follow the embedding.

In summary, the HDA methodology begins with some preliminary steps to obtain a network graph to be analyzed, either of the topology of the infrastructure, or of data dependencies. The graph is embedded in hyperbolic metric space(s) and distances/paths among/between node pairs are computed, as dictated by complex network analysis metrics of interest. These metrics are indicators of the structure of the network and also of its variation, in case of a dynamic system. They can be used directly for data analytics purposes or for monitoring and management of the networking system, as will be shown with some examples in the rest of the chapter.

The key idea behind HDA is that the hyperbolic space exhibits scaling features that suit well requirements posed by big data, e.g., data volume, velocity and variety increase, among others. For instance, the volume in hyperbolic space increases exponentially fast, compared to the polynomial increase of the volume of the Euclidean space, which means more data can be accommodated in fewer dimensions, thus further conserving resources while maintaining analytical strength. Also, networks of arbitrarily large size can be embedded in low-dimensional (even as small as two) hyperbolic spaces without sacrificing important information as far as network communication (e.g., routing) and structure (e.g., scale-free properties) are concerned [11]. Consequently, hyperbolic spaces are congruent with complex network topologies and are much more appropriate for representing and analyzing big network/networked data than traditionally employed Euclidean spaces.

A significant observation regarding the use of the presented framework for data analytics in general, is that frequently, massive data that take network form when their correlations are properly defined are anticipated to form a scale-free type of topology. This is due to the fact that such data are typically produced by online social networks, which are cyber-physical networked systems and represent the activity of users, who as shown extensively in the literature form complex (e.g., scale-free) networks most of the times [3,13]. Scale-free networks are characterized by heterogeneity regarding the node degree, due to their power-law degree distribution, implying a tree-like network organization [11]. On the other hand, the exponential scaling of a circle and an area of a disk in hyperbolic space coincides with the scaling of the number of nodes of a tree with respect to their distance from its root [11]. As a result, the underlying tree-like organization of scale-free topologies (representing either the cyber-physical network itself or dependencies of data produced by its users) is well suited by the hyperbolic space, since hyperbolic geometry is the geometry of trees, allowing for more convenient analysis from many perspectives.

9.2.2 Network embedding in hyperbolic space

Oftentimes, it is needed to analyze very large network graphs, either representing the underlying communication infrastructure, or the data dependency graph in big network data environments. The scales of these graphs are massive and are only expected to increase in the future, as networks and services further expand. Their analysis is already rather cumbersome and costly [14], if possible at all. One approach to handle such scales would be to transform the topology under analysis into a form that allows faster analysis without loss of accuracy, or at least sacrificing a small portion of accuracy for analysis speed. One such approach is network (graph) embedding in metric spaces. More formally,

Definition 9.1 Assume M a metric space. Given a finite, connected graph $G(V,E)$, with vertex set V, an *embedding* of G on M is a mapping $C(G) : V \rightarrow M$ that assigns to every vertex (node) $v \in V$ a virtual coordinate $C(v)$.

Thus, the embedding of G in M is a transformation from the original graph space (discrete) to M with the objective to potentially perform several computations of interest in a more scalable and efficient manner. The assignment of coordinates to network nodes can be completely random or follow specific rules. If the metric space M and the coordinate assignment rules are properly selected, it is possible that the embedding will have appealing properties and yield several benefits which can be decisive for the performance of the system.

The choice of hyperbolic space as the target embedding space versus other available ones, e.g., Euclidean spaces, is dictated by the properties of the hyperbolic space mentioned above and/or the potential hidden structure exhibited by the data analyzed. Regarding the first, the hyperbolic space provides nice scaling properties that address the requirements posed by big data. With respect to the second, several types of data following a hierarchical classification, exhibit tree-like dependencies (e.g., data originating in scale-free like networks). Such data graphs can be efficiently embedded in the hyperbolic space, since the hyperbolic geometry is the geometry of the trees [11].

In the following, we briefly present three state-of-the-art techniques for network embedding in the hyperbolic space. Other techniques may be found in the literature, but we focus on these three, which have been used in various relevant (mostly routing and search) applications [11,15,16].

9.2.2.1 Rigel

Rigel embedding [15] is based on the principle that the coordinates assigned to each node should be such that each node pair's metric distance in the embedding will be approximately equal to the length of the hop-based shortest path between the corresponding pair of nodes in the original graph. In order to achieve this, the methodology adopts a multidimensional scaling technique where some nodes are initially selected as *landmarks*. For the landmark nodes, Rigel computes the shortest path trees towards all other nodes. Firstly, the hyperbolic coordinates of the landmarks are computed with the aid of a global optimization algorithm aiming to achieve that the distances among the landmarks in the new metric space M (e.g., the hyperbolic one) are as close as possible to their matching hop-based distances in the graph G. In order to embed the rest of nodes a linear programming technique, e.g., Simplex [17], may be employed to assign to each of the rest of the nodes coordinates that optimize their metric space distance from landmark nodes. In the latter, optimization is meant in the sense that for non-landmark nodes, the coordinates are computed in a way that each node's distances from landmark nodes are preserved by as much as possible between the initial graph G (in hops) and the final metric space M. The property of Rigel embedding to preserve distances, renders it very efficient for the computation of distance-based metrics (Section 9.3.1).

9.2.2.2 Greedy

A greedy embedding of an undirected graph $G(V,E)$ in a metric space M with distance function d, is a mapping $f : V \to M$ with the property that for every pair of distinct vertices $s,t \in V$ there exists a vertex u neighboring to s, such that $d(f(u), f(t)) < d(f(s), f(t))$. Thus, if for every pair of nodes s,t there exists a neighbor of s closer to t than s, such embedding is called greedy. By definition, greedy embedding in general, i.e., in every metric space, ensures 100% success rate of greedy routing in the corresponding metric space. A very useful property that can be used to check if a greedy embedding exists for a graph is that every graph containing a 3-connected planar subgraph has a greedy embedding [18]. Furthermore, it is proven that every network graph has a greedy embedding in two-dimensional hyperbolic space [19], which is not true for the two-dimensional Euclidean space. That is why the greedy embedding in hyperbolic space should be preferred over the one in Euclidean space, allowing also for efficient visualization in the two-dimensional space. An efficient and distributed algorithm for the greedy embedding is proposed in Ref. [16], which is however more suitable for smaller network topologies with short diameter [15] due to implementation constraints.

9.2.2.3 HyperMap

In HyperMap [13], it is assumed that the network to be embedded is in a random geometric form (spatial graph). For each node, it computes a radial and angular coordinate. The radial corresponds to the "popularity" of the node, while the angular reflects the "similarity" between nodes. Thus, the smaller the radial coordinate is, the more popular the node is considered. Similarly, the smaller the angular distance between two nodes, the more similar the nodes are expected to be. This way, the distance becomes a representation of a combined popularity-similarity metric. The connection probability between two nodes becomes a decreasing function of their hyperbolic distance, which means that as the embedding of nodes proceeds in a sequential fashion, connections of nodes to be embedded with already embedded ones take place by optimizing the trade-off between popularity-similarity.

HyperMap applies statistical learning methods to embed a network graph in hyperbolic space by constructing a new network graph trying to mimic with high probability the initial graph structure. Initially it disintegrates the graph that is to be embedded into disconnected nodes. Then it processes each node one-by-one according to a specific sequence that has been also optimally decided. For each processed node, it assigns its radial coordinate and computes its angular coordinate through a localized maximum likelihood function. The latter estimates the connection probability for a new link, given the radial coordinate of the node and the already embedded subgraph of the network. It proceeds until the whole network is eventually embedded in the metric space.

9.3 Hyperbolic Data Analytics for Network Management

Complex network metrics [3,20], such as path-based centrality metrics, the clustering coefficient, etc., become very helpful tools for the analysis and optimization of network structure, while their evolution serves as efficient indicator of the network evolution itself (which will be analyzed in Section 9.4.1). In this section, we will leverage on HDA (briefly outlined in Section 9.2.1) for the efficient computation of complex network metrics. These computations are crucial for tracking network evolution and the impact of the role of its individual actors allowing for efficient network management within large network and big data environments.

9.3.1 *Complex network metrics for network management in big data environments*

Various complex and social network analysis metrics can be employed for efficient network management as sufficient indicators of the type of network structure and/or the role of each individual node in it [3]. The employed metrics can be split in two categories, regarding the network as a whole or indicating properties of individual nodes, e.g., node importance in terms of popularity, information control, etc., [21]. The most frequently employed network analysis metrics in the past have been the node degree (node-oriented) and the associated degree distribution (network-oriented), the average path length (network-oriented), the clustering coefficient (CC) (network/node-oriented) and the variants of centrality measures (network/node-oriented) [3,22], which will be concisely presented in the following.

The *degree* of each node is the number of its connections (neighbors), while the associated *node degree distribution* uniquely characterizes a specific type of network topology. For example, scale-free networks are characterized by power-law degree distributions [11,23], whereas random and small-world network structures have usually Poisson degree distributions [20]. As a result, computing the degree distribution of a network (e.g., by fitting the node degrees to several distributions and choosing the one with the smallest fitting error) reveals the actual underlying structure, which can be very important for network management decisions and application/service optimizations.

The *average path length* is computed as the average of the shortest paths in graph (hop) distances for all node-pairs in a network [3]. It indicates how close two randomly selected nodes of the network are, revealing for example how fast can information be communicated across the network. Small average path length allows performing more efficient centralized computations, whereas longer average path lengths may indicate the need for distributed network management (e.g., more surrogate servers in a content distribution network (CDN) [24]). Note that the average path length requires only knowledge of the shortest path lengths and not of the actual paths, thus it is a distance-based metric, not a path-based one.

The *clustering coefficient* (CC) and centrality metrics can be defined for individual nodes and also computed as network averages over all nodes. The CC is a measure of the degree to which nodes in a graph tend to cluster together, e.g., it can be used to choose locations (nodes) for distributed decision centers when this is decided according to the average path length metric. For a specific network node, the local CC is given as the fraction of the number of links existing between the nodes within its neighborhood to the maximum number of links that could possibly exist among them (to the maximum number of potentially existing links among them in the fully connected graph) [3]. Computation of CC takes place at node level and can be performed efficiently over large networks. The same is true also for the node degree computations. However, this is not the case for the computation of path-based metrics, such as the centrality metrics explained in the following or the average path length. The presented HDA framework is an appealing solution in this case.

Centrality is a popular measure of node importance in a network [21]. Since importance can be subjective in different application settings, there exist various centrality metrics, e.g., degree centrality (a normalized version of node degree), closeness centrality, routing betweenness centrality, eigenvector centrality, etc., [3]. In this chapter, we will focus on the efficient computation of the two most important of them, namely routing betweenness centrality, which is a path-based metric and its variants, and closeness centrality, which is a distance-based metric. Traditionally, node betweenness centrality (BC) is defined in terms of graph (hop) distance for each node s, as the (normalized) sum of its partial betweenness centralities for all other node pairs u, v in the graph. The partial betweenness of s with respect to a (u, v) pair is the fraction of all (u, v) shortest paths that pass through s to the number of all u, v shortest paths [5,25]. Such a computation requires exact knowledge for all the existing shortest paths, i.e., not only of their length (in hops), but the exact node sequence in each path. Thus, computing BC may become cumbersome in modern cyber-physical and data analysis networks, and various approaches have been employed for computing it efficiently, including variants of its definition [5]. Node BC is a key indicator for identifying the control that a node has over the exchanged network traffic. Large BC values indicate that many shortest paths traverse a specific node, allowing it to control the information passing through them and have a key role in network management [21,26]. Thus, node-hubs in scale-free networks are expected to attain large BC values, and so is the case for other scale-free structures [27]. Node BC is a very important metric for network management used in many applications, e.g., [26,28] (fraud management in networks), [29].

Node closeness centrality [21,26] is defined as the (normalized) reciprocal of the sum of distances of a node from all other nodes in the network. The distances employed in the definition of node closeness centrality are typically shortest path (hop) distances. In general, a high value of node closeness centrality indicates the particular node is very close to all other nodes in the network (hop-wise), which can be taken into account in network management and application/service design.

In the above description, node BC was defined over hop-based shortest path distances. However, routing in a network may not rely on hop-based shortest path metrics, for various reasons, e.g., complexity [6] and fault tolerance [27], etc. Thus, in Ref. [27], an extended concept of the traditional BC was defined, denoted as routing betweenness centrality. *Routing betweenness centrality* (RBC) is defined exactly as BC, where now the paths are not only shortest hop-based ones but they can be determined by a loop-free routing protocol as well. The latter may determine shortest paths either in a source-oblivious way such as greedy routing [11,16], or based on both the source and the destination, while multiple alternative paths between source and destination may exist. By definition, RBC, emerges as a very important factor for network management, with wider potential applicability than BC in the traditional hop-based shortest path sense.

Traffic load centrality (TLC) is another variant of BC that falls in the RBC classification of metrics, as it aims at identifying central nodes in terms of the traffic they handle/control with respect to the total network traffic. TLC assumes the following routing scheme: each node sends a unit amount of some commodity (e.g., traffic) to any other node. The commodity is transferred from one node to its neighbor closer hop-wise to the destination. In case that more than one such relays exist, the commodity is equally divided among them. Then, TLC is defined as the total amount of traffic passing through a vertex via these exchanges [5]. Similarly to BC, TLC is based on shortest paths in terms of graph (i.e., hop) distances, e.g., [5,27], but other routing methods can be also considered in the framework of RBC, thus leading to variants of TLC itself.

By the aforementioned definitions, all the metrics presented can be very important for network management purposes and application optimization. However, as modern information and communication networks dramatically increase in size, generating/transferring massive amounts of data, the above metrics should be computed efficiently in flexible and scalable ways, ensuring the required level of accuracy. Indeed, shortest paths based on graph distances reveal a lot of information for social communication networks and other complex networks, as information is carried primarily through them (e.g., seeking the more influential/central node in an online Social Network such as Facebook or Twitter). However, hop-distances are hard to compute for large-scale graphs such as online social networks with millions/trillions of nodes [2,14,15]. In the state-of-the-art, the most efficient algorithms for the exact computation of BC and TLC with respect to time and space complexity are those suggested by Brandes [5,25]. Brandes' approach requires $\Theta(N \cdot |E|)$ time on unweighted networks with N nodes and E edges and $\Theta(N + |E|)$ space. Two main improving directions have been suggested, i.e., those simplifying the exact computations by exploiting network structure properties, e.g., [30,31], and those performing approximations that reduce time/space complexity, e.g., exploiting sampling [32–34] or restricting the length of the examined paths, such as the computation of ego-centralities [35,36]. The first category of approaches have a worst time complexity equal to Brandes' algorithm, whereas the second category of approaches perform only approximations of the node centralities with various levels of accuracy.

In the following section, we present an approach for efficiently computing TLC, leveraging on the HDA framework (Section 9.2.1), i.e., on the network embedding in hyperbolic space and the greedy routing techniques. This approach can be also applied for BC in the same way but without the same benefits in reducing the time computational complexity as in TLC. Thus, we will focus on TLC although a similar methodology can be employed for BC. In addition, TLC as a close variant of BC reveals almost the same information with BC for each node's importance regarding network operations. In the following section, we will also describe how HDA can be applied for the efficient computation of closeness centrality and the average shortest path length. A similar approach is adopted by [13,15,16] for routing purposes, but not for computing TLC. It consists of employing network embedding algorithms, e.g., in Euclidean, spherical or hyperbolic spaces, etc., in order to efficiently approximate the original node graph distances (i.e., hop distances) via coordinate systems' distances that rely on simple algebraic computations. Extensive evaluations have shown that the hyperbolic space embedding emerges as the most suitable for the aforementioned purposes [15,37].

9.3.2 Efficient computation of complex network management metrics: Average path length, traffic load, betweenness, and closeness centralities

In this section we present how one can efficiently compute some of the metrics described above by leveraging on the HDA framework. For demonstration purposes we focus on the average path length, TLC, BC and closeness centralities.

Towards achieving a trade-off among flexibility-scalability-accuracy, as mentioned in Section 9.2, TLC can be approximated by the hyperbolic traffic load centrality (HTLC), which was defined in Ref. [6]. HTLC may be less accurate than TLC for hop-based shortest path routing applications, but allows for more flexible and scalable computation within the HDA framework. The definition of HTLC is inspired by RBC's definition. HTLC also belongs to the category of RBC metrics (Section 9.3.1). It differs from TLC in terms of the routing scheme employed to assess the node importance. Specifically, it assumes greedy routing over hyperbolic coordinates (and distances) instead of hop-based shortest path routing.

According to greedy routing, each node forwards traffic to one of its neighbors with hyperbolic distance to the destination smaller than itself. As a result, greedy routing is a non-deterministic approach that uses only local information, i.e., each node is required to know the hyperbolic coordinates of its neighbors and the destination. Thus, it bears salient features that make it suitable for large-scale topologies, by reducing the complexity imposed by hop-based shortest path computations [15,37]. We stress that in HLTC we assume greedy routing over geometric space coordinates and not over shortest graph (hop) distances as TLC does. Although both routing schemes are greedy, TLC demands pre-computation of shortest paths and their lengths among all node pairs that may be much harder to compute over large (e.g., social) networks than the hyperbolic distances. The latter can be computed by simple algebraic computations using the hyperbolic coordinates of nodes [8,15]. In the sequel, we denote as greedy a path paved by greedy routing, and as greedy neighbors, all possible next hop relays of a node under greedy routing.

In order to obtain the hyperbolic coordinates of the network nodes, HTLC employs the Rigel embedding [15] in hyperbolic geometry, which is more suitable in terms of complexity for large-scale topologies. The other two types of embedding (greedy and HyperMap) may be applied as well. For example, the greedy embedding ensures the success of greedy routing in hyperbolic space in finding a path between a source and a destination, which is not always true for the Rigel embedding applied in arbitrary graph types. On the other hand, Rigel embedding achieves a high success rate of greedy routing over hyperbolic coordinates for scale-free graphs [15]. HTLC can be applied in any network type, but it is capable to approximate TLC with high accuracy for hop-based shortest path routing applications in scale-free network topologies [6] under the Rigel network embedding. This is due to scale-free graphs, which are often regarded as having a hidden hyperbolic structure [11] (Section 9.2.1). Thus, HTLC leverages on the network structure for improving its accuracy.

Given the above, *hyperbolic traffic load centrality (HTLC)* is formally defined as [6]:

Definition 9.2 Assuming that (1) each node sends a unit amount of some commodity (traffic) to each other node and (2) from each node (except from the destination) the commodity is equally divided to its greedy neighbors, then, HTLC is defined as the total amount of commodity passing through a vertex via these exchanges.

It should be noted that greedy routing is more efficient than shortest path routing for topologies, and it is shown in the literature that the paths paved by greedy routing are close to the shortest paths in length for many complex networks of interest especially the scale-free ones [11,16,38]. Thus, greedy routing can be employed in application of information transfer and search in graphs, in order to reduce the associated computational complexity. In this case, HTLC will be a more accurate metric for assessing the importance of nodes than TLC, while also bearing several advantages, such as flexible and scalable computations.

Following this approach, the average path length metric can be replaced by the very efficiently computed *average hyperbolic distance* metric, which is equal to the average of the hyperbolic distances of all node pairs [15] (a metric exploited in the efficient computation of closeness centrality below). The hyperbolic distance metric which is based on algebraic computations is shown to achieve high precision for multiple real-world topologies [15]. Extending this approach, the average path length can be further replaced by an average greedy path length metric, which for example can be computed as the expected length of all greedy paths between a source-destination pair averaged over all possible such pairs.

With respect to closeness centrality, the computations of hop-based shortest path distances can be replaced by algebraic computations of hyperbolic distances over the hyperbolic coordinates of the embedded nodes. This technique has been tested in the literature and provided results very close to the ground truth (i.e., when using the hop-based shortest path distances) [15] for a wide range of real network topologies. Rigel achieved a high accuracy in identifying the node ranking with respect to closeness centrality and outperformed existing schemes. For completeness purposes, in Table 9.1 we summarize the formulas for computing BC, closeness centrality (CLC) and the average shortest path length (ASP) according to hop-based and hyperbolic distances (denoted as HBC, HCLC, HASP, respectively).

In Table 9.1, $\sigma_t(s)$ ($\sigma_t^G(s)$) is the number of hop-based shortest (greedy) paths with source node s and destination t and $\sigma_t^v(s)$ ($\sigma_t^{Gv}(s)$) the number of hop-based shortest (greedy) paths with source node s and destination node t that pass via

Table 9.1 BC, CLC (of a node v), and ASP computed in the initial graph and the embedded network

Centrality	Standard computation	HDA computation
BC (without normalization)	$HBC(v) = \frac{\sigma_t^v(s)}{\sigma_t(s)}$	$HBC(v) = \frac{\sigma_t^{Gv}(s)}{\sigma_t^G(s)}$
CLC	$CLC(v) = \frac{N-1}{\sum_j dist(v,j)}$	$HCLC(v) = \frac{N-1}{\sum_j dist^H(v,j)}$
ASP	$ASP = \frac{\sum_{v,j} dist(v,j)}{N(N-1)}$	$HASP = \frac{\sum_{v,j} dist^H(v,j)}{N(N-1)}$

$v \neq s,t$. Also, $dist(v,j)$ ($dist^H(v,j)$) is the hop-based (hyperbolic [6,8]) distance of nodes v, j and the summations extend to all the network nodes. Note that the greedy paths connecting a source-destination pair need not be all of the same length as the hop-measured shortest paths in the definition of BC [5].

9.3.2.1 Example of efficient computation of HTLC with the HDA framework

In order to demonstrate how one may compute HTLC more efficiently via the presented HDA framework, we will provide a diagrammatic description of HTLC (Figure 9.2) and compare it with TLC (Figure 9.3) in terms of time

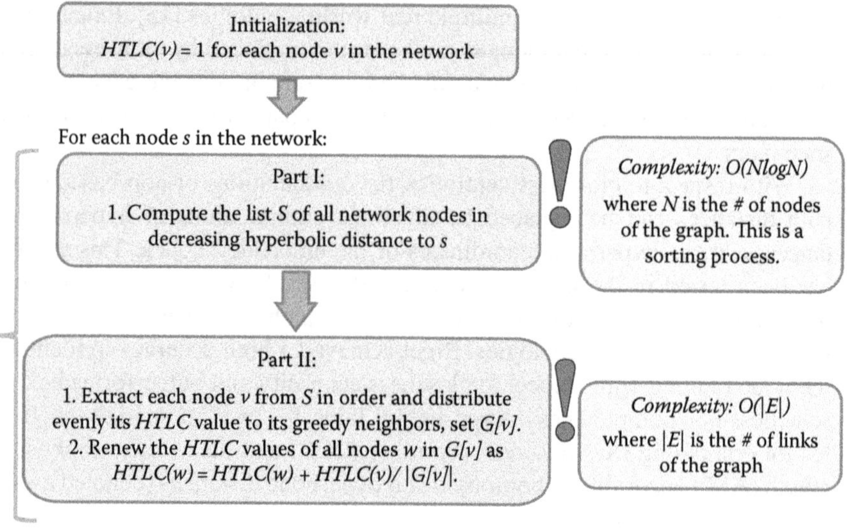

Figure 9.2: HTLC diagrammatic representation. Note that in this diagram we assume that the network is already embedded in hyperbolic space.

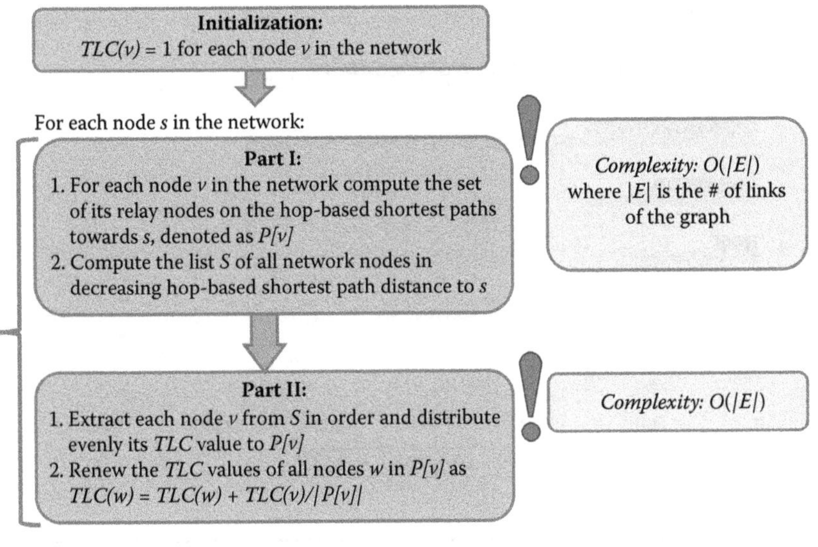

Figure 9.3: TLC diagrammatic representation.

computational complexity. A pseudo-code description of the algorithm is presented in Ref. [6]. We will not delve into the details of the algorithm as the goal of this chapter is to focus on the use of the framework for computing such metrics, aiding in network management, and not on the computations themselves.

In Figure 9.2, the sorting performed in Part I serves the purpose of examining the nodes in the correct order when computing the HTLC values in Part II. Specifically, since routing is greedy with respect to hyperbolic distances, if examining nodes in decreasing order of their hyperbolic distances towards the corresponding destination, a node that is already examined cannot be used again as a greedy neighbor of a next node. For comparison purposes, the diagrammatic computation of TLC, is presented in Figure 9.3 according to Brandes' approach [5,25]. The two approaches differ only in Part I. Part I in Figure 9.2 performs sorting and has a complexity equal to $O(NlogN)$ (if quicksort or heapsort is employed). Part I of Figure 9.3 has a complexity equal to $O(|E|)$ [25], where $|E|$ is equal to the number of links of the network graph. If also considering the outer loop, the complexity for Part I becomes $O(N^2 logN)$ and $O(N \cdot |E|)$ for HTLC and TLC, respectively.

Specifically, according to Ref. [39], the number of edges of a connected graph $|E|$ can be represented as N^a (where a is a real number that lies between 1 and 2). Then, we have a complexity of $O(NN^a)$ for Part I of TLC and $O(N^2 logN)$ for Part I of HTLC. Since $O(N^a) > O(NlogN)$, HTLC algorithm's complexity for Part I stays below the complexity limit imposed by $O(|E|)$ of TLC. For real graphs a

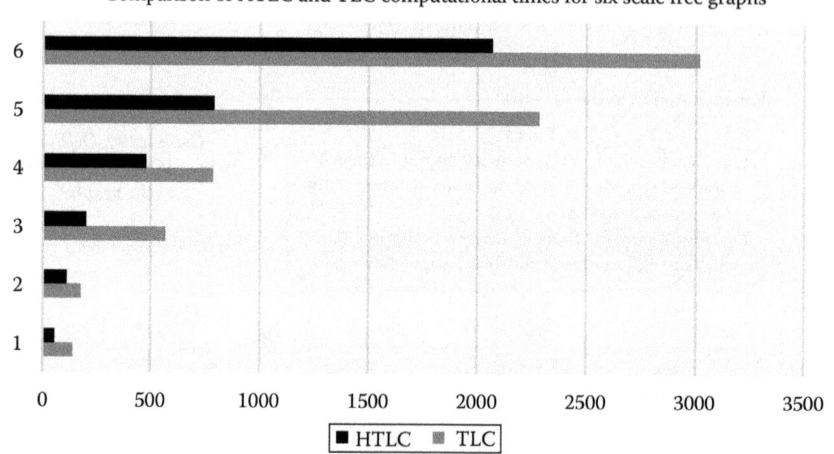

Figure 9.4: Comparison of HTLC and TLC with respect to computational time in six scale-free topologies with different densities and number of nodes and edges. The vertical axis shows the ID number of the scale-free topology and the horizontal axis shows the time in seconds for each approach in order to compute the HTLC and TLC values of all nodes. The topologies consist of 5000 up to 20,000 number of nodes and of 29,000 up to 400,000 number of links, respectively.

ranges from 1.16 for networks of autonomous systems up to 1.56 for citation networks [39] making this deviation more apparent.

In Figure 9.4, we show some numerical results confirming that while HTLC approximates closely TLC in terms of node ranking for scale-free topologies, it significantly reduces computational time. Node ranking refers to an absolute ordering of nodes according to their HTLC/TLC values and can be useful in many applications, e.g., in identifying most congested nodes. Specifically, HTLC coincides with TLC more than 65% in node ranking in all cases examined, while its computational time is more than 1.5 times lower than that required for TLC for dense graphs and more than 2.5 times lower for less dense graphs. More numerical evaluations and discussions for synthetic and real-world topologies are provided in Ref. [6].

As a synopsis, HDA can be leveraged on for computing efficiently CLC and TLC, and the average shortest path length. It can be also applied for BC. The computations of HTLC, HBC metrics become exact if routing/search is performed via greedy paths in hyperbolic coordinates, while they improve their precision for scale-free network topologies under Rigel embedding [6]. For CLC and the average path length, the precision achieved is high for topologies, as shown in Ref. [15]. Note that the clustering coefficient can be computed efficiently in any case for big data network topologies, due to the localized information required (on the extent of a node and its neighbors).

9.4 Computational Intelligence via Hyperbolic Analytics under Network Evolution

Modern networking systems do not remain static. They constantly evolve under the addition/deletion of users, physical links, protocols and services, etc. [40]. In this chapter we focus on those network modifications that lead to topological variations and can affect the physical or the cyber infrastructure, as well as the overlay applications and services. We show how the presented HDA framework can be used for creating computational awareness as the network evolves, which in turn can be used for optimizing the infrastructure and overlay applications/services. We first provide a concise picture of network evolution in typical networking systems, e.g., online social networks, mobile networks, etc., and then investigate the use of HDA for tracking large-scale network evolution via the topological metrics discussed previously. We investigate the potentials of exploiting HDA for more efficient analysis of network evolution and exploitation of the outcomes in network management.

9.4.1 Evolution of complex cyber-physical networked systems

Since the cyber-physical complex communication systems of the future will consist of various types of network topologies, they will exhibit rather diverse characteristics. The most important types of these topologies are the following: random (Erdõs–Rényi), scale-free (power-law degree distribution), small-world (small average shortest path length and relatively high clustering coefficient), lattice (nodes have certain/the same degree) and random geometric (multi-hop) topologies [3,41]. In this chapter, we focus on the first three, namely random graphs (RG), scale-free (SF) and small-world (SW), as they are the most frequently encountered ones in the cyber-physical networking systems of interest.

9.4.1.1 Impact of network evolution on topology and protocol mechanisms

The study of complex network structure and its properties has received considerable attention, especially in the past decade [20,22,41,42]. However, it was only recently realized that more realistic investigations are needed, addressing salient aspects of network structure, e.g., link distribution as network topology evolves in time [3,40]. The study of evolving networks is essential for developing more realistic applications.

Networks in general, and computer networks in particular, are characterized by various forms of topological and operational evolution [40]. For instance, different traffic patterns emerge as networks grow, or as user habits change over time. Several examples of real network evolution regarding the WWW or other prominent communication networks are included in Ref. [40]. Network evolution entails variations in the number of nodes/users, or most frequently variations of the number of connection links or changes in the interconnections of the nodes (i.e., the links). With respect to the latter, the authors in Ref. [43] proposed a continuum model for dynamic wireless networks, assuming that links change in a continuous fashion. They formulated network evolution through differential equations and obtained the long-term behavior of the average node degree. The work in Ref. [39] studied the evolution of real networks, implicitly focusing on power-law (scale-free) topologies, with respect to the metrics of the average path length (average node distance), network diameter (maximum node distance) and node degree (number of connections of each node). The evolution was analyzed under the regime of network growth, i.e., assuming that networks asymptotically increase in size rather than decrease, which is realistic for commercial communications networks. In [3,44] network evolution models for wireless multihop networks were considered, and especially, a methodology for adding features typical of social networks (e.g., short path length typical in small-world topologies, etc.) into multihop (random geometric) networks via network churn evolution mechanisms was proposed.

A network that does not change at all, or if the changes are taking place in a very slow manner so that the properties of the network are very slowly varying, is said to be in equilibrium. Examples include a random network with N nodes and $|E|$ edges, or a multihop topology on the same nodes and number of edges. On the other hand, non-equilibrium networks are those for which network evolution leads to variations of their properties, even though their original type remains the same, i.e., they remain RG if starting as RG. Examples include random networks where edges are added according to a specific rule, or nodes are deleted and added in a random fashion but connect to other nodes in a specific manner, e.g., the one defined for edge modification.

The most widely observed network evolution process is network growth, where new nodes or edges are introduced in the network [39,40]. The mechanism under which new nodes connect to existing ones or the edge addition process can be very critical for the evolution of the network as it grows. A direct outcome is that it affects the way various other mechanisms are designed and operate. For instance, in communication networks the addition of links might affect routing, while the addition of nodes (users) is expected to increase the volume of traffic transferred. Moreover, extreme topological modifications can have an adverse effect on the genuine character of each network. Consider for example the most popular rule for network growth, i.e., preferential attachment [3,20,22,41,42]. According to this, a new node will connect with higher probability with nodes that already have the most neighbors, i.e., they are most popular. This mechanism leads to the evolution of a regular lattice to a scale-free network when new nodes connect in this way to existing ones. Consequently, it becomes very critical to study the evolution of networks, according to the topological metrics of interest, i.e., the ones we presented in the previous sections, and determine the exact impact that evolutionary process are expected to have on communication systems and protocols employed. Furthermore, given the scale of current and future infrastructures, this will need to be done at a large scale. Addressing this with the presented HDA methodology will be the topic of the next section.

9.4.1.2 Network feature vector and network evolution tracking

In order to track and analyze network evolution, we adopt a new framework, recently proposed in Ref. [4]. It is based on the observation of network graph metrics of interest by introducing the notion of network feature vector. For that, assume a set of m metrics of interest of a network graph, denoted as $g_i, 1 \leq i \leq m$. The number m of available/employed network metrics can be arbitrary but finite, and depends on the application and problems emerging. For instance, the metrics used in Ref. [4] are sufficient for studying node importance under network evolution, while additional ones are required for, e.g., the study of resource allocation problems.

Network metrics can be also classified into node-oriented and edge-oriented ones. The first are characteristic of node properties, e.g., node centrality or node clustering coefficient. The second are characteristic of edge properties, e.g., average weight of links. Thus, the set of parameters employed can be split in two subsets, one with node-related features $\{g_i^{(n)}, 1 \leq i \leq m_1\}$ and a second with edge-related metrics $\{g_i^{(e)}, 1 \leq i \leq m_2\}$, $m_1 + m_2 = m$. The *network feature vector* (NFV), consists of all the employed network metrics arranged in vector form: $\mathbf{g}(t) = [g_1(t)\ g_2(t)\ \ldots\ g_m(t)]^T$, where in this compact expression we discard for simplicity the distinction of metrics as node-related and edge-related. If the topology varies with time, at least some of the features will be time-varying as well.

Through the feature vector $\mathbf{g}$, a specific network topology with its properties is mapped to a vector (point) in a metric space. As the topology evolves, so does the point in the metric space and the direction of the associated position vector $\mathbf{g}(t)$, i.e., the angle coordinates and measure of $\mathbf{g}(t)$ evolve in time. The dimension of the metric space depends on the number of metrics considered, so that different network feature spaces correspond to studying different properties of network evolution. The dimension of the feature vector (not its values) is independent from the size and order of the network graph.

The time-varying feature vector can be used to assess the similarity of different topologies, namely quantify how "close" the final topology is to the initial. Also, it can be used to assess the similarity of different types of topologies. Various distance or similarity metrics can be employed to quantify the distance/similarity between topologies [9]. In the special case that each component (metric) of the feature vector is independent of the rest, the network feature vector can be cast as a probability density function, and thus, in addition to distance, entropy-like measures can be employed as well [9]. For simplicity, in the following we are only concerned with distance and similarity metrics.

Distance metrics are more adequate to quantify the “magnitude” of network evolution, corresponding to the magnitude change of the network feature vector. On the other hand, inner product metrics (e.g., cosine metric) depict the “direction” of change (e.g., if a network changes drastically type) corresponding to the directional change of the network feature vector. One representative metric from each category is the Euclidean distance and cosine metric, quantifying the magnitude and direction of change, respectively, of two topology instances, $\mathbf{g}(t_1)$ and $\mathbf{g}(t_2)$:

$$d_e = \sqrt{\sum_{i=1}^{m} |g_i(t_1) - g_i(t_2)|^2} \tag{9.1}$$

$$s_c = \frac{\sum_{i=1}^{m} g_i(t_1) g_i(t_2)}{\sqrt{\sum_{i=1}^{m} g_i^2(t_1)}\sqrt{\sum_{i=1}^{m} g_i^2(t_2)}} \tag{9.2}$$

It should be noted that $\mathbf{g}(t)$ corresponds to the instance of a topology at time t, and $\mathbf{g}(t')$ denotes another instance, namely the evolved topology at time $t' > t$.

One of the most fascinating potentials of the NFV concept is the control capability over topology evolution. By properly defining a cost function of the form $J = h(\mathbf{g}(t_f), t_f) + \int_{t_0}^{t_f} k(\mathbf{g}(t), \mathbf{u}(t), t)dt$, where $[t_0, t_f]$ is the observation time interval, $h(\cdot), k(\cdot)$ properly defined continuous functions and $\mathbf{u}(t)$ a control function, one can potentially develop an optimal control problem on $\mathbf{g}(t)$ and exploit the constraints and controls for optimally balancing trade-offs relevant to network evolution and the benefit-cost relations of network processes emerging. The control function $\mathbf{u}(t)$ is related to the real mechanics of network evolution that determine how the topology evolves through the system of equation $\dot{\mathbf{g}}(t) = \mathbf{a}(\mathbf{g}(t), \mathbf{u}(t), t)$, where $\mathbf{a}(\cdot)$ determines the relation of the network feature with each control. Depending on the type of cost J, controls $\mathbf{u}(t)$ and relation between network feature vector-controls $\mathbf{a}(\cdot)$, various solution methodologies can be employed [45].

9.4.2 Network management under network evolution via hyperbolic data analytics

In evolving big data network topologies the NFV framework can leverage on HDA for tracking the network evolution in a scalable manner, trading-off scalability with precision. In this section we demonstrate this possibility with respect to some of the metrics presented previously.

In order to allow the HDA to aid in the analysis a large-scale evolving environment, the topology should be mapped in hyperbolic coordinates at each time instance of interest (via one of the embeddings listed in Section 9.2.2). Following, the metrics of interest that constitute the NFV components can be computed, as described in Section 9.3.2. The potential benefit comes from the fact that if the parameters of interest synthesizing the NFV can be computed more efficiently in the hyperbolic space, this will save significant resources and eventually allow more accurate tracking of network evolution.

In order to make this approach more concrete, if one selected as NFV components the metrics of TLC, closeness centrality and average path length described before, the time needed for the corresponding computations can be significantly reduced via HDA, as explained and indicatively shown in Section 9.3.2. This allows for real-time tracking of the network evolution, a fact that would be of significant importance for the management of the corresponding future networks. Note that, if one was interested in a wider set of parameters, their selection should be to strategically allow their computations to be accommodated, if possible, by the HDA framework, i.e., aim at performing the computations via hyperbolic coordinates/distances, thus reducing the associated computational complexity. As a counter-example, this approach might not be applicable for the computation of the clustering coefficient, which is computed based only on neighboring relations (Section 9.3.1). Figure 9.5 shows how HDA techniques can be integrated in the NFV framework, yielding efficient analytics for predictive and proactive management in evolving network topologies.

At each time instance, NFV tracks the evolution of complex network metrics in the corresponding NFV space. Due to the large scale of the considered

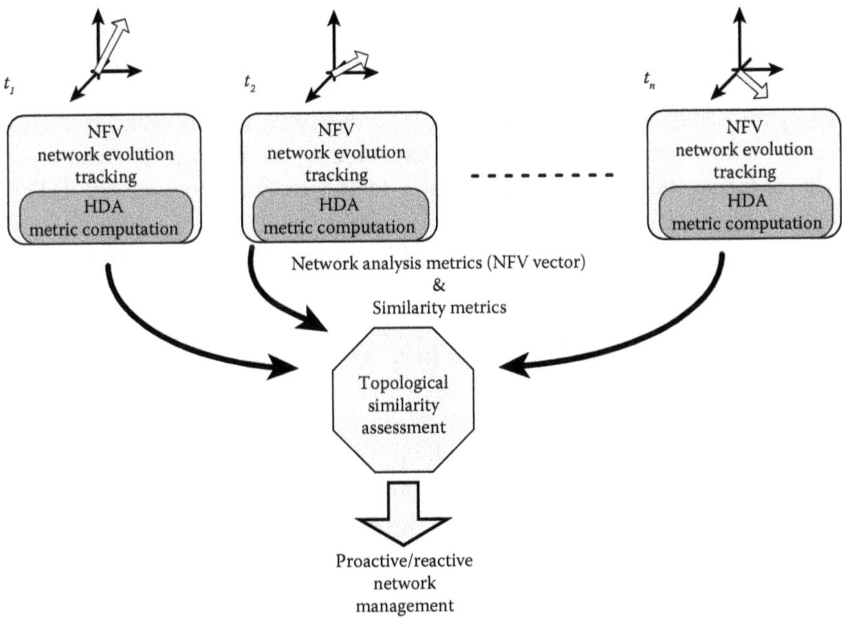

Figure 9.5: Exploiting HDA techniques in the NFV framework for predictive network management in evolving big network data environments.

evolving networks, HDA can aid in faster and more efficient computation of the components of NFV and thus provide a good idea of the network evolution without wasting many resources. This allows for more scalable prediction of the expected topology evolution, enabling predictive and proactive network management and control, when necessary.

The integration of HDA techniques in the NFV framework is not completely straightforward. Precision issues arise regarding the accuracy of computations. If routing/search/node importance decisions are based on hop-based shortest path routing, network evolution impacts the precision of HDA, requiring careful consideration of the HDA technique itself. This is due to the fact that HDA has a better precision in the computations of path-based centralities for scale-free topologies given the properties of hyperbolic space (Section 9.2.1), in case of shortest path routing, especially under the Rigel and HyperMap embeddings [13,15]. However, a scale-free network topology may evolve to a random one under certain evolutionary rules, as it was demonstrated in Ref. [4], e.g., after random edge additions/deletions. Thus, HDA will be expected to achieve high precision initially, which reduces as the network evolves. In this case, one should either sacrifice precision in computations for obtaining scalable computations in time and space, or investigate the application of other forms of network embedding that are more suitable for all types of networks. Note that the precision of metrics that are based on distances and not on paths, e.g., closeness centrality (CLC) and average shortest path length (ASP) will not be affected under the Rigel embedding, as in this case the precision achieved is due to the fact that Rigel preserves distances, as explained in Section 9.2.2. Furthermore, although HDA may not maintain its precision in nodes' path-based centrality computations under network evolution, it is expected to track network evolution, i.e., via capturing the change of HTLC of a scale-free graph towards the HTLC of a random graph. In the latter, the HTLC-based node ranking may differ from the corresponding TLC-based node ranking, a fact that will happen to a smaller extent in the former.

In the following, we present some indicative numerical results, illustrating the integration of HDA within NFV for tracking network evolution. The results are shown in Figures 9.6 through 9.8. We consider three initial topologies, namely one random graph (RG), one small-world (SW) and one scale-free (SF) with 500 nodes each and approximately 4000 links. At each of them we apply edge churn in a random manner, i.e., we randomly delete existing links and randomly add links between existing pairs of nodes that are not already connected, where both edge addition and deletion are performed with almost equal probabilities (addition takes place at a slightly higher probability to ensure network connectivity). The topologies indicated as evolved in Figures 9.6 through 9.8 correspond to the final topologies of RG, SW, SF after applying the random edge churn for multiple iterations. For HDA the Rigel embedding with 30 landmarks is applied over an eight-dimensional hyperbolic space.

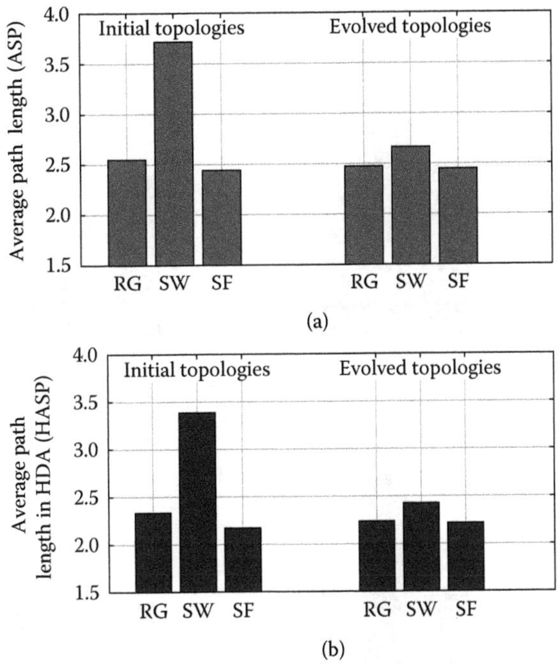

Figure 9.6: (a) ASP in initial and evolved topologies. (b) HASP in initial and evolved topologies. Comparison of the evolution of diverse topologies under edge churn via NFV and precisely the average path length metric with and without HDA.

Three metrics are chosen for tracking the network evolution, namely the average path length, the traffic load centrality and the closeness centrality. We chose these metrics as they can be computed via HDA, and our aim here is to exemplify the potential of integrating HDA in NFV and demonstrating the inherent trade-off offered between precision and scalability. By observing the results, the following important observations can be made. Firstly, with respect to the metrics of average path length and closeness centrality that are both distance-based, HDA achieves a very good precision in their computation for all topologies. This is basically due to the Rigel embedding that preserves graph (hop-based) distances in hyperbolic space. In other words, HASP, HCLC assume values very close to the ones of ASP, CLC for all topologies (initial and evolved topologies of all types). In addition, satisfactory precision is achieved for the computation of the traffic load centrality which is a path-based metric, i.e., HTLC approaches TLC for all types of topologies, although better approximation is achieved for the scale-free graphs (initial topology), as expected (Section 9.3.2). The most important observation is that the integration of HDA in NFV does not impact the tracking of the network evolution, even if not achieving high precision, as in the

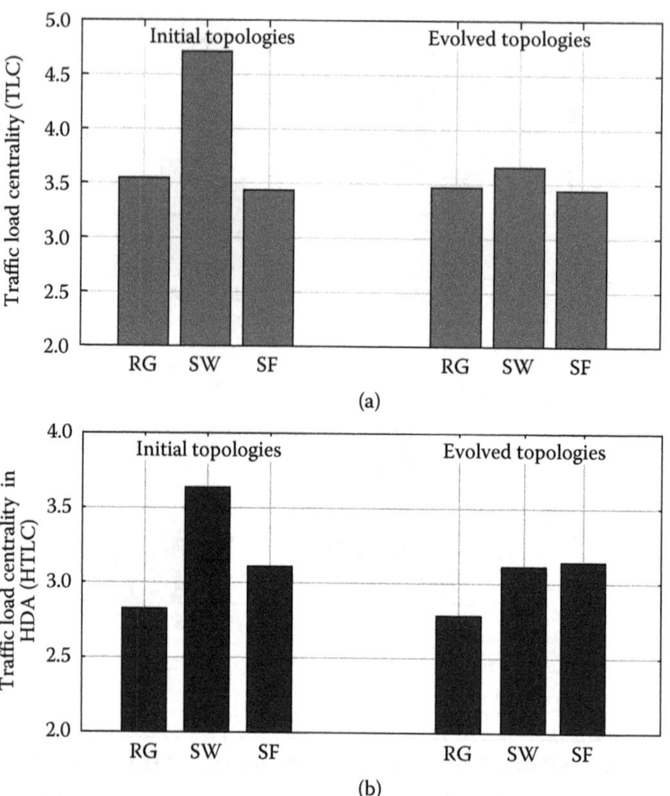

Figure 9.7: (a) TLC in initial and evolved topologies. (b) HTLC in initial and evolved topologies. Comparison of the evolution of diverse topologies under edge churn via NFV and precisely the traffic load centrality metric with and without HDA.

case of TLC, HTLC. This means that in all cases, the evolution of metrics (and even their quantitative variation) from the initial to the evolved topologies under HDA is very similar to the case where one would compute the metrics explicitly via their definitions.

At this point, we need to note that the initial and evolved RG topologies are expected to be similar, due to the random edge churn process (RG is a network in equilibrium under this specific evolution rule). Regarding the SF topology which has also similar initial and evolved topologies, these two topologies differ structurally, i.e., the evolved is more random since links are deleted from hub nodes and added randomly to other nodes with fewer connections. Also, note that we may need more metrics (e.g., clustering coefficient, betweenness centrality, degree distribution, etc.) to differentiate between different topologies,

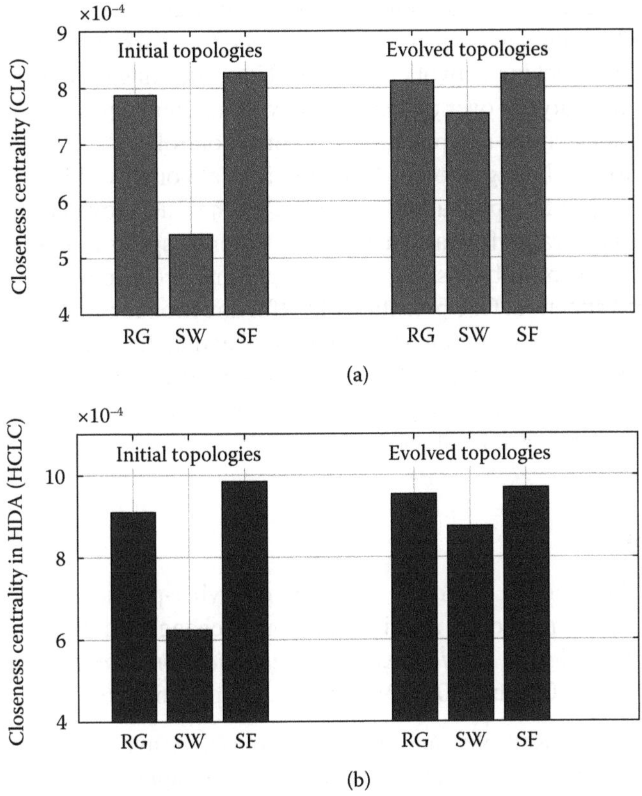

Figure 9.8: (a) CLC in initial and evolved topologies. (b) HCLC in initial and evolved topologies. Comparison of the evolution of diverse topologies under edge churn via NFV and precisely the closeness centrality metric with and without HDA.

i.e., using only the employed three metrics is typically not sufficient for differentiating between SF, RG topologies. However, it can be easily observed that the SW topology moves closer to a random one for all metrics. More relevant results on these aspects can be found in Ref. [4].

9.5 Discussion and Future Work

In this chapter we presented a framework (hyperbolic data analytics - HDA) for performing efficient network analytics in large-scale and complex cyber-physical networks. HDA allows computing efficiently and in a scalable manner topological metrics, such as the traffic load centrality and in general distance and path-based metrics, for complex networking topologies, or massive data dependency graphs. Furthermore, it was demonstrated that it is possible to integrate HDA techniques in another framework (network feature vector - NFV) employed for tracking network evolution. Thus, such integration allows performing efficient analytics over dynamic and evolving topologies, enabling proactive network management and potentially optimal control.

The proposed integration of HDA in NFV, although viable in principle, and feasible in specific application examples, as the one provided in the previous section, is not straightforward in any case. Several aspects require more research and various open problems, e.g., those regarding precision over the hyperbolic space, need attention. One potentially fruitful direction for addressing such issues is to investigate the potential use of other embedding approaches, different from the ones employed to date. The results presented in this chapter indicate that the proposed HDA-NFV integration is possible and that much more research is ahead for the interested audience.

References

[1] Q. Zhu and L. Bushnell. Networked cyber-physical systems: Interdependence, resilience and information exchange. In *Proceedings of 51st Annual Allerton Conference on Communication, Control, and Computing (Allerton)*, October 2013, Monticello, IL, pp. 763–769.

[2] E. Stai, V. Karyotis, and S. Papavassiliou. A hyperbolic space analytics framework for big network data and their applications. *IEEE Network Magazine*, 30(1):11–17, 2016.

[3] V. Karyotis, E. Stai, and S. Papavassiliou. *Evolutionary Dynamics of Complex Communications Networks*. CRC Press - Taylor & Francis Group, Boca Raton, FL, 2013.

[4] V. Karyotis, E. Stai, and S. Papavassiliou. On the impact of network churn on topology evolution in complex networks. In *Proceedings of the 14th International Conference on Wired and Wireless Internet Communications (WWIC)*, Thessaloniki, Greece, pp. 227–240, 2016.

[5] U. Brandes. On variants of shortest-path betweenness centrality and their generic computation. *Social Networks*, 30(2):136–145, May 2008.

[6] E. Stai, K. Sotiropoulos, V. Karyotis, and S. Papavassiliou. Hyperbolic traffic load centrality for large-scale complex communications networks. In *Proceedings of the International Conference on Telecommunications (ICT)*, Thessaloniki, Greece, pp. 153–157, May 2016.

[7] D. Boyd and K. Crawford. Six provocations for big data. In *A Decade in Internet Time: Symposium on the Dynamics of the Internet and Society*, Oxford Internet Institute, pp. 1–17, September 2011.

[8] J. W. Anderson. *Hyperbolic Geometry*. 2nd ed. Springer-Verlag, London, UK, 2007.

[9] S.-H. Cha. Comprehensive survey on distance/similarity measures between probability density functions. *International Journal of Mathematical Models and Methods in Applied Sciences*, 1(4):300–307, 2007.

[10] R. Lior and O. Maimon. *Clustering Methods: Chapter in Data Mining and Knowledge Discovery Handbook*. Springer Science+Business Media, 2005.

[11] F. Papadopoulos, D. Krioukov, M. Boguñá, and A. Vahdat. Greedy forwarding in dynamic scale-free networks embedded in hyperbolic metric spaces. In *IEEE INFOCOM*, San Diego, CA, pp. 2973–2981, 2010.

[12] I. Benjamini and Y. Makarychev. Dimension reduction for hyperbolic space. *American Mathematical Society*, 137(2):695–698, 2009.

[13] F. Papadopoulos, C. Psomas, and D. Krioukov. Network mapping by replaying hyperbolic growth. *IEEE/ACM Transactions on Networking*, 23(1):198–211, February 2015.

[14] A. Ching, S. Edunov, M. Kabiljo, D. Logothetis, and S. Muthukrishnan. One trillion edges: Graph processing at facebook-scale. In *International Conference on Very Large Data Bases (VLDB)*, Kohala Coast, HI, pp. 1804–1815, 2015.

[15] X. Zhao, A. Sala, H. Zheng, and B. Y. Zhao. Efficient shortest paths on massive social graphs. In *Proceedings of the 7th International Conference on Collaborative Computing: Networking, Applications and Worksharing (CollaborateCom)*, Orlando, FL, pp. 77–86, 2011.

[16] A. Cvetkovski and M. Crovella. Hyperbolic embedding and routing for dynamic graphs. In *IEEE INFOCOM*, Rio de Janeiro, Brazil, pp. 1647–1655, 2009.

[17] G. B. Dantzig and M. N. Thapa. *Linear Programming 1: Introduction*. Springer-Verlag LLC, New York, 1997.

[18] C. Papadimitriou and D. Ratajczak. On a conjecture related to geometric routing. *Theoretical Computer Science*, 344(1):3–14, 2005.

[19] R. Kleinberg. Geographic routing using hyperbolic space. In *Proceedings of the IEEE INFOCOM*, Anchorage, AK, pp. 1902–1909, 2007.

[20] R. Albert and A.-L. Barabási. Statistical mechanics of complex networks. *Reviews of Modern Physics*, 74(1):47–97, January 2002.

[21] S. P. Borgatti. Centrality and network flow. *Social Networks*, 27(1):55–71, 2005.

[22] M. Newman. The structure and function of complex networks. *SIAM Review*, 45(2):167–256, 2003.

[23] A.-L. Barabási and E. Bonabeau. Scale-free networks. *Scientific American*, 288(5):50–59, May 2003.

[24] B. Krishnamurthy, C. Wills, and Y. Zhangn. On the use and performance of content distribution networks. In *Proceedings of the 1st ACM SIGCOMM Workshop on Internet Measurement*, Burlingame, CA, 2001, pp. 169–182.

[25] U. Brandes. A faster algorithm for betweenness centrality. *Journal of Mathematical Sociology*, 25(2):163–177, 2001.

[26] E. M. Daly and M. Haahr. Social network analysis for information flow in disconnected delay-tolerant manets. *IEEE Transactions on Mobile Computing*, 8(5):606–621, May 2009.

[27] S. Dolev, Y. Elovici, and R. Puzis. Routing betweenness centrality. *Journal of the ACM*, 57(4):25:1–25:27, May 2010.

[28] V. Zizmond. Fraud management based on betweenness centrality. http://www.admiralondemand.com/applying-betweenness-centrality-to-our-fraud-management-strategy/ (accessed 26 September 2016).

[29] A. Papadimitriou, D. Katsaros, and Y. Manolopoulos. *Social Network Analysis and Its Applications in Wireless Sensor and Vehicular Networks*, pages 411–420. Springer, Berlin, 2010.

[30] R. Puzis, P. Zilberman, Y. Elovici, S. Dolev, and U. Brandes. Heuristics for speeding up betweenness centrality computation. In *International Conference on Privacy, Security, Risk and Trust (PASSAT) and International Conference on Social Computing (SocialCom)*, Boston, MA, pp. 302–311, 2012.

[31] M. Baglioni, F. Geraci, M. Pellegrini, and E. Lastres. Fast, exact and approximate computation of betweenness centrality in social networks. In F. Can, T. Özyer, and F. Polat (eds.), *State of the Art Applications of Social Network Analysis*, Part of the Series Lecture Notes in Social Networks, Springer, Heidelberg, pp. 53–73, 2014.

[32] U. Brandes and C. Pich. Centrality estimation in large networks. *International Journal of Bifurcation and Chaos*, 17(7):2303, 2007.

[33] D. A. Bader, S. Kintali, L. Madduri, and M. Mihail. Approximating betweenness centrality. In *5th International Conference on Algorithms and Models for the Web-Graph (WAW)*, San Diego, CA, pp. 124–137, 2007.

[34] R. Geisberger, P. Sanders, and D. Schultes. Better approximation of betweenness centrality. In *Proceedings of the 10th Workshop on Algorithm Engineering and Experiments (ALENEX)*, San Fransisco, CA, pp. 90–100, 2008.

[35] M. Everett and S. P. Borgatti. Ego network betweenness. *Social Networks*, 27(1):31–38, January 2005.

[36] J. Pfeffer and K. M. Carley. k-centralities: Local approximations of global measures based on shortest paths. In *Proceedings of WWW '12 Companion*, ACM, Lyon, France, pp. 1043–1050, 2012.

[37] X. Ban, J. Gao, and A. van de Rijt. Navigation in real-world complex networks through embedding in latent spaces. In *Proceedings of the 12th Workshop on Algorithm Engineering and Experiments (ALENEX)*, Austin, TX, pp. 138–148, 2010.

[38] D. Krioukov, F. Papadopoulos, M. Kitsak, A. Vahdat, and M. Boguñá. Hyperbolic geometry of complex networks. *Physical Review Letters*, 82(3):036106, September 2010.

[39] J. Leskovec, J. Kleinberg, and C. Faloutsos. Graphs over time: Densification laws, shrinking diameters and possible explanations. In *Proceedings of 11th ACM SIGKDD International Conference on Knowledge Discovery and Data Mining*, Chicago, IL, pp. 177–187, 2005.

[40] S. N. Dorogovtsev and J. F. F. Mendes. *Evolution of Networks: From Biological Nets to the Internet and WWW*. Oxford University Press, New York, 2003.

[41] T.G. Lewis. *Network Science: Theory and Applications*. Wiley, Hoboken, NJ, 2009.

[42] M. Newman. *Networks: An Introduction*. Oxford University Press, New York, 2010.

[43] S. Papavassiliou and J. Zhou. A continuum theory-based approach to the modeling of dynamic wireless sensor networks. *IEEE Communications Letters*, 9(4):337–339, April 2005.

[44] E. Stai, V. Karyotis, and S. Papavassiliou. Topology enhancements in wireless multihop networks: A top-down approach. *IEEE Transactions on Parallel and Distributed Systems*, 23(7):1344–1357, April 2012.

[45] D. E. Kirk. *Optimal Control Theory: An Introduction*. Dover Publications, New York, 1998.

Chapter 10

Predictive Analytics for Network Big Data Using Knowledge-Based Reasoning for Smart Retrieval of Data, Information, Knowledge, and Wisdom (DIKW)

Aziyati Yusoff, Norashidah Md. Din, and Salman Yussof
Universiti Tenaga Nasional
Selangor, Malaysia

Assad Abbas and Samee U. Khan
North Dakota State University
Fargo, North Dakota

CONTENTS

10.1 Introduction

The study of data science, analysis, and decision-making has evolved from translating the raw data, information sharing, and knowledge representation to the wisdom of the Web of Things. Starting from the idea of architecting a wisdom hierarchy, the base of the hierarchy is built upon a data, information, knowledge, and wisdom (DIKW) pyramid [1]. The pyramid or hierarchy as illustrated in Figure 10.1 consists of the components of DIKW. In addition, the recent trend in the needs of network big data has challenged this hierarchy to be redefined and implemented beyond the contemporary use of data analytics. If data on its own is raw, information is adding the context, knowledge is describing on how to use it and wisdom is explaining why to use it [2], then the big data is challenging the hierarchy to be in a more complex yet integrated structure.

In this chapter, the first section describes the background of DIKW and the challenges that it poses to the big data network. The second section deliberates

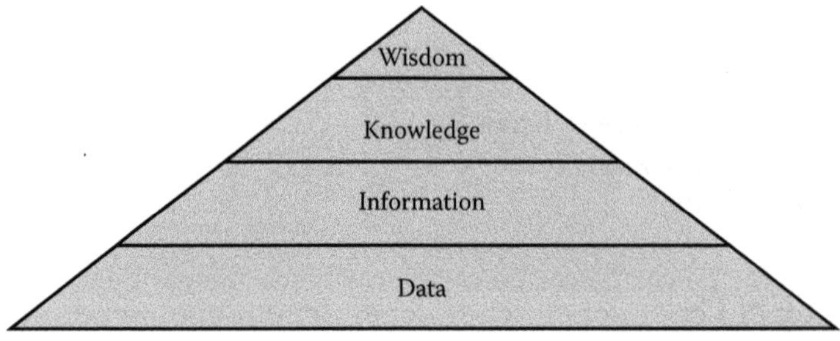

Figure 10.1: The DIKW hierarchy.

on the form that most big data takes in enterprises, such as the mathematical model, statistical inferences, machine learning, and decision-making techniques. Hypothesis testing was included to illustrate the engineering process of this statistical method. Section 10.3 discusses the knowledge-based reasoning that can be induced from the statistical method performed in the previous section. The integration of these two scopes of study is constructed by the technique of ontology and semantic network. Therefore, from this technique the predicate calculus, propositional logics, and knowledge representations are highly enumerated. The platform of ontology that is used throughout this study is by using the web ontology language (OWL). The OWL is used to design the big data feed and is expected to demonstrate a quality performance for use in the DIKW platform. Section 10.4 of this research demonstrates the smart retrieval that can benefit from the OWL design and performance described in the preceding section, and Section 10.5 concludes the chapter.

10.2 DIKW Hierarchy in Network Big Data

10.2.1 What is DIKW?

The term DIKW was introduced in the 1980s [3,4] where originally, the wisdom phase was not proven because it was inferred that wisdom would deal with values and judgments. The ability to deal with values and judgments was not foreseen in computer and automated machines at that time [5,6]. Data is an important element in the build of a computer [7]; from data, people found ways provide further information on a subject matter. For the past 15 years, there has been tremendous progress in computational knowledge management [8]. However, the mathematical and computational sciences never stop at knowledge-sharing methodologies; 5 years later, the wisdom of the DIKW hierarchy came into the limelight [9,10].

10.2.2 DIKW and the challenges in big data network

As big data is making waves in the 2010s, people are revisiting DIKW. When data was treated as the main subject for all computing machines, they were organized and architected such that they could be represented in a manageable way for storage and retrieval purposes. However, with the inception of Cloud computing as an alternative storage, the types of data have evolved from structured to semistructured and unstructured forms. This type of data is now known as big data.

The term "big data" is always associated with its characteristics generally called the 5Vs. The 5Vs are volume, velocity, variety, veracity, and value [11,12]. Data science was originally considered mostly as technical but as the enterprises demanded more in terms of data storage and processing power, big data-enabled methods started emerging rapidly. Therefore, the big data operator should have the ability to accommodate the variety of data structures, the volume it carries, the velocity of information retrieval, the veracity of its users' behavior, and the value that it represents.

In addition, if the big data is to be operated for the purpose of information sharing and knowledge management, then the DIKW hierarchy is best considered for the system architecture and smart retrieval engine. The aforementioned operational study is also known as network big data. The analytics among other things involve the intelligent phase, the design phase, and the choice phase. As a performance measure, the implementation of analytics depends on the success of the engine to validate and verify the problem for decision-making processes.

10.2.3 The network big data framework and architecture

The network big data in this chapter will be discussed in two case studies. Case study I is about flood information management in the state of Kelantan, Malaysia and case study II is about the demand and the skills qualifications of the labor market in Malaysia. The method of analysis for these two case studies will involve statistical inferences and knowledge-based reasoning in network big data prediction.

Figure 10.2 illustrates the general framework of network big data for DIKW smart retrieval. The framework consists of the input parameters, the process involved, and the output parameters. The input parameters are also known as the design parameters and are all the possible big data feeds. The process involved

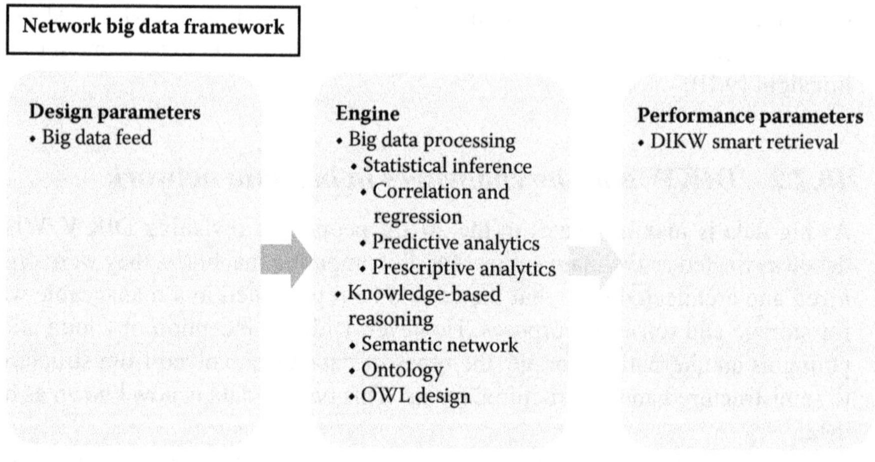

Figure 10.2: The network big data framework for DIKW smart retrieval.

is also referred to as the engine and consists of a statistical inference approach and knowledge-based reasoning methodology, while the output parameters are the performance parameters and are the objectives of this study, i.e., the DIKW smart retrieval.

The challenge in network big data is mainly about how the data is read, processed, and translated. Big data comprises all kinds of data types and are high in complexity. This complexity is also challenged by the anticipation of big data within the Internet technology. As a result, the environment of network big data is dynamic and should be able to transform the data feed into the desired form of data presentation. In this chapter, the method of handling network big data is deliberated by the approach of a smart retrieval engine. This engine is aimed to sort the data in accordance with the DIKW hierarchy.

In addition, the architecture for this network big data demonstrated in both of the case studies is illustrated in Figure 10.3. The network big data architecture is built upon three main parameters, i.e., methodology, design, and performance.

The methodology component comprises all forms of data readings including the types of *.txt* for text data, *.csv* for numerical data, *.kml* for geographic-based location data, and *.script* for online data services. The design component is built on all possible elements of a computing program including the algorithm, tools, and interface. The algorithm involved is a connotation to ontology engineering

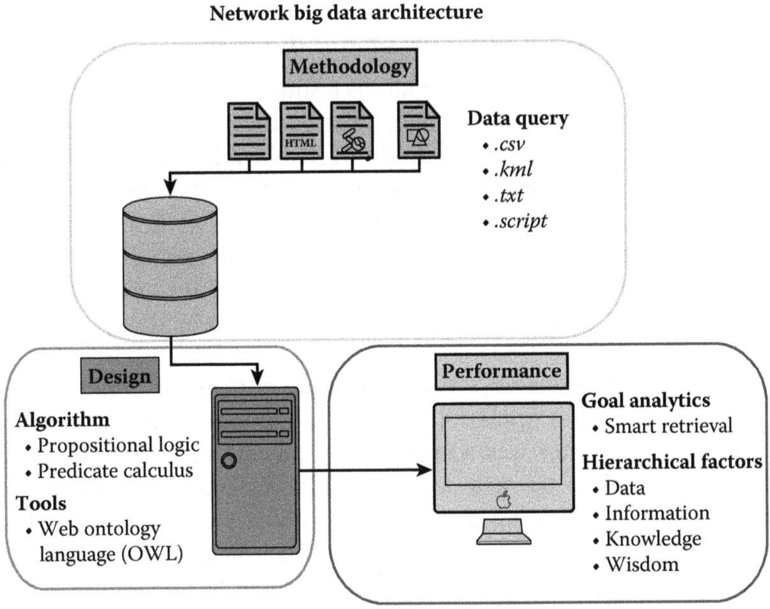

Figure 10.3: The network big data architecture for DIKW smart retrieval.

design and consists of propositional logic and predicate calculus. The tool used for this study is the OWL. The interface for this design is the uniform resource identifiers (URI) and the resource description framework (RDF). As for the performance of this study, the architecture is explicitly showing that the two main elements are the smart retrieval by using the hierarchical factor of DIKW.

10.3 Statistical Inferences and Analytics in Network Big Data

10.3.1 Hypothesis testing for big data

One of the methods that entrepreneurs, data scientists, and engineers usually apply for the decision-making process is statistical analysis. When a study involves the nature of the relationship to a certain subject matter, the differences among groups, or the independence of variability between two or more factors, the approach taken is usually hypothesis testing [13]. In light of the above, big data methods seem suitable to be evaluated for their relationship from one component to another, or from one class to another, or from one category to another. This is further proven by the need for the analytics on data collection, analysis, and its interpretation.

10.3.2 Correlation and regression analysis

To illustrate the application of hypothesis testing, two case studies were chosen. The hypotheses will concentrate on correlation and regression analysis. The correlation and regression analysis is done to study the relationships and the strength of the connections between the involved parameters. Therefore, it fits the study of data analysis toward the hierarchy in interpreting the information, knowledge, and wisdom of the findings. Case study I is about the findings in flood management in the state of Kelantan, Malaysia and case study II is about the findings in the demand and skills qualification of the labor market in Malaysia.

1. *Case Study I: Flood management in the state of Kelantan, Malaysia*

   A case study was carried out on the flood disaster in the state of Kelantan, Malaysia. This disaster was seen to be an annual event so many researchers keep coming back to the state to study its causes and implications. The flood is always happening during the northeast monsoon which usually takes place between October and February every year. One of the studies had suggested that the flood keeps happening due to the volume of the rainfall at that time of year which had caused the area to be under a constant downpour for several days which contributed to the rise of the water level. Hypothesis statements were made on this fact including the alternatives. However, the end result was quite surprising in that the flood was not totally relying on the amount of rainfall. The relationship measured for this hypothesis was showing a weak connection. This made the researchers investigate other factors further, that might trigger the cause of the flood [14].

The sample readings of correlation and regression for this case study illustrated the results during the flood period in the state of Kelantan [15]. However, the graphical representation of water level with respect to rainfall is showing some scattered data from the correlation readings. This did not represent a strong relationship between the two variables to deduce them as the cause of the flood incident.

2. *Case Study II: The demand and skills qualification of the labor market in Malaysia*

Another case study was done on best practices and a comparative analysis on the labor market in Malaysia, and the training institutions that are responsible to fulfill the industry needs and demands. Like most of developed and developing countries, Malaysia is also coping with the needs of highly skilled manpower resources to work at the plants and in industries. To administer the quality skilled workforce, Malaysia has its own government agency that manages the occupational and skills qualifications. The main aim of this agency is to accredit the skilled workers with the right level of certification.

The hypothesis made for this study was on the relationship of a good quality of skilled workforce and its dependency on the occupational analysis (OA) and the curricula that were founded and developed by the governing agency. The study was carried out by interview sessions with focus groups. As a result, most of the respondents agreed that to produce knowledgeable workers, the OA and strong curricula indeed have a high influence on the successful implementation of training institutions and should be able to fulfill the needs of industry [15]. This result is contrary when compared to the case study I because the regression value of the resulting computation is showing a strong relationship between the two variables.

The above two case studies demonstrated the use of correlation and regression on a hypothesis. This approach is usually dealing with numerous aspects of relationships in the social sciences field of studies. Though the parameters might be technical and scientific, this correlation and regression is used to prove the relationships in society's problem solving. However, correlation is not causation [16]. The study on correlation and regression does not provide insight to the analyzed data and information; knowledge might be extracted but is limited to some extent. Therefore, the hypothesis testing, correlation, and regression seem feasible at the foundation level of a wisdom abstraction. In consequence, further investigations, techniques, and a computational approach are needed to process the wisdom of the subject matter.

10.3.3 Predictive analytics

Before computers were created, perhaps the term "prediction" was more likely to be used by astrologers and clairvoyants [17]. It was considered a taboo to some cultures and a religious ritual to some others. In statistical analysis, data prediction can be performed by identifying the variables, parameters, and environments. Graphical representations usually involve the curve of a normal distribution. From the normal curve, the study on its properties and characteristics may lead the researcher to predict the next data reading. This prediction method is only carried out by comparing the pattern of previous data sets of the subject matter.

To illustrate the predictive analytics, case study I is referred. The study on predicting the flood in the state of Kelantan had been carried out over a long period due to the nature of its occurrence, which is almost annually. The state of Kelantan, Malaysia has an area of 117 km^2 of land bounded by the latitude from $6°7'$ N to $6°14'$ N, and longitude from $102°9 1/2'$ E to $102°14'$ E. The Kelantan River is the largest river of the state and has a delta built, but it is poorly drained [18].

Predicting the flood disaster from a statistical hypothesis is similar to forecasting computation by a normal distribution curve. However, the challenge to the data readings in this case is that the aim of the study is to reduce the disaster to 0. This is unlike the normal forecasting process that is used to maximize profits for specific business purposes.

In predicting the flood incident, several assumptions and limitations are made to define the scope of the study. The assumptions to this case study include: (1) the rainfall data readings are of normal distribution, (2) the water level has a very high dependency on the volume of rainfall, and (3) other relative independent variables are very small or negligible. In addition, the limitations to the research parameters should also consider other factors for the occurrence of this incident including wind movement, monsoon, global phenomena, tidal waves, and the gravitational force of moon and earth that affects the rise and fall of sea levels.

The above-mentioned assumptions and limitations to the case study are best presented in a similar geographical information system (GIS). Simultaneously, the result of the prediction will be illustrated in image format, such as geospatial mapping or keyhole markup language (KML). The simulation of the rise in water level is also expected to run if the calculation of the prediction is accurate by using accurate parameters of data prediction. On the other hand, such an application is seen as static and provides data solely to the disaster alert but contains less information, knowledge, and wisdom that would be able to aid not only the authorizing agencies but also the affect communities as a whole.

In the early 2000s Google Inc. started to use an engine known as Hadoop MapReduce [19]. Hadoop is an open-source Java-based programming language that aids the processing of massive data sets in a distributed environment [20].

This engine is also responsible for predicting the search term that is expected from the user input. As a comparison, the approaches of predicting the output by using Hadoop MapReduce in Java platform and statistical analysis differ in many aspects yet are able to be interconnected. Hence, this study is deliberating on the idea of integrating a source of statistical computation that can be applied to a machine-learning platform such as an ontology. This will be further discussed in the next sections.

10.4 Knowledge-Based Reasoning of Data Prediction in Network Big Data

10.4.1 Semantic network and ontology of big data

A semantic network is used to show the connections from one knowledge to another as a set of concepts. It has also been used as a graph structure to represent knowledge in patterns of interconnected nodes and arcs, which were first developed for artificial intelligence and machine translation [21,22]. The semantic network is favorably used for knowledge representation in ontologies; an ontology is a way to formally model the structure of a system. This includes the definitions of the relationships and concepts within the system and usually the representation of logic in the form of propositional logic and predicate calculus [23,24].

As an application for business websites and online enterprises, a semantic web can be created by using a formal ontology approach. This semantic web is able to extract, analyze, and manipulate the data in accordance with the business requirements [25]. One of the languages that is used widely for this purpose is the web ontology language (OWL). The OWL is a semantic markup language for publishing and sharing ontologies on the World Wide Web [26] and the common syntax includes the extensible markup language (XML) or RDF.

10.4.2 OWL design for online prediction

To illustrate the OWL design for online prediction, case study I is revisited. Defining its semantic network produces the OWL design for this case study. Classes and subclasses are identified and the relationships between one class to another are defined. This is illustrated in Ref. [27]. The semantic network of flood management is concentrated from the study of the big data it carries. The big data of this case is annotated by main classes and subclasses including hydrology data, tidal wave and monsoon data, telemetry data, and meteorology data.

From the classification modeling above, the properties of each of subclass with its main class and instances can be defined thereby illustrating the relationships of the model. The relationships of the above examples include object properties, subproperties, and functional properties such as:

1. *hasData* (NetworkBigData, (HydrologyData, TelemetryData, TidalWaveMonsoonData, MeteorologyData))

2. *hasData* (HydrologyData, (Rainfall, WaterLevel))

3. *providesAlert* (HydrologyData, WaterLevel) & *hasData* (WaterLevel, (GunungGagau, RantauPanjang, Jeli, Dabong, Laloh, GuaMusang, KualaKrai, Kusial, Tualang, Aring, Jenob, PasirPutih, KotaBharu))

4. *hasInformation* (NetworkBigData, HydrologyData) & *hasInformation* (HydrologyData, WaterLevel) & *hasInformation* (WaterLevel, (GunungGagau, RantauPanjang, Jeli, Dabong, Laloh, GuaMusang, KualaKrai, Kusial, Tualang, Aring, Jenob, PasirPutih, KotaBharu))

5. *mitigateAction* (FloodInformationManagement, NetworkBigData) & *emergencyResponse* (FloodInfomationManagement, (WaterLevel, (GunungGagau, RantauPanjang, Jeli, Dabong, Laloh, GuaMusang, KualaKrai, Kusial, Tualang, Aring, Jenob, PasirPutih, KotaBharu)))

Consequently, an ontology architecture of the above-mentioned semantic network is inferred as illustrated in Figure 10.4. The ontology is showing the relationships of the instances with the subclasses and the main class of the study. This ontology relationship is further translated to the predicate calculus. The predicate calculus for the above illustrated ontology among others include:

1. $\forall x1$: (HydrologyData $(x1)$) $\Rightarrow$ NetworkBigData $(x1)$

2. $\forall x2$: (TelemetryData $(x2)$) $\Rightarrow$ NetworkBigData $(x2)$

3. $\exists x3$: (MeteorologyData $(x3)$) $\Rightarrow$ NEONASAData $(x3)$

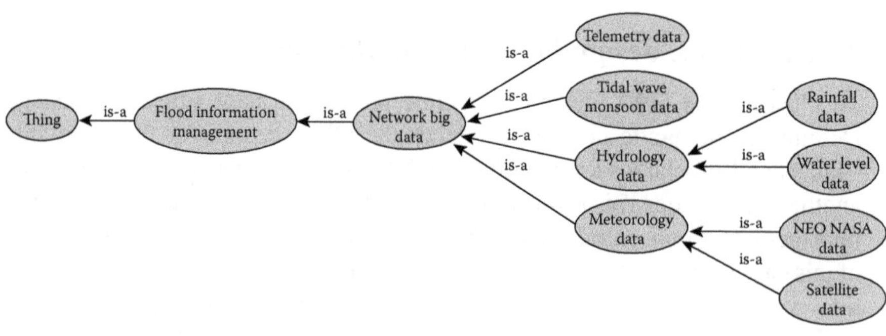

Figure 10.4: The ontology for network big data for flood information management.

4. $\exists x4$: (WaterLevelData ($x4$)) $\Rightarrow$ HydrologyData ($x4$)

5. $\forall x$ P (x) $\Leftrightarrow$ P ($x1$) $\wedge$ P ($x2$) $\wedge$ P ($x3$) $\wedge$ P ($x4$)

Hence, it is from this process of designing the semantic network that the identification of properties, subproperties and instances, the design of ontology relationships, and the translation of predicate calculus that the engine of smart retrieval is instructed and operated. In general, the translation of the above ontology engineering study is using the OWL method.

10.4.3 OWL performance for DIKW and beyond

The ultimate performance for an OWL design is to produce a semantic web application using XML or RDF syntax and data interchange. The advantages of using the OWL design for semantic network architecture include the ability to identify the conceptual modeling, the relationship representations, and the object properties.

As for case study I, the performance analysis is about the actions that are able to be implemented once the flood prediction is activated. This is as illustrated in Figure 10.5. The main aim of the study is to generate the wisdom that can be abstracted from the data, information, and knowledge of the flood readings at the respective reading stations. Consequently, the wisdom in action when this disaster happens will include: (1) provision of a clean water supply, (2) manageable evacuation sites, (3) continuous connections and communication network, (4) road access, and (5) continuation of food supply.

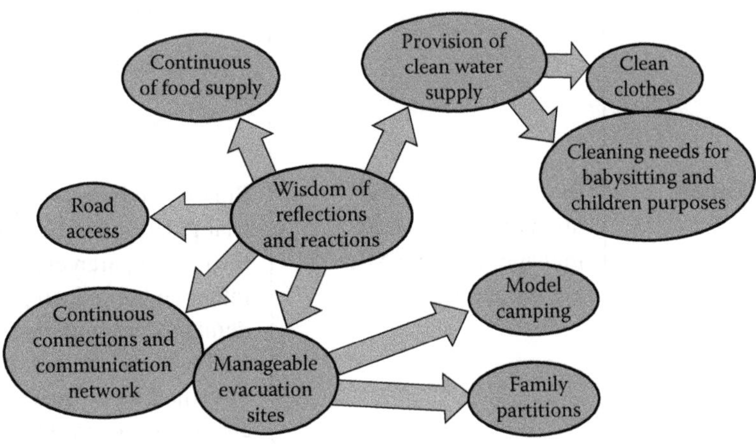

Figure 10.5: The wisdom of reflections and reactions to the flood incident.

Table 10.1 The generic details of big data, design, engine, and performance parameters of case study I and case study II

Case study	Case study I: Flood management in the state of Kelantan, Malaysia.	Case study II: The demand and skills qualification of the labor market in Malaysia.
Big data	Hydrology data (rainfall and water level), GIS data (geospatial mapping, location), meteorology data (longitude, latitude, monsoon).	Technical and vocational education training (TVET) data in selected countries i.e., Malaysia, Singapore, Australia, and Canada.
Design	OWL design which includes the following parameters: 1. Rainfall data 2. Water level data 3. Telemetry data 4. NEO NASA data 5. Tidal wave and monsoon data	OWL design which includes the following parameters: 1. Occupational framework 2. Occupational competency standard 3. TVET qualification 4. TVET standards & curriculum guide 5. TVET terms used 6. industry partnership 7. training institutions
Engine	Smart web using the taxonomy of disaster management in XML syntax and URI	Smart web based on the triangulation method using the design parameters to integrate the industry demands, training needs analysis, and the numbers of skilled workforce that are able to be produced.

(Continued)

Table 10.1 (Continued) The generic details of big data, design, engine, and performance parameters of case study I and case study II

Performance	OWL performance which includes the following parameters: 1. *Data*—water level readings 2. *Information*—alert on the flood to occur within hours or days 3. *Knowledge*—mitigation actions, emergency response and rescue from the authorities, access road, and evacuation centers 4. *Wisdom*—the number of nearby evacuation centers with details of distance, capacity, etc., the nearest access road, available transport, and the duration of moving	OWL performance which includes the following parameters: 1. *Data*—number of training institutions and occupational standards developed 2. *Information*—best practices of TVET by comparative analysis in selected countries, and recommendations on standard methodology 3. *Knowledge*—TVET implementation and curriculum developed that are able to fulfill the needs of labor and industry demand 4. *Wisdom*—standard methodology for occupational frameworks, and competency standards

As a summary, for both of the previous case studies, the OWL performance is expected to provide services which should comply with the initial objectives of the study. The design, performance, and engine for the case studies are illustrated in Table 10.1. The OWL performance is analyzed in the form of DIKW perspectives. This summary is also to illustrate that the integration of prediction analysis with the DIKW hierarchy can be performed successfully.

10.5 Smart Retrieval Prediction Engine in Network Big Data

In comparison to the study of information retrieval (IR), the issues that are affecting the performance of this area of study include the ability of crawlers, indexing, and ranking [28]. Designing a smart retrieval online prediction engine on an ontology platform is seen to be the next frontier to the available IR engine. The constraint of this application is to retrieve the alert of flood incident in the form of a DIKW hierarchy.

This is as illustrated in Figure 10.6. The network big data for this system involves the process of sentiment analysis for social media networks, statistical inferences, and web crawling from the available authorities' web applications. The analyzed data will undergo the architecture of semantic network, the OWL design, and identification of propositional logic in knowledge representation. These three processes are the fundamental structures of the online prediction engine. The syntax of XML or RDF from the OWL design is strengthening the operations of this engine. As an output, the engine is expected to be able to process the network big data to produce the DIKW of a flood incident.

Simultaneously, the graphical representation on how the DIKW of flood incident can be implemented is illustrated in Figure 10.7. This illustration is called a decision tree and depicted in accordance with the DIKW hierarchical level. The online prediction for big data should be able to produce a smart retrieval in this form of representation. Data is at the basic level, the most essential build of decision sciences engineering. However, data is smart when the analysis is able to interpret the information and knowledge from the studied materials. The data is at wisdom level when more than just knowledge representations can be abstracted.

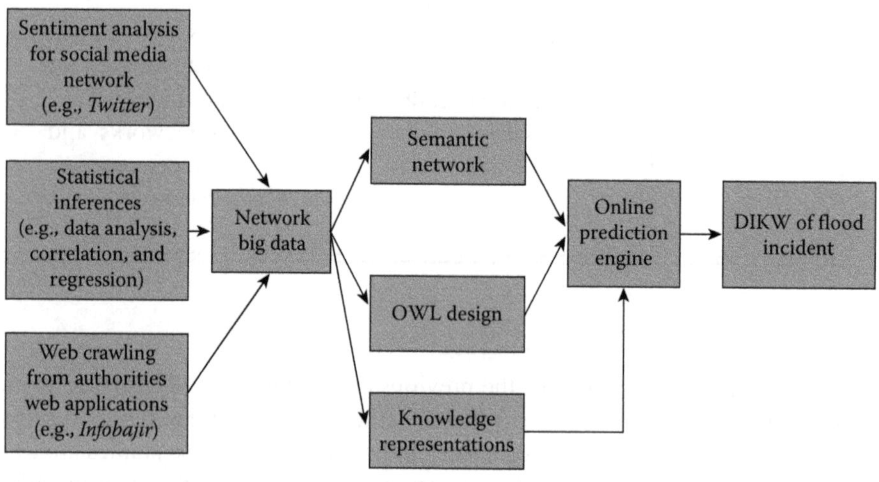

Figure 10.6: The network big data prediction engine for DIKW of a flood incident.

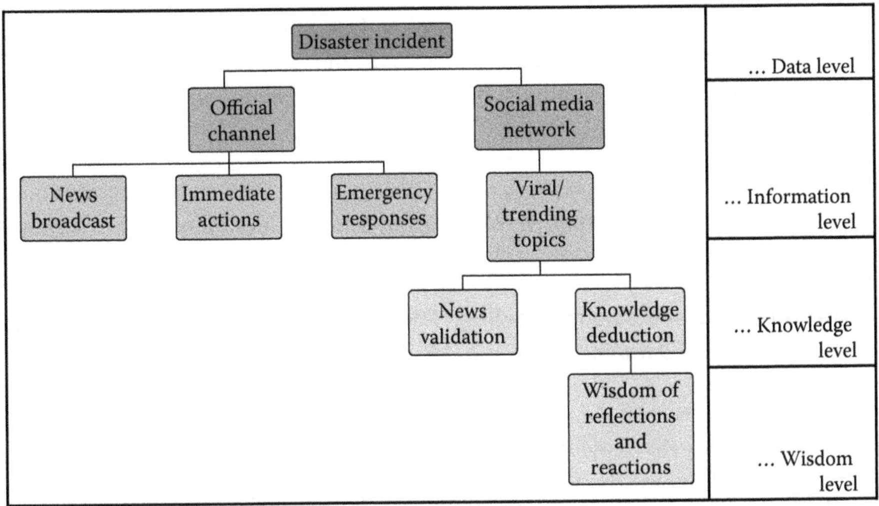

Figure 10.7: The decision tree and DIKW level of abstraction for a disaster incident.

10.6 Conclusion

Big data is always associated with its properties of 5Vs: volume, velocity, variety, veracity, and value. The challenge in this study was to utilize the network big data by producing a DIKW hierarchy to the product of its processes. As a comparison, the analytics approach was initially started with a statistical testing method. From the statistical analysis, the study can define the hypotheses, the data to be manipulated, the operations such as correlation and regression, and finally the prediction by a normal distribution forecasting method. However, this approach is further deliberated by defining the ontological relationships of the data and its propositional logic. The semantic network is defining the classes and subclasses of the research study; OWL design is chosen as the platform to design the parameters. The knowledge representations of the semantic web relationships are defined as the properties, subproperties, and functional properties to the classes. At the end of the process, an online prediction is expected to run. This online prediction engine is meant to produce DIKW hierarchical outputs for a specific case study that is performed.

References

[1] Aven, Terje. A conceptual framework for linking risk and the elements of the data–information–knowledge–wisdom (DIKW) hierarchy. *Reliability Engineering & System Safety* 2013; 111: 30–36.

[2] Baskarada, Sasa, and Andy Koronios. Data, information, knowledge, wisdom (DIKW): A semiotic theoretical and empirical exploration of the hierarchy and its quality dimension. *Australasian Journal of Information Systems* 2013; 18(1): 5–24.

[3] Sharma, Nikhil. *The origin of DIKW Hierarchy*, 2004. https://erealityhome.wordpress.com/2008/03/09/the-origin-of-dikw-hierarchy, 2008 (accessed July 12, 2017).

[4] Jifa, Gu, and Zhang Lingling. Data, DIKW, big data and data science. *Procedia Computer Science* 2014; 31: 814–821.

[5] Ackoff, Russell L. From data to wisdom. *Journal of Applied Systems Analysis* 1989; 16(1): 3–9.

[6] Zeleny, Milan. Management support systems: Towards integrated knowledge management. *Human Systems Management* 1987; 7(1): 59–70.

[7] Yusoff, Aziyati, Intan Shafinaz Mustafa, Salman Yussof, and Norashidah Md Din. Green cloud platform for flood early detection warning system in smart city, in *2015 5th National Symposium on Information Technology: Towards New Smart World (NSITNSW)*, February 17–19, Riyadh: IEEE, 2015, pp. 1–6.

[8] Wolfram, Stephen. *A New Kind of Science*. Vol. 5. Champaign, IL: Wolfram Media, 2002.

[9] Rowley, Jennifer E. The wisdom hierarchy: Representations of the DIKW hierarchy. *Journal of Information Science* 2007; 33(2): 163–180.

[10] Batra, Surinder. Big data analytics and its reflections on DIKW hierarchy *Review of Management* 2014; 4(1/2): 5.

[11] Katal, Avita, Mohammad Wazid, and R. H. Goudar. Big data: Issues, challenges, tools and good practices, in *2013 6th International Conference on Contemporary Computing (IC3)*, August 8–10. Noida, India: IEEE, 2013, pp. 404–409.

[12] Singh, Sachchidanand, and Nirmala Singh. Big data analytics, in *2012 International Conference on Communication Information Computing Technology (ICCICT 2012)*, October 19–20. Mumbai, India: IEEE, 2012, pp. 1–4.

[13] Sekaran, Uma, and Roger Bougie. *Research Methods for Business: A Skill-building Approach*. Chichester: Wiley, 2010.

[14] Yusoff, Aziyati, Norashidah Md Din, Salman Yussof, and Samee Ullah Khan. Big data analytics for Flood Information Management in Kelantan, Malaysia, in *2015 IEEE Student Conference on Research and Development (SCOReD)*, December 13–14. Kuala Lumpur, Malaysia:, IEEE, 2015, pp. 311–316.

[15] Asia-Pacific Economic Cooperation (APEC). *ANSSR: Enhancing the Quality and Relevance of Technical and Vocational Education and Training (TVET) for Current and Future Industry Needs*. Kuala Lumpur, Malaysia: APEC Publications, 2014.

[16] Navidi, William Cyrus. *Statistics for Engineers and Scientists*. Vol. 1. New York: McGraw-Hill, 2006.

[17] Shroff, Gautam. *The Intelligent Web: Search, Smart Algorithms, and Big Data*. Oxford: Oxford University Press, 2013.

[18] Zakaria, A.S. *The Geomorphology of Kelantan Delta (Malaysia)*, CATENA, volumn 2. Amsterdam, Netherlands: Elsevier, 1975, pp. 337–349.

[19] Nielsen, Lars. *Hadoop: The Engine That Drives Big Data*. New York: New Street Communications LLC, 2013.

[20] Mayer-Schönberger, Viktor, and Kenneth Cukier. *Big Data: A Revolution That Will Transform How We Live, Work, and Think*. Houghton Mifflin Harcourt, 2013.

[21] Hurwitz, Judith, Marcia Kaufman, and Adrian Bowles. *Cognitive Computing and Big Data Analytics*. Indianapolism, IN: John Wiley & Sons, 2015.

[22] Ohlhorst, Frank J. *Big Data Analytics: Turning Big Data Into Big Money*. Hoboken, NJ: John Wiley & Sons, 2012.

[23] Sowa, John F. Semantic networks, in S. C. Shapiro (ed.), *Encyclopedia of Cognitive Science*, New York, 2006.

[24] Guarino, Nicola, Daniel Oberle, and Steffen Staab. What is an Ontology? In Staab, Steffen, and Rudi Studer (eds.), *Handbook on Ontologies*, pp. 1–17, Berlin, Heidelberg: Springer, 2009.

[25] Aronson, Jaye E., Ting-Peng Liang, and Efraim Turban. Decision support systems and intelligent systems. *Yoyakarta: Andi*, pp. 51–71, New Jersey: Pearson-Prentice Hall, 2005.

[26] McGuinness, Deborah L., and Frank Van Harmelen. OWL web ontology language overview. *W3C Recommendation* 2004; 10(10): 1–22.

[27] Yusoff, Aziyati, Norashidah Md Din, Salman Yussof, and Samee Ullah Khan. The semantic network of flood hydrological data for Kelantan, Malaysia, in *IOP Conference Series: Earth and Environmental Science*, vol. 32, no. 1, p. 012021, Putrajaya, Malaysia: IOP Publishing, 2016.

[28] Thangaraj, M., and G. Sujatha. An architectural design for effective information retrieval in semantic web. *Expert Systems with Applications* 2014; 41(18): 8225–8233.

Chapter 11

Recommendation Systems

Joonseok Lee
Google Research
Mountain View, California

CONTENTS

In this chapter, we take an example of industrial applications of network big data focusing on computational intelligence. As the example, we take the *recommendation systems* or *recommender systems*. Recommendation systems refer to computational systems deployed for many users, analyzing each individual's taste on products and actively suggesting preferable items based on the analysis.

As readers are familiar, recommendation systems are already pervasive in our daily lives. First of all, production recommendation is the most popular form of recommendation systems. E-commerce sites such as Amazon or Home Depot collects each user's purchase history and page visits, and analyze those data to figure out their interest. Based on this analysis, personalized recommendations are made on the home page or each product page. Similarly, online contents providers such as Netflix (movies) or Pandora (music) take advantage of recommendation systems a lot. These services may be one of the most effective areas of recommendations, since cultural contents are consumed in very different patterns based on the individual's taste. Netflix hosted a recommendation system competition from 2006 to 2009 with 1 million dollars grand prize to improve their recommendation system. Another popular form of recommendations is in social networks, such as Facebook or LinkedIn. In social networks, users (and other entities, such as companies) are interconnected based on their social relationship. The connections in a social network are usually partially complete, so the service providers try to suggest "people you may know" to add a new connection, based on analysis of the graph. Personalized web search is another form of recommendation systems. In such a system, a web search result is tailed considering both data relevant to the search query and personal taste analyzed from their previous web search history. On smartphones, application recommendation is getting more and more popular. The mobile OS also analyzes the user's pattern of phone use, and recommends applications they may be interested in from the store.

Due to its nature, recommendation systems are usually deployed online, where many users can purchase items and interact with each other explicitly by leaving reviews or ratings, or implicitly by the system. Since the recommendation systems should deal with entire set of users and products in an online system, there are many challenges related to networking and large-scale data. For example, let us consider a music recommendation system. Apple claimed Apple Music service provides more than 10 million songs. In 2015, it is estimated that there were 75 million iPhone users. Although not all iPhone users actually use Apple Music service, we can imagine how potentially large the size of problem recommendation system may have to solve: 750 trillion pairs of a user and a song. Compared to the Netflix competition size, with 500,000 users and 20,000 items in 2006, the scale of commercial recommendation systems has skyrocketed within the last decade.

In this section, we will first overview what is a recommendation system. Then, we introduce several goals we want to achieve with it as well as how it is categorized. Lastly, we preview important challenges, which will be discussed further in the later sections.

11.1 Introduction

We have briefly listed some examples of recommendation systems, but what precisely is a recommendation system? We may think of it as any system that *recommends* something to the users. The term recommendation may indicate that the system is on the active side, which means the system initiates proposing something to the user, even without users' action. So, we would like to add *actively suggesting* to the definition:

Definition: Recommendation systems are information filtering software systems that actively suggests items that each user may like.

According to this definition, we may have a question. *Is an advertisement a recommendation?* Advertisements also actively suggest items to users to purchase or subscribe. Are these also recommendations? Are advertising engines also recommendation systems? In a broad sense, yes, as in the definition above. However, we would like to distinguish real recommendation systems from general advertisements in this chapter. Then, what is the key difference? It is *personalization*. When we recommend different items to individual users, we call it personalized, and this is the key difference distinguishing recommendation systems from general advertisements. So, here is a revised definition:

(Revised) Definition: Recommendation systems (or recommender systems) are information filtering software systems that predict the preference of users based on their and other users' explicit and implicit feedback on items and actively suggest items that each user may like.

To achieve personalization, it is essential to *learn* individual preference from available data, so machine learning and data mining techniques are widely used. In the following sections, we will learn more about such techniques.

11.1.1 Goals with recommendation systems

There are several goals or tasks with recommendation systems. Although these goals are inter-related, the most important goal can be different for each system or domain.

11.1.1.1 Goal 1: Recommending good items

First of all, one important goal with recommendation systems would be recommending good items to users. From the vendor perspective, proper recommendations will increase sales and revenue. From the customer perspective, users may be able to purchase good items they did not know about before they saw the recommendations. Proper recommendations will increase the customer's satisfaction and they may want to come back to purchase another item later.

Depending on the application, however, recommending good items may be in different forms. In some applications, it is important to show *all* relevant items, even if we may sometimes risk including irrelevant items. Citation recommendation for scientific papers is a good example. It is very important to include all relevant previous research in the paper, as the user may not want the system to miss any important previous works. Having some unnecessary citation recommendations may be okay; the user can easily exclude them. In information retrieval terms, high *recall* is required but the system may sacrifice precision.

On the other hand, some applications may not need to recall all relevant items, but just need to show *some* good items. Instead, in this case, having irrelevant items in the recommendation list can be a disaster. For example, cultural content recommendations such as music, movies, or books are in this category. The user usually does not expect to see *all* movies that they may like, but wants to just watch an interesting movie tonight. If the user watches a bad movie based on a recommendation, however, they may not trust the recommendation and might not come back to the website in the worst case. A dating partner recommendation is another example; when a man or a woman meets a partner based on a recommendation system, they meet just a few partners, not every potentially good partner registered in the system. If they meet someone not to their taste and waste time, however, they will not trust the system any more. These examples show that it is important to set proper measures for good recommendations depending on the application area.

11.1.1.2 Goal 2: Optimizing a utility function

A possible generalization of Goal 1 is optimizing an arbitrary utility function, for example, the profit function of a company. With Goal 1, recommending good items, the company may want to increase sales by recommending the most preferable items to each user. If this is done properly, the company's sales will increase (or ideally, maximized). However, maximizing the number of items sold does not necessarily mean that the company maximized profit from them. The margin or profit the company may earn can be very different by items, and the company may want to promote items with higher margin, even if there are fewer customers who are interested in these items. This can be seen as a generalization of Goal 1; in that recommending good items is maximizing the number of items that users like, without distinguishing them. In practice, however, it is hard to know exact utility functions, or even if it is possible, so the optimization can be usually very complex.

11.1.1.3 Goal 3: Predicting ratings

Another popular goal of recommendation systems is predicting unseen ratings on items by users. This is especially popular in research communities or in academia, since it is clearer to define quantitative performance. The Netflix grand prize competition was also designed to predict unseen movie ratings in Netflix.

The final goal of commercial services may be raising their profit anyway, but why do we care about ratings? Usually ratings are provided very sparsely. For instance, there are tens of thousands of movies in Netflix, but how many movies do you watch and rate? Typically users rate just a few movies a year. However, what if Netflix can estimate how many stars are you going to give for every movie? Then, it will be straightforward to generate a recommendation list for you, by just simply ranking every unseen movie and recommending the top 10 or so. Although this may not be the optimal way to recommend movies, this approach for recommendations has been shown to be effective.

11.1.2 Types of recommendation systems

Then, how can we build a recommendation system? What kind of data, model, and learning algorithm to use? Depending on answers to these questions, we can categorize recommendation systems into roughly three categories, shown in Figure 11.1: content-based filtering, collaborative filtering, and hybrid (combination of those two) approaches.

11.1.2.1 Type 1: Content-based filtering

Recommendation systems are basically connecting a user and an item based on preference. One intuitive approach is based on data about the users and the items, what we call *content*. The deployed recommendation systems may know about the user: who is this user? Is this user a man or a woman? How old is he/she? Where does this user live? Also, the system may have attributes of the products. For movies, what genre is it? Who is the director? Who are the main actor and actress? When was the movie released? How long is it? If the system possess

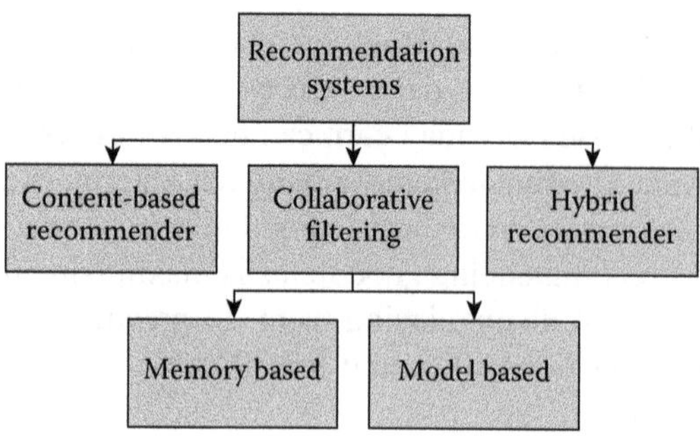

Figure 11.1: Types of recommendation systems.

information like these, we can generate recommendations as follows:

1. Given a target user, retrieve the list of movies this user liked before.
2. For each movie in the list, retrieve set of movies similar to them.
3. Rank by the similarity, and recommend the top k items to the target user.

Among the steps above, the most challenging part would be the second one, retrieving similar movies. For this part, a similarity metric is needed for the movie attributes. As we have a lot of movie attributes, we need to define how to represent the attributes, and how to compare them. If some of the attributes are categorical, we need to define similarity between different values of them.

Content-based filtering can be powerful, when the system can make use of abundant domain knowledge or data. However, it also has drawbacks; since the types of available features are different by domain or by data set, domain-specific modeling needs to be designed. In other words, it is hard to reuse a general model which is applicable to virtually every recommendation system. The learning algorithm may be also different domain by domain.

11.1.2.2 Type 2: Collaborative filtering

Unlike the situation in content-based filtering, what if we have no information about the content? Some systems do not collect data on who are the users. Item information also can be limited depending on applications. In such a case, how can we recommend?

Even though we do not have content information, we can still collect *feedback* from users. Users may give positive or negative feedback on items explicitly or implicitly. In Netflix, for example, users can rate movies from 1 star (worst) to 5 stars (best) based on how much they like them. This is a good example of explicit rating, since the user *explicitly* gives a rating to a movie. Also, in this case the user can express both positive and negative opinions about the item. Sometimes, the system may allow only positive feedback from users. For instance, Facebook has only a "Like" button, but no "Dislike" button. Using this setting, the system may collect only positive feedback from the users.

On the other hand, the system might collect implicit signals, such as page view or click on links. Although we are not 100% sure about the user's intent, we consider these as positive signals, since people usually click something because they are at least somewhat interested in it. These implicit ratings might be less precise, but usually are easier to collect. Due to the nature of implicit feedback, it is usually positive only.

In collaborative filtering, the system does not need to know features of users or contents of items. Instead, it just takes these kinds of user feedback on items. In practice, however, users give feedback only on a very small portion of items. In Netflix, for example, how many movies do you watch a year? For the last 10 years, how many movies have you watched? The answers may be different by users, but we can easily imagine that the average number of movies people watch in a year may be less than 10 or 20, so in most cases, people may rate at most 200 movies even in 10 years. However, there are millions of movies in the world. Even a movie fan can only see very small portion of them. Also, people do not rate most movies they watched. From the perspective of service providers like Netflix, it is curious how much a particular user would like to watch a particular movie, if the rating is not given. Collaborative filtering is a useful technique to fill out these missing ratings, from not only the target user's ratings on other movies, but also other users' ratings on all other movies.

According to the original definition of collaborative filtering [1], people *collaborate* to help one another perform *filtering*, by recording their reactions to products they consumed. In other words, users in the system may not seem actually collaborate, but their feedback or ratings into the system are useful to generate recommendations for other users. This is because collaborative filtering makes use of other users' feedback to fit an individual's preference, and vice versa.

We can represent this problem as a matrix completion problem. Figure 11.2 shows an example. Each row of the matrix represents a user, while each column denotes an item. This particular example has five users and five items in the system. In each cell (u, i), the rating on item i given by user u is written. This example takes a 1 star to 5 stars scale. For example, user 2 gave 3 stars on item 1, while user 3 gave 5 stars on item 5. As you see, there are many empty cells, with no ratings given yet. The goal of a recommendation system (or matrix completion) is assigning proper estimation of these missing ratings based on some reasonable assumptions about the domain. In the subsequent section, we will discuss detailed algorithms to solve matrix completion problems based on low-rank assumption.

The collaborative filtering method is categorized further to memory-based and model-based methods. Memory-based models contain the entire matrix in

Items

			3		
	3				5
		5		4	
Users			2	5	
	1			2	

Figure 11.2: An example of matrix representation of collaborative filtering problem.

the memory, and for each query (target user), it computes items to recommend based on the matrix. Model-based methods, on the other hand, learn a model generalizing (user, item) $\rightarrow$ score relation from the matrix, then use this model to predict unseen ratings without access to the raw rating matrix. We will discuss several widely used algorithms for both categories in the next section.

11.1.2.3 Type 3: Hybrid approach

The hybrid approach is a combination of content-based filtering and collaborative filtering. In many cases, the system may contain both content information and user feedback on items. There are many ways to combine both of these signals to improve performance of recommendation systems.

11.1.3 Challenges with recommendation systems

We chose the recommendation system as our industry application, since it represents several important challenges in network big data. First of all, the data scale is extremely large as in other big data problems. Nevertheless, another challenge comes from extreme sparsity of data collection, when we consider each individual user or item. Furthermore, the data is endlessly created; new users and new items are continuously added to the system. The recommendation system should be able to deal with this large-scale sparsity data smoothly. We briefly introduce these challenges here, and will discuss several methods to resolve them in the subsequent section.

11.1.3.1 Challenge 1: Extreme sparsity

As we discussed earlier, recommendation data is extremely sparse. For movie recommendations, we already estimated the average number of movies rated by a user. Even for a movie fan, it is not common to rate more than 1000 movies out of hundreds of thousands of movies. Most regular users rate just 10 or so movies.

Another example is online advertisements, which collect clicks by a user on any advertisement (ad) shown on the web page. How many times do you click an ad on a web portal site? Statistics says that the click-through rate on ads is at the 10^{-6} level. In other words, the ad is clicked roughly once per every 100,000 users. With this low density of the user-ad matrix, we need to fill out the other 99.999% empty cells.

Personalized web search is more open ended. The set of search queries is not even finite like a set of movies or ads. Only with hundreds or thousands of recent web searches in the history of a user, we need to recommend web pages to visit.

As these examples show, data collected for recommendation systems are usually very sparse. Therefore, an efficient way of handling sparse data is essential. Also, robust statistical methods are needed to avoid overfitting due to the noise in the collected data.

11.1.3.2 Challenge 2: Large scale

Another important challenge is the extremely large scale of the data set. For movie recommendations, the size of the matrix is given by the number of users times the number of movies in the system. If we have 1 million users and 100,000 movies, the matrix we want to fill contains 100 billion cells. Music recommendation is even bigger, as the number of songs in the system is usually far larger. Without an efficient algorithm, estimating each of these cells would take forever.

What about friend recommendation in a social network? Facebook claimed there are 1.71 billion monthly active users as of the second quarter in 2016. As the friend relationship is reciprocal, the matrix we handle here is 1.71 billion $\times$ 1.71 billion, i.e., 2.92 trillion. If we estimate the probability that user u knows another user v for all (u, v) pairs, how long will it take? Suppose we do not use a parallelism and we can process 1000 cells per second. To complete this matrix, we need 92.6 years (even longer than the expected lifetime)!

Dealing with this large-scale dataset requires very efficient learning algorithm. These days, making use of parallelism becomes essential, probably with GPU. We do not deal with details of GPGPU (general purpose GPU) in this chapter, but we will show some ideas on how to parallelize a learning algorithm in the next section.

11.1.3.3 Challenge 3: Cold-start problem

In addition to the extreme sparsity and large scale, recommendation systems suffer from another challenge: the cold-start problem. Recommendation systems are usually deployed as web applications, so new users and items are continuously added to the system. For those new users, how can we generate recommendations? If the system is purely collaborative filtering-based, previous feedback from the target user is essential. However, these new users do not have previous ratings or feedback, so it is impossible to figure out the user's preference. This is an innate limitation of collaborative filtering methods. To overcome cold-start, we usually adopt a hybrid approach, where we take advantage of user feedback as well as content information. We will discuss two basic approaches (hybrid approach and initial survey) in the next section.

Throughout this chapter, we will focus on collaborative filtering approaches. It is mainly because collaborative filtering-based methods can be applied to many data sets without lots of adaptation, since it is independent of the domain. In the next section, we start with basic collaborative filtering methods, which are easy to understand and implement. In the later sections, we will focus on how to resolve the challenges discussed above. With a cold-start problem, we may also briefly discuss how we can use content-based filtering. Lastly, we will review how recommendation systems are evaluated.

11.2 Basic Collaborative Filtering Approaches

We introduced collaborative filtering in a previous section. Recall that *collaborative filtering* means that users collaborate with each other for filtering preferable items by recording their own preference. In this section, we will introduce a couple of basic (memory-based) collaborative filtering methods which implement this idea directly. These methods are very simple, and so easy to understand and implement. Although they are not scalable, they can be still be reasonably used for small-size applications.

11.2.1 User-based collaborative filtering

Suppose we have a rating matrix M, and we are about to predict an unseen rating of item i by user u. In user-based collaborative filtering, we first seek *neighbors* of the user u. For this, we need a similarity measure between two users. At this point, we assume a black box computing similarity between two users. This will be discussed later. By calculating similarity between u and all other users, we can select k most similar users to u. To predict the rating $M_{u,i}$, we use ratings of these k similar users. The easiest way may be the simple average of available ratings on the item i by those similar users. A more sophisticated way is an weighted average, based on similarity between the target user u and its neighbors. Formally,

$$\hat{M}_{u,i} = \frac{\sum_{v \in \mathcal{U}} sim(u,v) M_{v,i}}{\sum_{v \in \mathcal{U}} sim(u,v)} \tag{11.1}$$

where $\mathcal{U}$ is the set of similar users with u, and sim is the similarity black box.

Let us illustrate this approach by an example, using Figure 11.3. Suppose we are about to predict a rating by user 5 on item 3. Let us assume that the neighbor size $k = 2$, the neighbor user set $\mathcal{U} = \{2, 3\}$, and user similarity is $sim(2,5) = 0.8$,

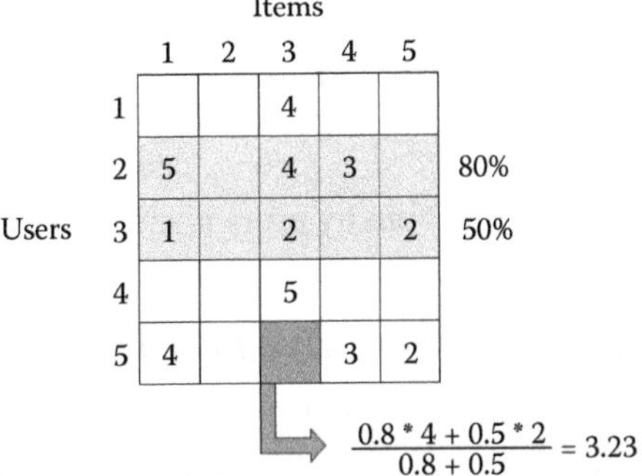

Figure 11.3: An example of user-based collaborative filtering.

$sim(3,5) = 0.5$, respectively. Then, we can compute Equation 11.1 as follows:

$$\hat{M}_{A,C} = \frac{0.8 \times 4 + 0.5 \times 2}{0.8 + 0.5} = \frac{4.2}{1.3} \approx 3.23 \tag{11.2}$$

That is, we predict that user 5 would have rated item 3 as score of 3.23.

Now, the only thing we need is how to create the black box computing similarity between two users. There are several ways to compute this, including the following:

Pearson Correlation

$$sim(u,v) = \frac{\sum_j (M_{u,j} - \bar{M}_u)(M_{v,j} - \bar{M}_v)}{\sqrt{\sum_j (M_{u,j} - \bar{M}_u)^2} \sqrt{\sum_j (M_{v,j} - \bar{M}_v)^2}} \tag{11.3}$$

where $\bar{M}_u$ and $\bar{M}_v$ are the average of ratings by user u and v, respectively, and the summation is only over observed ratings.

Cosine Similarity

$$sim(u,v) = \frac{M_u \cdot M_v}{|M_u||M_v|} \tag{11.4}$$

where M_u and M_v are the row vectors corresponding users u and v, respectively.

Mean Squared Difference

$$sim(u,v) = \frac{1}{|C|} \sum_{i \in C} (M_{u,i} - M_{v,i})^2 \tag{11.5}$$

where C is a set of items rated both by users u and v.

Mean Absolute Difference

$$sim(u,v) = \frac{1}{|C|}\sum_{i\in C}|M_{u,i} - M_{v,i}| \tag{11.6}$$

where C is a set of items rated both by users u and v.

11.2.2 Item-based collaborative filtering

Item-based collaborative filtering (CF) [2] resembles user-based CF, only the role of rows and columns is interchanged. To determine the rating of item i by user u, it seeks neighbors of the item i, rather than user u. By calculating similarity between i and all other items, we can select k most similar items to i, just as we did with users in the user-based method. The predicted rating can be calculated in the exact same way:

$$\hat{M}_{u,i} = \frac{\sum_{j\in\mathcal{I}} sim(i,j)M_{u,j}}{\sum_{j\in\mathcal{I}} sim(i,j)} \tag{11.7}$$

where $\mathcal{I}$ is the set of similar items to i and sim is the similarity function between two items. We can use similarity measures in Equation 11.3 through Equation 11.6 using column vectors i and j of rating matrix M, instead of row vectors.

Figure 11.4 shows a similar example to user-based CF. Now we estimate the rating on item 4 by user 3. Suppose we know that item 1 and 3 are similar to the target item 4, with similarity of 60% and 40%, respectively. We predict the target unseen rating by

$$\hat{M}_{A,C} = \frac{0.6\times 1 + 0.4\times 2}{0.6+0.4} = \frac{1.4}{1.0} = 1.40 \tag{11.8}$$

implying that the target user may not like the item so much.

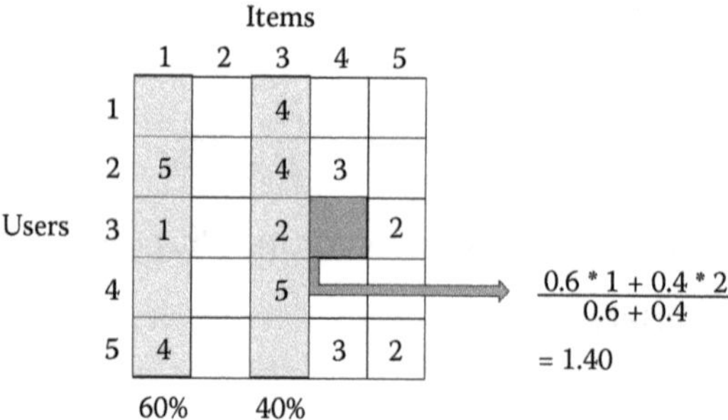

Figure 11.4: An example of item-based collaborative filtering.

Sarwar et al. [2] argue that the item-based approach performs more accurately than the user-based counterpart, because the item neighborhood relationship tends to be more stable than user relationships. That is, users tend to change their preference as time goes on, so the user neighbor group may not be accurate in many cases. (The success of temporal dynamics used by the Netflix winner [3] is also based on this observation.) An item relationship, on the other hand, tends to be more stable since the intrinsic property of items (e.g., genre) does not change as time goes by. The item-based approach can take advantage of this in the computational aspect as well, by precomputing item similarity offline.

11.2.3 Extensions to memory-based CF

There are some important extensions applicable to memory-based collaborative filtering approaches [4].

Instead of computing similarity only on observed ratings, we apply *default voting* for unseen ratings. This is effective especially when the rating matrix is very sparse, as we have a much smaller chance to find corated items or corating users. The default value may be determined differently depending on the type of dataset. For example, we may apply a neutral value for rating the matrix of movies, as we do not know the preference of unseen movies. For a purchase history data, however, we may give a negative preference on an unseen part, as it may indicate dislike.

Inverse user frequency is based on an observation that universally liked items are not that useful in capturing similarity. Inverse user frequency emphasizes less common items with higher weights, while degrading weights of popular items.

Case amplification is used to emphasize highly-weighted cases further, while make low-weighted cases negligible. This is effective to reduce noise in the dataset.

11.2.4 Complexity: Pros and cons

Both user-based and item-based CF belong to memory-based methods, since they maintain the whole rating matrix in memory and predict ratings when asked. As they do nothing but store the whole matrix in the memory, training time is negligible. If we precalculate user or item similarity offline, user-based CF takes $O(m^2n)$ and item-based CF takes $O(mn^2)$, respectively, where m is the number of users and n is the number of items. For querying time, it takes $O(m)$ searching time for user-based CF and $O(n)$ for item-based CF.

Memory-based collaborative filtering is simple and easy to understand, as well as implement. Since it uses similar users or items to predict a rating or to generate a recommendation list, it is also easy to *explain* why those items are recommended. This justification elevates the credibility of the recommendation system [5]. However, memory-based approaches are not as accurate as matrix factorization methods, discussed later. Also, memory-based CF is not that scalable, so it is not proper for large-scale systems requiring accurate prediction.

11.3 How to Overcome Sparsity: Matrix Factorization

The first challenge with recommendation systems we discussed was extreme sparsity of the data set. Because of this, memory-based models may not work for many users (or items) when they do not have enough corated items (or users). How can we provide more reliable similarity measures for pairs with just a few coratings?

Matrix factorization is a possible solution for this problem, since it reveals the latent structure of main factors determining preference on items by users. Recall that we have a sparse rating matrix $M \in \mathbb{R}^{m \times n}$, and we are going to fill in missing values in this matrix, based on observed entries.

Let us start with an example in Figure 11.5. In Figure 11.5a, we see the example matrix M with some of the ratings known. Our goal is factorizing this matrix into two 5-dimensional vectors (or 5×1 matrices), called U and V. Each dimension of U represents each user with one value, while each dimension of V represents each item with one value. Our goal is to find proper values in U and V, which approximate the known values in the matrix when we multiply corresponding values. For instance, user 2 gave 5 stars on item 1. In our matrix factorization, we want to have $U_2 V_1 \approx 5$. Many different combinations of U_2 and V_1 will achieve this; for instance, $U_2 = 5$ and $V_1 = 1$, or $U_2 = 2.5$ and $V_1 = 2$, and so on. However, U_2 also needs to be set properly for the rating on item 4 by user 2, which is 3. Similarly, V_1 needs to be set properly to reflect ratings by users 3 and 5 on item 1. There are some ways to find such values satisfying all known ratings, and we will discuss them later in this section. At this moment, just assume that we already found a satisfactory assignment for all values in U and V; this is shown in Figure 11.5b. When we multiply one value from U and one from V, it approximates the rating (if given) in the matrix. For instance, $U_2 = 1.6$ and $V_1 = 3$, giving 4.8 for the rating on item 1 by user 2, which is 5 stars. This is an approximation by our *model* U and V, and approximated ratings for all existing ratings are shown in Figure 11.5c. (Compare them against Figure 11.5a to check whether this is a good model.)

Now, we are ready to estimate all other unseen ratings, since we have all proper values in U and V. This gives estimated ratings for pairs of any user and any item, shown in Figure 11.5d. Based on the estimated ratings, we can select items to recommend to each user. What to recommend? We may want to recommend movies that the user may like, so we choose items with high estimated ratings. One more thing to consider is that we may not want to recommend a movie that the user already has seen. Thus, we exclude items in the training set

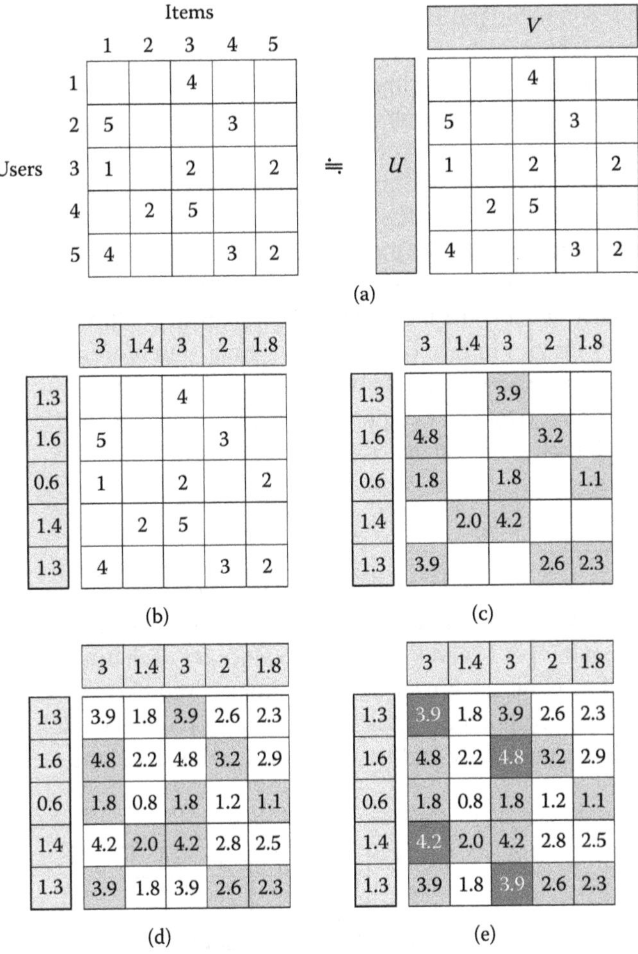

Figure 11.5: An example of a matrix factorization problem. (a) The left matrix M is to be factorized to $UV^\top$, where U and V contain one-dimensional user and item profiles, respectively. (b) Once we fit U and V *somehow*, we may get user and item profile scores like this. (How to get these scores will be explained later.) (c) With the fitted user and item profile, we reconstruct known values in M. We see that these ratings are similar to those in (a). (d) In addition to the known values, we can now estimate unknown values (white cells) using the user and profile scores. (e) With estimated ratings for all user-item pairs, we can recommend items with high estimated ratings to each user (darkest shading).

(i.e., the known ratings in M). We also may set some threshold in estimated rating to recommend. User 3 in Figure 11.5e, for example, has not seen movies 2 and 4, but the estimated scores are around 1 star, which means the user may not like those movies. Even though item 4 is the highest among the unseen movies, we do not recommend this item. In this way, we chose four movies to recommend to four users respectively: red-colored cells in Figure 11.5e.

Let us think about underlying meaning of this approach. We represented each rating as a multiplication of one score for the user and another score for the item. For this score to be high, both of these should be high. If one of these is low, the estimation will not be high. Of course, if both of these are low, the estimation will be low. Then, what would be the hidden meaning of item features V? It probably reflects how much people like the movie, or the popularity of the movie. In other words, the item feature is high only if most of the ratings given to the item are high. Similarly, what is the meaning of the values in U? It may reflect how much the user likes movies in general. If the user gave high scores to most movies, the corresponding user scores should be high, and vice versa.

In matrix factorization, we approximate the given matrix M with a product of two low-rank (say r), dense matrices $U \in \mathbb{R}^{m \times r}$ and $V \in \mathbb{R}^{n \times r}$:

$$M \approx UV^\top \tag{11.9}$$

where $r \ll \min(m, n)$.

In the above example we had only one value to represent each user and each item. What if we have more than one value to represent each user and item? Let us think about thicker U and V with three values for each user and item, as shown in Figure 11.6. Now, each user and each item is represented with three values, and the score is computed by taking the inner product (or dot product) of the corresponding user vector and item vector. For instance, the element at ($M_{3,2}$),

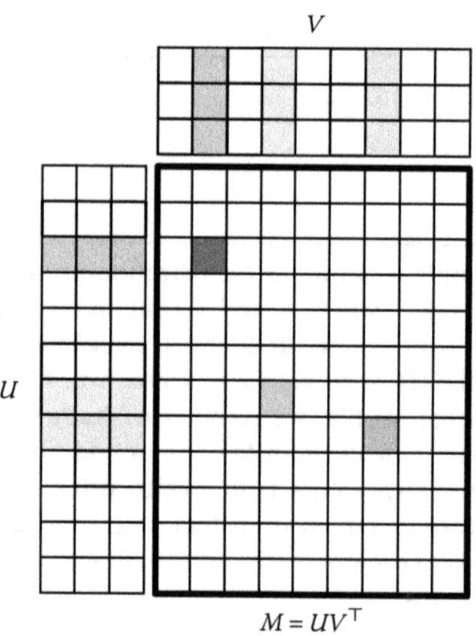

Figure 11.6: An example of matrix factorization.

is expressed as the inner product of the corresponding row vector of U, and the column vector of $V^\top$. The other two elements are also expressed in the same way.

The intuitive meaning of the user profile and the item profile is similar here: each dimension of user and item profiles represents the three most important factors determining how much users like items in M. When corresponding values are both high, the multiplied score will be higher. For instance, each dimension can be genres; say, action, melodrama, and science fiction. If a user likes action, the first dimension of the user profile will be a high value. When formed into an inner product with action movies, with high value in the first dimension, the multiplied value would be high. For other genre movies, however, the first dimension representing how much this movie is an action movie would be small, so the multiplied score would be also small. In reality, however, the actual meaning of each dimension in U and V is hard to interpret, but it has just automatically discovered the most important factors determining the preference of users on items in the data set. Because matrix factorization can automatically discover this structure, we can alleviate the data sparsity problem by making full use of other available ratings to discover the entire structure.

Let us mathematically define this problem now. Each entry in M is approximated as an inner product of two vectors, one row from U and one row from V. Specifically, $M_{u,i}$ is approximated by $U_u V_i^\top$. Our learning task is determining the value of matrices U and V by enforcing $U_u^\top V_i$ to be similar to $M_{u,i}$ for all observed entries. Although the rating matrix M is sparse, U and V would be dense matrices, provided that we have at least one observation for all users (rows) and all items (columns). As U and V are dense matrices, we can estimate unseen entries by taking the inner-product of two corresponding vectors from U and V. The exact way of learning U and V differs depending on algorithms. We introduce some representative methods below.

11.3.1 Regularized SVD

Singular value decomposition (SVD) decomposes a matrix $M \in \mathbb{R}^{m\times n}$ into

$$R = U\Sigma V^\top = \sum_{k=1}^{d} \sigma_k u_k v_k^\top \tag{11.10}$$

where $U \in \mathbb{R}^{m\times d}$ is a set of left singular vectors, $V \in \mathbb{R}^{n\times d}$ is a set of right singular vectors, and $\Sigma \in \mathbb{R}^{d\times d}$ is a diagonal matrix with singular values. Without loss of generality, we can sort singular vectors in decreasing order of σ_k. When we take singular vectors corresponding to r largest singular values, we get the best rank-r approximation to M:

$$\hat{M} = U\Sigma V^\top = \sum_{k=1}^{r} \sigma_k u_k v_k^\top \tag{11.11}$$

in terms of least squares.

Our goal in collaborative filtering is the opposite: given M, we want to find U and V, where this minimizes the squared error between M and $UV^\top$ on observed entries. The objective function $E(U,V)$ we want to minimize is given by

$$E(U,V) = \sum_{(u,i)\in\Omega} \left([UV^\top]_{u,i} - M_{u,i}\right)^2 = \sum_{(u,i)\in\Omega} \left(\sum_{k=1}^{r} U_{u,k}V_{i,k} - M_{u,i}\right)^2 \tag{11.12}$$

where Ω is a set of indices of observed entries. In addition to (11.12), we may need regularization to avoid overfitting. We add $R(U)$ and $R(V)$ to the end of (11.12), preventing values in U and V from being too large. Several different forms of regularization can be possible, but we use L_2-regularization (ridge regression) to make $E(U,V)$ differentiable. The modified objective function is then

$$E(U,V) = \sum_{(u,i)\in\Omega} \left([UV^\top]_{u,i} - M_{u,i}\right)^2 + \lambda R(U) + \lambda R(V) \tag{11.13}$$

$$= \sum_{(u,i)\in\Omega} \left(\sum_{k=1}^{r} U_{u,k}V_{i,k} - M_{u,i}\right)^2 + \lambda \sum_{u=1}^{m}\sum_{k=1}^{r} U_{u,k}^2 + \lambda \sum_{i=1}^{n}\sum_{k=1}^{r} U_{i,k}^2 \tag{11.14}$$

where λ controls the relative importance between least square fitting and regularization terms. (Note that we can use different regularization coefficients for U and V.)

To minimize (11.14), we use gradient descent, since the least square problem of a partially-observed matrix is nonconvex. Algorithm 11.1 describes the gradient-descent framework. Considering a single term in $E(U,V)$, we have

$$E_{u,i}(U,V) = \left(\sum_{k=1}^{r} U_{u,k}V_{i,k} - M_{u,i}\right)^2 + \lambda \sum_{k=1}^{r} U_{u,k}^2 + \lambda \sum_{k=1}^{r} U_{i,k}^2 \tag{11.15}$$

Partial derivatives of (11.15) with respect to single elements in U and V are given by

$$\frac{\partial E_{u,i}(U,V)}{\partial U_{u,k}} = 2V_{i,k}\left([UV^\top]_{u,i} - M_{u,i}\right) + 2\lambda V_{i,k} \tag{11.16}$$

$$\frac{\partial E_{u,i}(U,V)}{\partial V_{i,k}} = 2U_{u,k}\left([UV^\top]_{u,i} - M_{u,i}\right) + 2\lambda U_{u,k} \tag{11.17}$$

which are used for updating in Algorithm 11.1. The parameter μ in Algorithm 11.1 controls learning speed. It runs until $UV^\top$ converges to M over observed entries Ω. Due to the nonconvexity of the problem, the converged U and V may depend on initial values.

Algorithm 11.1 Regularized SVD

Input: $M \in \mathbb{R}^{n_1 \times n_2}, \mu$
while $\|M - UV^\top\| > \epsilon$ **do**
  for all $(u,i) \in \Omega, k = 1, \cdots, r$ **do**
    $U_{u,k} := U_{u,k} - \mu \frac{\partial E_{u,i}(U,V)}{\partial U_{u,k}}$
    $V_{i,k} := V_{u,k} - \mu \frac{\partial E_{u,i}(U,V)}{\partial V_{i,k}}$
  end for
end while
Output: U, V

11.3.2 Nonnegative matrix factorization

Nonnegative matrix factorization (NMF) is a matrix factorization technique approximating $M \approx UV^\top$ under the constraint that all entries in U and V should be nonnegative. This requirement can be important in some applications where the representation of each element is inherently nonnegative, or it seeks low-rank matrices which are enforced to have only nonnegative values. For example, a text document is represented as a vector of nonnegative numbers with the term-frequency encoding. Each element in this representation is the number of appearances of each term in the document, so it is nonnegative. Another example is image processing. Digital images are represented by a matrix of pixel intensities, which are inherently nonnegative. In natural sciences such as chemistry or biology, chemical concentrations or gene expressions are also nonnegative [6]. In recommendation systems, a rating matrix is also usually nonnegative. Although other matrix factorization methods may allow negative entries in factorized low-rank matrices, it still makes sense to enforce nonnegativity as the original data is nonnegative.

The objective function which is minimized in NMF is either Euclidean distance

$$E(U,V) = \sum_{(u,i)\in\Omega} \left([UV^\top]_{u,i} - M_{u,i}\right)^2 \tag{11.18}$$

or Kullback–Leibler divergence

$$E(U,V) = \sum_{(u,i)\in\Omega} \left(M_{u,i} \log \frac{M_{u,i}}{[UV^\top]_{u,i}} - M_{u,i} + [UV^\top]_{u,i} \right) \tag{11.19}$$

Lee and Seung [7] present multiplicative update rules for both Euclidean distance and Kullback–Leibler divergence objective functions. For Euclidean distance, the update rules are

$$V_{i,k} \leftarrow V_{i,k}\frac{[U^\top M]_{i,k}}{[U^U V^\top]_{i,k}} \tag{11.20}$$

$$U_{u,k} \leftarrow U_{u,k}\frac{[MV]_{u,k}}{[UV^\top V]_{u,k}} \tag{11.21}$$

For Kullback–Leibler divergence, the update rules are

$$V_{i,k} \leftarrow V_{i,k}\frac{\sum_u U_{u,k}M_{u,i}/[UV^\top]_{u,i}}{\sum_u U_{u,k}} \tag{11.22}$$

$$U_{u,k} \leftarrow U_{u,k}\frac{\sum_i V_{i,k}M_{u,i}/[UV^\top]_{u,i}}{\sum_i V_{i,k}} \tag{11.23}$$

which were proved to converge in Ref. [7]. Note that these multiplicative update rules are possible thanks to the nonnegativity constraints, and converge faster than additive update rules.

11.3.3 Other matrix factorization models

Besides several methods we introduced so far, there are hundreds of variations and extensions on matrix factorization methods for collaborative filtering. We list some of them before finishing this section.

Probabilistic matrix factorization (PMF) [8] is represented as a graphical model. Assuming Gaussian observation noise, conditional distribution over the observed ratings is represented as a probabilistic model. *Bayesian PMF* (BPMF) [9] further generalizes this idea by estimating the whole posterior probability distribution.

Maximum margin matrix factorization (MMMF) [10] resembles maximum margin classifiers such as support vector machines (SVM). It utilizes low-norm, instead of low-rank, factorizations by solving a semidefinite optimization problem. Ref. [11] improved original MMMF to a faster and more scalable version, by a direct gradient-based optimization algorithm. Ref. [12] proposed ensembles of MMMF models, achieving better prediction accuracy.

Nonlinear probabilistic matrix factorization (NLPMF) [13] proposed a nonlinear model for matrix factorization using Gaussian process latent variable models. Applying stochastic gradient descent, NLPMF is scalable to millions of observations without approximating methods. Rating prediction is done in a similar way with neighborhood-based methods discussed in the previous section.

Fast nonparametric matrix factorization [14] developed a fast optimization algorithm for the nonparametric matrix factorization method. Nonparametric models can be preferred to parametric low-rank models thanks to their flexibility, but the drawback is computational overhead and limited scalability. The fast nonparametric principal component analysis (NPCA) algorithm turns out to be efficient as well as achieving good accuracy.

11.4 For Scalability: Local Approach with Parallelism

Another challenge with recommendation systems is extremely large data size. Large-scale data makes it hard to use the algorithms we introduced in the previous section in many ways. First of all, it is hard to load the entire dataset on the memory. Most algorithms in the memory-based CF category require that all data should be loaded in the memory, since it does not learn anything in the training phase. Even with model-based methods, we still need to store user model and/or item model in the memory. With millions of users and items, this size might be still too large to load in memory. Even if we can have the model in memory, another problem is the training time. With extremely large training data, learning and fitting the model takes very long time.

There can be many approaches to deal with this scalability problem. In this section, we introduce one such idea, taking advantage of parallelism. Suppose we have too many users and too many items in the matrix. The entire matrix might not fit into memory in a single machine. However, we may think of a divide-and-conquer approach. When we consider only a subset of users and a subset of items, the submatrix created by these subsets may fit into a single machine. Once the submatrix fits into memory, we can learn a model-based CF model for those users and items. We repeat this with different sets of users and items. If we have more than one machine, we may run many of these training processes at the same time, taking advantage of parallelism. This completes the "conquer" part.

Then, how can we divide the matrix? One way may be to randomly choose a fixed number of users and items, which fit in memory. As the size of this submatrix is large enough, we may expect that it still has a similar distribution to the entire matrix, so it may be approximated by low-rank matrix factorization. However, we may do better than this. Suppose we have a metric to compute similarity or distance between two users (or two rows) and between two items (or two columns). Then, we may want to choose a set of similar users and a set of similar items to be in the same submatrix. When we factorize this small matrix, the observed principal component may follow quite different distribution from the entire set. In other words, this may be so more representative for the users and items in the submatrix.

Let us take a concrete example in the movie recommendation problem. We may collect movies from same genre; say, action movies. We also collect users based on some demographic data; say, male users from the age of 15 to 25. When we factorize this submatrix, it will contain the most important factors determining the preference of these young men for action movies. One possible factor may be "how much the action scenes are realistic." Obviously, this is not an important concern for other types of movies such as romantic comedy. This means that the model we learned for a particular submatrix may preserve more information if we select users and items from the same community.

Another issue is whether we allow for each user or item belonging to more than one submatrix, or local model. If we do not allow overlapping, we can run some clustering algorithm such as K-means to divide users and items. One advantage of this approach is that we guarantee that all users and items should belong to at least one group, so we can use our model for estimating any pair of user–item. On the other hand, we may allow more than one group for users or items to belong to. This approach may make more sense in many applications; for instance, suppose we divide movies by genre. Some movies have more than one genre applicable Titanic is a romance movie, but at the same time, it is a disaster film. It is also considered as a historical drama. Users are the same; a person may belong to a gender group, an age group, and a geographical location group at the same time. Allowing overlap actually improves performance, since we can consider multiple aspects of users and items.

Once we allow overlapping, some user-item pair may have more than one model applicable. We may combine estimation of each model to produce final estimation in several ways: simple average, weighted average, and so on.

11.4.1 Local low-rank matrix approximation

As an example of divide-and-conquer approach, we introduce local low-rank approximation (LLORMA) [15]. Figure 11.7 illustrates the divide-and-conquer idea. Assuming no content information is available, LLORMA computes similarity between users and between items by vector cosine distance between vectors computed by global SVD. It allows overlapping, and final estimation is computed by the weighted average of each model. Note that even though Figure 11.7 shows

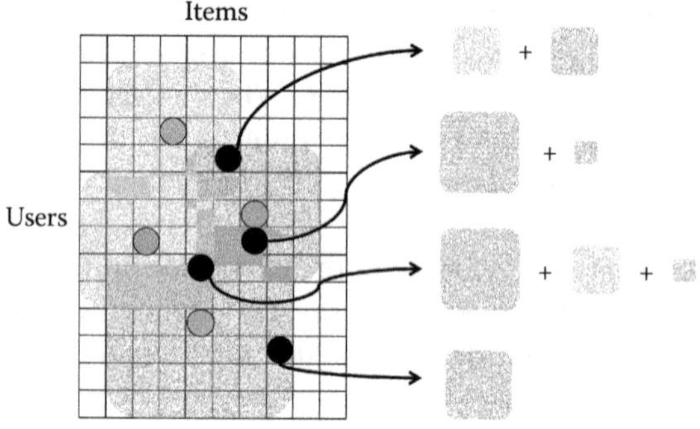

Figure 11.7: Overview of local low-rank matrix approximation (LLORMA).

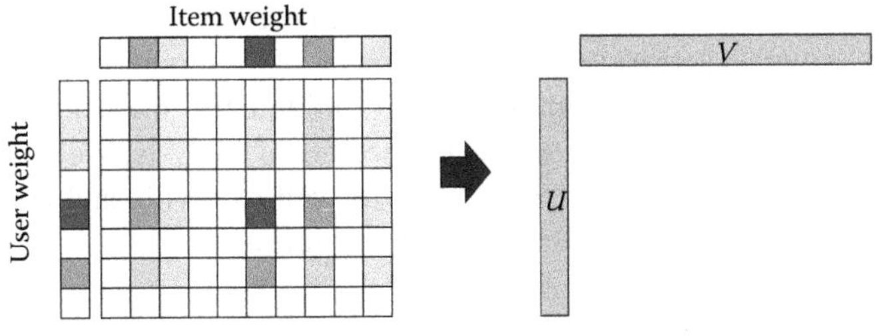

Figure 11.8: The LLORMA algorithm.

that adjacent rows or columns belong to the same local model, it is actually not, since we use a similarity measure to decide membership.

A more practical illustration of LLORMA is shown in Figure 11.8. For each local model, we randomly select a user and an item. The pair of these (user, item) becomes the *anchor point*. In Figure 11.8, user 5 and item 6 (darkest color) is the anchor point. Then, we compute the user weight (similarity) vector. Each cell reflects similarity between each row and the anchor user. For this, we apply kernel smoothing. The item weight vector is computed in a similar way. The weights applied to each cell are the outer product of user weights and item weights, as shown in the figure. In the figure, we see that the darker the color is, the higher the weight is. White color means the weight is 0, which means the corresponding user and item do not belong to the local model. Based on the weights, we solve a weighted regularized SVD problem to produce user and item embeddings, U and V, respectively. This entire process may run in parallel, since the training with different anchor points are independent of each other.

Mathematically, the parallel LLORMA algorithm above constructs q local models based on q different anchor points:

$$\begin{aligned} U^{(t)}, V^{(t)} \leftarrow \min_{U,V} & \sum_{(i,j)\in\Omega} [K^{(a_t)}]_i [K^{(b_t)}]_j \left([UV^\top]_{i,j} - M_{i,j}\right)^2 \\ & + \lambda_U \sum_{i,k} U_{i,k}^2 + \lambda_V \sum_{j,k} V_{j,k}^2 \end{aligned} \tag{11.24}$$

where K is kernel smoothing vector based on anchor point a_t and b_t. It then combines the models via kernel regression to produce $\hat{M}$ which yields the following approximation:

$$\hat{M}_{u,i} = \sum_{t=1}^{q} \frac{K(u_t,u)K(i_t,i)}{\sum_s K(u_s,u)K(i_s,i)} [U^{(t)} V^{(t)\top}]_{u,i} \tag{11.25}$$

where $K(\cdot,\cdot)$ is a smoothing kernel. That is, the algorithm learns each local model independently based on different subsets of the matrix (with some potential overlap).

To sum up, we introduced LLORMA as an example of highly parallelizable and thus scalable approach with the number of observations and the dimension of the problem. For simplicity, we omitted the mathematical detail of LLORMA, its experimental results, and theoretical analysis. We encourage readers to refer to the original paper [15,16] as well as divide-and-conquer matrix factorization [17], which is also along similar lines.

11.5 How to Recommend for Fresh Users/Items

Another important challenge with recommendation system is the cold-start problem. Once the recommendation service is launched, new users will join. We have no feedback or purchase history of these users, so pure collaborative filtering methods may not work. With memory-based collaborative filtering, for example, it is impossible to find neighbors of these users, since they do not have any preferred items, thus no copreferred items with any other user. Matrix factorization also suffers from the same problem. Starting with random assignment on the user profile (or embedding), it will never be updated since there is no available rating from the user on any item. Figure 11.9 illustrates how matrix factorization suffers from cold-start: rows and columns without rating will never be updated. Many recommendation systems also grow with new items released as well. We always have new movies, new music, and so on. A similar problem happens for new items. User-based CF may find similar users for a target user, but no neighbor users have seen this new item, so this new item will never be recommended to the target user.

In this section, we introduce two different approaches to resolve the cold-start problem: how should we recommend new items and/or to new users (without any feedback)? The first approach is leveraging external content information for users and items. Using extra information, we try to figure out better initialization of user and item profiles, and based on those we generate the initial recommendations. The second approach is an initial survey; asking users to answer some questions to identify his or her interest at the beginning. The key interest with this approach is what questions we should ask to effectively and quickly identify the user's preferences.

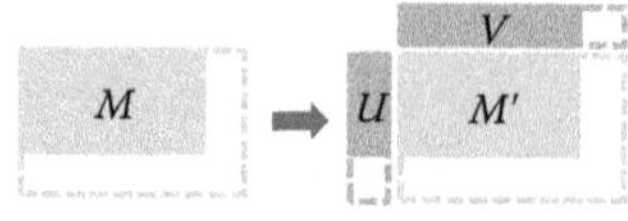

Figure 11.9: Illustration of the cold-start problem. The dotted part of users and items in *M* has no available rating (left), so the corresponding user and item profiles (dotted part of *U* and *V*) also contain random values.

11.5.1 Hybrid approach: Using content information

In some cases, we may have extra information about who are the users and what are the items in addition to the rating matrix. In movie recommendation systems, for example, we may know about the movies such as genre, the director, main actors, released year, and so on. Such information is usually available right away once the movie is released. Using these metadata, it is possible to find similar movies even in the case of cold-start cases; that is, even when nobody has watched the movie yet.

This is also true for users; even for a new customer, without any feedback or behaviors in the site, we still may have some demographic information we might get through the registration process. That is, we may ask gender, age, or address at sign-up, and based on these, we may cluster similar users even with the cold-start users.

We may alleviate the cold-start problem by leveraging these metadata. For memory-based CF, we first collect neighbors of the target user or item. This has been done by collecting those with a similar watch history or preference pattern shown in the rating matrix so far. With the metadata, however, we can do the same thing even without any entry in the matrix. For the case of users, we may define a distance metric based on available information; for instance

$$dist_{cold}(u,v) = \alpha|age_u - age_v| + \beta I(sex_u \neq sex_v) + \gamma d(addr_u, addr_v) \quad (11.26)$$

where u and v are users, $I(cond)$ is an indicator function returning 1 if the *cond* is true, 0 otherwise, and $d(\cdot,\cdot)$ is a distance between two vectors. This function computes distance between two users: the distance gets larger with age gap, different gender, and geographic distance between them. α, β, and γ are weights for each factor. Applying this function, we can compute distance between any two users (as long as we have age, gender, and address data), and it means we can find neighbors for cold-start users. For established users, having sufficient ratings, we may mix similarity or distance computed from preference pattern and metadata, with a larger coefficient with the increase in number of ratings.

In the case of matrix factorization, we can estimate embeddings for cold-start users or items by using metadata. Let us set X be the available metadata features for a user or an item, and Y be the embeddings for the corresponding user or item. We can learn a mapping $f: X \rightarrow Y$ from established users or items. This is a regression problem, mapping an input variable X to another continuous variable Y. We may use any regression method; for instance, linear regression, kernel regression, neural networks, or decision trees.

11.5.2 Initial survey

Another approach for resolving the cold-start issue is taking an initial survey to new users. Once a new user registers, we ask some questions to figure out his or her personal interests. For music recommendations, we may play several songs for 5–10 seconds, and ask how much the user likes it. For movies, it may be hard to show trailers, as they are already too long (2–3 minutes each). Thus, it may make more sense to list just title (or with a poster, a thumbnail, or a short description) and give an option to dismiss answering that question. For example, Figure 11.10 [18] shows such an example: listing movies and users may answer either like, dislike, or unknown, or a 5-star scale with an "unknown" option.

For this approach, the key question is what items (movies or musics) to ask to best figure out the person's preference. Asking too few questions may lead to inaccurate estimation of user profiles and the system is unable to provide satisfactory recommendations, while asking too many questions may cause users to abandon the interview. Thus, it is important to ask critical questions discovering user interests with minimum interactions. Intuitively, we may want to ask items from various types; for example, one item each from different genres. We may apply machine-learning techniques to make this process more accurate and effective.

In this section, we introduce an adaptive interview process, which is known to be effective to improve accuracy compared to a fixed set of questions. As the next question is dependent on the previous answers from the user, we represent the interview process as a decision tree. At each node, the new user is asked

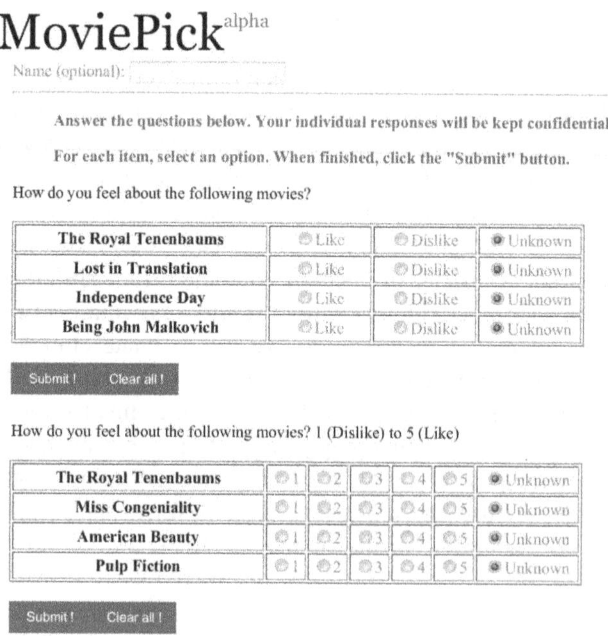

Figure 11.10: An example of initial survey website.

a question about an item, and depending on the user's answer (like, dislike, or unknown), we move down to the corresponding subtree. Once the user reaches a leaf, there are users with established watch history with similar taste to the new user, so we may recommend movies they liked. An example of a decision tree is shown in Figure 11.11 [19].

In the adaptive interview, our goal is learning a function that maps user responses to user preference profiles from training data. Formally, let $R_{u,i}$ denote the observed rating on item i by training user u. Taking a similar formulation to the matrix factorization we studied earlier, Zhou et al. [19] proposed functional matrix factorization:

$$\min_{T,V} \sum_{(u,i)\in O} (R_{u,i} - v_i^\top T(a_u))^2 + \lambda \|V\|^2 \tag{11.27}$$

where $T(a_u)$ is the function mapping the user response a_u to the user profile. We learn both T and V using a typical decision tree learning algorithm such as C4.5 or CART [20]. For more detailed optimization, please refer to the original paper [19]. Sun et al. [18] extended this work for asking more than one question in each stage with different kinds of questions.

11.6 Evaluation of Recommendation Systems

Recommendation systems can be evaluated in various ways. When a system is deployed as a real application, it may be tested with real users on a real situation. That is, one or more recommendation engines are implemented on a target system, and each user is directed to test those recommenders. From the system log, we can observe how users are influenced by the system. We may also survey them directly. This kind of user study is widely used in human computer interaction (HCI) or the computer-supported cooperative work (CSCW) research community. However, a user study is very costly in general. Also, we need to accept the burden of opening an imperfect version to real users. This may give a negative experience, making them avoid using the system in the future.

Instead of online experiments with real users, we can conduct offline experiments using previously gathered data sets. In this section, we focus on evaluation of *recommendation algorithms*, from a machine learning and data mining perspective. We introduce various evaluation metrics and strategies which have been used in the recommendation system research community [21,22] as well as that used throughout this chapter.

11.6.1 Metrics for prediction accuracy

When our main task is predicting unseen ratings, we usually want to quantify how accurate the predicted rating is. Formally, we define a recommendation

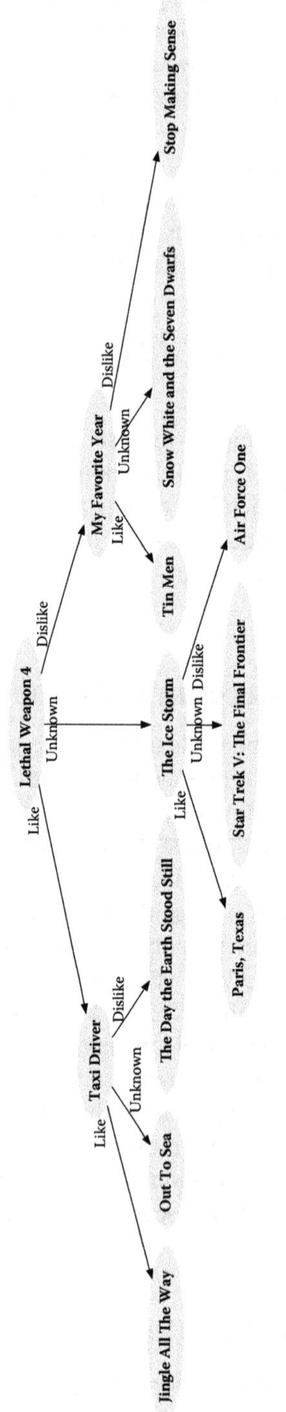

Figure 11.11: An example of initial survey, based on a decision tree. Each node has three children: like, dislike, and don't know.

system $f(u,i)$ as a function, returning predicted rating for item i by user u. For a set of indices Ω of m test entries, we compare the predicted rating and the observed true rating. This test set is not supposed to be seen by the recommendation system before it finishes the learning phase. The three most widely used metrics include

Mean absolute error (MAE)

$$MAE = \frac{1}{m} \sum_{(u,i)\in\Omega} |f(u,i) - M_{u,i}| \tag{11.28}$$

where $f(u,i)$ is our prediction on item i by user u, and $M_{u,i}$ is the ground truth.

Normalized mean absolute error (NMAE)

$$NMAE = \frac{MAE}{r_{max} - r_{min}} \tag{11.29}$$

where r_{max} and r_{min} indicate the maximum and minimum possible rating in the dataset, respectively. This measure surely scales between $[0,1]$.

Root mean squared error (RMSE)

$$RMSE = \sqrt{\frac{1}{m} \sum_{(u,i)\in\Omega} (f(u,i) - M_{u,i})^2} \tag{11.30}$$

$RMSE$ tends to give a higher penalty to big mistakes than MAE. Traditionally, MAE was used in general. Since the Netflix prize, $RMSE$ has become more popular.

Asymmetric Measures

In addition to these three metrics [23] introduced asymmetric measures, which have been widely used in classification problems. Asymmetric losses reflect the idea that false-positive and false-negative (see Table 11.1) may result in quite different situations. For example, diagnosing a patient with cancer as normal brings about a much more serious result than its opposite. In recommendation systems, the same problem can happen. Specifically, recommending an item which is not preferable may harm the trustworthiness more than missing an item which is preferable.

Formally, the metrics above can be generalized to the form

$$ASYM = \frac{1}{m} \sum_{(u,i)\in\Omega} L(f(u,i), M_{u,i}) \tag{11.31}$$

where L is defined by a matrix or a function returning a real number. Based on the spirit of the above, an example of asymmetric loss can be defined as

$$L(x,y) = \begin{bmatrix} 0 & 0 & 0 & 3 & 4 \\ 0 & 0 & 0 & 2 & 3 \\ 0 & 0 & 0 & 1 & 2 \\ 6 & 4 & 2 & 0 & 0 \\ 8 & 6 & 4 & 0 & 0 \end{bmatrix} \tag{11.32}$$

$L(x,y)$ in (11.32) indicates the penalty when the system predicts a rating as x (row) for real rating y (column), on a system with ordinal ratings between 1 and 5. For instance, predicting 1 as 2 or 2 as 1 does not give a penalty, since the item is not recommended to the user. This is same for the case of 4 as 5 or 5 as 4 as they are still recommended after all. When we predict 4 as 1, $L(x,y)$ gives a penalty corresponding to their difference as MAE. However, if it is the opposite way, it gives twice the penalty, as we believe recommending bad items will cause more serious problems. This kind of loss matrix or loss function can be defined arbitrarily based on our belief. We observe that MAE or RMSE can be seen as a special case of this asymmetric measure. Since all of these measures are *errors*, lower values mean better performance.

11.6.2 Metrics for classification accuracy

Another way of evaluating a recommendation algorithm is viewing the recommendation process as a classification problem. Based on the ground truth, we can classify each rating as one of {Preferred, Not-preferred}. We want to *recommend* preferred items, but *not to recommend* not-preferred. Among the four cases in Table 11.1, TP and TN are considered correct. Using the table, there are two important measures for accuracy of classifiers:

Precision measures the ratio of correct recommendations among the list of recommended items. If we have 6 items preferred by the user in the recommended list of 10 items, the precision is 0.6, for example.

$$Prec = \frac{\{\text{Recommended} \bigcap \text{Preferred}\}}{\{\text{Recommended}\}} = \frac{TP}{TP+FP} \tag{11.33}$$

Recall measures the ratio of the user's preferred items covered by the recommendation list. If there are 20 items preferred by the user in the system and

Table 11.1 Classification matrix for recommendation systems

	Recommended	Not-recommended
Preferred	True-Positive (TP)	False-Negative (FN)
Not-preferred	False-Positive (FP)	True-Negative (TN)

the system suggests 5 of them, the recall is 0.25, regardless of the length of recommendation list.

$$Recall = \frac{\{\text{Recommended} \bigcap \text{Preferred}\}}{\{\text{Preferred}\}} = \frac{TP}{TP+FN} \tag{11.34}$$

Recall has a property that it is monotonically nondecreasing with the increase of recommendations. An extremely foolish recommender suggesting all items to all users always achieves highest recall. However, increasing the number of recommended items in general reduces its precision. In other words, there is a trade-off between precision and recall.

F1 is a good measure taking both of them into account:

$$F1 = \frac{2 \cdot Prec \cdot Recall}{Prec + Recall} \tag{11.35}$$

The higher all these three measures are, the better the recommender system is. F1 is widely used since it provides a reasonable way to compare two or more systems with just one metric, considering both concepts of precision and recall.

11.6.3 Metrics based on ranks

Rank-based metrics use relative order of recommended items rather than exact scores of them. Below is a list of rank-based measures, which are also used in web search engine evaluation.

Half-life utility score (HLU) [4] is one of the most popular metrics based on ranking. Suppose we recommend an ordered list of items to a user. Naturally, we would expect that the user will see the list from the top to the bottom, and he may stop either when he finds an interesting one or when he feels the list is not useful to him. We want to estimate how likely the user will actually retrieve the recommended items. Assuming an exponential decay with a half-life α, HLU evaluates how many actually preferred items are located in the front of the recommended list. Overall score is in relative scale to the maximum possible score of the target user. Formally, an HLU score HLU_u for user u and overall score HLU is given by

$$HLU_u = \sum_{j=1}^{n_1} \frac{1}{2^{(idx(j)-1)/(\alpha-1)}} \tag{11.36}$$

$$HLU = \frac{\sum_u HLU_u}{\sum_u HLU_u^{max}} \tag{11.37}$$

where $idx(j)$ is the index of the item j in the recommended list, and α is the half-life, the number of items in the list where the probability of retrieval drops to half. For example, if $\alpha = 5$, we assume that users will see the item ranked in the sixth position with half the probability of the one in the first position. HLU_u^{max} is the maximum possible score for the user u. This is achieved when the recommended items are sorted by the user's actual preference. Ref. [22] argues that this is a proper measure when the recommender system is aimed to optimize utility.

Normalized discounted cumulative gain (NDCG) is a popular metric for measuring the effectiveness of a web search engine or other information retrieval applications. Discounted Cumulative Gain (DCG) measures the usefulness of an item based on its rank in a recommended list. NDCG normalizes the DCG in order to compensate for the varying length of the recommendation list. For this, the DCG score is divided by the maximum possible gain with the given list. This is conceptually similar to HLU, but gives slightly different result. Formal definition of DCG and NDCG with a list of p recommendations is given by

$$DCG_u = rel_1 + \sum_{i=2}^{p} \frac{rel_i}{\log_2 i} \tag{11.38}$$

$$NDCG_u = \frac{DCG_u}{DCG_u^{max}} \tag{11.39}$$

where rel_i is the relevance of the item in the index i in the recommended list to the target user. NDCG is the normalized version of DCG by the maximum possible one. This DCG_u^{max} is also achieved when the recommendation list is sorted by the user's actual preference.

Kendall's Tau is a distance measure, representing the number of discordant pairs among m items. Formally,

$$KT_u = \sum_{i=1}^{m} \sum_{j<i} I[(f(u,i) - f(u,j))(M_{u,i} - M_{u,j}) > 0] \tag{11.40}$$

where $F(u,i)$ is our prediction of rating on item i by user u, and $M_{u,i}$ is the ground truth of it. I is an indicator function returning 1 if the condition is true, and 0 otherwise.

Spearman's distance is the square of the Euclidean distance between two rankings interpreted as vectors. Formally, for a predicted ranking vector x and a ground truth ranking vector y over m items, Spearman's distance is

$$SP_u = \sum_{i=1}^{m} (x_i - y_i)^2 \tag{11.41}$$

Before finishing this section, we relate the two important categories of evaluation: rating prediction accuracy (Section 11.6.1) and ranking-based metrics (Section 11.6.3). One question we may have is whether reducing RMSE is really meaningful to users. This is a natural question, since reduction in RMSE seems almost negligible. For instance, the Netflix prize winner achieved RMSE of 0.8567, but so many participants failed to win the million dollar prize as their RMSE were slightly larger than 0.8567, such as 0.86 or so.

Ref. [3] conducted an interesting experiment to verify that reducing RMSE is actually a meaningful task, in a top-k recommendation situation. Assuming that we recommend k items to users, the order is important as we discussed in Section 11.6.3. Our goal in recommendation is therefore locating interesting items on the top (or relatively high rank) of the list. The experiment measured the place of interesting items (observed as highest score) within the recommendation list among 1000 randomly selected items. Comparing the location of interesting items in the recommended list, [3] found that a system with lower RMSE actually locates interesting items on a higher rank on average. This experiment proves that the efforts the research community made on reducing RMSE were actually meaningful in practice.

11.7 Summary and Further Reading

In this chapter, we took the recommendation system as an industry example for network big data. The recommendation problem shares some important challenges for networking, such as large-scale data, sparsity, and fresh entities such as new users or items. We focused on collaborative filtering methods, starting by introducing traditional memory-based methods including user-based and item-based collaborative filtering methods with some possible extensions. Then, we introduced possible solutions for three main challenges: matrix factorization-based advanced models to solve data sparsity problems, divide-and-conquer inspired parallel approaches for data scale issues, and taking advantage of user and item content information as well as an initial survey for cold-start problems. Last, we have briefly discussed how we usually evaluate recommendation systems, with some useful metrics.

For readers who are interested in this area, we recommend to read general survey papers. Adomavicius and Tuzhilin [24] categorized CF algorithms available as of 2006 into content-based, collaborative, and hybrid types and summarized possible extensions. Su and Khoshgoftaar [25] concentrated more on CF methods, including memory-based, model-based, and hybrid methods. A recent textbook on recommender systems introduces traditional techniques and explores additional issues like privacy concerns [26]. Lee et al. [23] compared state-of-the-art collaborative filtering methods experimentally, using open-source software PREA [27].

In addition to several matrix factorization methods we introduced in this chapter, there are many other model-based approaches: clustering-based methods [4,28–30], Bayesian networks [4], dependence network [31], and probabilistic latent variable models [14,32,33]. Slope-one [34] achieved fast and reasonably accurate prediction. Other examples include [7,35,36]. There are some recent efforts to model the recommendation problem as a ranking problem [15,37–41]. Also, there are some theoretical efforts such as deriving a bound on the performance, including [42–45].

More generally, interested readers are strongly encouraged to study machine learning and data mining further, to better understand underlying theory in most of the recommendation methods we introduced [46–50].

References

[1] D. Goldberg, D. Nichols, B. M. Oki, and D. Terry. Using collaborative filtering to weave an information tapestry. *Communications of the ACM*, 35(12):61–70, 1992.

[2] B. Sarwar, G. Karypis, J. Konstan, and J. Reidl. Item-based collaborative filtering recommendation algorithms. In *Proceedings of the International Conference on World Wide Web*, May 1–5, 2001, Hong Kong, pp. 285–295.

[3] Y. Koren, R. Bell, and C. Volinsky. Matrix factorization techniques for recommender systems. *Computer*, 42(8):30–37, 2009.

[4] J. Breese, D. Heckerman, and C. Kadie. Empirical analysis of predictive algorithms for collaborative filtering. In *Proceedings of Uncertainty in Artificial Intelligence*, July 24–26, 1998, Madison, WI, pp. 43–52.

[5] P. Symeonidis, A. Nanopoulos, and Y. Manolopoulos. Providing justifications in recommender systems. *IEEE Transactions on Systems, Man and Cybernetics, Part A: Systems and Humans*, 38(6):1262–1272, 2008.

[6] J. Kim. *Nonnegative Matrix and Tensor Factorizations, Least Squares Problems, and Applications*. PhD thesis, Georgia Institute of Technology, 2011.

[7] D. Lee and H. Seung. Algorithms for non-negative matrix factorization. In *Advances in Neural Information Processing Systems*, December 3–8, 2001, Vancouver, BC, pp. 556–562.

[8] R. Salakhutdinov and A. Mnih. Probabilistic matrix factorization. In *Advances in Neural Information Processing Systems*, December 8–14, 2001, Vancouver, BC, pp. 1257–1264.

[9] R. Salakhutdinov and A. Mnih. Bayesian probabilistic matrix factorization using markov chain monte carlo. In *Proceedings of the International Conference on Machine Learning*, July 5–9, 2008, Helsinki, Finland, pp. 880–887.

[10] N. Srebro, J. D. M. Rennie, and T. S. Jaakola. Maximum-margin matrix factorization. In *Advances in Neural Information Processing Systems 17*, pages 1329–1336, MIT Press, 2005.

[11] J. D. M. Rennie and N. Srebro. Fast maximum margin matrix factorization for collaborative prediction. In *Proceedings of the International Conference on Machine Learning*, August 7–11, 2005, Bonn, Germany, pp. 713–719.

[12] D. DeCoste. Collaborative prediction using ensembles of maximum margin matrix factorizations. In *Proceedings of the ICML*, June 25–29, 2006, Pittsburgh, PA, pp. 249–256.

[13] N. D. Lawrence and R. Urtasun. Non-linear matrix factorization with gaussian processes. In *Proceedings of the International Conference on Machine Learning*, June 14–18, 2009, Montreal, Canada, pp. 601–608.

[14] K. Yu, S. Zhu, J. Lafferty, and Y. Gong. Fast nonparametric matrix factorization for large-scale collaborative filtering. In *Proceedings of ACM SIGIR Conference*, June 14–18, 2009, Montreal, Canada, pp. 211–218.

[15] J. Lee, S. Bengio, S. Kim, G. Lebanon, and Y. Singer. Local collaborative ranking. In *Proceedings of the International World Wide Web Conference*, April 7–11, 2014, Seoul, Korea, pp. 85–96.

[16] J. Lee, S. Kim, G. Lebanon, Y. Singer, and S. Bengio. LLORMA: Local low-rank matrix approximation. *Journal of Machine Learning Research*, 17:1–24, 2016.

[17] L. W. Mackey, A. S. Talwalkar, and M. I. Jordan. Divide-and-conquer matrix factorization. In *Advances in Neural Information Processing Systems*, December 12–17, 2011, Granada, Spain, pp. 1134–1142.

[18] M. Sun, F. Li, J. Lee, K. Zhou, G. Lebanon, and H. Zha. Learning multiple-question decision trees for cold-start recommendation. In *Proceedings of the ACM International Conference on Web Search and Data Mining*, February 4–8, 2013, Rome, Italy, pp. 445–454.

[19] K. Zhou, S. Yang, and H. Zha. Functional matrix factorizations for cold-start recommendation. In *Proceedings of the ACM-SIGIR Conference*, July 24–28, 2011, Beijing, PRC, pp. 315–324.

[20] L. Breiman, J. Friedman, C. J. Stone, and R. A. Olshen. *Classification and Regression Trees*. Boca Raton, FL, CRC Press, 1984.

[21] J. L. Herlocker, J. A. Konstan, L. G. Terveen, and J. T. Riedl. Evaluating collaborative filtering recommender systems. *ACM Transactions on Information Systems*, 22(1):5–53, 2004.

[22] A. Gunawardana and G. Shani. A survey of accuracy evaluation metrics of recommendation tasks. *Journal of Machine Learning Research*, 10:2935–2962, 2009.

[23] J. Lee, M. Sun, and G. Lebanon. A comparative study of collaborative filtering algorithms. *ArXiv Report 1205.3193*, 2012.

[24] G. Adomavicius and A. Tuzhilin. Toward the next generation of recommender systems: A survey of the state-of-the-art and possible extensions. *IEEE Transactions on Knowledge and Data Engineering*, 17(6):734–749, 2005.

[25] X. Su and T. M. Khoshgoftaar. A survey of collaborative filtering techniques. *Advances in Artificial Intelligence*, 2009:1–19, 2009.

[26] D. Jannach, M. Zanker, A. Felfernig, and G. Friedrich. *Recommender Systems–An Introduction*. Cambridge University Press, Cambridge, 2011.

[27] J. Lee, M. Sun, and G. Lebanon. Prea: Personalized recommendation algorithms toolkit. *Journal of Machine Learning Research*, 13:2699–2703, 2012.

[28] L. H. Ungar and D. P. Foster. Clustering methods for collaborative filtering. In *AAAI Workshop on Recommendation Systems*, October 22–24, 1998, Orlando, FL, vol. 1, pp. 114–129.

[29] G. R. Xue, C. Lin, Q. Yang, W. S. Xi, H. J. Zeng, Y. Yu, and Z. Chen. Scalable collaborative filtering using cluster-based smoothing. In *Proceedings of ACM SIGIR Conference*, August 15–19, 2005, Salvador, Brazil, pp. 114–121.

[30] N. Mirbakhsh and C. X. Ling. Clustering-based matrix factorization. *ArXiv Report arXiv:1301.6659*, 2013.

[31] D. Heckerman, D. Maxwell Chickering, C. Meek, R. Rounthwaite, and C. Kadie. Dependency networks for inference, collaborative filtering, and data visualization. *Journal of Machine Learning Research*, 1:49–75, 2000.

[32] D. M. Pennock, E. Horvitz, S. Lawrence, and C. L. Giles. Collaborative filtering by personality diagnosis: A hybrid memory- and model-based approach. In *Proceedings of the Conference on UAI*, June 30–July 3, 2000, Palo Alto, CA, pp. 473–480.

[33] B. Marlin. Modeling user rating profiles for collaborative filtering. In *Advances in Neural Information Processing Systems*, December 13–18, 2004, Vancouver, BC, pp. 627–634.

[34] D. Lemire and A. Maclachlan. Slope one predictors for online rating-based collaborative filtering. *Society for Industrial Mathematics*, 5:471–480, 2005.

[35] Y. Koren. Factor in the neighbors: Scalable and accurate collaborative filtering. *ACM Transactions on Knowledge Discovery from Data*, 4(1):1–24, 2010.

[36] B. Lakshminarayanan, G. Bouchard, and C. Archambeau. Robust bayesian matrix factorisation. In *Proceedings of the International Conference on Artificial Intelligence and Statistics*, April 11–13, 2011, Ft. Lauderdale, FL, pp. 425–433.

[37] R. Herbrich, T. Graepel, and K. Obermayer. Large margin rank boundaries for ordinal regression. In *Advances in Neural Information Processing Systems*, MIT Press, Cambridge, MA, 2000.

[38] Y. Freund, R. Iyer, R. E. Schapire, and Y. Singer. An efficient boosting algorithm for combining preferences. *Journal of Machine Learning Research*, 4:933–969, 2003.

[39] J. Weston, S. Bengio, and N. Usunier. Wsabie: Scaling up to large vocabulary image annotation. In *Proceedings of the International Joint Conference on Artificial Intelligence*, July 16–22, 2011, Barcelona, Spain, pp. 2764–2770.

[40] Z. Chen and H. Ji. Collaborative ranking: A case study on entity linking. In *Proceedings of the Conference on Empirical Methods in Natural Language Processing*, July 27–31, 2011, Edinburgh, Scotland, pp. 771–781.

[41] A. Mohan, Z. Chen, and K. Q. Weinberger. Web-search ranking with initialized gradient boosted regression trees. *Journal of Machine Learning Research-Proceedings Track*, 14:77–89, 2011.

[42] E. J. Candès and T. Tao. The power of convex relaxation: Near-optimal matrix completion. *IEEE Transactions on Information Theory*, 56(5):2053–2080, 2010.

[43] S. Shalev-Shwartz, A. Gonen, and O. Shamir. Large-scale convex minimization with a low-rank constraint. In *Proceedings of the International Conference on Machine Learning*, June 28–July 2, 2011, Bellevue, WA, pp. 329–336.

[44] R. Foygel and N. Srebro. Concentration-based guarantees for low-rank matrix reconstruction. *ArXiv Report arXiv:1102.3923*, 2011.

[45] R. Foygel, N. Srebro, and R. Salakhutdinov. Matrix reconstruction with the local max norm. *ArXiv Report arXiv:1210.5196*, 2012.

[46] T. Mitchell. *Machine Learning*. New York City, NY, 1997.

[47] Y. Anzai. *Pattern Recognition & Machine Learning*. Elsevier, Amsterdam, Netherlands, 2012.

[48] K. P. Murphy. *Machine Learning: A Probabilistic Perspective*. MIT Press, Cambridge, MA, 2012.

[49] J. Friedman, T. Hastie, and R. Tibshirani. *The Elements of Statistical Learning*, volume 1. Springer Series in Statistics. Springer, Berlin, 2001.

[50] C. Manning, H. Schutze, and P. Raghavan. *Introduction to Information Retrieval*. Cambridge University Press, Cambridge, UK, 2008.

Chapter 12

Coordinate Gradient Descent Methods

Ion Necoara

University Politehnica Bucharest
Bucharest, Romania

CONTENTS

We start with some basic notations used in this chapter. For an integer $N > 0$ we denote by $[N] = \{1, 2, \cdots, N\}$. We work in the space $\mathbb{R}^N$ composed of column vectors. For $x, y \in \mathbb{R}^N$ we denote the inner product $\langle x, y \rangle = x^T y$ and the corresponding Euclidean norm $\|x\| = \sqrt{\langle x, x \rangle}$. We use the same notations $\langle \cdot, \cdot \rangle$ and

$\|\cdot\|$ for spaces of different dimensions. If we fix a norm $\|\cdot\|$ in $\mathbb{R}^N$, then its dual norm is defined by:

$$\|y\|^* = \max_{\|x\|=1} \langle y, x \rangle$$

Then, the Cauchy–Schwarz inequality holds: $\langle y, x \rangle \leq \|x\| \cdot \|y\|^*$ for all $x, y \in \mathbb{R}^N$. We assume that the entire space dimension is decomposable into n blocks $N = \sum_{i=1}^{n} n_i$. We denote by E_i the blocks of the identity matrix:

$$I_N = [E_1 \ \ldots \ E_n], \quad \text{where} \quad E_i \in \mathbb{R}^{N \times n_i}$$

When $n_i = 1$ for all $i \in [n]$, we have that $E_i = e_i$, the standard basis of the Euclidean space $\mathbb{R}^n$. For some vector $x \in \mathbb{R}^N$, we use the notation x_i for the ith block of the vector x, i.e.:

$$x_i = E_i^T x \in \mathbb{R}^{n_i}$$

We can also write $x = \sum_{i \in [n]} E_i x_i$. In the rest of this chapter we consider local Euclidean norms in all spaces $\mathbb{R}^{n_i}$, i.e., $\|x_i\| = \sqrt{x_i^T x_i}$ for all $x_i \in \mathbb{R}^{n_i}$ and $i \in [n]$. For a given nonnegative vector $u \in \mathbb{R}^n_{++}$, we define the following norm: $\|x\|_u = \sqrt{\sum_{i=1}^{n} u_i \|x_i\|^2}$.

For a continuously differentiable function $F : \mathbb{R}^N \to \mathbb{R}$, we define the partial gradient corresponding to the variables in the vector x_i as the ith block in the gradient of F at x,

$$\nabla_i F(x) = E_i^T \nabla F(x)$$

In this chapter we are mainly interested in network problems. This is due to the fact that networks of interconnected subsystems (agents) can be found in many applications such as resource allocation [1], electricity generation from renewable energies [2], distributed control (e.g., control for power system networks) [3], telecommunications [4], coordination in multiagent systems (e.g., satellite flight formation) [5], estimation in sensor networks [6], image processing [7], machine learning [8], network flow, and other areas [9]. In general, the performance of such networks can be improved if the separated subsystems are jointly optimized. Optimization methods have been always a powerful tool for solving large-scale network problems. There are basically two network optimization formulations, one associated to the subsystems (nodes) of the network and the other associated to the edges of the network. The first one is formulated as follows:

$$\min_{x \in \mathbb{R}^N} F(x) \quad \left(:= \sum_{i \in [m]} f_i(a_i^T x) \right) \tag{12.1}$$

where m denotes the number of subsystems (nodes) in the network, $f_i(\cdot)$ represents the local objective function associated to the ith subsystem and the goal is to jointly optimize the sum of these local objective functions, denoted F. Note that the previous objective function can be written compactly as $F(x) = f(Ax)$, where the jth row of matrix $A \in \mathbb{R}^{m \times n}$ is a_j, and includes as applications least-squares, logistic regression, lasso, and support vector machines. The second network optimization problem has the following formulation:

$$\min_{x \in \mathbb{R}^N} F(x) \quad \left(:= \sum_{(i,j) \in E} f_{ij}(x_i, x_j) \right) \tag{12.2}$$

where E are the edges in the graph associated to the network, and include as applications graph-based label propagation, probabilistic graphical models, etc. For large-scale networks, the associated problems (12.1) and (12.2) have the following features: *the decision variable* x is big so that usual methods based on whole gradient computations are prohibitive; moreover *the incomplete structure of the information*, e.g., the data are distributed over the nodes of the network, so that at a given time we need to work only with the data available then, may also be an obstacle for whole gradient computations; finally the decision variables are *unconstrained*. In this case, an appropriate way to approach these problems is through coordinate descent methods. These methods were among the first optimization methods studied in literature, but until recently they have not received much attention. The main differences in all variants of coordinate descent algorithms consist of the way we define the local approximation function over which we optimize and the criterion of choosing at each iteration the coordinate over which we minimize this local approximation function. For updating the block variable x_i, while keeping the other variables $(x_1, \cdots, x_{i-1}, x_{i+1}, \cdots, x_n)$ fixed, two basic choices for the local approximation function are usually considered:

(i) Exact approximation function, leading to *coordinate minimization methods*:

$$x_i^+ = \arg \min_{y_i \in \mathbb{R}^{n_i}} F(x_1, \cdots, x_{i-1}, y_i, x_{i+1}, \cdots, x_n) \tag{12.3}$$

Although the minimization of the function F over the whole variable x can be computationally expensive, it can happen that the exact minimization of F over the variable x_i, while keeping all the other variables fixed, can be easy. For example, the function F can be nonconvex, but the function $y_i \to F(x_1, \cdots, x_{i-1}, y_i, x_{i+1}, \cdots, x_n)$ can be convex and/or the minimization in y_i can have closed form solution. Indeed, let us consider the nonconvex function $F(x_1, x_2) = -x_1 x_2 + (x_1 - 1)_+^2 + (-x_1 - 1)_+^2 + (x_2 - 1)_+^2 + (-x_2 - 1)_+^2$, where $(a)_+ = \max(a, 0)$ for any scalar a. Then, the exact minimization in x_1, given x_2, is convex and has the following closed form expression: $x_1^+ = \text{sign}(x_2)\left(1 + \frac{1}{2}|x_2|\right)$.

(ii) Quadratic approximation function, leading to *coordinate gradient descent methods*:

$$\begin{aligned} x_i^+ &= \arg\min_{y_i \in \mathbb{R}^{n_i}} F(x) + \langle \nabla_i F(x), y_i - x_i \rangle + \frac{1}{2\alpha_i} \|y_i - x_i\|^2 \\ &= x_i - \alpha_i \nabla_i F(x) \end{aligned} \tag{12.4}$$

There are several strategies for determining the steplength α_i, such as performing an exact minimization along the ith component, or choosing a value of the steplength that satisfies some line-search conditions of sufficient decrease, or making a predefined choice of α_i based on prior knowledge of the gradient of F. Note that, usually, finding the partial gradient $\nabla_i F(x)$ represents the main computational bottleneck in the update (12.4). However, in many practical situations such partial gradient computations can be done very efficiently, as we will see later in this chapter (see Section 12.1.2).

Furthermore, three classical criteria for choosing the coordinate search i used often in these algorithms are the greedy, the cyclic, and the random coordinate search, which significantly differs by the amount of computations required to choose the appropriate index. Thus, the basic coordinate descent framework for the minimization problem $\min_{x \in \mathbb{R}^N} F(x_1, \cdots, x_n)$ is shown in algorithm CD below:

Algorithm CD:Choose $x^0 \in \mathbb{R}^N$.
For $k \geq 0$ **do**:

1. Choose an index $i_k \in [n]$ (greedy, cyclic, random)
2. Update $x_{i_k}^{k+1}$ as in (12.3) or (12.4), $x_j^{k+1} = x_j^k \ \forall j \neq i_k$

until a stopping criterion is satisfied.

For cyclic coordinate minimization methods, convergence rates are given in Ref. [9] under the assumption that the minimizer along any coordinate direction from any point is unique. Recently, a new coordinate minimization framework has been proposed in Ref. [10] and convergence results were given under more relaxed conditions. For coordinate gradient descent methods based on cyclic coordinate search, estimates on the rate of convergence were given recently in Ref. [11], for the greedy coordinate search (e.g., Gauss–Southwell rule) the convergence rate is given in Ref. [12], while for random coordinate search, convergence estimates were obtained recently in Refs. [13–15]. A detailed exposition of coordinate descent methods, together with variants and extensions and their convergence properties, has been also given recently in the survey paper [16]. In this chapter we present the fundamentals of coordinate gradient descent approach, based on the aforementioned choices for the coordinate search, for minimizing unconstrained convex problems and analyze their convergence behavior and computational cost per iteration under various assumptions on the optimization problem.

12.1 Motivation

Coordinate descent methods were among the first optimization algorithms suggested for solving unconstrained minimization problems. In this section we will provide strong arguments in the favor of coordinate gradient descent methods, such as the simplicity of each iteration and the existence of a general convergence theory, both aspects raising difficulties when coordinate descent methods based on exact minimization are used.

12.1.1 *Coordinate minimization versus coordinate gradient descent*

We start with a simple nonconvex example due to Powell [17], where he proved that coordinate descent with exact minimization based on cyclic search of coordinates fails to converge to a minimizer. Powell considered the following nonconvex, continuously differentiable function $F : \mathbb{R}^3 \to \mathbb{R}$ defined as follows:

$$
\begin{aligned}
F(x_1,x_2,x_3) = & -x_1x_2 - x_2x_3 - x_1x_3 + (x_1-1)_+^2 + (-x_1-1)_+^2 + (x_2-1)_+^2 \\
& + (-x_2-1)_+^2 + (x_3-1)_+^2 + (-x_3-1)_+^2
\end{aligned}
$$

where recall that $(a)_+ = \max(a,0)$ for any scalar a. It can be easily checked that this function has the minimizers $[1\ 1\ 1]^T$ and $[-1\ -1\ -1]^T$, which are vertices of the unit cube. Note that the optimal x_1 given fixed x_2 and x_3 has the following expression:

$$
x_1^+ = \arg\min_{y_1} F(y_1,x_2,x_3) = \operatorname{sign}(x_2+x_3)\left(1+\frac{1}{2}|x_2+x_3|\right)
$$

Now, suppose we start near, but outside, one of the other vertices of the cube, for example:

$$
\left[-1-\epsilon \quad 1+\frac{1}{2}\epsilon \quad -1-\frac{1}{4}\epsilon\right]^T \quad \text{with} \quad \epsilon > 0
$$

then the iterates of the cyclic coordinate descent method based on exact minimization (12.3) move around the other six vertices of the cube:

$$
\begin{aligned}
&\left[1+\frac{1}{8}\epsilon \quad 1+\frac{1}{2}\epsilon \quad -1-\frac{1}{4}\epsilon\right]^T && \left[1+\frac{1}{8}\epsilon \quad -1-\frac{1}{16}\epsilon \quad -1-\frac{1}{4}\epsilon\right]^T \\
&\left[1+\frac{1}{8}\epsilon \quad -1-\frac{1}{16}\epsilon \quad 1+\frac{1}{32}\epsilon\right]^T && \left[-1-\frac{1}{64}\epsilon \quad -1-\frac{1}{16}\epsilon \quad 1+\frac{1}{32}\epsilon\right]^T \\
&\left[-1-\frac{1}{64}\epsilon \quad 1+\frac{1}{128}\epsilon \quad 1+\frac{1}{32}\epsilon\right]^T && \left[-1-\frac{1}{64}\epsilon \quad 1+\frac{1}{128}\epsilon \quad -1-\frac{1}{256}\epsilon\right]^T
\end{aligned}
$$

For this example the gradient is not 0 at any vertex of the cube $[\pm 1 \ \pm 1 \ \pm 1]^T$, so that the previous iterates will not converge to some stationary point.

This example also shows that a cyclic coordinate minimization method can have a nonconvergent behavior for a nonconvex objective function, but a randomized coordinate minimization method applied to the same example would be expected to converge to the vicinity of a solution in a few steps. Therefore, we cannot expect a general convergence theory of coordinate descent methods for nonconvex objective functions and thus it is better to concentrate on coordinate gradient descent methods for minimizing smooth convex optimization problems.

12.1.2 Computational complexity for coordinate gradient descent

For problems of big dimension it is important to treat very carefully all the operations that need to be performed for the coordinate gradient descent scheme. Note that one of the main computational bottlenecks in updating x, according to (12.4), is to compute the full and the partial gradient $\nabla F(x)$ and $\nabla_i F(x)$, which usually requires an efficient handling of the problem structure. For example, let us consider the objective function defined in the optimization problem (12.1) with $n_i = 1$ for all i. Let us define the matrix $A \in \mathbb{R}^{m \times n}$ whose jth row is given by a_j. For simplicity of the exposition, we assume that matrix A is sparse having at most $p \ll \min(m,n)$ nonzero entries on each row and column. Then, the whole gradient vector has the following expression:

$$\nabla F(x) = \sum_{i \in [m]} f_i'(a_i^T x) a_i = A^T [f_1'(a_1^T x) \cdots f_m'(a_m^T x)]^T \tag{12.5}$$

which requires first the computation of the residual $r = Ax$. For the full gradient method, that is $x^+ = x + d$, with $d \in \mathbb{R}^n$, the update of the residual needs $\mathcal{O}(np)$ operations and thus the computation of the whole gradient vector requires $\mathcal{O}(2np)$ operations, since all the vectors a_i are sparse. However, the cost of computing the partial gradient $\nabla_i F(x)$ is small and the residual $r = Ax$ can be updated efficiently when algorithm CD, with update (12.4), is used. Indeed, knowing the residual $r = Ax$, then the coordinate gradient descent update:

$$x^+ = x + d_i e_i \quad \text{with} \quad d_i \in \mathbb{R}$$

results in the following change in the residual:

$$r^+ = Ax^+ = A(x + d_i e_i) = Ax + d_i A_i = r + d_i A_i$$

where A_i is the ith column of A. Thus the cost of updating the residual under the coordinate descent method is only of order $\mathcal{O}(p)$. Moreover, the computation of the ith component of the gradient $\nabla_i F(x)$ can also be performed efficiently in $\mathcal{O}(p)$ operations, according to (12.5). Therefore, for structured objective functions with sparse data the previous coordinate gradient descent update $x^+ = x + d_i e_i$ needs $\mathcal{O}(2p)$ operations, while the full gradient update needs

$\mathcal{O}(2np)$ operations, that is n times more computationally expensive. In particular, for the least square problem:

$$F(x) = \frac{1}{2}\|Ax-b\|^2$$

we have $\nabla f(x) = A^T(Ax-b)$. If the residual $r = Ax - b$ is known, then the computation of the whole gradient requires at most $\mathcal{O}(np)$ operations and of the ith component of the gradient needs $\mathcal{O}(p)$ operations, respectively. On the other hand, the coordinate update $x^+ = x + d_i e_i$ results in the following change in the residual:

$$r^+ = Ax^+ - b = A(x + d_i e_i) - b = (Ax - b) + d_i A_i = r + d_i A_i$$

so that we need $\mathcal{O}(p)$ operations for updating the residual in the coordinate descent framework. In conclusion, for large-scale structured optimization problems with sparse data, coordinate gradient descent schemes based on the update (12.4) need to compute a partial gradient which may be n times simpler than the computation of the whole gradient vector.

12.2 Problem Formulation

In this chapter, we are interested in solving unconstrained convex minimization problems with differentiable objective function $F : \mathbb{R}^n \to \mathbb{R}$ defined by a black-box oracle:

$$F^* = \min_{x \in \mathbb{R}^N} F(x) \tag{12.6}$$

We denote by X^* the optimal set of the previous convex problem, i.e.,

$$X^* = \arg\min_x F(x)$$

We make the standard assumption that the optimal set X^* is nonempty and the optimal value F^* is finite. For a given constant $c \in \mathbb{R}$ we also define the sublevel set:

$$\mathcal{L}_c = \{x \in \mathbb{R}^N : F(x) \le c\}$$

We consider the following assumptions on the objective function F:

Assumption 12.1 (i) *Function F is strongly convex, i.e., there is a constant $\sigma \ge 0$ such that:*

$$F(x) \ge F(y) + \langle \nabla F(y), x - y\rangle + \frac{\sigma}{2}\|x-y\|^2 \quad \forall x, y \in \mathbb{R}^N$$

(ii) *Function F has (block) componentwise Lipschitz continuous gradient, i.e., there are constants $L_i > 0$ such that:*

$$\|\nabla_i F(x + E_i s_i) - \nabla_i F(x)\| \le L_i \|s_i\| \quad \forall x \in \mathbb{R}^N, s_i \in \mathbb{R}^{n_i}, i = 1:n$$

If the objective function F satisfies Assumption 12.1(i) with $\sigma = 0$, then we say that F is simply convex, otherwise if $\sigma > 0$, then we say that F is σ strongly convex. Note that if the objective function satisfies Assumption 12.1(i) with $\sigma > 0$, then minimizing both hand sides over x, for fixed y, that is:

$$\min_{x\in\mathbb{R}^N} F(x) \geq \min_{x\in\mathbb{R}^N} \left[F(y) + \langle \nabla F(y), x-y\rangle + \frac{\sigma}{2}\|x-y\|^2\right]$$

we obtain the following useful relation:

$$F(y) - F^* \leq \frac{1}{2\sigma}\|\nabla F(y)\|^2 \quad \forall y \in \mathbb{R}^N \tag{12.7}$$

Furthermore, Assumption 12.1(ii) is typical for convex optimization and covers many applications, see e.g., [12,13,15,16]. Coordinatewise Lipschitz continuity of the gradient of function F implies that F can be upper bounded by a quadratic function along the ith coordinate. Indeed, using the mean value theorem in the integral form, we have:

$$\begin{aligned}
F(x+E_is_i) &= F(x) + \int_0^1 \langle \nabla F(x+\delta E_ix_i), E_is_i\rangle\, d\delta \\
&= F(x) + \int_0^1 \langle \nabla_i F(x+\delta E_ix_i), s_i\rangle\, d\delta \\
&= F(x) + \langle \nabla_i F(x), s_i\rangle + \int_0^1 \langle \nabla_i F(x+\delta E_ix_i) - \nabla_i F(x), s_i\rangle\, d\delta \\
&\leq F(x) + \langle \nabla_i F(x), s_i\rangle + \int_0^1 \|\nabla_i F(x+\delta E_ix_i) - \nabla_i F(x)\|\|s_i\| d\delta \\
&\leq F(x) + \langle \nabla_i F(x), s_i\rangle + \int_0^1 \delta L_i\|s_i\|^2 d\delta
\end{aligned}$$

and thus we obtain the so-called descent lemma:

$$F(x+E_is_i) \leq F(x) + \langle \nabla_i F(x), s_i\rangle + \frac{L_i}{2}\|s_i\|^2 \quad \forall x \in \mathbb{R}^N, s_i \in \mathbb{R}^{n_i} \text{ and } i \in [n] \tag{12.8}$$

From Assumption 12.1(ii) we can also derive an estimation of the global Lipschitz constant L based on the block-coordinatewise Lipschitz constants L_is (see Ref. [13, Lemma 2]):

$$\|\nabla F(x) - \nabla F(y)\| \leq \left(\sum_{i=1}^{n} L_i\right)\|x-y\| \qquad \forall x,y \in \mathbb{R}^N$$

From previous discussion, it follows that the global Lipschitz constant L can be bounded as:

$$\max_{i\in[n]} L_i \leq L \leq \sum_{i\in[n]} L_i \tag{12.9}$$

We also define the following two vectors $\mathbb{1} = [1 \cdots 1]^T \in \mathbb{R}^n$ and $\mathbb{L} = [L_1 \cdots L_n]^T \in \mathbb{R}^n$. In the remainder of this chapter, we present coordinate gradient descent methods based on greedy, cyclic, and random coordinate search for solving the optimization problem (12.6), and we derive the corresponding convergence results.

12.3 Greedy Coordinate Gradient Descent Method (G-CGD)

In this section we introduce a greedy (block) coordinate gradient descent algorithm for solving the unconstrained optimization problem (12.6). The method chooses at each iteration $k \geq 0$ an index $i_k \in [n]$ for which the corresponding component of the gradient is maximum in some norm (also called the Gauss–Southwell rule) and then performs a gradient update along the i_kth coordinate:

Algorithm G-CGD

1. Choose the index $i_k = \arg\max_{i \in [n]} \dfrac{\|\nabla_i F(x^k)\|}{\sqrt{L_i}}$
2. Update $x^{k+1} = x^k - \dfrac{1}{L_{i_k}} E_{i_k} \nabla_{i_k} F(x^k)$

Note that the algorithm moves along the direction $E_{i_k} d_{i_k} = E_{i_k}\left(-\frac{1}{L_{i_k}} \nabla_{i_k} F(x^k)\right)$, which represents the solution of the following local optimization subproblem:

$$d_{i_k} = \arg\min_{s_{i_k} \in \mathbb{R}^{n_{i_k}}} F(x^k) + \langle \nabla_{i_k} F(x^k), s_{i_k} \rangle + \frac{L_{i_k}}{2} \|s_{i_k}\|^2$$

coming from the descent lemma (12.8). Moreover, in algorithm G-CGD the most expensive operation is finding the active index i_k based on the Gauss–Southwell rule, which requires computation of the whole gradient vector ∇F. Thus, the greedy coordinate gradient descent method may be as expensive as the full gradient. However, there are special cases of structured objective functions with sparse data, in the form of those given in Section 12.1.2, where algorithm G-CGD is n times faster than the full gradient. For example, if the network problem has the structure given in (12.2) so that the maximum degree is comparable to the average degree, then we can track the gradients efficiently and use a max-heap data structure (see Ref. [18] for more details). Moreover, Section 12.1.2 provides an efficient procedure for the computation of the gradient ∇F for structured objective functions of the form $F(x) = f(Ax)$ given in (12.1), when the rows and columns of matrix A have $\mathcal{O}(\log n)$ nonzeros.

We further analyze the convergence rate of algorithm G-CGD under different assumptions on the objective function. For this, we first introduce the following pair of dual norms:

$$\|x\|_{\mathbb{L}}^2 = \sum_{i \in [n]} L_i \|x_i\|^2 \quad \text{and} \quad \|y\|_{\frac{1}{\mathbb{L}}}^2 = \sum_{i \in [n]} \frac{1}{L_i} \|x_i\|^2$$

which satisfy the Cauchy–Scawarz inequality: $\langle x, y \rangle \leq \|x\|_{\mathbb{L}} \cdot \|y\|_{\frac{1}{\mathbb{L}}}$ for all $x, y \in \mathbb{R}^N$. Furthermore, we define the following quantity:

$$R_{\mathbb{L}}(\bar{x}) = \max_{x^* \in X^*} \max_{x \in \mathcal{L}_{F(\bar{x})}} \|x - x^*\|_{\mathbb{L}}$$

which we assume is finite. For example, $R_{\mathbb{L}}(\bar{x})$ is finite if the sublevel set $\mathcal{L}_{F(\bar{x})}$ is compact.

12.3.1 Convergence rates for G-CGD

We first analyze the convergence behavior of the algorithm G-CGD under the Lipschitz gradient assumption on the objective function.

Theorem 12.1

Let the objective function F satisfy Assumption 12.1 with $\sigma = 0$. Then, the sequence x^k generated by algorithm G-CGD satisfies the following sublinear convergence rate in the objective function values:

$$F(x^k) - F^* \leq \frac{2nR_{\mathbb{L}}^2(x^0)}{k} \tag{12.10}$$

Proof. Based on (12.8) we have the following decrease in the objective function:

$$F(x^k) - F(x^{k+1}) \geq \frac{1}{2L_{i_k}} \|\nabla_{i_k} F(x^k)\|^2 \geq \frac{1}{2n} \|\nabla F(x^k)\|_{\frac{1}{\mathbb{L}}}^2 \tag{12.11}$$

This shows that algorithm G-CGD is a descent method and consequently $x^k \in \mathcal{L}_{F(x^0)}$ for all $k \geq 0$. In particular, $\|x^k - x^*\|_{\mathbb{L}} \leq R_{\mathbb{L}}(x^0)$ for all $k \geq 0$. On the other hand, using convexity of F and the Cauchy–Schwarz inequality for the pair of dual norms $\|\cdot\|_{\mathbb{L}}$ and $\|\cdot\|_{\frac{1}{\mathbb{L}}}$, we obtain:

$$\begin{aligned} R_{\mathbb{L}}(x^0) \|\nabla F(x^k)\|_{\frac{1}{\mathbb{L}}} &\geq \|x^k - x^*\|_{\mathbb{L}} \|\nabla F(x^k)\|_{\frac{1}{\mathbb{L}}} \geq \langle \nabla F(x^k), x^k - x^* \rangle \\ &\geq F(x^k) - F(x^*) \end{aligned}$$

Combining the previous two relations, we get:

$$F(x^k) - F(x^{k+1}) \geq \frac{(F(x^k) - F^*)^2}{2nR_{\mathbb{L}}^2(x^0)}$$

If we denote $\Delta^k = F(x^k) - F^*$, we further obtain:

$$\Delta^k - \Delta^{k+1} \geq \frac{(\Delta^k)^2}{2nR^2_{\mathbb{L}}(x^0)}$$

If we divide in both sides by $\Delta^{k+1}\Delta^k$ and use $\Delta^{k+1} \leq \Delta^k$, we get:

$$\frac{1}{\Delta^{k+1}} \geq \frac{1}{\Delta^k} + \frac{1}{2nR^2_{\mathbb{L}}(x^0)} \geq \cdots \geq \frac{1}{\Delta^0} + \frac{k+1}{2nR^2_{\mathbb{L}}(x^0)}$$

This relation immediately implies the statement of our theorem. □

Let us now assume that we know some upper bounds $R_i > 0$ on $\|x_i - x_i^*\|$, that is:

$$\|x_i - x_i^*\| \leq R_i \quad \forall x \in \mathcal{L}_{F(x^0)},\ i \in [n]$$

Then, we get from Theorem 12.1 rate of convergence for algorithm G-CGD of order:

$$\mathcal{O}\left(\frac{\sum_{i\in[n]}(nL_i)R_i^2}{k}\right)$$

For the full gradient method, with the update

$$x^{k+1} = x^k - \frac{1}{L}\nabla F(x^k)$$

the convergence rate in the smooth case is of order [19]:

$$\mathcal{O}\left(\frac{\sum_{i\in[n]} LR_i^2}{k}\right)$$

Note that there may be situations where $nL_i \approx L$ for all i, see (12.9), so that in the worst case the convergence rates of algorithms G-CGD and full gradient are comparable. Moreover, the complexity per iteration of both algorithms is similar, since both require computation of the whole gradient of F. However, if the whole gradient is available, it seems better to apply the usual full gradient method.

Furthermore, for first-order methods better convergence rates can be attained if the objective function additionally satisfies a strong convexity condition. Therefore, we further prove that under the additional strong convexity assumption, the algorithm G-CGD has linear convergence rate in the function values.

Theorem 12.2

Let the objective function F satisfy Assumption 12.1 with $\sigma > 0$. Then, the sequence x^k generated by algorithm G-CGD satisfies the following linear convergence rate in the objective function values:

$$F(x^k) - F^* \leq \left(1 - \frac{\sigma}{n\max_{i\in[n]} L_i}\right)^k (F(x^0) - F^*) \tag{12.12}$$

Proof. Combining (12.11) and (12.7) we obtain the following relation:

$$F(x^k) - F(x^{k+1}) \geq \frac{1}{2n} \left\| \nabla F(x^k) \right\|_{\frac{1}{L}}^2 \geq \frac{1}{2n \max_{i \in [n]} L_i} \left\| \nabla F(x^k) \right\|^2$$
$$\overset{(12.7)}{\geq} \frac{\sigma}{n \max_{i \in [n]} L_i} \left(F(x^k) - F^* \right)$$

which leads to the linear convergence rate from the theorem. □

From Theorem 12.2 we get rate of convergence for algorithm G-CGD of order:

$$\mathcal{O}\left(\left(1 - \frac{\sigma}{n \max_{i \in [n]} L_i} \right)^k \right)$$

For the full gradient method the convergence rate for smooth strongly convex objective functions is of order [19]:

$$\mathcal{O}\left(\left(1 - \frac{\sigma}{L} \right)^k \right)$$

From (12.9), we get that in the worst case the global Lipschitz constant L can be as large as $n \max_{i \in [n]} L_i$. Thus, we can conclude that the convergence rates of algorithms G-CGD and full gradient are comparable also when we have a smooth strongly convex objective function. Moreover, both algorithms require computation of the whole gradient vector. Therefore, also in the smooth strongly convex case it seems better to apply the full gradient method. However, there are special cases of structured objective functions where greedy coordinate descent updates are faster than full gradient updates, see e.g., [18] for more details.

12.4 Cyclic Coordinate Gradient Descent Method (C-CGD)

In this section we introduce a cyclic (block) coordinate gradient descent algorithm for solving the optimization problem (12.6). The method chooses at each iteration $k \geq 0$ the index $i_k \in [n]$ in a cyclic fashion and then performs a gradient update along the i_kth coordinate:

Algorithm C-CGD

1. Choose the index $i_k = [i_{k-1} \bmod n] + 1$, starting with $i_0 = 1$
2. Update $x^{k+1} = x^k - \frac{1}{L_{i_k}} E_{i_k} \nabla_{i_k} F(x^k)$

The direction $E_{i_k} d_{i_k} = E_{i_k} \left(-\frac{1}{L_{i_k}} \nabla_{i_k} F(x^k) \right)$ in the algorithm C-CGD has the same interpretation as for algorithm G-CGD. Moreover, in algorithm C-CGD the most expensive operation is the computation the partial gradient $\nabla_i F(x)$. Note that Section 12.1.2 provides for the coordinate descent framework an efficient procedure for the computation of the partial gradient of structured objective functions with sparse data. In the sequel we analyze the convergence rate of algorithm C-CGD. We use the same notations as in Section 12.3.

12.4.1 Convergence rates for C-CGD

We first analyze the convergence rate of algorithm C-CGD under the smooth assumption on the objective function. Our analysis here is similar to the one in Ref. [11]. The convergence rates will be given in the iterates of the form kn.

Theorem 12.3

Let the objective function F satisfy Assumption 12.1 with $\sigma = 0$. Then, the sequence x^k generated by algorithm C-CGD satisfies the following sublinear convergence rate in the objective function values:

$$F(x^{kn}) - F^* \leq \frac{4n\left(1 + n\frac{L^2}{\min_{i\in[n]} L_i^2}\right) R_{\mathbb{L}}^2(x^0)}{kn} \tag{12.13}$$

Proof. As for algorithm G-CGD (see (12.11)), we also get for algorithm C-CGD the same decrease in the objective function F at each cyclic iteration:

$$F(x^k) - F(x^{k+1}) \geq \frac{1}{2L_{i_k}} \left\|\nabla_{i_k} F(x^k)\right\|^2$$

Thus, algorithm C-CGD is also a descent method and consequently $\left\|x^k - x^*\right\|_{\mathbb{L}} \leq R_{\mathbb{L}}(x^0)$ for all $k \geq 0$. Summing over an epoch of n consecutive iterations, we get:

$$F(x^{kn}) - F(x^{(k+1)n}) \geq \sum_{i=1}^{n} \frac{1}{2L_i} \left\|\nabla_i F(x^{kn+i-1})\right\|^2$$

Now, we need to bound from below $\sum_{i=1}^{n} \frac{1}{L_i} \left\|\nabla_i F(x^{kn+i-1})\right\|^2$ by the norm of the whole gradient $\sum_{i=1}^{n} \frac{1}{L_i} \left\|\nabla_i F(x^{kn})\right\|^2$. Indeed, using Assumption 12.1(ii), we get:

$$\begin{aligned}
\left\|\nabla F(x^{kn})\right\|_{\frac{1}{\mathbb{L}}}^2 &= \sum_{i=1}^{n} \frac{1}{L_i} \left\|\nabla_i F(x^{kn})\right\|^2 \\
&\leq \sum_{i=1}^{n} \frac{1}{L_i} \left(\left\|\nabla_i F(x^{kn}) - \nabla_i F(x^{kn+i-1})\right\| + \left\|\nabla_i F(x^{kn+i-1})\right\|\right)^2 \\
&\leq \sum_{i=1}^{n} \frac{2}{L_i} \left(\left\|\nabla_i F(x^{kn}) - \nabla_i F(x^{kn+i-1})\right\|^2 + \left\|\nabla_i F(x^{kn+i-1})\right\|^2\right)
\end{aligned}$$

$$\leq \sum_{i=1}^{n} \frac{2}{L_i} \left(\left\| \nabla F(x^{kn}) - \nabla F(x^{kn+i-1}) \right\|^2 + \left\| \nabla_i F(x^{kn+i-1}) \right\|^2 \right)$$

$$\leq \sum_{i=1}^{n} \frac{2}{L_i} L^2 \left\| x^{kn} - x^{kn+i-1} \right\|^2 + \sum_{i=1}^{n} \frac{2}{L_i} \left\| \nabla_i F(x^{kn+i-1}) \right\|^2$$

where recall that L denotes the global Lipschitz constant of the gradient ∇F. We also have the following recurrence in algorithm C-CGD:

$$x^{kn+i} = x^{kn} - \sum_{j=1}^{i} \frac{1}{L_j} E_j \nabla_j F(x^{kn+j-1}) \quad \forall i \in [n]$$

which used in the previous derivations, leads to:

$$\begin{aligned}
\left\| \nabla F(x^{kn}) \right\|_{\frac{1}{\mathbb{L}}}^2 &\leq 2L^2 \sum_{i=1}^{n} \frac{1}{L_i} \left\| \sum_{j=1}^{i-1} \frac{1}{L_j} E_j \nabla_j F(x^{kn+j-1}) \right\|^2 \\
&\quad + 2 \sum_{i=1}^{n} \frac{1}{L_i} \left\| \nabla_i F(x^{kn+i-1}) \right\|^2 \\
&= 2L^2 \sum_{i=1}^{n} \frac{1}{L_i} \left(\sum_{j=1}^{i-1} \frac{1}{L_j^2} \left\| \nabla_j F(x^{kn+j-1}) \right\|^2 \right) \\
&\quad + 2 \sum_{i=1}^{n} \frac{1}{L_i} \left\| \nabla_i F(x^{kn+i-1}) \right\|^2 \\
&\leq 2 \frac{L^2}{\min_{i \in [n]} L_i^2} \sum_{i=1}^{n} \sum_{j=1}^{i-1} \frac{1}{L_j} \left\| \nabla_j F(x^{kn+j-1}) \right\|^2 \\
&\quad + 2 \sum_{i=1}^{n} \frac{1}{L_i} \left\| \nabla_i F(x^{kn+i-1}) \right\|^2 \\
&= 2 \frac{L^2}{\min_{i \in [n]} L_i^2} \sum_{i=1}^{n} (n-i) \frac{1}{L_i} \left\| \nabla_i F(x^{kn+i-1}) \right\|^2 \\
&\quad + 2 \sum_{i=1}^{n} \frac{1}{L_i} \left\| \nabla_i F(x^{kn+i-1}) \right\|^2 \\
&\leq 2 \left(1 + n \frac{L^2}{\min_{i \in [n]} L_i^2} \right) \sum_{i=1}^{n} \frac{1}{L_i} \left\| \nabla_i F(x^{kn+i-1}) \right\|^2
\end{aligned}$$

Finally, we get the following inequality:

$$F(x^{kn}) - F(x^{(k+1)n}) \geq \frac{1}{4\left(1 + n \frac{L^2}{\min_{i \in [n]} L_i^2}\right)} \left\| \nabla F(x^{kn}) \right\|_{\frac{1}{\mathbb{L}}}^2 \tag{12.14}$$

The rest of the proof follows similar steps as in the proof of Theorem 12.1. Indeed, from the convexity of F and the Cauchy–Schwarz inequality, we get:

$$R_{\mathbb{L}}(x^0)\left\|\nabla F(x^{kn})\right\|_{\frac{1}{\mathbb{L}}} \geq \langle \nabla F(x^{kn}), x^{kn} - x^* \rangle \geq F(x^{kn}) - F(x^*)$$

Combining the previous two relations, we get:

$$F(x^{kn}) - F(x^{(k+1)n}) \geq \frac{(F(x^{kn}) - F^*)^2}{4\left(1 + n\frac{L^2}{\min_{i\in[n]} L_i^2}\right) R_{\mathbb{L}}^2(x^0)}$$

If we denote $\Delta^k = F(x^{kn}) - F^*$, we further obtain:

$$\Delta^k - \Delta^{k+1} \geq \frac{(\Delta^k)^2}{4\left(1 + n\frac{L^2}{\min_{i\in[n]} L_i^2}\right) R_{\mathbb{L}}^2(x^0)}$$

If we divide in both sides by $\Delta^{k+1}\Delta^k$ and use $\Delta^{k+1} \leq \Delta^k$, we get:

$$\frac{1}{\Delta^{k+1}} \geq \frac{1}{\Delta^k} + \frac{1}{4\left(1 + n\frac{L^2}{\min_{i\in[n]} L_i^2}\right) R_{\mathbb{L}}^2(x^0)} \geq \cdots \geq \frac{1}{\Delta^0} + \frac{k+1}{4\left(1 + n\frac{L^2}{\min_{i\in[n]} L_i^2}\right) R_{\mathbb{L}}^2(x^0)}$$

This relation immediately implies the statement of our theorem. □

Comparing the complexity bound for the cyclic variant C-CGD (12.13), with the corresponding bound proved in Theorem 12.1 for the greedy variant G-CGD, we see that in general, the numerator in (12.13) is $\mathcal{O}(n^2)$, in contrast to $\mathcal{O}(n)$ term in (12.10). However, the cost per iteration of the greedy algorithm is usually n times more expensive than the cost per iteration of the cyclic algorithm, since the first one needs the whole gradient vector ∇F while the other needs only the partial gradient $\nabla_i F$.

We further prove linear convergence rate in the function values for the algorithm C-CGD when the objective function is smooth and strongly convex.

Theorem 12.4

Let the objective function F satisfy Assumption 12.1 with $\sigma > 0$. Then, the sequence x^k generated by algorithm C-CGD satisfies the following linear convergence rate in the objective function values:

$$F(x^{kn}) - F^* \leq \left(1 - \frac{\sigma}{2(\max_{i\in[n]} L_i)\left(1 + n\frac{L^2}{\min_{i\in[n]} L_i^2}\right)}\right)^k (F(x^0) - F^*) \quad (12.15)$$

Proof. Combining (12.14) and (12.7) we obtain the following relation:

$$
\begin{aligned}
F(x^{kn}) - F(x^{(k+1)n}) &\geq \frac{1}{4\left(1+n\frac{L^2}{\min_{i\in[n]} L_i^2}\right)} \|\nabla F(x^{kn})\|^2_{\frac{1}{\mathbb{L}}} \\
&\geq \frac{1}{4(\max_{i\in[n]} L_i)\left(1+n\frac{L^2}{\min_{i\in[n]} L_i^2}\right)} \left\|\nabla F(x^{kn})\right\|^2 \\
&\overset{(12.7)}{\geq} \frac{\sigma}{2(\max_{i\in[n]} L_i)\left(1+n\frac{L^2}{\min_{i\in[n]} L_i^2}\right)} \left(F(x^{kn}) - F^*\right)
\end{aligned}
$$

which leads to the linear convergence rate from the theorem. □

Comparing again the complexity bound for the cyclic variant C-CGD (12.15), with the corresponding bound for the greedy variant G-CGD (12.12), an additional factor $\mathcal{O}(n)$ appears again in (12.15), since we have $(1-\alpha)^{1/n} \approx 1 - \frac{\alpha}{n}$ for small values of α. On the other hand, the cost per iteration of algorithm G-CGD is usually n times more expensive than the cost per iteration of algorithm C-CGD.

12.5 Randomized Coordinate Gradient Descent Method (R-CGD)

In this section we introduce a random (block) coordinate gradient descent algorithm for solving the unconstrained optimization problem (12.6). The method chooses randomly at each iteration $k \geq 0$ a (block) index $i_k \in [n]$ with respect to a prespecified probability distribution $\mathcal{P} = (p_i)_{i\in[n]}$ for which the probability mass function takes nonzero values, i.e., $p_i > 0$ for all $i \in [n]$, and then performs a gradient update along the i_kth coordinate:

Algorithm R-CGD
1. Choose randomly an index $i_k \in [n]$ with probability p_{i_k}
2. Update $x^{k+1} = x^k - \frac{1}{L_{i_k}} E_{i_k} \nabla_{i_k} F(x^k)$

Note again that the i_kth direction $d_{i_k} = -\frac{1}{L_{i_k}} \nabla_{i_k} F(x^k)$ in the previous update law is chosen as the solution of the following optimization subproblem:

$$
d_{i_k} = \arg \min_{s_{i_k} \in \mathbb{R}^{n_{i_k}}} F(x^k) + \langle \nabla_{i_k} F(x^k), s_{i_k} \rangle + \frac{L_{i_k}}{2} \|s_{i_k}\|^2
$$

In algorithm R-CGD two operations are important for updating x: the random generation of the active index and the computation of the partial gradient $\nabla_i F$.

Let us analyze how we can perform these operations very efficiently. First, procedures for the efficient computations of the partial gradient $\nabla_i F$ for structured objective functions in the coordinate descent framework have been already given in Section 12.1.2. Further, since the algorithm R-CGD is based on choosing at each iteration one (block) coordinate, we need a fast procedure to generate random coordinates that are distributed according to a given probability distribution. In a straightforward way, this random generation of coordinates can be implemented in $\mathcal{O}(n)$ operations. However, it is known that we can have a much cheaper procedure for generating a random coordinate for a given discrete probability distribution $(p_i)_{(i)\in[n]}$:

$$\Pr[i = \ell] = p_\ell$$

We first construct a sequence of sorted numbers by dividing interval $[0,\ 1)$ into n subintervals:

$$[0,\ p_1),\ [p_1,\ p_1 + p_2),\ \cdots,\ \left[\sum_{\ell=1}^{n-1} p_\ell,\ 1\right)$$

where we used that $\sum_{\ell=1}^{n} p_\ell = 1$. Clearly, the width of ℓth interval equals the probability p_ℓ. Note that the preliminary computations for the subintervals consists of $n-2$ additions. Then, we can construct our random index procedure:

Random index generator:

Input : a uniformly distributed random number $u \in [0,\ 1]$

Use the binary search algorithm to determine the index ℓ_u for which

$$\sum_{\ell=1}^{\ell_u - 1} p_\ell \leq u < \sum_{\ell=1}^{\ell_u} p_\ell$$

Output : the coordinate ℓ_u.

Clearly, this procedure correctly implements the random index generator. Since the sampling algorithm described above is based on binary search [20], which halves the search interval at each iteration, it has complexity $\mathcal{O}(\ln(n))$ and requires generating only one uniform random number. There exist also random sampling algorithms with constant computational time, based on some precomputed sequences, but the time required for the initialization of these sequences is $\mathcal{O}(n)$, see e.g., [21]. Other procedures for generating random coordinates, with the same $\mathcal{O}(\ln(n))$ complexity, can be found in Ref. [13].

In the next sections we analyze the rate of convergence of the algorithm R-CGD in expectation. We use the following notations for the random set of indexes and for the expected values of the objective function up to the iteration k:

$$\omega^k = \{i_0, \ldots, i_k\} \quad \text{and} \quad \mathbb{E}[F(x^k)]$$

Further, we define the vector of probabilities $\mathbb{P} = [p_1 \cdots p_n]$. Then, we introduce the following pair of dual norms:

$$\|x\|^2_{\frac{\mathbb{L}}{\mathbb{P}}} = \sum_{i \in [n]} \frac{L_i}{p_i} \|x_i\|^2 \quad \text{and} \quad \|y\|^2_{\frac{\mathbb{P}}{\mathbb{L}}} = \sum_{i \in [n]} \frac{p_i}{L_i} \|x_i\|^2$$

which satisfy the Cauchy–Schwarz inequality: $\langle x, y \rangle \leq \|x\|_{\frac{\mathbb{L}}{\mathbb{P}}} \cdot \|y\|_{\frac{\mathbb{P}}{\mathbb{L}}}$ for all $x, y \in \mathbb{R}^N$. We also define the following quantity:

$$R_{\frac{\mathbb{L}}{\mathbb{P}}}(\bar{x}) = \max_{x^* \in X^*} \max_{x \in \mathcal{L}_{F(\bar{x})}} \|x - x^*\|_{\frac{\mathbb{L}}{\mathbb{P}}}$$

which we assume to be finite for any fixed $\bar{x}$.

12.5.1 Convergence rates for R-CGD in expectation: Convex case

We derive below the convergence rate in the expected values of the objective function for algorithm R-CGD under different assumptions on the objective function. Our analysis from this section follows similar lines as in Ref. [13]. We start analyzing the convergence behavior of the algorithm under the Lipschitz gradient assumption on F.

Theorem 12.5
Let the objective function F satisfy Assumption 12.1 with $\sigma = 0$. Then, the sequence x^k generated by algorithm R-CGD satisfies the following sublinear convergence rate in the expected values of the objective function:

$$\mathbb{E}[F(x^k)] - F^* \leq \frac{2R^2_{\frac{\mathbb{L}}{\mathbb{P}}}(x^0)}{k + R^2_{\frac{\mathbb{L}}{\mathbb{P}}}(x^0)/(F(x^0) - F^*)} \tag{12.16}$$

Proof. Based on (12.8) we have the following decrease in the objective function:

$$F(x^{k+1}) \leq F(x^k) - \frac{1}{2L_{i_k}} \|\nabla_{i_k} F(x^k)\|^2$$

This shows that algorithm R-CGD is a descent method and moreover $x^k \in \mathcal{L}_{F(x^0)}$ for all $k \geq 0$. Taking expectation with respect to i_k in both sides, we have:

$$\begin{aligned}\mathbb{E}[F(x^{k+1})|\omega^k] &\leq F(x^k) - \sum_{i \in [n]} \frac{p_i}{2L_i} \|\nabla_i F(x^k)\|^2 \\ &= F(x^k) - \frac{1}{2} \|\nabla F(x^k)\|^2_{\frac{\mathbb{P}}{\mathbb{L}}} \end{aligned} \tag{12.17}$$

On the other hand, using the convexity of F and the Cauchy–Schwarz inequality for the pair of dual norms $\|\cdot\|_{\frac{\mathbb{L}}{\mathbb{P}}}$ and $\|\cdot\|_{\frac{\mathbb{P}}{\mathbb{L}}}$, we obtain:

$$\begin{aligned} R_{\frac{\mathbb{L}}{\mathbb{P}}}(x^0)\left\|\nabla F(x^k)\right\|_{\frac{\mathbb{P}}{\mathbb{L}}} &\geq \left\|x^k - x^*\right\|_{\frac{\mathbb{L}}{\mathbb{P}}}\left\|\nabla F(x^k)\right\|_{\frac{\mathbb{P}}{\mathbb{L}}} \geq \langle \nabla F(x^k), x^k - x^*\rangle \\ &\geq F(x^k) - F(x^*) \end{aligned}$$

The above relation clearly implies:

$$\frac{1}{R_{\frac{\mathbb{L}}{\mathbb{P}}}(x^0)}\left(F(x^k) - F(x^*)\right) \leq \left\|\nabla F(x^k)\right\|_{\frac{\mathbb{P}}{\mathbb{L}}} \tag{12.18}$$

Further, from (12.17) and (12.18) we have:

$$\mathbb{E}[F(x^{k+1}) - F^*|\omega^k] \leq F(x^k) - F^* - \frac{(F(x^k) - F^*)^2}{2R^2_{\frac{\mathbb{L}}{\mathbb{P}}}(x^0)} \tag{12.19}$$

Taking expectation with respect to ω^k and denoting $\Delta^k = \mathbb{E}[F(x^k)] - F^*$, we obtain:

$$\Delta^{k+1} \leq \Delta^k - \frac{(\Delta^k)^2}{2R^2_{\frac{\mathbb{L}}{\mathbb{P}}}(x^0)}$$

If we divide in both sides by $\Delta^{k+1}\Delta^k$ and use $\Delta^{k+1} \leq \Delta^k$ we get:

$$\frac{1}{\Delta^{k+1}} \geq \frac{1}{\Delta^k} + \frac{1}{2R^2_{\frac{\mathbb{L}}{\mathbb{P}}}(x^0)} \geq \cdots \geq \frac{1}{\Delta^0} + \frac{k+1}{2R^2_{\frac{\mathbb{L}}{\mathbb{P}}}(x^0)}$$

This relation immediately implies the statement of the theorem. □

Let us assume again that we know some upper bounds $R_i > 0$ on $\|x_i - x_i^*\|$ for all $x \in \mathcal{L}_{F(x^0)}$ and $i \in [n]$. Then, if we choose Lipschitz dependent probabilities $p_i = L_i / \sum_{j\in[n]} L_j$, we get from Theorem 12.5 a rate of convergence for algorithm R-CGD of order:

$$\mathcal{O}\left(\frac{\sum_{i\in[n]}(\sum_{j\in[n]} L_j)R_i^2}{k}\right)$$

On the other hand, for an uniform probability distribution $p_i = \frac{1}{n}$, the convergence rate of algorithm R-CGD is of order:

$$\mathcal{O}\left(\frac{nR^2_{\mathbb{L}}(x^0)}{k}\right) = \mathcal{O}\left(\frac{\sum_{i\in[n]}(nL_i)R_i^2}{k}\right)$$

Recall that for the full gradient method the convergence rate is of order:

$$\mathcal{O}\left(\frac{\sum_{i\in[n]} LR_i^2}{k}\right)$$

However, there are situations where $\sum_{j\in[n]} L_j \approx L$, see (12.9), which means that the convergence rates of algorithms R-CGD and of full gradient may be comparable in the worst case. However, the cost per iteration of algorithm R-CGD is usually much lower than that of the full gradient method (see the discussions on the efficient computation of the partial gradient from Section 12.1.2 and on the random index generator we have provided in this section), implying a much better arithmetical complexity for the first one (in a worst case scenario even n times better). Furthermore, if we compare the complexity bound for the cyclic variant C-CGD (12.13), with the corresponding bound proved in Theorem 12.5 for the randomized variant R-CGD with uniform probabilities, that is $\frac{2nR^2_{\mathbb{L}}(x^0)}{k}$, we see in the numerator of (12.13) a term $\mathcal{O}(n^2)$, in contrast to $\mathcal{O}(n)$ term for R-CGD, although the costs per iteration of both methods are comparable. However, the bounds in Theorem 12.5 are on expected function values, rather than being deterministic, as in Theorem 12.3.

We further prove that under the additional strong convexity assumption on F, the algorithm R-CGD has linear convergence rate in expectation.

Theorem 12.6

Let the objective function F satisfy Assumption 12.1 with $\sigma > 0$. Then, the sequence x^k generated by algorithm R-CGD satisfies the following linear convergence rate in the expected values of the objective function:

$$\mathbb{E}[F(x^k)] - F^* \leq \left(1 - \sigma \min_{i\in[n]} \frac{p_i}{L_i}\right)^k (F(x^0) - F^*) \tag{12.20}$$

Proof. Combining (12.17) and (12.7) we obtain the following relation:

$$F(x^k) - \mathbb{E}[F(x^{k+1})|\omega^k] \geq \frac{1}{2}\left\|\nabla F(x^k)\right\|^2_{\frac{\mathbb{P}}{\mathbb{L}}} \geq \frac{1}{2}\min_{i\in[n]}\frac{p_i}{L_i}\left\|\nabla F(x^k)\right\|^2$$
$$\overset{(12.7)}{\geq} \sigma \min_{i\in[n]} \frac{p_i}{L_i}\left(F(x^k) - F^*\right)$$

Taking expectation with respect to ω^k, the previous relation implies:

$$\Delta_k - \Delta_{k+1} \geq \sigma \min_{i\in[n]} \frac{p_i}{L_i} \Delta_k$$

which leads to the linear convergence rate from the theorem. □

Note that, if we choose Lipschitz dependent probabilities $p_i = L_i / \sum_{j\in[n]} L_j$, we get from Theorem 12.6 a rate of convergence for algorithm R-CGD of order:

$$\mathcal{O}\left(\left(1 - \frac{\sigma}{\sum_{i\in[n]} L_i}\right)^k\right)$$

On the other hand, for an uniform probability distribution $p_i = \frac{1}{n}$, the convergence rate of algorithm R-CGD is of order:

$$\mathcal{O}\left(\left(1 - \frac{\sigma}{n \max_{i\in[n]} L_i}\right)^k\right)$$

Recall that for the full gradient method the convergence rate is of order:

$$\mathcal{O}\left(\left(1 - \frac{\sigma}{L}\right)^k\right)$$

From (12.9) we have that the global Lipschitz constant L can be as large as $n \max_{i\in[n]} L_i$ in the worst case. Thus, we conclude that the convergence rates of algorithms R-CGD and of full gradient are also comparable in the smooth strongly convex case. However, the arithmetical complexity of algorithm R-CGD is usually much lower than that of the full gradient method, typically n times better. Moreover, comparing the complexity bound for the cyclic variant C-CGD (12.15), with the corresponding bound for the randomized variant R-CGD (12.20), an additional factor $\mathcal{O}(n)$ appears again in (12.15), since we have $(1-\alpha)^{1/n} \approx 1 - \frac{\alpha}{n}$ for small values of α. However, for the algorithm R-CGD we have obtained convergence rates on expected function values, rather than deterministic. We should notice however, that we can also derive convergence rate results for algorithm R-CGD showing that the problem is approximately solved with high probability in both situations, smooth and strongly convex cases, see e.g., Refs. [13–15] for more details.

12.5.2 Convergence rate for R-CGD in expectation: Nonconvex case

Now, we still assume coordinatewise Lipschitz gradient for the objective function F, i.e., Assumption 12.1(ii) holds, but we do not impose any convexity condition on F. Therefore, we analyze further the behavior of algorithm R-CGD on the structured unconstrained optimization problem (12.6) with nonconvex smooth objective function F.

Theorem 12.7
Let the nonconvex objective function F satisfy Assumption 12.1(ii). Then, the algorithm R-CGD generates a sequence x^k satisfying the following sublinear convergence rate for the expected values of the norm of the gradient:

$$\min_{0\leq l\leq k} \mathbb{E}\left[\left\|\nabla F(x^l)\right\|^2_{\frac{\mathbb{P}}{\mathbb{L}}}\right] \leq \frac{2(F(x^0)-F^*)}{k+1}$$

Proof. From (12.17) we get the following decrease:

$$\mathbb{E}[F(x^{k+1})|\omega^k] \leq F(x^k) - \frac{1}{2}\|\nabla F(x^k)\|^2_{\frac{\mathbb{P}}{\mathbb{L}}}$$

Now, taking the expectation in both sides with respect to ω^k, we obtain:

$$\frac{1}{2}\mathbb{E}\left[\|\nabla F(x^k)\|^2_{\frac{\mathbb{P}}{\mathbb{L}}}\right] \leq \mathbb{E}[F(x^k)] - \mathbb{E}[F(x^{k+1})]$$

Summing with respect to the entire history, we have:

$$\frac{1}{2}\sum_{l=0}^{k}\mathbb{E}\left[\|\nabla F(x^l)\|^2_{\frac{\mathbb{P}}{\mathbb{L}}}\right] \leq \mathbb{E}[F(x^0)] - \mathbb{E}[F(x^{k+1})] \leq \mathbb{E}[F(x^0)] - F^* = F(x^0) - F^*$$

which leads to the statement of the theorem. □

Note that, if we choose Lipschitz dependent probabilities $p_i = L_i / \sum_{j\in[n]} L_j$, we get from Theorem 12.7 a rate of convergence for algorithm R-CGD of order:

$$\mathcal{O}\left(\frac{2\sum_{i\in[n]} L_i(F(x^0) - F^*)}{k}\right)$$

On the other hand, for an uniform probability distribution $p_i = \frac{1}{n}$, the convergence rate of algorithm R-CGD is of order:

$$\mathcal{O}\left(\frac{2n\max_{i\in[n]} L_i(F(x^0) - F^*)}{k}\right)$$

For the full gradient method the convergence rate is of order [22]:

$$\mathcal{O}\left(\frac{2L(F(x^0) - F^*)}{k}\right)$$

Looking again at (12.9), we conclude that there may be situations when the convergence rates of algorithms R-CGD and full gradient are also comparable in the smooth nonconvex case. However, the arithmetical complexity of algorithm R-CGD is usually lower than that of the full gradient method.

12.6 Previous Work and Extensions

In the last decade we can observe an increasing interest into optimization problems of a very big size coming from networks, machine learning, the Internet, telecommunications, and traffic applications. In these applications, even the evaluation of the objective function at some point needs substantial computational efforts. Such problems require simple and scalable optimization algorithms. One of the most popular methods that fit into these requirements is the coordinate descent. However, due to its low efficiency on big problems and lack of convergence results, it has not received much attention until recently. This attention has returned due to the recent theoretical results and applications in networks [9], machine learning [8,23], compressed sensing [24], protein loop closure [25], optimal control [3,26] and optimization [27]. More specifically, for coordinate minimization convergence rates were given in Ref. [9] and recently new variants and extensions were presented and analyzed e.g., in Ref. [10]. The first global convergence rate for a randomized coordinate gradient descent method on smooth convex optimization was given in a seminal paper [13]. The generalization of this convergence rate analysis to composite convex optimization has been extensively studied, under different assumptions on the objective function, in Refs. [14,15,28]. Composite nonconvex optimization has been studied in Ref. [29], and ℓ_0 regularized convex optimization has been studied in Refs. [26,30]. Convergence rate results for randomized variants of coordinate gradient descent methods for linearly constrained convex optimization were given in Refs. [31,32] and for linearly constrained nonconvex optimization were given in Ref. [29]. For coordinate gradient descent methods based on cyclic coordinate search bounds on the rate of convergence were given recently in Ref. [11] and based on greedy coordinate search (e.g., Gauss–Southwell rule) bounds on the convergence rate were given in Refs. [12,27]. Accelerated variants, based on the Nesterov fast gradient method [19], have also been proposed in the literature, see e.g., [13,33,34].

We can also notice that coordinate descent methods are adequate to different kinds of parallel implementation, which involves multiple instances of a basic coordinated descent algorithm to run in parallel on multiple processors in synchronous or asynchronous fashion. A detailed analysis of convergence and implementation of coordinate minimization was given in Ref. [9]. Recently, a more thorough investigation regarding the ways in which the convergence of coordinate gradient descent methods can be accelerated through parallelization was undertaken in Refs. [15,35–38], where it is shown theoretically and/or practically that speedup can be achieved through this approach.

Finally, a numerical comparison between variants of coordinate descent methods is beyond the scope of this chapter, but the interested reader can consult several papers that report detailed numerical tests and applications to real problems, such as Refs. [11,15,29,38]. In particular, detailed numerical tests on least-square problems were performed in Ref. [11] for comparing the performances of cyclic versus random coordinate gradient descent algorithms and showed that first one usually works better. In Ref. [18], the authors compare the performance of greedy versus random coordinate gradient descent algorithms and showed that if greedy and random schemes have similar costs per iteration, then the greedy method works better.

As we have seen from our presentation and from the list of references of this chapter, coordinate descent methods have become one of the most important optimization tools for solving big data applications that arise in networks, the Internet, traffic, and in general in data analysis. In the next years we expect a growing interest in these methods, in particular new variants and extensions to be given, adaptation to various parallel and distributed platforms to be realized, and application to new big data areas.

Acknowledgments

The research leading to these results has received funding from UEFISCDI Romania: PNII-RU-TE 2014, project MoCOBiDS, no. 176/01.10.2015; PNIII-PCE 2016, project ScaleFreeNet, no. 39/2017.

References

[1] L. Hurwicz, The design of mechanisms for resource allocation, *American Economic Review*, 63: 1–30, 1973.

[2] R. Banos, F. Manzano-Agugliaro, F. Montoya, C. Gil, A. Alcayde and J. Gomez, Optimization methods applied to renewable and sustainable energy: A review, *Renewable and Sustainable Energy Reviews*, 15(4): 1753–1766, 2011.

[3] I. Necoara, V. Nedelcu and I. Dumitrache, Parallel and distributed optimization methods for estimation and control in networks, *Journal of Process Control*, 21(5): 756–766, 2011.

[4] P. Tsiaflakis, I. Necoara, J. Suykens and M. Moonen, Improved dual decomposition based optimization for DSL dynamic spectrum management, *IEEE Transactions on Signal Processing*, 58(4): 2230–2245, 2010.

[5] A. Nedic, A. Ozdaglar and P. Parrilo, Constrained consensus and optimization in multi-agent networks, *IEEE Transactions on Automatic Control*, 55(4): 922–938, 2010.

[6] M. Rabbat and R. Nowak, Distributed optimization in sensor networks, *Proceedings of the International Symposium on Information Processing in Sensor Networks*, April 26–27, Berkeley, California, pp. 20–27, 2004.

[7] P. Combettes, The convex feasibility problem in image recovery, in *Advances in Imaging and Electron Physics*, P. Hawkes Ed., vol. 95, pp. 155–270, Academic Press, Cambridge, MA, 1996.

[8] S. Shalev-Shwartz and T. Zhang, Stochastic dual coordinate ascent methods for regularized loss minimization, *Journal of Machine Learning Research*, 14: 437–469, 2013.

[9] D. Bertsekas and J. Tsitsiklis, *Parallel and Distributed Computation: Numerical Methods*, Athena Scientific, Nashua, HN, 1997.

[10] M. Razaviyayn, M. Hong and Z.Q. Luo, A unified convergence analysis of block successive minimization methods for nonsmooth optimization, *SIAM Journal on Optimization*, 23(2): 1126–1153, 2013.

[11] A. Beck and L. Tetruashvili, On the convergence of block coordinate descent type methods, *SIAM Journal on Optimization*, 23(4): 2037–2060, 2013.

[12] P. Tseng and S. Yun, A block-coordinate gradient descent method for linearly constrained nonsmooth separable optimization, *Journal of Optimization Theory and Applications*, 140: 513–535, 2009.

[13] Yu. Nesterov, Efficiency of coordinate descent methods on huge-scale optimization problems, *SIAM Journal on Optimization*, 22(2): 341–362, 2012.

[14] P. Richtarik and M. Takac, Iteration complexity of randomized block-coordinate descent methods for minimizing a composite function, *Mathematical Programming*, 144(1–2): 1–38, 2014.

[15] I. Necoara and D. Clipici, Parallel coordinate descent methods for composite minimization: Convergence analysis and error bounds, *SIAM Journal on Optimization*, 26(1): 197–226, 2016.

[16] S. Wright, Coordinate descent algorithms, *Mathematical Programming*, 151(1): 3–34, 2015.

[17] M. Powell, On search directions for minimization algorithms, *Mathematical Programming*, 4: 193–201, 1973.

[18] J. Nutini, M. Schmidt, I. Laradji, M. Friedlander and H. Koepke, Coordinate descent converges faster with the Gauss–Southwell rule than random selection, *Proceedings of the International Conference on Machine Learning*, July 7–9, Lille, France, pp. 1632–1641, 2015.

[19] Yu. Nesterov, *Introductory Lectures on Convex Optimization: A Basic Course*, Kluwer Academic Publisher, Dordrecht, Netherlands, 2004.

[20] D. Knuth, *The Art of Computer Programming*, Addison-Wesley, Boston, MA, 1981.

[21] M. Vose, A linear algorithm for generating random numbers with a given distribution, *IEEE Transactions on Software Engineering*, 17(9): 972–975, 1991.

[22] Yu. Nesterov, Gradient methods for minimizing composite objective functions, *Mathematical Programming*, 140: 125–161, 2013.

[23] K. Chang, C. Hsieh and C. Lin, Coordinate descent method for large-scale l2-loss linear support vector machines, *Journal of Machine Learning Research*, 9: 1369–1398, 2008.

[24] Y. Li and S. Osher, Coordinate descent optimization for l1 minimization with application to compressed sensing: A greedy algorithm, *Inverse Problems and Imaging*, 3: 487–503, 2009.

[25] A. Canutescu and R. Dunbrack, Cyclic coordinate descent: A robotics algorithm for protein loop closure, *Protein Science*, 12: 963–972, 2003.

[26] A. Patrascu and I. Necoara, Random coordinate descent methods for l0 regularized convex optimization, *IEEE Transactions on Automatic Control*, 60(7): 1811–1824, 2015.

[27] P. Tseng and S. Yun, A coordinate gradient descent method for nonsmooth separable minimization, *Mathematical Programming*, 117(1): 387–423, 2008.

[28] Z. Lu and L. Xiao, On the complexity analysis of randomized block-coordinate descent methods, *Mathematical Programming*, 152(1): 615–642, 2015.

[29] A. Patrascu and I. Necoara, Efficient random coordinate descent algorithms for large-scale structured nonconvex optimization, *Journal of Global Optimization*, 61(1): 19–46, 2015.

[30] Z. Lu, Iterative hard thresholding methods for l0 regularized convex cone programming, *Mathematical Programming*, 147(1): 125–154, 2014.

[31] I. Necoara, Random coordinate descent algorithms for multi-agent convex optimization over networks, *IEEE Transactions on Automatic Control*, 58(8): 2001–2012, 2013.

[32] I. Necoara and A. Patrascu, A random coordinate descent algorithm for optimization problems with composite objective function and linear coupled constraints, *Computational Optimization and Applications*, 57(2): 307–337, 2014.

[33] O. Fercoq and P. Richtarik, Accelerated, parallel, and proximal coordinate descent, *SIAM Journal on Optimization*, 25(4): 1997–2023, 2015.

[34] Y. Lee and A. Sidford, Efficient accelerated coordinate descent methods and faster algorithms for solving linear systems, *Annual Symposium on Foundations of Computer Science*, October 26–29, Berkeley, CA, pp. 147–156, 2013.

[35] J. Bradley, A. Kyrola, D. Bickson and C. Guestrin, Parallel coordinate descent for l1-regularized loss minimization, *Proceedings of the International Conference on Machine Learning*, June 28–July 2, Bellevue, WA, pp. 321–328, 2011.

[36] J. Liu and S. Wright, Asynchronous stochastic coordinate descent: Parallelism and convergence properties, *SIAM Journal on Optimization*, 25(1): 351–376, 2015.

[37] I. Necoara and D. Clipici, Efficient parallel coordinate descent algorithm for convex optimization problems with separable constraints: Application to distributed mpc, *Journal of Process Control*, 23(3): 243–253, 2013.

[38] P. Richtarik and M. Takac, *Parallel coordinate descent methods for big data optimization*, Technical report, University of Edinburgh, Edinburgh, UK, 2012.

Chapter 13

Data Locality and Dependency for MapReduce

Xiaoqiang Ma
Huazhong University of Science and Technology
Wuhan, China

Xiaoyi Fan and Jiangchuan Liu
Simon Fraser University
Burnaby, British Columbia, Canada

CONTENTS

Recent years have witnessed a surge of new generation applications involving big data, and the emergence of MapReduce as a convenient computation tool for data-intensive applications has greatly changed the landscape of large-scale distributed data processing [1]. Harnessing the power of large clusters of tens of thousands of servers with high fault-tolerance, such practical MapReduce implementations as the open-source Apache Hadoop project* have become a preferred choice in both academia and industry in this era of big data computation at terabyte and even petabyte scales.

A typical MapReduce workflow consists of two major phases, as shown in Figure 13.1. First, the map processes (mappers) on slaves read the input data from the distributed file system and transform the input data to a list of intermediate key-value pairs (known as the map phase); the reduce processes (reducers) then merge the intermediate values for the distinct keys, which are stored in the local disks of slaves, to form the final results that are written back to the distributed file system (known as the reduce phase). This distributed paradigm of MapReduce effectively partitions and distributes computation workloads to a cluster of servers, facilitating today's big data processing; yet it also inevitably incurs a large amount of network traffic within/across MapReduce clusters. Given the massive data to be dispatched, and the intermediate results to be collected and aggregated, it is highly desirable to colocate computation with data, making them as close as possible to achieve *data locality*.

In this chapter, we first present DALM (dependency-aware locality for MapReduce) [2,3] for processing the real-world input data that can be highly skewed and dependent. DALM accommodates data dependency in a data-locality framework, organically synthesizing the key components from data reorganization, replication, and placement. Besides algorithmic design within the framework, we have also closely examined the deployment challenges, particularly in public virtualized Cloud environments.

Second, we present vLocality [34], a comprehensive and practical solution toward data locality in virtualized environments. It incorporates a novel storage architecture that efficiently mitigates the shared disk contention, and an enhanced task scheduling algorithm that prioritizes colocated VMs.

*Apache Hadoop http://hadoop.apache.org

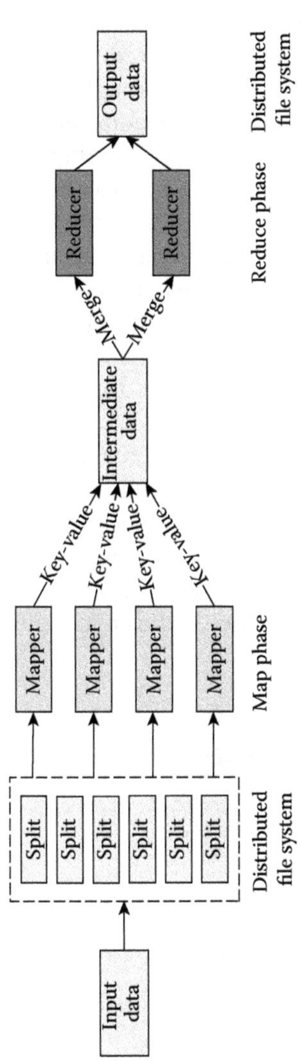

Figure 13.1: A typical MapReduce workflow.

13.1 Dependency-Aware Data Locality for MapReduce

Colocating computation with data, namely, *data locality*, largely avoids the costly massive data exchange crossing switches, thereby reducing the job finish time of MapReduce applications [4]. By default, MapReduce achieves data locality via data replication, which divides data files into blocks of fixed size (e.g., 64 MB) and stores multiple replicas of each block on different servers. Real-world systems, e.g., Google's MapReduce and Apache Hadoop, have attempted to achieve better *data locality* through replicating each file block on multiple servers. This simple uniform replication approach reduces cross-server traffic as well as job finish time for inputs of uniform popularity, but is known to be ineffective with skewed input [5,6]. It has been observed that in certain real-world inputs, the number of accesses to popular files can be ten or even one hundred times more than that to less popular files, and highly popular files thus still experience severe contention with massive concurrent accesses.

There have been a series of works on alleviating *hot spots* with popularity-based approaches. Representatives include Scarlett [5], DARE [6] and PACMan [7], seeking to place more replicas for popular blocks/files. Using the spare disc or memory for these extra replicas, the overall completion time of data-intensive jobs can be reduced. The inherent relations among the input data, however, have yet to be considered. It is known that many of the real-world data inherently exhibit strong *dependency*. For example, Facebook relies on the Hadoop distributed file system (HDFS) to store its user data, which, in a volume over 15 petabytes [8], preserves diverse social relations. A sample social network graph with four communities is shown in Figure 13.2. The dependency

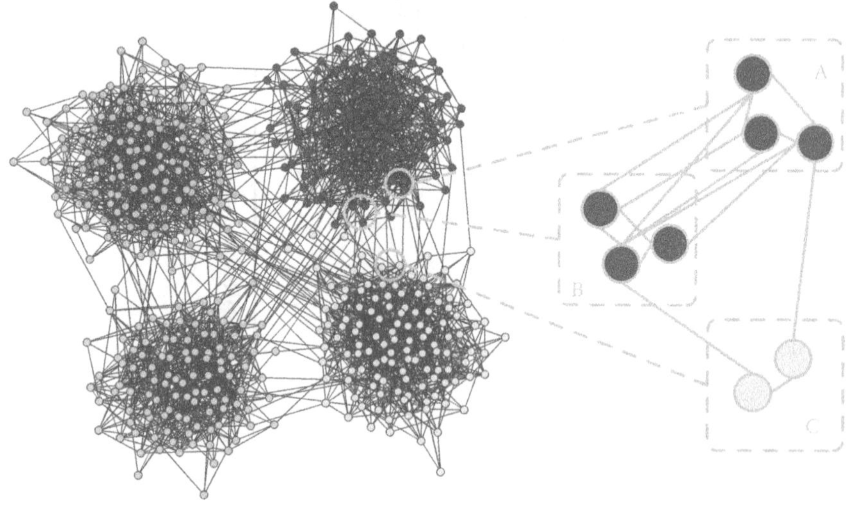

Figure 13.2: A social network graph with four communities.

between data files is determined by the size of cut (the count of edges) between them. Here subsets A and B have very strong dependency (as compared to subsets A and C, as well as B and C), since their users are in the same community, thus being friends to each other with higher probability. As such, accesses to these two subsets are highly correlated. The dependency can be further aggravated during mapping and reducing: many jobs involve iterative steps, and in each iteration, specific tasks need to exchange the output of the current step with each other before going to the next iteration; in other words, the outputs become highly dependent.

To understand the impact of dependency in data replication and the necessity of joint optimization with popularity and dependency, we take Figure 13.3 as an example, where files A and B are popular, and files C, D, E, F are not. Now assume that there is strong data dependency between each of the file pairs (A,B), (C,D), and (E,F), weak dependency between (A,C), (A,E), and (D,F), and no dependency otherwise. We try to find a good storage strategy to minimize the traffic overhead, according to the dependency among files, as well as the file popularity.

As Figure 13.3a shows, the default replication strategy of Hadoop uniformly spreads files over all the servers, which achieves good fault tolerance and scalability. Yet it does not consider file popularity and dependency, and thus would incur high cross-server traffic. Figure 13.3b demonstrates the efforts of more advanced solutions with min-cut based partitioning techniques to balance computation and communication [9]. Since files with strong dependency are stored together, a large amount of cross-server traffic among workers can be avoided. Unfortunately, without considering file popularity, they suffer from imbalanced workload on individual servers. For example, server 1 would become the hotspot since it hosts more popular files, as compared to other servers. (Server 4 even has no jobs to schedule).

On the other hand, the popularity-based replication strategies, e.g., Scarlett [5], work well only if the original data-intensive job can be evenly distributed, and each computation node can work in parallel. In practice, ultra-high parallelization is often hindered by data dependency among files. A basic popularity-based strategy would create two replicas for the popular files, namely A1, A2 for file A, and B1, B2 for file B, and one for each of the remaining files. The replicas of the popular files can then be evenly to distributed to four servers, each accompanying a replica of an unpopular file (see Figure 13.3b). This strategy, however, would incur frequent cross-server traffic when highly dependent files are stored separately. For example, since files A and B have strong dependency, there will be frequent communications between servers 1 and 2, so will be servers 3 and 4.

Hence, a better replication strategy should consider both file popularity and dependency, as shown in Figure 13.3d. We can replicate files based on file popularity and place the files with strong dependency in close vicinity. Not only the

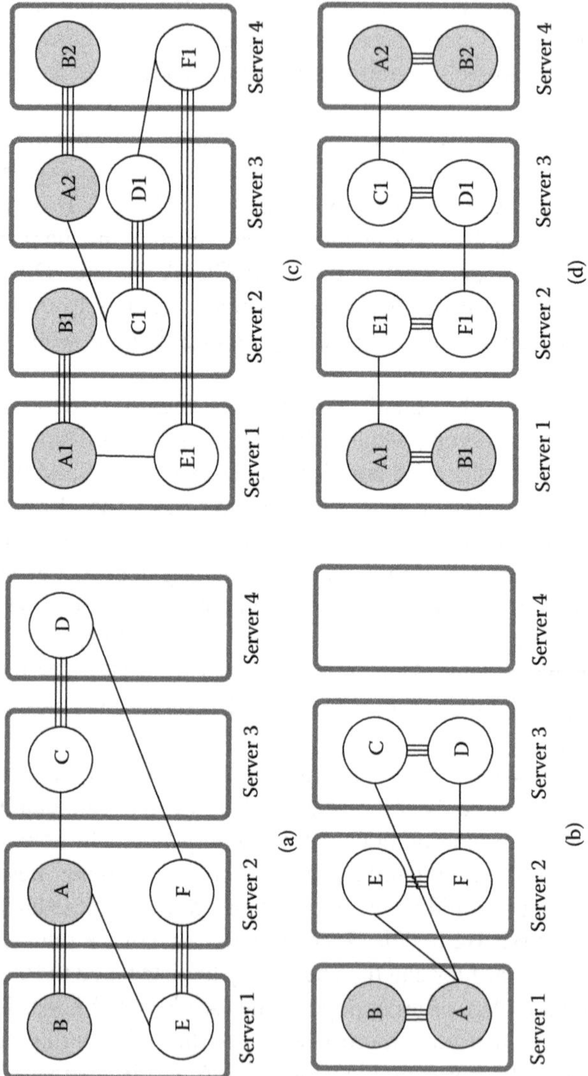

Figure 13.3: An example of different replication strategies based on (a) Hadoop only; (b) graph partition approach only; (c) data popularity only; and (d) both data popularity and dependency. The number of edges between nodes denotes the level of dependency.

cross-server traffic can be largely reduced, but also the imbalanced computation workloads can be relieved.

It is worth noting that a dependency-aware strategy may result in less-balanced workload of individual servers, as shown in Figure 13.3d. The side effect however is minimal: (1) the popular files still have more replicas, which remain to be stored on different servers, thereby mitigating the hotspot problem and (2) for the servers storing popular files, e.g., servers 1 and 4, most of the data I/O requests can be serviced locally, resulting in higher I/O throughput and thus lower CPU idle time. In other words, a good dependency-based strategy should strive to localize data access as much as possible while avoiding potential hotspots through replicating popular files.

13.1.1 DALM: Design and optimization

Our dependency-aware locality for MapReduce (DALM) addresses the challenges above under a coherent framework. Figure 13.4 provides a high level description of the DALM workflow. A *data preprocess* module first operates on the raw data to identify the dependency in the data, and reorganize the raw data accordingly; A *popularity* module built on HDFS then records the access counters for each data block, and dynamically modifies the replication factors of individual files using an adaptive replication strategy. If a block has a higher replication factor than the actual number of the replicas, the *popularity* module inserts replicated blocks in the HDFS triggered by remote-data accesses. These series of modular operations ensure that DALM can accommodate both data popularity and dependency with minimized overhead. We next present detailed design and optimization of DALM.

13.1.1.1 Dependency-aware data reorganization

In the existing HDFS, when the raw input data, which is either a single file or a set of files, is sequentially loaded into the distributed file system, the raw data

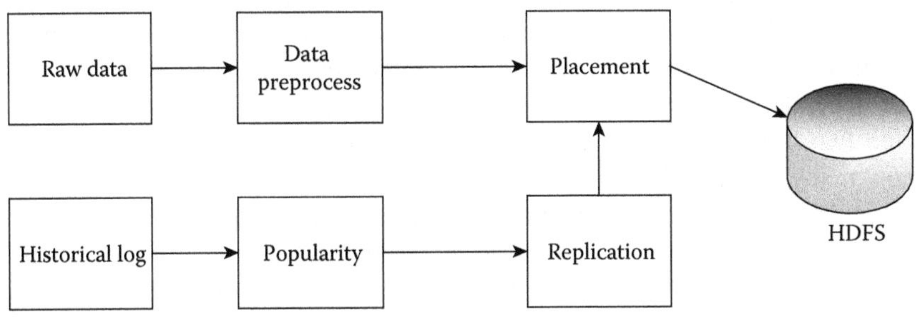

Figure 13.4: DALM workflow.

will be segmented into data blocks of equal size, which are then distributed to individual slave nodes. Thus the dependency among data will be hardly preserved. For example, a large connected component will be divided into a number of subgraphs and then stored on different servers. When specific tasks need to process this connected component, the states of all the servers storing data need to be synchronized, which may incur considerable communication overhead. Instead of loading the raw data files directly into the underlying distributed file system, DALM first identifies data dependency in its preprocessing module through graph partitioning, which helps to place dependent data as close as possible. The key observation here is that the data points in the same cluster have a high degree of self-similarity among them, and a proper graph partitioning will divide the raw data into k partitions of almost equal size, where k is the user-defined parameter which can adapt to the storage system and system scale. In this way, the highly dependent data will be kept in the same file, and the dependency between a pair of files can be easy obtained by normalizing the size of cut of the considered two files. There have been extensive studies on rapidly achieving good quality partitioning for large-scale graphs [10–13]. DALM is not confined to work with a particular partitioning algorithm, and such popular tools as ParMETIS [11] and SCOTCH [13] all can be incorporated. The algorithms implemented in ParMETIS are based on the parallel multilevel K-way graph-partitioning, adaptive repartitioning, and parallel multiconstrained partitioning schemes.

Figure 13.4 shows how the preprocessing step is gracefully integrated into HDFS. DALM balances its workload by detecting the dependency in the graph data, placing dependent data blocks together, and then determining the replication factors of individual data blocks based on the file popularity as shown below.

13.1.2 Minimizing cross-server traffic: Problem formulation

After reorganizing the raw data based on dependency, DALM aims at reducing the cross-server traffic by placing dependent data on nearby servers, as formulated in the following. Consider that there are n different files, and that for file i, denoting its popularity by p_i and its size s_i. The value of the element d_{ij} of the matrix D refers to the dependency degree between files i and j. In DALM, the dependency degree is obtained by normalizing the size of cut of the considered two files. In the first step, we need to determine the replication factor, or how many replicas that each file has, which is denoted by r_i. Then we need to place these replicas on m independent servers, where for each server j, denote the storage space by c_j. We use ρ_i^k to represent the k_{th} replica of file i, then for a replica placement strategy, $\rho_i^k = j$ indicates that the k_{th} replica of file i is stored in server j.

In the following we discuss the constraints in the considered data replication and placement problem.

To ensure that the total file size on any server does not exceed the storage capacity of the server, we must have:

$$\sum_{i=1}^{n}\sum_{k=1}^{r_i} I_j(\rho_i^k)s_i \leq c_j \tag{13.1}$$

where I_j is the indicator function such that $I_j(\rho_i^k)$ is equal to 1 if $\rho_i^k = j$ holds, and 0 otherwise.

In off-the-shelf MapReduce-based systems, e.g., Hadoop, all files have the same replication factor, which is three by default, and can be tuned by users. In our considered problem, the replication factor of each file can vary from the lower bound (r_L) to the upper bound (r_U) based on the file popularity to balance the workload.

Naturally, the extra replicas beyond the lower bound provide higher data availability, which also call for additional storage space. A user-set parameter δ controls the percentage of the total storage capacity reserved for extra replicas, which trades off the data locality and storage efficiency. Let $S = \sum_{1\leq i} s_i r_L$ be the total storage capacity of storing r_L replicas for each file. Then the replication factor should satisfy the following constraints:

$$\sum_{i=1}^{n}(r_i - r_L)s_i \leq \delta S \tag{13.2}$$

$$r_L \leq r_i \leq r_U \text{ for } i = 1,\ldots,n \tag{13.3}$$

The basic idea of the popularity-based replication approach is to adapt the replication factor of each file according to the file popularity in order to alleviate the hotspot problem and improve the resource utilization. Let P_j be the aggregate file popularity of server j, which is the sum of the popularity of all the replicas stored in this server, and $\bar{P}$ the average of aggregate file popularity of all servers. Further, the replica placement should prevent any single server from hosting too many popular files. Hence we have the following constraints,

$$P_j = \sum_{i=1}^{n}\sum_{k=1}^{r_i} I_j(\rho_i^k)\frac{p_i}{r_i} \leq (1+\eta)\bar{P} \tag{13.4}$$

where η is the threshold of the deviation of P_j from $\bar{P}$. We divide p_i by r_i by assuming that the access to file i evenly spreads over all of its replicas.

In our considered problem, we aim at minimizing the remote access. In the current Hadoop system, the computation node will access the replicas as close as possible. Similar to the popularity-based strategy [5,6], we consider a *file* as the replica granularity, and our dependency-aware replication strategy is then divided into two successive steps. The first is to calculate the replication factor of each file based on its popularity, and the second is to decide which server to store each replica, such that the replicas of highly dependent files are stored as close as possible while not exceeding the storage budget and preventing potential hotspots.

13.1.2.1 Replication strategy

We compute the replication factor r_i of file f_i based on the file popularity and size, as well as the storage budget given by δ. Denote the observed number of concurrent accesses by p_i. The files with larger size have a higher priority of getting its desired number of replicas, since it has been shown that large files are accessed more often [5].

Following is the optimization problem to obtain the file replication factor:

$$\min \left\| \frac{\mathbf{r}}{R} - \mathbf{p} \right\|^2 \tag{13.5}$$

$$s.t. \quad \sum_{i=1}^{n} (r_i - r_L) s_i \leq \delta S$$

$$r_L \leq r_i \leq r_U, \text{ for } i = 1,..,n$$

where $\mathbf{r} = (r_1, \ldots, r_n)$, $R = \sum_{i=1}^{n} r_i$, and $\mathbf{p} = (p_1, \ldots, p_n)$.

To solve it, we start from the Lagrangian function:

$$f(\mathbf{r}) = \left\| \frac{\mathbf{r}}{R} - \mathbf{p} \right\|^2 + \alpha \left[\sum_{i=1}^{n} (r_i - r_L) s_i - \delta S \right] + \sum_{i=1}^{n} \beta_i (r_L - r_i) + \sum_{i=1}^{n} \gamma_i (r_i - r_U) \tag{13.6}$$

where α, β_i and γ_i are the Lagrange multipliers. Now the Lagrangian dual becomes

$$f_{LD} = \max_{\substack{\alpha \geq 0, \\ \beta_i \geq 0, \\ \gamma_i \geq 0}} \min_{r_L \leq r_i \leq r_U} f(\mathbf{r}) = f_\Delta$$

Since the objective function in (13.5) is convex, and the constraints are linear, according to the Slater's condition, we have

$$\Delta_{r_i} = 2\left(\frac{r_i}{R} - p_i\right)\frac{1}{R} + \alpha s_i - \beta_i + \gamma_i = 0$$

Namely,

$$r_i = Rp_i - \frac{R^2}{2}(\alpha s_i - \beta_i + \gamma_i) \tag{13.7}$$

Combining Equations (13.6) and (13.7), the Lagrange dual problem becomes:

$$\begin{aligned}
\max \quad g(\alpha,\boldsymbol{\beta},\boldsymbol{\gamma}) = & \sum_{i=1}^{n} \left(\frac{R(\alpha s_i - \beta_i + \gamma_i)}{2} \right)^2 \\
& + \alpha \left[\sum_{i=1}^{n} (Rp_i + \frac{R^2}{2}(\alpha s_i - \beta_i + \gamma_i) - r_L)s_i - \delta S \right] \\
& + \sum_{i=1}^{n} \beta_i \left(r_L - Rp_i + \frac{R^2}{2}(\alpha s_i - \beta_i + \gamma_i) \right) \\
& + \sum_{i=1}^{n} \gamma_i \left(Rp_i - \frac{R^2}{2}(\alpha s_i - \beta_i + \gamma_i) - r_U \right) \\
s.t. \quad & \alpha \geq 0, \ \beta_i \geq 0, \ \gamma_i \geq 0, \ \text{for } i = 1, \ldots, n
\end{aligned}$$

This is a quadratic programming (QP) optimization problem with linear constraints. Rather than adopting the time-consuming numerical QP optimization, here we use the sequential minimal optimization (SMO) technique [14] to solve the above problem to find r_i. The main idea of SMO is as follows. SMO breaks the original QP problem into a series of smallest subproblems, which have only two multipliers and can be solved analytically. The original problem is solved when all the Lagrange multipliers satisfy the Karush–Kuhn–Tucker (KKT) conditions. In other words, SMO consists of two components: solving the subproblems with two Lagrange multipliers through an analytic method, and choosing which pair of multipliers to optimize, through heuristics in general. The first multiplier is selected among the multipliers that violate the KKT conditions, and the second multiplier is selected such that the dual objective has a large increase. SMO is guaranteed to converge, and various heuristics have been developed to speed up the algorithm. Compared to numerical QP optimization methods, SMO scales better and runs much faster.

13.1.2.2 Placement strategy

After obtaining the replication factor of each file, replicas are to be placed on a set of candidate servers, which is equivalent to finding a mapping from replicas to servers, so that the replicas with strong dependency can be assigned to the same server or nearby ones. This is related to the clustering problem that the replicas are partitioned into m groups, where m is the numbers of servers. The popular K-means clustering [15] (including its variations, e.g., K-median) however does not work in this context for it requires the data points being coordinated in a feature space. In our scenario, only the distance information between data points are available, which reflect the data dependency. As such, we resort to a K-medoids algorithm [16] that relies on distance information only and is reliable to outliers. The original K-medoids works as follows. Suppose that there are n data points to be divided into k clusters. In the first step, k data points are randomly selected as the medoids (*initialization*). In the second step, associate each of the remaining data points to the closest medoid based on the distance information. In the third step, for each medoid m and each nonmedoid data point o associated to m, swap m and o and compute the total cost of this new configuration. Select the configuration with the lowest cost and update the corresponding medoid. Then repeat the second and third steps until there is no change in the medoid, namely the total cost converges. Yet in DALM, we need to further incorporate the following constraints:

- Only one replica of the same file can be placed in the same server.
- The aggregated popularity of each server cannot exceed $(1+\eta)\bar{P}$.
- The total file/replica size on any server cannot exceed the storage capacity of the server.

To accommodate these constraints, a modified K-medoids algorithm is developed (pseudo code shown in Algorithm 13.1). It takes the dependency matrix D as the input, and returns a partition of replicas that minimizes the cross-server dependency while satisfying all the constraints. It is worth noting that this algorithm assumes that all the servers are in the same layer, e.g., interconnected by a single core switch. For a multilevel tree-topology cluster, this algorithm should be modified in a hierarchical way, which means that the data replicas are iteratively partitioned from the top level to the bottom level, such that dependent data is placed as close as possible.

Algorithm 13.1 The modified K-medois algorithm for replica placement

```
1: Randomly select m replicas be the initial cluster centers, namely medoids.
2: For each of the remaining replicas i, assign it to the cluster with the most
   dependent files if the constraints are satisfied.
3: for each medoid replica i do
4:     for each non-medoid replica j do
5:         Swap i and j if the constraints are satisfied.
6:         Memorize the current partition if it preserves more data dependency
7:     end for
8: end for
9: Iterate between steps 3 and 8 until convergence.
10: return m clusters
```

13.1.3 Implementation and deployment issues

So far we have outlined the design of DALM and laid its algorithmic foundations. We now discuss the practical challenges toward deploying DALM in the real-world Cloud environment.

To reduce the cross-server network traffic during the job execution, the MapReduce task scheduler on the master node usually places a task onto the slave, on which the required input data is available if possible. This is not always successful since the slave nodes having the input data may not have free slots at that time. Recall that the default replication factor is three in the Hadoop systems, which means that each file block is stored on three servers—two of them are within the same rack and the remaining one is in a different rack. Hence, depending on the distance between DataNode and TaskTracker, the default Hadoop defines three levels of data locality, namely, *node-local*, *rack-local*, and *off-switch*. Node-local is the optimal case that the task is scheduled on the node having data. Rack-local represents a suboptimal case that the task is scheduled on a node different from the node having data; the two nodes are within the same rack. Rack-local will incur cross-server traffic. Off-switch is the worst case, in which both the node-local and rack-local nodes have no free slots, and thus the task needs to retrieve data from a node in a different rack, incurring cross-rack traffic. When scheduling a task, the task scheduler takes a priority-based strategy: node-local has the highest priority, whereas off-switch has the lowest.

DALM can be easily incorporated into this conventional three-level design with a physical machine cluster. Such machine virtualization tools as Xen, KVM, and VMware allow multiple *virtual machines* (VMs) running on a single *physical machine* (PM), offering highly efficient hardware resource sharing and effectively reducing the operating costs of Cloud providers. They have not only become a foundation for today's modern Cloud platforms, but also affect the notion of data locality [17–20]. For illustration, consider the overall architecture of a typical Xen-based virtualized system in Figure 13.5. For a file block stored on VM 1-a, scheduling the task on VM 1-b or VM 2-b are considered identical by the task scheduler, for both are rack-local. The data exchanges between colocated VMs (e.g., VM 1-a and VM 1-b), however, are much faster than those between remote VMs (e.g., VM 1-b and VM 2-b), and hence the two cases should have different scheduling priorities.

To understand the impact to locality with highly-dependent data, we set up a MapReduce cluster consisting of three physical machines: one acts as the master node, and the other two each runs three VMs. As such, our cluster has six slave nodes in total. For the file block placement strategy, we consider the following three representatives: (1) first, divide the whole graph into two partitions, and then further divide each partition into three smaller partitions, which are placed on the colocated three VMs, respectively; (2) divide the graph into six partitions, and randomly place each partition on each VM; and (3) uniformly place the graph data on all VMs.

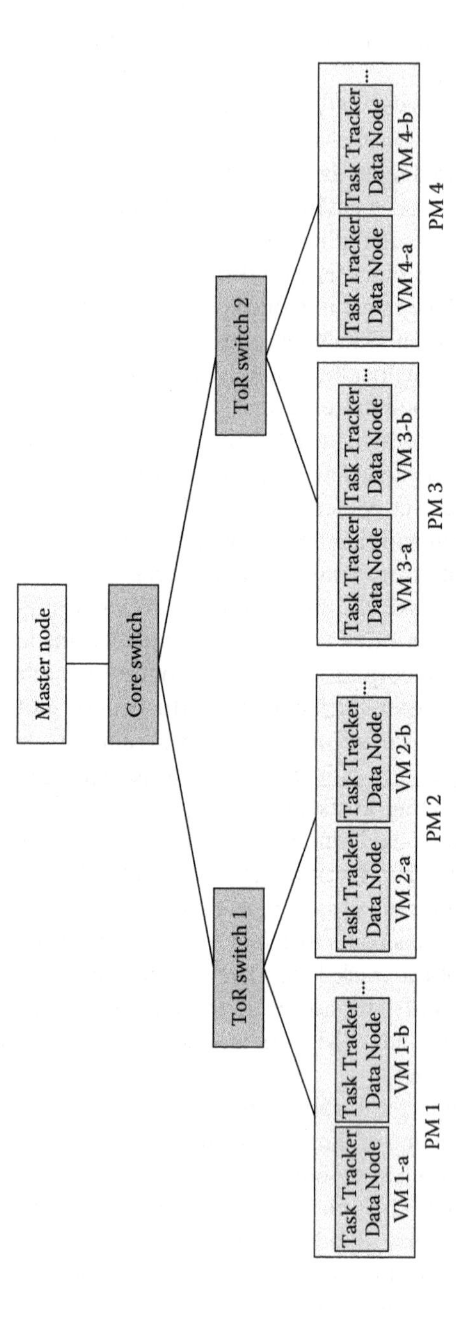

Figure 13.5: A typical virtual MapReduce cluster. A core switch is a high-capacity switch interconnecting top-of-rack (ToR) switches, which have relatively low capacity.

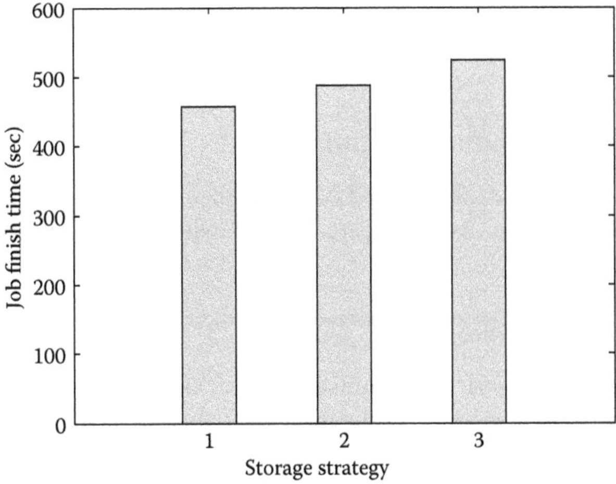

Figure 13.6: Job finish time with different storage strategies.

We extract 3.5 GB Wikipedia data from the Wikimedia database,* and then run the *Shortest Path* application in the widely used Giraph system as the microbenchmark. Figure 13.6 reports the average job finish time over five runs. The first storage strategy achieves the best performance since it matches well with the underlying server topology. As compared with the second strategy, it can significantly reduce the cross-server traffic by placing dependent data on the same PM, which on the other hand, is offloaded to the much more efficient communication among colocated VMs.

As such, it is necessary to modify the original three-level priority scheduling strategy by splitting node-local into two priority levels, namely, *VM-local* and *PM-local*. A task is VM-local if its required data is on the same virtual machine, while a task is PM-local if its required data is on two colocated virtual machines. At the beginning of running a MapReduce job, DALM launches a topology configuration process that identifies the structure of the underlying virtualized clusters from a configuration file. The points in the same or nearest communities in the graph are able to be placed on the same data block, so that they will be dealt with in the same computation node. A VM is associated with a unique ID, in the format of *rack-PM-VM*, such that the degree of locality can be easily obtained. The scheduling algorithm then schedules tasks in a virtualized MapReduce cluster based on the newly designed priority levels. The key change in this scheduling algorithm is that, when a VM has free slots, it requests new tasks from the master node through a heartbeat, and the task scheduler on the

*Available at http://dumps.wikimedia.org/

master node assigns tasks according to the following priority order: VM-local, PM-local, rack-local, and off-switch.

13.1.4 Performance evaluation

In this section, we evaluate DALM through extensive simulations and testbed experiments. We also compare DALM with state-of-the-art data locality solutions.

13.1.4.1 Simulations

We first conduct a series of simulations to examine the effectiveness of the proposed dependency-based replication strategy. As in previous studies [21], we assume that the file popularity exhibits a Pareto distribution [22], although DALM works with other popularity distributions as well. The probability density function (PDF) of a random variable X with a Pareto distribution is

$$f_X(x) = \begin{cases} \frac{\alpha x_m^\alpha}{x^{\alpha+1}} & x \geq x_m \\ 0 & x < x_m \end{cases}$$

where x_m is the minimum possible value of x, and α is a positive parameter that controls the skewness of the distribution. We plot the relative file popularity (the percentage of accesses of each file in the total accesses of all the files) as a function of the rank of the file for a sample set of 50 files in Figure 13.7. We can see that with larger α, the most popular files will have more accesses.

We generate data dependency based on the file popularity since the dependent files will be accessed together with high probability, and thus the dependent files may have similar popularity. To reflect this fact, we randomly pick up a dependency ratio for each pair of files between 0 and the popularity of the less popular file such that popular files will have strong mutual dependency with higher probability.

We compare our dependency-based replication strategy (DALM) with a representative popularity-based system, Scarlett [5]. The basic Hadoop system serves as the baseline. In the simulation, there are 50 different files with equal size and each file has at least three replicas. We examine the sensitivity of such system parameters as the extra storage budget ratio, the upper bound of replication factor, the number of servers, and the Pareto index α, with the default value of 20%, 5, 10, and 4.0, respectively.

The simulation results are shown in Figures 13.8 through 13.11, for each of the above system parameters, respectively. In general, we find that DALM outperforms the other two approaches with significantly reduced remote accesses. In the following we present our detailed analysis with respect to each system parameter.

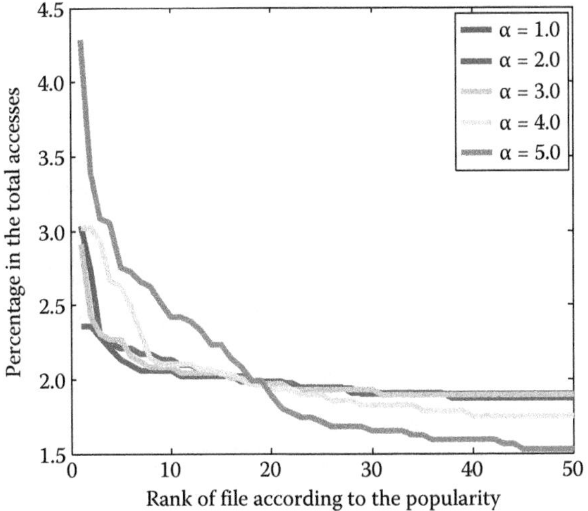

Figure 13.7: File rank ordered by relative popularity.

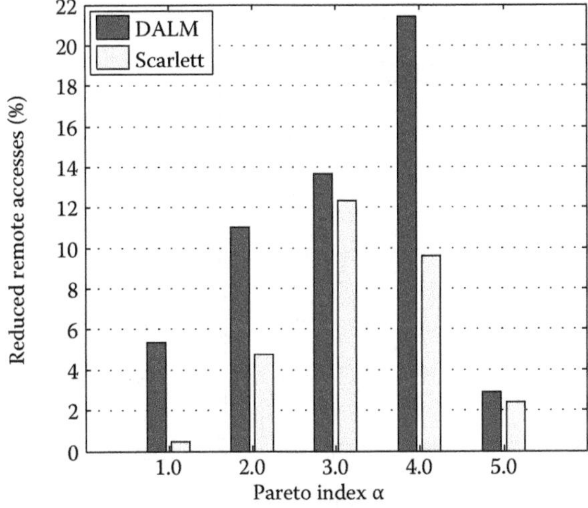

Figure 13.8: Impact of the skewness of file popularity.

Figure 13.8 shows the impact of the skewness of file popularity on the reduction of remote access, with the Pareto index α varying from 1.0 to 5.0. We can see that, with increased skewness, the data exchanges between the popular files will be more frequent, and thus DALM can reduce more remote accesses by putting highly dependent files together. However, when $\alpha = 5.0$, the popularity

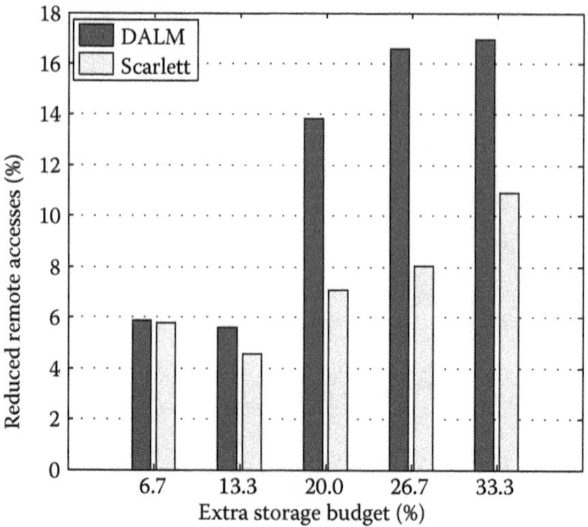

Figure 13.9: Impact of the extra storage budget ratio.

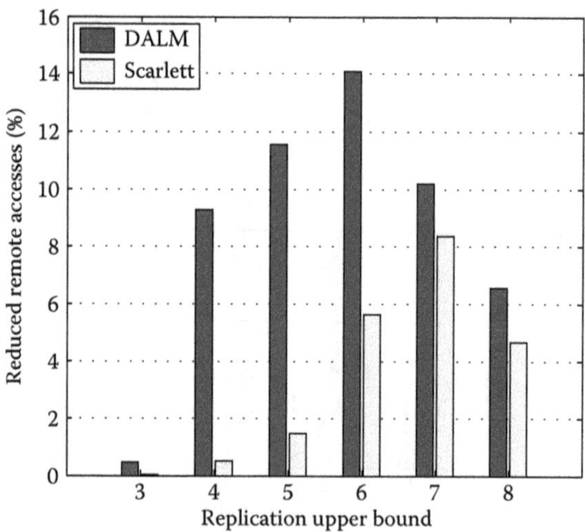

Figure 13.10: Impact of the upper bound of the replication factor.

of the most popular files is extremely high, such that the replicas of the highly dependent files cannot be stored together if both of them are very popular, due to the constraint of aggregated popularity. Scarlett also experiences a similar trend, with less improvement over the baseline.

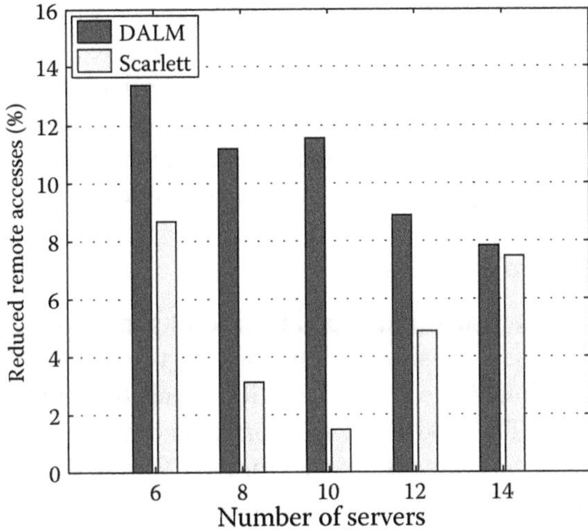

Figure 13.11: Impact of system scale.

Figure 13.9 illustrates the impact of the extra storage budget ratio. We can see that when the budget ratio is low, say 6.6% and 13.3%, the reduction of remote access is limited. The reason is that with limited extra storage, only a small number of the most popular files have a lot of replicas, while the other popular files do not have any replicas. Therefore, a lot of data access/exchange requests need to seek remote servers. The improvement of DALM becomes remarkable when the budget ratio reaches 20%, which reduces the remote access substantially by 22%, compared with 7% of Scarlett. It is worth noting that the gap between DALM and Scarlett will slightly decrease when the budget ratio keeps growing. The reason is that with more extra storage, Scarlett will have more replicas, and thus dependent files would be stored together with higher probability.

With a storage budget of 20%, the impact of the upper bound of the replication factor is shown in Figure 13.10. The improvement of DALM becomes more significant when the replication factor grows from 3 to 6, since a higher upper bound can give more opportunities to alleviate frequent access of the popular files; on the other hand, when the upper bound is too high, the improvement goes down since the most popular files will have excessive replicas while few of the other files have more than three replicas. Intuitively, this imbalance of the number of replicas maximizes the locality of the most popular files while sacrificing the locality of other files that occupy a large portion of the whole accesses.

Figure 13.11 shows the impact of the number of servers. Interestingly, the improvement of DALM becomes less with more servers, though DALM still noticeably outperforms Scarlett in most cases. The reason is that, with more servers, the replicas have to spread over all servers such that the deviation of popularity of each server does not exceed a predefined value, namely η, in which case the data dependency cannot be perfectly preserved. We expect to smartly adapt our strategy to the number of servers. In particular, when the servers are abundant, the imbalance of the servers' aggregated popularity is allowed, and thus more popular files with strong dependency can be placed on the same server without causing tangible hardware resource contention.

13.1.4.2 Test-bed experiments

We next present the real-world experiment results in a typical virtualized environment. Our testbed consists of four Dell servers (OPTIPLEX 7010), each equipped with an Intel Core i7-3770 3.4 GHz quad core CPU, 16 GB 1333 MHz DDR3 RAM, a 1 TB 7200 RPM hard drive, and a 1 Gbps network interface card (NIC). Hyper-threading is enabled for the CPUs so that each CPU core can support two threads. All physical machines are interconnected by a NETGEAR 8-port gigabit switch. This fully controllable test-bed system allows the machines to be interconnected with the maximum speed, and enables us to closely examine the impact of data dependency and data locality.

We use a separate physical machine as the master node, which, as the central controller, involves heavy I/O operations and network communications to maintain the state of the whole cluster and schedule tasks. Using a dedicated physical machine, rather than a virtual machine, ensures fast response time with minimized resource contention, and accordingly enables a fair comparison with fully nonvirtualized systems. Other physical machines that host virtual slave nodes run the latest Xen Hypervisor (version 4.1.3). On each physical machine, besides the Domain0 VM, we configure three identical DomainU VMs, which act as slave nodes. For the operating systems running on VMs (both Domain0 and DomainU), we use the popular Ubuntu 12.04 LTS 64 bit (kernel version 3.11.0-12). All the VMs are allocated two virtual CPUs and a 4 GB memory. We use the popular *logical volume management* (LVM) system for on-demand resizing, and allocate each DomainU VM a 100 GB disk space in default. We use the open source monitoring system Ganglia* 3.5.12 to monitor the system running conditions.

We compare DALM with Scarlett and Surfer, as well as the basic Hadoop system, in terms of job finish time, and cross-server traffic. We use a public social network data set [23], which contains 8,164,015 vertices and 153,112,820 edges, and the volume is 2.10 GB. There are roughly five communities in the graph, and we select one of them as the popular one. The default system settings are as follows: the block size is 32 MB, and the replication factor is 2 in the basic Hadoop system; the extra storage budget ratio is 20%, with the replication lower bound of 2 and the upper bound of 4 for both DALM and Scarlett. We allocate 32 workers in total, with 8 map workers on each slave server, and 7 map workers

*Ganglia Monitoring System, http://ganglia.sourceforge.net

and 1 reduce worker on the master server. We run two representative applications to evaluate the performance of these systems, namely, *Shortest Path* and *PageRank*. The *Shortest Path* application finds the shortest path for all pairs of vertices; the *PageRank* application ranks the vertices according to the PageRank algorithm.

We first compare the job finish time of different systems. For each system, we run each benchmark application five times, and plot the average improvement of job finish time in Figure 13.12. Again, the basic Hadoop system serves as the baseline.

It can be observed that DALM significantly improves the system performance in the job finish time over the other systems. Compared with the basic Hadoop, Scarlett, Surfer, our proposed DALM on average improves the job finish time by 10.74%, 12.40%, and 28.09% for *Shortest Path*, respectively. For *PageRank*, the improvements are 6.74%, 16.37%, and 17.80%, respectively. These results clearly demonstrate all the three systems can significantly reduce the job finish time over the basic Hadoop system. Scarlett improves data locality by smartly replicating popular blocks, while Surfer can reduce cross-server traffic with dependency-aware placement. DALM achieves the shortest job finish time by integrating the dependency-aware placement strategy of Surfer, and the popularity-based replication strategy of Scarlett. Further, DALM adapts the task scheduling algorithm to be virtual aware, which has the potential to further improve job finish time in larger-scale systems.

We now take a closer look at how DALM achieves the best performance. Data locality is an important metric in MapReduce systems, since it largely reflects the data traffic pressure on the network fabric. Data locality is highly desirable for

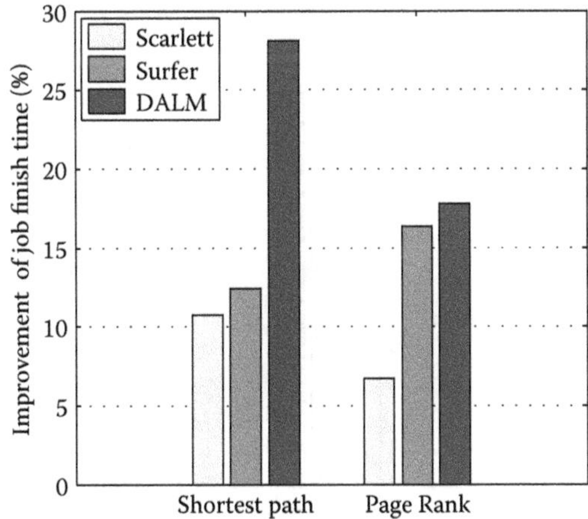

Figure 13.12: Average job finish time.

MapReduce applications, especially in commercial data centers where the network fabrics are highly oversubscribed, and the communications across racks are generally costly. Figure 13.13 shows that DALM achieves remarkable improvement in data locality, as compared to Scarlett and Surfer for both benchmark applications. Since Scarlett has more replicas for popular data blocks than Surfer, the data locality of Scarlett is higher. With both popularity and dependency-based schemes, DALM is able to provide 100% data locality.

Figure 13.14 explains the advantages of DALM over Hadoop, Scarlett, and Surfer, from the perspective of cross-server traffic. In the basic Hadoop, only half of the tasks are localized, which means there is considerable overhead caused by remote task executions and communications. Scarlett and Surfer successfully reduce the cross-server traffic with more replications and dependency-aware data placement, respectively. Yet Scarlett can evict strong dependent tasks on remote VMs, leading to increased task finish time. Surfer, on the other hand, successfully reduces a large amount of remote communications by placing dependent tasks on nearby VMs, but incurs the hotspot problem for popular data blocks. In DALM, most tasks are assigned to the appropriate VMs storing the necessary data blocks, minimizing the out-of-rack tasks. The hot spot problems are also largely mitigated through data replication.

13.1.5 Discussion

It is worth noting that cross-server traffic still exists in DALM. For example, if the VMs on one PM are all busy and have no free slots, while some VMs on other PMs have free slots, the task scheduler has to allocate the pending tasks.

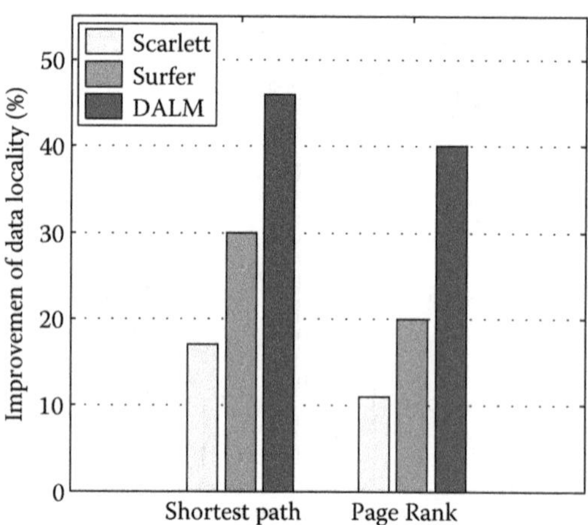

Figure 13.13: Data locality of jobs.

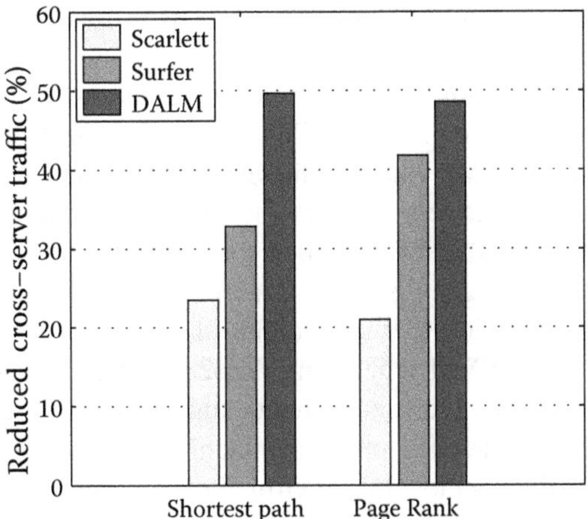

Figure 13.14: Cross-server traffic.

This could be improved through incorporating delay scheduling [24] into DALM. DALM also needs the topology information of the underlying clusters for data placement. If such information is not available, a topology inference algorithm might be needed, e.g., through bandwidth/latency measurement between VM pairs. DALM could be further improved by incorporating the prioritization technique [25].

13.2 Data Locality for MapReduce in Virtualized Clouds

MapReduce has been increasingly embraced by both academic and industrial users; yet not all MapReduce users or potential users have dedicated MapReduce clusters due to various reasons, e.g., the costly upfront investment on hardware/software, and the lack of expertise on cumbersome configuration, not to mention the challenges on expanding the cluster when the application scale escalates. Fortunately, the readily available Clouds provide an alternative solution for big data analytics. The Cloud users can rent machines from public Cloud providers, say Amazon Web Services (AWS),* and deploy the Hadoop stack as well as other standard/customized tools. As such, they can enjoy the convenient and flexible *pay-as-you-go* billing option, as well as the on-demand resource scaling. For example, Yelp, a famous business rating and review site, successfully

* Amazon Web Services, http://aws.amazon.com

saved 55,000 dollars in upfront hardware costs by using MapReduce on the AWS, processing 3 TB of data per day.*

As one of the most important technical foundations of modern Clouds, virtualization techniques (e.g., Xen, KVM, and VMware) allow multiple VMs running on a single PM, which achieves highly efficient hardware resource multiplexing, and effectively reduces the operating costs of Cloud providers. It has been identified that MapReduce jobs running on virtual machines can take a significantly longer finish time, as compared with directly running on physical counterparts due to such unique characteristics of VMs as resource sharing/contention and VM scheduling [26–28], which is also confirmed by our real-world experiments. Our experiments suggest that the conventional notion of data locality designed for physical machines needs substantial revision to accurately reflect the data locality in virtualized environments.

13.2.1 When data locality meets virtualization

Real-world MapReduce systems, such as Hadoop and Google's MapReduce, attempt to achieve better data locality through replicating each file block on three servers, so that two of them are within the same rack and the remaining one is in a different rack. More advanced data locality solutions have also been developed [5,6,24], though mostly working for physical machine clusters.

Similarly, in a virtual machine cluster, each virtual machine serving as a slave also has a DataNode and a TaskTracker by default. This balanced architecture is very straightforward, and is supposed to provide the best performance since each virtual machine can access data locally, achieving the maximum data locality. On the other hand, a single DataNote can be set up on only one virtual machine to serve all the other colocated virtual machines. Intuitively, this imbalanced architecture incurs more remote accesses and has a lower degree of data locality, since the virtual machines without DataNodes need to fetch data remotely.

We have conducted a series of experiments in a test-bed Cloud platform to understand and compare the performance of data locality under the different configurations above. Our experimental results reveal the distinct characteristics when data locality meets virtualization, which indeed contradict our intuition, suggesting that the conventional data locality strategies working for physical machines should be revised.

Our test-bed consists of three state-of-the-art Dell servers (OPTIPLEX 7010), each equipped with an Intel Core i7-3770 3.4 GHz quad core CPU, 8 GB 1333 MHz DDR3 RAM, a 1 TB 7200 RPM hard drive, and a 1 Gbps ethernet NIC. Hyper-threading is enabled for the CPU so that each CPU core can support two threads. All the physical machines are interconnected through a gigabit switch. This cluster of controlled scale allows the machines to be interconnected

*AWS Case Study: Yelp, http://aws.amazon.com/solutions/case-studies/yelp/

with the maximum speed and enables us to closely examine the interplay among all of them, without concerning the background interference from many other machines. We use a widely adopted open source virtualization tool, Xen [29], in which a Xen Hypervisor provides the resource mapping between the virtual hardware and the underlying real hardware of the physical machine. A privileged VM, namely, the *Domain0*, is created at boot time and is allowed to use the control interface. The hypervisor works together with the *host OS* running on the Domain0 to provide system management utilities. The OS running on an unprivileged domain (*DomainU*) VM is called the *guest OS*, which can only access the resources that are allocated by the hypervisor. The DomainU VMs cannot directly access the I/O devices; rather, the Domain0 VM handles all of the I/O processing. Xen uses the shared memory mechanism for data transfer between colocated VMs [29].

We use a separate physical machine as the master node to ensure fast response time with minimized resource contention, and accordingly enable a fair comparison with fully nonvirtualized systems. On each of other physical machines, besides the Domain0 VM, we configure three identical DomainU VMs (2 virtual CPUs and 2 GB RAM for each) as slave nodes. We use the LVM system, which is convenient for resizing, to allocate each DomainU VM a 100 GB disk space by default. We use the popular Ubuntu 12.04 LTS 64 bit as the operating system, and run the Hadoop 1.2.1 on the VMs. Our test-bed is configured similarly to the public Cloud,* as well as the setting in Ref. [30], with high-end Intel multicore CPUs, Linux-based operating systems, and the Xen virtualization tool. Hence, the observations in our test-bed experiments can be reproducible in typical virtualized Clouds.

13.2.1.1 DataNode placement: Less is better

Our first observation is that the number of DataNodes per physical machine has a remarkable impact on MapReduce's performance. We start from a simple cluster, in which two physical machines are interconnected through the switch, one serving as the master node and the other hosting three VMs. The three VMs act as slaves, each having a TaskTracker. We extract 3.5 GB Wikipedia data from the Wikimedia database,† and select the widely used `Sort` application as our benchmark, which arranges the lines of text in the input files in alphabetical order. For the DataNode placement, we examine three representative configurations: (1) setting up a DataNode on only one VM; (2) randomly selecting two VMs and setting up a DataNode on each; and (3) setting a DataNode on each VM. When there is more than one DataNode, the input data will be almost evenly stored on them.

*For example, a Rackspace *General1-2* instance has 2 virtual CPUs and 2 GB RAM.

†Available at http://dumps.wikimedia.org/

We run the benchmark application five times for each configuration, and the average job finish times of the above three configurations are 458.0, 487.0, and 524.5 seconds, respectively. It can be seen that, the fewer DataNodes per physical machine, the shorter the job finish time. This contradicts to the observation with traditional physical machine MapReduce clusters. In a physical machine cluster, the highest data locality will be achieved when all tasks can access the input data from local nodes (*node local*), and the job finish time is generally shorter than with a lower-degree data locality. For virtualized clusters, our results however indicate that achieving complete VM locality can be harmful.

A closer look shows that the reasons are threefold. First, many MapReduce tasks, say `Sort` in the example, are both computation and I/O intensive; considering the contention for the shared resources, more DataNodes will significantly increase the burden of VMs and the extent of inter-VM interference. Second, both reading data from and writing data to the HDFS, involve metadata exchange with the master node; having multiple DataNodes also increases the overhead of such information exchange. Third, besides HDFS involved I/O operations, each VM also generates massive intermediate data, which is generally several times more than the amount of input and output data; the intermediate data needs to be written to and read from the local disk of each VM to bridge the map and reduce phases. Yet the concurrent I/O operations of HDFS and local disks will aggravate the intra- and inter-VM contention for the disk.

The observations suggest that selecting one VM hosting the DataNode to serve all co-located VMs can be a better choice. This architecture overcomes the above drawbacks of one DataNode per VM, and thus mitigates the contention for disk. To understand this, we use the `iotop` tool, which is available in most Linux distributions, to measure the real-time disk read/write throughput during the process of two experiments (one DataNode per VM and one DataNode per PM), and plot the total disk read/write throughput of the three VMs in Figure 13.15. We can see that the one-DataNode-per-PM setting has a noticeably higher average disk read/write throughput (read: 19.03 MBps vs. 15.19 MBps, write: 27.39 MBps vs. 21.23 MBps) and lower variation.* Further, the data exchange between colocated VMs is very efficient, which has been validated using the `iperf` tool. The measurement results show that the network bandwidth between two colocated VMs exceeds 15 Gbps, indicating that colocated VMs directly use the memory bus for data exchange. Hence, the added latency caused by remote access across colocated VMs is negligible.

13.2.1.2 Virtual locality: Nearest is not the best

To further verify that remote data access across colocated VMs does not add noticeable performance penalty, our other set of experiments uses two physical

*It is worth noting that `iotop` itself introduces some overhead and thus the job finish time becomes slightly longer, which however exists for all the cases and thus will not affect the relative differences.

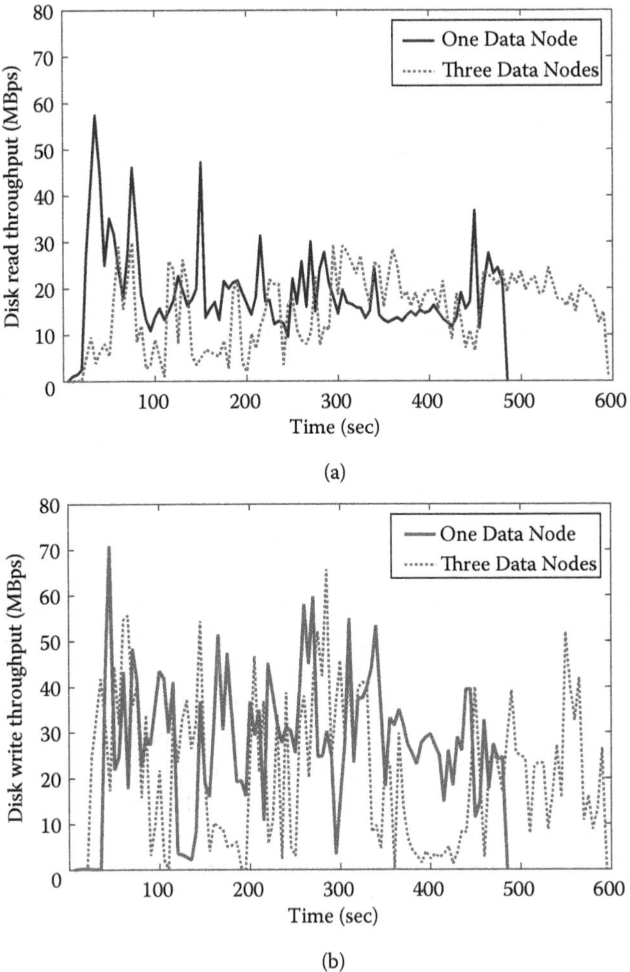

Figure 13.15: (a) Total disk read throughput during MapReduce running time and (b) Total disk write throughput during MapReduce running time.

machines, which are connected through a switch. For the nonmaster physical machine, we have two configurations: in configuration (a), we boot up only one DomainU VM, which has both TaskTracker and DataNode; in configuration (b), we boot up two DomainU VMs: one has a TaskTracker only and the other has a DataNode only. Other experimental settings are the same as in the previous experiment. We again run each experiment five times for each configuration. The average job finish times of configurations (a) and (b) are 799.0 and 433.3 seconds, respectively. The result is very interesting. In configuration (a), the VM can access all the data from its local disk; while in configuration (b), all the input/output data needs to be transmitted between the two VMs. Yet the latter is much more efficient in terms of MapReduce job finish time, which not only verifies our previous conjecture that remote access across colocated VMs does not add noticeable performance penalty, but also indicates that the MapReduce can significantly benefit from decoupling TaskTracker and DataNode.

13.2.2 vLocality: Architecture design

Given the observations above, it is necessary to revisit the notation of data locality for MapReduce in virtualized Clouds. This inspires our design and development of vLocality, which seeks to improve the effectiveness of locality in the virtualized environment, yet with minimized modifications to the existing MapReduce implementations. Figure 13.16 illustrates the architecture of vLocality. For the VMs colocated on the same PM, we only set up a single DataNode on one of them; all the other VMs on this PM each had a TaskTracker only.

To reduce the cross-server network traffic during the job execution, the task scheduler on the master node usually places a task onto the slave, on which the required input data is available if possible. Yet this is not always successful since the slave nodes having the input data may not have free slots at that time. Recall that the default replication factor is three in the Hadoop systems, which means that each file block is stored on three servers two of them are within the same rack and the remaining one is in a different rack. Hence, depending on the distance between DataNode and TaskTracker, the default Hadoop defines three levels of data locality, namely, *node-local*, *rack-local*, and *off-switch*. Node-local is the optimal case that the task is scheduled on the node having data. Rack-local represents a suboptimal case that the task is scheduled on a node different from the node having data; yet the two nodes are within the same rack. Rack-local will incur cross-server traffic. Off-switch is the worst case, in which all the node-local and rack-local nodes are busy, and thus the task needs to retrieve data from a node in a different rack, incurring cross-rack traffic. When scheduling a task, the task scheduler takes a priority-based strategy: node-local has the highest priority, whereas off-switch has the lowest.

In virtualized MapReduce clusters, however, the three-level design is not enough to accurately reflect the data locality. For example, in Figure 13.16, for a file block stored on VM 1-a, scheduling the task on VM 1-b or VM 2-b are considered identical by the task scheduler, for both are rack-local. Yet data exchanges between colocated VMs (e.g., VM 1-a and VM 1-b) are much faster than those between remote VMs (e.g., VM 1-b and VM 2-b), and hence the two cases should have different scheduling priorities. To this end, we modify the original three-level priority scheduling strategy by splitting node-local into two priority levels, namely, *VM-local* and *PM-local*, in virtualized MapReduce clusters, defined as follows: **VM-local**—a task and its required data are on the same

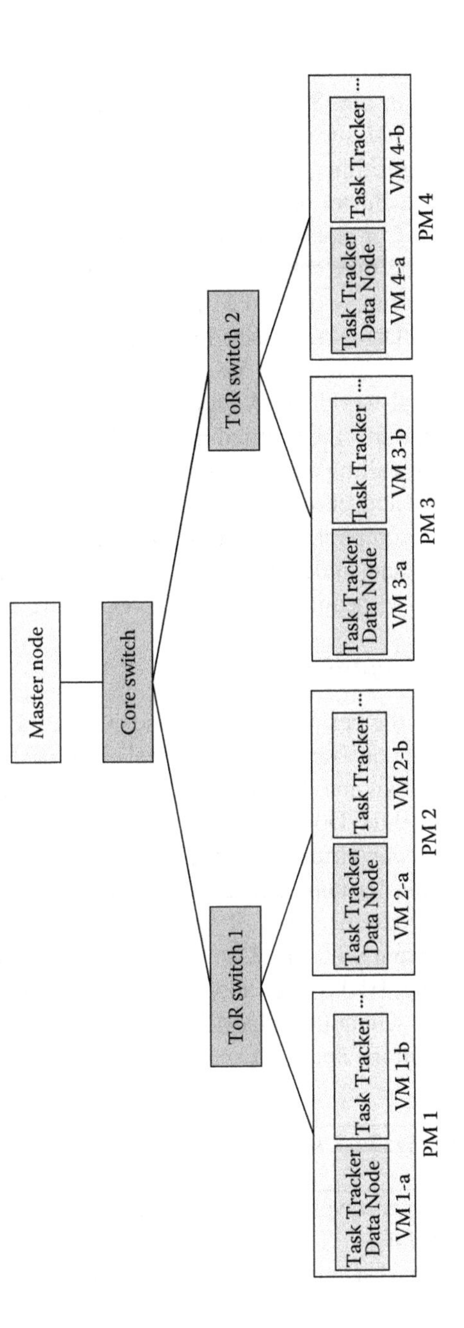

Figure 13.16: vLocality architecture design. A core switch is a high-capacity switch interconnecting top-of-rack (ToR) switches, which have relatively low capacity.

virtual machine; **PM-local**—a task and its required data are on two colocated virtual machines, respectively.

At the beginning of running a MapReduce job, vLocality launches a topology configuration process that identifies the structure of the underlying virtualized clusters from a configuration file. Then a VM is associated with a unique ID, in the format of *rack-PM-VM* such that the degree of locality can be easily obtained. A vScheduling algorithm (see Algorithm 13.2) then schedules the tasks in a virtualized MapReduce cluster based on the newly designed priority-levels as follows. When a VM has free slots, it requests new tasks from the master node through a heartbeat, and the task scheduler on the master node assigns tasks according to the following priority order: PM-local if this VM has no DataNode (VM-local if this VM has a DataNode), rack-local, and off-switch.

The above high-level description provides a sketch of the vLocality's workflow. Implementing it in real-world MapReduce systems however is nontrivial. In particular, we need to modify the original priority level as well as the corresponding scheduling policy, calling for careful examination of the whole Hadoop package to identify the related classes and methods. We also need to ensure that our modifications are compatible with other modules. To demonstrate the practicability of vLocality and understand its practical performance, we have implemented a prototype of vLocality based on Hadoop 1.2.1.

13.2.3 Performance evaluation

In this section, we evaluate the performance of vLocality based on a virtualized Cloud test-bed. Our test-bed consists of eight physical machines, which are interconnected through a gigabit switch. We use one dedicated physical machine as the master node, and create three DomainU VMs on each of the remaining seven physical machines. Hence, our virtualized MapReduce cluster has 22 nodes in total, namely, 1 physical master node and 21 virtual slave nodes. We compare vLocality with two other systems, *Default* and *HDFS-only*. Default runs the standard Hadoop 1.2.1 system with one DataNode on each virtual slave node, which serves as the baseline; HDFS-only adopts the one-DataNode-per-PM setting with the original task scheduling algorithm. We select three widely used Hadoop benchmark applications `Sort`, `ShortestPath`, and `PageRank`. We use

---

Algorithm 13.2 vScheduling: Task scheduling in vLocality MapReduce systems

---

when the task scheduler receives a heartbeat from node v:
    if v has a free slot **then**
        sort the pending tasks according to the priority policy and obtain a list T
        schedule the first task to node v
    end if

---

the 3.5 GB Wikipedia data as the input for `Sort`, and process the data to the input format (directed graph) of `ShortestPath` and `PageRank`.* The `PageRank` application ranks the vertices according to the PageRank algorithm, and the `ShortestPath` application finds the shortest path for all pairs of vertices in the input file.

It is worth noting that in all the experiments, all the file blocks are evenly distributed on all VMs, and thus on all PMs as well. In each experiment, the file access pattern is uniform, which means that each file block is accessed once. In this scenario, the Default system already achieves the optimal node-local data locality, as discussed in Ref. [5,31]. Since vLocality takes the major efforts on minimizing the interference of colocated VMs, as well as differentiating between PM-local and rack-local, our test-bed platform, where all the nodes are connected with one switch, focuses on the improvements in the rack level. The results are representative, and the conclusion can be extended to larger systems since cross-rack scheduled tasks only account for a marginal portion of the total tasks [20].

We first compare the job finish time of different systems. For each system, we run each benchmark application five times, and plot the average job finish time in Figure 13.17.

It is observed that vLocality significantly improves the performance of all the selected MapReduce applications over the other systems. Compared with Default, HDFS-only improves the job finish time by 9.6% on average for `Sort`, which again verifies the effectiveness of revising the DataNote placement strategy. vLocality, by adapting the task scheduling algorithm to be virtual aware, can further improve the job finish time by 16.3% on average, as compared with

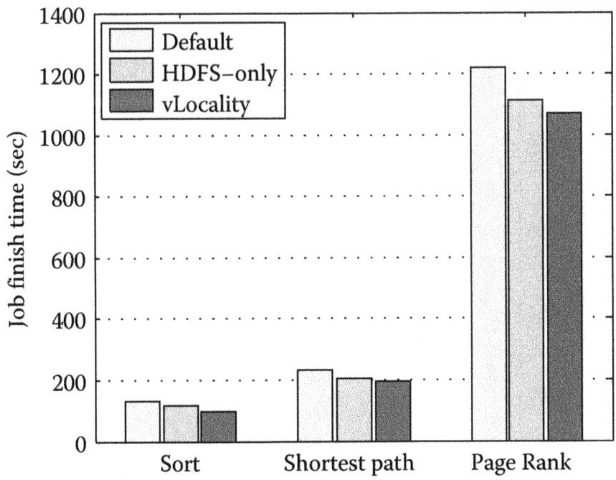

Figure 13.17: Comparison of job finish time.

*Each URL in the file is represented by a vertex, and each hyperlink is represented by a directed edge.

HDFS-only (24.3% as directly compared with Default). The improvements on `ShortestPath` and `PageRank` are less significant (16.2% and 12.3% as compared with Default, respectively), since the number of reducers in these two applications is less than that in `Sort`, and thus the reduce phase, in which data locality has less impact, accounts for most of the running time. Further, these two applications involve iterative steps, which incur a lot of communication overhead.

Since data locality is mainly related to the map phase, we plot the empirical CDF of the map task finish time in Figure 13.18, which gives a much more clearer picture of the impressive improvements of vLocality over Default. We can see that the system design has a remarkable impact on the finish time of individual map tasks. Taking `Sort` as an example, in the Default system, all the map tasks take more than 20 seconds, and nearly 30% of tasks need more than 40 seconds. On the other hand, in both HDFS-only and vLocality, more than 70% of tasks can be finished in less than 18 seconds, indicating that the reduced number of DataNodes can effectively mitigate the interference and speed up task execution. The remaining tasks, accounting for about 20% of the total, have divergent finish time distributions in HDFS-only and vLocality: all the remaining tasks can be finished within 40 seconds in vLocality, while most of them need more than 40 seconds in HDFS-only, implying that vScheduling significantly reduces rack-local (cross-PM) tasks.

We further calculate the distribution of different degrees of data locality for each system running the benchmark applications, and report the results of `Sort` in Table 13.1. The results are similar for `ShortestPath` and `PageRank`, which are omitted for the sake of conciseness.

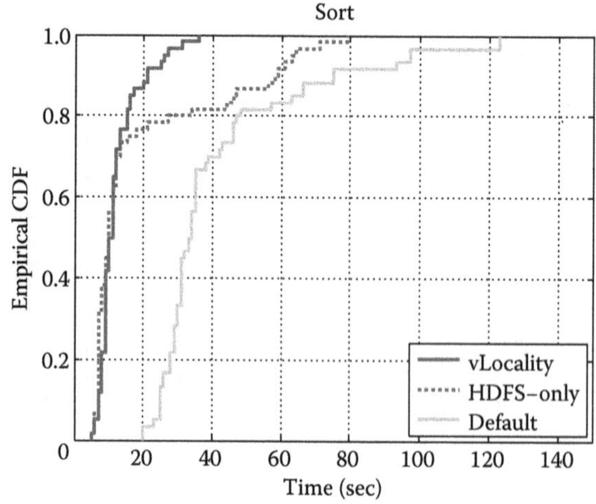

Figure 13.18: Empirical CDF of map task finish time of different systems.

Table 13.1 Degrees of data locality in different systems

	VM-local	PM-local	Rack-local
Default	90.0%	1.7%	8.3%
HDFS-only	31.7%	38.3%	30.0%
vLocality	25.0%	71.7%	3.3%

Table 13.1 explains the advantages of vLocality over Default and HDFS-only. In Default, most tasks are VM-local, a few are rack-local, and the PM-local cases are very rare. Concurrent running VM-local tasks on colocated VMs will incur severe inter-VM interference, leading to increased task finish time. HDFS-only successfully reduces VM-local tasks by reducing the number of DataNodes per PM, yet it incurs many rack-local tasks since the original task scheduler regards PM-local and rack-local as identical. In vLocality, most tasks are assigned to the appropriate VMs, minimizing the nonnecessary rack-local tasks. It is worth noting that vLocality cannot completely eliminate the rack-local tasks. To identify the root cause, we analyze the log files, and find that in some cases, the VMs on one PM are all busy and have no free slots, while some VMs on other PM have free slots. Hence, the task scheduler has to allocate the pending tasks, which are rack-local to these VMs; otherwise the slot resources would be wasted.

13.2.4 Discussion

Data locality is critical to the performance of MapReduce tasks, and there have been significant studies toward improving data locality [4]. Scarlett [5] and DARE [6] adopt a popularity-based strategy, which smartly place more replicas for popular file blocks. There have also been substantial efforts on directly scheduling tasks close to data, e.g., [24,32,33].

These works on data locality have yet to address the distinguished challenges from virtual machines in a public Cloud. In the virtualized environment, a location-aware data allocation strategy was proposed in Ref. [31], which allocates file blocks across all physical machines evenly and the replicas are located in different physical machines. DRR [19] enhances locality-aware task scheduling through dynamically increasing or decreasing the computation capability of each node. An interference and locality-aware (ILA) scheduling strategy has been developed for virtualized MapReduce clusters, using a task performance prediction model to mitigate inter-VM interference and preserve task data locality [20].

Our vLocality improves the data locality in a virtualized Cloud environment by observing that directly applying the conventional data locality strategies in physical machine clusters to virtual machine clusters, namely, achieving complete VM-locality, can be harmful to the MapReduce performance given the shared resource contention nature. We have revised the underlying data placement strategy and accordingly propose a customized virtual-aware task scheduling algorithm. The existing improvements, e.g., delay scheduling [24], DRR [19], and interference-aware scheduling [20], can be further incorporated into vLocality after being customized for the new architecture of vLocality. We plan to work on this issue in the future work.

The virtualization performance overhead in Cloud scenarios has attracted a lot of attention from researchers [28]. In general, the causes of overhead stem from different levels of Cloud infrastructure: from single-server virtualization, a single-site mega data center, to multiple geo-distributed data centers. In this chapter, we investigated the single-server virtualization overhead for MapReduce-based big data processing, and vLocality is also beneficial to mitigate the overhead of data center scale by reducing cross-server traffic.

The dynamics of virtualized Cloud platforms, e.g., VM migration [28,30], is also very important for load balancing, power saving, and fault tolerance. In big data processing, VM migration can be very costly since a large volume of data also need to be migrated besides VM images. The data center network would be overloaded during migration, and the performance interference on migration source and destination PMs can be severe. vLocality is able to reduce the migration overhead since migrating a VM without DataNode incurs much less data transfer as compared with migrating a fully functional VM, while the data availability is not affected. The iAware strategy [30] can be also adapted to vLocality, e.g., considering the data locality issue when selecting destination PMs, to further minimize the overhead of live migration.

13.3 Conclusion

As an important practice to improve MapReduce's performance, data locality has been extensively investigated in the literature. In this chapter, we first showed strong evidence that data dependency, which exists in many real-world applications, has a significant impact on the performance of typical MapReduce applications. We developed DALM, a comprehensive and practical solution toward dependency-aware locality for MapReduce. DALM first leverages the graph partition technique to identify the dependency of the input data, and reorganizes the data storage accordingly. It then replicates data blocks according to the historical data popularity, and smartly places data blocks across VMs subject to such practical constraints as storage budget, replication upper bound, and the underlying network topology. Through both simulations and real-world deployment of the DALM prototype, we illustrated the superiority of DALM against state-of-the-art solutions.

We then showed strong evidence that the conventional efforts on improving data locality can cause a negative impact on typical MapReduce applications in virtualized Clouds. We suggested to adapt the existing storage architecture to be virtual-machine-aware, which offloads a large portion of congested disk I/O to the highly efficient network I/O with memory sharing. This new storage design demands revision on the traditional three-level data locality, so does the task scheduling. We developed vLocality, a systematic solution to improve data locality in virtualized MapReduce clusters, and demonstrated the superiority of vLocality against state-of-the-art systems.

References

[1] J. Dean and S. Ghemawat, MapReduce: Simplified data processing on large clusters, *Communications of the ACM*, vol. 51, no. 1, pp. 107–113, 2008.

[2] X. Fan, X. Ma, J. Liu, and D. Li, Dependency-aware data locality for MapReduce, in *Proceedings of IEEE International Conference on Cloud Computing (CLOUD)*, 2014.

[3] X. Ma, X. Fan, J. Liu, and D. Li, Dependency-aware data locality for MapReduce, *IEEE Transactions on Cloud Computing*, DOI: 10.1109/TCC.2015.2511765.

[4] Z. Guo, G. Fox, and M. Zhou, Investigation of data locality in MapReduce, in *Proceedings of IEEE/ACM International Symposium on Cluster, Cloud and Grid Computing (CCGRID)*, May 13–16, 2012, Ottawa, Canada, pp. 419–426.

[5] G. Ananthanarayanan, S. Agarwal, S. Kandula, A. Greenberg, I. Stoica, D. Harlan, and E. Harris, Scarlett: Coping with skewed content popularity in MapReduce clusters, in *Proceedings of European Conference on Computer Systems (EuroSys)*, 2011.

[6] C. L. Abad, Y. Lu, and R. H. Campbell, Dare: Adaptive data replication for efficient cluster scheduling, in *Proceedings of IEEE International Conference on Cluster Computing (CLUSTER)*, 2011.

[7] G. Ananthanarayanan, A. Ghodsi, A. Wang, D. Borthakur, S. Kandula, S. Shenker, and I. Stoica, Pacman: Coordinated memory caching for parallel jobs, in *Proceedings of USENIX Symposium on Networked Systems Design and Implementation (NSDI)*, 2012.

[8] A. Thusoo, Z. Shao, S. Anthony, D. Borthakur, N. Jain, J. Sen Sarma, R. Murthy, and H. Liu, Data warehousing and analytics infrastructure at facebook, in *Proceedings of ACM SIGMOD International Conference on Management of Data (SIGMOD)*, June 6–11, 2010, Indianapolis, IN, pp. 1013–1020.

[9] R. Chen, M. Yang, X. Weng, B. Choi, B. He, and X. Li, Improving large graph processing on partitioned graphs in the cloud, in *Proceedings of ACM Symposium on Cloud Computing (SoCC)*, 2012.

[10] G. Karypis and V. Kumar, Analysis of multilevel graph partitioning, in *Proceedings of ACM/IEEE Conference on Supercomputing*, 1995.

[11] G. Karypis and V. Kumar, Parallel multilevel k-way partitioning scheme for irregular graphs, in *Proceedings of ACM/IEEE Conference on Supercomputing*, 1996.

[12] K. George and V. Kumar, A fast and high quality multilevel scheme for partitioning irregular graphs, *SIAM Journal on Scientific Computing*, vol. 20, no. 1, pp. 359–392, August 1998.

[13] F. Pellegrini and J. Roman, Scotch: A software package for static mapping by dual recursive bipartitioning of process and architecture graphs, in *Proceedings of International Conference and Exhibition on High-Performance Computing and Networking*, 1996.

[14] P. John, Sequential minimal optimization: A fast algorithm for training support vector machines, in B. Schölkopf, C. J. C. Burges, and A. J. Smola (eds.), *Advances in Kernel Method: Support Vector Learning*, MIT Press, Cambridge, MA, 1999, pp. 185–208.

[15] A.K. Jain, M.N. Murty, and P.J. Flynn, Data clustering: A review, *ACM Computing Surveys*, vol. 31, no. 3, pp. 264–323, September 1999.

[16] H.S. Park and C.H. Jun, A simple and fast algorithm for k-medoids clustering, *Expert Systems with Applications*, vol. 36, no. 2, Part 2, pp. 3336–3341, March 2009.

[17] H. Kang, Y. Chen, J.L. Wong, R. Sion, J. Wu, Enhancement of Xen's scheduler for MapReduce workloads, in *Proceedings of International Symposium on High Performance Distributed Computing (HPDC)*, 2011.

[18] B. Palanisamy, A. Singh, L. Liu, and B. Jain, Purlieus: Locality-aware resource allocation for MapReduce in a cloud, in *Proceedings of International Conference for High Performance Computing, Networking, Storage and Analysis*, 2011.

[19] J. Park, D. Lee, B. Kim, J. Huh, and S. Maeng, Locality-aware dynamic VM reconfiguration on MapReduce clouds, in *Proceedings of International Symposium on High Performance Distributed Computing (HPDC)*, 2012.

[20] X. Bu, J. Rao, and C. Xu, Interference and locality-aware task scheduling for MapReduce applications in virtual clusters, in *Proceedings of International Symposium on High Performance Distributed Computing (HPDC)*, 2013.

[21] J. Lin, The curse of zipf and limits to parallelization: A look at the stragglers problem in MapReduce, in *Workshop on Large-Scale Distributed Systems for Information Retrieval*, 2009.

[22] M. Newman, Power laws, pareto distributions and zipf's law, *Contemporary Physics*, vol. 46, no. 5, pp. 323–351, 2005.

[23] J. Yang and J. Leskovec. Defining and evaluating network communities based on ground-truth, in *Proceedings of ACM SIGKDD Workshop on Mining Data Semantics*, 2012.

[24] M. Zaharia, D. Borthakur, J. Sen Sarma, K. Elmeleegy, S. Shenker, and I. Stoica, Delay scheduling: A simple technique for achieving locality and fairness in cluster scheduling, in *Proceedings of European Conference on Computer Systems (EuroSys)*, 2010.

[25] Y. Zhang, Q. Gao, L. Gao, and C. Wang, PrIter: A distributed framework for prioritizing iterative computations, *IEEE Transactions on Parallel and Distributed Systems*, vol. 24, no. 9, pp. 1884–1893, September 2013.

[26] S. Ibrahim, H. Jin, L. Lu, L. Qi, S. Wu, and X. Shi, Evaluating MapReduce on virtual machines: The Hadoop case, in *Proceedings of IEEE International Conference on Cloud Computing Technology and Science (CloudCom)*, 2009.

[27] Y. Yuan, H. Wang, D. Wang, and J. Liu, On interference-aware provisioning for cloud-based big data processing, in *Proceedings of IEEE/ACM International Symposium on Quality of Service (IWQoS)*, 2013.

[28] F. Xu, F. Liu, H. Jin, and A.V. Vasilakos, Managing performance overhead of virtual machines in cloud computing: A survey, state of the art, and future directions, *Proceedings of the IEEE*, vol. 102, no. 1, pp. 11–31, January 2014.

[29] P. Barham, B. Dragovic, K. Fraser, S. Hand, T. Harris, A. Ho, R. Neugebauer, I. Pratt, and A. Warfield, Xen and the art of virtualization, in *Proceedings of ACM Symposium on Operating Systems Principles (SOSP)*, 2003.

[30] F. Xu, F. Liu, L. Liu, H. Jin, B. Li, and B. Li, iAware: Making live migration of virtual machines interference-aware in the cloud, *IEEE Transactions on Computers*, vol. 63, no. 12, pp. 3012–3025, December 2014.

[31] Y. Geng, S. Chen, Y. Wu, R. Wu, G. Yang, and W. Zheng, Location-aware MapReduce in virtual cloud, in *Proceedings of International Conference on Parallel Processing (ICPP)*, 2011.

[32] X. Zhang, Z. Zhong, S. Feng, B. Tu, and J. Fan, Improving data locality of MapReduce by scheduling in homogeneous computing environments, in *Proceedings of IEEE International Symposium on Parallel and Distributed Processing with Applications (ISPA)*, 2011.

[33] M. Hammoud and M.F. Sakr, Locality-aware reduce task scheduling for MapReduce, in *Proceedings of IEEE International Conference on Cloud Computing Technology and Science (CloudCom)*, 2011.

[34] X. Ma, X. Fan, J. Liu, H. Jiang, and K. Peng, vLocality: Re-visiting data locality for MapReduce in virtualized clouds, *IEEE Network*, vol. 31, no. 7, pp. 28–35, 2017.

Chapter 14

Distributed Machine Learning for Network Big Data

Seunghak Lee
Human Longevity, Inc.
Mountain View, California

CONTENTS

Machine learning typically involves an optimization problem with an objective function. For large-scale machine learning problems, the optimization is challenging because a large amount of computation or memory is required. In this chapter, we review the challenges associated with large-scale machine learning and the existing approaches to address them. Specifically, we categorize the large-scale machine learning problems into two types: big data and big models. In the former, a problem involves a large number of samples; in the latter, a problem involves a large number of model parameters (e.g., number of latent features for matrix factorization), although not necessarily with a large number of samples. In both cases, assuming that the CPU or the memory size for a single worker is insufficient to solve an optimization problem at hand, we should turn to parallel optimization approaches in distributed settings, which involve issues including (1) how to parallelize parameter updates on multiple workers and (2) how to synchronize concurrent parameter updates performed by multiple workers. In the context of the above issues, for big data problems, we review data-parallel approaches for parallelizing computations (e.g., gradients of the objective function of interest) of partitioned data using multiple workers. For big model problems, we consider model-parallel approaches for parallelizing computations of partitioned model parameters. We then discuss a combined approach that uses both data- and model-parallel approaches.

14.1 Machine Learning Models for Network Inference

Machine learning has been widely used for network data. Examples include latent Dirichlet allocation (LDA) [1] for social network analysis [2], graphical lasso [3], neighborhood selection [4], and penalized logistic regression for estimation of gene–gene interaction networks [5]. In network data analysis, one of the fundamental problems is to discover conditional independencies from data. To this end, machine learning methods such as graphical lasso and neighborhood selection have been developed to estimate an inverse covariance matrix. Let $\mathbf{\Sigma}^{-1}$ be an inverse covariance matrix, and Σ_{ij}^{-1} is the entry at the ith row and the jth column of $\mathbf{\Sigma}^{-1}$. Note that inverse covariance matrix encodes conditional independencies (i.e., if $\Sigma_{ij}^{-1} = 0$ then node i and node j are conditionally independent, given all the other nodes [3]). For example, in Figure 14.1, $\Sigma_{41}^{-1} = 0$ because X_4 is conditionally independent of X_1 given the rest.

The graphical lasso aims to find the maximum likelihood solution for an inverse covariance matrix with ℓ_1 penalty. The ℓ_1 regularization not only introduces sparsity in the inverse covariance matrix (i.e., the estimated undirected graph is sparse) but also allows us to apply this algorithm on the cases where the number of features is larger than the number of samples. Let us assume that we have N observations following p-dimensional multivariate Gaussian with mean μ and covariance $\mathbf{\Sigma}$, and define $\mathbf{\Theta} = \mathbf{\Sigma}^{-1}$. The graphical lasso [3] maximizes

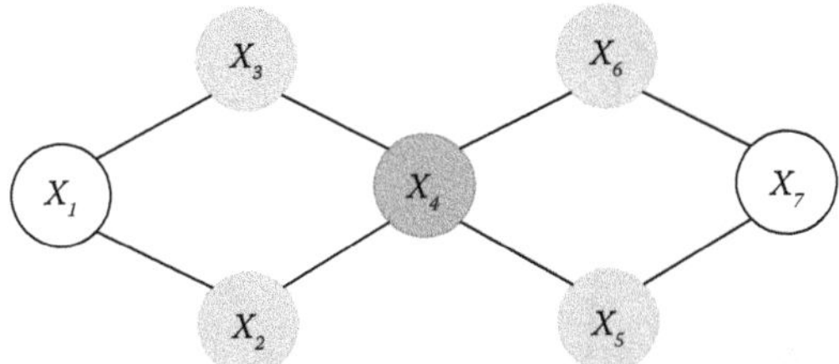

Figure 14.1: An example of a graph, where X_4 is conditionally independent from X_1 (or X_7), given X_4's neighbors, i.e., $\{X_2, X_3, X_5, X_6\}$. Zero elements in the inverse covariance matrix of X, defined by $\boldsymbol{\Sigma}^{-1}$, encode conditional independence (e.g., $\boldsymbol{\Sigma}_{41}^{-1} = 0$).

log-likelihood with ℓ_1 penalty:

$$\max_{\boldsymbol{\Theta} \succ \mathbf{0}} (\log \det \boldsymbol{\Theta} - \text{tr}(\mathbf{S}\boldsymbol{\Theta}) - \lambda \|\boldsymbol{\Theta}\|_1) \tag{14.1}$$

where $\mathbf{S}$ is an empirical covariance matrix, and λ determines the degree of the sparsity in $\boldsymbol{\Theta}$. Equation 14.1 is an instance of semidefinite programming (SDP), and thus can be solved by SDP algorithms such as the interior point method [6]. However, the interior point method requires a computationally expensive Hessian matrix, which makes it undesirable for large-scale data. Interestingly, an optimal $\boldsymbol{\Theta}$ can also be found by iteratively solving a series of lasso problems [7], if $\boldsymbol{\Theta}$ is initialized with a positive definite matrix (please refer to Ref. [3] for the details of the algorithm). As an example, we estimated a graph by graphical lasso using scikit-learn [8] Wisconsin breast cancer data [9,30]. Taking ten features from the breast cancer data as an input, the graphical lasso estimated the sparse inverse covariance matrix. Figure 14.2 visualizes the estimated inverse covariance matrix, where nodes represent the features and edges represent the node dependencies.

Although (14.1) finds an exact solution for the sparse inverse covariance matrix, the neighborhood selection is an algorithm to find an approximation of the graphical lasso. To find edges between node i and its neighbors, the neighborhood selection solves the following lasso problem [4]:

$$\hat{\boldsymbol{\beta}} = \underset{\boldsymbol{\beta}:\beta_i=0}{\text{argmin}} \frac{1}{2} \|\mathbf{X}_i - \mathbf{X}\boldsymbol{\beta}\|_2^2 + \lambda \sum_j |\beta_j| \tag{14.2}$$

where λ determines the sparsity in the set of edges between the node i and the rest, and the neighbors of the node i are chosen by $\{X_j | \hat{\beta}_j \neq 0\}$. For example, in Figure 14.1, to find the neighbors of X_4, we need to solve a lasso problem, where X_4 is an output, and $\{X_k\}_{k \neq 4}$ are input variables. Under certain assumptions, it has been proven that the probability of finding correct neighbors by neighborhood

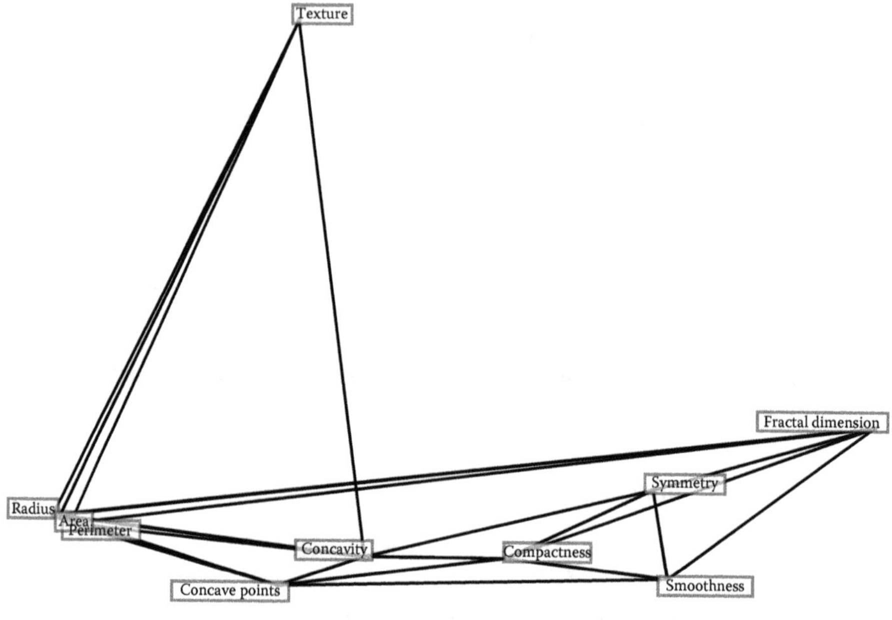

Figure 14.2: An example of graph estimation by graphical lasso on the Wisconsin breast cancer data [9,30]. The nodes represent the features and the edges represent the relationships between the nodes. This plot was generated using scikit-learn [8].

selection converges to one as the sample size approaches infinity [4]. In both the exact and approximate graph estimations described, solving lasso problems plays an important role in identifying conditional independencies.

As discussed, regularized regression (e.g., lasso) is a fundamental technique for network data analysis. However, given big data, it is nontrivial to solve the problems using a sequential algorithm because data can be too big to store in memory or the problems can take too long to solve. Below, we review popular optimization algorithms for regularized regression, including proximal gradient and coordinate descent. We then discuss how to efficiently solve the models in distributed settings using data parallelization, model parallelization, or both.

14.2 Background: Regularized Regression

Regularized regression is a popular regression model, used to shrink parameters to avoid overfitting, or discover a small subset of features that are relevant to an output $\mathbf{y}$. For example, in computational biology, lasso [7] has been used to detect genetic variants associated to a phenotype, where genetic variants are input variables and the phenotype is an output variable. Regularized regression solves the following optimization problem:

$$\min_{\boldsymbol{\beta}} \ell(\mathbf{X}, \mathbf{y}, \boldsymbol{\beta}) + \lambda h(\boldsymbol{\beta}) \tag{14.3}$$

where λ denotes a regularization parameter that determines the level of sparsity in parameters $\boldsymbol{\beta}$, $\ell(\cdot)$ is a nonnegative convex loss function such as squared-loss or logistic-loss, and $h(\boldsymbol{\beta})$ is a regularization (e.g., for lasso, $\ell(\mathbf{X}, \mathbf{y}, \boldsymbol{\beta}) = \frac{1}{2}\|\mathbf{y} - \mathbf{X}\boldsymbol{\beta}\|_2^2$ and $h(\boldsymbol{\beta}) = \|\boldsymbol{\beta}\|_1$). We assume that $\mathbf{X}$ and $\mathbf{y}$ are standardized and consider (14.3) without an intercept. The ℓ_1 penalty not only shrinks the size of $\boldsymbol{\beta}$ but also can set many parameters in $\boldsymbol{\beta}$ to exactly 0, which allows for feature selection. Algorithms to solve (14.3) will be discussed below.

Another instance of (14.3) is ℓ_2 regularized matrix factorization (MF), often used for collaborative filtering. The goal of MF is to predict a user's unknown preferences, given his/her known preferences and the preferences of others. The input data are modeled as an incomplete matrix $\mathbf{A} \in \mathbb{R}^{N \times M}$, where N is the number of users, and M is the number of items/preferences. The idea is to discover smaller rank-K matrices $\mathbf{W} \in \mathbb{R}^{N \times K}$ and $\mathbf{H} \in \mathbb{R}^{K \times M}$ such that $\mathbf{WH} \approx \mathbf{A}$. Thus, the product $\mathbf{WH}$ can be used to predict the missing entries (user preferences). Formally, let Ω be the set of row and column indices of observed entries in $\mathbf{A}$, a_j^i be the entry at the ith row and the jth column of $\mathbf{A}$, $\mathbf{w}^i$ be the ith row of $\mathbf{W}$, and $\mathbf{h}_j$ be the jth column of $\mathbf{H}$. Then, ℓ_2 regularized MF is defined as an optimization program:

$$\min_{\mathbf{W},\mathbf{H}} \sum_{(i,j)\in\Omega} (a_j^i - \mathbf{w}^i \mathbf{h}_j)^2 + \lambda(\|\mathbf{W}\|_F^2 + \|\mathbf{H}\|_F^2) \tag{14.4}$$

where $\|\mathbf{W}\|_F^2$ is a square of Frobenius norm, defined by $\|\mathbf{W}\|_F^2 = \sum_i \sum_j (w_j^i)^2$. Now let us discuss how to optimize (14.3) using proximal gradient or coordinate descent algorithms. Furthermore, we investigate parallelization errors, which may occur if multiple parameters are updated concurrently.

14.2.1 Proximal gradient descent algorithm

The regularized regression may involve a nondifferentiable term (e.g., ℓ_1 penalty), and thus a gradient descent algorithm is often inapplicable. However, a proximal gradient descent algorithm [10] can be used, which solves problems in the form of:

$$f(\boldsymbol{\beta}) = l(\boldsymbol{\beta}) + h(\boldsymbol{\beta}) \tag{14.5}$$

where $l(\boldsymbol{\beta})$ is convex and differentiable and $h(\boldsymbol{\beta})$ is convex but possibly nondifferentiable. Roughly speaking, proximal gradient descent works by iteratively updating (14.5) in two steps: (1) update parameters to minimize $l(\boldsymbol{\beta})$ based on a gradient descent algorithm and (2) apply proximal operator for $h(\boldsymbol{\beta})$ on the parameters. The second step can be considered as a generalization of the projection of $\boldsymbol{\beta}$ on $h(\cdot)$. The proximal gradient descent algorithm terminates when a stopping condition is met (e.g., objective function or parameter change per iteration is less than a fixed threshold). Note that if $f(\boldsymbol{\beta}) = l(\boldsymbol{\beta})$, proximal gradient becomes a simple gradient descent. Specifically, proximal gradient descent iteratively updates parameters using the update function of

$$\boldsymbol{\beta}^{(k)} = \mathbf{prox}_h\left(\boldsymbol{\beta}^{(k-1)} - t_k \nabla l(\boldsymbol{\beta}^{(k-1)})\right) \tag{14.6}$$

where k represents the iteration count and t_k is a step size. When $h(\boldsymbol{\beta}) = \lambda \sum_j |\beta_j|$, the proximal operator becomes soft-thresholding:

$$\mathbf{prox}_h(\boldsymbol{\beta})_j = \begin{cases} \beta_j - \lambda & \text{if } \beta_j \geq \lambda \\ 0 & \text{if } |\beta_j| \leq \lambda \\ \beta_j + \lambda & \text{if } \beta_j \leq -\lambda \end{cases} \tag{14.7}$$

The above proximal operator for $h(\boldsymbol{\beta}) = \lambda \sum_j |\beta_j|$ was found as follows. Note that given $h(\boldsymbol{\beta})$, a proximal operator is defined by: $\text{prox}_h(\boldsymbol{\beta}) = \text{argmin}_{\mathbf{t}}\, h(\mathbf{t}) + \frac{1}{2}\|\mathbf{t} - \boldsymbol{\beta}\|_2^2 = \text{argmin}_{\mathbf{t}}\, \lambda \sum_j |t_j| + \frac{1}{2}\|\mathbf{t} - \boldsymbol{\beta}\|_2^2$. To obtain an optimal solution for $\text{prox}_h(\boldsymbol{\beta})$, we compute its subgradient with respect to t_j, and set it to 0:

$$\lambda s_j + t_j - \beta_j = 0 \tag{14.8}$$

where $s_j = \text{sign}(t_j)$ if $t_j \neq 0$ and $s_j \in [-1, 1]$ if $t_j = 0$. Based on optimality conditions via subgradients, an optimal t_j can be found by (14.7) for all j.

For the proximal gradient descent, we can parallelize: (1) computation of gradients $\nabla l(\boldsymbol{\beta}^{(k-1)})$ on multiple data partitions and (2) computation of a partition of parameters, each of which will be explained in Sections 14.3.3 and 14.3.4. The former is called data-parallel, where multiple workers perform computations on data partitions concurrently, followed by their aggregation. The latter is called model-parallel, where multiple workers perform computations on parameter partitions concurrently; however, it may induce errors in parameter updates if one parameter update depends on other parameters which are concurrently updated. In the next section, we will discuss potential errors generated in model-parallel approaches in the context of a coordinate descent algorithm.

14.2.2 Coordinate descent algorithm

A coordinate descent algorithm is another popular algorithm to optimize (14.3). The key idea behind this is to update each coefficient at a time iteratively, while fixing the rest of the parameters until the objective converges. It is simple to implement, and in practice, it converges as fast as the proximal gradient descent using bookkeeping illustrated in Ref. [11], which will be described below.

Taking lasso as a running example, let us review the coordinate descent. The update rule of the coordinate descent for lasso [11] is as follows:

$$\beta_j^{(k)} = S\left(\sum_{i=1}^{N} x_{ij}(y_i - \hat{y}_i), \lambda\right) \tag{14.9}$$

where $S(\gamma,\lambda) = \text{sign}(\gamma)(|\gamma| - \lambda)_+$ and $\hat{y}_i = \sum_{m \neq j} x_{im}\beta_m^{(k-1)}$. We iterate (14.9) for all $j = 1, \ldots, J$ in a cyclic fashion until the lasso objective or $\boldsymbol{\beta}$ converges.

In practice, lasso coordinate descent is implemented with the following bookkeeping trick [11]. We compute $\alpha = \sum_i^N x_{ij}y_i$ only once, and let $\gamma = \sum_{i=1}^N x_{ij} \sum_{m=1}^J x_{im}\beta_m^{(k-1)}$. Then (14.9) can be written as:

$$\beta_j^{(k)} = S\left(\alpha - \gamma + \sum_{i=1}^{N} x_{ij}^2 \beta_j^{(k-1)}, \lambda\right) \tag{14.10}$$

After computing $\beta_j^{(k)}$ based on the above rule, if $\beta_j^{(k)} = 0$, we do not change γ, and move the next parameter; if $\beta_j^{(k)} \neq 0$, we set $\gamma = \gamma - \sum_{i=1}^N x_{ij}^2(\beta_j^{(k-1)} - \beta_j^{(k)})$, and move to the next parameter. The computational complexity of (14.10) is $O(N)$. Furthermore, only when $\beta_j^{(k)} \neq 0$, the update of γ requires $O(N)$. In contrast, (14.9) requires $O(NJ)$ for a parameter update. Therefore, this trick makes each parameter update fast, and it is particularly useful when $\boldsymbol{\beta}$ is sparse.

Now let us see how (14.9) was derived. For a simple demonstration, features are assumed to be standardized such that $\sum_i x_{ij} = 0$ and $\sum_i x_{ij}^2 = 1$ for all j. We start taking the subgradient of the objective of (14.3), defined by J, with respect to β_j, and set it to 0:

$$\frac{\partial J}{\partial \beta_j} = -\sum_{i=1}^{N} x_{ij}(y_i - \mathbf{x}_i^T\boldsymbol{\beta}) + \lambda s_j = 0 \tag{14.11}$$

where s_j is a subgradient of the ℓ_1 penalty, given by $s_j = \text{sign}(\beta_j)$ if $\beta_j \neq 0$, and $s_j \in [-1, 1]$ if $\beta_j = 0$. Thus,

$$\frac{\partial J}{\partial \beta_j} = -\sum_{i=1}^{N} x_{ij}\left(y_i - x_{ij}\beta_j - \sum_{m \neq j} x_{im}\beta_m\right) + \lambda s_j = 0 \tag{14.12}$$

$$\Rightarrow \quad \beta_j = \sum_{i=1}^{N} x_{ij}(y_i - \hat{y}_i) - \lambda s_j \tag{14.13}$$

From above, we can see that if $\beta_j > 0$ and $\sum_{i=1}^N x_{ij}(y_i - \hat{y}_i) > \lambda$, then $\beta_j = \sum_{i=1}^N x_{ij}(y_i - \hat{y}_i) - \lambda$; if $\beta_j < 0$ and $\sum_{i=1}^N x_{ij}(y_i - \hat{y}_i) < -\lambda$, then $\beta_j = \sum_{i=1}^N x_{ij}(y_i - \hat{y}_i) + \lambda$; if $\left|\sum_{i=1}^N x_{ij}(y_i - \hat{y}_i)\right| \Leftarrow \lambda$, then $\beta_j = 0$. Summarizing this, the solution for lasso becomes (14.9).

As previously mentioned, when multiple parameters are concurrently updated, there can be errors in parameter updates. Suppose β_q and β_r are updated in parallel using the coordinate descent (14.9), and the update rules for them are as follows:

$$\beta_q = S\left(\sum_{i=1}^{N} x_{iq}(y_i - x_{ir}\beta_r - \sum_{m\notin\{q,r\}} x_{im}\beta_m), \lambda\right) \text{ and } \tag{14.14}$$

$$\beta_r = S\left(\sum_{i=1}^{N} x_{ir}(y_i - x_{iq}\beta_q - \sum_{m\notin\{q,r\}} x_{im}\beta_m), \lambda\right) \tag{14.15}$$

Clearly, (14.14) shows that β_q is updated with the term $\mathbf{x}_q^T\mathbf{x}_r\beta_r$. If β_r is not up-to-date (i.e., $\beta_r^{(k-1)} \neq \beta_r^{(k)}$) and $\mathbf{x}_q^T\mathbf{x}_r \neq 0$, the update for β_q will have an error. Note that when $\mathbf{X}$ is standardized, i.e.,$\sum_i x_{ij} = 0$ and $\sum_i x_{ij}^2 = 1$ for all j, $\mathbf{x}_q^T\mathbf{x}_r$ is identical to the Pearson correlation coefficient. Therefore, if $\mathbf{x}_q$ and $\mathbf{x}_r$ are highly correlated (either negatively or positively), the error incurred by concurrent updates for them is likely to be high. To reduce the parallelization errors, various scheduling methods have been developed [12–14], where the main idea is to dispatch a set of parameters only if they are not strongly coupled. In an extreme case, if $\mathbf{x}_q$ and $\mathbf{x}_q$ independent, they can be safely updated simultaneously.

MF optimization (14.4) can also be solved via a parallel coordinate descent [15], with the following update rules for $\mathbf{W}$ and $\mathbf{H}$:

$$w_t^i \leftarrow \frac{\sum_{j\in\Omega^i}(r_j^i + w_t^i h_j^t)h_j^t}{\lambda + \sum_{j\in\Omega^i}(h_j^t)^2} \tag{14.16}$$

$$h_j^t \leftarrow \frac{\sum_{i\in\Omega_j}(r_j^i + w_t^i h_j^t)w_t^i}{\lambda + \sum_{i\in\Omega_j}(w_t^i)^2} \tag{14.17}$$

where Ω^i be the set of observed column indices in the ith row of $\mathbf{A}$, Ω_j be the set of observed row indices in the jth column of $\mathbf{A}$, and $r_j^i = a_j^i - \mathbf{w}^i\mathbf{h}_j$ for all $(i, j) \in \Omega$. To solve the MF problem, it iterates through each rank $t \in \{1\ldots K\}$, parallelizing the updates $\{w_t^i\}$ over blocks of rows i in $\mathbf{A}$, and parallelizing the updates $\{h_j^t\}$ over blocks of columns j in $\mathbf{A}$. We note that in this parallelization of coordinate descent for MF, each parameter can be independently updated without errors.

14.3 Distributed Machine Learning

In distributed machine learning, one should consider (1) how to parallelize computations on multiple workers and (2) how to synchronize parameters between

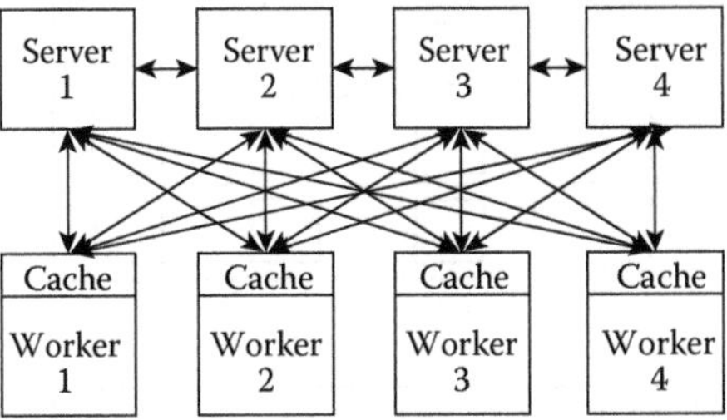

Figure 14.3: An architecture of parameter servers. To share global parameters, workers communicate with parameter servers, which store the parameters in a distributed fashion. Each worker uses a cache (process/thread cache) to minimize network communications, while allowing for less strict synchronization across different workers.

different workers, among others. Workers refer to processes or threads in distributed settings. In this chapter, we assume a parameter server [16] which stores global parameters shared across multiple workers in a distributed fashion. An example of parameter server architecture is shown in Figure 14.3. For the former, we usually parallelize the computation of gradients of parameters or the computation of a block of parameters. The latter determines communication protocol across multiple workers, and can be largely categorized into three consistency models: (1) bulk synchronous parallel (BSP) [17], (2) asynchronous parallel (AP) [18,19], and (3) stale synchronous parallel (SSP) [20], each of which is illustrated in Figure 14.4.

14.3.1 Parameter servers

So far, we assumed a parameter server (PS) to share global parameters for distributed machine learning. There are multiple implementations for parameter servers [16,21–23]. While details of their system designs are different, they share server-client architecture. For example, Petuum PS [16] attempts to reduce network communications using hierarchical cache policies and various consistency models, and Li et al.'s PS [22] supports elastic scalability and fault tolerance for Cloud computing environments. Here we describe an instance of parameter server.

Petuum PS (www.petuum.com) is designed to support various consistency policies. It implements variants of SSP including clock-bounded asynchronous parallel (CAP), value-bounded asynchronous parallel (VAP), and clock-value-bounded asynchronous parallel (CVAP). Briefly, CAP is the same as SSP except that servers can send parameters to workers whenever possible depending on the network bandwidth availability, rather than synchronization phase. VAP synchronizes model replicas such that their differences are less than

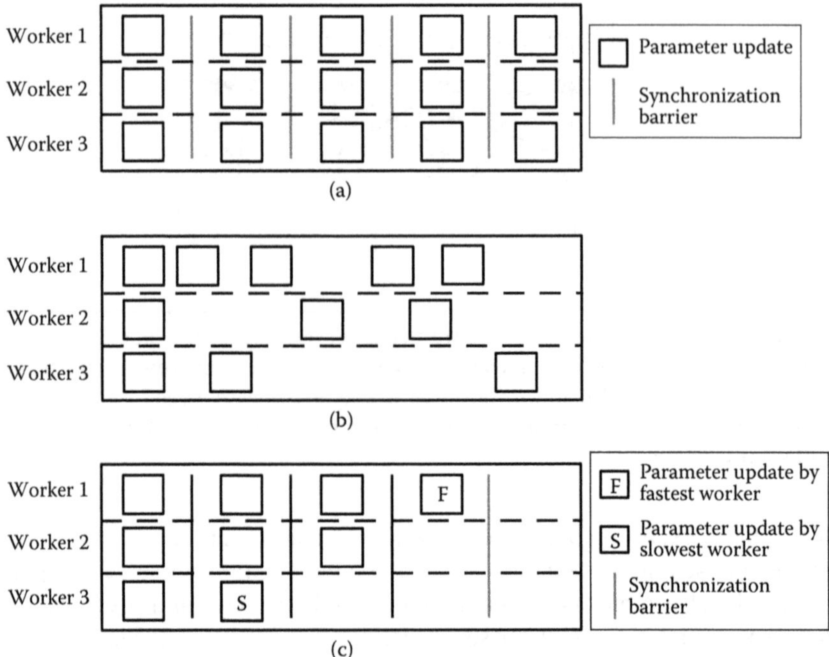

Figure 14.4: Illustration of consistency policies for (a) bulk-synchronous-parallel (BSP); (b) asynchronous-parallel (AP); and (c) stale-synchronous-parallel (SSP) with staleness parameter $s = 2$. Vertical bars represent the point where a clock increases and light gray bars represent synchronization barriers. In BSP, every worker shares updated parameters in every iteration, while AP has no synchronization barriers. In SSP, the fastest worker can be faster than the slowest worker up to s iterations.

a user-defined threshold, and CVAP is the scheme that combines both CAP and VAP. Furthermore, Petuum PS implemented a two-level cache that consists of process and thread caches in each worker machine. In the first-level, each thread has a thread cache; in the second-level, multiple threads in the same process share a process cache. Therefore if the thread cache misses, workers look for queried parameters in a process cache. If the process cache misses, they find the parameters from servers and the up-to-date parameters are transferred via network communication.

To implement various consistency models, Petuum PS maintains the clocks of threads, as well as the clocks of processes, where a thread corresponds to a logical worker, and a process is a group of them. Each thread is responsible to maintain its thread clock by incrementing it after updating parameters, and a process clock is determined by the minimum of the thread clocks involved in each process. The servers keep track of process clocks to enforce a consistency model. For end-users, Petuum PS provides the following interfaces:

- `Get(table_id, row_id, column_id)`: Retrieve the parameter stored in the corresponding table, row, and column.
- `Inc(table_id, row_id, column_id, delta)`: Increase the parameter stored in the corresponding table, row, and column by delta.
- `Clock()`: Increment the clock of the worker that runs its corresponding thread by 1.

Internally Petuum PS accesses elements in the tables by table id, row id, and column id, and the parameters are distributed in multiple servers via hash partitioning.

14.3.2 Consistency models of parameter servers

The consistency models (i.e., synchronization policy among workers) are important because communication among workers significantly affects the effectiveness of each parameter update and CPU utilization due to expensive network costs. We will explain each consistency model and discuss their positive and negative effects. Let us assume that we have three workers. In Figure 14.4a, BSP [17] sets a synchronization barrier in every parameter update computed from workers, and forces them to share updated parameters. In a distributed setting, workers update parameters, and push them to the parameter server. Then, the servers should wait until all workers push their updated parameters. When a master server receives all updates from the workers, it aggregates them, and the servers push the updated parameters to the workers. This step iterates until the objective function value (or parameters) converges. Obviously workers frequently share their updates, and thus errors due to concurrent parameter updates can be small, resulting in effective parameter updates (i.e., a parameter update by BSP can improve the objective better than an update by other consistency models); however, the frequent parameter synchronization generates straggler problem. If some workers are significantly slower than others, they become the bottleneck in parameter synchronization, which can be detrimental for heterogeneous Cloud computing.

In contrast to BSP, AP [18,19] (Figure 14.4b) asynchronously updates parameters. When a worker sends updated parameters, it receives the most up-to-date parameters from a parameter server with no wait. Since there is no synchronization barrier, there is no straggler problem, and it is the most effective way to keep worker CPUs busy. However, no control on synchronization may generate high errors in concurrent parameter updates, resulting in ineffective parameter updates in each iteration (i.e., after parameter updates, AP may not improve the objective as much as the other consistency models).

Recently, SSP [20] (Figure 14.4c) has been developed to attempt to find a sweet spot between BSP and AP. The key idea is to relax AP to the point where the fastest and slowest workers are not too far apart. Specifically, SSP considers the following scenario, where parameters are iteratively updated by δs computed from multiple workers (e.g., one δ is computed from a worker with a data partition and a local copy of parameters θ). Each worker's δ is applied to the global copy of parameter θ by $\theta \leftarrow \theta + \delta$. Under this setting, SSP assigns a clock (iteration counter) to each worker c, and enforces that the difference between the slowest and the fastest worker's clock is not greater than s. Thus, fast workers do not have to wait for slow workers as long as the difference of the iterations is tolerable (i.e., $\leq s$), which alleviates the straggler problem. Furthermore, it ensures that each worker contains a local copy of θ that contains all updates from 0 to $c-s-1$ iterations, which is helpful to manage errors due to concurrent parameter updates. Thus with a proper s, SSP gives better convergence rate than BSP and AP.

When the size of problem is small enough to be fitted in a single machine (i.e., data and parameters fit into memory and no computational bottleneck exists), we can solve (14.3) using the update function for proximal gradient descent. In practice, accelerated proximal gradient descent [24] is applicable for faster convergence. However, when a single machine is insufficient, we should turn to distributed solutions. Distributed solutions can be categorized into data- and model-parallel approaches [16]. In data-parallel approaches, data are partitioned and each worker shares all model parameters; in the case of model-parallel, model parameters are partitioned and data are not necessarily partitioned. Therefore when the size of data (or model parameters) is large, data-parallel (or model-parallel) is desirable. If both are large, we may use a combined approach, i.e., data-model-parallel, where data are partitioned across multiple workers and a partition of models are updated by all workers [25]. The parallelization schemes are illustrated in Figure 14.5.

14.3.3 Data-parallel optimization

Here we describe an example of the data-parallel approach (Figure 14.5a), where data are partitioned to multiple workers and gradients are computed in each worker using its partition in parallel. We note that our description of data-parallel is a simplified version of Ref. [25], where both data and models are partitioned and parallelized. For simplicity, let us assume that we use a parameter server to share all parameters across all workers, and use BSP.

Recall that sequential proximal gradient descent updates parameters based on (14.6) in each iteration. In a distributed setting, parameters are updated as follows: Workers compute $\boldsymbol{\delta}$s and send them to the parameter servers. When a parameter server receives $\boldsymbol{\delta}$s from all T workers, it updates the parameters by:

$$\boldsymbol{\beta}^{(k)} = \boldsymbol{\beta}^{(k-1)} + \sum_{i=1}^{T} \boldsymbol{\delta}(i)^{(k-1)} \tag{14.18}$$

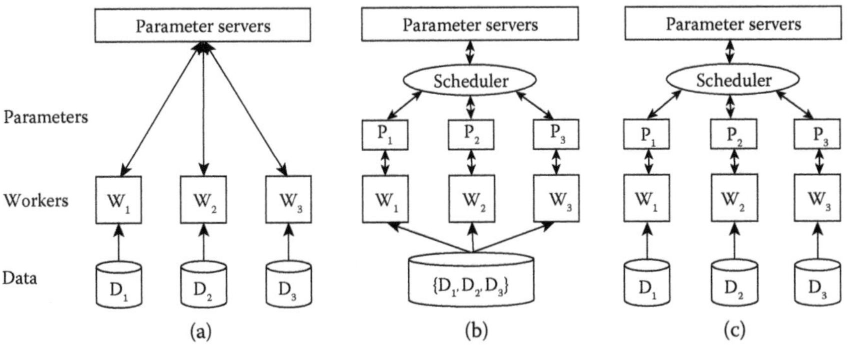

Figure 14.5: Various parallelization schemes including (a) data-parallel, (b) model-parallel, and (c) data-model-parallel. Data-parallel partitions data across multiple workers, but each worker processes all the parameters. In model-parallel, each worker processes a partition of parameters on all the shared data. Data-model-parallel partitions data and all workers update a partition of parameters, chosen by a scheduler.

where $\boldsymbol{\delta}(i)^{(k-1)}$ is computed from worker i given its data partition and the local copy of $\boldsymbol{\beta}^{(k-1)}$, and $\boldsymbol{\delta}(i)^{(k-1)}$ is defined by:

$$\boldsymbol{\delta}(i)^{(k-1)} = \mathbf{prox}_h\left(\boldsymbol{\beta}^{(k-1)} - t_k \nabla l_i(\boldsymbol{\beta}^{(k-1)})\right) - \boldsymbol{\beta}^{(k-1)} \tag{14.19}$$

where $\nabla l_i(\boldsymbol{\beta}^{(k-1)})$ is the gradient of $l(\cdot)$ based on the data partition for worker i and $\boldsymbol{\beta}^{(k-1)}$. After the parameter server updates the parameters, it sends the updates to all workers. This step iterates until a stopping condition is met.

In the case of AP, the synchronization barriers above are removed. In other words, when the parameter server receives an update from worker i, it updates the parameter without waiting for other workers. For SSP, the update function is not changed but the parameter server needs to have SSP protocol, implemented with a cache.

14.3.4 Model-parallel optimization

Unlike data-parallel optimization, the model-parallel approach (Figure 14.5b) partitions parameters, say, $\boldsymbol{\beta}_b$ for $b = 1, \ldots, B$, which is a set of parameters indexed by b. For simplicity, let us assume a small data, stored in all workers, and use BSP. In a model-parallel scheme, worker i computes updates $\boldsymbol{\delta}_b$ for a block of parameters $\boldsymbol{\beta}_b$, where b is the index set assigned to worker i. Then the parameter server updates $\boldsymbol{\beta}_b$ by:

$$\boldsymbol{\beta}_b^{(k)} = \boldsymbol{\beta}_b^{(k-1)} + \boldsymbol{\delta}_b^{(k-1)} \tag{14.20}$$

where $\boldsymbol{\delta}_b^{(k-1)} = \{\delta_j^{(k-1)}\}_{j \in b}$ and

$$\delta_j^{(k-1)} = \mathbf{prox}_h \left(\beta_j^{(k-1)} - t_k \nabla_j l(\boldsymbol{\beta}^{(k-1)}) \right) - \beta_j^{(k-1)} \tag{14.21}$$

where $\delta_j^{(k-1)}$ is the jth component of $\boldsymbol{\delta}^{(k-1)}$, and $\nabla_j l$ is the jth component of the gradients of $\nabla l(\cdot)$. Note that $\boldsymbol{\delta}^{(k-1)}$ is computed based on all the data. When all workers send $\{\boldsymbol{\delta}_b^{(k-1)}\}$ to the parameter server, it updates the parameters using (14.20), and then sends the updated parameters to all workers. Model-parallel optimization using AP or SSP can be implemented in a similar fashion to the data-parallel case. However, model-parallel is usually more sensitive to parallelization errors than data-parallel due to interdependencies among parameters (i.e., features are correlated with each other). For data-parallel, we rely on a milder assumption of independent and identically distributed samples.

Now let us consider model-parallel approaches using coordinate descent algorithms. Various model-parallel coordinate descent algorithms have been developed to solve (14.3) including Shotgun [26], block-greedy coordinate descent (BCD) [12], and lasso with STRADS [13]. The parallelization schemes of these methods are illustrated in Figure 14.6. Briefly, for concurrent updates of parameters, Shotgun and BCD randomly select individual or groups of parameters, while lasso with STRADS uses a scheduler to determine a set of parameters to be updated in parallel.

More specifically, Shotgun (Figure 14.6a) is a parallel coordinate descent for ℓ_1-regularized regression in a shared memory setting. Shogun randomly

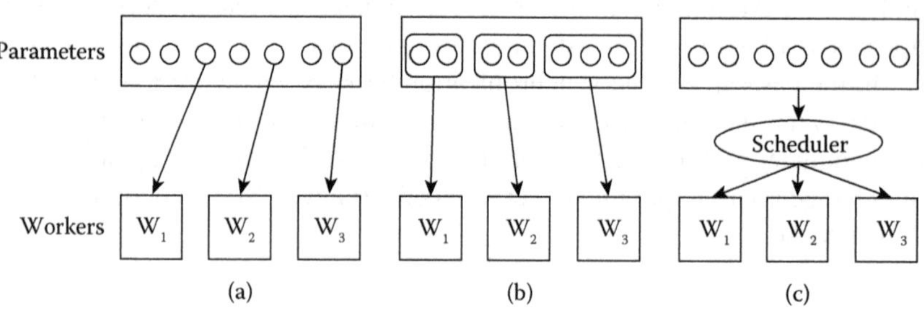

Figure 14.6: Three different model-parallel coordinate descent algorithms for ℓ_1 regularized regression that include (a) Shotgun [26], (b) block-greedy coordinate descent (BCD) [12], and (c) lasso with STRADS [13]. Shotgun and BCD dispatch randomly selected individual parameters and groups of parameters, respectively. Lasso with STRADS uses a dedicated scheduler which dispatches parameters to be updated based on the size of parameter values and correlations among features for dispatched parameters for better improvement in the objective function and to reduce the errors from parallel updates.

selects T parameters, and assigns them to T workers for parallel updates. After that, the updates are copied to global parameters in BSP fashion. However, the objective may not effectively decrease (or even diverge) if parameters, whose corresponding features are highly correlated, are selected and updated concurrently.

Another approach is BCD (Figure 14.6b) which dispatches groups of parameters rather than individual ones to workers, and each worker evaluates how much each parameter update can improve the objective function value. Then each worker selects only one parameter to be updated among the group of parameters, and they are copied to global parameters. BCD assumes that groups of parameters are determined in such a way that parameters in different groups are not highly correlated with each other. A heuristic was proposed to find such groups greedily [12]. Under the assumption, workers can update a set of parameters effectively in terms of optimizing the objective function value without much interference.

STRADS (STRucture-Aware Dynamic Scheduler) (Figure 14.6c) is a distributed model-parallel machine learning framework. STRADS involves a scheduler which selects T parameters to be updated with two criteria: (1) parameters that are substantially changed in the previous iteration should be picked with high probability and (2) the features corresponding to the selected parameters should not be highly correlated. More precisely, the first condition is that the scheduler selects the jth parameter to be updated with probability $p(j) \propto \delta(\beta_j^{(k-1)})^2$. This condition is useful to update some parameters more frequently that require more iterations to converge because typically, different parameters are converged with different rates [14]. The second condition is to mitigate the parallelization errors. Decoupled parameters can safely be updated with small errors (or no errors) caused by concurrent updates. Note that the scheduler can also be distributed, and the scheduler has been applied to various machine learning models including ℓ_1 regularized logistic regression, latent Dirichlet allocation (topic modeling), and matrix factorization. For the details of system implementations, we refer readers to Ref. [14].

14.3.5 Data-model-parallel optimization

Let us consider extremely large problems with big data and big models, where the size of parameters and the size of data are too big to store in a single machine memory. Taking into account such scenarios, a distributed delayed proximal gradient method [25] has been developed that adopts a delayed synchronization for faster convergence and updates a block of parameters at a time, rather than all parameters. The block of parameters to be dispatched is selected by a scheduler [13,14], and one of the simple schedulers is round robin. Furthermore, each worker computes gradients on a partition of data, and thus it is a data-model-parallel approach (Figure 14.5c).

Specifically, each worker computes $\nabla_b l_i(\boldsymbol{\beta}^{(k-1)})$ on a partition of data assigned to the ith worker for a partition of parameters $\boldsymbol{\beta}_b$. After all workers compute the gradients, the parameter servers aggregate $\boldsymbol{\delta}_b(i)^{(k-1)}$ from all workers, and update the bth partition of the global parameters as follows:

$$\boldsymbol{\beta}_b^{(k)} = \boldsymbol{\beta}_b^{(k-1)} + \sum_{i=1}^{T} \boldsymbol{\delta}_b(i)^{(k-1)} \tag{14.22}$$

where $\boldsymbol{\delta}_b(i)^{(k-1)} = \{\delta_j(i)^{(k-1)}\}_{j\in b}$ and

$$\delta_j(i)^{(k-1)} = \mathbf{prox}_h\left(\beta_j^{(k-1)} - t_k \nabla_j l_i(\boldsymbol{\beta}^{(k-1)})\right) - \beta_j^{(k-1)} \tag{14.23}$$

After the updates by the servers, the updated parameters are sent to the workers. Under this strategy, each worker stores only a partition of data and computes gradients for a partition of parameters. Therefore, it scales well with respect to both the size of data and model parameters.

14.4 Discussions

In this chapter, we discussed distributed machine learning with an example of regularized regression and its optimization algorithms, such as proximal gradient descent and coordinate descent algorithms. In particular, under a parameter server architecture, we reviewed various consistency models, including bulk-synchronous parallel, asynchronous parallel, and stale-synchronous parallel, as well as data-, model-, and data-model-parallel approaches for distributed optimization. In practice, implementing such systems is nontrivial, and one may use a distributed machine learning framework such as Petuum [16], TensorFlow [27], and Spark [28], among others. Petuum is a distributed framework, consisting of parameter servers, a multi-GPU deep learning framework, and a scheduler for model-parallel machine learning that allows for intelligent job dispatches to multiple workers. TensorFlow is an open source framework for large-scale machine learning (including neural networks), that can be run on heterogeneous systems, including mobile devices and a cluster of machines. Spark has been developed to support iterative algorithms and interactive data analysis tools by fixing the the issue of acyclic data flow by MapReduce. For machine learning applications under Spark, MLlib [29] has been developed to provide diverse machine learning models including logistic regression, decision trees, and K-means clustering. Because large-scale network data are becoming more prevalent, use of distributed machine learning is becoming commonplace. To effectively take advantage of distributed machine learning, it would be critical to consider issues such as the straggler problem, the effective use of CPU and network resources, and the algorithmic correctness of parallel optimizations.

References

[1] D. M. Blei, A. Y. Ng, and M. I. Jordan. Latent dirichlet allocation. *Journal of Machine Learning Research*, 3:993–1022, 2003.

[2] Y. Cha and J. Cho. Social-network analysis using topic models. In *SIGIR*, August 12–16, pp. 565–574, ACM, OR, 2012.

[3] J. Friedman, T. Hastie, and R. Tibshirani. Sparse inverse covariance estimation with the graphical lasso. *Biostatistics*, 9(3):432–441, 2008.

[4] N. Meinshausen and P. Bühlmann. High-dimensional graphs and variable selection with the lasso. *The Annals of Statistics*, 34(3):1436–1462, 2006.

[5] M. Park and T. Hastie. Penalized logistic regression for detecting gene interactions. *Biostatistics*, 9(1):30–50, 2008.

[6] C. Helmberg, F. Rendl, R. J. Vanderbei, and H. Wolkowicz. An interior-point method for semidefinite programming. *SIAM Journal on Optimization*, 6(2):342–361, 1996.

[7] R. Tibshirani. Regression shrinkage and selection via the lasso. *Journal the Royal Statistical Society. Series B (Methodological)*, 58(1):267–288, 1996.

[8] F. Pedregosa et al. Scikit-learn: Machine learning in python. *Journal of Machine Learning Research*, 12:2825–2830, 2011.

[9] W. N. Street, W. H. Wolberg, and O. L. Mangasarian. Nuclear feature extraction for breast tumor diagnosis. *IS&T/SPIE International Symposium on Electronic Imaging: Science and Technology*, 1905:861–870, 1993.

[10] N. Parikh et al. Proximal algorithms. *Foundations and Trends in Optimization*, 1(3):127–239, 2014.

[11] J. Friedman, T. Hastie, H. Höfling, and R. Tibshirani. Pathwise coordinate optimization. *The Annals of Applied Statistics*, 1(2):302–332, 2007.

[12] C. Scherrer, A. Tewari, M. Halappanavar, and D. Haglin. Feature clustering for accelerating parallel coordinate descent. In *NIPS*, December 3–8, pp. 28–36, Lake Tahoe, CA, 2012.

[13] S. Lee et al. On model parallelization and scheduling strategies for distributed machine learning. In *NIPS*, December 8–13, pp. 2834–2842, Montréal, Canada, 2014.

[14] J. Kim et al. STRADS: A distributed framework for scheduled model parallel machine learning. In *EuroSys*, April 18–21, p. 5, ACM, London, UK, 2016.

[15] H. Yu, C. Hsieh, S. Si, and I. Dhillon. Scalable coordinate descent approaches to parallel matrix factorization for recommender systems. In *ICDM*, December 10–13, pp. 765–774, IEEE, Brussels, Belgium, 2012.

[16] E. P. Xing et al. Petuum: A new platform for distributed machine learning on big data. *IEEE Transactions on Big Data*, 1(2):49–67, 2015.

[17] J. Dean and S. Ghemawat. MapReduce: Simplified data processing on large clusters. *Communications of the ACM*, 51(1):107–113, 2008.

[18] Y. Low et al. Distributed graphlab: A framework for machine learning and data mining in the cloud. *PVLDB*, 5(8):716–727, 2012.

[19] B. Recht, C. Re, S. Wright, and F. Niu. Hogwild: A lock-free approach to parallelizing stochastic gradient descent. In *NIPS*, December 12–17, pp. 693–701, Granada Spain, 2011.

[20] Q. Ho et al. More effective distributed ml via a stale synchronous parallel parameter server. In *NIPS*, December 5–10, pp. 1223–1231, Lake Tahoe, CA, 2013.

[21] M. Li, D. G. Andersen, A. J. Smola, and K. Yu. Communication efficient distributed machine learning with the parameter server. In *NIPS*, December 8–13, pp. 19–27, Montréal, Canada, 2014.

[22] M. Li et al. Parameter server for distributed machine learning. In *Big Learning NIPS Workshop*, December 9, Lake Tahoe, CA, 2013.

[23] M. Li et al. Scaling distributed machine learning with the parameter server. In *OSDI*, October 6–8, vol. 14, pp. 583–598, Broomfield, CO, 2014.

[24] Y. Nesterov. Smooth minimization of non-smooth functions. *Mathematical Programming*, 103(1):127–152, 2005.

[25] M. Li, D. G. Andersen, and A. Smola. Distributed delayed proximal gradient methods. In *NIPS Workshop on Optimization for Machine Learning*, December 9, Lake Tahoe, CA, 2013.

[26] J. K. Bradley, A. Kyrola, D. Bickson, and C. Guestrin. Parallel coordinate descent for l1-regularized loss minimization. *ICML*, June 28–July 2, Bellevue, WA, 2011.

[27] M. Abadi et al. Tensorflow: A system for large-scale machine learning. In *12th USENIX Symposium on Operating Systems Design and Implementation*, November 2–4, pp. 265–283, USENIX Association, Savannah, GA, 2016.

[28] M. Zaharia, M. Chowdhury, M. J. Franklin, S. Shenker, and I. Stoica. Spark: Cluster computing with working sets. *HotCloud*, June 22–25, Boston, MA, 2010.

[29] X. Meng et al. Mllib: Machine learning in apache spark. *Journal of Machine Learning Research*, 17(34):1–7, 2016.

[30] M. Lichman. *UCI Machine Learning Repository*. University of California, School of Information and Computer Science, Irvine, CA, 2013.

Chapter 15

Big Data Security: Toward a Hashed Big Graph

Yu Lu and Fei Hu
University of Alabama
Tuscaloosa, Alabama

CONTENTS

15.1 Introduction

15.1.1 What is big graph?

Big graph, also known as large-scale graph-structured database, is a popular solution for representing social networks [1], healthcare records, and Internet of Things (IoT) data. The basic components of a graph are vertexes and edges, and it can be represented as $G = (V, E)$; here V is the set of all vertexes and E is the set of all edges. In a graph-structured database, the vertexes are the basic data points which can be any type of data, and the edges reflect the relationships among these data points. An edge $e(v1, v2, w)$ in E is a link from vertex $v1$ to $v2$ with the weight w. An edge in an undirected graph can be represented as two directional edges. In Figure 15.1a there is a simple graph with only two vertexes and

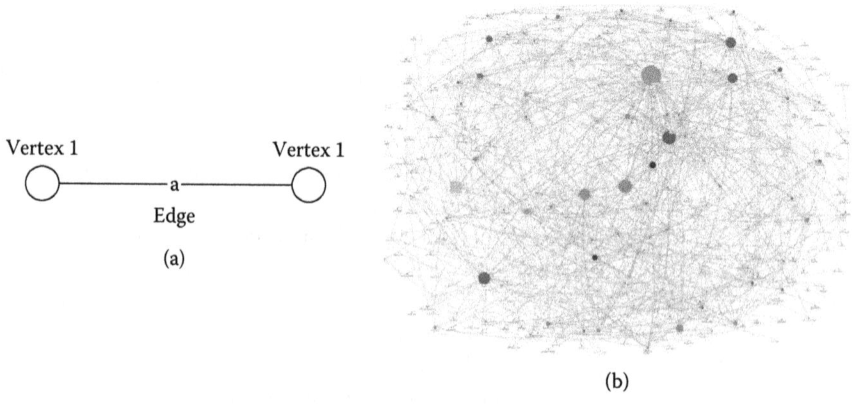

Figure 15.1: (a) Simple graph and (b) Large-scale graph [2].

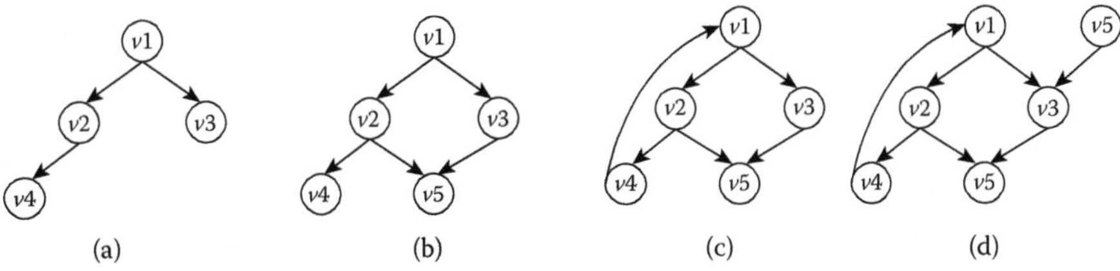

Figure 15.2: Graphs: (a) Tree; (b) DAG; (c) Graph with cycles; and (d) Graph with multiple sources.

one edge. This graph is easy to store and process. However, in Figure 15.1b we can see that as the numbers of edges and vertexes increase, the graph eventually becomes very complex.

There are mainly four types of graphs, i.e., the tree, the directed acyclic graph (DAG), the graph with cycles, and the graph with multiple source vertexes (a source vertex is a node without incoming edges). The simple cases of each type are shown in Figure 15.2. The real-world graphs could be the combinations of these four types of graphs.

15.1.2 Big graph and machine learning

Many machine learning and data mining (MLDM) problems such as target marketing and social network analysis, are performed on graph-structure data [3]. However, existing relational database management systems (RDBMS) have poor performance while handling complex relations among massive data points, especially when those data points and relations are frequently updated. Since a graph with billions of edges obviously may exceed the capability of a single machine, a distributed scheme is required to process the graph. In table-based big data, MapReduce is a popular method for distributed processing. But it may not be suitable for some applications. For example, data processing algorithms with graph-like data representations are beyond its capability. Therefore, several new large-scale graph-structured database processing methods, such as *GraphLab* [3] and *Pregel* [4], are proposed. These schemes use *think like a vertex* (TLAV) frameworks to implement user-defined machine learning tasks from the perspective of each vertex. It can improve the locality and scalability of the whole program.

15.1.2.1 TLAV frameworks [5]

The basic philosophy behind TLAV is to iteratively execute the graph algorithms over vertexes, which means that a vertex program only handles data from its adjacent vertices and incident edges. All programs in different vertexes can be executed synchronously or asynchronously, and they will stop execution after a predefined number of iterations or until the results of all vertex programs have converged into a stable status. Although TLAV frameworks are local and bottom-up schemes, they are able to generate provable global results with appropriate synchronicity and communication mechanisms. Because it tries to execute everything locally and performs the communications among the vertexes only when it is needed, TLAV can significantly reduce the time and resources consumed when processing a large-scale graph-structured database. Later on we will use two popular TLAV frameworks to illustrate how it works.

15.1.2.2 Pregel: Bulk synchronous message passing abstraction [4]

In Pregel all vertex programs run simultaneously through a sequence of supersteps. In each superstep a vertex first receives all messages from the last superstep, then executes and sends new messages to all neighbors in the next superstep. During this process a barrier is used to ensure the synchronicity. The whole program halts while there are no messages remaining and all vertexes "vote" to terminate. The following example [6] shows how a page-rank algorithm works in Pregel. The page-rank algorithm [5] is designed by Google to determine the importance of websites. A vertex program can receive the messages from all of its in-edge neighbors which contain the combination of all page ranks [10]. Then it computes the new page rank and sends it to all neighbors reached via its outgoing edges.

15.1.2.3 GraphLab [3]*: Asynchronous, distributed, shared memory abstraction*

Different from Pregel, in a GraphLab structure all vertex programs are executed *asynchronously*. All vertexes share the access to all distributed graphs, and each vertex program may use the data from itself, its neighbors, or the edges. In order to ensure serialization, the programs in neighboring vertexes cannot run simultaneously. GraphLab enables a multiversion scheme to help users precisely distinguish between permanent data (vertex data) and temporary data from specific neighbors (edge data).

15.1.2.4 GAS (gather, apply, and scatter) model

In both Pregel and GraphLab, the vertex program can be represented in a GAS model. In the *gather* phase, the data in neighbors and edges is collected, then in the *apply* phase the data in the center vertex is updated. Finally, in the *scatter* phase it uses the new value in the central vertex to update the values of all edges. However, GraphLab and Pregel implement the GAS model quite differently; Pregel uses a message combiner to implement the *gather* phase and the remaining two phases are done in a vertex program. GraphLab implements communication schemes in gather/scatter phases by making any updates of the data content in vertexes and edges that are visible to all adjacent vertexes.

15.1.3 Security issues in big graph

In graph-based machine learning algorithms, the data in the graph is frequently accessed and updated. Thus the most important security requirements in a graph-structured database are access management and integrity tests. Here we will focus on the integrity issue. In order to prevent database from unwanted changes, a hash scheme for a graph-structured database is required. Since the hash scheme will be used in a large-scale machine learning scenario, it should be efficient while ensuring data integrity.

15.2 Hash Scheme for Graphs

The hash function is an essential element of modern cryptography. Verifications of data integrity, message authentication codes (MAC), and digital signature techniques are all based on hash functions. Substantially, the hash function is a scheme to transform a random-size message into a unique fixed-length bit string: H: $\{0,1\}$^$n \to \{0,1\}$^l. The original hash function handles the data on the block level. For table-based databases the hashes of different blocks can be organized according to their columns and rows. Merging all block hashes bottom up can build a unique root hash for the whole database. However, this scheme cannot be simply applied to a graph-structured database.

For a graph $G(V,E)$, it seems that we may simply build one vertex table for all the vertexes and one edge table for all the edges, then hash them in the same way. In a vertex table the process is straightforward, since each vertex is an independent unit. However, the edges in the edge table are not independent; their relative positions determine the structure of the whole graph. The data stored in graph-structure databases is often privacy sensitive. Therefore, an additional requirement of a graph hashing scheme is that the hash value should not leak any information of the plaintext. This requirement involves two aspects: first, the hash function itself should be a perfect one-way function; second, when computing the root hash in a Merkle hash tree (MHT) scheme, some hash values of the data contents may be sent together. Thus a perfect collision-resistant hash scheme for the graph should also be robust against preimage attacks based on the plaintext cryptology analysis.

Verifications of the integrity of large-scale datasets are primarily carried out by the MHT. In the next section we will briefly introduce MHT and integrity verification issues associated with the MHT.

15.2.1 What is a Merkle hash tree?

A Merkle hash tree (MHT) is a widely used cryptographic technology for large-scale database hash management. The basic idea of MHT is redacting hashes of all data units in the dataset to generate one or multiple root hashes. This allows efficient verifications and updates. We can illustrate the procedure of

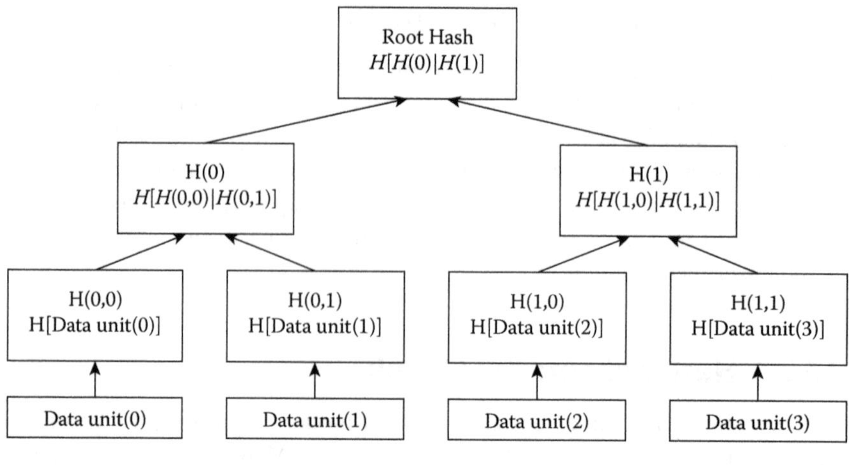

Figure 15.3: A simple binary MHT.

MHT construction with a simple but useful case of MHT, called the binary hash tree (BHT). As shown in Figure 15.3, the BHT works in bottom up. The whole datasets are handled as small data unions. The leaf level of the MHT has the hashes of all data blocks Each nonleaf-level node contains the hash of the concatenations of all hashes in its children nodes (in BHT each node has two children). In general BHTs, it computes node hashes as follows: let's denote the leaf node as $NH(n) = H(data\text{-}union_n)$, and nonleaf node as $NH(m) = H(NH(m_1)||NH(m_2))$. NH denotes node hash, m is the ID of a nonleaf node while m_1, m_2 are its two children's IDs. The BHT is only a special case of MHT, and the form of MHT can be adjusted in different scenarios; for example the fanout can be changed. For efficient update and query we can combine balance tree or B+ tree with the MHT.

15.2.2 Security of an MHT

Ideally, the security of an MHT depends on the cryptographic hash function that it uses. However, in practice, the structure of an MHT and the content of the data also play important roles. Fine-tuned MHT structure and data content can help with the security if implemented with some light-weighted hash functions. We will review the security definitions of cryptographic hash functions, and introduce some popular hash functions. We will describe how the structure of an MHT and the content of the data affect the security level of the MHT.

15.2.2.1 Security of cryptographic hash function

Hash function is an essential block of modern cryptography [7]. MAC and digital signature techniques are based on hash functions. Ideally a hash function is a scheme to transform any random-sized message into a unique fixed-length bits string: H: $\{0,1\}^{\wedge n} \rightarrow \{0,1\}^{\wedge l}$.

A standard hashing scheme contains three parts, $H = (KG, HG,\ and\ HV)$.

KG: a key-generation algorithm. *KG* takes as the input a security parameter 1^p and generates a security key k: $k = KG(1^p)$.

HG: a hash generation algorithm. *HG* takes as the input the security key k generated by KG and uses a basic union of data to generate a hash value $HG^k(data) \in \{0,1\}^{p_0(p)}$, where p_0 is a polynomial, and p is the value of the security parameter chosen in KG.

HV: a deterministic function to verify the integrity of data. This takes as the input the hash value of data and the data that needs to be verified. Then it compares the received hash with the computed hash based on the received data to generate a value, which can determine the integrity of data.

The security of a cryptographic hash function is determined by the following three properties of a hash function:

1. Computationally infeasible to find data content that has been mapped to specific hash (preimage property)

2. Computationally infeasible to find two data contents to the same hash (the second preimage resistance property)

3. Computationally infeasible to find any pair of data contents with the same hash value (strict collision resistance property)

Figure 15.4 shows the relationships of these properties. Strict collision resistance is the strongest notion and subsumes second preimage resistance and part of preimage property. The preimage property ensures that the process of a hash function cannot be reversed. A collision-finding experiment can be used to test the collision resistance performance of hash functions. In this test, generally the attacker A is a probabilistic polynomial-time (PPT) adversary.

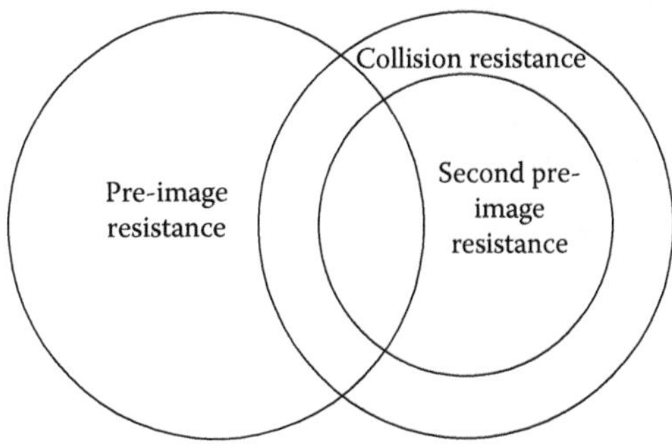

Figure 15.4: The relationships among security properties of a hash function.

Collision-finding Experiment: Col-$F_H(p)$

1. *Key* $k = Generate(1^p)$.

2. A can access k and hash function H, and generates two output x_1 and x_2.

3. The experiment will compare the hash result of x_1 and x_2. If $x_1 \neq x_2$, and $H(x_1) = H(x_1)$, a collision is found; otherwise, the hash function passes the collision-finding experiment.

4. A hash function is collision-resistant if for all A it has a negligible function that meets:

$$\Pr[Col - FH(p)] \leq \text{negl}(p)$$

So far the known attacks to hash operations can be classified into two types:

1. Brute-force attack: the attackers utilize powerful computers to find the collision pairs or the original message of a specific hash value. The strength of a hash code against brute-force attacks is determined by its length m. Cryptographically it takes $2^{m/2}$ steps.

2. Cryptanalysis attack: the attackers analyze the hash algorithms and data contents, to come up with some skillful methods aiming at specific vulnerability they found to reduce the computation required for attacking, and thus make it possible to attack the brute-force resistant hash schemes. One typical case of cryptanalysis attack toward hash functions is the birthday attack; it is based on the *birthday paradox* and works as follows:

    a. Assume a user prepares to sign a valid message x. An attacker generates $2^{m/2}$ variations x' of x with essentially the same meaning and saves them. Then he also generates $2^{m/2}$ variations y' of a desired fraudulent message y.

    b. The attacker searches two sets of messages to find a pair with the same hash value (probability > 0.5 by birthday paradox).

    c. The attacker captures the valid message signed by the user, then substitutes it with the forgery which also has a valid signature to launch a man-in-the-middle attack.

The above two kinds of attacks indicate that a secure hash scheme should have large hash value and good one-way propriety. In practice the data contents in datasets need to be reinforced with some randomness to avoid cryptanalysis attacks.

15.2.2.2 Security impact of MHT structure and data contents

The utilization of MHT can make hash management and update more efficient. However, the MHT structure itself has some security issues. One obvious case is that the original root hash of MHT does not indicate the depth of the MHT, and this will lead to a second preimage attack. Using the MHT in Figure 15.3 as an example, an adversary can substitute the block of $H(0) = H[H(0,0) \mid H(0,1)]$ with $H(0) = H[\mathit{Data\ unit}\ (0)]$, where $\mathit{Data\ unit}\ (0) = H(0,0) \mid H(0,1)$. In this way the database is modified while the root hash still remains unchanged. To solve this issue one possible way is to use *certificate transparency*: when computing leaf node hashes, we can prepend a 0×00 byte to the hash data, and a 0×01 byte should be prepended when computing internal node hashes. Limiting the hash tree size is a prerequisite of some formal security proofs, and helps with making some proofs tighter. Another solution is to use a radix path identifiers (RPI) scheme together with the MHT. The RPI works as below:

$$RPI = \begin{cases} 0 & n == 0 \\ rpi_{parent} * r + i & n \geq 0 \end{cases}$$

where n is the sequence number of a node in MHT, for root hash node $n = 0$; r is the radix between the parent and the children, and i is the sequence number of a node in its siblings. In some large-scale graph-structured databases, a user can only access a particular part of the database.

Implementing MHT in such database will introduce some other security issues. One is the data confidentiality problem. As we described before, the root hash of MHT contains the all the hash information of a database. Therefore, the users may get some hash values of the data content they do not have authority to access. This requires that the hash function used in MHT should be a perfect one-way function. Even if we use common one-way hash functions such as SHA3-512, we still cannot achieve the perfect one-way property. For example, if the attackers are internal users who can access part of the database, they will know the basic format of data content. Therefore, they can utilize their knowledge to narrow down the scope of possible data contents. Thus it makes it computationally possible to obtain the original data from the hash value via a brute-force search.

For example, assume MHT in Figure 15.3 is used for managing a database used by two entities Alice and Bob who run their businesses in the same city. In each data unit it stores a customer's address. For an external attacker, it is computationally impossible to deduce any data from the root hash. However, if Bob has the access to half of all data units stored in database and also has the most recent root hash, it is computationally possible to determine all addresses in the rest of data units belonging to Alice. In order to protect a database using MHT from this type of internal attacks, the relationship between different data units should be eliminated. Generally, this can be achieved by appending data content in each data union with some large random number. In Bob's case, if a 128-bit random number is appended, it becomes computationally impossible for Bob to deduce the addresses belonging to Alice.

15.2.2.3 Existing solutions for graph-structure data hashing (search_DAG, PCHFG)

There are several existing hashing schemes for trees and graphs: original MHT [8], search-DAG [6], and perfectly collision-resistant hash functions for graphs (PCHFG) [9]. The original MHT scheme can handle tree-structured graphs under the assumption that any update will not change the graph type from tree to any nontree types. Similar to the original MHT method, search-DAG can only handle DAG, and thus it is not capable of managing other types of graphs. To address this problem, Muhammad et al. proposed PCHFG to serve as a universal solution to all types of graphs. PCHFG uses graph traversal schemes to obtain labels which can represent the structure of the graph (edges), and appends them to the vertexes. In this way the hashes of vertexes contain the information of the edges, and thus can ensure the integrity of vertexes and edges. However, this scheme cannot work on the weighted graphs. The attackers can change an edge's weight without affecting any hash value. However, in large-scale graphs the data contents in vertexes may be frequently updated; then this scheme is inefficient.

The idea of using graph traversal to create labels that can represent the structure of a graph in PCHFG is feasible. Based on it we propose a new hash scheme which can be implemented on any type of graph, and is quite efficient in a large-scale graph machine learning scenario. The following section provides the details.

15.3 Implementation of Hash Scheme for Graphs

15.3.1 Graph traversal

The first step of our hashing scheme is to generate labels for all the edges by traveling through the whole graph. A graph $G(V,E)$ can be traveled either by *depth-first* traversal or *breadth-first* traversal. Then it will be represented as a depth-first tree (DFT) or a breadth-first tree (BFT). Here we choose breadth-first traversal. During the traversal we will assign some labels to the vertexes to indicate their relative positions in the whole graph. For example, as shown in Figure 15.5a the vertex $v1$ will have the label (1, 0, 1). For all of the children nodes of node $v1$, we can sort them in nondecreasing order of their contents. The labels will be $(2,1,N)$ $(N = 1,2,3\ldots)$, in which N indicates the sequence number defined in the sorting. For a vertex, its label is (l,p,N). Here l indicates the level this vertex is in, and p is the sequence number of its parent node (for a source vertex, p is 0). The table in Figure 15.5b shows the traversal label of each node, and the BFT format of the graph is shown in Figure 15.5a.

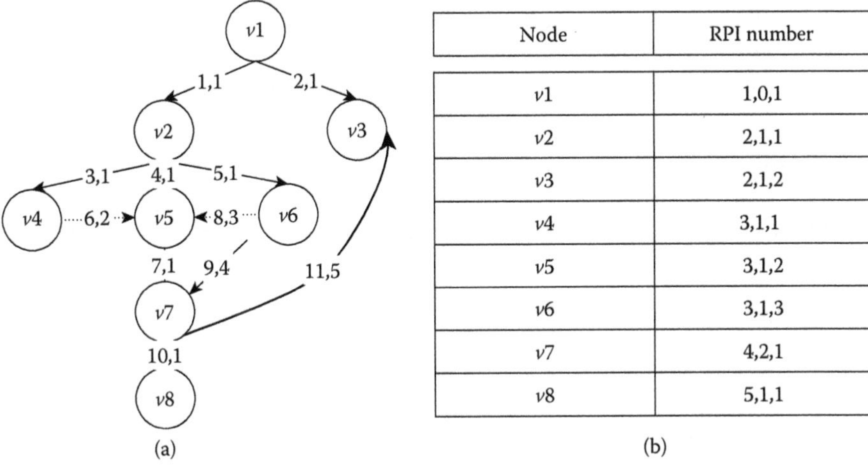

Node	RPI number
$v1$	1,0,1
$v2$	2,1,1
$v3$	2,1,2
$v4$	3,1,1
$v5$	3,1,2
$v6$	3,1,3
$v7$	4,2,1
$v8$	5,1,1

Figure 15.5: A graph with (a) BFT and (b) RPI traversal.

Properties of traversal labels: Vertexes in the same level have the same level number l, and p indicates the parent of a node in last level. The following lemma tells us that the traversal labels can be used to represent the relative positions of all vertexes in a graph.

Lemma 15.1
The traversal labels of all vertexes in a graph can represent their relative positions uniquely. Here the position of a vertex is defined by the level it belongs to, its parents' position and its order among its siblings.

Proof. The proof is straightforward. With all traversal labels we can reconstruct the BFT easily by a simple tree traversal.

15.3.2 Edge labels

In the shared database, the traversal labels may leak some sensitive information. For instance, in the BFT of Figure 15.5a, an internal attacker can use the traversal labels of $v7$ and $v6$ to deduce the traversal label of $v5$. Therefore, we prefer to use an edge-order number (EON) scheme based on the traversal labels to represent the graph structure.

The various types of edges in the graph are defined below using the notion of traversal labels. Here we use the BFT in Figure 15.5a and its traversal labels in Figure 15.5b as an example to illustrate our scheme. Edge $e(v1, v2)$ is a tree edge, edge $e(v4, v5)$ is a cross-forward edge, edge $e(v6, v5)$ is a cross-backward edge, edge $e(v6, v7)$ is a forward edge and edge $e(v7, v3)$ is a back edge. The tree edge is the edge between a parent and its children. Such an edge can be easily captured by the RPI numbers. However, to capture all types of edges, the relationship between RPI numbers and edges should be defined.

Definition 15.1 Let T be the BFT representation of a graph $G = (V, E)$, and $A, B \in V$ are two vertexes in the graph. (l_1, p_1, N_1) and (l_2, p_2, N_2) are the traversal labels corresponding to $v1$, $v2$. In the structure of BFT T, $e(a,b)$ could be one of the following cases:

1. tree edge, iff $l_1 + 1 = l_2$ and $N_1 = p_2$;
2. forward edge, iff $l_1 + 1 = l_2$ and $N_1 > p_2$;
3. backward edge, iff $l_1 > l_2$;
4. cross-forward edge, iff $l_1 = l_2$ and $N_1 < N_2$;
5. cross-backward edge, iff $l_1 = l_2$ and $N_1 > N_2$;
6. self-connect edge, iff $l_1 = l_2$ and $N_1 = N_2$.

In this *EON* scheme each edge has an *EON* (N, T), here N indicates the sequence number of the edge among all edges in no-decreasing order, and T represents the type of this edge (1 means tree edge, 2 means cross-forward edge, 3 means cross-backward edge, 4 means forward edge, and 5 means backward edge).

Lemma 15.2
The EON for an edge in a graph can represent the positions of its vertexes uniquely, where the position and relationship of nodes in an edge can be defined by the order and type of the edge.

Proof. With EONs and edge contents we can correctly reconstruct the structure that we obtained in BFS traversal (Figure 15.6).

15.3.3 Procedure of hashing graph

Here we define the basic procedure of our hash scheme

HG and graph traversal:
Input: a graph $G(V, E)$, and a key k

1. Find and sort all source nodes in the order of their constant labels.
2. Let x be the first source node in the sorted order. If there are no source nodes in $G(V, E)$, choose the first node as the source node.

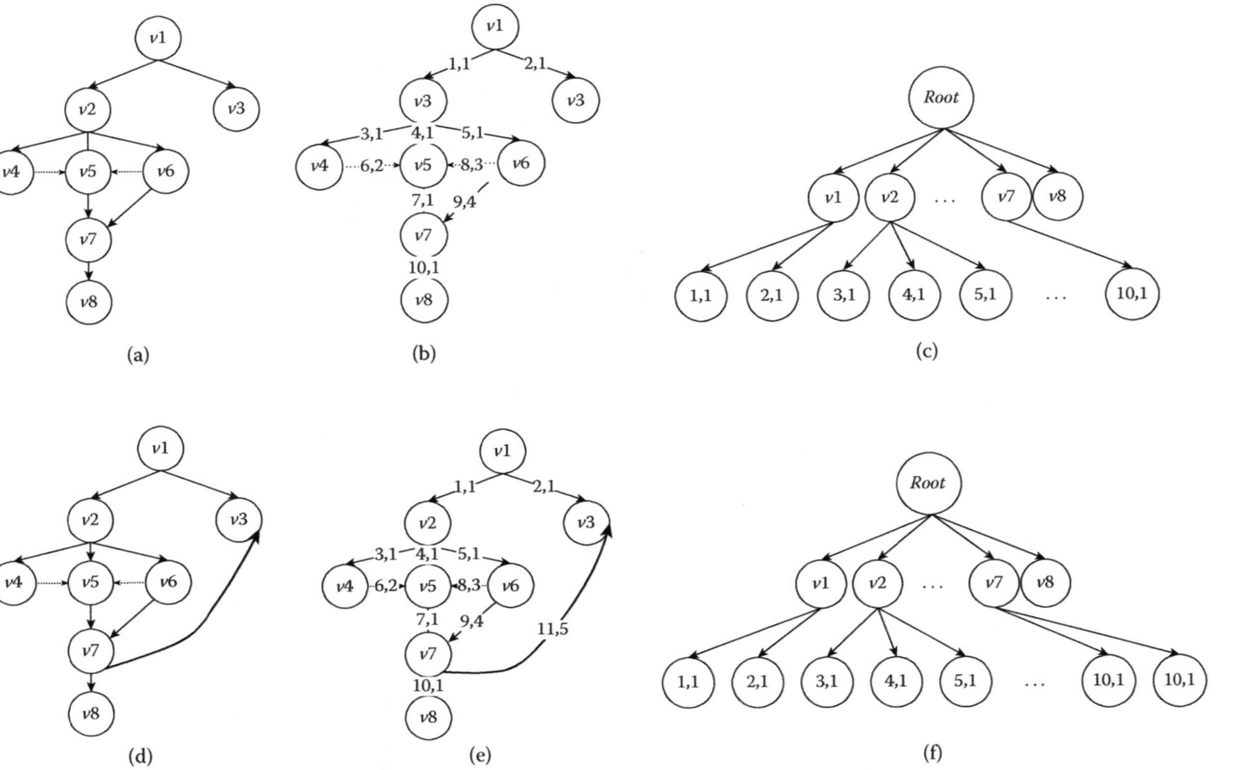

Figure 15.6: BFT and edge-order tree (ET) representations of DAG and graphs with cycles. The trees in (b and e) are BFT representations of graphs in (a and d); each edge in BFT contains its EN. Trees in (c and f) are ET representations for graphs in (a and d)—each edge contains an EON (an edge node has both the RPI number of the destination node and the start node), together with the hash value of their content.

3. Use the breadth-first traversal on the graph $G(V,E)$ from the source node x as follows:
   a. If node y is visited in BFS, assign its RPI number to it (called RPI y).
   b. Find an edge $e(y,z)$ such that $e(y,z) \in E$ and $z \in V$.
   If $e(y,z)$ is a tree edge, then assign the edge as $(EON)\|(1)\|(e(y,z))$
   If it is a forward edge: $(EON)\|(2)\|(e(y,z))$
   If it is a backward edge: $(EON\|(3)\|(e(y,z))$
   If it is a cross-forward edge: $(EON)\|(4)\|(e(y,z))$
   If it is a cross-backward edge: $(EON)\|(5)\|(e(y,z))$
   If it is a self-connect edge: $(EON)\|(6)\|(e(y,z))$
4. Remove x from the sorted order of source nodes if it exists.
5. If there are nodes in $G(V,E)$ that are not yet visited, then repeat from 2.
6. Compute the hashes of all edges and nodes with a standard hash function.

MHTB: Set the fan out of MHT and build it based on all hashes computed from the bottom up. Generate a root hash gH for the graph.

15.3.4 Pre-image resistance hashing for graph

Data contents in an edge are EON, type, source vertex, destination vertex, and weight, which are usually less than 24 bytes. In our scheme all edges from the same source vertex will have similar *EONs*. Therefore, an attacker can deduce an unknown edge with its hash value and one of its adjacent edges within 2^32 steps. This means that the scheme is not a perfect one-way function. To make it a perfect one-way function, we should diffuse the relationship between the contents of different edges. Hence, we should add some random redundancy into the edge content. We add one operation into our scheme: appending a unique random key (128 bits) to each edge. Referring to steps in Section 15.2.2.3, we implement this operation as below:

1. In step 3(a), it generates a unique random key $K_{e(y,z)}$ for each edge.
2. In step 6 we compute the hash of an edge and also compute the hash of the edge appended with a random key as follows:

   $$H_{re(y,z)} \leftarrow H((EON)\,||Type|\,|e(y,z)\,||Weight|\,|K_{e(y,z)}$$

   The EONs of edges will leak some information of the graph, such as the total number of edges in the graph. Therefore, an order-preserving encryption scheme is required. A randomized traversal number scheme proposed by A. Kundu in Ref. [9] had the feature we need, and it can transfer the EON into a random edge-order number (REON) to make it leakage free while keeping the order unchanged.

15.3.4.1 MHT construction scheme for graph query

In a binary MHT, generating a verification object (VO) needs a time of $O(E)$; here, E is the number of edges. The VO size is $O(E-M)$, M is the number of edges queried by a client. Therefore, when only a small subgraph with M edges (M << E) is queried the VO size is unacceptably large. Wei et al. [11] proposed a two-level Merkel tree (TL-MT) scheme for big table integrity protection. In this TL-MT scheme they partitioned the original MHT into two levels, and could thus significantly reduce the construction time and the size of VO. Here we modify this scheme to make it suitable for a big graph. Figure 15.7 shows the TL-MT structure for a graph. The top level is the index tree which stores the root hash of the edge table and root hash of the vertex table. As we discussed before, vertexes tables can be managed as table-based data, which has been well studied. Therefore, here we focus on the construction of the edge MHT:

1. Store edge hashes in small blocks, combine all hashes $(h_1, h_2, \ldots h_q)$ in one block to generate a block hash $BH = HG(h_1 \| h_2 \| \cdots h_q)$. These block hashes $(BH_1, BH_2, \ldots, BH_n)$ are on the bottom level of the edge MHT.

2. From the bottom up, we build MHT on a set fanout f.

This MHT will be stored in the client side. To generate a VO set for subgraph query verification, the server first finds all edge hash blocks spanned by the subgraphs, and redacts the hashes of edges in the blocks but not in the subgraphs. Equation 15.1 below denotes the VO set size of subgraphs query, in which q denotes the size of each block; m is the number of blocks in this subgraph query; and s_{sub} denotes the size of subgraphs queried. Since in regular graph query the subgraphs are always connected graphs, the subgraphs will span a

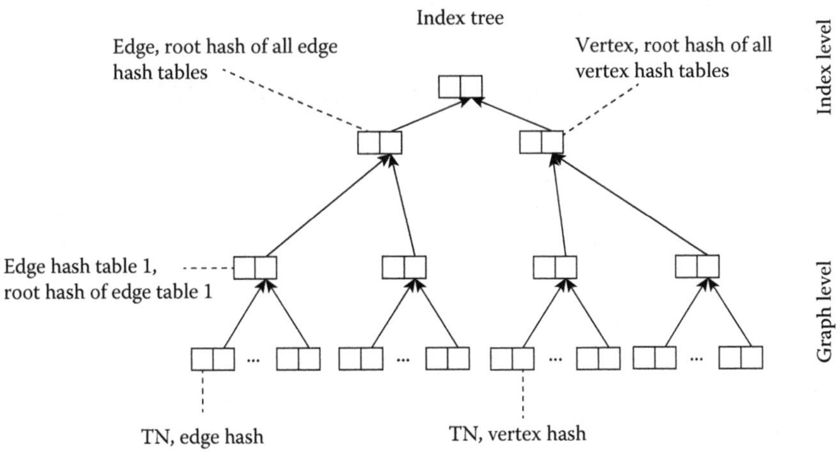

Figure 15.7: TL-MT for a graph.

small number of tables. Therefore the VO set size can be reduced. Even in the worst case that subgraphs span many blocks (even equal to its size), it can perform well.

$$S_{vo_{subquery}} = (q * m - s_{sub}) \tag{15.1}$$

$$H \approx \log_f(N) \tag{15.2}$$

$$S_{VO\_update}(f) = (f-1)\log_f(N) \tag{15.3}$$

$$S'_{VO\_update}(f) = In(N) * \left(\frac{1}{f * (In(f))^2} + \frac{1}{In(f)} - \frac{1}{(In(f))^2}\right) \tag{15.4}$$

$$S_{total}(f) = 1 + f + f^2 + \cdots + f^{\log_f(N)} \tag{15.5}$$

$$S_{total}(f) = \frac{1 - f * N}{1 - f} \tag{15.6}$$

$$S'_{total}(f) = \frac{1 - N}{(1-f)^2} \tag{15.7}$$

As we mentioned above, the MHT will be stored in both the client and server side. Equations 15.5 and 15.6 tell the total size of the MHT based on the fanout f and the number of data blocks N. Equation 15.7 is the differential format of Equation 15.6. As we can see, S'_{total} is negative, which means that by increasing the fanout, the size of MHT can be reduced. However, for an MHT another important feature is update efficiency. In Equation 15.3 we calculate the size of VO sets required to update one block hash in MHT. Equation 15.4 is the differential result of Equation 15.3 when $f > 3$, $(Inf) < (Inf)$; thus $S'_{VO\_update}(f) > 0$, which means that the size of VO set increases as the fanout f increases. Since the bottleneck of a computer system often exists in bus communications and CPU calculations rather than in memory storage spaces, the fanout of MHT should be minimized to maintain efficient update.

15.3.5 Data operations and corresponding MHT updates

Given a BFT labeled with an RPI number, we describe how clients can ensure the integrity of the main data operations of the graph data. We address several challenges, including regular subgraph queries and efficient updates. Since the vertexes can be operated as table-based data, we focus on edge MHT operations.

15.3.5.1 Graph query

We start our discussions from regular subgraph range queries. Here we will use a running example to further illustrate the whole procedure. Figure 15.8 shows a running example for data query on a graph. Initially, the graph has 10 edges and 8 vertexes.

Subgraphs query across hash blocks. We have discussed subgraphs query in Section 15.5.6. Using the graph in Figure 15.4 as an example, assume we want to

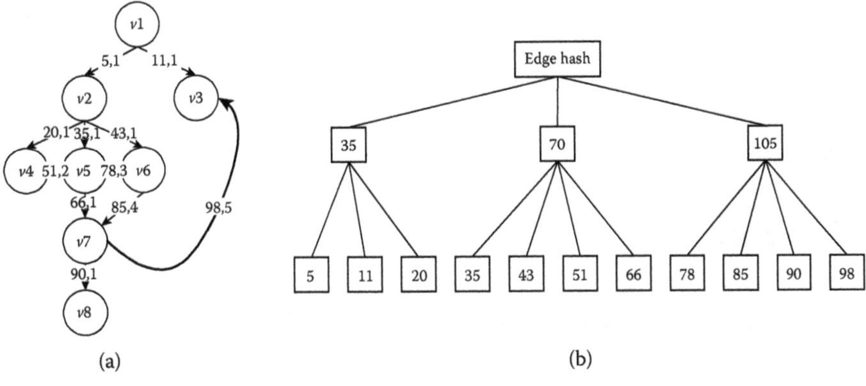

Figure 15.8: (a) Initial graph and (b) edge MHT.

query the edge $e(v1,v2)$, $e(v1,v3)$, $e(v2,v5)$, and $e(v4,v5)$. A VO set containing the hash of edges with REON 20, 35, and 66 will be returned from the server.

Efficient updates. All graph edge updates can be the combination of three types of operations: delete, insert, and weight change. In order to achieve efficient updates, we need to limit the influence of updates inside the blocks; and for those updates that will change the BFT results, we can use some update operations without changing the BFT structure, as follows:

- *Weight change* operations only involve the edges that need to be updated and will not change the BFT structure. Therefore it can be easily updated.
- *Deletion operation* may change the BFT structure. Thus instead of deleting the edge we can change the type of edge to 0, which denotes that the edge has been deleted. In this way, the structure of BFT can be maintained. Next time when we update the whole graph, the edge can be deleted.
- *Insertion operation* refers to inserting six types of edges we defined in Section 15.5. For all edges except the tree edges, the insertion will not change the BFT structure. Inserting a tree edge at leaf level will not change the BFT structure, thus it can be done inside the hash block. However, the insertion of a tree edge at the root level will totally change the BFT structure while the order of edges can be maintained.

15.4 Chapter Summary

In this chapter, we have introduced the basic concept of big graph, a special type of big data. We have proposed an efficient scheme to decompose a large graph into subgraphs, and suggested a Merkel tree-based hashing scheme. Such a scheme is especially suitable to real-time, large-scale graph processing. We have also discussed the hashing tree update process. In future work, we will study the hash operations for other types of big data such as big sensor data stream and big database.

References

[1] Jagadish, H. V., & Olken, F. Database management for life sciences research. *ACM SIGMOD Record* vol. 33, no. 2 (2004): 15–20.

[2] Shilovitsky, O. Why graph analyzes will rule plm in the future? http://beyondplm.com/2013/08/23/why-graph-analyzes-will-rule-plmin-the-future/ (2013).

[3] Low, Y., et al. Distributed GraphLab: A framework for machine learning and data mining in the cloud. *Proceedings of the VLDB Endowment*, vol. 5, no. 8 (2012): 716–727.

[4] Malewicz, G., Austern, M. H., Bik, A. J., Dehnert, J. C., Horn, I., Leiser, N., & Czajkowski, G. (2010, June). Pregel: A system for large-scale graph processing. In *Proceedings of the 2010 ACM SIGMOD International Conference on Management of data* (pp. 135–146). ACM, Indianapolis, IN.

[5] McCune, R. R., Weninger, T., & Madey, G. Thinking like a vertex: A survey of vertex-centric frameworks for large-scale distributed graph processing. *ACM Computing Surveys (CSUR)*, vol. 48, no. 2 (2015): 25.

[6] Kim, S. C., & Lee, S. (2005, June). Push-pull: Guided search dag scheduling for heterogeneous clusters. In *2005 International Conference on Parallel Processing (ICPP'05)* (pp. 603–610). IEEE, Oslo.

[7] Canetti, R. (1997, August). Towards realizing random oracles: Hash functions that hide all partial information. In *Annual International Cryptology Conference* (pp. 455–469). Springer, Berlin.

[8] Kundu, A., & Bertino, E. (2012). On hashing graphs. *IACR Cryptology ePrint Archive*, 2012, 352.

[9] Arshad, M. U., Kundu, A., Bertino, E., Madhavan, K., & Ghafoor, A. (2014, March). Security of graph data: Hashing schemes and definitions. In *Proceedings of the 4th ACM Conference on Data and Application Security and Privacy* (pp. 223–234). ACM, San Antonio, TX.

[10] Page, L., Brin, S., Motwani, R., & Winograd, T. (1999). The PageRank citation ranking: Bringing order to the web, Technical Report. Stanford InfoLab.

[11] Wei, Wei, Ting Yu, and Rui Xue. iBigTable: Practical data integrity for bigtable in public cloud. In *Proceedings of the 3rd ACM Conference on Data and Application Security and Privacy*. ACM, San Antonio, Texas, 2013.

Further Reading

Boldyreva, A., Chenette, N., Lee, Y., & O'neill, A. (2009, April). Order-preserving symmetric encryption. In *Annual International Conference on the Theory and Applications of Cryptographic Techniques* (pp. 224–241). Springer, Berlin.

Canetti, R., Micciancio, D., & Reingold, O. (1998, May). Perfectly one-way probabilistic hash functions (preliminary version). In *Proceedings of the 30th Annual ACM Symposium on Theory of Computing* (pp. 131–140). ACM, Dallas.

Katz, J., & Lindell, Y. *Introduction to modern cryptography*. CRC Press, Boca Raton, 2014. ISBN: 9781466570269.

Kundu, A., Atallah, M. J., & Bertino, E. (2012, February). Leakage-free redactable signatures. In *Proceedings of the 2nd ACM Conference on Data and Application Security and Privacy* (pp. 307–316). ACM, San Antonio.

Merkle, R. C. (1987, August). A digital signature based on a conventional encryption function. In *Conference on the Theory and Application of Cryptographic Techniques* (pp. 369–378). Springer, Berlin.

Merkle, R C. (1989). A certified digital signature. In *Conference on the Theory and Application of Cryptology* (pp. 218–238). Springer, New York.

Zhou, Y., Cheng, H., & Yu, J. X. Graph clustering based on structural/attribute similarities. *Proceedings of the VLDB Endowment*, vol. 2, no. 1 (2009): 718–729.

Further Reading

IV

EMERGING APPLICATIONS OF NETWORKED BIG DATA

Chapter 16

Mobile Augmented Reality to Enable Intelligent Mall Shopping by Network Data

Vincent W. Zheng

Advanced Digital Sciences Center
Singapore

Hong Cao

Analytics & Enterprise Intelligence
Ernst & Young Advisory Pte. Ltd
Singapore

CONTENTS

16.1 Introduction

Shopping is an important part of our daily life and today's vibrant economy. According to the Year 2013 Singapore government report (as shown in Figure 16.1a)*, among receipts totaling S$23.56 billion, 27% (~S$6.38 billion) is for shopping, food, and beverages. With the proliferation of smartphones and ubiquitous supporting of 3G/4G/LTE networks, we have the opportunity to enhance the shopping experience through mobile technology. In this chapter, we demonstrate *IntelligShop*, a novel location-based augmented reality application, for intelligent shopping in malls. We leverage both the shopping mall infrastructure of wireless networks for indoor localization and the World Wide Web for retailer content aggregation. With these networks, we manage to provide an immersive and informative shopping experience to the mobile users in the city.

System functionality. The key functionality of IntelligShop, as shown in Figure 16.1b, is to provide an augmented reality interface—people can simply use ubiquitous smartphones to face the retailers (e.g., Pastamania, Starbucks), then IntelligShop will automatically recognize the retailers (i.e., it is Pastamania or Starbucks) and bring their online reviews from various sources (including blogs, forums, and publicly accessible social media) to display on the phones. It is worth noting that IntelligShop provides seamless location-based augmented reality, which makes the review searching and aggregation process automatic—the user now does not need to type the retailer name or browse through some catalog; instead they just simply raise the phone camera facing the retailer to immediately get its reviews displayed at the right place on the mobile screen.

Network data in use. We summarize two types of network data we use to build IntelligShop, including the ***wireless network data*** and the ***Web data***, in Figure 16.2.

*https://www.stb.gov.sg/statistics-and-market-insights/marketstatistics/stb%20tourism%20statistics_fa%20as%20of%2002262016%20(lowres%20res).pdf

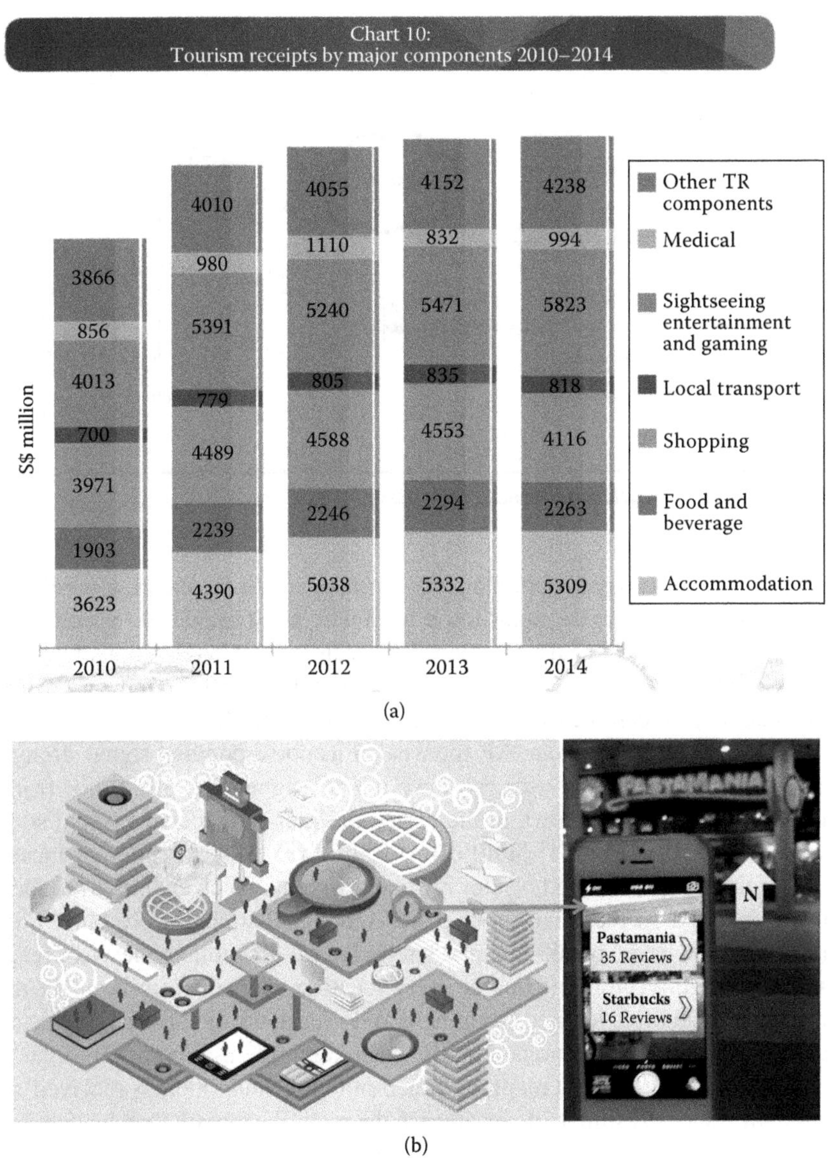

Figure 16.1: (a) Motivation and (b) application scenario for IntelligShop.

First, we rely on the wireless network data to enable the retailer recognition. Our idea is to estimate the user location and then combine it with the user orientation information to identify which retailer the user is currently looking at. Because the shopping malls are often in an indoor environment, where GSP

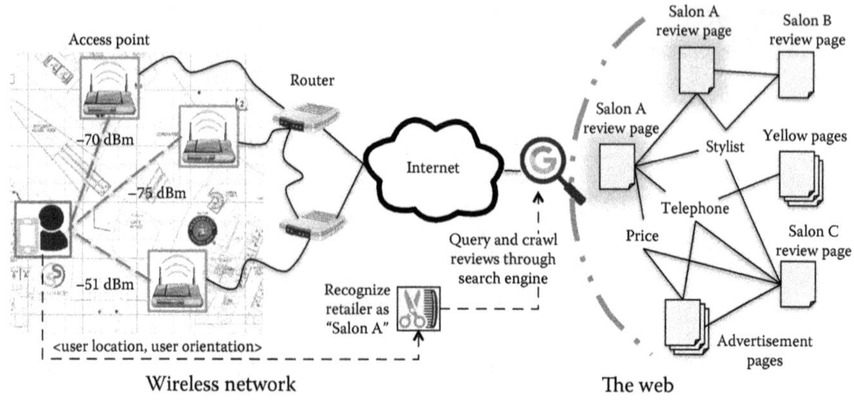

Figure 16.2: Network data in use.

signals are weak, our system manages to make use of the existing wireless network infrastructure in the malls to perform wireless localization. Specifically, as shown in Figure 16.2, a user's smartphone can receive WiFi signals from a network of multiple access points (APs) in the mall's wireless network. For each WiFi signal, we can measure its signal strength (unit: dBm). In general, the farther a user is away from one AP, the weaker its corresponding signal strength is. Thus at each location, a user can have a WiFi signal strength vector from the multiple APs; e.g., as shown in the figure, the user can receive a signal strength vector of $[-70, -75, -51]$ (unit: dBm) from three APs. At different locations, the received signal strength vector is often different, which enables us to localize the user based on the smartphone's received signal strengths. To build a localization model based on WiFi signal strengths, we first collect the WiFi received signal strength vectors off-line at every location of interest in the mall; then a mapping function is learned from these WiFi received signal strength vectors to their corresponding locations. Finally, when a mobile user comes into the mall, we can apply the learned mapping function to the smartphone's received signal strength vector to estimate its location in the mall. We remark that, by using wireless network data for localization our system is able to leverage the existing mall infrastructure without requiring any additional location sensing infrastructures such as iBeacon.* More details are provided in Section 16.2.

Second, we rely on Web data to provide the retailer reviews. Once we identify the mobile user's location and their orientation in the mall, we can infer which retailer they are currently looking at based on the mall's floor plan. To assist intelligent shopping, we try to provide more information, in particular reviews, of the retail shops to the mobile users. In practice, the retailer's reviews are often

* https://developer.apple.com/ibeacon/

spread all over the Web. We try to aggregate the reviews for a retailer from different sources on the Web, so as to consolidate a more complete view about that retailer and avoid potential opinion bias. Because the Web has been indexed by search engines, our system manages to make use of the search engine interface to query and crawl the reviews from the Web. Therefore, the problem becomes how to find the right queries to ask the search engine, so as to find as many reviews as possible for a given retailer. As shown in Figure 16.2, after a retailer "Salon A" is recognized by using the wireless network data, we try to find its reviews. In general, we do not know what kinds of queries are good in advance, thus we first collect some Web pages off-line for the same domain retailers (e.g., "Salon B" and "Salon C" in this case). Among these off-line Web pages for "Salon B" and "Salon C," there can be review pages and irrelevant pages such as yellow pages and advertisement pages. As a result, based on these Web pages, we can analyze what kinds of keywords and phrases are useful in retrieving the reviews. As shown in Figure 16.2, the keywords and the Web pages are connected into a network. Based on the network, we can observe that, both "Salon B" and "Salon C" have their review pages linked to some stylists, while their irrelevant pages hardly linked to any stylist. We can then conclude that "stylist" can be a good query to search for salon reviews. Finally, for our target "Salon A," we use "sylist" to construct queries to search for reviews. We remark that by using a search engine to retrieve the retailer reviews our system is able to utilize the search engine's Web indexing capability. More details are provided in Section 16.3.

System architecture. The system architecture of IntelligShop is illustrated in Figure 16.3. We designed IntelligShop with: (1) an Android client app that runs in the user's smartphone, (2) a localization server that supports location lookup, and (3) a retailer server that crawls, stores, and indexes the reviews for each retailer in the mall. First, the client app will read the context, such as RSS values from the APs and the orientation. By sending the $\langle$AP, RSS$\rangle$ tuples to the localization server, the mobile device will get to know its location through the robust feature learning model and a location estimation function. Second, the location and the orientation together can be sent to the retailer server, so as to rank the possible retailers according to the mall layout. We developed a retailer ranking algorithm, based on the overlap degree between the phone's angle of view and the retailers in the view. Once the retailers are ranked, their corresponding reviews can be queried through the augmented reality engine. The retailer reviews are crawled periodically by the iterative learning to query model and saved into the retailer DB. Finally, for smooth content display in augmented reality, the client app keeps detecting changes with respect to the phone location and its orientation. If there is any change, the augmented reality engine will be called to update the localization and retailer ranking results for display of the relevant information.

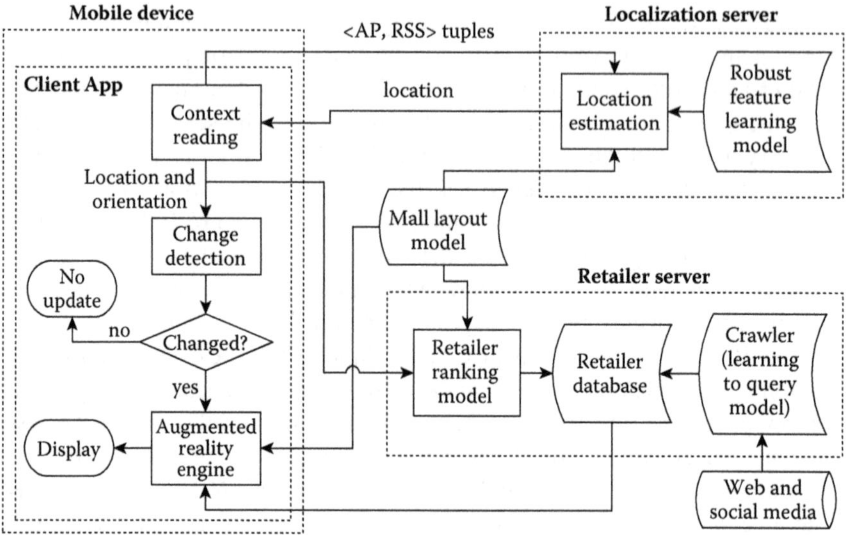

Figure 16.3: IntelligShop system architecture.

System novelty. To the best of our knowledge, IntelligShop is the first indoor location-based augmented reality application that integrates heterogeneous-device wireless localization and automatic online content crawling for intelligent shopping. IntelligShop is different from other notable location-based augmented reality applications in the market. For example, Monocle* is a feature provided by Yelp.com's mobile app; it allows users to view the nearby businesses by using the camera on the phone and pointing it at the surroundings. However, Monocle only supports outdoor (by GPS) augmented reality, and its content is solely from Yelp's reviews. Similarly, for location-based augmented reality, Junaio† also focuses on the outdoor scenario, and its content mainly comes from either user contributions or Google maps. It is worth noting that GPS does not work indoors; hence, IntelligShop is clearly different from Yelp's Monocle and Junaio in supporting indoor location-based augmented reality. There are a few location-based augmented reality systems that can support indoor use. The most notable one is Navvis,‡ which mainly relies on image recognition to perform indoor localization and manual editing to provide digital content for augmented reality. However, similar to Yelp's Monocle and Junaio, Navvis also suffer from: (1) cold start in user generated content and (2) content bias from a single source. In contrast, IntelligShop is able to *automatically crawl* the online review content

* http://www.yelp-support.com/article/What-is-Yelp-s-Monocle-feature

† http://www.junaio.com/

‡ https://www.navvis.com/

from *diverse sources*, and thus successfully avoids the cold start and content bias problems. Finally, IntelligShop is also different from the applications in Refs. [1,2], which do not even support the shopping scenario.

Technically, IntelligShop is a data mining application, novelly addressing two challenging data mining problems on cold start: (1) supporting heterogeneous smartphones in a wireless network localization and (2) collecting retailer content from the Web for augmented reality. We shall discuss these two data mining problems with details in Sections 16.2 and 16.3.

16.2 Leverage Wireless Network for Localization

The state of the art in wireless localization is the learning-based approach [3,4]. In an environment with $d_1 \in \mathbb{Z}^+$ access points (APs), a mobile device receives wireless signals from these APs. The received signal strength (RSS) values at one location are used as a feature vector $\mathbf{x} \in \mathbb{R}^{d_1}$, and the device's location is a label $y \in \mathcal{Y}$, where $\mathcal{Y}$ is the set of possible locations in the environment. In an off-line training stage, given sufficient labeled data $\{(\mathbf{x}_i, y_i)\}$, we learn a mapping function $f : \mathbb{R}^{d_1} \to \mathcal{Y}$. In an online testing stage, we use f to predict the location for a new $\mathbf{x}$.

16.2.1 *Cold-start challenge*

Most of the existing models work under the data homogeneity assumption, which is impractical given the prevalent *device heterogeneity*. Specifically, the assumption requires the data used in training f to have the same distribution as that used in testing. However, in practice, users carry a variety of heterogeneous mobile devices, which are different from the device used to collect data in training f. Due to different sensing chips, these heterogeneous devices easily receive different RSS values even in the same location, thus failing the model f. Denote a *surveyor device* as S, on which we collect labeled data for training the f. Denote a *target device* as T, on which we have test data to predict the labels. In Figure 16.4, we show that the localization accuracy can drop significantly, if we apply the model trained on S's training data to T's test data (denoted as $S \to T$), other than the same S's test data (denoted as $S \to S$).

Ideally, to address the device heterogeneity issue, one would require the users to be willing to help collect a sufficient amount of calibration data [3,4] to tune their models, before localization service is provided. Such an assumption is impractical—in fact, we often face the *cold start*, i.e., no calibration data is available for the new device at a new place.

As a result, we consider the heterogeneous-device localization with cold start task as a *robust feature learning* problem. Specifically, without asking users to calibrate their devices, we try to learn a device-robust feature representation $g : \mathbb{R}^{d_1} \to \mathbb{R}^{d_2}$, such that for two RSS vectors $\mathbf{x}_s$ and $\mathbf{x}_t$ collected at the same

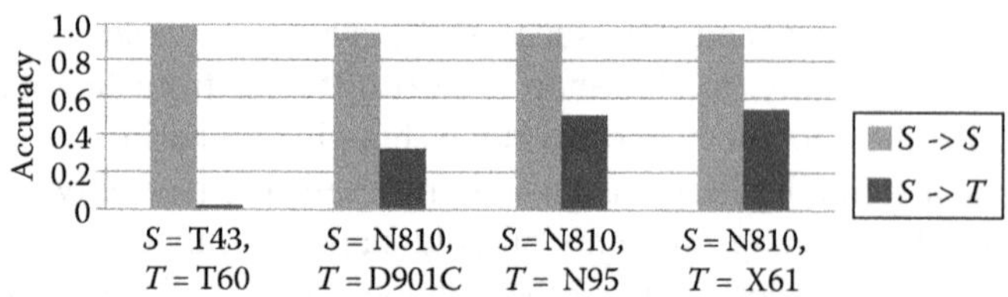

Figure 16.4: Accuracy drops from same-device ($S \to S$) to heterogeneous-device ($S \to T$) localization, on four pairs of devices. Data details are given in the experiment. We used SVM [5] as the localization model.

location $\tilde{y} \in \mathcal{Y}$ by any device S and device T, we have:

$$g(\mathbb{E}[\mathbf{x}^s]|y^s = \tilde{y}) = g(\mathbb{E}[\mathbf{x}^t]|y^t = \tilde{y}) \tag{16.1}$$

where the expectation is taken over each dimension of $\mathbf{x}$ to account for the randomness in the received signal strength from each AP. Finally, given this $g(\cdot)$, we build a new $f : \mathbb{R}^{d_2} \to \mathcal{Y}$ to locate the heterogeneous devices. Note that, finding a $g(\cdot)$ to satisfy Equation 16.1 is challenging—because of the unknown y_t, we cannot align $\mathbf{x}_t$ with $\mathbf{x}_s$, and thus can only directly learn a mapping function between them as g, as in Ref. [3]. Is it possible to find a device-robust feature representation only from $\mathbf{x}_s$? Interestingly, our answer is yes, as we show this through the insights below.

16.2.2 Our insight—HOP features

First, a pairwise feature that compares RSS values from two APs is robust to device heterogeneity. We are motivated by the observation that RSS value is often inversely proportional to the distance between AP and device; i.e., the closer the device is to the AP, the larger the RSS value is. Formally, this observation is characterized by a *log-normal shadowing model* [6] in radio propagation theory. Denote $x_{k|\ell}$ as a RSS value at an arbitrary distance ℓ from AP_k, then according to shadowing model,

$$x_{k|\ell} = x_{k|\ell_0} - 10\beta \log\left(\frac{\ell}{\ell_0}\right) + \psi_k \tag{16.2}$$

where $x_{k|\ell_0}$ is an RSS value at a constant reference distance ℓ_0 from AP_k. This $x_{k|\ell_0}$ is unique to the device, which explains why different devices receive different RSS values at the same location. ψ_k is a Gaussian noise with zero mean. β is a constant denoting the path loss exponent. According to Equation 16.2, if a device S can observe a larger RSS value from AP_1 than that from AP_2, then S is generally closer to AP_1 than AP_2* (e.g., in Figure 16.5, S is at location y_1, receiving signals

*By expectation, ψ_k becomes 0, and $x_{k|\ell_0}$ cancels if APs are similar.

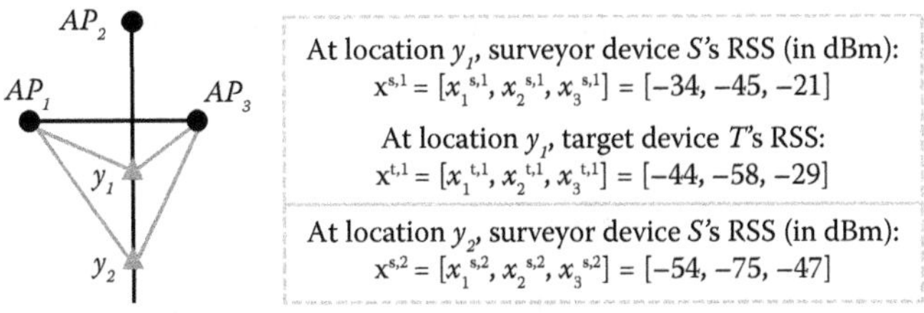

AP2
AP1
AP3
y1
y2
At location y1, surveyor device S's RSS (in dBm):
x^{s,1} = [x1^{s,1}, x2^{s,1}, x3^{s,1}] = [−34, −45, −21]
At location y1, target device T's RSS:
x^{t,1} = [x1^{t,1}, x2^{t,1}, x3^{t,1}] = [−44, −58, −29]
At location y2, surveyor device S's RSS (in dBm):
x^{s,2} = [x1^{s,2}, x2^{s,2}, x3^{s,2}] = [−54, −75, −47]

Figure 16.5: An example of two devices (S, T) receiving signals from three APs (AP_1, AP_2, AP_3) at two locations (y_1, y_2). The received signal strengths (RSS) are denoted as x vectors.

from AP_1 with -34 dBm and AP_2 with -45 dBm). Hence, another device T in the same location will (by expectation) also observe a larger RSS value from AP_1 than from AP_2 (e.g., in Figure 16.5, T is also at location y_1, receiving signals from AP_1 with -44 dBm and AP_2 with -58 dBm). Hence, if we use this boolean pairwise RSS comparison between AP_1 and AP_2 (e.g., $x_1^{s,1} - x_2^{s,1} > 0$ and $x_1^{t,1} - x_2^{t,1} > 0$ both hold in Figure 16.5) as a new feature, it is *robust* to both S and T.

Second, the pairwise feature is unfortunately not expressive enough for differentiating different locations, and we want to extend it to a high-order comparison feature.* The pairwise features are not discriminative to differentiate locations. For example, we can find in Figure 16.5 that $\delta(x_{k_1}^{s,1} - x_{k_2}^{s,1} > 0) = \delta(x_{k_1}^{s,2} - x_{k_2}^{s,2} > 0)$ for any AP_{k_1} and AP_{k_2} (e.g., try $k_1 = 3$, $k_2 = 1$). This means the pairwise RSS comparison feature cannot differentiate y_1 and y_2. Such a limitation is caused by the feature being only second-order and inexpressive. To enable the discriminativeness, we try to involve more APs in the comparison, but still evaluate the relative closeness between two APs. For example, in Figure 16.5, we can see $x_3^{s,1} - x_1^{s,1} > x_1^{s,1} - x_2^{s,1}$ for y_1, while $x_3^{s,2} - x_1^{s,2} < x_1^{s,2} - x_2^{s,2}$ for y_2. In other words, a third-order pairwise feature $(x_3^{e,j} - x_1^{e,j}) - (x_1^{e,j} - x_2^{e,j}) > 0$ is discriminative for y_1 and y_2. Such discriminativeness is due to our comparing (1) a location y_j's relative closeness between AP_3 and AP_1 and (2) y_j's relative closeness between AP_1 and AP_2.

16.2.3 Problem formulation

We generalize our intuition of combining multiple pairwise RSS comparisons together to formulate high-order pairwise (HOP) features. In Figure 16.5, the third-order pairwise feature $(x_3^{e,j} - x_1^{e,j}) - (x_1^{e,j} - x_2^{e,j}) > 0$ is a linear combination of two pairwise RSS differences. To use more APs, we consider more pairwise RSS differences. Denote a pairwise RSS difference as $(x_{k_1}^{e,j} - x_{k_2}^{e,j})$ for AP_{k_1} and AP_{k_2}. For notation simplicity, we omit the superscript ^{e,j} and only use

*Here the order is the number of APs used in comparison.

$(x_{k_1} - x_{k_2})$ in our feature representation. Then, we linearly combine multiple pairwise RSS differences:

$$\sum_{(k_1,k_2)} c_{k_1,k_2}(x_{k_1} - x_{k_2}) > 0 \tag{16.3}$$

where $c_{k_1,k_2} \in \mathbb{R}$ can be seen as the *normalized* number of times that $(x_{k_1} - x_{k_2})$ is used to construct the linear combination. The summation in Equation 16.3 is over all the possible (k_1, k_2), which means Equation 16.3 is capable of providing the highest-order representation by using all the APs in one feature. As RSS value is noisy (c.f., the shadowing model), Equation 16.3 may not always hold for different RSS samples collected over time. To deal with this random noise, we introduce $b \in \mathbb{R}$ as a "slack" to Equation 16.3. Finally, we have

Definition 16.1 (HOP feature). A HOP feature h is defined as

$$h = \delta\left(\sum_{(k_1,k_2)} c_{k_1,k_2}(x_{k_1} - x_{k_2}) + b > 0\right) \tag{16.4}$$

The HOP feature is expressive, thanks to using more APs in our high-order representation.

16.2.4 Our model—HOP feature learning and robustness

There are many possible h's that meet Definition 16.1, due to the infinite choices for parameter (c_{k_1,k_2}, b)'s. However, not all of them can represent the data well. Some h can be trivial; e.g., when all the $c_{k_1,k_2} = 0$ and b is any real value, h is still robust as different $\mathbf{x}$'s are transformed to the same value. But such a h is not discriminative for locations, and thus cannot represent the data well. We propose to learn a set of h's, such that they are representative for the data:

$$\max_{\mathbf{h} \in \{0,1\}^{d_2}} \sum_{k=1}^{n_L} \log P(\mathbf{x}^{(k)}; \mathbf{h}) \tag{16.5}$$

where $\mathbf{h} = [h_1, \ldots, h_{d_2}]$ is a vector of d_2 HOP features; $P(\mathbf{x}; \mathbf{h})$ is the data likelihood (to define later) with $\mathbf{h}$.

Directly learning $\mathbf{h}$ leads to optimizing an excessive number of parameters. Based on Equation 16.4, to learn h's parameters (c_{k_1,k_2}, b), we shall enumerate all the $(x_{k_1} - x_{k_2})$'s, which are quadratic to the number of APs. As a result, in all we have to optimize at least $O(d_1^2 \times d_2)$ parameters. Fitting more parameters generally requires more data, thus increasing the labeling burden. We can reduce the number of parameters by rewriting Equation 16.4 to an equivalent form, which avoids the explicit pair enumeration. As $\sum_{(k_1,k_2)} c_{k_1,k_2}(x_{k_1} - x_{k_2}) + b$ admits a linear form over different x_i's, we can organize:

$$\sum_{(k_1,k_2)} c_{k_1,k_2}(x_{k_1} - x_{k_2}) + b = \sum_{i=1}^{d_1} \alpha_i x_i + b \tag{16.6}$$

where $\alpha_i = \sum_{(k_1,k_2)} [c_{k_1,k_2}\delta(k_1 = i) - c_{k_1,k_2}\delta(k_2 = i)]$. The weights for each x_{k_1} and x_{k_2} are c_{k_1,k_2} and $-c_{k_1,k_2}$. Therefore, by summing up weights for all the (k_1,k_2) pairs, the sum becomes 0. In other words, $\sum_{i=1}^{d_1} \alpha_i$ is 0:

$$\begin{aligned}\sum_{i=1}^{d_1} \alpha_i &\overset{1}{=} \sum_{i=1}^{d_1} \sum_{(k_1,k_2)} [c_{k_1,k_2}\delta(k_1 = i) - c_{k_1,k_2}\delta(k_2 = i)] \\ &\overset{2}{=} \sum_{(k_1,k_2)} \left[\sum_{i=1}^{d_1} c_{k_1,k_2}\delta(k_1 = i) - \sum_{i=1}^{d_1} c_{k_1,k_2}\delta(k_2 = i) \right] \\ &\overset{3}{=} \sum_{(k_1,k_2)} (c_{k_1,k_2} - c_{k_1,k_2}) = 0 \end{aligned} \tag{16.7}$$

where at step 1 we plug in the definition of α_i; at step 2, we swap the summations over i and (k_1,k_2); step 3 holds, because each x_{k_1} always corresponds to one x_i. Equation 16.7 implies that a HOP feature of Equation 16.4 corresponds to a special feature transformation function with constraint:

$$h = \delta\left(\sum_{i=1}^{d_1} \alpha_i x_i + b > 0 \right), \quad s.t. \sum_{i=1}^{d_1} \alpha_i = 0 \tag{16.8}$$

As a result, to learn HOP features, we only need to focus on learning linear weights for each individual RSS value x_i, subject to a zero-sum constraint. In this case, we only need to optimize $O(d_1 \times d_2)$ parameters, which are several orders of magnitude smaller than the brute-force learning's $O(d_1^2 \times d_2)$ (as d_1 is often hundreds in practice).

16.2.4.1 Constrained restricted Boltzmann machine

Although there have been many feature learning methods, none of them can be directly applied to learn HOP features. According to Equation 16.5 and Equation 16.8, we need a generative model to learn **h**, such that: (1) each $h \in \mathbf{h}$ has a binary output, based on a δ-function of a linear transformation over the numeric input x_i's and (2) the linear transformation weights α_i's have a zero-sum constraint. These two requirements for learning **h** fail the existing feature learning methods, including classic dimensionality reduction such as principle component analysis [7], kernel methods [8,9] and deep learning such as the convolution network [10]. As a result, we propose a novel *constrained* restricted Boltzmann machine (RBM) to learn our HOP features.

First, because (Gaussian-Bernoulli) RBM [11] is well known as a generative model for feature learning with numeric input, binary output and linear mapping, we use RBM to instantiate the data likelihood $P(\mathbf{x};\mathbf{h})$ in Equation 16.5. In particular, RBM considers the data likelihood as

$$P(\mathbf{x};\mathbf{h}) = \frac{1}{Z}\sum_{\mathbf{h}} e^{-E(\mathbf{x},\mathbf{h})} \tag{16.9}$$

where $E(\mathbf{x},\mathbf{h}) = \sum_{i=1}^{d_1} \frac{(x_i-a_i)^2}{2\pi_i^2} - \sum_{j=1}^{d_2} b_j h_j - \sum_{i,j} \frac{x_i}{\pi_i} h_j w_{ij}$ is an energy function. The first term of $E(\mathbf{x},\mathbf{h})$ models a Gaussian distribution over each x_i, where a_i and π_i are the mean and standard deviation. The second term models the bias b_j for each h_j. The third term models the linear mapping between $\mathbf{x}$ and h_j. Finally, $Z = \sum_{\mathbf{x},\mathbf{h}} e^{-E(\mathbf{x},\mathbf{h})}$ is a partition function. In RBM, each h_j can be seen as $h_j = \delta(\sum_{i=1}^{d_1} \frac{x_i}{\pi_i} w_{i,j} + b_j > 0)$, and it is sampled by a conditional probability [12]:

$$P(h_j = 1|\mathbf{x}) = \sigma\left(\sum_{i=1}^{d_1} \frac{x_i}{\pi_i} w_{i,j} + b_j\right) \tag{16.10}$$

where $\sigma(r) = \frac{1}{1+e^{-r}}$ is a sigmoid function.

Second, we extend RBM to incorporate the zero-sum constraint. We emphasize that, as this zero-sum constraint guarantees robustness and it has never been studied, our constrained RBM is a novel robust feature-learning model. To take the zero-sum constraint into account, we compare Equation 16.10 and Equation 16.8, and set each $\alpha_i = \frac{1}{\pi_i} w_{ij}$. Denote the parameters as $\Theta = \{w_{ij}, a_i, b_j\}$. Finally, our robust feature learning minimizes:

$$L_1(\Theta) = -\frac{1}{n_L}\sum_{k=1}^{n_L} \log P(\mathbf{x}^{(k)}) \text{ s.t.} \sum_{i=1}^{d_1} \frac{1}{\pi_i} w_{ij} = 0, \forall j \tag{16.11}$$

As h_j is sampled by $P(h_j = 1|\mathbf{x})$, to take this uncertainty into account, we define our robust feature representation as:

$$g(\mathbf{x}) \triangleq [P(h_1 = 1|\mathbf{x}), \ldots, P(h_{d_2} = 1|\mathbf{x})] \tag{16.12}$$

As $g(\mathbf{x})$ is differentiable for Θ, Equation 16.12 also makes it possible to integrate with localization model training for getting more discriminative HOP features, as shown later.

We can prove that Equation 16.12 meets the robustness requirement in Equation 16.1. The detailed proof can be found at Ref. [13].

16.2.4.2 Integration with localization

To make our HOP features more discriminative for localization, we are inspired by Ref. [14] to consider integrating robust feature learning with location classifier

f's learning. Specifically, as we have multiple locations, we define f as a multi-class classifier and train it with the popular *one-vs-one* setting. We let $f = \{f'_{m_1,m_2} | m_1 \in \mathcal{Y}, m_2 \in \mathcal{Y}\}$, where each $f'_{m_1,m_2} = \mathbf{v}_{m_1,m_2} \cdot g(\mathbf{x})$ is a binary classifier for locations m_1 and m_2, with $\mathbf{v}_{m_1,m_2} \in \mathbb{R}^{d_2}$ as the parameter. We emphasize that how to best design f'_{m_1,m_2} is not the focus of this paper. For each f'_{m_1,m_2}, we generate a set of labels $\{y'_1, \ldots, y'_{n_{m_1,m_2}}\}$, where each $y'_k \in \{1, -1\}$ depends on whether an instance in D_s has its label to be m_1 or m_2. Finally, we consider a hinge loss to optimize f'_{m_1,m_2}:

$$\tilde{L}_2(f'_{m_1,m_2}) = \sum_{k=1}^{n_{m_1,m_2}} \max\left(1 - y'_k f'_{m_1,m_2}(g(\mathbf{x}^{(k)}), 0\right)$$

Given Θ for $g(\mathbf{x})$, we define the total loss for f as:

$$L_2(f;\Theta) = \sum_{m_1} \sum_{m_2: m_2 \neq m_1} \tilde{L}_2(f'_{m_1,m_2})$$

We use voting of the f'_{m_1,m_2}'s to perform the location prediction.
In all, we optimize the following objective function:

$$\min_{\Theta,f} L_1 + \lambda_2 L_2 \text{ s.t. } \sum_{i=1}^{d_1} \frac{1}{\pi_i} w_{ij} = 0, \forall j \tag{16.13}$$

where $\lambda_2 > 0$ is a parameter to tune. Recall that in Equation 16.12 we define $g(\mathbf{x})$ as differentiable to Θ, then we can optimize Equation 16.13 by doing a gradient descent on L_2. In practice, for computational convenience, we relax the constraint in Equation 16.13 as a regularization term $R_1 = \frac{1}{2}\sum_{j=1}^{d_2}\left(\sum_{i=1}^{d_1}\frac{1}{\pi_i}w_{ij}\right)^2$. Then, we optimize the regularized objective function:

$$\min_{\Theta,F} L_1 + \lambda_1 R_1 + \lambda_2 L_2 \tag{16.14}$$

In training, we optimize Equation 16.14 iteratively with Θ and F. For Θ we use contrast divergence to compute the gradient for optimization. For F we compute the subgradient for the hinge loss for optimization. Due to space limits, we skip the details.

16.3 Leverage the Web for Review Crawling

16.3.1 Cold-start challenge

To the best of our knowledge, the existing applications, such as Junaio and Navvis, require manually edited and uploaded content, to provide the content for augmented reality. However, when a new application launches, there is often

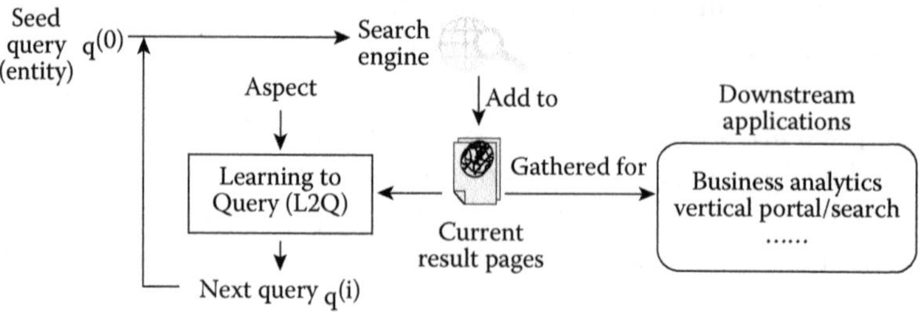

Figure 16.6: High-level flow to harvest pages for entity aspects.

very limited user-generated content (i.e., cold start), which stops people from using that application. We try to address this cold start issue by automatically crawling online content for the retailers. To avoid bias, we aim to crawl content from diverse sources from the Web and social media (e.g., public Facebook pages).

Our crawling is largely inspired by search engine users. Suppose the target is a hair salon. Users often start with a target identifier query like `salon name + branch` (e.g., "Salon Vim in Orchard"), and obtain a few initial pages. From these pages, they learn more about the salon, e.g., it is famous for some stylists. Then in the next round, users can use a stylist name (e.g., "Alice") together with the salon identifier to search for more reviews. In summary, users iteratively expand their search to gather relevant information until they run out some budget of iteration number. The key to our crawling is to ask right queries, and we aim to learn these queries automatically.

We can summarize the above iterative querying process in Figure 16.6. In each iteration, the core task is to select the best query among a pool of candidate queries based on current result pages. We call this core task *learning to query* (L2Q).

16.3.2 Our insight for learning to query

First, to select the best query, we must quantify what is considered a good query, by estimating the *utility* of each candidate query. Since the ultimate purpose of a query is to retrieve relevant pages (e.g., pages containing reviews) from the Web, the utility of a query should reflect how well it can accomplish this purpose, such as the precision and recall (or some combination of them) of the retrieved pages with respect to the target entity and aspect. Of course, the utility should be inferred *without* actually firing any candidate query.

Second, an entity does not exist in isolation. There are often a large number of peer retailers, which can reveal useful insights of the domain. Imagine we are gathering reviews for a hair salon (e.g., "Salon Vim" in Orchard). By analyzing the domain data (i.e., Web pages) of other hair salons, we can easily learn many useful patterns such as `salon name + stylist name`. We can use these useful patterns to guide what kind of queries we should choose (e.g., "Salon Vim in Orchard, Alice"), to maximize the utility. Thus, it is necessary to be *domain aware*: leveraging the domain of an entity to bootstrap at the beginning when little about the target entity is known, as well as to enhance learning during the entire querying process.

Third, a query does not exist in isolation. Multiple queries are needed to gather more target pages. That is, there exists a context of past queries that were already fired for the target retailer. Given the time, bandwidth and sometimes financial costs to query through a commercial search engine, it is imperative to become *context-aware*: accounting for the past queries to eliminate redundancy between queries. Consider an example for getting hair salon A's review. `Alice` and `service` are both useful queries on their own, but their respective top result pages from Google may overlap. Such redundancy implies that a set of individually best queries is not necessarily the best set of queries collectively. Thus, it is imperative to become *context aware*: accounting for the context of past queries to eliminate redundancy between queries.

16.3.3 Problem formulation

While a few existing crawling approaches [15–18] also use queries, they are not designed for entity aspects. Moreover, many of them have incomplete or ad hoc utility models, and often fail to leverage the domain or context. In the following, we formalize the problem of L2Q, which boils down to domain and context-aware utility inference.

Data model. We view each page and each query as a bag of words, respectively. Each word is a term or phrase depending on the tokenization. Moreover, a query can retrieve a set of pages through an information retrieval model, such as a commercial search engine.

Input. Our goal is to gather pages for a target entity, focused on a given aspect. The *target entity* is given by a *seed query* q^0 that uniquely identifies it. Note that the seed query is not only the initial query to bootstrap the entire process, but also appended to subsequent queries when submitting them to the search engine, in order to focus on the target entity.

The *target aspect* is given by a function $Y : P \rightarrow \{1, 0\}$, which maps each page $p \in P$ to relevant (1) or irrelevant (0). Essentially, we classify entity pages based on the interest. For instance, if we are only interested in researchers' RESEARCH and EDUCATION, their pages about HOBBY would be perceived as irrelevant. More generally, Y can map a page to a real-valued relevance score, but for ease of discussion we keep to the binary function for now.

Output. In each iteration of Figure 16.6, we form the candidate query set $\mathbf{Q}$ for the target entity. We then select the best query

$$q^* = \arg\max_{q \in \mathbf{Q}} \mathcal{U}^Y(q) \tag{16.15}$$

where $\mathcal{U}^Y(q)$ measures the utility of query q with respect to aspect Y. We will omit the superscript ^{Y} and only write $\mathcal{U}(*)$ hereafter to implicitly assume a target aspect Y. $\mathcal{U}(*)$ will be inferred in a domain and context-aware manner, as follows.

Subproblem 1: Domain-aware L2Q. We are given the additional input of already gathered pages of other entities in the same domain, which we call *domain pages*. Useful queries for one entity do not necessarily align with another entity in the same domain. Thus, instead of directly learning queries from domain pages, we propose to learn some "templates," which are query abstractions consistent across entities. Based on these templates, we need to further infer the utilities of candidate queries for the target entity.

Subproblem 2: Context-aware L2Q. In the ith iteration of Figure 16.6, there is a context of past queries $q^{(0)}, q^{(1)}, \ldots, q^{(i-1)}$, which were fired in previous iterations. Thus, in addition to the candidate queries themselves, we propose to account for the context of past queries, in order to capture the effect of redundancy.

16.3.4 Our model—Learning to query for cold-start review crawling

16.3.4.1 Utility inference

We hinge on the intuition of mutual reinforcement between pages and queries. In general, a "useful" page for the target aspect Y contains useful queries for Y, and a useful query can retrieve useful pages for Y. Thus, our measure of "usefulness," or utility $\mathcal{U}(*)$, will uniformly apply to both pages and queries alike. That is, for a page p and a query q, high $\mathcal{U}(p)$ implies high $\mathcal{U}(q)$ if p contains q, and vice versa. The mutuality can be formalized to relate and estimate $\mathcal{U}(p)$ and $\mathcal{U}(q)$ in a unified model.

As the first step, we must quantify the usefulness of pages and queries. Given the ultimate goal to gather pages, we can measure two complementary forms of utility: precision and recall of the retrieved pages with respect to Y. From the utilities (precision or recall) of these pages, we can further infer the corresponding utilities of related queries.

Let $\mathcal{M}$ denote a mapping from each of the following notions to a set of pages in the domain, i.e., $\mathcal{M}(*) \subseteq P$.

- $\mathcal{M}(Y)$, pages that are relevant to the target aspect Y.

- $\mathcal{M}(q)$, pages that can be retrieved by query q.
- $\mathcal{M}(p)$, the page p itself, i.e., $\mathcal{M}(p) = \{p\}$.

In Ref. [19], we develop the probabilistic precision and recall as our two utility measures, denoted $\mathcal{P}$ and $\mathcal{R}$ respectively. That is, $\mathcal{U}$ can be instantiated as either $\mathcal{P}$ or $\mathcal{R}$.

$$\mathcal{P}(v) \triangleq P(\omega \in \mathcal{M}(Y) | \omega \in \mathcal{M}(v)) \tag{16.16}$$

$$\mathcal{R}(v) \triangleq P(\omega \in \mathcal{M}(v) | \omega \in \mathcal{M}(Y)) \tag{16.17}$$

where ω is a random page from $\mathcal{M}(*)$. For brevity, we have omitted ^{Y} from the notations and only write $\mathcal{P}$ or $\mathcal{R}$, to implicitly mean that we are measuring the utilities with respect to the target aspect Y.

Interestingly, we can show that the precision of a query q is the average precision of the pages that q can retrieve, weighted by q's probability of retrieving each page, i.e.,

$$\mathcal{P}(q) = \sum_{p \in N_q} \frac{W_{p,q}}{\sum_{p' \in N_q} W_{p',q}} \mathcal{P}(p) \tag{16.18}$$

and the recall of a query q is the sum of weighted recalls of the pages that q can retrieve, such that each page only contributes a part of its recall according to its probability of being retrieved by q, i.e.,

$$\mathcal{R}(q) = \sum_{p \in N_q} \frac{W_{p,q}}{\sum_{q' \in N_p} W_{p,q'}} \mathcal{R}(p) \tag{16.19}$$

In symmetry, $\mathcal{P}(p)$ or $\mathcal{R}(p)$ can be expressed in terms of $\mathcal{P}(q)$ or $\mathcal{R}(q)$, $\forall q \in N_p$. Their derivations are similar to Equations 16.18 and 16.19.

$$\mathcal{P}(p) = \sum_{q \in N_p} \frac{W_{p,q}}{\sum_{q' \in N_p} W_{p,q'}} \mathcal{P}(q) \tag{16.20}$$

$$\mathcal{R}(p) = \sum_{q \in N_p} \frac{W_{p,q}}{\sum_{p' \in N_q} W_{p',q}} \mathcal{R}(q) \tag{16.21}$$

Regardless of precision or recall and whether for page or query, we can unify the above reinforcement rules (Equations 16.18 through 16.21) into one equation below. We have $\forall v \in V$ (where v can be either a page or a query),

$$\mathcal{U}(v) = F(\{\mathcal{U}(v') | v' \in N_v\}) \tag{16.22}$$

where F represents an aggregation function over the neighbors' utilities $\{\mathcal{U}(v') | v' \in N_v\}$, which instantiates differently for precision and recall. As a result, pages (or queries) that connect to similar neighboring queries (or pages) tend to have similar utilities.

Finally, we incorporate the page relevance as the regularization into the utility function by:

$$\mathcal{U}(v) = (1-\alpha)F(\{\mathcal{U}(v')|v' \in N_v\}) + \alpha\hat{\mathcal{U}}(v) \tag{16.23}$$

where $\hat{\mathcal{U}}(v)$ is the known utility for node v (particularly for the pages), $\alpha \in (0,1)$ is the regularization parameter, and $\hat{\mathcal{U}}(v)$ is the utility regularization for v representing either $\hat{\mathcal{P}}(v)$ or $\hat{\mathcal{R}}(v)$.

16.3.4.2 Domain-aware L2Q

As discussed earlier, an entity does not exist in isolation. There often exist many peer entities in the same domain (we call them *domain entities*). We must learn what kind of queries are useful from these domain entities, not only to bootstrap from the beginning when we know little about the target entity, but also to enhance the entire querying process.

More specifically, for a given domain we can prepare some domain entities, and further collect their pages (*domain pages*) in advance. Building upon the utility inference model, we address the subproblem of domain-aware L2Q, which naturally consists of two phases, below.

- *Domain phase (D)*. Learn what kind of queries are useful from domain pages P_D. This phase is only executed once.

- *Entity phase (E)*. Choose the best query for the target aspect of the given entity, based on both current result pages P_E and "knowledge" learned from P_D in the domain phase. This phase is executed once for every query selection (i.e., for each iteration in Figure 16.6).

Note that we use subscripts $_D$ and $_E$ to differentiate the corresponding notions in the two phases. Accordingly, we concretize Equation 16.15 to formalize domain-aware L2Q, as follows.

$$q^* = \arg\max_{q \in Q_E} \mathcal{U}_E(q|P_E, P_D) \tag{16.24}$$

where $\mathcal{U}_E(q|P_E, P_D)$ denotes that P_E, P_D are given as input, which we will henceforth omit to only write $\mathcal{U}_E(q)$ for brevity.

We bridge the domain phase and entity phase by using templates. We first define template:

Definition 16.2 Template Consider a universe of words $\mathcal{W}$, and a set of types $\mathcal{C} = \{C_1, C_2, \ldots, C_m\}$ where each type contains a subset of words, i.e., $C_i \subset \mathcal{W}$. Then, for a given *maximum query length L*, and some $\ell \leq L$,

- a *query* is a sequence of words $q = (w_1, w_2, \ldots, w_\ell)$ such that each word $w_i \in \mathcal{W}$;

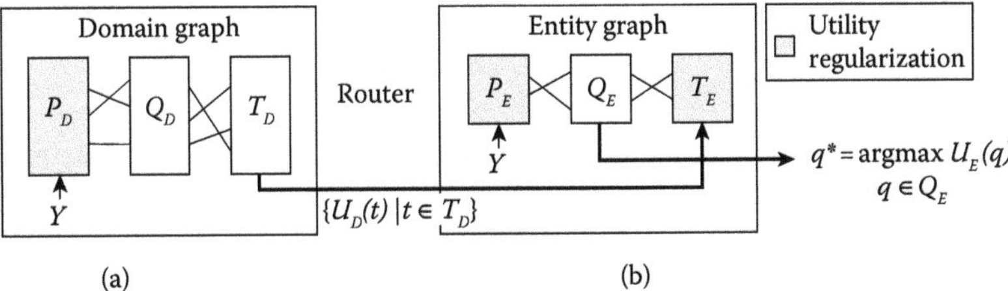

Figure 16.7: (a, b) Pipeline of domain-aware L2Q.

- a *template* is a sequence of units $t = (u_1, u_2, \ldots, u_\ell)$ such that each unit u_i is either a word $w \in \mathcal{W}$ or a type $C \in \mathcal{C}$;
- We say that t can abstract q if $w_i = u_i$ when u_i is a word, or $w_i \in u_i$ when u_i is a type, $\forall i \in \{1, \ldots, \ell\}$.

We summarize our pipeline of using domain phase and entity phase in Figure 16.7. In the domain phase, we induce useful queries Q_D from domain pages P_D, and further generalize them into templates T_D. In the entity phase, we adopt those templates T_E that also appear with the target entity to match target queries Q_E, and further regularize them with target pages P_E. In each phase, there is utility regularization for pages with respect to Y. Moreover, the utilities of templates from the domain phase, $\{\mathcal{U}_D(t) | t \in T_D\}$, provide additional regularization for the target entity, as we will elaborate in the entity phase.

Then in the domain phase, we estimate the utilities of the templates by linking templates with queries. Similar to our estimating the utilities of a query from its linked pages, we estimate the utility of a template by its linked queries. Consider a template universe T, which can be enumerated from queries with a given set of types. Denote $\mathcal{M}(t)$ as the set of pages that can be indirectly "retrieved" by a template t through any of its abstracted queries. Thus, the utility of a template can be derived as Ref. [19]:

$$\mathcal{P}(t) = \sum_{q \in N_t} \frac{\mathcal{W}_{q,t}}{\sum_{q' \in N_t} \mathcal{W}_{q',t}} \mathcal{P}(q) \tag{16.25}$$

$$\mathcal{R}(t) = \sum_{q \in N_t} \frac{\mathcal{W}_{q,t}}{\sum_{t' \in N_t q} \mathcal{W}_{q,t'}} \mathcal{R}(q) \tag{16.26}$$

Besides, since a query now can link to both templates and pages, we estimate its utility by:

$$\mathcal{P}(q) = \frac{1}{2} \sum_{t \in N_q} \frac{\mathcal{W}_{q,t}}{\sum_{t' \in N_t q} \mathcal{W}_{q,t'}} \mathcal{P}(t) + \frac{1}{2} \sum_{p \in N_q} \frac{W_{p,q}}{\sum_{p' \in N_q} W_{p',q}} \mathcal{P}(p) \tag{16.27}$$

$$\mathcal{R}(q) = \frac{1}{2}\sum_{t\in N_q}\frac{\mathcal{W}_{q,t}}{\sum_{q'\in N_t}\mathcal{W}_{q',t}}\mathcal{R}(t) + \frac{1}{2}\sum_{p\in N_q}\frac{W_{p,q}}{\sum_{q'\in N_p}W_{p,q'}}\mathcal{R}(p) \tag{16.28}$$

Finally, by incorporating the supervision in the domain data (as the pages and their relevance are known), we can estimate the utility of each $v \in \mathcal{V}$, where v can be either a page, a query, or a template:

$$\mathcal{U}_D(v) = (1-\alpha)F(\{\mathcal{U}_D(v')|v' \in N_D(v)\}) + \alpha\,\hat{\mathcal{U}}_D(v) \tag{16.29}$$

In the entity phase, we will leverage the relevance of the utilities of templates and some popular queries (we choose the queries that occur with at least 50 domain entities in our experiments) as the regularization to estimate the utilities of new queries unique to each test entity. Thus, we can estimate

$$\mathcal{U}_E(v) = (1-\alpha)F(\{\mathcal{U}_E(v')|v' \in N_E(v)\}) + \alpha\,\hat{\mathcal{U}}_E(v) \tag{16.30}$$

where $\hat{\mathcal{U}}_E(v)$ is the utility value learned from the domain data, if v is either a template or a popular query. Besides, $\hat{\mathcal{U}}_E(v)$ is the relevance score if v is a current page that has been retrieved. Therefore, based on Equation 16.27 and Equation 16.28, we estimate the utility of a candidate query from Equation 16.30. Finally, we output the query with maximum utility.

16.3.4.3 Context-aware L2Q

Due to the redundancy between queries, measuring the utility of each candidate query without accounting for the context queries is hardly promising.

Thus, we address the subproblem of context-aware L2Q: selecting the best query based on the utility of each candidate query in conjunction with the context. We further extend Equation 16.24 as follows. (As usual, we omit P_E, P_D from the utility notation for brevity.)

$$q^* = \arg\max_{q\in Q_E} \mathcal{U}_E(\mathcal{Q} \cup \{q\}|P_E, P_D) \tag{16.31}$$

In other words, we measure the *collective* utility for a set of queries consisting of both the candidate query q and the context queries $\mathcal{Q}$.

Parallel to the probabilistic utilities of one query (Equations 16.16 and 16.17), we define below the collective utilities of a set of queries probabilistically, where $\mathcal{M}(Q) \equiv \bigcup_{q\in Q}\mathcal{M}(q)$.

$$\mathcal{P}_E(\mathcal{Q}\cup\{q\}) \triangleq P(\omega \in \mathcal{M}(Y) \mid \omega \in \mathcal{M}(\mathcal{Q}\cup\{q\})) \tag{16.32}$$

$$\mathcal{R}_E(\mathcal{Q}\cup\{q\}) \triangleq P(\omega \in \mathcal{M}(\mathcal{Q}\cup\{q\}) \mid \omega \in \mathcal{M}(Y)) \tag{16.33}$$

16.3.4.4 Collective recall

We can decompose $\mathcal{R}_E(\mathcal{Q}\cup\{q\})$ into simpler components, including $\mathcal{R}_E(q)$ and $\mathcal{R}_E(\mathcal{Q})$, as well as the redundancy between q and $\mathcal{Q}$. Such a decomposition

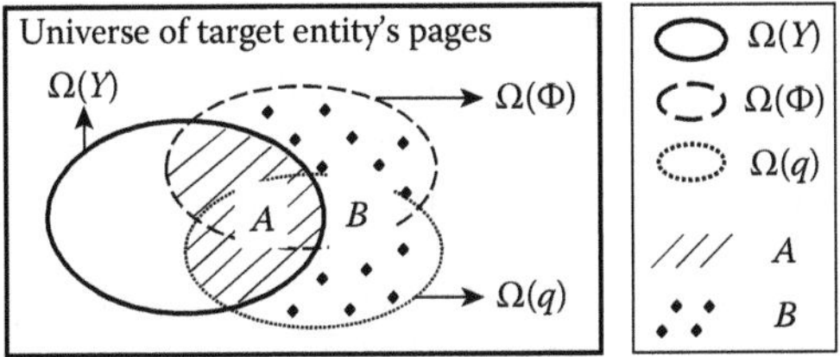

Figure 16.8: Venn diagram to illustrate collective utilities.

is desirable, because we have already established the inference of $\mathcal{R}_E(q)$ earlier, and we can compute $\mathcal{R}_E(\mathcal{Q})$ recursively using the same decomposition. Thus, to compute the collective recall, we only have to focus on minimizing the redundancy between q and $\mathcal{Q}$.

Consider the Venn diagram in Figure 16.8. We focus on three subsets that define collective utilities: (1) $\mathcal{M}(\mathcal{Q})$, pages retrieved by any query in the context $\mathcal{Q}$; (2) $\mathcal{M}(q)$, pages retrieved by a candidate query q; (3) $\mathcal{M}(Y)$, the relevant pages (i.e., pages that contain relevant information with respect to Y). These subsets interact with each other, forming subset A consisting of relevant pages by $\mathcal{Q}$ and q collectively, and subset B consisting of irrelevant pages (i.e., pages that do not contain any relevant information with respect to Y) by them collectively.

In particular, A can be aggregated from relevant pages of $\mathcal{Q}$ and those of q, if we only count their overlap (relevant pages of both $\mathcal{Q}$ and q) once. Correspondingly, $\mathcal{R}_E(\mathcal{Q} \cup \{q\})$ is the sum of $\mathcal{R}_E(\mathcal{Q})$ and $\mathcal{R}_E(q)$ if we further subtract their overlap. This intuition can be formalized and derived as below [19]:

$$\mathcal{R}_E(\mathcal{Q} \cup \{q\}) = \mathcal{R}_E(\mathcal{Q}) + \mathcal{R}_E(q) - \Delta(\mathcal{Q}, q) \tag{16.34}$$

where $\Delta(\mathcal{Q}, q)$ denotes the redundancy between $\mathcal{Q}$ and q:

$$\Delta(\mathcal{Q}, q) = P(\omega \in \mathcal{M}(\mathcal{Q}), \omega \in \mathcal{M}(q) \mid \omega \in \mathcal{M}(Y))$$

i.e., the probability that a relevant page can be retrieved by both of them. We skip the details of estimating $\Delta(\mathcal{Q}, q)$, and interested readers can refer to Ref. [19].

16.3.4.5 Collective precision

To optimize collective precision, $\mathcal{Q}$ and q should collectively retrieve many relevant pages (i.e., A in the Venn diagram), but at the same time few total pages (i.e., $A \cup B$). As our major insight, the collective precision can be decomposed into two components that correspond to A and $A \cup B$, respectively. In particular, $|A|$ is the coverage of relevant pages by $\mathcal{Q}$ and q collectively. $|A \cup B|$ is the coverage of all pages by $\mathcal{Q}$ and q collectively. Because we have known how to compute collective recall, we try to link the estimation of $|A|$ and $|A \cup B|$ with collective recall.

Specifically, $|A|$ is proportional to the collective recall of $\mathcal{Q}$ and q when we see the pages containing information of Y as relevant. $|A \cup B|$ is proportional to the collective recall of $\mathcal{Q}$ and q when we see all the pages as relevant. Thus, we can compute collective precision by way of collective recall:

$$\begin{aligned}\mathcal{P}_E(\mathcal{Q} \cup \{q\}) &\overset{1}{=} \frac{P(\omega \in \mathcal{M}(\mathcal{Q} \cup \{q\}) \mid \omega \in \mathcal{M}(Y))}{P(\omega \in \mathcal{M}(\mathcal{Q} \cup \{q\}))} P(\omega \in \mathcal{M}(Y)) \\ &\overset{2}{\propto} \frac{P(\omega \in \mathcal{M}(\mathcal{Q} \cup \{q\}) \mid \omega \in \mathcal{M}(Y))}{P(\omega \in \mathcal{M}(\mathcal{Q} \cup \{q\})) \mid \omega \in \mathcal{M}(Y^*))} \\ &\overset{3}{=} \frac{\mathcal{R}_E(\mathcal{Q} \cup \{q\})}{\mathcal{R}_E^{(Y^*)}(\mathcal{Q} \cup \{q\})}\end{aligned} \tag{16.35}$$

where $\mathcal{R}_E(\mathcal{Q} \cup \{q\})$ is the recall of $\mathcal{Q} \cup \{q\}$ for retrieving relevant pages; $\mathcal{R}_E^{(Y^*)}(\mathcal{Q} \cup \{q\})$ is the recall of $\mathcal{Q} \cup \{q\}$ for retrieving all the possible pages (regardless of being relevant or irrelevant). $\mathcal{R}_E(\mathcal{Q} \cup \{q\})$ is estimated by Equation 16.34, and $\mathcal{R}_E^{(Y^*)}(\mathcal{Q} \cup \{q\})$ can be estimated similarly, except that the target pages set becomes all the possible pages.

16.4 System Evaluation

16.4.1 Evaluation with wireless network-based localization

Data sets: We use two public real-world data sets HKUST data set [4] and MIT data set* [20], as shown in Tables 16.1 and 16.2. For each data set, we follow the previous work [4,20] to choose the source device S and the target devices T's. Totally, we have four pairs of heterogeneous devices for experiments: (1) $S = \text{T43}, T = \text{T60}$, (2) $S = \text{N810}, T = \text{D901C}$, (3) $S = \text{N810}, T = \text{N95}$, (4) $S = \text{N810}, T = \text{X61}$.

In each pair of devices, for S, we randomly selected 50% of its data at each location as the labeled training data. We used the other 50% of S's data as test data in Figure 16.4 to demonstrate the device heterogeneity. For T, we used 100% of its data as test data. We repeated the above process five times, and report results with mean and standard deviation (depicted as error bars in Figure 16.9).

Baselines: As our cold-start problem requires no data from the target domain, in the experiment we only compare with the baselines that also fall into this setting. First, we compare with SVM [5], which ignores device heterogeneity. Second, we compare with several transfer learning methods that require no data from the target device, including HLF [21] and ECL [22], as discussed in our related work section.

*We do not use the devices N810(2) and EEE900A due to their low heterogeneity to N810 as reported in Ref. [20].

Table 16.1 Description for our data sets

	#(SAMPLE)	#(LOC.)	#(AP)	#(DEVICE)	ENVIRONMENT
HKUST	4,280	107	118	2	$64m \times 50m$
MIT	13,658	18	202	4	$39m \times 30m$

Table 16.2 Description for the devices

	DEVICE	CATEGORY	WIRELESS CHIPSET	ROLE
HKUST	T43	IBM laptop	Intel PRO/W 2200BG	Source
	T60	IBM laptop	Intel PRO/W 3495BG	Target
MIT	N810	Nokia phone	Conexant CX3110X	Source
	X61	IBM laptop	Intel 4965AGN	Target
	D901C	Clevo laptop	Intel 5300AGN	Target
	N95	Nokia phone	TI OMAP2420	Target

Evaluation metric: Following the convention of localization study [3,23,24], we evaluated the *accuracy under an error distance* (i.e., the accuracy when the prediction is within a certain distance to its ground truth). We will study the impact of error distance later in Figure 16.9a. Unless specified, we set the error distance as 4 meters in evaluation.

Comparison with Baselines: We first compare with the baselines by using all the training data of S, and evaluate the localization accuracy under different error distances. As shown in Figure 16.9a, our model is consistently better than the baselines. Besides, we compare with the baselines by using different amount of training data from S, and evaluate the localization accuracy under a 4-meter error distance. As shown in Figure 16.9b, our model is also in general consistently better than the baselines. In summary, by using all the training data of S and under the error distance of 4 meters, our model can achieve 23.1%–91.3% accuracy improvement than the best baseline (i.e., ECL) across different pairs of devices. Such improvements are all statistically significant—according to our student t-tests, the one-tailed test $p_1 < 0.01$.

Our model is better than SVM, as we address device heterogeneity by robust feature learning. Our model is better than HLT, because HLT only uses pairwise RSS ratio features, which are not discriminative (as we discussed in the example of Figure 16.5) and are sensitive to the RSS values. In fact, we observe that HLT is sometimes even worse than SVM. Our model is also better than ECL, since ECL is still limited in using pairwise comparison (in contrast with our using higher-order pairwise features). Finally, we emphasize both HLT and ECL lack robustness guarantee as we do.

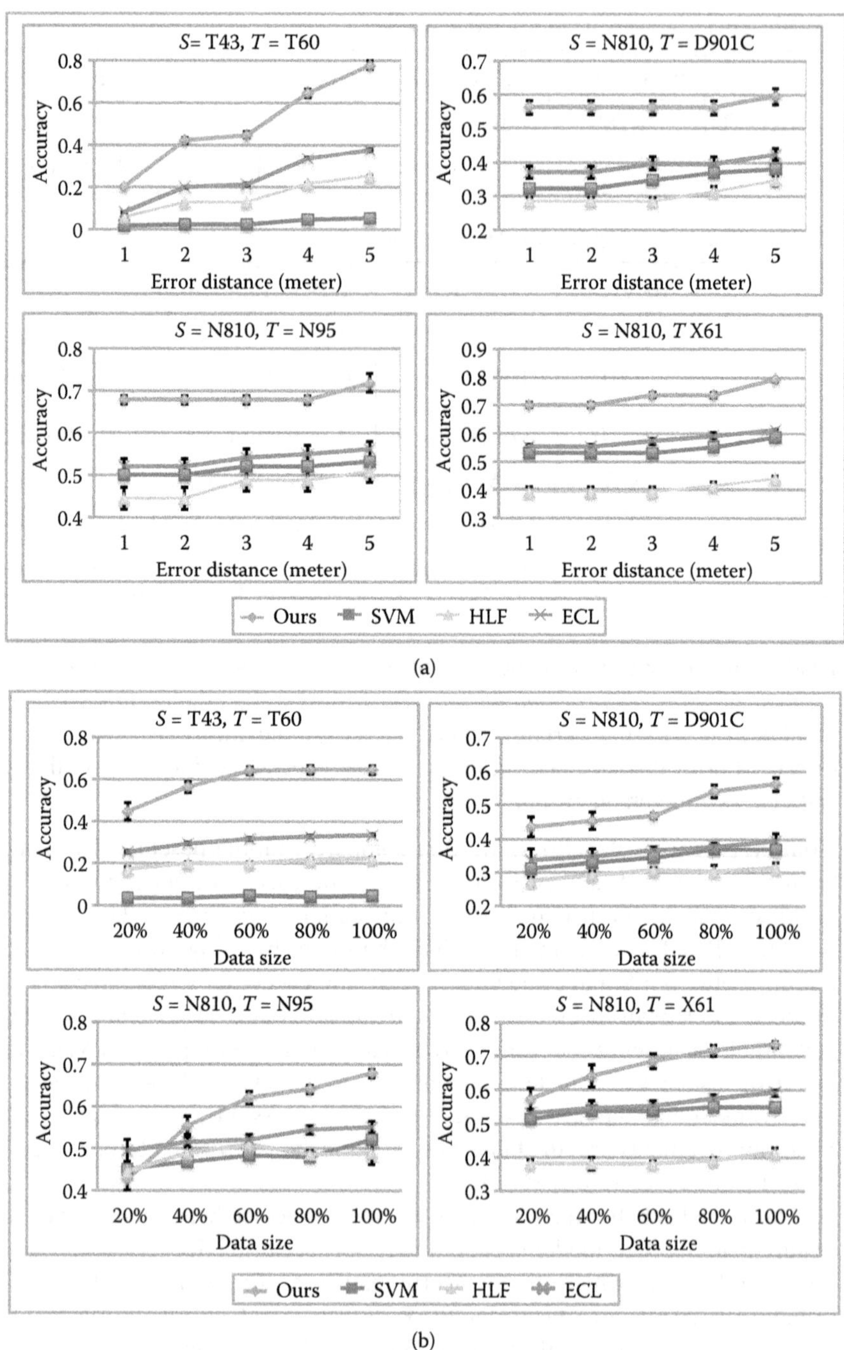

Figure 16.9: Comparison with baselines. (a) Impact of error distance and (b) impact of training data size.

16.4.2 Evaluation with web-based review crawling

Data sets: For reproducibility, we conduct experiments over a corpus collected from the Web in advance, and all queries will retrieve pages from this corpus only. We prepared data sets for two domains: *researchers* and *cars*. To retrieve pages from the corpora, we used a language model with Dirichlet smoothing [25] as the search engine. For each query, pages in the corpus are ranked and the top five are returned. As such, we can measure the performance of our approach against an ideal but otherwise infeasible solution (to be explained in evaluation methodology).

To construct the types for enumerating templates, we resorted to three options. First, we constructed a dictionary to map a keyword or phrase to a type based on Freebase* and Microsoft Academic Search (MAS),† such as mapping "data mining" to `topic`. Freebase is an open and general database containing a huge number of types across many different domains. Thus, we can rely on it to devise templates for many real-world applications. In addition, we used MAS to supplement types for the researcher domain. Second, we relied on Stanford CoreNLP [26] to recognize the named entities as types, such as `organization`, `person` and `location`. Third, we devised regular expressions to tag well-formed texts, such as `phonenum`, `url` and `email`.

We tested seven target aspects (Y's) on each domain as shown in Table 16.3. To enable finer granularity of evaluation, we segmented each page into paragraphs, and we looked at the relevance of each paragraph with respect to each given Y. (Note that query selection is independent with the retrieval units used.) Specifically, we trained one classifier for each Y based on conditional random fields, which can classify a paragraph as relevant to Y or not. Our aspect classifiers can achieve a high level of accuracy on both domains as shown in Table 16.3, and thus their output is taken as the ground truth.

Table 16.3 Entity aspects and accuracy of their classifiers

Researchers			Cars		
Aspects	**Frequency**	**Accuracy**	**Aspects**	**Frequency**	**Accuracy**
BIOGRAPHY	8K	0.99	VERDICT	7K	0.91
PRESENTATION	10K	0.99	INTERIOR	7K	0.96
AWARD	11K	0.97	EXTERIOR	5K	0.97
RESEARCH	107K	0.85	PRICE	8K	0.92
EDUCATION	11K	0.99	RELIABILITY	2K	0.97
EMPLOYMENT	3K	0.94	SAFETY	2K	0.99
CONTACT	7K	0.97	DRIVING	16K	0.89

*https://www.freebase.com/

†http://academic.research.microsoft.com/

To enumerate candidate queries from a page, we first tokenize the page into words. Each word is either a single keyword, or a phrase (e.g., "data mining") that can be mapped to a type. Subsequently, we applied a sliding window of ℓ words over the page for each $\ell \in \{1,2,\ldots,L\}$. Note that L is the maximum query length in Definition 16.2. The ℓ words in each window are taken as a candidate query. In particular, we set $L = 3$, i.e., only queries containing 1, 2, or 3 words are enumerated from pages. This maximum length is generally sufficient to capture various semantic units, as choosing a larger value for L results in no notable improvement in the effectiveness, but increases the query space and thus computational cost.

Evaluation methodology. In each domain, we randomly reserved half of the entities as domain entities, and the remaining as target entities. One of our experiments also varied the number of domain entities used to showcase the effect of domain size. Target entities were further divided into two equal splits, such that one of the splits is reserved for parameter validation, and the other for testing. We repeated the split randomly, 10 times.

On the testing set, we evaluate the retrieved pages in terms of their actual precision and recall (and eventually F-score) for every target entity and aspect. We then normalize the results against an *ideal* solution, for two reasons. First, as different entities entail varying degrees of difficulty, normalization makes results comparable across entities. Second, the ideal solution, which supposedly achieves a performance upper bound, enables us to evaluate the actual gap with the best achievable performance. Note that, for each entity, the same normalization factor is applied to all methods (i.e., our approach and the baselines) without biasing toward any method—a better method is still better after normalization.

We thus design an ideal solution as the upper bound to measure against. Ideally, we would select queries that cover as many relevant pages as possible, and achieve a high precision over the covered pages. We then select queries to maximize the product of their *actual* coverage and precision, which can be obtained by feeding each candidate query to the search engine. Thus, it is clearly infeasible in real applications, and only acts as a performance upper bound for normalization.

Given multiple target entities and test splits, we report the average results over all entities and splits. We further average the results across aspects, omitting the detailed performance for every aspect due to space constraints.

Settings. In the experiments, we varied the number of queries (i.e., number of iterations in Figure 16.6) between 2 and 5, excluding the initial seed query. When we do not mention the number of queries used, our default is set as 3. We selected the seed query parameter r_0 by cross validating on the validation set. We set the regularization parameter to $\alpha = 0.15$ in Equation 16.23, which is a typical value robust to random walks on most graphs. Lastly, we set the adaption parameter $\lambda = 10$, which turns out to be generally effective and stable in our experiments.

Effect of domain and context awareness. We first validate the significance of the two subproblems, namely, domain-aware and context-aware L2Q. Thus, we devised and compared several strategies below, in order to highlight the usefulness of the domain entities and the context queries. As we proposed two measures of utility, namely precision $\mathcal{P}$ and recall $\mathcal{R}$, each strategy (except the random method RND) has two variants: one optimizes $\mathcal{P}$ and the other optimizes $\mathcal{R}$. We then evaluate each variant using the metric that it intends to optimize.

- RND, which randomly selects a query from all the candidates, to establish a reference point for other strategies.
- P or R, which optimizes precision or recall as Section 16.3.4 discussed, i.e., without domain and context awareness.
- P+q or R+q, which directly uses *queries* (+q) of best precision or recall learned from the domain phase, to show the problem of entity variations.
- P+t or R+t, which optimizes precision or recall with *template*-based learning (+t), but without context awareness.
- L2QP or L2QR, which optimizes precision or recall with both domain and context awareness (i.e., the full approach).

Domain awareness. The results in Figure 16.10 demonstrate that, while domain entities can be beneficial to L2Q, we must employ templates according to entity variations. Evidently, P+t is superior to P in precision, given that P+t learn from domain entities with templates and P does not utilize the domain at all. Similarly, R+t outperforms R in recall for the same reason. However, if we do not abstract queries into templates, we cannot leverage the domain to the fullest

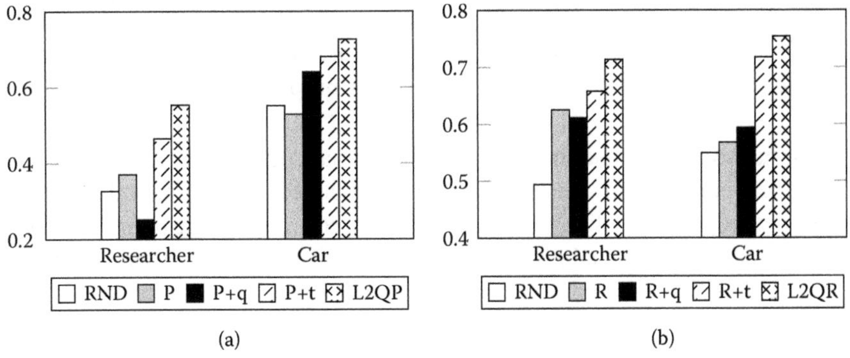

Figure 16.10: Validation of domain and context awareness: (a) comparison of precision and (b) comparison of recall.

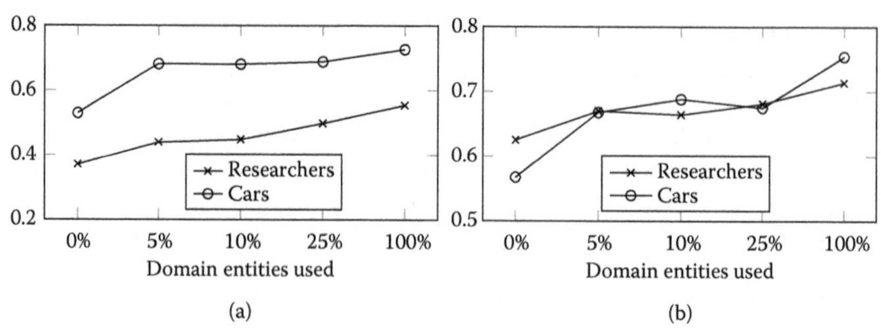

Figure 16.11: Effect of domain size on full approaches: (a) precision for L2QP and (b) recall for L2QR.

extent. In particular, P+q directly uses queries with the best precision among domain entities, but its performance is worse than the template-based P+t. We observe a similar outcome between R+q and R+t in recall. That means, entity variations do exist and it is necessary to adopt templates. Naturally, when entity variations are more severe, P+q and R+q could even become worse than P and R, as in the case of "researchers."

We also investigate the effect of domain size. As reported in Figure 16.11, we use between 0% and 100% domain entities. In general, using more domain entities results in better precision for L2QP and better recall for L2QR. The improvement is especially substantial when we increase from 0% to 5%, meaning that even a small number of domain entities can be quite useful.

Context awareness. The results also show that it is important to account for the past queries through collective utilities. In Figure 16.10, our full approach L2QP outperforms P+t in precision. Note that both L2QP and P+t learn from domain entities through templates, but L2QP is aware of the context of past queries whereas P+t is not. Likewise, L2QR is superior to R+t in terms of recall.

Comparison with baselines. We further compare our approaches L2QP, L2QR, and their combination (to obtain a balance between precision and recall) with four independent baselines below. The first three baselines are *algorithmic* methods adapted from related problems, since there is no previous work on our exact setting. The fourth baseline is a *manual* approach based on a user study.

- *Language Model* (LM), based on the language feedback model [27]. In each iteration, it chooses the query with maximum likelihood on the k most relevant current pages. In particular, we use $k = 1$, which results in the best performance on our corpora.

- *Adaptive Querying* (AQ), based on the adaptive query selection policy [18]. It was designed to crawl text databases, using query statistics adaptive to the current results. As it lacks the notion of relevance, to adopt it for our purpose the query statistics are only computed over relevant pages instead of all pages.

- *Harvest Rate* (HR), based on the harvest rate heuristic [15]. It was originally meant for crawling structured databases, using query statistics from current results and domain data. We first modify its query and record model as a bag of words, and incorporate the notion of relevance just as we did for AQ. We then apply templates: the statistics of each query are computed as the average over its templates. (We only use templates in HR but not the others, since only HR exploits domain data.)

- *Manual Querying* (MQ), based on human designed queries. For each domain and aspect, we asked nine graduate students to provide five queries that they would use to search for the target entity aspect. For instance, for researchers' AWARD aspect, sample queries given by the user study include "award," "distinguished," "award won," and so on. We observed that there is generally good interuser agreement, and thus only report the average performance of the users. Note that manually designing queries that are specific to each entity does not scale up, and thus is not a viable baseline in real-world applications.

Precision and recall. We first compare L2QP and L2QR to the baselines in terms of precision and recall, with varying number of queries (i.e., iterations). The results are reported in Figure 16.12.

In terms of precision as Figure 16.12a shows that L2QP achieves the best performance, surpassing not only the baselines, but also L2QR, since L2QP is designed to optimize precision. This observation is consistent in both domains across different numbers of queries. On average, L2QP outperforms the best algorithmic baselines by 28%, and beats the manual baseline by 14%. Note that, as we use more queries, L2QP and MQ tend to suffer a minor decrease in precision since there only a limited number of pages exist that are relevant to the target aspect of each entity.

In terms of recall as Figure 16.12b shows, L2QR likewise outperforms all the other methods, as it is designed to optimize recall. On average, L2QR outperforms the best algorithmic baseline by 11%, and beats the manual baseline by 14%.

Combining L2QP **and** L2QR. Although L2QP and L2QR perform the best in their corresponding utilities, we often seek a trade-off in the real world, which is usually measured by the F-score. Therefore, we combined the collective precision score from L2QP and the collective recall score from L2QR into a collective F1 score by $\mathcal{F}_1(\mathcal{Q} \cup q) = \frac{2\times\mathcal{P}(\mathcal{Q}\cup q)\times\mathcal{R}(\mathcal{Q}\cup q)}{\mathcal{P}(\mathcal{Q}\cup q)+\mathcal{R}(\mathcal{Q}\cup q)}$. This results in a new query

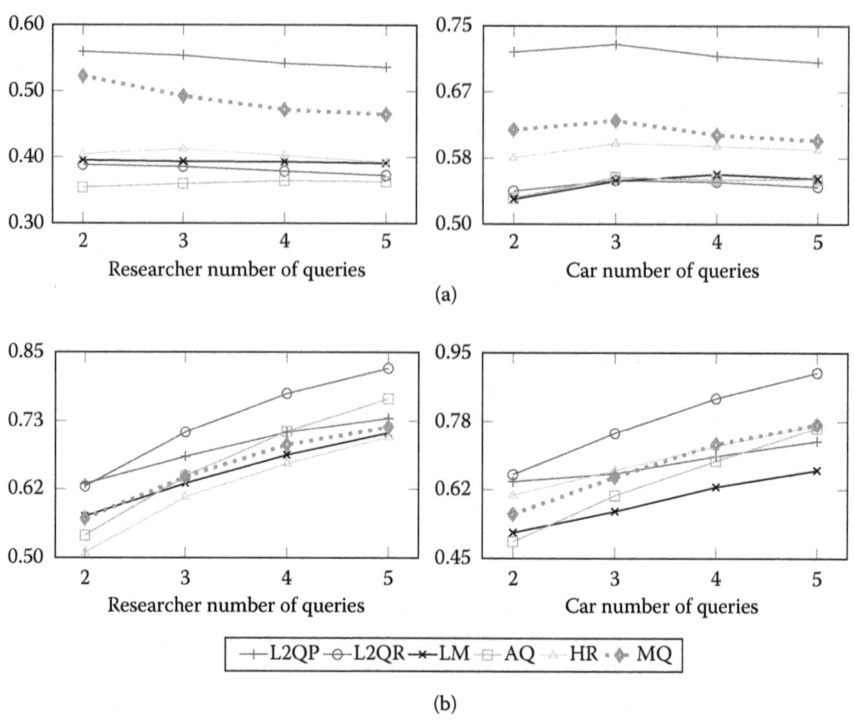

Figure 16.12: Comparison of (a) precision and (b) recall.

selection method L2QBAL that balances precision and recall. Specifically, we select queries based on the geometric mean of the collective precision and recall. We do not optimize the harmonic mean given that our utilities are probabilistic in nature, which means the estimated precision and recall have incomparable scales.

We verified that L2QBAL indeed outperforms L2QP and L2QR in F-score. Subsequently, we compare L2QBAL with the baselines in terms of F-score. As shown in Figure 16.13, L2QBAL is consistently better than all the baselines for various numbers of queries. On average, it beats the best algorithmic baseline by 16%, and exceeds the manual baseline by 10%. In other words, it is feasible to combine L2QP and L2QR. As L2QBAL is only a trivial combination, we expect that a more thorough and principled approach would give even better results, which is left to future work.

16.4.3 Evaluation of IntelligShop system in a real-world test-bed

We deployed IntelligShop in a real mall of Singapore, as shown in Figure 16.14. Take the first floor of the mall as an example. The public space outside the retailers is 45×36 m^2. It has in total six retailers, and it is equipped with WiFi.

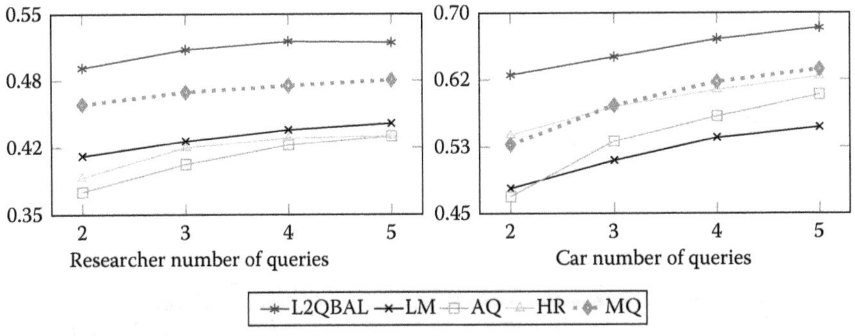

Figure 16.13: Comparison of F-scores with balanced strategy.

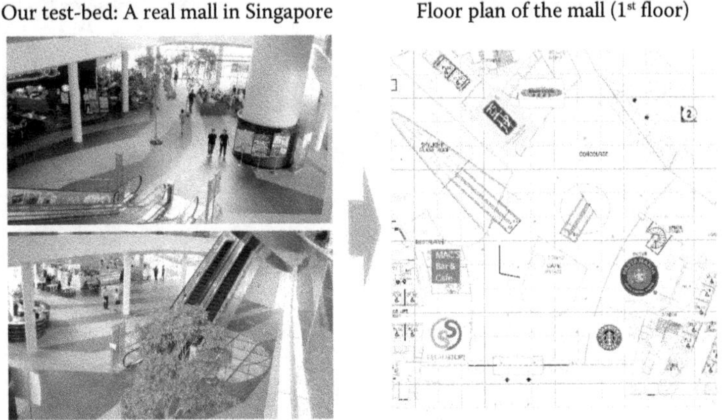

Figure 16.14: A real mall in Singapore.

For the client side, IntelligShop is published as an Android app. We consider that the user already has the IntelligShop app installed on their smartphone. The phone is equipped with basic sensors (i.e., WiFi, camera, and compass) and is able to connect to the Internet (for connecting to the IntelligShop backend server). The user is in a mall, interested in getting reviews about the retailers. In the following, we describe how the user will interact with the IntelligShop app.

1. The user starts the IntelligShop app, and points the phone camera toward the interested retailer(s), as shown in Figure 16.15a.

2. The user will see some text boxes with the retailers' names on the screen. Hopefully, each retailer name appears right in front of its corresponding

retailer in the camera. For example, as shown in Figure 16.15b, a text box "PastaMania" appears in front of the real Pastamania restaurant.

3. The user can click on any retailer name to see its reviews, as shown in Figure 16.15c. Each review consists of: (1) a star rating based on the content sentiment, (2) a URL indicating where this review comes from,

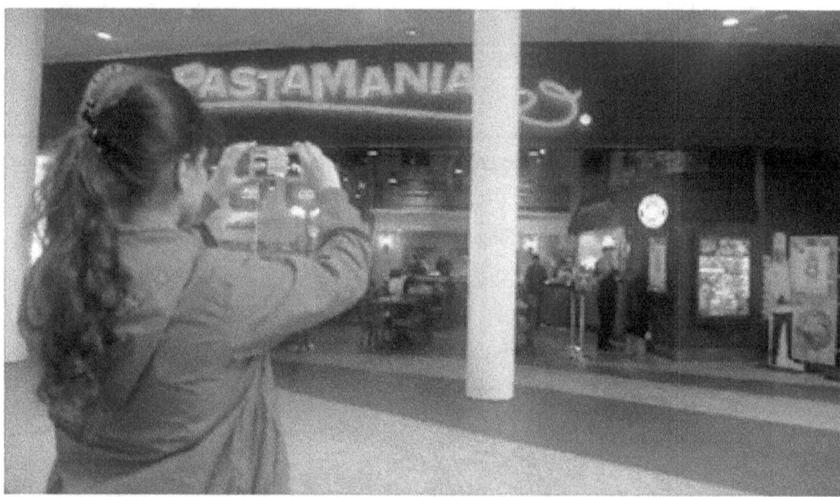

(a)

(b)

Figure 16.15: Using the IntelligShop in a real mall of Singapore: (a) user faces the camera to the retailer, (b) retailers are recognized. *(Continued)*

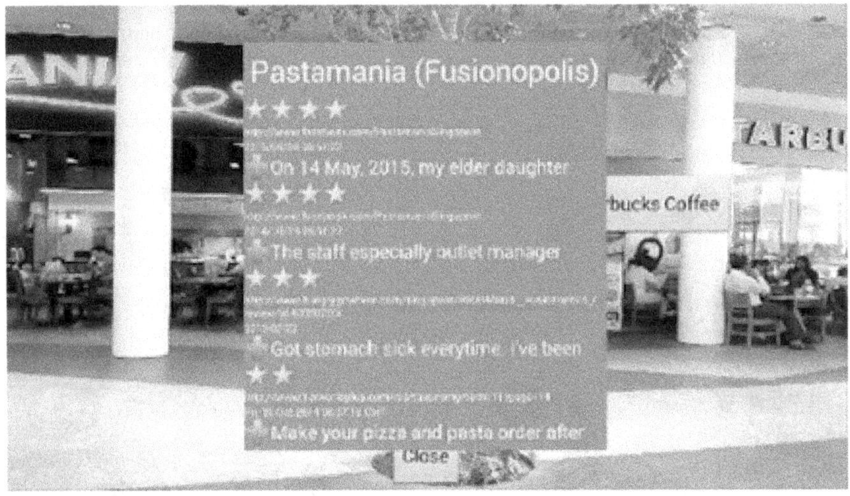

(c)

(d)

Figure 16.15 (Continued): Using the IntelligShop in a real mall of Singapore: (c) user clicks to see the reviews, and (d) retailers change as the camera moves.

(3) a piece of review content (displayed in a collapse view, and the user can click the "+" button to unfold the content).

4. The user can stop the app, or continue to move the camera to check for other retailers, which goes back to Step 2. As the camera moves, the IntelligShop will automatically add the retailers that newly appear in the camera and remove the retailers that are no longer visible in the camera.

For localization, we sampled 16 locations and used a Samsung S3 phone to collect data. The localization model was built and tested with a Samsung S4 phone. According to our experiments, our wireless network localization algorithm can achieve a 73% absolute localization accuracy under a 7-meter

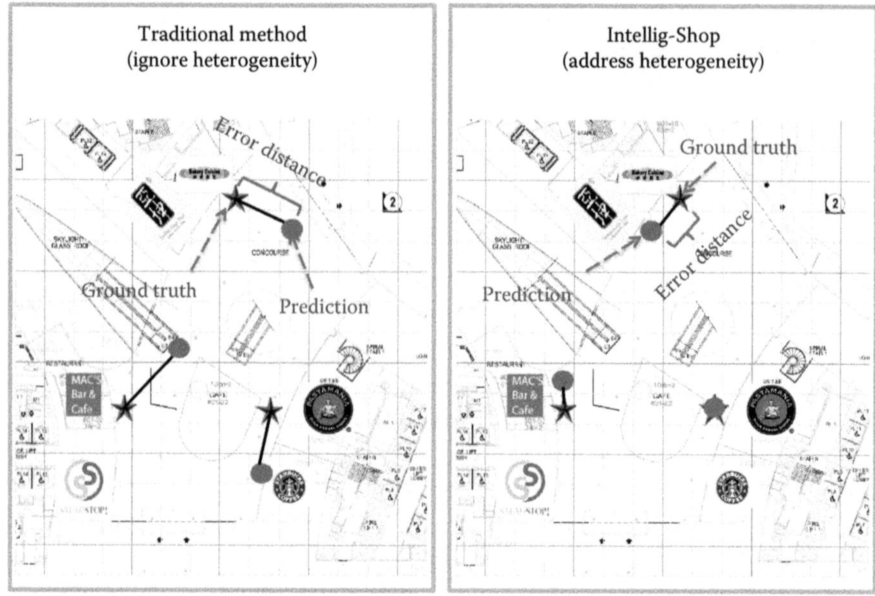

Figure 16.16: Localization result demonstration in the mall.

error distance,* and a 34% relative localization accuracy improvement from the traditional baseline method SVM, which ignores the device heterogeneity. A demonstration of the localization result comparison is given in Figure 16.16.

For review crawling, we gathered reviews for the six retailers. Figure 16.17 shows the reviews we crawled for a restaurant retailer "Pastamaina" in the mall. Our reviews for that restaurant are crawled from diverse online sources, including social media (13%), review sites (25%), forums (37%) and blogs (25%). This helps demonstrate the advantage of our review crawling algorithm in generating more representative reviews from versatile sources than from a single dedicated source.

16.5 Conclusion and Future Work

We presented IntelligShop, a novel location-based augmented reality application that uses network data to enable intelligent shopping in the malls. IntelligShop provides a good demonstration of: (1) the usefulness of the ubiquitous network data and (2) the nontriviality of turning the real-world network data into useful applications. Technically, we manage to address two challenging network data mining problems in IntelligShop: (1) robust feature learning in the

*We choose 7 meters, because 85% of our test locations are farther than 7 meters from each other.

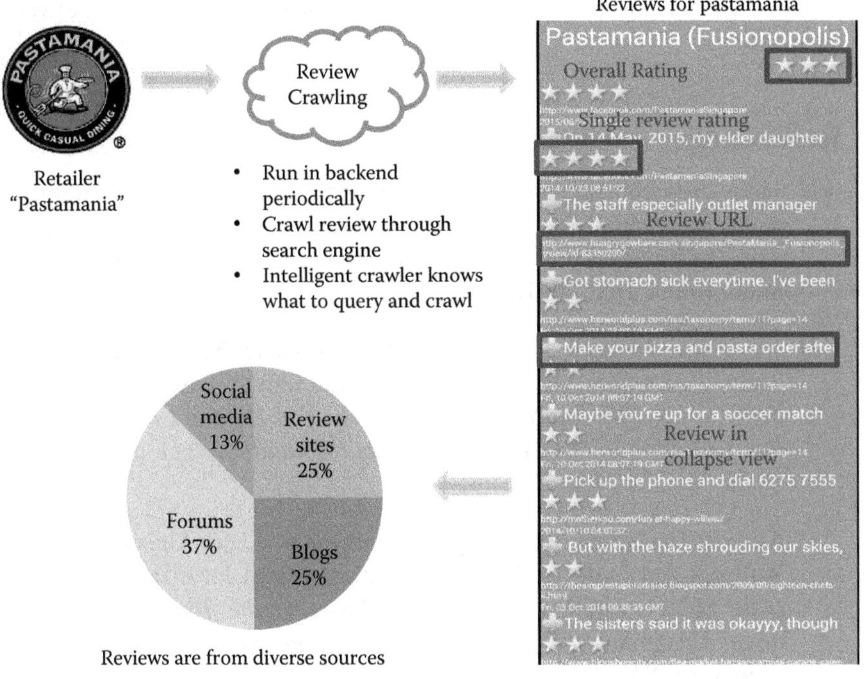

Figure 16.17: Review demonstration for a retailer in the mall.

cold-start heterogeneous-device localization with the wireless network data and (2) learning to query in the cold-start retailer content gathering from the Web. We empirically evaluate our solutions to these two network data mining tasks with many real-world data sets. For the wireless network localization task, we achieve 23.1%–91.3% relative accuracy improvement than the best baseline across different pairs of heterogeneous devices. For the Web crawling task, we achieve on average 16% relative F1-score improvement than the best algorithmic baseline, and 10% relative F1-score improvement than the manual baseline. We also deployed IntelligShop in a test-bed established in a real mall of Singapore. We showed how to achieve a 34% relative localization accuracy improvement over the baseline ignoring the device heterogeneity, and collected reviews from versatile Web sources, including social media, blogs, forums and review sites.

In the future, we plan to investigate deeper into the network data along the following directions: (1) solve the wireless network's data sensitivity to the time and the environment change; (2) combine different approaches to access the Web in a more effective manner (e.g., we can access the Web not only through search engine queries, but also through URL links on the Internet and various APIs on social media); and (3) explore the possibility to incorporate other types of network data such as bluetooth network (e.g., iBeacon) and cellular network in localization.

References

[1] Junho Ahn and Richard Han. Rescue me: An indoor mobile augmented-reality evacuation system by personalized pedometry. In *Proc. of IEEE Asia-Pacific Services Computing Conference (APSCC)*, pages 70–77, Jeju, South Korea, Dec. 2011.

[2] Alessandro Mulloni, Hartmut Seichter, and Dieter Schmalstieg. Handheld augmented reality indoor navigation with activity-based instructions. In *Proc. of the 13th International Conference on Human Computer Interaction with Mobile Devices and Services (MobileHCI '11)*, pages 211–220, Stockholm, Sweden, 2011.

[3] Andreas Haeberlen, Eliot Flannery, Andrew M. Ladd, Algis Rudys, Dan S. Wallach, and Lydia E. Kavraki. Practical robust localization over large-scale 802.11 wireless networks. In *Proc. of the 10th Annual International Conference on Mobile Computing and Networking*, pages 70–84, New York, NY, 2004.

[4] Vincent W. Zheng, Sinno J. Pan, Qiang Yang, and Jeffrey J. Pan. Transferring multi-device localization models using latent multi-task learning. In *Proc. of the 23rd AAAI Conference on Artificial Intelligence*, AAAI '08, pages 1427–1432, Chicago, IL, 2008.

[5] Chih-Chung Chang and Chih-Jen Lin. Libsvm: A library for support vector machines. *ACM Trans. Intell. Syst. Technol.*, 2(3):27:1–27:27, May 2011.

[6] Theodore S. Rappaport. *Wireless communications: Principles and practice.* Prentice Hall PTR, Upper Saddle River, NJ, 1999.

[7] Ian Jolliffe. *Principal component analysis.* 2nd Edition, Springer-Verlag, New York, 2002.

[8] Jiayuan Huang, Alex Smola, Arthur Gretton, Karsten M. Borgwardt, and Bernhard Schölkopf. Correcting sample selection bias by unlabeled data. In *Advances in Neural Information Processing Systems 20*, NIPS '07, pages 601–608, Vancouver, B.C., Canada, 2007.

[9] Kai Zhang, Vincent W. Zheng, Qiaojun Wang, James Kwok, Qiang Yang, and Ivan Marsic. Covariate shift in hilbert space: A solution via surrogate kernels. In *Proc. of the 30th International Conference on Machine learning*, ICML '13, pages 388–395, Atlanta, GA, 2013.

[10] Alex Krizhevsky, Ilya Sutskever, and Geoffrey E. Hinton. Imagenet classification with deep convolutional neural networks. In *Advances in Neural Information Processing Systems 25*, NIPS '12, pages 1097–1105, Lake Tahoe, Nevada, 2012.

[11] Geoffrey Hinton. *A practical guide to training restricted boltzmann machines*. Technical report, University of Toronto, 2010.

[12] Alex Krizhevsky and Geoffrey Hinton. *Learning multiple layers of features from tiny images*. Technical report, Computer Science Department, University of Toronto, 2009.

[13] Vincent W. Zheng, Hong Cao, Shenghua Gao, Aditi Adhikari, Miao Lin, and Kevin Chen-Chuan Chang. Cold-start heterogeneous-device wireless localization. In *Proc. of the 30th AAAI Conference on Artificial Intelligence*, pages 1429–1435, Phoenix, AZ, 2016.

[14] Jason Weston, Frédéric Ratle, and Ronan Collobert. Deep learning via semi-supervised embedding. In *Proc. of the 25th International Conference on Machine Learning*, ICML '08, pages 1168–1175, Helsinki, Finland, 2008.

[15] Ping Wu, Ji-Rong Wen, Huan Liu, and Wei-Ying Ma. Query selection techniques for efficient crawling of structured web sources. In *Proc. of IEEE 22nd International Conference on Data Engineering*, pages 47, Atlanta, GA, 2006.

[16] William W Cohen and Yoram Singer. Learning to query the Web. In *AAAI Workshop on Internet-Based Information Systems*, pages 16–25, Portland, Oregon, 1996.

[17] Eugene Agichtein and Luis Gravano. Querying text databases for efficient information extraction. In *Proc. of IEEE 19th International Conference on Data Engineering*, pages 113–124, Bangalore, India, 2003.

[18] Petros Zerfos, Junghoo Cho, and Alexandros Ntoulas. Downloading textual hidden web content through keyword queries. In *Proc. of the 5th ACM/IEEE-CS Joint Conference on Digital Libraries*, pages 100–109, Denver, CO, 2005.

[19] Yuan Fang, Vincent W. Zheng, and Kevin Chen-Chuan Chang. Learning to query: Focused web page harvesting for entity aspects. In *Proc. of IEEE Interantional Conference on Data Engineering*, pages 1002–1013, Helsinki, Finland, 2016.

[20] Jun-Geun Park, Dorothy Curtis, Seth J. Teller, and Jonathan Ledlie. Implications of device diversity for organic localization. In *Proc. 30th IEEE*

International Conference on Computer Communications, INFOCOM '11, pages 3182–3190, Shanghai, China, 2011.

[21] Mikkel Baun Kjaergaard and Carsten Valdemar Munk. Hyperbolic location fingerprinting: A calibration-free solution for handling differences in signal strength. In *Proc. of 6th Annual IEEE International Conference on Pervasive Computing and Communications*, PerCom '08, pages 110–116, Hong Kong, 2008.

[22] Kiran Yedavalli, Bhaskar Krishnamachari, Sharmila Ravula, and Bhaskar Srinivasan. Ecolocation: A sequence based technique for RF localization in wireless sensor networks. In *Proc. of the Fourth International Symposium on Information Processing in Sensor Networks*, IPSN '05, pages 285–292, Los Angeles, CA, 2005.

[23] Hyuk Lim, Lu-Chuan Kung, Jennifer C. Hou, and Haiyun Luo. Zero-configuration, robust indoor localization: Theory and experimentation. In *Proc. of the 25th IEEE International Conference on Computer Communications*, INFOCOM '06, pages 1–12, Barcelona, Catalunya, Spain, 2006.

[24] Nuo Xu, Kian Hsiang Low, Jie Chen, Keng Kiat Lim, and Etkin Baris Ozgul. Gp-localize: Persistent mobile robot localization using online sparse gaussian process observation model. In *Proc. of the 28th AAAI Conference on Artificial Intelligence*, AAAI '14, pages 2585–2593, Quebec City, Quebec, Canada, 2014.

[25] Chengxiang Zhai and John Lafferty. A study of smoothing methods for language models applied to ad hoc information retrieval. In *Proc. of the 24th Annual International ACM SIGIR Conference*, pages 334–342, New Orleans, LA, 2001.

[26] Christopher D. Manning, Mihai Surdeanu, John Bauer, Jenny Finkel, Steven J. Bethard, and David McClosky. The Stanford CoreNLP natural language processing toolkit. In *ACL: System Demonstrations*, pages 55–60, Baltimore, Maryland, 2014.

[27] Chengxiang Zhai and John Lafferty. Model-based feedback in the language modeling approach to information retrieval. In *Proc. of the 10th International Conference on Information and Knowledge Management*, pages 403–410, Atlanta, GA, 2001.

Chapter 17

Toward Practical Anomaly Detection in Network Big Data

Chengqiang Huang, Yulei Wu, Zuo Yuan, and Geyong Min

University of Exeter
Exeter, United Kingdom

CONTENTS

17.1 Introduction

With the advent of the 21st century, different kinds of networks, e.g., data centers, mobile networks, sensor networks, etc., have witnessed unprecedented demands from network users. As concrete examples, the desire for faster downloading, the expectation of stable video calls, etc. have never stopped since the popularization of personal digital devices. The proliferation of Internet users and mobile users has excited a tremendous number of network applications and services, which greatly boost the generation of different data in various aspects of the networks. For instance, the intense utilization and periodical maintenance of the networks have led to the rocketing amount of heterogeneous network operational data, e.g., performance metrics, device logs, and network topology, which could be generated in the magnitude of gigabyte per second, terabyte per second, or even higher according to specific networks. As we notice, this simple example has revealed the three salient aspects of the network big data, i.e., the tremendous *volume*, the unpredicted *velocity*, and the enormous *variety*.

Under the presence of network big data, a network administrator could still maintain the conservative position and follow traditional ways of running the network regardless of the immense potential value that the data brings. Nevertheless, to automatize the operation of the network and gain network intelligence, the analysis of network big data is inevitable and it is releasing its power in different aspects of network management, e.g., network anomaly detection, prediction, and localization. Nonetheless, due to the aforementioned properties, the analysis of network big data is not trivial. The nature of network big data, i.e., big volume, high velocity, wide variety, has caused principle challenges, which weaken the effects of the traditional methods used for network operation and management, as well as optimization.

To support the utilization of network big data, numerous researches have been undertaken in the last decade to effectively mine the knowledge inside network big data and further employ the discovered knowledge in network operations. In this chapter, we will focus on discussing the most fundamental application of network management, i.e., *network anomaly detection*, and presenting existing related solutions. Conceptually, network anomaly detection is a broad topic concerning the detection of anomalous behaviors within a target network. According to different types of data sources, methods for network anomaly detection vary.

In what follows, we will firstly illustrate three common data types that one would encounter in network anomaly detection.

17.1.1 Network key performance indicators

As an essential source of information for detecting anomalies of network operations, network key performance indicators (KPIs) have drawn a significant amount of attention from researchers. Normally, a KPI is a time series that represents one particular metric of the performance of a specific network device/service. Figure 17.1, as an example, demonstrates a KPI with various anomalies [1], i.e., point anomaly, contextual anomaly, and collective anomaly.

As shown in Figure 17.1, a single KPI could contain different anomalies that are hard to detect using only a single method. Besides the original difficulties, the enormous numbers of KPIs in the network, the streaming nature of them, e.g., periodic pattern, range, and other contexts, all contribute to additional challenges of online anomaly detection of network KPIs under the network big data environment.

17.1.2 Network traffic flow packets

Traffic flow analysis is another significant area concerning the performance of network services. Through analyzing the network flows of a specific service, the network administrator could gain access to various KPIs concerning the

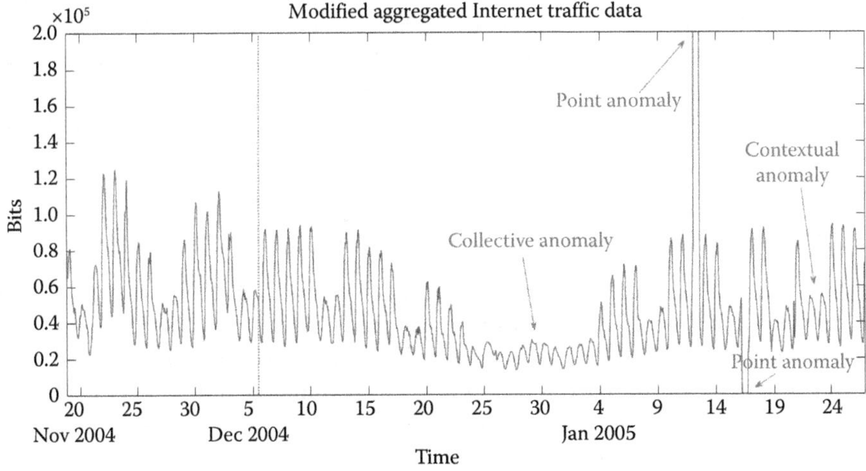

Figure 17.1: Different anomalies in a network KPI.

Table 17.1 A sample from the KDD Cup 1999.

Duration	Protocol	Service	Flag	Src_Bytes	Dst_Bytes
0	TCP	HTTP	SF	181	5450
0	TCP	HTTP	SF	239	486
0	TCP	HTTP	SF	235	1337
0	TCP	HTTP	SF	219	1337
0	TCP	HTTP	SF	217	2032
0	TCP	HTTP	SF	217	2032
0	TCP	HTTP	SF	212	1940
0	TCP	HTTP	SF	159	4087
0	TCP	HTTP	SF	210	151
0	TCP	HTTP	SF	212	786

service and, at the same time, directly perform anomaly detection, e.g., intrusion detection, based on the traffic packets/connections.

Table 17.1 illustrates a small sample from the KDD Cup 1999 [2], which is a dataset used for the competition task of building a network intrusion detector. Each row of the table corresponds to a network connection that may be labeled as "normal" or "abnormal" based on whether the connection is a network attack. The size of the original dataset is 743 megabytes and it contains categorical data that should be treated differently. This specific anomaly detection problem is essentially a classification problem that identifies good connections from bad ones.

In practice, a network intrusion detection system normally deals with a higher volume of streaming heterogeneous dataset, which requires the utilized method to be very efficient and capable of leveraging heterogeneous information for high accuracy. Besides the higher requirements, the existence of the training dataset is another issue that a practical network anomaly detection method should take into account.

17.1.3 Network operational logs of devices or services

Network log is another kind of critical information that a network management system spends much effort on. Different from network KPI and traffic information, network logs cannot be easily turned into data vector and consume much more effort in data preprocessing and feature extraction. A typical log of network devices/services could look like that in Figure 17.2, where the headers of log entries have been removed [3].

What is shown above is only a very small sample of the logs that a network administrator may investigate in his/her daily work. In reality, the volume of the logs could be enormous so that identifying any possible anomalies within

```
CE sym 8, at 0x18127fc0, mask 0x10
total of 16 ddr error(s) detected and corrected
1 ddr errors(s) detected and corrected on rank 0, symbol 5, bit 6
13 ddr errors(s) detected and corrected on rank 0, symbol 3, bit 0
CE sym 5, at 0x00722c80, mask 0x02
3 L3 EDRAM error(s) (dcr 0x0157) detected and corretced
2 ddr error(s) detected and corrected on rank 0, symbol 19, bit 2
CE sym 3, at 0x07d02da0, mask 0x80
total of 1 ddr error(s) detected and corrected
CE sym 19, at 0x057c7e00, mask 0x20
CE sym 3, at 0x07d02da0, mask 0x80
CE sym 19, at 0x057c7e00, mask 0x20
CE sym 3, at 0x07d02da0, mask 0x80
total of 2 ddr error(s) detected and corrected
CE sym 3, at 0x07d02da0, mask 0x80
CE sym 3, at 0x07d02da0, mask 0x80
CE sym 3, at 0x07d02da0, mask 0x80
CE sym 3, at 0x07d02da0, mask 0x80
total of 13 ddr error(s) detected and corrected
1 ddr errors(s) detected and corrected on rank 0, symbol 12, bit 7
4 ddr errors(s) detected and corrected on rank 0, symbol 16, bit 3
1 ddr errors(s) detected and corrected on rank 0, symbol 3, bit 0
1 ddr errors(s) detected and corrected on rank 0, symbol 21, bit 1
1 ddr errors(s) detected and corrected on rank 0, symbol 23, bit 3
27 ddr errors(s) detected and corrected on rank 0, symbol 15, bit 6
1 ddr errors(s) detected and corrected on rank 0, symbol 23, bit 5
```

Figure 17.2: A sample of LANL data. (From USENIX, *CFDR Data*, 2016, https://www.usenix.org/cfdr-data)

millions of log entries is a very challenging task for current anomaly detection methods. If anomalies were to be discovered by manual identification, it would be practically impossible. Considering also the high speed of the generation of these logs in networks, building an efficient and accurate online log anomaly detector remains a very challenging task.

17.1.4 Summary

Based on a report provided by CISCO in April 2016 [4], by the end of 2019, the global data center IP traffic will reach 863 exabytes per month. The IP traffic will grow threefold in the next 5 years. In other words, the metrics that record the properties, e.g., packet loss, average delay of IP traffic packets, the content of the IP packets, and the logs produced by IP traffic in network devices are all explosively generated within the network. Network management systems witness an unprecedented era when the abundant network big data presents great chances for network administrators to deeply understand their network and network users, yet at the same time poses great challenges of designing appropriate methods to mine the underlying knowledge.

In next section, a review of some existing data analysis methods for data anomaly detection will first be presented. Due to the impracticality of exhausting all the data analysis methods, we summarize a review of four novel methods (not in Ref. [5]) for network big data anomaly detection and later in this chapter, emphasize support vector data description (SVDD) as a more mature tool. We will present the origin and most up-to-date research outcomes concerning how SVDD could be employed in anomaly detection and how it could be revised to tackle the aforementioned challenges brought by network big data.

17.2 Novel Methods for Big Data Anomaly Detection

As has been shown earlier, network data has various types, e.g., time series, categories, and texts. Accordingly, many anomaly detection methods have been devised specifically according to different types of targeted dataset. However, in this chapter, we will focus on reviewing general unsupervised anomaly detection methods that can be adopted for general datasets. All the methods reviewed have their specific advantages in analyzing network big data, which will be clear in later sections. Note that, other than general datasets, datasets with specific properties including spatial datasets and temporal datasets, all pose different anomalies according to different contextual information [5]. Especially, time series anomaly detection [6] has become a large research domain and is intensely related to time series data mining, a comprehensive survey of which can be found in Ref. [7]. For anomaly detection in graph datasets, [8] is recommended for interested readers.

17.2.1 Taxonomy of anomalies

Different from other taxonomy [5,6], which categorizes anomalies into point anomaly, collective anomaly, and contextual anomaly, we categorize anomalies into two main classes: *point anomaly*, i.e., a data instance that is too much different from other data instances, and *group anomaly*, i.e., a group of data whose patterns or properties deviate significantly from groups of other data, and further consider the contextual information as an extra criteria for extending a point anomaly to a *contextual point anomaly*, and a group anomaly to *a contextual group anomaly*. A concrete example of a contextual point anomaly could be the high electricity consumption of a building at midnight, where the context is midnight, while an example of contextual group anomaly could be the absence of all the students in one class on a Monday morning during term time.

This categorization tries to emphasize the way in which data instances are treated, i.e., as a single data instance or a part of a data group, and particularly stress contextual information as an extra factor that should be taken into consideration when anomaly detection is performed upon different types of dataset, e.g., time series, graphs, texts. Therefore, the purpose of the general unsupervised anomaly detection in this chapter is to identify point anomalies under the situations where contextual information is rarely provided.

17.2.2 Novel anomaly detection methods

For anomaly detection methods, a very informative review has been reported in Ref. [5]. In this chapter, we provide a supplement set of new promising methods emerging in recent years and point out their advantages and disadvantages in anomaly detection under the presence of network big data. These new methods are Gaussian process [9], matrix factorization [10–12], local sensitive hashing [13,14], and isolation-based anomaly detection [15]. For other methods related to anomaly detection, such as soft computing methods, graph anomaly detection, please refer to Refs. [6,8,16,17].

17.2.2.1 Gaussian process

A Gaussian process (GP) has long been well known as an approach for regression and classification [18]. Nevertheless, rare work has been reported concerning the utilization of GP in anomaly detection. In 2013, Kemmler et al. [9] investigated the task of using GP to achieve one-class classification and discussed theoretical connections between GP and other methods in terms of mathematical relations.

Essentially, GP relaxes the assumption that a given dataset is generated by a certain parametric family of functions and proposes that a specific probability distribution of functions gives rise to the generation of given dataset, where the function values are assumed to follow a GP. With a further assumption of Gaussian white noise between a real value and its corresponding function value, the predictive value for a new data instance can be estimated using another Gaussian distribution denoted here by $p(y_* \mid X,Y,x_*) = N(y_* \mid \mu_*,\sigma_*^2)$, where X and Y are the feature values and labels of the training dataset respectively, x_* and y_* are the feature value and label of the target dataset respectively, and μ_* and σ_*^2 are the mean and variance of the target label respectively corresponding to the given target feature value x_*. For one-class classification, typically a zero mean of the GP is used, labels of all training data are set to 1, and four criteria are suggested as scores for anomaly detection: (1) mean of predicted value μ_*, (2) negative variance value $-\sigma_*^2$, (3) the probability of normal target label $N(y_* \mid \mu_*,\sigma_*^2)$, and (4) a heuristic score $\frac{\mu_*}{\sigma_*}$. It is reported that the second criterion seems to be the best among the four.

As an elegant method for anomaly detection, an important potential problem that may hinder the utilization of GP may also be the assumptions that it makes, which are the Gaussian process the function values follow and the Gaussian white noise. One could imagine that if the assumptions do not hold under some specific situations, the performance of GP would be heavily degraded. On the other hand, the explosive growth of the size of the covariance function matrix, which is a matrix required for calculating μ_* and σ_*^2, is another potential issue for practical application of GP in anomaly detection. Despite these, the method itself provides probabilistic output for each testing of data, which is desirable for big data cleaning. It is reported to provide comparable or superior performance to other techniques in different application domains, which makes this method very promising and attracts research efforts for further investigation.

17.2.2.2 Matrix factorization

As reported in Ref. [5], spectral anomaly detection methods form a critical research direction, in which matrix decomposition plays a significant role. Recent years have witnessed the increasing interest in anomaly detection through matrix factorization, e.g., robust principle component analysis (RPCA) [19] and nonnegative mätrix factorization (NMF) [10,12,20]. Here, we concisely introduce direct robust matrix factorization (DRMF) [11] in anomaly detection due to its generality in terms of matrix factorization.

The central idea of DRMF is neat and formulated as the following matrix factorization problem:

$$\begin{aligned} &\min_{L,S} \|(X-S)-L\|_F \\ &\text{s.t. } rank(L) \leq K \\ &\|S\|_0 \leq e \end{aligned}$$

where X is the original data matrix, S is the matrix of outliers, L is the low-rank approximation of matrix X, K is the rank, and e denotes the maximum number of nonzero entries in matrix X, i.e., the maximum number of outliers in the dataset. $\|\cdot\|_F$ and $\|\cdot\|_0$ represent L_2 norm, i.e., Frobenius norm, and L_0 norm respectively.

Through iteratively updating L and S, DRMF is able to obtain a robust approximation of the original matrix with all identified outliers in S, which is a major advantage of this method—the conciseness and effectiveness. The dimension reduction effect of DRMF also contributes directly to the efficiency of processing a high-dimensional big dataset. However, a major drawback of DRMF is that it is an offline method that works with static matrices. To achieve online anomaly detection, there is still much work to do, e.g., incremental matrix factorization.

17.2.2.3 Local sensitive hashing

Local sensitive hashing (LSH) is a type of hashing that maintains the similarity among data instances even after dimension reduction [21]. Thus, LSH is mainly utilized by applications in which similarities among data instances of high dimensionality need to be measured. As a concrete example, SimHash [22], a well-known method of LSH, has been practically employed by Google for removal of duplicate web pages, which normally contain hundreds or thousands of features. LSH is a very good candidate for data approximation and dimension reduction, all of which point out its capability of anomaly detection with network big data. However, it is only lately [13,14] that LSH has attracted major research interest.

Note that there have been various ways of using LSH for anomaly detection. Here we present the very first example of SimHash, which is based on calculating the hamming distance among hashed data instances. In SimHash, a hash value of a data instance is formulated as:

$$h_w = sig(w^T x)$$

where h_w is the hash value with projection vector w, x is the data instance with value 1 in its first dimension, T represents the transpose of a vector/matrix, and function $sig(\cdot)$ is a sign function that output 1 if the input value is not less than 0, and 0 otherwise. With a number of projection vectors uniformly selected from a Gaussian distribution, the final hash of a data instance is the concatenation of the corresponding hash values. In a naïve case, anomaly detection could be simply achieved by examining the hamming distance among data instances.

To summarize, LSH is essentially a dimension reduction method with binary outputs. Its great properties help with constant detection time and low memory requirement, as well as simple implementation. A large set of anomaly detection methods may benefit from LSH.

17.2.2.4 Isolation-based method

Another very promising anomaly detection method for network big data is isolation-based method called iForest, proposed in Ref. [15]. The idea of isolation for anomaly detection arises from the observation that anomalies in a given dataset can always be easily isolated from other normal data instances. Therefore, to identify an anomaly, iteratively random divisions of the input space is performed to construct division trees called isolation forest (iForest) for anomaly detection.

iForest starts with sampling subdatasets from the original dataset. For each sample, it randomly selects a feature of the subdataset and randomly selects a value for the feature to form a node of a binary tree, called iTree. The left child and the right child of the node are determined afterward. Thus, the whole tree is constructed iteratively until any of the leaf nodes, nodes that have no children, represent only one data instance in the subdataset. The anomaly score for a data instance is measured according to the average length of the traversing paths in all iTrees when searching for the data.

As the process of iForest indicates, the anomaly detection in iForest does not require any explicit similarity measurements, e.g., density measurement and distance measurement, among data instances. This property significantly simplifies the process of anomaly detection and contributes greatly to its high efficiency. The distributed nature of iTrees helps with enabling distributed anomaly detection, which further lowers the time complexity of the method. It is also reported in Ref. [15] that iForest outperforms many other methods in terms of accuracy and robustness. However, a potential issue of iForest may arise from the size of the iTrees when the size of the given dataset is immense and updating the iTrees with incoming new data instances is another important research direction that has not been largely explored.

17.2.3 Summary

In this chapter, we surveyed four methods that are very promising for achieving big data anomaly detection. As one may notice, all the above-mentioned methods are good candidates for handling big data situations. From some specific perspectives, these methods provide promising solutions. However, to work practically with a heterogeneous massive streaming dataset, a rounded method is currently more desirable. In next part, a comparatively mature and rounded method, support vector data description (SVDD), from the research domain of one-class classification (OCC) is detailed in terms of its theoretical enhancements over the past decade, especially the improvements that boost its applicability in dealing with network big data. For a broad review of OCC, interested readers are recommended to refer to Ref. [23] for details.

17.3 A Sparse Model for Anomaly Detection—SVDD

In machine learning, a prestigious method for classification is the support vector machine (SVM) [24]. It is especially well known because it is a sparse kernel model, which has sparse solutions so that maintaining a subset of the dataset, i.e., support vectors, for model training is sufficient for model testing. SVM has been extended for multiclass classification and regression, as well as novelty detection. In anomaly detection, which is essentially similar to novelty detection, one-class SVM and support vector data description (SVDD) [25–28] are considered as two branches from SVM even though they have been proven to be identical under the utilization of the Gaussian kernel.

In this chapter, SVDD is considered as the main tool for big data anomaly detection due to its easy-to-understand geometrical interpretation. We will detail its improvements over the last decade and aim at discussing its applicability in processing network big data with the purpose of anomaly detection.

Especially, the methods that help with processing massive heterogeneous streaming network dataset will be emphasized.

SVDD was invented after one-class SVM in 2004. Its applications spread through all the possible applicable areas that are under the umbrella of clustering, anomaly detection, and novelty detection. Different from the idea of SVM, which strives for separating two sets of different data instances, SVDD endeavors to describe existing data instances using an area, i.e., a hypersphere in high-dimensional space. The formulation of SVDD is as follows:

$$\begin{gathered}\min_{a,R} R^2 + C\sum_{t} \xi_i \\ \text{s.t. } \forall i, \|x_i - a\|^2 \leq R^2 + \xi_i \\ \xi_i \geq 0\end{gathered}$$

where a hypersphere is found by minimizing the sum of the square of its radius R and the weighted (by a factor C) slack variables ξ_i of all the data instances x_i according to the constraints that the distance from a data instances x_i to the center of the hypersphere a should be smaller than the sum of the square of the radius R and the positive slack variable ξ_i.

In Figure 17.3, a simple demonstration of utilizing SVDD in describing a random sample of banana set in two-dimensional space is depicted. Data instances are marked as blue crosses, and the boundary of data description is in red.

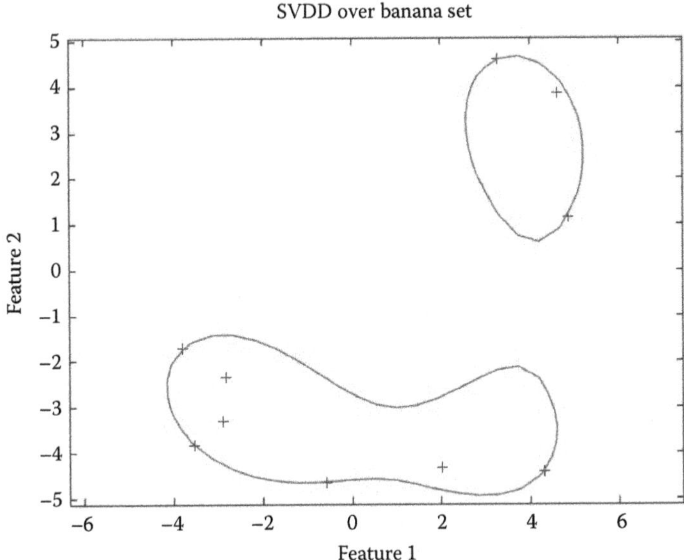

Figure 17.3: An example of an SVDD over a banana dataset.

Essentially, the entire boundary is determined only by the data instances that lie on the boundary. These data instances are called support vectors. In Figure 17.3, the boundary is not a strict sphere that one would expect. This is due to the transformation of the data instances from input space to the so-called feature space, which is denoted by $\Phi(x_i)$ and eventually leads to the utilization of kernel functions (please see Ref. [26] for details):

$$k(x_i, x_j) = \langle \Phi(x_i), \Phi(x_j) \rangle$$

With the obtained boundary for normal data instances, SVDD detects anomalies if they are outside the boundary. The detection is solely based on the testing data instances, the support vectors, and the radius of the hypersphere. The small number of support vectors thus helps with boosting the testing process. Due to this high effectiveness and the high accuracy of SVDD, it has been heavily investigated. SVDD has fruitful research outcomes that spread through four main research directions: (1) theoretical improvement and discovery, improving the (2) accuracy and (3) efficiency of SVDD, and (4) exploring its general application in different problems and areas.

Originally, SVDD led to an underlying quadratic programming problem. Over the last decade, numerous research has helped better understand the problem. In Ref. [29], Chang et al. provide a thorough analysis of the quadratic programming problem and discuss the feasibility of the solution under different settings. In Ref. [30], Campbell and Bennett devise a linear programming SVDD instead of quadratic programming. A unified model of SVM and SVDD is proposed in Ref. [31].

Besides the development of SVDD in terms of the basic theory, much of the previous research focuses on the developing of data description under the presence of noise or imbalance data [32–34]. Developing SVDD under probabilistic input is another important research direction, some work of which includes Fuzzy SVDD [35] or the like [36]. In addition, elliptical SVDD [37,38] and multisphere SVDD [39,40] are investigated to enhance the accuracy in describing inputs with a specific shape.

From the perspective of applications, SVDD has been extended for clustering [28], and binary/multiclass classification problems [41]. The application of SVDD in novelty detection and anomaly detection has also led to research efforts in different domains, such as image processing [42], process control [43], machinery fault diagnosis [44], wireless sensor networks [45], and many others [46,47].

In what follows, we will concentrate on the discussion of why SVDD is suitable for network big data anomaly detection. Specifically, we will investigate what methods have enabled SVDD in processing network datasets with high volumes, how incremental SVDD supports the processing of stream network dataset, and why SVDD is applicable in integrating and processing heterogeneous network datasets.

17.3.1 SVDD with high-volume network dataset

In current networks, the volume of the generated data is always massive. So typical machine learning methods would take a long time to process. However, SVDD has an intrinsic advantage over other methods in that it is a sparse model, thus able to provide comparative performance with little information during the testing phase. However, the training phase of SVDD still takes a considerable amount of time. Therefore, many researches focus on boosting the process of model training [30,48,49], while others try to further improve SVDD in the testing phase [50].

In 2000, Campbell and Bennett proposed to train one-class SVM through linear programming [30]. The essential method can be directly employed in designing linear programming SVDD. The utilization of linear programming over the original quadratic programming problem in SVDD greatly enhances the training effectiveness of SVDD. A further improvement of SVDD [48] considers the utilization of the coreset in SVDD, which takes into consideration that the data instances in the training dataset, which are unlikely to be inliers, have little contribution to the boundary that is described by SVDD. Therefore, the training of SVDD could start with describing a coreset of the dataset and incrementally including important data to redescribe the dataset. The description is finished when the amount of the data instances outside the described boundary is below a predefined threshold for outliers. It is reported that the time complexity of SVDD using coreset is linear in the size of the input dataset.

Both of the methods mentioned above concern the process of model training. Fast SVDD [50], on the other hand, concentrates on speeding up the process of model testing. In original SVDD, the time for testing a new data instance is in proportion to the number of support vectors due to the calculations of the inner products between the new data and the support vectors. In Fast SVDD, the method tries to find the preimage of the scaled center of the hypersphere in feature space and thus replace the utilization of the center with the preimage during testing. Because the preimage can be represented as a data instance in the input space, the testing time can be reduced to constant time without hindering the accuracy of anomaly detection.

These methods mentioned are among the very good candidates [51–53] for improving the efficiency of SVDD. All these methods are heading toward enabling the real-time SVDD training and testing. In the presence of network big data, i.e., high volume of network datasets, better utilization of specific methods will help with anomaly detection in real time.

17.3.2 SVDD with streaming network dataset

Different from a high-volume dataset, a streaming network dataset places higher requirements for the anomaly detection methods. Constant processing time for each incoming data, constant/low memory utilization of the method, and maintaining the original accuracy are three prior requirements. In Refs. [54–56], the ideas for incremental SVDD had been fulfilled to meet the above requirements. In incremental SVDD, when a new data instance comes, it is first assigned a zero weight (Lagrangian multiplier) and added to the original dataset afterward by adjusting all the Lagrangian multipliers of the existing data instances according to a constraint, which maintains the validity of data description. The incremental SVDD is also capable of removing existing data instances with a similar procedure. Therefore, with incremental SVDD, the data description is incrementally maintained by adding/removing new/old data instances.

Figure 17.4 shows the utilization of incremental SVDD in a sample of a two-dimensional banana dataset [57]. The cross points denote the data in the original dataset, and the areas circled by black curves are the legitimate areas inside which data are not considered as outliers. While new data is added to the dataset, the areas are slightly changed and turned into the areas that are circled by the dash line. This is done through incremental SVDD without recalculating the legitimate areas for the entire dataset. When existing data is deleted, it follows the same process and the resulting area is surrounded by the dash-and-dot lines in Figure 17.4.

By refraining from solving a quadratic programming problem every time a new data instance comes, incremental SVDD achieves almost constant time complexity for updating the model. This enhancement greatly improves the

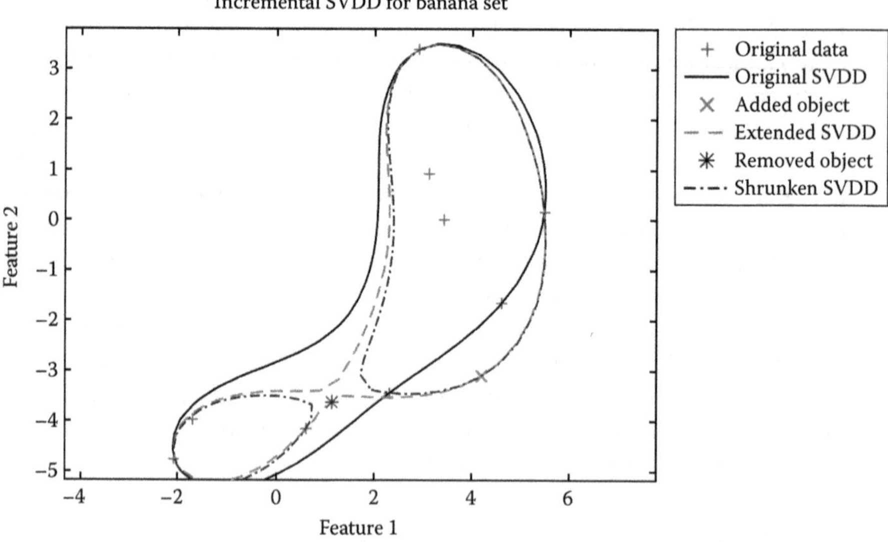

Figure 17.4: An example of incremental SVDD over a banana dataset. (From Tax, D. M. J., *DDtools, the Data Description Toolbox for Matlab*, 2015.)

applicability of SVDD in a streaming dataset. Generally speaking, incremental SVDD is a preeminent method for streaming data anomaly detection. With few modifications according to practical scenarios, it is capable of producing high-quality anomaly detection results in real time.

17.3.3 SVDD with heterogeneous network dataset

Besides the improvement of efficiency, SVDD is also capable of incorporating extra/latent information within the dataset to provide a more accurate and robust solution for anomaly detection. On one hand, extra information can help with identifying the significance of data instances. Thus by placing different weights for the slack variable of different data instances, SVDD is able to construct a more accurate data description, excluding the data instances that have low weights (noise). This method or the like [32,58–60] results in shrinking the boundary of SVDD, which ensures that the data inside the boundary are normal. On the other hand, extra information could help expand the boundary of SVDD that reduces the false alarm rate of the method. The validity of the expansion lies on the observations in various datasets that, typically, data instances that are very close to the boundary are very likely to be normal. Therefore, by leveraging extra information to expand the boundary, false alarms are largely reduced. This research direction has leaded to fruitful outcomes [33,34,41,61–63].

In network anomaly detection, heterogeneous datasets come from different aspects of the network. They are helpful in enhancing the accuracy and robustness of the final result. For a specific task, e.g., network time series anomaly detection, heterogeneous information may cover periodic information of the time series, special events that happened during the period, the growing trend of the time series, etc. Integrating the information into the formulation of SVDD aims at easing the negative effect caused by noisy and untrusted data, reducing false alarms due to the tight boundary, and performing anomaly detection according to specific contexts. This topic has been investigated thoroughly as mentioned above—SVDD could seamlessly integrate the heterogeneous information and refine the result for a specific task. Typically, the heterogeneous information used covers data density and similarity, different data related to the same task, etc.

Another critical example that emerged in 2009 and utilizes heterogeneous information is named *learning using hidden information* (LUHI) [64], and presents a new research direction for learning SVDD with a heterogeneous dataset. LUHI denotes a new learning paradigm in which an extra set of information is available only during the training phase of the model, not in the testing phase. The extra information is reported to be fundamentally different from the original dataset, such as the textual captions of images in image processing. A deep investigation of this new paradigm is promising to provide more research outcomes concerning the processing of heterogeneous information in SVDD.

17.3.4 Summary

In this section, we reviewed the existing methods of SVDD for anomaly detection under the presence of network big data. As shown above, different methods and improvements have extended SVDD for handling massive heterogeneous streaming data. New research directions and topics are emerging to further optimize SVDD, which will all contribute to the successful utilization of SVDD in network anomaly detection. Therefore, we hold the view that SVDD is indispensable on the way toward practical anomaly detection in network big data.

17.4 Conclusion

Throughout this chapter, we consider the task of anomaly detection under the presence of network big data. Specifically, three exemplary common data types in networks are illustrated to discuss how the characteristics of network big data have fundamentally challenged previous methods and strategies for network anomaly detection. To present some promising and novel methods, the second part of the chapter emphasizes four distinct methods for anomaly detection, each of which has individual advantages that are beneficial in analyzing network big data. In the third part of the chapter a very well developed method, SVDD, is detailed, explaining how researchers have developed the method for processing data with high efficiency and accuracy. We discuss the most promising solutions to the theoretical and practical challenges in processing heterogeneous streaming network big data and present the most up-to-date research trends in SVDD. It is believed that SVDD will broadly benefit network operation and management in the task of network big data anomaly detection.

References

[1] DataMarket, *Aggregated Traffic in the United Kingdom Academic Network Backbone*, https://datamarket.com/data/set/232g/, 2014.

[2] University of California Irvine, *KDD Cup 1999 Data*, 1999, http://kdd.ics.uci.edu/databases/kddcup99/kddcup99.html, 1999.

[3] USENIX, *CFDR Data*, https://www.usenix.org/cfdr-data, 2016.

[4] Cisco, *Cisco Global Cloud Index: Forecast and Methodology, 2014–2019 White Paper*, https://www.cisco.com/c/dam/m/en_us/service-provider/ciscoknowledgenetwork/files/547_11_10-15-DocumentsCisco_GCI_Deck_2014-2019_for_CKN_10NOV2015_.pdf, 2016.

[5] V. Chandola, A. Banerjee, and V. Kumar, Anomaly detection: A survey, *ACM Computing Surveys (CSUR)*, vol. 41, no. 3, pp. 15–58, 2009.

[6] O. Ibidunmoye, F. Hernández-Rodriguez, and E. Elmroth, Performance anomaly detection and bottleneck identification, *ACM Computing Surveys (CSUR)*, vol. 48, no. 1, 2015.

[7] P. Esling and C. Agon, Time-series data mining, *ACM Computing Surveys (CSUR)*, vol. 45, no. 1, pp. 12–34, 2012.

[8] L. Akoglu, H. Tong, and D. Koutra, Graph based anomaly detection and description: A survey, *Data Mining and Knowledge Discovery*, vol. 29, no. 3, pp. 626–688, 2015.

[9] M. Kemmler, E. Rodner, E. S. Wacker, and J. Denzler, One-class classification with Gaussian processes, *Pattern Recognition*, vol. 46, no. 12, pp. 3507–3518, 2013.

[10] E. G. Allan, M. R. Horvath, C. V. Kopek, B. T. Lamb, T. S. Whaples, and M. W. Berry, Anomaly detection using nonnegative matrix factorization, *Survey of Text Mining*, vol. II, no. 11, pp. 203–217, 2008.

[11] L. Xiong, X. Chen, and J. G. Schneider, *Direct Robust Matrix Factorization for Anomaly Detection*, ICDM, 2011.

[12] X. Guan, W. Wang, and X. Zhang, Fast intrusion detection based on a non-negative matrix factorization model, *Journal of Network and Computer Applications*, vol. 32, no. 1, pp. 31–44, 2009.

[13] E. A. Manzoor, S. Momeni, V. N. Venkatakrishnan, and L. Akoglu, *Fast Memory-Efficient Anomaly Detection in Streaming Heterogeneous Graphs*, KDD, 2016.

[14] Y. Wang, S. Parthasarathy, and S. Tatikonda, *Locality Sensitive Outlier Detection: A Ranking Driven Approach*, ICDE, pp. 410–421, 2011.

[15] F. T. Liu, K. M. Ting, and Z. H. Zhou, Isolation-Based Anomaly Detection, *ACM Transactions on Knowledge Discovery from Data (TKDD)*, vol. 6, no. 1, pp. 3–39, 2012.

[16] M. Xie, S. Han, B. Tian, and S. Parvin, Anomaly detection in wireless sensor networks: A survey, *Journal of Network and Computer Applications*, vol. 34, no. 4, pp. 1302–1325, 2011.

[17] M. H. Bhuyan, D. K. Bhattacharyya, and J. K. Kalita, Network anomaly detection: Methods, systems and tools, *Communications Surveys & Tutorials*, vol. 16, no. 1, pp. 303–336, 2014.

[18] C. Williams and C. E. Rasmussen, *Gaussian Processes for Machine Learning*, MIT Press, Cambridge, MA, 2006.

[19] E. J. Candès, X. Li, Y. Ma, and J. Wright, Robust principal component analysis? *Journal of the ACM (JACM)*, vol. 58, no. 3, pp. 11–37, 2011.

[20] D. D. Lee and H. S. Seung, Learning the parts of objects by non-negative matrix factorization, *Nature*, vol. 401, no. 6755, pp. 788–791, 1999.

[21] M. Slaney and M. Casey, Locality-sensitive hashing for finding nearest neighbors, *IEEE Signal Processing Magazine*, vol. 25, no. 2, pp. 128–131, 2008.

[22] G. S. Manku, A. Jain, and A. D. Sarma, *Detecting Near-Duplicates for Web Crawling*, WWW, pp. 141–150, 2007.

[23] S. S. Khan and M. G. Madden, One-class classification: Taxonomy of study and review of techniques, *The Knowledge Engineering Review*, vol. 29, no. 3, pp. 345–374, 2014.

[24] K. P. Bennett and C. Campbell, Support vector machines: Hype or hallelujah? *ACM SIGKDD Explorations Newsletter*, vol. 2, no. 2, pp. 1–13, 2000.

[25] B. Schölkopf, R. C. Williamson, and A. J. Smola, *Support Vector Method for Novelty Detection*, NIPS, 1999.

[26] D. M. J. Tax and R. P. W. Duin, Support vector data description, *Machine Learning*, vol. 54, no. 1, pp. 45–66, 2004.

[27] D. M. J. Tax and R. P. W. Duin, Support vector domain description, *Pattern Recognition Letters*, vol. 20, no. 11, pp. 1191–1199, 1999.

[28] A. Ben-Hur, D. Horn, H. T. Siegelmann, and V. Vapnik, Support vector clustering, *The Journal of Machine Learning Research*, vol. 2, pp. 125–137, 2002.

[29] W. C. Chang, C. P. Lee, and C. J. Lin, *A Revisit to Support Vector Data Description*, Technical Report, Department of Computer Science, National Taiwan University, 2013.

[30] C. Campbell and K. P. Bennett, *A Linear Programming Approach to Novelty Detection*, NIPS, 2000.

[31] T. Le, D. Tran, W. Ma, and D. Sharma, A unified model for support vector machine and support vector data description, in *IJCNN*, pp. 1–8, 2012.

[32] G. Chen, X. Zhang, Z. J. Wang, and F. Li, Robust support vector data description for outlier detection with noise or uncertain data, *Knowledge-Based System*, vol. 90, pp. 129–137, 2015.

[33] S. M. Guo, L. C. Chen, and J. S. H. Tsai, A boundary method for outlier detection based on support vector domain description, *Pattern Recognition*, vol. 42, no. 1, pp. 77–83, 2009.

[34] M. Wu and J. Ye, A small sphere and large margin approach for novelty detection using training data with outliers, *IEEE Transactions on Pattern Analysis and Machine Intelligence*, vol. 31, no. 11, pp. 2088–2092, 2009.

[35] T. Le, D. Tran, T. Tran, K. Nguyen, and W. Ma, Fuzzy entropy semi-supervised support vector data description, in *IJCNN*, pp. 1–5, 2013.

[36] Q. Fan, Z. Wang, D. Li, D. Gao, and H. Zha, Entropy-based fuzzy support vector machine for imbalanced datasets, *Knowledge-Based Systems*, vol. 115, pp. 87–99, 2016.

[37] K. Teeyapan, N. Theera-Umpon, and S. Auephanwiriyakul, Ellipsoidal support vector data description, *Neural Computing and Applications*, pp. 1–11, 2016.

[38] K. Wang, H. Xiao, and Y. Fu, Ellipsoidal support vector data description in kernel PCA subspace, in *2016 3rd International Conference on Digital Information Processing, Data Mining, and Wireless Communications (DIPDMWC)*, pp. 13–18, 2016.

[39] Y. Xiao, B. Liu, L. Cao, X. Wu, C. Zhang, Z. Hao, F. Yang, and J. Cao, Multi-sphere support vector data description for outliers detection on multi-distribution data, in *2009 IEEE International Conference on Data Mining Workshops (ICDMW)*, pp. 82–87, 2009.

[40] T. Le, D. Tran, W. Ma, and D. Sharma, *Fuzzy Multi-Sphere Support Vector Data Description*, FUZZ-IEEE, pp. 1–5, 2012.

[41] T. Mu and A. K. Nandi, Multiclass classification based on extended support vector data description, *IEEE Transactions on Systems, Man, and Cybernetics, Part B (Cybernetics)*, vol. 39, no. 5, pp. 1206–1216, 2009.

[42] A. Banerjee, P. Burlina, and C. Diehl, A support vector method for anomaly detection in hyperspectral imagery, *IEEE Transactions on Geoscience and Remote Sensing*, vol. 44, no. 8, pp. 2282–2291, 2006.

[43] S. Mahadevan and S. L. Shah, Fault detection and diagnosis in process data using one-class support vector machines, *Journal of Process Control*, vol. 19, no. 10, pp. 1627–1639, 2009.

[44] L. Duan, M. Xie, T. Bai, and J. Wang, A new support vector data description method for machinery fault diagnosis with unbalanced datasets, *Expert Systems with Applications*, vol. 64, pp. 239–246, 2016.

[45] N. Shahid, I. H. Naqvi, and S. Bin Qaisar, One-class support vector machines: Analysis of outlier detection for wireless sensor networks in harsh environments, *Artificial Intelligence Review*, vol. 43, no. 4, pp. 515–563, 2015.

[46] V. A. Sindagi and S. Srivastava, Domain adaptation for automatic OLED panel defect detection using adaptive support vector data description, *International Journal of Computer Vision*, vol. 122, no. 2, pp. 193–211, 2017.

[47] M. Wytock, S. Salapaka, and M. Salapaka, Preventing cascading failures in microgrids with one-sided support vector machines, in *IEEE 53rd Annual Conference on Decision and Control (CDC)*, pp. 3252–3258, 2014.

[48] C. S. Chu, I. W. Tsang, and J. T. Kwok, Scaling up support vector data description by using core-sets, in *IJCNN*, vol. 1, pp. 425–430, 2004.

[49] C. Campbell and Y. Ying, *Learning with Support Vector Machines*, Morgan & Claypool, San Rafael, CA, pp. 1–95, 2011.

[50] Y. H. Liu, Y. C. Liu, and Y. J. Chen, Fast support vector data descriptions for novelty detection, *IEEE Transactions on Neural Networks*, vol. 21, no. 8, pp. 1296–1313, 2010.

[51] C. Hu, B. Zhou, and J. Hu, Fast support vector data description training using edge detection on large datasets, in *IJCNN*, pp. 2176–2182, 2014.

[52] X. Peng and D. Xu, Efficient support vector data descriptions for novelty detection, *Neural Computing and Applications*, vol. 21, no. 8, pp. 2023–2032, 2012.

[53] A. Chaudhuri, D. Kakde, M. Jahja, W. Xiao, H. Jiang, S. Kong, and S. Peredriy, *Sampling Method for Fast Training of Support Vector Data Description*, arXiv preprint arXiv:1606.05382, 2016.

[54] P. Laskov, C. Gehl, S. Krüger, and K. R. Müller, Incremental support vector learning: Analysis, implementation and applications, *The Journal of Machine Learning Research*, vol. 7, pp. 1909–1936, 2006.

[55] J. Ma, J. Theiler, and S. Perkins, Accurate on-line support vector regression, *AAAI Fall Symposium Artificial Intelligence*, vol. 15, no. 11, pp. 2683–2703, 2003.

[56] D. M. J. Tax and P. Laskov, Online SVM learning: From classification to data description and back, presented at the *IEEE XIII Workshop on Neural Networks for Signal Processing*, 2003, pp. 499–508.

[57] D. M. J. Tax, *DDtools, the Data Description Toolbox for Matlab*, http://prlab.tudelft.nl/david-tax/dd_tools.html, 2015.

[58] B. Liu, Y. Xiao, L. Cao, Z. Hao, and F. Deng, SVDD-based outlier detection on uncertain data, *Knowledge and Information Systems*, vol. 34, no. 3, pp. 597–618, 2013.

[59] J. Zhou, W. Fu, Y. Zhang, H. Xiao, J. Xiao, and C. Zhang, Fault diagnosis based on a novel weighted support vector data description with fuzzy adaptive threshold decision, *Transactions of the Institute of Measurement and Control*, 2016.

[60] M. Cha, J. S. Kim, and J. G. Baek, Density weighted support vector data description, *Expert System Application*, vol. 41, no. 7, pp. 3343–3350, 2014.

[61] P. Phaladiganon, S. B. Kim, and V. C. P. Chen, A density-focused support vector data description method, *Quality and Reliability Engineering International*, vol. 30, no. 6, pp. 879–890, 2014.

[62] K. Lee, D. W. Kim, D. Lee, and K. H. Lee, Improving support vector data description using local density degree, *Pattern Recognition*, vol. 38, no. 10, pp. 1768–1771, 2005.

[63] K. Lee, D. W. Kim, K. H. Lee, and D. Lee, Density-induced support vector data description, *IEEE Transactions on Neural Networks*, vol. 18, no. 1, pp. 284–289, 2007.

[64] V. Vapnik and A. Vashist, A new learning paradigm: Learning using privileged information, *Neural Networks*, vol. 22, no. 5, pp. 544–557, 2009.

Chapter 18

Emerging Applications of Spatial Network Big Data in Transportation

Reem Y. Ali and Shashi Shekhar
University of Minnesota
Minneapolis, Minnesota

Venkata M.V. Gunturi
Indraprastha Institute of Information Technology
Delhi, India

Zhe Jiang
University of Alabama
Tuscaloosa, Alabama

CONTENTS

Routing and navigation services are a set of ideas and technologies that transform lives by understanding the physical world, knowing and communicating relations to places in that world, and navigating through those places. From Google Maps (maps.google.com) to consumer global positioning system (GPS) devices, society is benefiting immensely from transportation services. However, the size, variety, and update rate of spatial network data sets are increasingly exceeding the capacity of commonly used spatial computing and database technologies to learn, manage, and process the data with reasonable effort. We believe that this data, which we call spatial network big data (SNBD), represents the next frontier in transportation services. Examples of emerging spatial big data (SBD) data sets include temporally detailed (TD) road maps that provide speeds every minute for every road segment, GPS track data from cell phones, and engine measurements of fuel consumption, greenhouse gas (GHG) emissions, etc.

SNBD has transformative potential. For example, a 2011 McKinsey Global Institute report estimates savings of "about $600 billion annually by 2020" by helping vehicles avoid traffic congestion via next-generation routing services such as *eco-routing* [1,2]. While today's route-finding services are based on shortest historical average travel time or distance, eco-routing may leverage various forms of SBD to compare alternative routes by typical travel speed, fuel consumption, or greenhouse gas emissions for the precise departure time(s) of interest. Preliminary evidence for the value proposition of SNBD includes the experience of UPS, which saves millions of gallons of fuel by simply avoiding left turns and associated engine idling when selecting routes [3]. Similarly, other pilot studies with TD road maps [4] and congestion information derived from GPS traces [5] showed that indeed, travelers can save up to 30% in travel time compared with approaches that assume a static network. Thus, it is conceivable that immense savings in fuel cost and greenhouse gas emissions are possible if other consumers avoided hot spots of idling, low fuel-efficiency, and congestion. Eco-routing has the potential to significantly reduce the United States' consumption of petroleum, the dominant source of energy for transportation. It may even reduce the gap between domestic petroleum consumption and production, helping bring the nation closer to the goal of energy independence [6].

In this chapter, we present recent advances of SNBD techniques in transportation applications such as eco-routing. The rest of the chapter is organized as follows: In Section 18.1 we define SNBD and compare it to traditional spatial data sets. Then, we discuss the challenges posed by SNBD in transportation applications. In Section 18.2, we introduce current work toward developing novel approaches for addressing these challenges. Section 18.3 discusses some future directions for research in eco-routing services.

18.1 Introduction

18.1.1 What is spatial network big data?

Generally, SNBD refers to spatial network data sets that exhibit one or more of the following characteristics: a large volume, variety, and/or velocity that exceeds the capabilities of current computing technologies. However, SNBD cannot be completely defined without reference to the user experience which can be expressed in terms of the computational platform, use case, and data set at hand [7]. When dealing with SNBD, users may experience unacceptable response times, due to the high data volume in a computationally expensive operation such as correlation. Users may also experience frequent data loss due to the high data velocity relative to the data ingest capacity of the computational platform, or they may find themselves expending large amounts of effort to preprocess or postprocess SNBD due to its high variety. For example, Cloud computers that can process 10^9 million instructions per second (MIPS) may be able to handle data volumes of 10^{12} for use cases of n^2 complexity. However, clusters that are capable of processing 10^6 MIPS would not be able to handle these use cases. Therefore, in such a case, the same 10^{12} data volume represents spatial big data for the cluster, but not for the Cloud computer.

SNBD versus Spatial Data: Types of traditional spatial data include point data sets (e.g., disease reports), linear data (e.g., road centerline), graphs (e.g. road maps) and raster data (e.g., satellite imagery). An example of use cases of such data might be mapping crime reports in a region during a specific time interval, or mapping presidential voter preferences across the country during an election year. On the other hand, examples of SNBD include GPS track data, temporally detailed (TD) road maps, spatio-temporal and engine measurement data, Waze, and Open Street Map. Use cases for SNBD can include displaying a (near) real-time map for disaster-related tweets or displaying (near) real-time traffic maps using Waze (waze.com) user-generated content. In this subsection we describe GPS track data and TD road maps in more detail.

- **GPS Track Data:** GPS trajectories are becoming available for a larger collection of vehicles due to the rapid proliferation of cell phones and in-vehicle navigation devices. Such GPS tracks allow indirect estimation of fuel efficiency and GHG emissions via estimation of vehicle speed, idling, congestion, synchronized traffic lights, and turn delays. They also make it possible to offer personalized route suggestions to users to reduce fuel consumption and emissions. The data set size can reach 10^{13} items per year given constant minute-by-minute resolution measurements for all 100 million US vehicles.

- **TD Road maps:** New data sets from companies such as NAVTEQ [8] use probe vehicles (e.g., GPS tracks) and highway sensors (e.g., loop detectors) to compile travel time information across road segments for all times of the day and week at fine temporal resolutions (seconds or minutes). While traditional road maps have only one scalar value of speed for a given road segment (e.g., EID 1), TD road maps may potentially list speed/travel time for a road segment (e.g., EID 1) for thousands of time points (Figure 18.1a) in a typical week. This level of detail allows a commuter to compare alternate start times in addition to alternate routes. For example, route ranking may differ across rush hour and non-rush-hour periods and in general across different start times. Compared to traditional road maps whose size is in the order of gigabytes of data, TD road maps are big and their size may exceed 10^{13} items per year for the 100 million road segments in the United States when associated with per-minute values for speed or travel time. Thus, industry is using speed profiles, a lossy compression based on the idea of a typical day of a week, as illustrated in Figure 18.1b, where each road segment–day of the week pair is associated with a time series of speed values for each hour of the day.

18.1.2 Challenges posed by spatial network big data

SNBD raises big challenges for a potential realization of the next generation of routing services in road networks. For example, its voluminous nature of SNBD, which allows us to compare candidate routes for thousands of departure times in a week, violates the stationary-ranking-(across departure times)-of-candidate-solutions assumption behind classical dynamic programming (DP) based techniques. In other words, we observe a nonstationary ranking (across departure times) of candidate solutions in spatial big data. Furthermore, SNBD captures several properties of n-ary relations which cannot be completely decomposed into properties of binary relations without losing their semantic meaning [9].

State-of-the-art methods for navigational technologies may either become inapplicable (lose correctness) or nonpreferable (lose semantic meaning) in the face of SBD. For example, Dijkstra's algorithm—a classical algorithm for shortest path computation—assumes DP property, i.e., stationary ranking of candidate routes across departure times, which is violated in a temporally detailed road map. Similarly, static graphs, time-aggregated graphs [10], and time-expanded

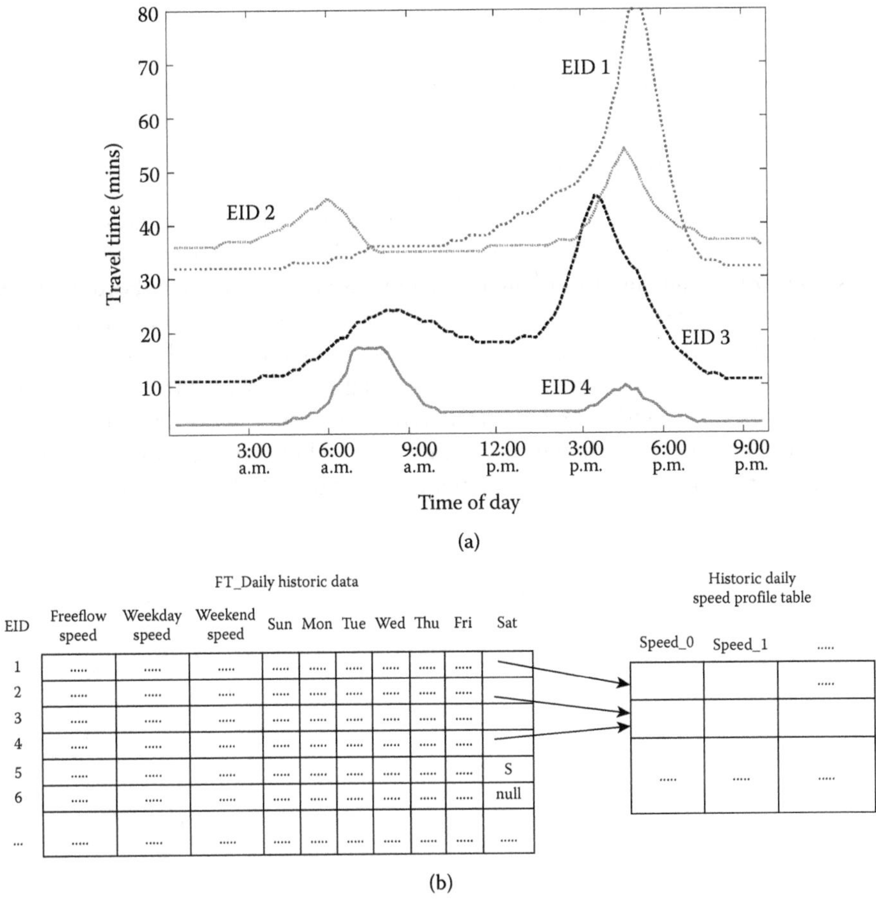

Figure 18.1: Temporally detailed roadmaps using historical speed profiles. (a) Travel time along four road segments over a day. (b) Schema for daily historic speed data.

graphs [11]—the classical underlying data representational models for querying or knowledge discovery on transportation networks—and the algorithms developed for them (by association) assume complete decomposability of properties recorded in the data [9].

18.2 Computational Accomplishments

In this section, we describe recent advances made toward addressing the above-mentioned challenges posed by SNBD. First, we present the logical models for SNBD. Then, we summarize current state of the art techniques for physical models. Finally, we introduce routing queries on SNBD. Particularly, we introduce the work [12] done on addressing the nonstationary ranking of candidate paths across departure times.

18.2.1 Spatial network big data: Logical model

Time-Aggregated Graph: A logical model called the time-aggregated graph (TAG) has been proposed [10,13] suitable for TD road maps and extended classical shortest path algorithms such as Dijkstras and the Bellman–Ford algorithm for TD road maps. TAG is based on associating a time series of attributes to nodes and edges of the graph representing the underlying topological road maps. Consider a series of snapshots of a sample TD road map as shown in Figure 18.2a for start times 1, 2, 3, and 4. An alternative representation, namely the time-expanded graph (TEG) [11], is shown in Figure 18.2c, which stitches all snapshots via edges representing not only start node and end node but also start time and

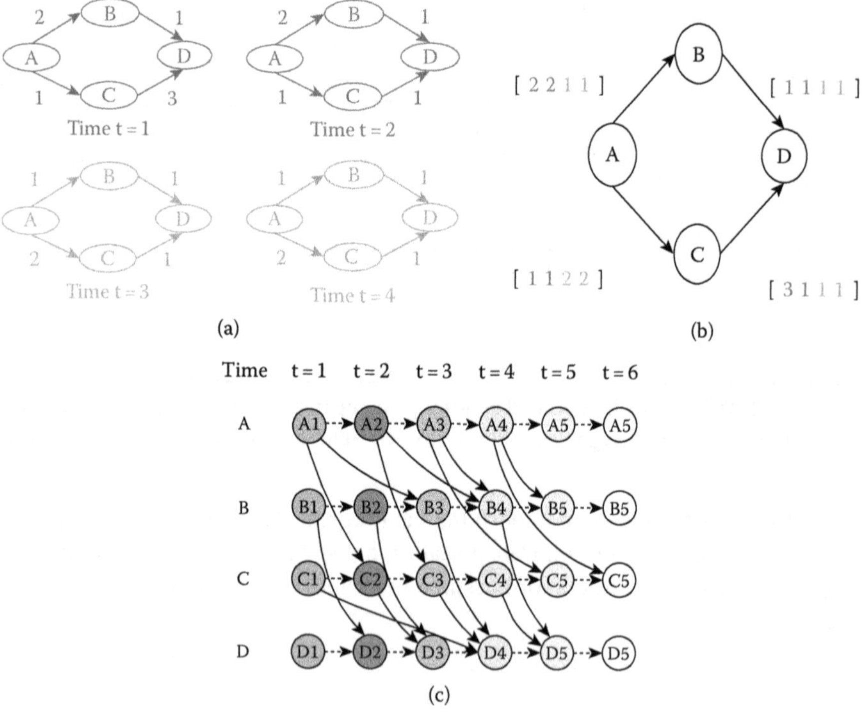

Figure 18.2: Spatiotemporal network model (shading indicates start time). (a) Snapshots of a sample TD road map. (b) Time aggregated graph. (c) Time expanded graph.

end time. In the time-aggregated graph representation shown in Figure 18.2b, edge (A,C) would be associated with time series [1,1,2,2], representing the travel times at start times t = 1, t = 2, t = 3, and t = 4, respectively. The time-aggregated graph is a more concise representation relative to the snapshot and TEG model as it does not replicate nodes and edges across time points. It also facilitates longitudinal reasonings and design of efficient algorithms.

Lagrangian X-Graph: The challenge of nondecomposable properties of n-ary relations manifests while designing a unified logical data model which can integrate multiple travel related data sets in SNBD (e.g. travel speed detailed road maps, GPS traces and traffic signal data) seamlessly so they all can be used simultaneously while comparing candidate itineraries for querying or knowledge discovery purposes.

Examples of nondecomposable properties of n-ary relations include travel time and fuel use during a journey on a route with a sequence of coordinated traffic signals. In case of coordinated traffic signals, the cycle lengths and phase gap between signals (belonging to the same system) are set in such a way that a platoon of vehicles moving toward a common destination (within a certain speed limit) would typically wait only at the first signal before being smoothly transferred through others without any waiting. This kind of coordination is common in big cities for the goal of reducing overall idling traffic at red lights. For instance, recently about 4400 traffic signals in Los Angeles were coordinated [14] in order to increase traffic speeds by about 16%.

Consider the problem of modeling a route R with n road intersections and $n+1$ road segments where the series of n traffic signals (at road intersections) are coordinated. A typical journey (J1) on this route starting at the first road segment would wait only on the first signal before being smoothly transferred through the second, third ... and n^{th} traffic signals without any waiting. However, another typical journey (J2) starting at the nth road segment would typically have to wait at the nth traffic signal. In other words, the waiting time experienced at the nth traffic signal depends on where the journey started. In such a scenario, if we represent R as an aggregation of typical experience along its individual component $n+1$ road segments and n traffic signals (as the current related work on spatial and spatio-temporal networks [10,11,15,16] would do), we would completely lose the semantics of signal coordination. Similar losses can be seen in the case of modeling a GPS trace [9], where the travel time experienced on a road segment depends on the speed and acceleration with which the vehicle entered the road segment under consideration.

To this end, a novel logical data model, called Lagrangian Xgraphs, has been proposed [9], which would model the route as a series of overlapping subjourneys, each representing a single atomic unit which retains the required semantics (signal coordination or initial speed for a GPS trace). Some sample overlapping subjourneys for the previous signal coordination example include: {experience of a journey containing first road segment and first signal (some wait)}, {experience of a journey containing first road segment, first signal (some wait), second road segment and second signal (no wait)}, {experience of a journey containing first road segment, first signal (some wait), second road segment, second signal (no wait), third road segment and third signal (no wait)}, ..., {experience of a journey containing second road segment and second signal (some wait)}, etc.

18.2.2 Spatial network big data: Physical model

Current Cloud computing infrastructure for supporting big spatial data includes the work on distributed systems for geometric data (e.g., lines, points, and polygons) [17–26]. These works consider the spatial aspect of data and use spatial index structures such as R-tree, R+-tree, or Quadtree indexes [27]. Thus, these techniques cannot capture the ST graph-based notions such as spatial and ST (Lagrangian) connectivity. Other related work for STG big data includes graph-based Cloud computing systems such as Giraph [28], GraphLab [29], and Pregel [30]. These works consider only the connectivity aspect of the data without any regard to spatial or temporal features.

Another physical storage model [31] is proposed that stores network nodes and edges in different disk partitions according to Lagrangian path, which is suitable for TD road maps and extended classical shortest path algorithms such as Dijkstras and Bellman–Ford algorithms for TD road maps.

18.2.3 Spatial network big data: Routing queries

Routing algorithms have been explored [10,32] for time-aggregated graphs via adaptation of both Dijkstras and Bellman–Ford algorithms. The adapted Dijkstras algorithm, called SP-TAG, determined the shortest travel time path for a source–destination pair for a given start time. The adapted Bellman–Ford algorithm, called BEst Start Time, recommended a route and a suitable start time such that total time spent in the network was minimized. Both SP-TAG and BEST showed superior performance [10] when compared to existing counterparts based on time-expanded graphs.

Another challenge in routing queries on SNBD is the nonstationary ranking across departure times. This challenge of SNBD was investigated in the context of the all start-time Lagrangian shortest path (ALSP) problem. In this problem, given a TD road map, a source, a destination and a departure time interval, a collection of routes is determined which includes the shortest path (between the source and destination) for every departure time in the given departure time interval. Consider an ALSP problem instance with the University of Minnesota as the source, the Minneapolis–Saint Paul Airport as the destination and a desired departure time interval of [7:30 a.m. 9:15 a.m.]. Figure 18.3 illustrates (on the left) two candidate routes between the university (Point A in Figure 18.3) and the airport (Point B in Figure 18.3) and their costs for different departure times

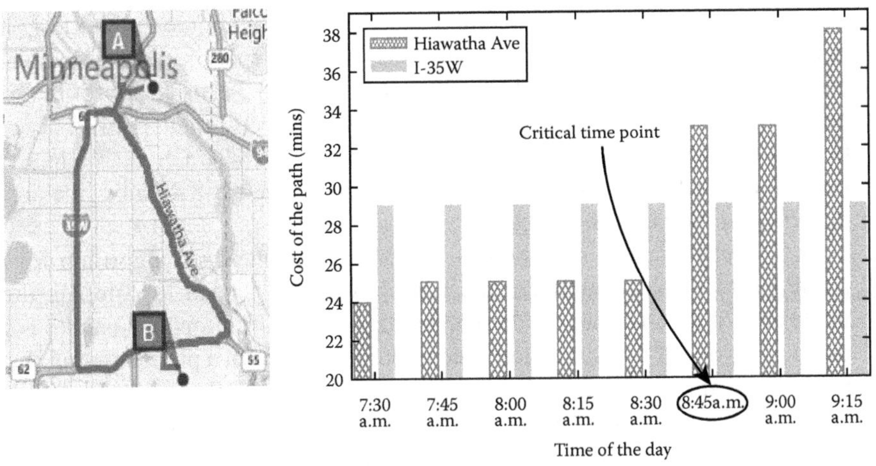

Figure 18.3: Candidate routes between university and airport and their travel costs.

(on the right) in the interval [7:30 a.m. 9:15 a.m.]. Figure 18.3 shows that the Hiawatha route is faster for departure times in the interval [7:30 a.m. 8:30 a.m.], whereas I35W was preferable for the interval [8:45 a.m. 9:30 a.m.]. The ALSP output includes both of these paths and the corresponding set of departure time instants when they are optimal.

A computationally efficient algorithm for the ALSP problem is important in the face of SNBD. This is because SNBD magnifies the impact of partial information and the ambiguity of a traditional routing query specified by a start location and an end location. Traditional routing queries were defined to identify a unique (or a small set of) route(s), given historical and current travel times. However, ALSP can leverage SNBD to identify a much larger set of solutions, e.g., one route each for thousands of possible departure times in a week. This gives the commuters an opportunity to make a more informed choice by providing them an option to compare alternative routes for multiple departure times of their choice.

A naïve approach for the ALSP problem could be to repeatedly recompute the shortest path for each departure time. However, this would incur redundant recomputation across departure times sharing a common solution, leading to a severe computational bottleneck in case of long departure time intervals. To reduce this computational cost, the notion of critical-time-points (CTP) has been proposed in Ref. [12] which divide the given departure time interval into a set of disjoint subintervals where the ranking among alternative routes is stationary. Now, within these intervals, the shortest path can be computed using a single run of a dynamic programming (DP)-based approach. The main advantage of such an approach is that it would avoid computing the shortest path for many departure times in the given interval. Instead, it will recompute the shortest path only at the critical-time-points without missing any departure time in the given interval where the shortest path can change. Figure 18.3 also illustrates the proposed idea of critical-time-points. The shortest path between the university and the airport changed at some instant inside the interval [8:31 a.m. 8:45 a.m.]. For sake of simplicity, it assumes the shortest path changed at 8:45 a.m., making it the critical-time-point in this case.

A key challenge in designing a critical-time-point based algorithm for an ALSP problem is to minimize the amount of time needed to compute them while ensuring correctness and completeness. Critical-time-points can be computed using one of two strategies, precomputing or lazy. In a precomputing based method, all the candidate solutions (routes) are enumerated and compared to determine the best route for each departure time. This approach, however, may become a bottleneck in the case of a temporally detailed road map, as there can be large number of candidate routes connecting a source–destination pair. To this end, the lazy technique was investigated for the ALSP problem. This approach computes a superset of critical-time-points on the fly while exploring candidate routes. The key insight in the lazy approach is that immediately after the computation of the shortest path for the earliest (n^{th}) departure time, one has adequate information to forecast a lower bound on the first (n^{th}) critical-time-point. In our university–airport example, this would mean that, after computing the shortest path at 7:30 a.m. we could forecast, e.g., 8:15 a.m. (a time point between 7:45 a.m. and 8:45 a.m.) as the next critical-time-point for the recomputation to start. In other words, a single logical work unit of the proposed algorithm was: "compute the shortest path for one departure time and forecast a lower bound on the next critical-time-point for recomputation."

A critical-time-point is forecast through the use of a modified priority queue, called a TD priority queue. In this kind of priority queue [32,33], there are multiple time series of values as its elements. This is in contrast to a regular priority queue which has scalar values as its elements. A time series in this queue contains the cost along a path to a node in the open list for the departure times under consideration. The queue is ordered on the current departure time under consideration. For instance, in our previous university–airport example, we would order the queue based on the costs for 7:30 a.m. for the first logical work unit and then for the forecasted critical-time-point for the second one, and so on. Apart from the standard priority queue operations such as insert, extract-min, update-key, there is a new operation called a forecast-critical-time-point. This operation is called at the end of each extract-min, when it compares the resulting time series (obtained via extract-min) with the other time series in the queue to determine the maximum duration (#departure times beyond the current one) for which the chosen time series has the lowest value. This value is stored in an auxiliary data structure as a potential critical-time-point. At any stage during the execution, there exists the following loop invariant: "The choices (i.e., results of extract-mins from the TD priority queue) made during the execution hold their validity for all the departure times between the time for which the queue is ordered (trivially) and the min{potential critical-time-points observed so far} [12]." Using this loop invariant and exploring the paths in a greedy fashion (similar to Dijkstra's enumeration style), when we expand (extract-min + forecast critical-time-point) a path to the destination, there is a shortest path between the source and destination which is optimal for all the departure times between the current one (on which the queue was ordered) and the min{potential critical-time-points}. This min{potential critical-time-point} becomes the forecasted critical-time-point where the recomputation starts.

Based on this idea of forecasting critical-time-points on the fly, critical-time-point ALSP solver (CTAS) [12] was proposed for the ALSP problem. The CTAS algorithm follows the above-mentioned procedure for a search starting from the source and terminates when all the desired departure times are covered. This algorithm was evaluated both theoretically and experimentally. The analysis showed that the proposed approach outperformed the related work particularly when the numbers of CTPs were less. This is because the additional cost associated with the computation of potential critical-time-points creates a trade-off.

18.3 Future Trends and Research Needs

In this section we discuss new trends in spatial network big data science. We also present several related data science and engineering challenges that need to be addressed before we can fully realize the potential of SNBD.

18.3.1 Trends

One example of data patterns that can be discovered from engine measurement data sets is noncompliant window co-occurrence patterns [34]. Given a set of trajectories annotated with measurements of physical variables, the noncompliant window co-occurrence (NWC) pattern discovery problem aims to determine temporal signatures in the explanatory variables which are highly associated with windows of undesirable or noncompliant behavior in a target variable (e.g., low fuel efficiency or high emission). The co-occurrence patterns are considered in a Lagrangian frame of reference since they are experienced by a moving observer (e.g., a moving vehicle) during its trip rather than a static observer (e.g., a stationary sensor). Figure 18.4 shows an example that when a vehicle climbs up (Figure 18.4 top) a highway ramp with constant acceleration (Figure 18.4 middle), the NO_x emissions (Figure 18.4 bottom) within that timewindow (between t = 2 and t = 6) exceeds the US EPA standard of 0.267 gm/kW-h. Hence, the pattern representing the high acceleration together with the increase in

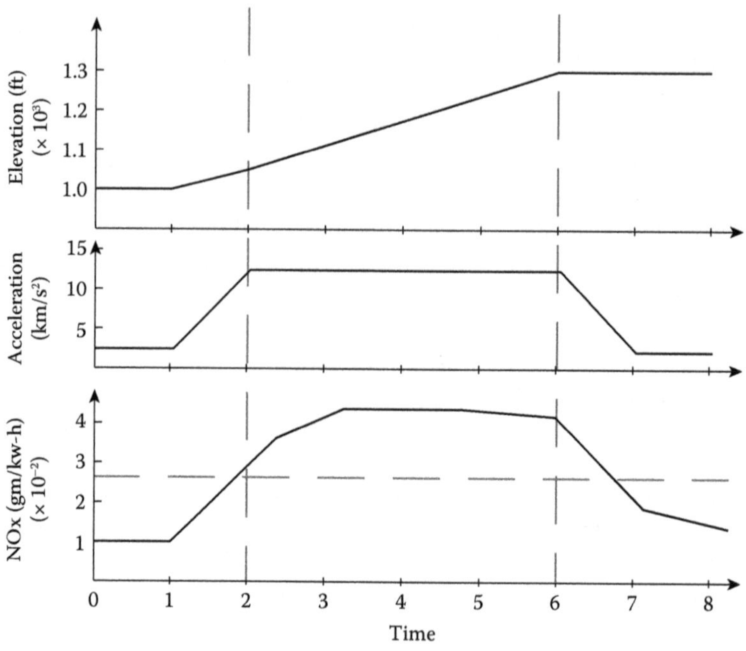

Figure 18.4: An example of a noncompliant window of NOx emissions.

elevation is considered as a candidate co-occurrence pattern which might explain this noncompliant engine emission behavior.

Discovering NWC patterns is challenging for several reasons. From a computational perspective, domain-preferred spatio-temporal statistical association measures (e.g., cross-K function) lack monotonicity. This means that a pattern representing an engine signature over multiple engine variables may be interesting although its component single-variable signatures may not. For instance, the doubling of both engine speed and brake torque might be more associated with a doubling in NO_x emissions than just the doubling of engine speed. This property renders a priori-based pruning inapplicable. Second, there is a huge number of candidate patterns to consider. For each noncompliant window, the number of associated candidate patterns is exponential in the number of variables. Third, the data volume is potentially huge due to the large number of variables over a long time series.

A naïve approach to discover such patterns would start by identifying all noncompliant windows in the data set. For each noncompliant window, the algorithm would enumerate all possible combinations of variable variations that co-occur with this noncompliant window. That would result in an exponential number of candidate patterns for each noncompliant window which is computationally very expensive. In Ref. [34], these computational challenges have been addressed by the proposed two novel upper-bounds for the cross-K function, the statistical interest measure used for evaluating how much the association of a pattern to noncompliant windows deviates from the assumption of independence. The proposed upper bounds are cheaper to compute than the computation of the exact value of the cross-K function. Thus, whenever an upper bound of a pattern does not exceed the given cross-K function threshold, the pattern is eliminated without the need to calculate its actual cross-K function value. One of the proposed upper bounds also had a special monotone property which allows the pruning of a pattern's subsets without even calculating their upper bounds. A multiparent tracking approach was used to traverse the lattice of all possible patterns. In the first step, all leaf patterns are enumerated by counting their occurrences in the dataset and their occurrences within a noncompliant window. Then, a top-down, breadth-first traversal starts from the top of the lattice where the upper bounds are calculated for each node using the counts of the lattice lead nodes. The algorithm also keeps track of the number of parents visited for each node to avoid duplicate enumeration of a node and to allow the enumeration of a node only after all its parents have been visited.

18.3.2 Research needs

In the previous subsection, we presented an example of pattern discovery from engine measurement data sets. In this section, we discuss some of the challenges that still need to be addressed when dealing with SNBD to fully realize the potential of these data sets. These challenges are discussed from the perspectives of spatial network query processing, data science, and data engineering [35].

18.3.2.1 Spatial network query processing

Novel Preference Functions for Routing Services: Traditional routing services are geared toward identifying a set of routes that satisfy limited user preference functions such as the path with the least travel distance or the path with the least travel time. However, emerging SNBD such as TD road maps allow the identification of routes for a much richer and larger set of preference functions. For instance, using these data sets, users can start comparing routes based on their fuel efficiency or greenhouse gas emissions. However, identifying these eco-friendly routes poses several challenges and research questions. For instance, how does the computational structure of shortest path queries differ from queries identifying the most fuel-efficient route or the route with the least greenhouse gas emissions? Will greedy or dynamic programming strategies work for these kind of queries? One of the main challenges of these new emerging queries is that these preference functions (e.g., fuel consumption) are nondecomposable in nature. This means that given the measurements of fuel consumption over a long route (i.e., a sequence of traversed edges), these measurements cannot be simply broken down into corresponding measurements for each edge. This behavior violates the assumptions behind traditional shortest path algorithms [9]. For instance, the amount of fuel consumption or greenhouse gas emissions that a vehicle experiences on a road segment would depend on factors such as the initial velocity/acceleration of that vehicle before actually entering the segment [9]. Similarly, a vehicle with a hybrid engine that is decelerating toward a stop sign might use the excess kinetic energy to charge its battery. Thus, when accelerating after the stop sign, the vehicle might be using its charged battery instead of any fuel consumption.

18.3.2.2 Spatial network big data science

Lagrangian Pattern Mining on Road Networks: The availability of engine measurement data sets will allow designing smarter electronic control units (ECUs) for future vehicles. Traditionally, ECUs calibrate the engine performance using a set of preselected rules that are designed in the laboratories and added by the manufacturer so that the vehicles can meet fuel efficiency and greenhouse gas regulations. However, by analyzing engine measurement data sets, new vehicles can rely on a dynamic set of rules that are being learned in real time based on the historical performance and current readings of the engine on-board sensors as well as other environmental variables (e.g., weather and real-time traffic conditions) to adapt and optimize the engine behavior for the current real-world conditions. For example, using these data sets, it can be useful to discover hotspots of high engine emissions or high fuel consumption and calibrate the engine to adapt to these conditions. However, these hotspot patterns are usually sensitive to many factors such as the type of vehicle or the driver's driving style. For instance, while a road segment might represent a hotspot of emissions for an aggressive acceleration or braking pattern, it might not be a hotspot of emissions for a gentler driving style. Thus, discovering these patterns from engine measurements data sets will require analyzing the data from a traveler's frame of reference (i.e., Lagrangian frame of reference). However, current related work has only focused on linear hotspots of aggregated counts such as hotspots of road fatalities or crime incidents [36]. Other challenges include the need for real-time algorithms for learning these rules from SNBD and exploring whether the search space of these rules can be reduced by leveraging physical engine science constraints that govern the engine behavior.

18.3.2.3 Spatial network big data engineering

Cloud computing platforms play an essential role in scaling up data analytic methods for handling the huge volumes of SNBD. However, most spatial Cloud computing platforms (e.g., ESRI GIS Tools for Hadoop [37], SpatialHadoop [19], HadoopGIS [17]) assume that the data is embedded in a geometric space rather than a network space. Hence, these platforms only support simple data types such as points, lines, and polygons. However, SNBD are usually modeled using more sophisticated graph objects (e.g., time-aggregated graphs, Lagrangian X graphs, etc.) which makes it inconvenient to represent SNBD operations using the current spatial Cloud computing programming models (e.g., SpatialHadoop Pigeon [38], Pregel [30], GraphLab [29]). Moreover, the data partitioning methods used in these platforms only account for the spatial and temporal closeness of the data points/nodes. However, these methods ignore the connectivity aspect of the data which have a great importance when dealing with network operations such as shortest path queries. Thus, current partitioning methods could suffer from a reduced load balancing and a large amount of I/O operations.

References

[1] Shashi Shekhar, Viswanath Gunturi, Michael R Evans, and KwangSoo Yang. Spatial big-data challenges intersecting mobility and cloud computing. In *MobiDE*, Scottsdale, AZ, May 20, pp. 1–6, ACM, 2012.

[2] Computing Community Consortium funded workshop. From gps and virtual globes to spatial computing - 2020: The next transformative technology, a community whitepaper, 2012. http://cra.org/ccc/events/spatial-computing-workshop/ (accessed August 22, 2017).

[3] Joel Lovell. Left-hand-turn elimination, December 9, 2007. *New York Times*. http://www.nytimes.com/2007/12/09/magazine/09left-handturn.html (accessed August 22, 2017).

[4] Ugur Demiryurek, Farnoush Banaei-Kashani, and Cyrus Shahabi. A case for time-dependent shortest path computation in spatial networks. In *Proceedings of the ACM SIGSPATIAL International Conference on Advances in GIS*, GIS '10, San Jose, CA, November 2–5, pp. 474–477, 2010.

[5] Jing Yuan, Yu Zheng, Chengyang Zhang, Wenlei Xie, Xing Xie, Guangzhong Sun, and Yan Huang. T-drive: Driving directions based on taxi trajectories. In *Proceedings of the SIGSPATIAL International Conference on Advances in GIS*, GIS '10, San Jose, CA, November 2–5, pp. 99–108, 2010.

[6] US Congress. Energy independence and security act of 2007. *Public Law*, (110–140), 2007. http://en.wikipedia.org/wiki/Energy_Independence_and_Security_Act_of_2007 (accessed August 22, 2017).

[7] Michael R Evans, Dev Oliver, KwangSoo Yang, Xun Zhou, Shashi Shekhar. Enabling Spatial Big Data via CyberGIS: Challenges and Opportunities. In S. Wang and M. Goodchild (Eds.), *CyberGIS: Fostering a New Wave of Geospatial Innovation and Discovery*, Springer, 2017 (expected).

[8] NAVTEQ. www.navteq.com (accessed August 22, 2017).

[9] Venkata MV Gunturi and Shashi Shekhar. Lagrangian xgraphs: A logical data-model for spatio-temporal network data: A summary. In *Advances in Conceptual Modeling*, Atlanta, GA, October 27–29, pp. 201–211, Springer, 2014.

[10] Betsy George, Sangho Kim, and Shashi Shekhar. Spatio-temporal network databases and routing algorithms: A summary of results. In *Proceedings of the 10th International Conference on Advances in Spatial and Temporal Databases*, SSTD'07, Seoul, South Korea, July 16–18, pp. 460–477, Springer-Verlag, Berlin, 2007

[11] Ekkehard Kohler, Katharina Langkau, and Martin Skutella. Time-expanded graphs for flow-dependent transit times. In *Algorithms ESA 2002*, vol. 2461, pp. 49–56, 2002.

[12] Venkata MV Gunturi, Ernesto Nunes, KwangSoo Yang, and Shashi Shekhar. A critical-time-point approach to all-start-time lagrangian shortest paths: A summary of results. In *Advances in Spatial and Temporal Databases: 12th International Symposium, SSTD 2011*, Minneapolis, MN, August 24–26, pp. 74–91, Springer, 2011.

[13] Betsy George and Shashi Shekhar. Time-aggregated graphs for modeling spatio-temporal networks. In *Journal on Data Semantics XI*, pp. 191–212. Springer, 2008.

[14] Ian Lovett. To Fight Gridlock, Los Angeles Synchronizes Every Red Light, April 1, 2013. *The New York Times*. http://www.nytimes.com/2013/04/02/us/to-fight-gridlock-los-angeles-synchronizes-every-red-light.html (accessed August 22, 2017).

[15] Erik G. Hoel, Wee-Liang Heng, and Dale Honeycutt. High performance multimodal networks. In *Advances in Spatial and Temporal Databases*, pp. 308–327, 2005. Springer. LNCS 3633.

[16] Ralf Hartmut Güting. Graphdb: Modeling and querying graphs in databases. In *Proceedings of the 20th International Conference on Very Large Data Bases*, San Francisco, CA, September 12–15, pp. 297–308, 1994.

[17] Ablimit Aji, Fusheng Wang, Hoang Vo, Rubao Lee, Qiaoling Liu, Xiaodong Zhang, and Joel Saltz. Hadoop GIS: A high performance spatial data warehousing system over MapReduce. *Proceedings of the VLDB Endowment*, 6(11):1009–1020, 2013.

[18] Ariel Cary, Zhengguo Sun, Vagelis Hristidis, and Naphtali Rishe. Experiences on processing spatial data with MapReduce. In *International Conference on Scientific and Statistical Database Management*, New Orleans, LA, June 2–4, pp. 302–319, Springer, 2009.

[19] Ahmed Eldawy and Mohamed F Mokbel. SpatialHadoop: A MapReduce framework for spatial data. In *2015 IEEE 31st International Conference on Data Engineering*, Seoul, South Korea, April 13–17, pp. 1352–1363, IEEE, 2015.

[20] Ahmed Eldawy and Mohamed F Mokbel. A demonstration of spatial-Hadoop: An efficient MapReduce framework for spatial data. *Proceedings of the VLDB Endowment*, 6(12):1230–1233, 2013.

[21] Jiamin Lu and Ralf Hartmut Güting. Parallel secondo: A practical system for large-scale processing of moving objects. In *2014 IEEE 30th International Conference on Data Engineering*, Chicago, IL, March 31–April 4, pp. 1190–1193, IEEE, 2014.

[22] Jiamin Lu and Ralf Hartmut Güting. Parallel secondo: Boosting database engines with Hadoop. In *IEEE 18th International Conference on Parallel and Distributed Systems (ICPADS)*, Singapore, December 17–19, pp. 738–743. IEEE, 2012.

[23] Jiamin Lu and Ralf Hartmut Güting. Parallel secondo: Practical and efficient mobility data processing in the cloud. In *2013 IEEE International Conference on Big Data*, Silicon Valley, CA, October 6–9, pp. 107–125, IEEE, 2013.

[24] Qiang Ma, Bin Yang, Weining Qian, and Aoying Zhou. Query processing of massive trajectory data based on MapReduce. In *Proceedings of the First International Workshop on Cloud Data Management*, Hong Kong, China, November 2, pp. 9–16, ACM, 2009.

[25] Shoji Nishimura, Sudipto Das, Divyakant Agrawal, and Amr El Abbadi. MD-HBase: Design and implementation of an elastic data infrastructure for cloud-scale location services. *Distributed and Parallel Databases*, 31(2):289–319, 2013.

[26] Randall T Whitman, Michael B Park, Sarah M Ambrose, and Erik G Hoel. Spatial indexing and analytics on Hadoop. In *Proceedings of the 22nd*

ACM SIGSPATIAL International Conference on Advances in Geographic Information Systems, Dallas, TX, November 4–7, pp. 73–82, ACM, 2014.

[27] Hanan Samet. *Applications of Spatial Data Structures*, Addison-Wesley Longman, Boston, MA, 1990.

[28] Ching Avery. *Giraph: Large scale graph processing infrastructure on Hadoop*, Hadoop Summit, Santa Clara, CA, June 29, 2011. https://www.slideshare.net/averyching/20110628giraph-hadoop-summit (accessed August 22, 2017).

[29] Yucheng Low, Joseph E Gonzalez, Aapo Kyrola, Danny Bickson, Carlos E Guestrin, and Joseph Hellerstein. Graphlab: A new framework for parallel machine learning. *arXiv preprint*, Available https://arxiv.org/ftp/arxiv/papers/1408/1408.2041.pdf (accessed August 22, 2017).

[30] Grzegorz Malewicz, Matthew H Austern, Aart JC Bik, James C Dehnert, Ilan Horn, Naty Leiser, and Grzegorz Czajkowski. Pregel: A system for large-scale graph processing. In *Proceedings of the ACM International Conference on Management of Data*, Indianapolis, IN, June 06–11, pp. 135–146, 2010.

[31] Michael R Evans, KwangSoo Yang, James M Kang, and Shashi Shekhar. A lagrangian approach for storage of spatio-temporal network datasets: A summary of results. In *Proceedings of the 18th SIGSPATIAL International Conference on Advances in Geographic Information Systems*, San Jose, CA, November 2–5, pp. 212–221, ACM, 2010.

[32] Sarnath Ramnath, Zhe Jiang, Hsuan-Heng Wu, Venkata MV Gunturi, and Shashi Shekhar. A spatio-temporally opportunistic approach to best-start-time lagrangian shortest path. In *International Symposium on Spatial and Temporal Databases*, HKUST, Hong Kong, August 26–28, pp. 274–291, Springer, 2015.

[33] Venkata MV Gunturi, Shashi Shekhar, and KwangSoo Yang. A critical-time-point approach to all-departure-time lagrangian shortest paths. *IEEE Transactions on Knowledge and Data Engineering*, 27(10):2591–2603, 2015.

[34] Reem Y Ali, Venkata MV Gunturi, Andrew J Kotz, Shashi Shekhar, and William F Northrop. Discovering non-compliant window co-occurrence patterns: A summary of results. In *International Symposium on Spatial and Temporal Databases*, HKUST, Hong Kong, August 26–28, pp. 391–410, Springer, 2015.

[35] Reem Y Ali, Venkata Gunturi, Shashi Shekhar, Ahmed Eldawy, Mohamed F Mokbel, Andrew J Kotz, and William F Northrop. Future connected vehicles: Challenges and opportunities for spatio-temporal computing. In *Proceedings of the 23rd SIGSPATIAL International Conference on Advances in Geographic Information Systems*, Seattle, WA, November 3–6, p. 14, ACM, 2015.

[36] Dev Oliver, Shashi Shekhar, Xun Zhou, Emre Eftelioglu, Michael R Evans, Qiaodi Zhuang, James M Kang, Renee Laubscher, and Christopher Farah. Significant route discovery: A summary of results. In *Geographic Information Science*, Vienna, Austria, September 24–26, pp. 284–300, Springer, 2014.

[37] ESRI GIS. Tools for Hadoop: Big data spatial analytics for the Hadoop framework. http://esri.github.io/gis-tools-for-hadoop/ (accessed August 22, 2017).

[38] Ahmed Eldawy and Mohamed F Mokbel. Pigeon: A spatial MapReduce language. In *Data Engineering (ICDE), 2014 IEEE 30th International Conference on*, pp. 1242–1245, IEEE, 2014.

Chapter 19

On Emerging Use Cases and Techniques in Large Networked Data in Biomedical and Social Media Domain

Vishrawas Gopalakrishnan and Aidong Zhang

State University of New York
Buffalo, New York

CONTENTS

19.1 Background on Big Data

Over the last two decades the tremendous growth of the Internet has resulted in large-scale generation of digital content. This has excited analysts and researchers to further the technological capabilities to store, represent, and analyze this voluminous data. To illustrate the magnitude of data explosion, specifically in last four years, consider the figures reported in Ref. [1]. The article suggests that we generated around 5 exabytes of data from the time data was earliest recorded to year 2003, while we now produce the same amount in a matter of just 2 days! Apart from social media and related domains, advances in biological, medical, and healthcare technologies, along with development in high-throughput biomedical technologies such as omic (e.g., genomic, metabolomics, proteomics, and next generation sequencing), imaging (e.g., behavior monitoring), wearable and portable medical sensors, yield vast amounts of highly complex biomedical data on a daily basis. Thus, paucity of data is no longer a bottleneck for data analysis. On the contrary, this rate and size of generated data not only compels us to think of effective ways for data management and content presentation for conveying good quality information to the end users but also of effective and efficient techniques in data analyses and pattern extraction.

19.1.1 Graph as a representation schema for big data

Toward this cause, researchers are now investigating efficient data representation techniques to enable quicker and more "interpretive" learning [2]. One such data representation that has garnered significant attention is graph. While graph representation of a data has been in usage from 1960s (e.g., IBM IMS uses hierarchical data structures), their usefulness, particularly their storage capacity, and their dexterity in handling different types of graphs and graph operations were restricted. However, with advancements in NoSQL solutions in the late 1990s and early 2000s, property store graph database products like Neo4J and Titan have gained traction in database market. Coupled with the availability of products like Apache Spark GraphX, Apache Spark MLib, etc., not only do users get the advantages of transaction-oriented database systems but also the flexibility to model explicit relationships and perform machine learning tasks. Compared to traditional relational forms of representation (e.g., RDBMS), graph-based representation provides several advantages. A major one is that the query/analysis latency in a graph is proportional to the subset one chooses to explore in a query, and is not proportional to the amount of data stored; thus, defusing the "join bomb" [3]. Apart from other efficiency-related arguments, another major advantage in graph representation is the inherent ability to provide "interpretable" inferences or analyses to facilitate semantic understanding and deduction. As an example, consider a network of people with different edge labels like "friend," "works-with," "spouse." In such a graph, it is not only possible to predict the links between any two unconnected nodes but also generate a sequence of intermediary inference steps that allows us to predict the edge labels/types. Furthermore, many data or events occurring in the real world are inherently captured better in a graph due to the causal and interactive nature of the participants—e.g., people interacting over social media, proteins interacting with each other, or computers connected and communicating over the network. Modeling such interactions using graph also allows us to use established graph techniques in knowledge discovery and at the same time provides us with interesting opportunities to adapt machine learning algorithms to graph models [4–7].

19.1.2 Example applications of graph-based analyses

Due to data explosion described earlier, the number of participants in a network has increased manifold, and consequently, the information passed over the edges. Furthermore, the high data velocity results in more frequent and sizeable interactions between the participants of the graph. This has motivated many researchers to try understand the changing influence on the network structure over time [8–10], predict the possible bridge nodes between given two nodes (concepts) in a graph (aka hypotheses generation in biomedical text mining) [11,12,41], etc. While these use cases contain a time aspect (dynamic) and represent evolving relationships that need to be factored in during analyses, there are many cases where the temporal element is ignored and the graph-based model is used simply to represent the relationship between concepts in a static setting—e.g., given a snapshot of a knowledge base of entities, an entity relationship graph is created to depict relatedness between the concepts. In this chapter, we will be discussing some use cases from both static and temporal domains. As example use case of static scenario, we will discuss topics related to coreference resolution and collective entity resolution in large corpora. Since temporal aspect occurs naturally in biological datasets, we talk in detail about few applications involving link prediction and biomedical text mining. We will also briefly discuss few works that adapts and ports methods/approaches popularly used in one domain (e.g., social media analyses) to comparatively more recent application domains (e.g., biomedical settings).

19.2 Graph-Based Models and Approaches in Social Text Mining for Entity Resolution

With the growth of social networks in last decade and worldwide penetration of the Internet in households, the amount of diverse media content generated by users has grown exponentially over the years. The variety of content generated, ranging from pictures to text posts provide a wealth of opportunity to mine and extract useful information. However, this is easier said than done, as there are variety of challenges like extracting the concept/subjects referred in the text (named entity recognition), identifying them and linking to an external knowledge base for semantic enrichment (named entity disambiguation and linking), word sense disambiguation, word dependency extraction, understanding the text semantics, etc. Much of these tasks are highly interrelated and advancements in one of these fields eventually furthers the advancements in others. This is primarily because much of the performance in these fields hinges upon the effective capturing and understanding of the context and semantics of the text. Once identified, these semantics can be passed on to remaining tasks or the semantic extraction process can be incorporated in the other approaches to improve their performance.

Let us begin our discussion from the most basic and yet pivotal task in text mining framework—entity resolution (ER). The task of entity resolution is to disambiguate and state whether two entities represented differently refer to the same underlying physical object. For example, in the e-commerce domain, if t_1 represents a product title *EOS 600D* and t_2 refers to *Rebel T3i*, the disambiguation task is to state whether t_1 and t_2 refer to the same physical object. Unlike the string similarity problem, this task is more nuanced as even though the surface form of the objects might be different (as in this case), they might actually be the same product (true in this case, the former is the name used in the European market, while the latter is the title used in the American market). There are similar parallel problems in other domains like determining if the string *JLo* and *Jennifer Lopez* refer to the same person or whether the bibliographic entry *Jerry Baulier, Philip Bohannon, S. Gogate, S. Joshi, C. Gupta, A. Khivesera, Henry F. Korth, Peter McIlroy, J. Miller,*

P. P. S. Narayan, M. Nemeth, Rajeev Rastogi, Abraham Silberschatz, S. Sudarshan, ***DataBlitz: A High Performance Main-Memory Storage Manager*** and *P. P. S. Narayan, S. Joshi, M. Nemeth, Abraham Silberschatz, Henry F. Korth, A. Khivesera, Jerry Baulier, S. Sudarshan, Philip Bohannon, Peter McIlroy, J. Miller, S. Gogate, Rajeev Rastogi, C. Gupta* refer to the same literature (the text in bold is the name of the paper) [13]. Such problems arise due to lack of standardization in the representation. This problem not only occurs in free-form unstructured domains like e-commerce where each website or reseller rewrites the name to improve his sale but also in scientific domains like chemical and biological names [14–16]. Resolving these ambiguous strings is important as it affects the recall of a search system and affects the performance of data analysis. To illustrate the practical importance of these kinds of matching problems, consider the e-commerce domain in the UK, where Web searches on this sector alone constituted 6.06% of Web traffic—next only to social networking—7.3% [17]. Losing search hits due to an inability to resolve the ambiguity could result in a heavy loss for the resellers. There are four distinct categories to the matching problem [13]:

1. *Matching entities with high degree of token overlap*: The input strings represent the same physical entity, and their token sets have high overlap. This is arguably the easiest case, which can be solved using any reasonable similarity function such as the Jaccard coefficient.

2. *Matching entities with low degree of token overlap*: These include entities that are regarded as synonyms and need specific domain knowledge for disambiguation.

3. *"Softly-matched" entities*: The inputs represent variations of the same object (in physical characteristics or configuration). Distinguishing between an exactly matched input and a softly-matched input using similarity measures can be very tricky.

4. *Unmatched entities with high degree of token overlap*: The strings do not represent the same physical entity, but their token sets have many elements in common. This happens, for example, when one is a subcategory of the other (e.g., a product vs. its accessory). Comparison under this category can be differentiated easily by humans but requires semantic understanding on the part of machines.

5. *Unmatched entities with low degree of token overlap*: This is symmetric to Category 1, and it is easily solved by a naïve similarity measure-based approach.

For an example of each category listed above, please refer to Table 19.1, which also provides the normalized output of two widely used string similarity approaches.

Table 19.1 Examples of input instances to the entity title matching problem

Category	Title 1	Title 2	Jaccard Coefficient	TF-IDF + cosine
1	Sony dvd-r recordable camcorder media 3DMR3011H	Sony mini dvd-r media 3DMR3011H	0.57	0.72
2	Rebel T3i	EOS 600D	0	0
3	Speck seethru green hard shell case for 15' Macbook - MB15GRNSEEV2	Speck Products seethru case for Apple 15' Macbook pro - MB15-blu-see-v2	0.42	0.59
4	FE-140 digital camera battery charger replacement for 4 aa NiMH 2800mah rechargeable battery	Olympus FE-140	0.07	0.47
5	Canon 2gb sd secure digital card - 3505b001	Sony Alpha DSLR-A350 digital slr camera - DSLRA350	0.083	0.1

Having firmly established that the ER problem is more generic and much harder than a string similarity problem, we now discuss a few graph-based approaches toward solving it. There are two distinct classes of approaches toward ER—(1) pair-wise and (2) collective. The difference in the two approaches stems from the level of access to the dataset. In the former case, the ER system is only provided with a pair of input strings (entity candidates) which need to be disambiguated, while in the latter, the system has access to all different candidates beforehand, i.e., the decision on whether a pair of input entities refers to the same object or not is not just based on one input at a time. Consequently, such approaches (collective entity resolution) are not suitable for online streaming with cold start-based disambiguation settings.

In this chapter, we will be discussing two works on graph-based entity resolution. The work *Matching Titles with Cross Title Web-Search Enrichment and Community Detection* published in VLDB 2014 [13] (CTE+CDAM) is a hybrid graph-based approach that solves the ER problem under a pair-wise setting.

An explanation on how a collective ER solution operates is provided through a review and a brief discussion of a technical report authored by Indrajit Bhattacharya and Lise Getoor, which was later published [18].

19.2.1 Graph-based approach for online pair-wise entity resolution

In this section, we describe the method proposed in Ref. [13]. Note the usage of term "hybrid" in describing this approach earlier. This is because the approach models the problem as a community detection task based on "strength of ties" and uses a Web search engine to generate reference corpora. In this way it leverages classical IR techniques in conjunction with graph/network mining principles.

The Web being a vast repository of documents containing information on virtually every possible entity or topic, from the very esoteric to the extremely common, is an ideal corpus for a range of datasets—bibliography to e-commerce. Thus, we can use the different representations of a given entity on the web, and also the keywords that occur in the vicinity of entity references within web pages to establish the extended context for the entity [19]. Thus, the authors use a Web search engine to swiftly and efficiently gather ranked set of pages that act as a reference corpora. Furthermore, the Web search engine also uses multiple signals like font, size, and position of query keywords within a page, presence of query keywords in anchor text for the page, PageRank, and query and page categories (e.g., electronics, music, apparel), for ranking.

19.2.1.1 Overview of the approach

The key problem which is to be addressed is the following. We are given two titles representing some physical entities such as commercial products, bibliographic entries, locations, or people. Each title is a string of words. The two titles typically come from different sources, such as product titles from `Amazon` and `BestBuy`, or bibliographic entries from `ACM` and `DBLP`, etc. Consider accessory vs. its corresponding product as an example:

$$t_1 = \text{"Optio S60 camera Battery Charger Replacement"}$$

$$t_2 = \text{"Pentax Optio S60 Digital Camera"}$$

We need to determine whether t_1 and t_2 represent the same physical entity or not. In some cases, t_1 and t_2 might be "almost" the same—this is the "softly matched" case discussed as Category 3 in Table 19.1. The output is a score, representing the confidence in marking the two titles identical.

The authors of Ref. [13] begin by turning the titles into two sets of words.

$$T_1 = \{\text{optio, s60, camera, battery, charger, replacement}\}$$

$$T_2 = \{\text{pentax, optio, s60, digital, camera}\}$$

Then the following two components acts on these sets as follows:

- The first component called *cross-title enrichment* (CTE) aims to use a small number of Web searches to enhance the quality of T_1 and T_2. In particular, using Web searches one enriches T_1 and T_2 by adding/deleting tokens to them in such a way that the enriched T_i still represents the same physical entity as the original T_i (for $i \in \{1,2\}$), and yet the enriched versions make it easier to tell whether t_1 and t_2 refer to the same physical object. By rewriting the titles as stated above, one "hopes" that the basic similarity measures like Jaccard coefficient or cosine similarity that were ineffective earlier can be reused now. The motivation for this is drawn from "query rewriting," a classic IR technique. However, their approach and use case is different from the traditional IR sense where query/user logs are used to perform this task [20,21].

- The second component called *community detection for approximate matching* (CDAM) is responsible for computing the distance between (enriched) T_1 and T_2 in cases where CTE could not resolve the ambiguity. This distance is computed based on the strength of the constructed "social" network between the private tokens, i.e., $(T_1 \setminus T_2) \cup (T_2 \setminus T_1)$. If these tokens form a network with separate "communities," then they are deemed far apart; otherwise if the strong ties give way to a single close-knit community, then the corresponding titles are deemed a match.

The motivation for CTE lies in the following facts: (1) not all tokens have the same discriminatory power, (2) even powerful tokens like model number get their distinguishing power only in conjunction with other tokens like brand name, and (3) for matching titles, the set of shared tokens between the two titles are the ones that have most semantic correlation with a title's private tokens. So then, if we have a method that is able to "expand" the token set shared by the titles and they are a mismatch, then the expansion will only increase the distinguishing power of the private tokens. On the other hand if the titles are a match, by this expansion one can "hope" to subsume all or part of the private tokens. So if C refers to shared context $(T_1 \cap T_2)$, then from previous example we get:

$$C = \{\text{optio, s60, camera}\}$$
$$T_1 \setminus C = T_1 \setminus T_2 = \{\text{battery, charger, replacement}\}$$
$$T_2 \setminus C = T_2 \setminus T_1 = \{\text{pentax, digital}\}$$

Thus, the objective of CTE is to "expand" C, so that if t_1 and t_2 are really nonmatching titles then discriminatory power of $T_1 \setminus C$ and $T_2 \setminus C$ increases, i.e., in this case, "battery," "charger," and "replacement." On the other hand, if the private tokens are not significant then their powers will fade away, since C would tend to subsume them as it should in the case of "pentax" and "digital."

Note the use of word “hope” when describing the expected behavior of CTE. This is due to errors that are introduced by a Web search engine; thus, the need for CDAM. Apart from that, CDAM is also expected to handle the situations of semantic correlation as in Categories 2 and 3 of Table 19.1. Thus, if even after expansion, $T_1 \setminus C$ and $T_2 \setminus C$ are not equal to $\emptyset$, then CDAM measures the semantic equivalence of the private tokens across the two titles.

One can conclude from the above discussion that the role of CTE is to try and make the pair of titles compact and precise, and check if they are an exact match. CDAM on the other hand quantifies the dissimilarity in cases where CTE is not able to make a decision. Thus, CDAM can handle all the cases which CTE can but vice versa is not true, making CDAM the core module. CTE can be considered as performance booster as, apart from just adding contextually relevant tokens to aid CDAM, it also helps in reducing the Web query firing by removing tokens that are contextually redundant, thus pruning out private tokens for CDAM.

To get a holistic view of an end-to-end system with all the presented algorithms, we can visualize the matching task as a sequence of three stages—refer Figure 19.1:

1. **Querying and blocking stage**—Responsible for issuing one Web query for each title and storing the obtained result set. This is then used for blocking and also CTE. Blocking helps in the first level of filtering where outright mismatches are removed from comparison.

2. **CTE**—Responsible for reranking the result set tokens based upon the compared title. It identifies new relevant tokens and removes unimportant tokens. For example, in comparison between *EOS 600D* vs. *Rebel T3i*,

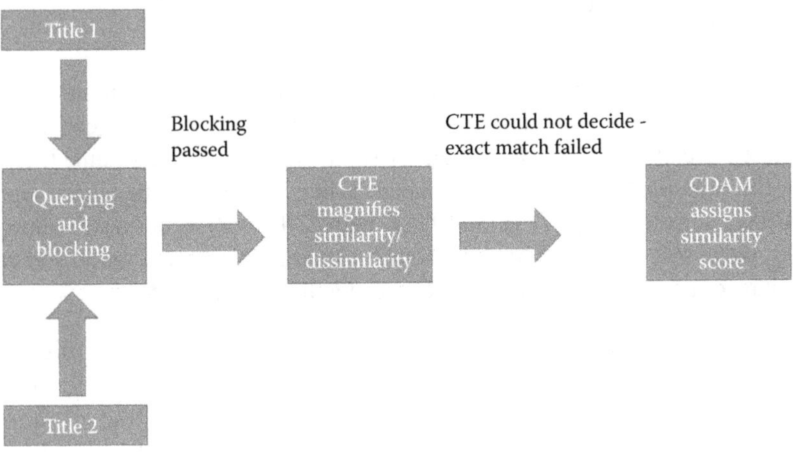

Figure 19.1: Component level flow diagram with algorithms.

canon & *camera* get added to both the titles due to their high frequencies in the search results. However, *eos* which has a lower frequency is still added to T_2 because of its presence in the enriched set of T_1. This process is called rescaling.

3. **CDAM**—Responsible for disambiguating two enriched titles that are not exactly similar after CTE, for example quantifying the dissimilarity between {600D} and {Rebel, T3i,} under the shared context of {Canon, EOS, Camera}.

The modules of this framework are presented in bottom-up fashion, starting from bare minimum to complete system. As the bare minimum system is CDAM, we begin our discussion from there.

19.2.1.2 Community detection for approximate matching—CDAM

Going by the notation introduced, the task of this section is to measure the semantic relatedness between the private tokens of T_1 and T_2 and quantify if the difference is substantial enough to be labeled a mismatch. As discussed earlier, the authors model this as a graph of private tokens $((T_1 \setminus C) \cup (T_2 \setminus C))$ where the edges represent the relationship of "can replace." Furthermore, because each token in $T_1 \setminus C$ and $T_2 \setminus C$ derives its power only in conjunction with tokens in C, the authors pair each of them with C and issue a Web query. The result of the Web query is used to create an adjacency matrix **A** for a directed graph G, where the weight of an edge from node a to b represents the frequency of b in the result set, when a is a part of the query—this depicts the implied association between the tokens. Typically a Web search API returns an XML with three fields for each result: title, abstract, and the URL of the Web page. Based upon the level of granularity, one can choose any of them for selecting the tokens—the choice dictates the level of complexity.

On the obtained matrix **A**, the authors use the concept of symmetric equivalence and domination to identify tokens that form a phrase and tokens that can be ignored because they are dominated by some other token in the same title. Thus, for the example "Optio S60" introduced earlier, we generate the query set, Q, by pairing each element in $T_1 \setminus C$ and $T_2 \setminus C$ with C. Thus, Q ={optio s60 camera battery, optio s60 camera charger, optio s60 camera replacement, optio s60 camera pentax, optio s60 camera digital}. Correspondingly, we get **A** as:

$$A = \begin{bmatrix} \text{Tokens} & \text{battery} & \text{replacement} & \text{charger} & \text{pentax} & \text{digital} \\ \text{battery} & 0 & 3 & 5 & 0 & 0 \\ \text{replacement} & 3 & 0 & 3 & 0 & 0 \\ \text{charger} & 8 & 3 & 0 & 0 & 0 \\ \text{pentax} & 0 & 0 & 0 & 0 & 4 \\ \text{digital} & 0 & 0 & 0 & 8 & 0 \end{bmatrix}$$

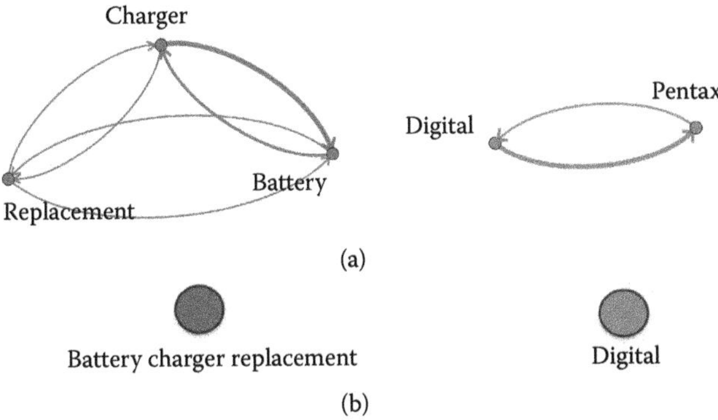

Figure 19.2: (a) Original graph. (b) Collapsed graph. Example of graph collapsing.

Based on the principles of equivalence and dominance, the original graph (Figure 19.2a) is collapsed into Figure 19.2b.

Obtaining a collapsed graph allows us to narrow our focus onto important private tokens that are unique to a given title. Having identified these, the next step is to quantify the strength of correlation between the private tokens of this collapsed graph. To do so, one can formulate the problem as one of graph clustering/community detection that measures the strength of cohesion and finds the number of communities. The intuition is that if the strength of cohesion is high enough to result in a single community, then it implies that the reduced private tokens share high semantic dependency; if so, we can term the two entities as a match, otherwise a mismatch. Modularity detection algorithms on such small graphs can give misleading results [22]. Furthermore, edges between tokens across titles need to be interpreted differently compared to traditional community detection. Assume that the two titles create two dense subgraphs and an edge connects them. According to edge-betweenness and other community detection algorithms, there are at least two communities [23]. However, this interpretation fails if an edge connects two important tokens across the two titles, as depicted in Figure 19.3, implying there is a high likelihood that the two titles are equivalent and the graph has just one community. Thus, the number of communities is a function of intertitle edges and their respective nodes. This is formulated as:

$$\max\left\{ (f(g(a),g(b),w(a,b)) - \lambda) \;\middle|\; \begin{smallmatrix} a\in T_1\setminus T_2 \\ b\in T_2\setminus T_1 \\ \exists E(a,b) \end{smallmatrix} \right\} \tag{19.1}$$

where:

$g(.) =$ avg weight of out-edges(.)$-$avg weight of in-edges(.)
if in-degree(.) $= 0$, avg. weight of in-edges(.) $= -1$

$f(.) =$ any aggregating function like addition

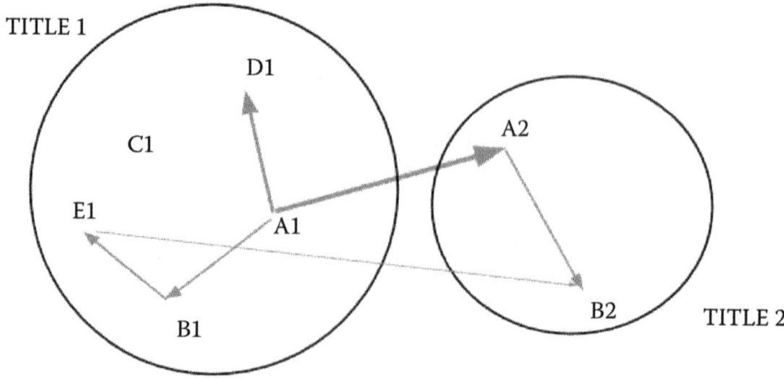

Figure 19.3: Example graphical relationship between tokens (represented as nodes) of two titles.

λ = penalty value for isolated nodes (nodes with no edges)

$w(a,b)$ = edge weight between a and b

The logic behind Equation 19.1 is to weigh an edge by factoring in the importance of the participating vertices. The importance of a vertex is directly proportional to its weighted out-degree and is inversely proportional to its weighted in-degree. This is consistent with the hypothesis that nodes with high discrimination power tend to identify more nodes and are rarely identified by others, i.e., high out-degree and a low in-degree. As it has an upper bound of 1, a node with no incoming edges is assigned a value of 1. As the maximum value of g(.) can be 1, the maximum value of f(.) can be 3 (if f is addition function). If the result of Equation 19.1 > threshold τ, T_1 and T_2 are said to be a match.

Continuing our example: since after graph collapsing we get only two nodes—*battery charger replacement* and *digital* which are isolated, as per Equation 19.1 we obtain two communities inferring the products are different.

To illustrate a walk-through for CDAM, consider the example of Category 2 of Table 19.1. Let t_1 be "rebel t3i" and t_2 be "eos 600d." In this example $C = \phi$ and $T_1 \setminus C = \{rebel, t3i\}$ and $T_2 \setminus C = \{eos, 600d\}$ and by proceeding exactly in the same way like the earlier example, we get **A** as:

$$A = \begin{bmatrix} \text{Tokens} & \text{rebel} & \text{t3i} & \text{eos} & \text{600D} \\ \text{rebel} & 0 & 0 & 0 & 0 \\ \text{t3i} & 8 & 0 & 5 & 0 \\ \text{eos} & 1 & 0 & 0 & 0 \\ \text{600D} & 3 & 5 & 7 & 0 \end{bmatrix}$$

After "graph collapsing," the adjacency matrix **A** reduces to two nodes—$t3i$ and $600d$. The intertitle edge along with the weight (for number of Web results = 10) is: (600d, $t3i$) = 0.5. Since the nodes $t3i$ and 600d do not have any inlinks from their own title tokens, they get the in-degree score of -1 to signify high importance; thus, making out-degree scores inconsequential. The resultant score is thus dependent only on the intertitle edge whose score is 0.5. Based on appropriate threshold, one can make the right decision.

19.2.1.3 Cross title enrichment—CTE

While the above section is responsible for disambiguation resolution, the objective of this section, as mentioned earlier, is to improve the shared context between the titles so as to magnify the semantic relatedness. This would not only improve the performance of CDAM but at the same time improve its efficiency by identifying and removing unimportant tokens. This task involves observing the titles under comparison and then adding or removing tokens that would amplify the similarity (or dissimilarity).

Algorithm 19.1 describes the CTE process. The input to the algorithm is the result set of the two comparable titles, t_1 and t_2. As a Web search engine returns a set of results sorted by relevance, this notion of relevancy needs to be propagated into the token selection mechanism. Since the results are ranked from highest to lowest, the authors apply a monotonically decreasing function—discounted cumulative gain (DCG). The weighted frequency of tokens is then calculated using this modified discount. The authors use two support thresholds in pruning out the candidate set of tokens. These are dependent on the weighted frequencies rather than on the number of results. The first support (dependent on η) is more liberal in nature and is primarily responsible for adding new tokens. The second threshold (dependent on μ) is the average of weighted frequencies obtained from

Algorithm 19.1 Cross Title Enrichment

Input: Result set for title t_1 and t_2 - $R(t_1)$ and $R(t_2)$, support threshold η, support threshold for self determination μ
Output: Enriched title $E(t_1)$ and $E(t_2)$
For each token w_i in the ith ranked result in $R(t_1)$, let $freq(w_{t_{1_i}})$ be the weighted frequency of the token, calculated using DCG
Similarly compute $freq(w_{t_{2_i}})$ for all w_i in $R(t_2)$
Let $w_{t_{1_1}}, w_{t_{1_2}}, \ldots, w_{t_{1_q}}$ be tokens of set $\{freq(w_{t_1})\}$ arranged in decreasing order of weighted frequency
$\Omega_{t_1} := w_{t_{1_i}}$ **if** $freq(w_{t_{1_i}}) > \eta \times freq(w_{t_1})$
Perform similar operation for Ω_{t_2}
Let avg_s & avg_t be average of frequencies in Ω_{t_1} & Ω_{t_2}
For each tok $\in \Omega_{t_1} \wedge T_1$ **if** $freq(tok) < \mu \times avg_s$**:** delete
Perform similar operation for Ω_{t_2}
Using Algorithm 19.2 calculate gain and update Ω_{t_1} & Ω_{t_2}
return $E(t_1) := \Omega_{t_1}$ and $E(t_2) := \Omega_{t_2}$

the previous step and is responsible for pruning tokens. Since search engines tend to return results that cover as many query tokens as possible, the secondary threshold acts as a regularizer and prevents uncontrolled preference to tokens from higher ranked results.

Now consider the example where for title 1 the token set obtained from the previous step was $\{canon, eos, 600d, camera\}$ and for title 2 $\{canon, rebel, t3i, camera\}$. Furthermore, consider the token *eos* that was found during enriching title 2, but was pruned out due to low support. We thus want to boost frequencies for all such tokens that (1) did not make it to the final set, (2) were close to their support cut-off, and (3) are present in the final set of the compared title. The boost percentage added depends on the contribution of that token to the dissimilarity between these intermediate enriched titles. Thus, the authors boost the frequency for *eos* in proportion to its contribution in the dissimilarity. If the modified frequency now meets the support threshold, this token is added to the set—refer to Algorithm 19.2.

Based on the enrichment result thus obtained, there are three possible situations that can occur:

1. The two sets are exactly identical and in that case the two product titles are said to be a match.

2. One set is a subset of other (subsumption). This case commonly occurs when a product is compared with its accessory.

3. The case which does not fall in either of the above two is handled by the algorithms in Section 19.2.1.2.

19.2.1.4 Handling a subsumption case

Prima facie, comparisons under (2) should be labeled as a mismatch. However, if we delve further, we can see that this need not always be true due to the various

Algorithm 19.2 Calculate Gain

Input: Weighted frequency of tokens from t_1 and t_2 i.e., $w_{t_{1_i}}$ & $w_{t_{2_i}}$, and Ω_{t_1} & Ω_{t_2}
Output: Gained weighted frequency for $w_{t_{1_i}}$ & $w_{t_{2_i}}$
repeat
    for each $tok \in \{(\Omega_{t_2} \setminus \Omega_{t_1}) \wedge w_{t_{1_i}}\}$ **do**
        calculate contribution of tok toward the dissimilarity between Ω_{t_1} & Ω_{t_2}
        increase weight of tok in $w_{t_{1_i}}$ proportionately
    end for
until All tokens are processed
Repeat for all tokens $\in \{(\Omega_{t_1} \setminus \Omega_{t_2}) \wedge w_{t_{2_i}}\}$
return $w_{t_{1_i}}$ and $w_{t_{2_i}}$

characteristics of a search engine. Consider the queries "Dell vostro 1400" and "Dell vostro 1400 laptop" in Google. The results we get are quite different from each other leading to a scenario where one enriched title is a subset of other. Handling this scenario becomes straightforward when we go deeper into page level processing of the results obtained from issuing the smaller title as the query and checking the coverage of the private tokens.

19.2.1.5 Experiments

This section presents selected results published by the authors, demonstrating the performance of the described method against various baselines. The authors used five real world data sets. The first four data sets are publicly available benchmark data sets [24].*

The fifth data set is created by the authors, comprising pairs from heterogeneous domains. The matches described in the first four data sets are "exact matches" and fall predominantly under categories 1 and 5 of Table 19.1 with some them in being in category 4, whereas those in the fifth belong to categories 2, 3, and 4.

1. **Abt-Buy dataset** contains 1097 matching product titles. This dataset comprises of electronic products and usually has unique identifiers in each title.

2. **Amazon-Google dataset** has 1300 matching product titles and unlike the Abt-Buy dataset, the titles do not always have discriminatory tokens.

3. **ACM-DBLP dataset** is made up of 2224 matching article titles. This dataset is subjected to extensive manual at curing source level.

4. **DBLP-Scholar dataset** has around 5347 matching article titles. Compared to ACM-DBLP dataset, this is fairly more difficult to process.

5. **Heterogeneous dataset** has 500 pairs, equally divided into matches and mismatches. It is a result of aggregation from domains like bibliographies, celebrities and their short-forms, locations and airport codes, products, etc.

As can be seen from Table 19.2, CTE+CDAM has the best results in product domain and also works decently in other domains like bibliography. This is despite using a generic Web search engine rather than something specific such as Google Scholar. All the Web searches were done with Yahoo! Boss API. For the heterogeneous dataset, the authors compare their method with top three performers from Table 19.2—refer to Table 19.3.

To demonstrate the efficacy of community detection formulation, the authors compared their formulation with two other state-of-the-art baselines—edge

*http://dbs.uni-leipzig.de/en/research/projects/object_matching/fever/benchmark_datasets_for_entity_resolution

Table 19.2 F1-Score comparison of various baselines

	Dataset			
	Abt-Buy	**Amazon-Google**	**DBLP-ACM**	**DBLP-Scholar**
Learning Based Approaches				
(Labelling effort 500)				
FEBRL SVM Winkler	~19%	~30%	~96%	~ 62%
FEBRL SVM Tokenset	~43%	46.5%	97.3%	~75%
FEBRL SVM Trigram	44.5%	46.5%	97.3%	~81%
FEBRL SVM Comb	44.5%	46.5%	97.3%	81.9%
MARLIN ADTree Cosine	~10%	~42%	96.4%	~72%
MARLIN ADTree Edit Distance (1 step learning)	~10%	~21%	96.4%	~80%
MARLIN ADTree Edit Distance (2 step learning)	~18%	~35%	96.4%	82.6%
MARLIN ADTree Comb	18.4%	45%	96.4%	82.6%
MARLIN SVM Cosine	~54.5%	~50%	~96%	~68%
MARLIN SVM Edit Distance (1 step learning)	~5%	~40%	~96%	~82%
MARLIN SVM Edit Distance (2 step learning)	~20%	~42%	~96%	~82%
MARLIN SVM Comb	54.8%	50.5%	96.4%	82.6%
Non-Learning Based Approaches				
FellegiSunter TokenSet	~40%	~45%	~97.5%	~50%
FellegiSunter Trigram	44.5%	48.4%	97.6%	57.2%
FellegiSunter Winkler	~18%	~48%	~50%	~55%
PPJoin+Cosine	~47%	~40%	91.9%	77.8%
PPJoin+Jaccard	47.4%	41.9%	91.9%	77.8%
IDF+Cosine	57%	52.9%	Not Applicable	Not Applicable
EN+IMP	62%	36.4%	68.62%	70.26%
CTE+CDAM	**59.8%**	**54.4%**	**96.99%**	**82.77%**

Table 19.3 Comparison for heterogeneous dataset

Methods	IDF	EN+IMP	CTE+CDAM
F1-score	50.4%	53.5%	**69.43%**

Table 19.4 Comparison of community detection algorithms

Dataset	Edge Betweenness	Blondel's Algorithm	CDAM
Abt-Buy	29.8%	37.8%	**49.41%**
Amazon-Google	26.8%	31.6%	**41.06%**
Heterogeneous	58.48%	63.2%	**69.43%**

betweenness [23] and Blondel's modularity [25]. Table 19.4 shows the F1-score of the system with CDAM and compares it with the system under an identical setting, replaced with corresponding baselines. In fact the CDAM results reported for Abt-Buy and Amazon-Google refer to the results of CDAM under the worst parameter setting. As can be seen, even the worst results of CDAM's community detection algorithm are better than those of the baselines.

Through various parameter tuning experiments and ablation-type testing, the authors show that CTE by itself is capable of handling most of the entity resolution cases when exact matching is required and CDAM is more useful when one is interested in soft matches. A major contribution in this work is the different interpretation of the intertitle edge tailored to suit the ER problem.

In this way, the authors interpreted the edge-betweenness approach differently to suit the task for ER. Coupled with the formulation of Equation 19.1, the authors present a graph-based formulation for pair-wise entity resolution that can be adapted for a generic setting. For instance, the authors show that the proposed method successfully resolves the case of "Sea-Tac" vs. "Seattle–Tacoma International Airport" and can also be used for phrase detection, e.g., for "linksys dual-band wireless-n gaming adapter–wga600n" the phrases identified are $\{$*wga600n linksys, dual- band wireless-n, gaming adapter*$\}$.

19.2.2 Graph-based approach for collective entity resolution

Unlike the previous technique wherein the system had access to only a pair of entities at a time, the following techniques [18,26–29] assume to have the entire corpus beforehand and the task is to perform collective entity resolution. In such approaches, it is generally assumed that there exists a reference graph, which essentially represents a known set of different "references" for entities and the relationship among themselves. Such a graph may contain hyperedges due to multiple relationship types between the reference entities. From this graph, we would like to extract and create an entity graph where each node in the entity graph represents a unique physical object which has corresponding mappings to the reference graph. Thus, the relation between the reference graph and entity graph is many-to-one. As a concrete example, consider that there are multiple names of a city (possibly abbreviations and airport codes like New York, New York City, NYC, etc.). Now based on the usage, one can have edges between NYC and NY state, or New York City and Shanghai, etc. Together these form the reference graph, where for the same entity "New York City," one has multiple references and there are hyperedges between the references that indicate a form of relationship among the subset of references. Note the links/edges are not complete for the references of a given entity, i.e., the edge NYC and NY state might have a label that is not the same as the New York City and Shanghai. The goal of the collective entity resolution is to make this subset complete by reconciling the references to a single entity and thereby also reconciling and completing/propagating the relationship among the references pointing to the same entity. While that is the objective, the fact there is already a partial information between references can also be leveraged to disambiguate the mapping between relationships and entities.

In this discussion, the authors focus primarily on the bibliographic domain [29] stored in relational data format; consequently, each entity can belong to one of the following three types of entities: author, paper, and venue. This results in two types of relationships—*writes* and *published_in*; authors write papers which get published in venues. Because there can be a reference involved in multiple hyperedges and the fact that there is a label associated to each such hyperedge which is known beforehand (e.g., *writes*, *published_in*), the hyperedges help us in providing both positive as well as negative evidences for entity resolution between two concepts in the reference graph. In this way, this formulation breaks away from the constraint of individual, pair-wise deduplication and focuses on predicting entity labels for the references collectively. To explain further, since the references for an entity are not observed individually, but rather as a member of hyperedges, the entity label $r.E$ of any reference r is directly influenced by the choice of its corresponding entity's label $r'.E$ for another reference r' if they are associated with the same hyperedge i.e., $r.H = r'.H$.

This entire process naturally lends itself to the task of clustering in graphs such that the entity labels in a cluster are identical. Consequently, agglomerative-based clustering approaches work best as they start from each reference being assigned as individual clusters and gradually, based on some similarity notion, they are aggregated to form different levels. Thus, one can slice the resulting dendrogram at different levels to find coreference resolutions at various thresholds. The most important aspect to this clustering is the similarity measure employed. The authors use a similarity measure which is a combination of both attribute-based and the relation similarity. Because the task is collective entity resolution, the authors also factor in the decisions of previous entity resolution tasks. Thus, at each step, based on the similarity measure, the entity clusters at a particular level in the dendrogram are evaluated for intercluster similarity and merged together based on threshold.

19.2.2.1 Similarity measures for entity resolution

Having established the motivation for clustering, the next step in the process is to select an effective notion of similarity between clusters. Since each data point in the graph has an associated set of attribute values, one needs to consider attribute values as well as the topological structure of the graph. Thus if c_i and c_j are the two entity clusters, the similarity between them is defined as

$$sim(c_i, c_j) = (1-\alpha) \times sim_{attr}(c_i, c_j) + \alpha \times sim_{graph}(c_i, c_j) \text{ where } 0 \leq \alpha \leq 1 \tag{19.2}$$

where $sim_{attr}()$ is the similarity of the attributes and $sim_{graph}()$ is the graph-based similarity between two entity clusters, and they are linearly combined with weights α and 1-α.

Attribute Similarity: The objective of defining attribute similarity is to capture the attribute level similarity between the members of each cluster and compare it with those of the other. Consequently, it is necessary that the computation process is not pair-wise as the performance will quickly degrade with growing cluster sizes. Hence, the authors recommend using a single link metric as it avoids similarities to be recomputed on merging or the addition of new members to a cluster. Furthermore, instead of considering all the references within an attribute, focusing on just the distinct references significantly reduces the similarity computation and allows incremental updates when clusters are merged. To reduce the computation even further, the authors suggest identifying representative attributes for each cluster. For example, given the references "A. Aho," "Alfred V. Aho," "A. V. Aho" for an entity whose correct attribute value is "Alfred V. Aho," it would be highly advantageous if this correct attribute value is identified as the *representative cluster attribute* for the cluster, then comparing two clusters boils down to comparing the representative cluster attributes.

Graph-Based Similarity: Now, we will discuss the graph-based similarity measures proposed by the authors that leverage the relationships between references. The network topology is defined by edges between nodes and the neighbors of given nodes.

1. *Edge Detail Similarity*: The authors begin by defining a similarity measure for a pair of edges, which can then be used in conjunction with linkage metrics like a single link to measure relational similarity between two clusters. It should be noted that just as in the case of attribute similarity, each entity cluster is associated with set of edges to which references contained in it belong. As each reference r is associated with an observed hyperedge $r.H$, the edge set $c.H$ for an entity cluster c is defined as $c.H = \{ h \mid r.H{=}h, r \in C\}$. In graph-based similarity, we are interested in the cluster label for

references. Thus, the authors define the similarity between h_i and h_j using the Jaccard coefficient:

$$sim(h_i,h_j) = \frac{|label(h_i) \cap label(h_j)|}{|label(h_i) \cup label(h_j)|} \tag{19.3}$$

Given this pair-wise similarity measure for edges, one can employ aggregation operators like *max* to calculate graph-based similarity between two entity clusters.

$$sim_{graph}(c_i,c_j) = max_{(h_i,h_j)}\{sim(h_i,h_j)\} \texttt{ where } h_i \in c_i.H, h_j \in c_j.H \tag{19.4}$$

2. *Neighborhood Similarity*: The above-described edge detail similarity is computationally expensive, especially since it is not trivial to adapt to handle incremental updates. Another significant issue with edge detail summary can be best explained through an example: Say we want to disambiguate between entities e_1 and e'_1. If e_1 participates in an edge with entities $\{e_1,e_2,e_3,e_4\}$ and e'_1 participates with the same entities, but in pair-wise fashion—$\{e'_1,e_2\}$, $\{e'_1,e_3\}$,$\{e'_1,e_4\}$, the latter has a totally different edge structure when compared to the former. Consequently, their edge detail similarity is also different due to the Jaccard of the labels on the edges. However, such inferences need not be true. In other words, regardless of whether two entity clusters with similar attributes have the same edge structure or not, if they have the same neighbor clusters to which they have edges, that is a sufficient graph-based evidence, at least in the bibliographic domain. That is, in the example of coauthorship above, it is not necessary for both e_1 and e'_1 to coauthor a paper with entities $e2, e3$, and $e4$ together, so long as they have a common neighborhood.

   Formally, if c represents the entity cluster, $c.N$ represents the neighborhood of the cluster and $c.H$ represents the set of edges associated to it, then

$$c.N = \bigcup_m label(h_i) | h_i \in c.H \tag{19.5}$$

   Note that $c.N$ is a multiset because the *label* function is a multiset due to the presence of hyperedges. In other words, there can be multiple edges to the same node emerging from the same source node, and thus the multiset neighborhood of a node is the collection of all the cluster labels occurring in all the edges associated to that node. Now, the Jaccard coefficient is extended to the multisets as:

$$sim_{graph}(c_i,c_j) = \frac{|c_i.N \cap c_j.N|}{|c_i.N \cup c_j.N|} \tag{19.6}$$

   In this way, the authors define the neighborhood similarity between two entity clusters.

19.2.2.2 Experiments

In this section, we present important results put forth by the authors. They focus only on bibliographic data sets with an objective of demonstrating the superiority of a graph-based entity resolution algorithm (*GBC*) over other attribute-based methods ($ATTR$). The authors use soft-TFIDF coupled with various similarity measures like scaled levenshtein (SL), Jaro (JA), and Jaro–Winkler (JW). As $ATTR$ provides only pair-wise matching results and since the duplication results are transitive, transitive closure is used to remove any results which have inconsistencies—this additional processing is referred to as $ATTR^*$.

As can be seen from Table 19.5, graph-based similarity consistently performs better than attribute-based approaches. Furthermore, for a similarity measure, JW acts as the most suitable candidate. Between GBC (neighbor) and GBC (edge), the difference is not significant, despite the fact that GBC (neighbor) is computationally less intensive.

To further convince the reader about the efficacy of the approach, the authors provide a few examples for which attribute-based methods were unable to disambiguate successfully. Examples include (liu j, lu j) and (chang c, chiang c). GBC correctly predicts that these are not duplicates. At the same time, there are other pairs that are not any more similar in terms of attributes than the examples above and yet are duplicates. These are also correctly predicted by GBC using the same similarity threshold by leveraging common collaboration patterns. Examples include (john m f, john m st), (reisbech c, reisbeck c k), (shortliffe e h, shortcliffe e h).

To summarize the topics discussed until now, we have introduced two contrary approaches to solve the entity resolution problem. While the first approach provides us the benefits of performing the deduplication in an online streaming environment, the second approach illustrates the benefits of using relationships between multiple references of the same entity and provides a methodology to gather this information in a systematic fashion. While both are a form of clustering, it is essentially the problem formulation and the interpretation behind

Table 19.5 F1 Score of ATTR vs. GBC-based approaches across three similarity-based measures

	CiteSeer			HEP		
	SL	**JA**	**JW**	**SL**	**JA**	**JW**
ATTR	0.98	0.981	0.980	0.976	0.976	0.972
ATTR*	0.989	0.991	0.990	0.971	0.968	0.965
GBC(Neighbor)	0.994	0.994	0.994	0.979	0.981	0.981
GBC(Edge)	0.995	0.995	0.995	0.982	0.983	0.982

the edges that distinguish the two approaches. As mentioned earlier, another advantage of graph formulation is that it allows interpretation of the decision. To illustrate that, consider Figure 19.3, where as explained in the formulation of Equation 19.1, the decision is made on the strength of ties between A_1 and A_2. Similarly, neighborhood-based or edge detail similarity introduced in the context of collective entity resolution also enables us to trace the inference procedure. This advantage and ability to interpret the inference procedure is also evident in use cases and techniques introduced in Section 19.3.2. Having discussed a ubiquitous preprocessing step in databases and data analyses of texts, we now talk about a few data mining tasks that are formulated as a graph problem in another emerging application domain—bioinformatics.

19.3 Graph-Based Models in Bioinformatics and Biomedical

Many of the use cases and scenarios that occur in the biological domain can be naturally modeled as a graph. This modeling of interactions between biological concepts can be effectively analyzed with a variety of techniques much of which is analogous to those employed in a social network setting [4]. In this section, we will first briefly talk about commonality and adaptation of approaches between social network and bioinformatics domains.

19.3.1 Commonality between social and biomedical network analyses

Guilt by association (GBA) is a common approach used in social network analyses, where new associations with a node in the graph are determined based on its existing associations and the associations of candidate nodes. This principle has been widely adopted in the biological domain. For example, Ref. [30] constructed a gene network based on association with the same genes and Ref. [31] combined protein interactions, genetic interactions, and gene expression correlation. At the same time, walk-based approaches have also gained popular support in determining relationships or link prediction [32]. Refs. [4,33] attempt to train a classifier to determine the validity of a new link between two concepts. Such link prediction tasks are formulated as PU learning tasks (positive unlabelled learning). Under such learning, one has limited access to a set of positive samples and treats randomly obtained unlabeled samples as negative. It then trains a biased SVM where it penalizes false negatives more heavily than false positives. The underlying principle is that since the positive samples are known to be true and the negative ones are created from the unlabeled set, getting the positive ones incorrect is more serious and cannot be condoned. Such PU-based learning has also been extensively used in social network settings. Furthermore, analogous to collaborative filtering where nodes/entities similar to the query node/entity are identified for profile enrichment of the latter and determining and recommending friends [34] or movies [35], works like [4,5,36] extend that principle to gather evidence from diverse, but related species and create a heterogeneous network for analyses. For instance, the human neural crest related developmental disorder Waardenburg syndrome shares gene modules with gravitropism (the ability to detect up and down) in plants, and mammalian angiogenesis has been found to involve the same pathways as lovastatin sensitivity in yeast. In this way, graph modeling of a data set enables us to leverage existing approaches and practices from one domain to other new and relatively less investigated areas.

In the next section, we introduce an interesting and very important problem of hypotheses generation in biomedical text mining and a relatively new hybrid approach that leverages and combines principles from the information retrieval (IR) field, and graph traversal to generate high quality, reliable postulates. While the broader objective is to say if two terms/nodes are linked (or would be linked) to each other, hypothesis generation goes a step further and provides evidence that leads to the two terms getting connected. This is particularly important in the biomedical area as merely stating two terms should be connected or interact with each provides incomplete information for doctors and clinicals scientist to validate this claim. In the next few paragraphs, we will introduce the problem of hypotheses generation and why it is important.

19.3.2 Hypotheses generation in biomedical texts

Even though technological advances have reduced the time of experimental verification of postulates and hypotheses in biological areas [37], the cost of performing the experiments is still considerably high. Hence most of the experiments are performed after a rigorous planning and analyses—most of which includes significant manual labor. Thus, although we have faster (but expensive) ways of verifying the hypotheses, there is a major bottleneck in the discovery process, viz. the task of analyzing and generating high-confidence viable postulates. At the same time, there has been a consistent growth in the amount of peer-reviewed articles submitted and accepted in the biomedical domain. Given the cost of experiments, many text mining researchers are interested in coming up with effective approaches to predict/generate high-quality hypotheses and postulates for medical practitioners and researchers.

Initially formulated as an IR problem [38], literature-based discovery (LBD) has grown to be one of the foremost tasks in text mining [39,40] in the biological domain. To explain the problem in a line, the objective of LBD is to uncover implicit relations between two terms using a corpora. There are two distinct variations in LBD closed discovery and open discovery. The former refers to the discovery process wherein two query terms are provided and the objective is to identify the relationship between them, if any. As an example, consider the task stated in Ref. [38], the first task that pioneered LBD in the biological domain—determining the relationship between fish oil and Raynaud's disease and how they are related. As opposed to this, in the open discovery approach only one term is provided and the task is to identify all the other terms that meet certain input criteria (e.g., the semantic of the second term). In this section, we restrict our discussion to closed discovery.

In this section, we will be discussing how to leverage limited textual concepts from biomedical publications to answer queries on possible interactions and relations between them. Thus, the problem statement is very much similar to link prediction; however, there are two added tasks: (a) Model and incorporate the semantics of the concepts to ensure that the links generated are meaningful. (b) Provide an explanation through intermediary terms on why there is a relation between two nodes. Toward that end, many approaches use tertiary knowledge bases to enrich the concepts with labels that aid in the discovery task. While there are few purely IR-based approaches for ranking the link terms between two query concepts, the naïve approach of focusing on immediate neighbors' neighbor (thus, restricting the search to depth 2) leads to identifying associations between only those terms that are well researched and pretty late in their discovery phase, i.e., whose association gap is reducing over the years due to continuous research in that domain. This was one of the reasons why graph-based approaches have gained traction in this area [41–44].

In the following section, we will discuss a recently proposed graph-based LBD technique published in Ref. [11], which combines IR and graph theory to perform discovery in a completely unsupervised way and without any human input or domain expertise.

19.3.2.1 Brief overview of the task and the approach

The problem that is addressed is the following. The system is given two input query terms representing medical concepts and a date; the latter acts as a constraint in the search space. The output of the system is a ranked list of relationships between the input query terms using all the knowledge that existed until that given date. As a source of knowledge, the authors use the entire dump of MEDLINE citation records (year 2015). Additionally, the authors restrict themselves in describing the concepts by using only the MeSH (medical subject heading) terms. The reasons for this are manifold: The terms in the MeSH vocabulary are a focused, finite collection of keywords that have been peer-reviewed before being incorporated into the dictionary. At the same time it is comprehensive enough to describe most of the articles present in MEDLINE and hence is used for indexing purposes. Thus, if a term is of importance in the discovery process, it is safe to assume it would be present in the MeSH vocabulary. Consequently, if the article is important for that MeSH term, it would be indexed with that term.

The system has two distinct phases: discovery phase and ranking phase. While the former is responsible for generating all the relationships between the query terms under the given date constraint, the latter, using various features and characteristics learned from the output of the discovery phase, generates a set of ranked results.

19.3.2.2 Transforming literature data into graph

In order to generate a comprehensive knowledge base for discovery, the authors focus on extracting three key features from the MEDLINE dump—the name of the article in each citation, the date of publication and the set of descriptor names in the collection of MeSH terms. The MeSH terms are divided into two types—descriptors and qualifiers. Qualifiers being refined subtopics within descriptors are important only in conjunction with descriptors. Hence, they filter to retain only descriptors. The extracted MeSH terms along with the article in which they occurred are represented as nodes in a graph, yielding a bipartite graph of MeSH terms and the articles in which those MeSH terms appeared. The edge between a MeSH vertex and an article has an attribute denoting the publication date of the article. It should be noted that while the MeSH vocabulary is constantly updated with new terms added every year, the past documents are never re-indexed with a newer vocabulary. The graph-based modeling of the knowledge base allows us the flexibility of finding relationships that span more than one implicit term.

Along with the data extracted, the authors use the MeSH tree code and MetaMap (a NLP toolkit by NLM) [45] to obtain additional characteristics of the MeSH terms. These data sources correspond to the tertiary knowledge bases that aid the discovery process by enriching the concepts with semantic labels. The MeSH tree code is a systematic hierarchical tree layout, representing an arrangement of descriptors. The MeSH descriptors are organized into 16 categories: category A for anatomic terms, B for organisms, C for diseases, etc. Each of these is again broken down into subcategories wherein terms are arranged hierarchically from generic to specific. For example, congenital abnormalities has tree code C16.131 and abnormalities, drug induced has a tree code C16.131.42. We will see in Section 19.3.2.3 how the tree codes play a role in ranking phase.

Apart from this, one also needs to quantify the possibility of a pair of MeSH terms occurring together to yield a relationship. For this, simply relying on co-occurrence at term level may severely reduce the number as well as the confidence in the candidate bridge terms. This usually occurs when the terms are still under extensive research or there are many specific terms under an umbrella of a type, thus reducing their individual support in the underlying literature. Hence, the authors map the terms to their corresponding semantic types using Metamap. Then, using it in conjunction with the co-occurrence matrix at term level (created using the bipartite graph), the authors generate a co-occurrence matrix of semantic types—a weighted matrix representing which semantic type co-occurs with a given semantic type.

Thus at the end of the knowledge-based creation process, we have created two knowledge bases: A bipartite graph depicting occurrences of MeSH terms inside an article (along with the publication date and the corresponding tree code of the MeSH term) and a co-occurrence matrix of semantic types. The authors use Neo4j to store and represent the humongous bipartite graph ($\sim$ 140 GB). All the nodes are indexed by id in the case of articles and by name in the case of MeSH terms. Edges are indexed by the date so as to facilitate faster retrieval. Please refer to Figure 19.4 that shows a snapshot of our bipartite graph.

19.3.2.3 Algorithms

As mentioned earlier, the system operates under two phases. In phase 1, the discovery phase, the authors identify all the intermediary link terms connecting the two query terms. This is performed by graph traversal on the bipartite graph. Once all the intermediary terms are collected, phase 2 is responsible for ranking them based on some global and local characteristics of the terms.

19.3.2.3.1 Discovery phase

Enrichment: This phase begins by accepting a pair of terms and a date from the user. Since MeSH terms are controlled vocabulary, and a query term can be too specific to have enough support in the literature for discovery, the authors perform query enrichment (the motivation is similar to cross-title enrichment described earlier for entity resolution of product titles). The principle behind the enrichment of the MeSH term is similar to subset candidate generation. However, there is an additional condition which leverages the MeSH tree code.

Before describing the process of enrichment, we should note that the relation between MeSH term and its tree code is one-to-many. This is because the tree code represents the categories/branches in which a MeSH term fits, e.g., ear occurs in the body sub-category as well as in sensory organs. The process begins by identifying the MeSH terms which are lexically most similar to the input query—m_l. This MeSH term is added to the set of enriched query terms. At the same time, it also extracts the corresponding set of MeSH tree categories—$\{c_l\}$. The system then generates the subsets of m_l by iteratively removing the last token and checking (1) if the resultant is a MeSH name and (2) if the corresponding set of tree category at the highest level has anything in common with $\{c_l\}$. If yes, the generated candidate is accepted in $E(q)$. For example, in the case of calcium independent phospholipase A2, we get three enriched terms—(1) phospholipases A2, calcium-independent, (2) phospholipases A2, and (3) phospholipases, each of which belongs to the category D08. Algorithm 19.3 describes the process.

Intermediary Nodes Generation: Once the system has computed the two sets of enriched vertices, it then identifies all the paths of length k (a user input) between them such that every edge in that path has a date less than or equal to d. Considering there are in all 26,944 nodes of type MeSH, 23,343,329 nodes of type

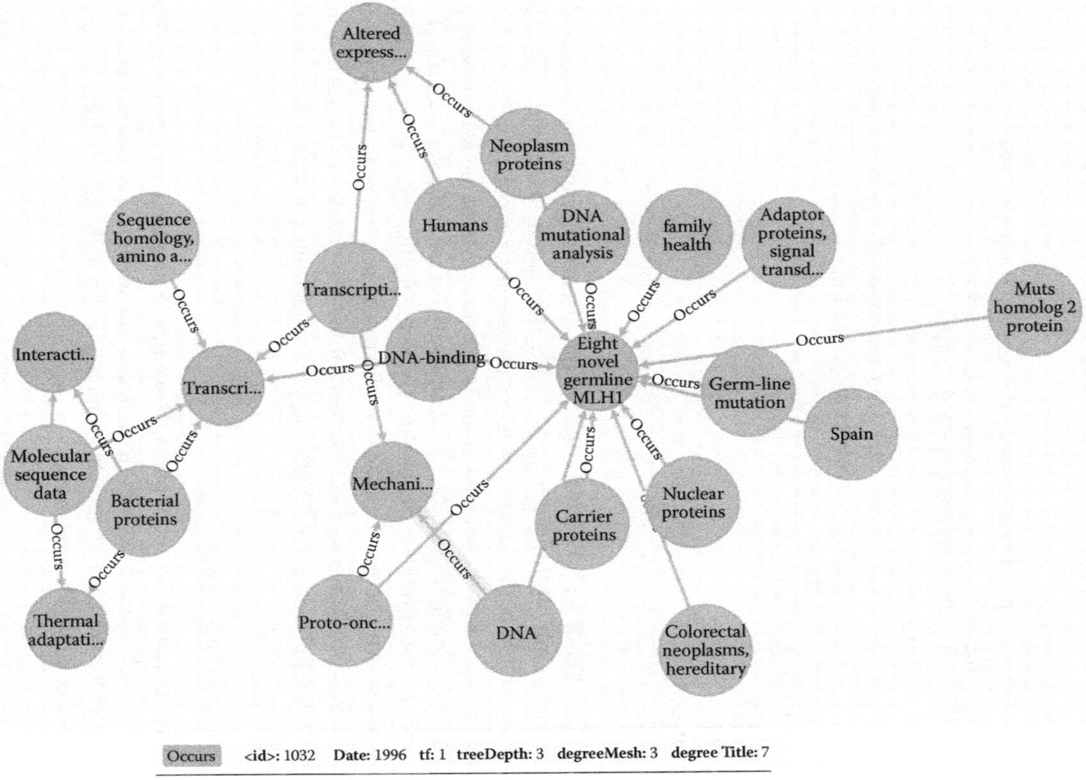

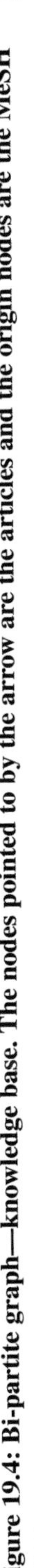

Figure 19.4: Bi-partite graph—knowledge base. The nodes pointed to by the arrow are the articles and the origin nodes are the MeSH terms.

Algorithm 19.3 Query Enrichment

Input: Query terms q and MeSH tree code Dictionary D:<Name,{Tree-code}>
Output: Enriched MeSH term set: $E(q)$
$m_l \leftarrow$ Extract the MeSH term from D that has most token overlap with q
$E(q) \leftarrow E(q) \cup m_l$
$\{c_l\} \leftarrow$ Extract the highest level categories from the tree codes corresponding to m_l
Let $\{m_l\} \leftarrow$ Tokenize m_l preserving the order
for n:- $1 \cdots |\{m_l\}|$ **do**
    $m_n \leftarrow$ Set of tokens from $\{m_l\}$ after removing the last n elements
    $c_{m_n} \leftarrow$ Extract the highest level category of m_n
    if $c_{m_n} \cap c_l \neq \phi$ **then**
        $E(q) \leftarrow E(q) \cup m_n$
    end if
end for
return $E(q)$

articles and a total of 417,492,542 edges in the bi-partite graph, the authors use a bidirectional graph [46] traversal to negotiate the search space explosion. This is because at each hop, the search space for the traverser exponentially increases and the many edges this do not lead to the target node. Mathematically speaking, if b is the average branching factor, the complexity for the traverser is $O(b^k)$. This is where bidirectional traversal is useful. By reducing the traversal to $k/2$ depth from each of the two query nodes, the complexity of each traverser vastly reduces to $O(b^{k/2})$. Once we have output from each of the traversers, we perform a join operation on the paths to get a complete path of maximum length k between the two nodes.

19.3.2.3.2 Ranking phase

Once we have obtained the set of paths, P, we need to rank each path p in it. This ranking needs to be locally as well as globally sensitive to the properties of the nodes in the path. We assume the characteristics of a path are exhibited only by the MeSH nodes in it. Thus we have

$$\{f(X) \mid X \subseteq p\} \tag{19.7}$$

where f is a ranking function such that given a vector of X MeSH terms (x_1, $x_2, \cdots, x_{\frac{|p|}{2}+1}$), $f : X \rightarrow R$.

We apply Equation 19.7 for each path p in P and obtain a vector of scores, which is then ranked in descending order to extract the top n paths. The function

f is expected to have following four fundamental characteristics:

1. It should take into consideration the overall (global) properties exhibited by the nodes in the graph.
2. It prevent awarding undue importance to a frequently co-occurring term without determining its relevance or importance in the context of discovery (local).
3. It focuses on identifying novel and contextually meaningful concepts.
4. At the same time, it is not aggressive in concluding relationships and recommending the linkage terms.

Global Features:

1. *Global Node Importance (GNI)*: Degree centrality of a node is equal to the number of its ties. Degree centrality, in this context, represents the frequency of the MeSH term with respect to the articles. It is equivalent to document frequency (DF) in IR. High DF is usually associated with common terms and in this context implies that the MeSH term is generic and has little novelty. Thus, one obtains novel MeSH terms by taking the inverse of the degree centrality. While this gives novel terms from a frequency perspective, one also needs enough confidence in a MeSH term to consider it as a bridge node between the query terms. This antithesis is resolved by incorporating betweenness centrality described in local features.
$$GNI(v) = 1/(Deg(v)) \tag{19.8}$$
2. *Tree Depth (TD)*: While GNI calculates the novelty from a topological perspective, it fails to capture the categorical importance behind the node. Thus, the authors use the MeSH tree codes. As mentioned earlier, tree codes denote a categorical hierarchy from generic to specialized concepts. Thus, lower the tree depth value, more generic is the concept. This tree code information of a MeSH term is used to measure the relative importance of a node within a particular category. This measure is a supplement to GNI which is agnostic of category importance. We normalize the tree depth within each category since the maximum tree depth within each category can differ quite drastically.

Local Features:

1. *Semantic co-occurrence (SC)*: Through the above features, the authors characterize a node irrespective of the query or its path neighbors. While they give an holistic characteristic of the node and also help in the determination of the rank of a node, they fail to factor in the context in which

they appear. Though co-occurrence plays an important role in determining the context, as mentioned earlier, by focusing only on co-occurrence at the term level we are narrowing our statistics-gathering to instance level. Instead, by projecting the MeSH term to its semantic type and then aggregating the co-occurrences, we are better able to generalize the relationship by including candidate intermediary MeSH terms which by itself have low co-occurrence frequency.

2. *Betweenness centrality (BC)*: As explained under global features, GNI tends to be aggressive and we need a measure that computes the confidence in a MeSH node to be a bridge node. This measure should be local to the paths between the query nodes. In other words, BC measures the probability of the node to occur in the set of paths P.

$$BC(v) = \Sigma_{s \neq v \neq t} \frac{\text{\#paths between s and t with v in it}}{\text{\# paths between s and t}} \qquad (19.9)$$

Once we have gathered these statistics for each MeSH term in P, the function f in Equation 19.7 is defined as:

$$f(X) = \Sigma_{x \in X}(GNI(x) \times TD(x) \times SC(x) \times BC(x)) \qquad (19.10)$$

We sort and take the top-n paths based on this value.

19.3.2.4 Experiments

Here, we describe the experimental analyses performed by authors on four golden test cases. Each of these test cases has a list of intermediary (connecting) terms put forth by Swanson. However, these are not an exhaustive set of terms, i.e., there can be valid terms which are not present in this list. Thus, the authors look for Swanson's *most important* bridge nodes within the top-n ranked paths generated by the system. At the same time they also check the veracity of other higher-ranked terms that were not part of Swanson's initial discovery or in previous LBD researches. They do this by manually checking the relationship between the intermediary terms and the query terms. Thus, precision is calculated for $n = 5$, 10, and 15. Because there is no user intervention or user knowledge to aid in search and ranking, one cannot perform a focused search and retrieval. Hence, the authors just report the terms that intersect in their finding with those of Swanson and other researchers (using the prefix GT) rather than treating their list as a "must cover set" to measure recall.

The list of golden test cases are as follows:

1. Fish oil (FO) and Raynaud's disease (RD).

2. Migraine (MIG) and magnesium (MG).

3. Somatomedin C (IGF1) and arginine (ARG).
4. Indomethacin (INN) and Alzheimer's disease (AD).

To illustrate the superiority of their approach in overcoming the limitation of other methods, where the discovery search space is restricted to only one hop, the authors evaluate the proposed method under two parameter settings—$k = 4$ and $k = 6$ ($k = 2$ means immediate neighbor due to the bipartite nature of the graph and hence not considered). In the interest of space, we discuss the analysis with $k = 6$ only for the FO-RD case.

19.3.2.4.1 Discovery with path length $k = 4$

Table 19.6 summarizes the number of paths between the terms, the upper limit on the date of discovery, and the set of enriched query terms obtained during the discovery phase. Note that somatomedin C (SmC) has another name—insulin-like growth factor I (IGF 1).

Rank Analysis: Table 19.7 tabulates the results of the intermediary MeSH nodes for a path of length 4. We also discuss in brief the expected bridge terms from Swanson's result [38,47–50].

1. **Fish oil (FO)—Raynaud's disease (RD)**: Swanson found three generic pathways between FO and RD—**platelet aggregation, blood viscosity, and vascular reactivity** (epoprostenol). As can be seen from Table 19.7, all these terms are covered within the top five. The other terms that were identified also were related to these pathways.
2. **Migraine (MIG)—magnesium (MG)**: Swanson found 11 pathways connecting MIG and MG. In absence of any user input (e.g., semantic types), the authors were unable to obtain as high a recall as in the previous case. Nonetheless, they covered major pathways like **vascular function**, **calcium channel blocker** and **neuroreactive substance**—serotonin. It is worthwhile to note that this is a difficult test case [51].
3. **Indomethacin (INN)—Alzheimer disease (AD)**: The most important terms in this relationship are **acetylcholine** and **membrane fluidity**. The results include a acetylcholine and terms related to concepts such as inflammation and proteins which are affiliated to membrane fluidity. One should note that in the top results, certain associations such as interleukin-1 and norepinephrine were published as late as 2001 (cited through the PMID), whereas the KB date was restricted to 1994.
4. **Insulin-like growth factor I (IGF1)—arginine (ARG)**: Swanson identified IGF1 and ARG to be related to each other through growth hormone—**somatotropin (growth hormone) and somatostatin**—both of which were identified in the top five. He also pointed out the relatedness of

Table 19.6 Path discovery of length (k) 4 (uni-directional depth is 2 ($k/2$))

Query Term 1	Enriched Query 1 EQ1	Query Term 2	Enriched Query 2 EQ2	# of paths from EQ1	# of paths from EQ2	# of paths from EQ1 to EQ2	Date
Fish Oils	Fish Oils	Raynaud's Disease	Raynauds Disease	8,049	26,897	912,651	1985
Migraine	Migraine	Magnesium	Magnesium	56,759	473,014	74,252,986	1988
Indomethacin	Indomethacin	Alzheimer's Disease	Alzheimer's Disease	226,708	165,449	177,497,732	1994
Insulin-Like Growth Factor I	Insulin-Like Growth Factor I	Arginine	Arginine	35,428	148,842	19,902,310	1989

Table 19.7 Top 15 intermediary MeSH terms for each test

FO-RD	Observation and Inference	MIG-MG	Observation and Inference	INN-AD	Observation and Inference	IGF1-ARG	Observation and Inference
Epo-prostenol	Epoprostenol is a Prostaglandins	propranolol	It is a β blocker Affect Vascular Mechanism	Anti-inflammatory agents, non-steroidal (NSAID)	True INN is NSAID NSAIDs protects against the development of AD PMID:12869452	Somatomedins	True (GT) PMID: 2406696
Prosta-glandins	True (GT) PMID: 3797213	Humans	False Too Generic	Humans	False par Too Generic	Somato-statin	True (GT) PMID: 2406696
Blood viscosity	True (GT) PMID: 3797213	Adenosine triphos-phate (ATP)	True PMID: 11306197 and PMID: 14979884	Interleukin-1	True INN controls Il-1 which is over-expressed in AD PMID:11754997	Growth hormone releasing hormone	True (GT) PMID: 2406696
Platelet aggregation	True (GT) PMID: 3797213	Calcium	True (GT) PMID: 3075738	Somato statin (SRIF)	False No concrete evidence between SRIF and INN	Dwarfism, pituitary	Non-Informative but true. (See A-PG)
Humans	False Too Generic	Ergotamine	True (GT) PMID: 3075738 Acts as Vasoconstriction	Norepinephrine (NE)	Emerging: Loss of NE triggers neurotoxic proinflammation PMID:23634965 and INN is NSAID	Kinetics	False Too Generic

(Continued)

Table 19.7 (Continued) Top 15 intermediary MeSH terms for each test

FO-RD	Observation and Inference	MIG-MG	Observation and Inference	INN-AD	Observation and Inference	IGF1-ARG	Observation and Inference
Lupus erythe matosus, systemic	Weak Association Sec. Phenomenon PMID: 7655867	Caffeine	Unsure association Caffeine reduces Magnesium but no definite positive or negative relation to MIG	Adreno cortico tropic hormone	False: Not conclusive in literature	Acromegaly (AC)	AC characterized by high production of IGF1 PMID 1906 0447. ARG increases GH in AC patients PMID:8492725
Vitamin a	False Too Generic	Kinetics	False Too Generic	Cyclo-oxygenase inhibitors	True INN inhibits COX thus slowing progression & onset of ADP-MID:10560656	Thyrotropin releasing hormone (TRH)	TRH is related to PRL (See PRL)
Beta-thrombo-globulin	True A protein released during platelet activation	Lithium (Li)	False: Li related to MIG No meaningful relationship with Mg	Prosta-glandins (PG)	True: INN inhibits PG production which initiates brain damageP-MID:12432919	Glucagon	Glucagon and IGF-1 control each other ARG stimulates release of Glucagon PMID:22623885
Arthritis, rheumatoid	Fish oil treats arthritis PMID:7639807 Arthritis is a major risk factor for Raynaud's disease	Serotonin	True (GT) PMID: 3075738	Acetyl-choline	True (GT) PMID: Padmini	Prolactin (PRL)	IGF 1 causes PRL cell proliferation PMID:19696100 ARG stimulates release of PRL PMID:22623885
Blood pressure	False: Too Generic	Potassium (K)	False: Too generic relationship between Mg and K	Arginine vasopressin	False: Not conclusive in literature	Radioimmuno-assay	False: Too Generic

Table 19.7 (Continued) Top 15 intermediary MeSH terms for each test

FO-RD	Observation and Inference	MIG-MG	Observation and Inference	INN-AD	Observation and Inference	IGF1-ARG	Observation and Inference
Endarteritis	Weak Association through inflammation of artery lining	Norepine-phrine	True: PMID: 14979884	Hydro-cortisone (HC)	False: HC and INN are different drugs for same purpose	Binding, competitive	False: Too Generic
Prostagla ndins e	True Specific type of prostaglandins	Sodium (Na)	False: Too generic relationship between Mg and Na	Receptors, adrenergic, beta	True: Triggers norepinephrine	Pituitary gland anterior (A-PG)	IGF-1 prepared in A-PG ARG goes to A-PG to produce ACTH
Alprostadil	True Specific type of prostaglandins	Methys-ergide	False: No concrete evidence found in top result for Magnesium and methysergide	Physo-stigmine	True: It is a cholinesterase inhibitor and reduces acetylcholine	Adreno cortico tropic hormone (ACTH)	IGF-I produced in ACTH cellsPMID: 17241280and ARG stimulates the pituitary release of ACTH PMID:9149290
Adult	False Too Generic	Adenine nucleotides	True Indirectly related through ATP	Aged	False Too Generic	Receptor, insulin	False: Too Generic
Thrombo-xanes	Weak Association-thromboxanes is vasoconstrictor-leading to RD regulated throughFO	Epinephrine	True: Lack of Mg reduces epinephrine which is β blocker PMID:10328182 PMID:16548139	Substance p	Weak and emerging research of possible association PMID:1711654 PMID 7686103	Follicle stimulating hormone (FSH)	Indirectly related by secretion location. No study with direct relationships found

Table 19.8 Precision for length 4

	n = 5		n = 10		n = 15	
Queries	**Strict**	**Lenient**	**Strict**	**Lenient**	**Strict**	**Lenient**
FO-RD	4	4	6	7	8	11
MIG-MG	4	4	5	6	8	9
INN-AD	3	3	6	6	8	9
IGF1-ARG	3	3	7	7	9	10

body weight and cancer to them which they were able to indirectly cover through ACTH and pituitary dwarfism (people with pituitary dwarfism have a lesser tendency to get cancer PMID:21459318). Similar to the previous cases, they have a very high precision in the top 15 results.

Precision Analyses: Table 19.8 shows the precision of our method for the top 5, 10, and 15 results. The precision is measured under two settings—strict and lenient. Under strict, any weak associations or emerging associations with low support were treated as false positives. As can be observed, the system has a high precision as well as covering many GT terms in the top five.

19.3.2.4.2 Discovery with path length $k = 6$

With $k = 6$, there are now two intermediary MeSH terms. As explained earlier, each hop increases the search space exponentially. As an illustration for $k = 6$, the file with a unidirectional path of length 3 from fish oils has a size of 200 GB as opposed to 542 KB for a path of length 2, and that of Raynaud's disease is 1.3 TB as opposed to 1.73 MB. Taking a join of these files is time-consuming. The authors report that in a map-reduce environment it took approximately 2 weeks to perform the join.

Though the task is not under an online setting, such high running time is not acceptable. The authors argue that certain nodes, like humans, are inherently noninformative but have a high degree resulting in search space explosion. Consequently, the authors employ a pruning step where they use heuristic cut-off of 13,000 as the degree limit (based on the top 10 results from Table 19.7). This results in much smaller and tractable file sizes—364 MB and 1.67 GB respectively.

One can observe from the results below that the increase in path length aids in better understanding of the connection and at the same time provides an opportunity for early discovery. However, it should be noted that an increase in the path length leads to more generic intermediary nodes—an expected behavior.

The top five intermediary MeSH terms filtered to retain only the first occurrence of a MeSH term in a path are: (a) diet, sodium-restricted and epoprostenol, (b) immunoglobulin fragments and thromboxanes, (c) receptors, adrenergic, alpha and beta-thromboglobulin, (d) dermatitis, occupational and pantothenic acid, (e) blood viscosity and graft occlusion, vascular. The additional filtering is done to prevent repetition of a dominant intermediary node that co-occurs with many weaker ones. It is interesting to note that while the longer paths provide more context to interpretation of intermediary terms (e.g., sodium salt levels are higher in a Raynaud's patient which is regulated via epoprostenol present in fish oils), it also provides a chance of early discovery as in the case of (c), discovered by 1983, as opposed to discovery of beta-thromboglobulin as an intermediary node in 1985 in the case of path length 4. Also, there are valid results which were not present in path length 4—e.g., (d).

In this way, the authors combine graph techniques with concepts from IR to generate high-quality intermediary terms without any human interventions. In some cases, they have been able to identify a bridge well in advance of actual discovery; thus, demonstrating the effectiveness of the ranking scheme, which factors both local and global characteristics. Furthermore, unlike previous approaches, this work makes no use of domain expertise or simplifying assumption. Despite that, the authors have been able to identify high-quality intermediary terms in top-K.

19.4 Further Reading

In this chapter, we have discussed the specific application of graph theory and techniques for entity resolution and hypothesis generation. One of the major common themes across the methodologies mentioned earlier, is the use of individual token(s) as a node in the graph. However, it is also possible to consider a phrase as a node, for instance the title of a web page. Such modeling is frequently employed in tasks where one wants to depict relationships between concepts or entities, like in collective ER. For more example in other related application areas, we would like to refer the readers to these works [52–54], where the objective of the authors is that given an input text, the system should link tokens to corresponding entries in a given knowledge base. As an example, given the text "Paris is a beautiful city," the system should identify that the word "Paris" refers to the city *Paris* and not an individual named *Paris*. It should then link this token to the appropriate entry in the knowledge base. This task is called entity linking and is an important task when attempting a semantic analysis. For instance in the papers [55,56] and also the ones mentioned earlier in the paragraph, the authors provide various mechanisms based on graph topology and traversal techniques (e.g., random walk) to determine relatedness, similarity, and matching.

Large-scale graphs also naturally arise in the biomedical domain. For instance there are works [41,44] that leverage the output generated by SemRep and create a graph of medical concepts. SemRep [57] is an NLP tool that accepts a string and identifies medical concepts and predicates that connect these concepts. Thus, one can create a graph of these concepts with edges representing the predicate type between any two nodes. Such works exploit these graphs to generate hypotheses that satisfy certain constraints over the predicates. For instance, in Ref. [41], the authors use subgraph generation in conjunction with a clustering algorithm to identify subsets of related paths that connect the given input query terms. The ranked subsets of related paths provide the necessary evidence of hypotheses that connects the input terms. At the same time, authors like Goodwin [58] use classical graph theoretic methods along with the theoretical foundation of information foraging theory [59,60] for performing literature-based discovery. In their work, for a given initial concept, a ranked subgraph is presented to the user by mining a semantic network of over 26 million object-relation-object triples from 7.8 million MEDLINE citations. In Ref. [61], the authors used co-occurrence data as input and the concepts are mapped to a multidimensional space by using a Hebbian learning algorithm [62]. The knowledge base is modeled as a graph of MeSH descriptors. Then, A* algorithm is used to find the paths between nodes in the graph.

19.5 Conclusion

Thus, there are several applications and potential benefits of modeling a problem as a graph. In this chapter, we have provided details about a few use cases where graph modeling of the task provides us with the flexibility to adapt existing techniques with ease on large-scale data. As discussed in the previous sections, it is interesting to note that there are many other graph-based approaches to solve other related tasks [52,63,64]. While some of them formulate the task as a subgraph identification problem, and mining patterns and interesting subgraphs within a large graph [65–67], the recent surge in computational capability has triggered use of machine learning techniques on large networked data [68–70]. We hope that the application settings discussed in this chapter provide the reader with a flavor of the variety of tasks to which a graph-based approach could be employed and convince him/her that graph as a data structure is a feasible option not only for representing large interactive or causal data but also for analyses.

Acknowledgment

We would like to thank the PVLDB and ISCA committees for allowing us to reuse the contents published in their proceedings.

References

[1] John Gantz and David Reinsel. The digital universe decade-are you ready. *IDC iView*, 2010.

[2] Nathan Robert Andrysco. *Data Structures for Efficient Analysis of Large-scale Unstructured Datasets*. PhD thesis, West Lafayette, IN, 2011. AAI3479292.

[3] Rik Van Bruggen. *Demining the join bomb with graph queries*, 2013. http://blog.bruggen.com/2013/01/demining-join-bomb-with-graph-queries.html (accessed August 21 2017).

[4] U Martin Singh-Blom, Nagarajan Natarajan, Ambuj Tewari, John O Woods, Inderjit S Dhillon, and Edward M Marcotte. Prediction and validation of gene-disease associations using methods inspired by social network analyses. *PLoS One*, 8(5):e58977, 2013.

[5] Nan Du, Jing Gao, Vishrawas Gopalakrishnan, and Aidong Zhang. De-noise biological network from heterogeneous sources via link propagation. In *Bioinformatics and Biomedicine (BIBM), 2012 IEEE International Conference on*, pp. 1–6, IEEE, 2012.

[6] Liang Ge and Aidong Zhang. Pseudo cold start link prediction with multiple sources in social networks. In *SDM*, pp. 768–779, SIAM, 2012.

[7] Marco Frasca. Automated gene function prediction through gene multifunctionality in biological networks. *Neurocomputing*, 162:48–56, 2015.

[8] Nan Du, Yuan Zhang, Kang Li, Jing Gao, Supriya D Mahajan, Bindukumar B Nair, Stanley A Schwartz, and Aidong Zhang. Evolutionary analysis of functional modules in dynamic ppi networks. In *Proceedings of the ACM Conference on Bioinformatics, Computational Biology and Biomedicine*, pp. 250–257, ACM, 2012.

[9] Derek Greene, Donal Doyle, and Padraig Cunningham. Tracking the evolution of communities in dynamic social networks. In *2010 International Conference on Advances in Social Networks Analysis and Mining (ASONAM)*, pp. 176–183, IEEE, 2010.

[10] Lei Tang, Huan Liu, Jianping Zhang, and Zohreh Nazeri. Community evolution in dynamic multi-mode networks. In *Proceedings of the 14th ACM SIGKDD International Conference on Knowledge Discovery and Data Mining*, pp. 677–685, ACM, 2008.

[11] V Gopalakrishnan, K Jha, A Zhang, and W Jin. Generating hypothesis: Using global and local features in graph to discover new knowledge from medical literature, pages 23–30, 2016.

[12] Scott Spangler, Angela D Wilkins, Benjamin J Bachman, Meena Nagarajan, Tajhal Dayaram, Peter Haas, Sam Regenbogen, Curtis R Pickering, Austin Comer, Jeffrey N Myers, et al. Automated hypothesis generation based on mining scientific literature. In *Proceedings of the 20th ACM SIGKDD International Conference on Knowledge Discovery and Data Mining*, pp. 1877–1886, ACM, 2014.

[13] Nikhil Londhe, Vishrawas Gopalakrishnan, Aidong Zhang, Hung Q Ngo, and Rohini Srihari. Matching titles with cross title web-search enrichment and community detection. *Proceedings of the VLDB Endowment*, 7(12):1167–1178, 2014.

[14] Tiago Grego, Catia Pesquita, Hugo P Bastos, and Francisco M Couto. Chemical entity recognition and resolution to chebi. *ISRN Bioinformatics*, 619427, 2012.

[15] Safaa Eltyeb and Naomie Salim. Chemical named entities recognition: A review on approaches and applications. *Journal of Cheminformatics*, 6(1):1, 2014.

[16] Peter Corbett, Colin Batchelor, and Simone Teufel. Annotation of chemical named entities. In *Proceedings of the Workshop on BioNLP 2007: Biological, Translational, and Clinical Language Processing*, pp. 57–64, Association for Computational Linguistics, 2007.

[17] Daniel Buchuk. UK online porn ban: Web traffic analysis of Britains porn affair. *SimilarWeb Blog*, 2013.

[18] Indrajit Bhattacharya and Lise Getoor. Collective entity resolution in relational data. *ACM Transactions on Knowledge Discovery from Data (TKDD)*, 1(1):5, 2007.

[19] Vishrawas Gopalakrishnan, Suresh Parthasarathy Iyengar, Amit Madaan, Rajeev Rastogi, and Srinivasan Sengamedu. Matching product titles using web-based enrichment. In *Proceedings of the 21st ACM International Conference on Information and Knowledge Management*, pp. 605–614, ACM, 2012.

[20] Wei Vivian Zhang and Rosie Jones. Comparing click logs and editorial labels for training query rewriting. In *WWW 2007 Workshop on Query Log Analysis: Social And Technological Challenges*, 2007.

[21] Andrei Broder, Peter Ciccolo, Evgeniy Gabrilovich, Vanja Josifovski, Donald Metzler, Lance Riedel, and Jeffrey Yuan. Online expansion of rare queries for sponsored search. In *Proceedings of the 18th International Conference on World Wide Web*, pp. 511–520, 2009.

[22] Santo Fortunato and Marc Barthelemy. Resolution limit in community detection. *Proceedings of the National Academy of Sciences*, 104(1):36–41, 2007.

[23] Michelle Girvan and Mark EJ Newman. Community structure in social and biological networks. *Proceedings of the National Academy of Sciences*, 104(1):7821–7826, 2002.

[24] Hanna Köpcke, Andreas Thor, and Erhard Rahm. Evaluation of entity resolution approaches on real-world match problems. *Proceedings of the VLDB Endowment*, 3(1–2):484–493, 2010.

[25] Vincent D Blondel, Jean-Loup Guillaume, Renaud Lambiotte, and Etienne Lefebvre. Fast unfolding of communities in large networks. *Journal of Statistical Mechanics: Theory and Experiment*, 2008(10):P10008, 2008.

[26] Parag Singla and Pedro Domingos. Entity resolution with markov logic. In *6th International Conference on Data Mining (ICDM'06)*, pp. 572–582, IEEE, 2006.

[27] Vibhor Rastogi, Nilesh Dalvi, and Minos Garofalakis. Large-scale collective entity matching. *Proceedings of the VLDB Endowment*, 4(4):208–218, 2011.

[28] Maximilian Nickel, Volker Tresp, and Hans-Peter Kriegel. A three-way model for collective learning on multi-relational data. In *Proceedings of the 28th International Conference on Machine Learning (ICML-11)*, pp. 809–816, 2011.

[29] Indrajit Bhattacharya and Lise Getoor. Entity resolution in graphs. *Mining Graph Data*, p. 311, 2006.

[30] Kwang-Il Goh, Michael E Cusick, David Valle, Barton Childs, Marc Vidal, and Albert-László Barabási. The human disease network. *Proceedings of the National Academy of Sciences*, 104(21):8685–8690, 2007.

[31] Weidong Tian, Lan V Zhang, Murat Taşan, Francis D Gibbons, Oliver D King, Julie Park, Zeba Wunderlich, J Michael Cherry, and Frederick P Roth. Combining guilt-by-association and guilt-by-profiling to predict saccharomyces cerevisiae gene function. *Genome Biology*, 9(1):1, 2008.

[32] Mohammad Al Hasan and Mohammed J Zaki. A survey of link prediction in social networks. In *Social network data analytics*, Charu C. Aggarwal (ed.), pp. 243–275, Springer, 2011.

[33] Fantine Mordelet and Jean-Philippe Vert. Prodige: Prioritization of disease genes with multitask machine learning from positive and unlabeled examples. *BMC Bioinformatics*, 12(1):1, 2011.

[34] Li Bian and Henry Holtzman. Online friend recommendation through personality matching and collaborative filtering. *Proc. of UBICOMM*, pp. 230–235, 2011.

[35] Prem Melville, Raymond J Mooney, and Ramadass Nagarajan. Content-boosted collaborative filtering for improved recommendations. In *AAAI/iaai*, pp. 187–192, 2002.

[36] Kriston L McGary, Tae Joo Park, John O Woods, Hye Ji Cha, John B Wallingford, and Edward M Marcotte. Systematic discovery of nonobvious human disease models through orthologous phenotypes. *Proceedings of the National Academy of Sciences*, 107(14):6544–6549, 2010.

[37] Hagit Shatkay and Mark Craven. *Mining the biomedical literature*. MIT Press, 2012.

[38] Don R Swanson. Fish oil, Raynaud's syndrome, and undiscovered public knowledge. *Perspectives in Biology and Medicine*, 30(1):7–18, 1986.

[39] Ronald N Kostoff. Method for data and text mining and literature-based discovery, April 26 2005. US Patent 6,886,010.

[40] Aaron M Cohen and William R Hersh. A survey of current work in biomedical text mining. *Briefings in Bioinformatics*, 6(1):57–71, 2005.

[41] Delroy Cameron, Ramakanth Kavuluru, Thomas C. Rindflesch, Amit P Sheth, Krishnaprasad Thirunarayan, and Olivier Bodenreider. Context-driven automatic subgraph creation for literature-based discovery. *Journal of Biomedical Informatics*, 54:141–157, 2015.

[42] Rui Zhang, Michael J Cairelli, Marcelo Fiszman, Graciela Rosemblat, Halil Kilicoglu, Thomas C Rindflesch, Serguei V Pakhomov, and Genevieve B Melton. Using semantic predications to uncover drug–drug interactions in clinical data. *Journal of Biomedical Informatics*, 49:134–147, 2014.

[43] Vit Novacek. Formalising hypothesis virtues in knowledge graphs: A general theoretical framework and its validation in literature-based discovery experiments. *arXiv preprint arXiv:1503.09137*, 2015.

[44] Bartłomiej Wilkowski, Marcelo Fiszman, Christopher M Miller, Dimitar Hristovski, Sivaram Arabandi, Graciela Rosemblat, and Thomas C Rindflesch. Graph-based methods for discovery browsing with semantic predications. *AMIA Annual Symposium Proceedings*, 2011:1514–23, 2011.

[45] Alan R Aronson. Effective mapping of biomedical text to the umls metathesaurus: The metamap program. In *Proceedings of the AMIA Symposium*, p. 17, American Medical Informatics Association, 2001.

[46] I Pohl. *Bi-directional and heuristic search in path problems*. Technical Report 104, SLAC (Stanford Linear Accelerator Center, Stanford, CA, 1969.

[47] Don R Swanson. Migraine and magnesium: Eleven neglected connections. *Perspectives in Biology and Medicine*, 31(4):526–557, 1988.

[48] Neil R Smalheiser and Don R Swanson. Indomethacin and alzheimer's disease. *Neurology*, 46(2):583–583, 1996.

[49] Don R Swanson. Somatomedin c and arginine: Implicit connections between mutually isolated literatures. *Perspectives in Biology and Medicine*, 33(2):157–186, 1990.

[50] Neil R Smalheiser and Don R Swanson. Calcium-independent phospholipase a2 and schizophrenia. *Archives of General Psychiatry*, 55(8):752–753, 1998.

[51] Padmini Srinivasan. Text mining: Generating hypotheses from medline. *Journal of the American Society for Information Science and Technology*, 55(5):396–413, 2004.

[52] Andrea Moro, Alessandro Raganato, and Roberto Navigli. Entity linking meets word sense disambiguation: A unified approach. *Transactions of the Association for Computational Linguistics*, 2:231–244, 2014.

[53] Anna Lisa Gentile, Ziqi Zhang, Lei Xia, and José Iria. Graph-based semantic relatedness for named entity disambiguation. 2009.

[54] Yuhang Guo, Wanxiang Che, Ting Liu, and Sheng Li. A graph-based method for entity linking. In *IJCNLP*, vol. 1010, p. 1018, Citeseer, 2011.

[55] Eric Yeh, Daniel Ramage, Christopher D Manning, Eneko Agirre, and Aitor Soroa. Wikiwalk: Random walks on Wikipedia for semantic relatedness. In *Proceedings of the 2009 Workshop on Graph-based Methods for Natural Language Processing*, TextGraphs-4, pp. 41–49, Stroudsburg, PA, Association for Computational Linguistics, 2009.

[56] Ian Witten and David Milne. An effective, low-cost measure of semantic relatedness obtained from Wikipedia links. In *Proceeding of AAAI Workshop on Wikipedia and Artificial Intelligence: An Evolving Synergy*, AAAI Press, Chicago, IL, pp. 25–30, 2008.

[57] Thomas C. Rindflesch and Marcelo Fiszman. The interaction of domain knowledge and linguistic structure in natural language processing: Interpreting hypernymic propositions in biomedical text. *Journal of Biomedical Informatics*, 36(6):462–477, 2003.

[58] J Caleb Goodwin, Trevor Cohen, and Thomas Rindflesch. Discovery by scent: Discovery browsing system based on the information foraging theory. In *2012 IEEE International Conference on Bioinformatics and Biomedicine Workshops (BIBMW)*, pp. 232–239, 2012.

[59] Peter Pirolli and Stuart Card. Information Foraging. *Psychological Review*, 106(4):643, 1999.

[60] Peter Pirolli. Rational analyses of information foraging on the web. *Cognitive Science*, 29(3):343–373, 2005.

[61] C Christiaan van der Eijk, Erik M van Mulligen, Jan A Kors, Barend Mons, and Jan van den Berg. Constructing an associative concept space for literature-based discovery. *Journal of the Association for Information Science and Technology*, 55(5):436–444, 2004.

[62] Jan Van Den Berg and Martijn J Schuemie. Information retrieval systems using an associative conceptual space. In *ESANN*, pp. 351–356, 1999.

[63] Huy Pham, Cyrus Shahabi, and Yan Liu. Ebm: An entropy-based model to infer social strength from spatiotemporal data. In *Proceedings of the 2013 ACM SIGMOD International Conference on Management of Data*, pp. 265–276, ACM, 2013.

[64] Fei Tan, Yongxiang Xia, and Boyao Zhu. Link prediction in complex networks: A mutual information perspective. *PLoS One*, 9(9):e107056, 2014.

[65] Jian Pei, Daxin Jiang, and Aidong Zhang. On mining cross-graph quasi-cliques. In *Proceedings of the 11th ACM SIGKDD International Conference on Knowledge Discovery in Data Mining*, pp. 228–238, ACM, 2005.

[66] Haiyan Hu, Xifeng Yan, Yu Huang, Jiawei Han, and Xianghong Jasmine Zhou. Mining coherent dense subgraphs across massive biological networks for functional discovery. *Bioinformatics*, 21(suppl 1):i213–i221, 2005.

[67] Mohammed Elseidy, Ehab Abdelhamid, Spiros Skiadopoulos, and Panos Kalnis. Grami: Frequent subgraph and pattern mining in a single large graph. *Proceedings of the VLDB Endowment*, 7(7):517–528, 2014.

[68] Robert Burbidge, Matthew Trotter, B Buxton, and S Holden. Drug design by machine learning: Support vector machines for pharmaceutical data analysis. *Computers & Chemistry*, 26(1):5–14, 2001.

[69] Duen Horng Chau, Aniket Kittur, Jason I Hong, and Christos Faloutsos. Apolo: Making sense of large network data by combining rich user interaction and machine learning. In *Proceedings of the SIGCHI Conference on Human Factors in Computing Systems*, pp. 167–176, ACM, 2011.

[70] Yucheng Low, Danny Bickson, Joseph Gonzalez, Carlos Guestrin, Aapo Kyrola, and Joseph M Hellerstein. Distributed graphlab: A framework for machine learning and data mining in the cloud. *Proceedings of the VLDB Endowment*, 5(8):716–727, 2012.

Chapter 20

Big Data Analysis for Smart Manufacturing

Z. Y. Liu and Y. B. Guo
University of Alabama
Tuscaloosa, Alabama

CONTENTS

20.1 Introduction

20.1.1 Smart manufacturing

The emerging paradigm of smart manufacturing creates and uses data and information throughout the product life cycle with the goal of rapid manufacturing of new products, dynamic response to product demand, and real-time optimization of manufacturing production and supply chain networks. Smart manufacturing has the potential to fundamentally change how products are designed, manufactured, supplied, used, remanufactured, and eventually retired. Smart manufacturing utilizes big data analytics, to refine complicated processes and manage supply chains [1]. Big data analytics refers to a method for gathering and understanding large data sets in terms of velocity, variety, and volume. Big data analytics allows an enterprise to use smart manufacturing to shift from reactionary practices to predictive ones, a change that targets improved efficiency of the process and performance of the product [2].

20.1.2 Big data characteristics in manufacturing

The advances of sensor and communication technologies enable manufacturing to be monitored continuously with sensor networks. The acquired sensory data such as force, temperature, power, acoustics, vibration, pressure, current, and voltage can be collected in real time. The large-scale heterogeneous sensor network with high sampling rate produces a huge size of data at a very high speed, which makes the data beyond the ability of commonly used software tools to capture, curate, manage, and process in a reasonable time frame.

In the case of a manufacturing company with numerous CNC machines in its factories, the CNC machines are being monitored for uptime, internal alarms, operational status such as speeds, feeds, tool paths, coolant conditions, energy usage, etc. The cutting tools used in the machine tools are being monitored for when, where, and how it was used. All the collected process data is streamed into massive online databases in the Cloud. Besides the data collected in the manufacturing processes, the company also receives feedback from customers and information from the supply chain. The acquired sensor data, supply chain data, and customer feedback data as well as the accumulated historical data will construct the big data in manufacturing. By analyzing the massive data, manufacturing companies may find undiscovered trends to improve productivity and reduce cost.

Big data is generally characterized in three Vs, that is, volume, variety, and velocity.

- *Volume*: The large volume of generated and stored data. The size of the data determines the value and potential insight and whether it can actually be considered big data or not.

- *Variety*: The various types and nature of the data. In the case of manufacturing industry, the data has extremely high diversity since the data are collected from different machines, sensors, and different departments. Furthermore, the collected data from different sources speak different languages and have different structures.
- *Velocity*: In this context, the high speed at which the data are generated and processed to meet the demands and challenges that lie in the path of growth and development. The difference between manufacturing and other applications is that the manufacturing industry controls production facilities and machinery in production lines in real time. Therefore, big data consisting of further automated production lines' log data, various information from sensors, and environmental information within and outside the plant are generated at extremely high speed.

20.1.3 Benefits of using big data in manufacturing

A better use of the collected data could improve productivity and reduce cost. At the manufacturing process level, the application of big data analytics discovers hidden trends to establish the relationship between manufacturing processes, cost, productivity, and quality, which can help operation managers select optimal process conditions. At the manufacturing system level, big data analytics provides an infrastructure for transparency in the manufacturing industry, which is the ability to unravel uncertainties such as inconsistent component performance and availability. Predictive manufacturing as an applicable approach toward near-zero downtime, energy and resource utilization, and transparency requires vast amounts of data and advanced prediction tools for smart manufacturing.

20.2 Big Data Collection in Manufacturing

20.2.1 Data types

Figure 20.1 outlines the big data variety dimension of a manufacturing system. The data can be classified into three types—structured data of the manufacturing operation, sensor data, and unstructured data of the marketing and social networking [3].

As for a manufacturing process, it is essential to build a process traceability system to record all the detailed information on exactly how one part is made. Manufacturing-induced defects impair product quality significantly. Engineers need all the data generated during manufacturing processes to determine how and when the defect was introduced in Ref. [4]. To achieve that goal, the following data are needed:

- *Identity data*. Identity data are the most basic type of data for part traceability, including the information on what is being made, how many parts

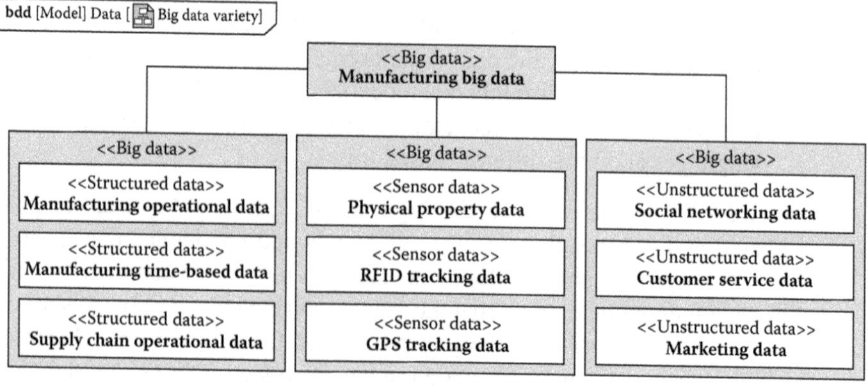

Figure 20.1: Big data variety in a manufacturing system [3].

are made, and when it is made. Examples include part ID, batch ID, operator ID, machine ID, tool ID.

- *Process data.* Process data reveal the detailed process conditions of how a component is being made. In the case of mold machining, the process data includes cutting speed, feed rate, tool path, etc. It should be noted that the process data are real-time data which are usually collected from the machine controllers.
- *Sensor data.* Modern machines are usually integrated with sensors to monitor the key process attributes during operation. For instance, a machine tool is equipped with sensors to monitor many signals such as force, temperature, power, vibration, and acoustic emission during a machining operation. Sensor data are also real-time collected data.
- *Product data.* Product data reveal the detailed information of the product being made. For example, after a machining step, part dimension accuracy and surface integrity are examined to check if they meet the product requirements. These data are usually collected by the quality assurance department.

20.2.2 Real-time data collection

As mentioned in the previous section, various data are collected in manufacturing. In contrast to other applications, process data and sensor data are collected in real time. Furthermore, sensors and machine controllers from different companies speak different languages. In this section, discussion is focused on the collection of high speed, real-time data from heterogeneous sources and data transformation into standardized formats.

Sensors are needed to measure the key attributes in the manufacturing process. Those key attributes (e.g., force, temperature, power, pressure, acoustic emission) reflect the response of a workpiece to the applied load during the manufacturing process, thus providing information on the product quality. Based on the characteristics of a specific manufacturing process, different sensors can be integrated into the machines. Sensors must be minimally invasive and capture without interrupting or influencing the phenomena being measured.

Real-time ethernet and wireless networks (IEEE 802.11 and IEEE 802.15.1) provide the bandwidth, speed, and common data structure to exchange data with low latency. A variety of data formats can be accessed immediately and analyzed to extract filtered data from the existing internal and external data sources [5].

Standardization of the collected data is essential for further data mining since the sensors and controllers from different companies may use different data structures. MTConnect is proved to be an effective standard to transform data from different data sources into a uniform format. MTConnect is an open, royalty-free standard that presents data from shop-floor devices in XML format. This standard is gaining increasing support from machine tool manufacturers. Furthermore, the interoperability of MTConnect enables third party solution providers to develop software and hardware to improve manufacturing processes [6]. Figure 20.2 shows the integration of a data collection system using MTConnect.

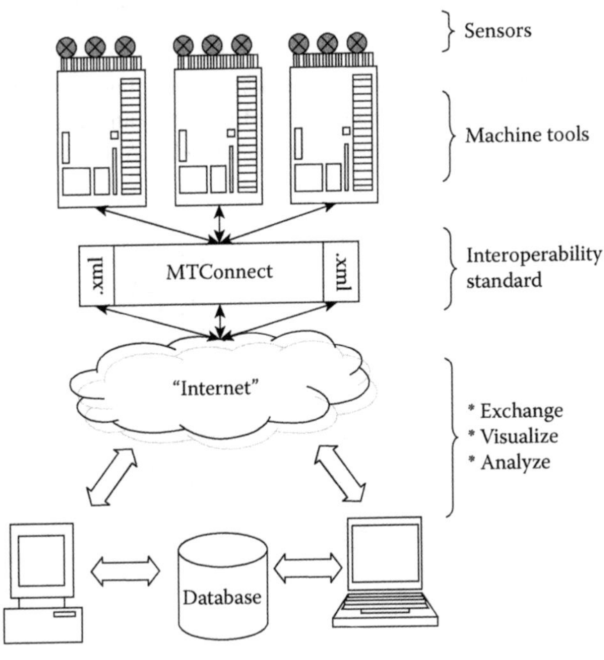

Figure 20.2: Integration of data collection system using MTConnect [6].

20.3 Data Mining in Manufacturing

These data collected from a manufacturing system offer enormous potential as sources of new knowledge. Data mining is the process of discovering patterns and transforming the data into useful knowledge. The extracted knowledge can be used to model, classify, and make predictions for numerous manufacturing applications. Several researchers have produced state-of-the-art reviews on this subject [7–10]. The knowledge discovery in databases (KDD) is commonly defined in several stages, e.g., data collection, data cleaning, data transformation, data mining, and interpretation/evaluation. The complete steps for KDD in manufacturing are illustrated in Figure 20.3.

20.3.1 Data mining tasks

Data mining in manufacturing involves five common classes of tasks [9]:

- *Concept (characterization and discrimination) description.* Descriptive data mining provides a description of the data set in a concise and summative manner and presentation of interesting general properties of the data. Characterization describes the data collection in a concise way, while discrimination provides a comparison for two or more data collections. For instance, characterization can be used to identify the most significant feature that impacts the quality of a printed circuit board.
- *Classification.* Classification is the task of generalizing a known structure to apply to new data. Classification is generally performed in two steps. The first step (supervised learning) is to analyze the database tuples described by attributes and develop a model to describe a predetermined

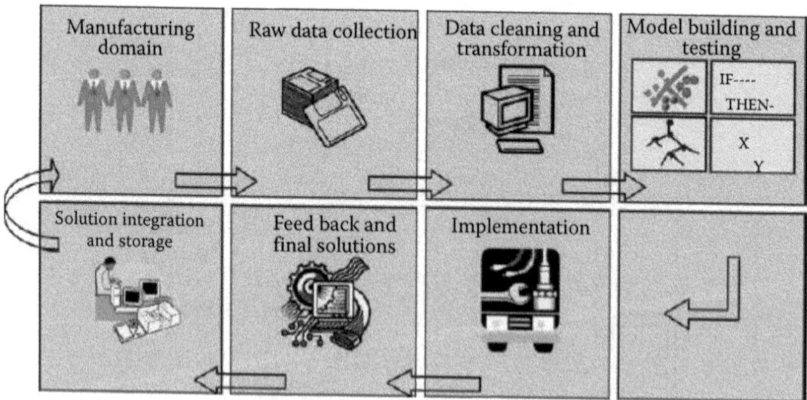

Figure 20.3: Data mining for knowledge discovery in manufacturing [9].

set of data classes. In the second step, the developed model is used to classify the future data set. For example, in the semiconductor industry, defects are classified to find patterns and derive the rules for future productivity improvement.

- *Clustering (unsupervised learning).* Clustering is the task of discovering groups and structures in the data that are in some way or another similar without using known structures in the data. For example, principal component analysis and fuzzy c-means clustering can be used to identify operational spaces in a manufacturing process.
- *Prediction.* Prediction is to find a function that models the data with the least error. For example, a neural network can be used to construct the relationship between cutting conditions, cutting time, and tool wear.
- *Association.* Association is used to identify the dependency relationship between a set of items in a database. In manufacturing, association rules can be used for failure analysis by identifying what events will occur before a failure.

20.3.2 Data mining techniques in manufacturing

A variety of data mining methods have been applied in manufacturing. Several techniques and their corresponding advantages/disadvantages are listed in Table 20.1. Data scientists can select a suitable data mining methods based on the specific applications.

20.4 Applications of Big Data in Manufacturing

20.4.1 Improving manufacturing processes

The application of big data can overcome one of the biggest challenges for manufacturing process optimization, i.e., the identification of the relationship between process conditions and product quality. For the case of a gear manufacturing company, every gear goes through a process chain (e.g., forging, machining, heat treatment, grinding, and polishing). Each process step has many independent process parameters. The relationship between process conditions and the final product quality is very difficult to identify.

The sensor networks installed on machines in a manufacturing system will generate a huge amount of data. Big data technologies provide an opportunity to aggregate these data sets and data from other units such as the quality assurance department. Operation managers can access those data sets easily and use big

Table 20.1 Data mining techniques [11]

Data mining techniques	Characteristics and advantages/disadvantages
Query tools	■ Used for extraction of "shallow" knowledge ■ SQL is used to extract information
Statistical techniques	■ SPC tools are used to extract deeper knowledge from databases ■ Limited but can outline basic relations between data
Visualization	■ Used to get a rough feeling of the quality of the data being studied
Online analytical processing	■ Used for multidimensional problems processing ■ Cannot acquire new knowledge ■ Database cannot be updated
Case-based learning	■ Uses K-nearest neighbor algorithm ■ A search technique rather than a learning algorithm ■ Better suited for small problems
Decision trees	■ Good for most problem sizes ■ Gives true insight into nature of the decision process ■ Hard to create trees from a complex problem
Neural networks	■ Mimics human brain ■ Algorithm has to be trained during encoding phase ■ Complex methodology
Genetic algorithms	■ Uses Darwin's evolution theory ■ Robust and reliable method for data mining ■ Requires a lot of computing power to achieve anything of significance

data analytics to take deep mining into process data. The data from the quality assurance department will identify patterns and relationships between process parameters and product quality, and then optimize the factors that prove to have the greatest effect on yield (Figure 20.4).

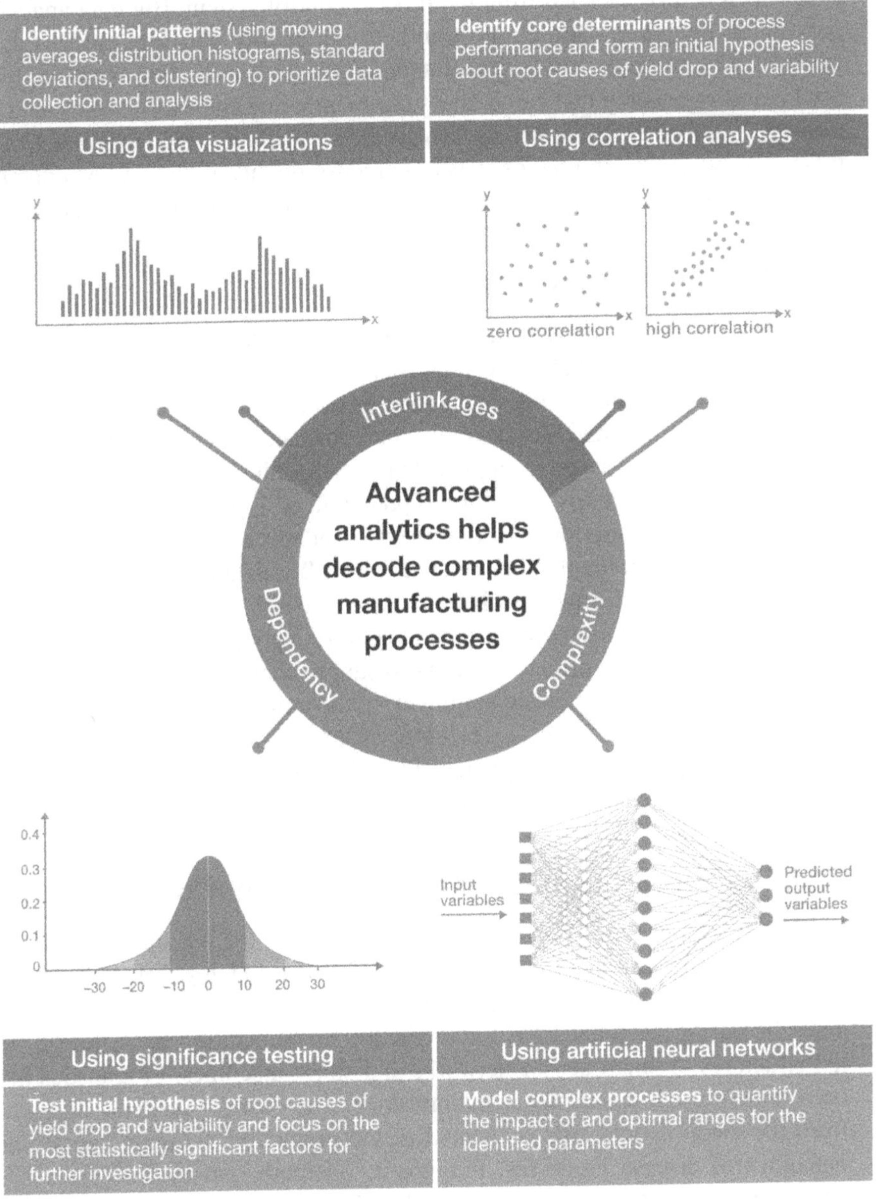

Figure 20.4: Improving manufacturing preprocess with big data analytics [12].

20.4.2 Quality control

Historically, quality control is achieved by planned sampling or event-driving sampling. Samples are sent to the laboratory and various tests are performed to qualify the samples. The quality is usually saved in a separated quality data system, which is disassociated from the process control system. Big data analytics provide an integration and connection between quality data and process data, which can improve the efficiency of sampling significantly. For example, Intel used to test every chip that came off its production line and each chip needed go through 19,000 tests. By using big data predictive analytics, Intel was able to significantly reduce the number of tests required for quality assurance. A reduction of $3 million in manufacturing costs can be achieved for a single production line.

20.4.3 Supply chain management

Waller and Fawcett addressed the importance of big data and data analytics for supply chain management [13]. The term *supply chain management data science* is defined as application of big data analytics combined with supply chain management theory to solve relevant supply chain management problems and predict outcomes. A detailed assessment provided by Schoenherr and Speier-Pero investigated the current status and future potential of big data in supply chain management [14]. More than 40% of the respondents actively used data analytics to optimize their supply chain management. Big data can help supply chain managers improve informed decision-making capability and supply chain efficiency, enhance demand planning capability and supply chain cost reduction, and increase visibility. The primary barriers to supply chain management predictive analytics include inexperienced employees, time constraints, lack of integration with current systems, and cost. Hazen et al. investigated the influence of data quality on supply chain management [15]. It is suggested that application of statistical process control can be used to control data quality in the supply chain.

20.4.4 Prognostics and health management (PHM)

Machinery maintenance is an important application for big data in manufacturing. The application of the Internet of Things and big data provides an opportunity for the machines and systems with "self-aware" capabilities, which helps in laying the foundation for predictive manufacturing by setting essential structures of smart sensor networks and smart machines. Prognostics have been widely used in machinery maintenance. The concept of PHM originated from the medical field, and is defined as the prediction of future courses and outcomes of disease processes. Prognostics methods and systems have been developed for machinery maintenance [16]. Insights into future equipment performance and estimation of time to failure predicted by big data analytics will reduce the impacts of production uncertainties. The conceptual framework of a

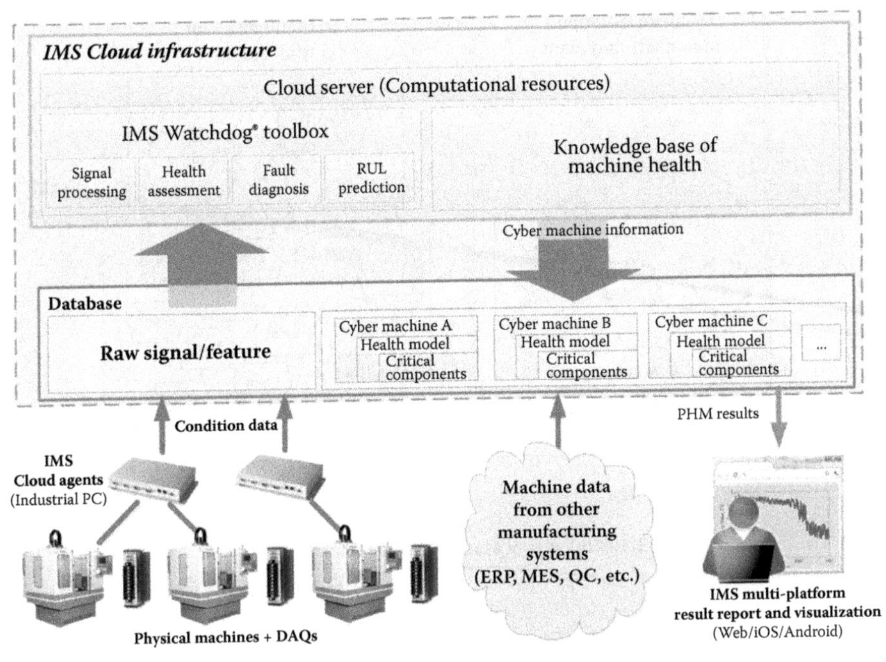

Figure 20.5: Cyber-physical model for an enhanced predictive manufacturing system [17].

PHM system is shown in Figure 20.5, in which various signals such as vibration, pressure, acoustics, and current can be collected with sensors installed on the machines. The controller signals can be recorded with the help of communication protocols, such as MTConnect and OPC. All the data are aggregated and stored in the Cloud. Predictive analytics tools such as Watchdog Agent® can be used to process the big data to discover useful information. The analytical procedures include signal processing and feature extraction, health assessment, performance prediction, and fault diagnosis. By integrating the calculated health information to the company management system, the equipment can be managed cost effectively with just-in-time maintenance [17].

20.4.5 *Smart manufacturing in the steel industry*

Steel manufacturing consumes the most energy (~6%) among all the US industrial sectors [18]. It is critical to minimize the energy use while ensuring high productivity/quality. A typical steel manufacturing system includes multiple highly energy-intensive process chains from furnace melting, casting, to hot rolling and cold rolling. The dynamic high energy demand in steel production as well as in facility heating, ventilation, and air-conditioning (HVAC) systems

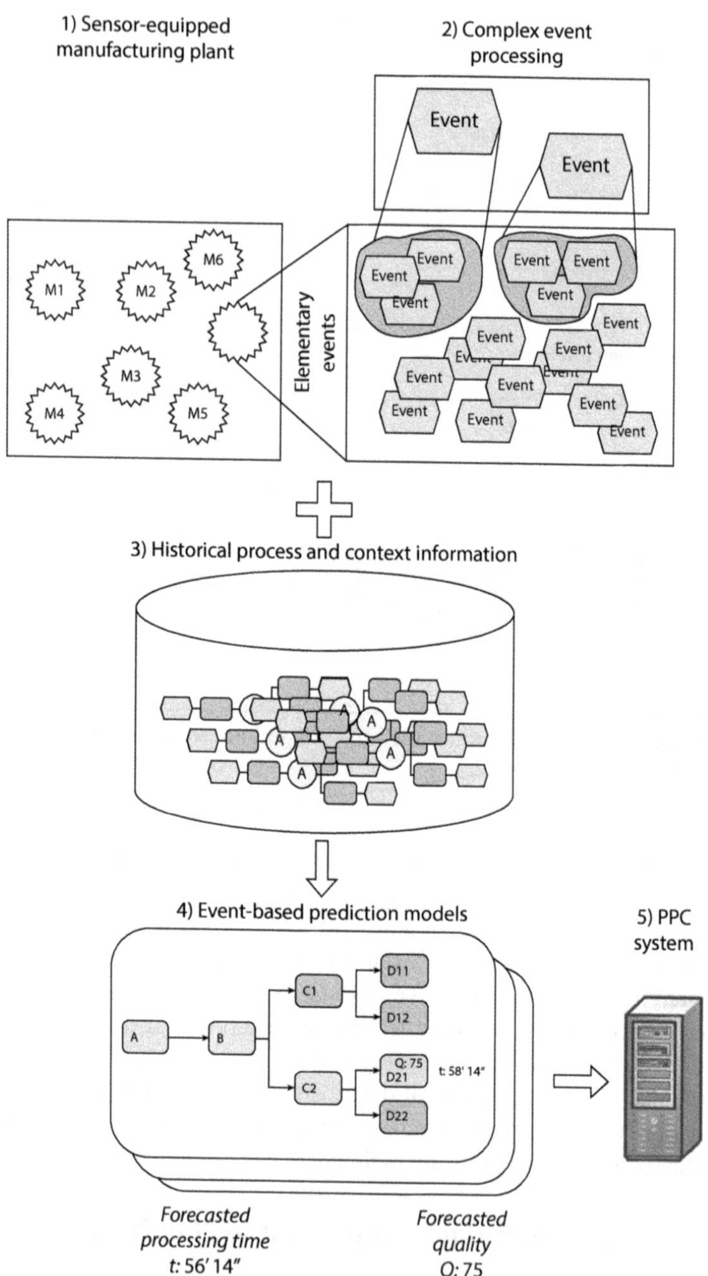

Figure 20.6: Basic concept for an event-based process forecast and control [19].

largely determines the total factory energy consumption. Because a significant amount of energy is not efficiently utilized (or even wasted) in steel manufacturing, energy efficiency of current steel plants is strikingly low. Therefore, transformative advances to smartly and adaptively improve the overall energy efficiency while not sacrificing product quality are imperative.

A big data analysis provides a case study in steel manufacturing [19,20], in which an optical surface defect sensor alone generates at least several hundred terabytes of data annually. In addition, the high data diversity continuously collected by different sensors and sensor networks throughout the process chain places high demands on an analysis by big data principles. Furthermore, process data (exceeding 50 terabytes) from a long period must be used for the model formation and forecasting. At present, however, such an amount of data can hardly be processed in real time. A direct compression of the data is impossible because of the variety to be considered. As of now, due to its big data characteristics, the manufacturing process is short of the envisioned optimum in terms of planning and control.

As the case analysis of steel manufacturing shows, the overall challenge of accurate predictions has shifted from being able to capture current context situations—as the baseline for deriving forecasts—to being able to manage and adequately consider this mass of data. In addition, the case study illustrates that the mass of data is progressively growing, possessing the necessity of having a scalable platform (Figure 20.6) for integrating sensor technology. The big data is potentially available for predictive planning and control of manufacturing processes. However, the analysis of this data showed that its full potential cannot be utilized without dedicated approaches of big data analytics.

20.5 Conclusions

Smart manufacturing has the potential to enable flexibility in physical processes to address a dynamic and global market. Big data analytics is a key enabling tool for smart manufacturing. This chapter presented big data types, collection, characteristics, and potential benefits in manufacturing. Big data mining methods to discover patterns and transform the data into useful knowledge are detailed. In addition, five case studies on the application of big data for smart manufacturing have been presented and discussed.

References

[1] Rachuri, S., 2014. *Smart manufacturing systems design and analysis.* Technical Report, National Institute of Standards and Technology. https://www.nist.gov/programs-projects/smart-manufacturing-systems-design-and-analysis-program (accessed August 22, 2017).

[2] Davis, J., Edgar, T., Porter, J., Bernaden, J., Sarli, M., 2012, Smart Manufacturing, Manufacturing Intelligence and Demand-Dynamic Performance, *Computers & Chemical Engineering*, 47, 145–156.

[3] Babiceanu, R.F., Seker, R., 2016, Big Data and Virtualization for Manufacturing Cyber-Physical Systems: A Survey of the Current Status and Future Outlook, *Computers in Industry*, 81, 128–137.

[4] Cutler, T.R., 2014, The Internet of Manufacturing Things, *Industrial Engineering*, 46(8), 37–41.

[5] Flammini, A., Ferrari, P., Marioli, D., Sisinni, E., Taroni, A., 2009, Wired and Wireless Sensor Networks for Industrial Applications, *Microelectronics Journal*, 40(9), 1322–1336.

[6] Vijayaraghavan, A., Sobel, W., Fox, A., Dornfeld, D., Warndorf, P., 2008, Improving Machine Tool Interoperability using Standardized Interface Protocols: MTConnect, *Proceedings of 2008 ISFA*, Atlanta, GA, June 23–26.

[7] Harding, J., Shahbaz, M., Kusiak, A., 2006, Data Mining in Manufacturing: A Review, *Journal of Manufacturing Science and Engineering*, 128(4), 969–976.

[8] Kusiak, A., 2006, Data Mining: Manufacturing and Service Applications, *International Journal of Production Research*, 44(18–19), 4175–4191.

[9] Choudhary, A.K., Harding, J.A., Tiwari, M.K., 2009, Data Mining in Manufacturing: A Review Based on the Kind of Knowledge, *Journal of Intelligent Manufacturing*, 20(5), 501–521.

[10] Köksal, G., Batmaz, İ, Testik, M.C., 2011, A Review of Data Mining Applications for Quality Improvement in Manufacturing Industry, *Expert Systems with Applications*, 38(10), 13448–13467.

[11] Gonzalez, R., Kamrani, A., 2001. A survey of methodologies and techniques for data mining and intelligent data discovery. In *Data mining for design and manufacturing*, pp. 41–59, Springer US.

[12] Auschitzky, E., Hammer, M., Rajagopaul, A., 2014. *How big data can improve manufacturing*. McKinsey & Company. http://www.mckinsey.com/business-functions/operations/our-insights/how-big-data-can-improve-manufacturing (accessed August 22, 2017).

[13] Waller, M.A., Fawcett, S.E., 2013, Click here for a Data Scientist: Big Data, Predictive Analytics, and Theory Development in the Era of a Maker Movement Supply Chain, *Journal of Business Logistics*, 34(4), 249–252.

[14] Schoenherr, T., Speier-Pero, C., 2015, Data Science, Predictive Analytics, and Big Data in Supply Chain Management: Current State and Future Potential, *Journal of Business Logistics*, 36(1), 120–132.

[15] Hazen, B.T., Boone, C.A., Ezell, J.D., Jones-Farmer, L.A., 2014, Data Quality for Data Science, Predictive Analytics, and Big Data in Supply Chain Management: An Introduction to the Problem and Suggestions for Research and Applications, *International Journal of Production Economics*, 154, 72–80.

[16] Lee, J., Wu, F., Zhao, W., Ghaffari, M., Liao, L., Siegel, D., 2014, Prognostics and Health Management Design for Rotary Machinery systems—Reviews, *Methodology and Applications, Mechanical Systems and Signal Processing*, 42(1–2), 314–334.

[17] Lee, J., Lapira, E., Bagheri, B., Kao, H., 2013, Recent Advances and Trends in Predictive Manufacturing Systems in Big Data Environment, *Manufacturing Letters*, 1(1), 38–41.

[18] U.S. Energy Information Administration. 2006 Manufacturing energy consumption survey (MECS); steel industry analysis brief. https://www.eia.gov/Consumption/Manufacturing/Briefs/Steel/ (accessed August 22, 2017).

[19] Krumeich, J., Werth, D., Loos, P., Schimmelpfennig, J., Jacobi, S., 2014, Advanced Planning and Control of Manufacturing Processes in Steel Industry through Big Data Analytics: Case Study and Architecture Proposal, *2014 IEEE International Conference on Big Data (Big Data)*, Washington, DC, October 27–30, pp. 16–24.

[20] Krumeich, J., Jacobi, S., Werth, D., Loos, P., 2014, Big Data Analytics for Predictive Manufacturing Control-A Case Study from Process Industry, *2014 IEEE International Congress on Big Data*, Anchorage, AK, June 27–July 2, pp. 530–537.

Index

N

S

Milton Keynes UK
Ingram Content Group UK Ltd.
UKHW021926071024
449327UK00022B/1709

9 780367 572440